"The annals of rock are famously filled ...... strange anecdotes, and this tirelessly researched book — a vivid chronicle of the under-investigated field of indie rock in the 1980s, from Black Flag and Mission of Burma to Sonic Youth, the Replacements, the great Hüsker Dü, the sort-of-scary Big Black, and the intransigently idealistic Fugazi — adds a whole bunch more to the canon. A must-read for anyone who thinks rock stopped signifying after 1977." — Kurt Loder, MTV

"Azerrad's book is a portrait of the world before Nirvana, a vanished age when 'indie' referred to music, not film. . . . Azerrad details the physical violence and ideological controversies that swirled around hardcore bands." — Alexander Star, *Nation*

"Azerrad's book stands as a reminder that music is indeed often worth fighting for, and that even the constraints of big corporations can't always withstand the power of pure adulation and a strong support network." — Joshua Klein, *In These Times*

"More than just an invaluable source of knowledge of many of the greatest rock & roll bands of the past twenty years, Azerrad's work offers a glimpse into the angry, spirited, us-against-the-world thump of the Minor Threats and Hüsker Düs of the land, lamenting that 'the revolution had been largely successful, but . . . the struggle was much more fun than the victory.'" — Michael Chamy, *Austin Chronicle*

"Fascinating. . . . An essential read for anyone intrigued by the motivations that drive earnest rock music." — Chuck Klosterman, *Beacon Journal*

"An exceptional look at some of the alt-rock nation's pioneers. . . . An extremely entertaining tale of bands at odds with the mainstream, yet able to connect with the pockets of kids that related to them the way their older brothers and sisters related to the Beatles, the Stones, Led Zeppelin, and Alice Cooper." — Mike Villano, *Billboard Review*

"Azerrad's new book finally gives an entire generation of influential and fiercely independent bands their due. . . . *Our Band Could Be Your Life* effectively captures what is now commonly referred to as indie rock in all its intensely passionate, do-it-yourself glory." — Jason Gargano, *Cincinnati City Beat*

"One of 'Our 25 Favorite Books of 2001.'"  — *Village Voice*

"A substantial, elegantly rendered assessment of the indie rock era.... A well-done, thoroughly detailed look at the stories behind the music that captures both the heart and the eccentricity of outsider rock's golden age."
  — *Kirkus Reviews*

"An important document.... Until now, no one has really told the story of how these bands got to these statesman-like positions. Azerrad does a fine job doing just that, detailing each band and its ensuing scene — not just the events and happenings, but the whole mindset that made them possible."  — Joe S. Harrington, *New York Press*

"Azerrad's focus on the bands' collective sense of independence — their refusal to knuckle under to commercial considerations — is laserlike, and his descriptions of the music are occasionally sublime."  — *Book* magazine

"*Our Band Could Be Your Life* is an exhaustive history by one of the indie scene's most diligent documentarians.... An invaluable guide for younger fans who don't know the history.... Azerrad's book reverently and unobtrusively bears witness to the time before Riot Grrrl, before Nirvana went Platinum, before hardcore punk noise played in the background of Mountain Dew commercials, before the dream broke down and had to be repaired."  — Emily White, *Newsday*

"Michael Azerrad is brilliant at uncovering the real stories of these artists, the unsung heroes of the alternative movement. It's great stuff."
  — Matt Pinfield, host of Farmclub.com

"*Our Band Could Be Your Life* is not only an essential musical encyclopedia for anyone who claims to enjoy indie rock, but also a great starting point for anyone interested in discovering music made for music, not music made for money."  — Jeremy Hedges, *The Pitt News*

"A solid historical compendium.... *Our Band Could Be Your Life* is a pointed requiem and testimonial to a movement that, like a good song, burns white-hot for only so long, and then dies."
  — Chris Lenz, *Privy Magazine*

(*continued on inside back cover*)

# OUR BAND COULD BE YOUR LIFE

## SCENES FROM THE AMERICAN INDIE UNDERGROUND 1981–1991

# MICHAEL AZERRAD

BACK BAY BOOKS

LITTLE, BROWN AND COMPANY  NEW YORK • BOSTON • LONDON

## ALSO BY MICHAEL AZERRAD

*Come as You Are: The Story of Nirvana*
*Screaming Life: A Chronicle of the Seattle Music Scene*

Back Bay Books / Little, Brown and Company
Hachette Book Group
1290 Avenue of the Americas, New York, NY 10104
www.hachettebookgroup.com

Originally published by Little, Brown and Company, July 2001
First Back Bay paperback edition, July 2002

Back Bay Books is an imprint of Little, Brown and Company. The Back Bay Books name and logo are trademarks of Hachette Book Group, Inc.

The publisher is not responsible for websites (or their content) that are not owned by the publisher.

The Hachette Speakers Bureau provides a wide range of authors for speaking events. To find out more, go to www.hachettespeakersbureau.com or call (866) 376-6591.

Library of Congress Cataloging-in-Publication Data
Azerrad, Michael.
Our band could be your life : scenes from the American indie underground 1981–1991 / by Michael Azerrad. — 1st ed.
p. cm.
ISBN 978-0-316-06379-7 (hc)/978-0-316-78753-6 (pb)
1. Alternative rock music — United States — History and criticism. 2. Alternative rock musicians — United States. 3. Rock groups — United States. I. Title.
ML3534.3 A94 2001
781.66'0973 — dc21          2001029052

20  19  18

LSC-C

Designed by Iris Weinstein
Printed in the United States of America

# CONTENTS

"I MUST CREATE A SYSTEM OR BE ENSLAVED
BY ANOTHER MAN'S."

— WILLIAM BLAKE

# INTRODUCTION

On September 24, 1991, an album called *Nevermind* by a band called Nirvana came out, went gold in a matter of weeks, bumped Michael Jackson off the number one spot on the *Billboard* album charts soon afterward, and prompted music journalist Gina Arnold to proclaim, "We won." But who was "we"? And why were "we" so different from "them"?

"We" was a sprawling cooperative of fanzines, underground and college radio stations, local cable access shows, mom-and-pop record stores, independent distributors and record labels, tip sheets, nightclubs and alternative venues, booking agents, bands, and fans that had been thriving for more than a decade before the mainstream took notice.

Beneath the radar of the corporate behemoths, these enterprising, frankly entrepreneurial people had built an effective shadow distribution, communications, and promotion network — a cultural underground railroad. "In an age of big entertainment conglomerates/big management/big media, touring the lowest-rent rock clubs of America in an Econoline is the equivalent of fighting a ground war strategy in an age of strategic nuclear forces," wrote Joe Carducci in *Rock and the Pop Narcotic*. And Nirvana, ground war strategy and all, had miraculously emerged as the victor.

**T**en years before *Nevermind,* Sonic Youth formed, the Minutemen and the Replacements released their first albums, Hüsker Dü released their first single, Henry Rollins joined Black Flag, Mission of Burma and Minor Threat both released their first EPs, and R.E.M. released their epochal "Radio Free Europe"/"Sitting Still" debut single on tiny Hib-Tone Records. And Ronald Reagan, the figurehead for so much of the discontent in America's underground culture, began his first term as president. The year 1981 was truly seminal for modern American underground rock. But it would be years before anyone realized what had been planted.

This book is by no means a complete history of the American indie movement from 1981–1991. It pays particular attention to the SST, Dischord, Touch & Go, and Sub Pop record labels, but those are far from the only labels that made the revolution happen. There was also Slash, Taang!, Frontier, Posh Boy, Coyote, Alternative Tentacles, Dangerhouse, Bar/None, Pitch-a-Tent, Wax Trax, and countless others. It would have been impossible to write about all of them.

The same could be said for the house organs of the indie scene, the fanzines. Most of them started as photocopied rants by people who were frustrated at the way the mainstream music magazines largely ignored this exciting new music. Some of them grew quite large and influential — including *Flipside, Maximumrocknroll,* and *Forced Exposure* — but there were literally hundreds of smaller zines that collectively framed the indie aesthetic.

And of course the American independent scene in the Eighties contained many, many bands, from those that made a mark on the national stage to bands that began obscure and stayed that way, sometimes by design. Many of the bands known only to a very few are personal favorites, but it was a matter of either excluding them or turning this book into an encyclopedia. My humblest apologies to those bands and their fans. There are plenty more books to be written about this subject; I invite you to write one of them.

Instead, this book profiles a series of bands who not only represented a musical innovation, a philosophy, a region or label, or contributed a noted character to the community, but illustrated a particular point in the evolution of the American indie scene in the Eighties, from aggressive pioneer days to a diverse scene struggling with its own success. And it's about giving credit where credit is overdue. These bands are legendary, but many folks don't know why. So merely telling the Minutemen story, or introducing readers to a band as great as Mission of Burma, or pointing out the profound debt the alternative rock boom of the Nineties owed to bands like Hüsker Dü and the Replacements would be rationale enough.

This book is devoted solely to bands who were on independent labels. So R.E.M., for instance, didn't make the cut, since the band's pre-Warner albums were recorded for I.R.S. Records, whose releases were manufactured and distributed by A&M (which in turn had a business relationship with RCA) and later, MCA. Correspondingly, the stories trail off when and if a band signed to a major label. Virtually every band did their best and most influential work during their indie years; and once they went to a major label, an important connection to the underground community was invariably lost.

Note also that the book concentrates on the bands' stories rather than their music. If you'd like to know more about the music, you should listen to it — as of this writing, virtually every record referred to in the book is still in print. And if you *really* need to read more about the music, check out some of the books listed in the bibliography, particularly the *Trouser Press Record Guide*, fourth edition, edited by my friend and distinguished colleague Ira Robbins.

"I ndependent" has several definitions, but the one this book uses is the crucial question of whether a label distributes its records through one of the corporate music behemoths — in the period in question they were the so-called Big Six: Capitol, CBS, MCA, PolyGram, RCA, and WEA — which allows them entrée to vastly more stores than the smaller, independent distributors. All kinds of advantages stem from this distinction, from access to commercial radio to the ability to attract name artists. Indie labels had to develop obscure artists on a grassroots level, essentially functioning with one or more arms tied behind their back.

American independent labels are nothing new: legendary labels like Motown, Stax, Chess, Sun, and Atlantic were all once independent, but by the mid-Seventies, most of the key ones had been swallowed up by the majors. A lot of rock indie records of that time were one-offs like the 1974 "Hey Joe"/"Piss Factory" single on Mer Records, recorded by a visionary New Jersey woman named Patti Smith and paid for by her photographer friend Robert Mapplethorpe.

But taking their cue from pioneering English indie punk labels like Stiff and Chiswick, more and more people realized that calling up a

pressing plant and getting their own record manufactured wasn't the mysterious, exclusive privilege of the giant record companies on the coasts. A
door was opened and a small trickle of people stepped through it. Independent record labels began springing up all around the United States in
the late Seventies in order to document punk rock and its offshoots.

It all started simply because there were great bands that would never
be signed to major labels. In true capitalist tradition, entrepreneurs recognized a need, however small, and catered to it. Suddenly there were indie labels all over the map: 99 in New York; Black Vinyl in Zion, Illinois;
Frontier in Los Angeles; Twin/Tone in Minneapolis; dB in Atlanta; and
on and on.

But doing an end run around the Powers That Be will always have an
inherent ideological spin. A lot of forward thinkers had seen how the major labels had devoured the first generation of British punks, particularly
the Sex Pistols, and resolved to retain control of their own destiny. As
writer Mike O'Flaherty has pointed out, early British post-punk labels
such as Rough Trade were "part of the tide of political radicalism that
swept Britain in 1978–79. . . . Political radicalism was built into the post-
punk model, and its implications would reverberate through American
indie in the political big sleep of the Reagan years like a half-remembered
promise."

To begin with, the key principle of American indie rock wasn't a circumscribed musical style; it was the punk ethos of DIY, or do-it-yourself.
The equation was simple: If punk was rebellious and DIY was rebellious,
then doing it yourself was punk. "Punk was about more than just starting
a band," former Minutemen bassist Mike Watt once said, "it was about
starting a label, it was about touring, it was about taking control. It was
like songwriting; you just do it. You want a record, you pay the pressing
plant. That's what it was all about."

The breakthrough realization that you didn't have to be a blow-dried
guitar god to be a valid rock musician ran deep; it was liberating on many
levels, especially from what many perceived as the selfishness, greed, and
arrogance of Reagan's America. The indie underground made a modest
way of life not just attractive but a downright moral imperative.

At first, though, a pragmatic stance was a necessity more than a statement. "It wasn't a PR move, it was the best we could do at the time," says
former Hüsker Dü singer-guitarist Bob Mould. "It was real simple: When
you're a fish going downstream and all you see is sharks at every tributary
and you see this one spot where another fish got through, you go that way.
You're not sure what that fish looked like, but you know it didn't get eaten,

so you just go that way. And one thing leads to another and people follow you and that's how it goes."

"People realized there was a way to do it in a very underground, low-key way that still counted and was still important," says Sonic Youth's Lee Ranaldo. "People got this idea that ultimately what mattered was the quality of what you were doing and how much importance you gave to it, regardless of how widespread it became or how many records it sold."

This realization turned the fate of the innovator — typically a constant uphill battle through obscurity, poverty, and frustration — upside down. In the microcosm of the independent label world, innovators could flourish, enjoy respect and admiration for their work, and actually be applauded and even rewarded for sticking with their vision. Lowering your sights was raising your sights.

In some ways, artists like the Beatles, Stevie Wonder, and Bob Dylan were precursors to DIY — while their careers were extensively stage-managed, they did demand and receive unprecedented amounts of control over their music, a radical development at the time. In their wake, musicians asserted their right to create without outside meddling, and how strongly they did so became key to their credibility. This concept loomed large in the Eighties indie scene.

In fact, the Sixties legacy had a lot to do with underground rock in the Eighties. Asked in 1980 what the L.A. punk scene was like, KROQ DJ Rodney Bingenheimer replied, "It's like living in the Sixties again." Sonic Youth's Thurston Moore once said of punk, "It was like a nihilist hippie movement, that's all it was." Virtually every artist in this book acknowledges the influence of the Sixties musical counterculture.

And no wonder — the earliest citizens of the indie nation had grown up on bands like the Beatles, the Who, and the Rolling Stones, groups that fostered the now nearly antiquated idea that rock & roll was an intrinsic part of a young person's soul, an engine of social change and not just a consumer commodity. "That decade was one where people felt enormously committed and enormously identified with music and culture, where people felt like it wasn't just a background, it was your *life*," says Fugazi's Guy Picciotto. "It was part of the fiber of what you did."

But the indie community saw what had happened to the Sixties dream. And they knew they didn't have the demographic strength for such a cultural overthrow, nor did they want to replicate the baby boomers' egregious sellout. So they just made sure they weren't part of the problem and fought the good fight, knowing they'd never prevail. And that was very punk. "Understand that we're fighting a war we can't win!" wrote Black Flag's Greg Ginn in the band's epochal song "Police Story."

In the indie scene, labels cultivated distinct identities through their own unique aesthetics, which extended through many manifestations — music, album art, even catalog copy. The best labels inspired as much loyalty as bands, sometimes more, because the bands on the label could be expected not only to be good, but good in a certain way. It was very common to see someone wearing an SST T-shirt, but few wore T-shirts that read "Columbia Records."

All of this led up to 1984, a year that yielded a spate of bona fide classics: the Meat Puppets' *Meat Puppets II*, Hüsker Dü's *Zen Arcade*, the Minutemen's *Double Nickels on the Dime*, the Replacements' *Let It Be*, and Black Flag's lesser but no less influential *My War*. It was an annus mirabilis for indie, thrust into even deeper relief by the fact that at the time, acts like Kenny Loggins, Yes, Phil Collins, and Lionel Richie were ruling the mainstream charts. It was abundantly clear that the best rock music in the world was being made in this circumscribed little community.

And thanks to that plethora of great albums, the music was now being noticed by mainstream audiences, critics, and record labels. A couple of key bands defected to major labels and suddenly Pandora's box was opened. A few other key bands valiantly tried to preserve the autonomy of the scene, but they were only delaying the inevitable. As it had ten years before, the late Eighties music industry tried to lift itself out of a slump by taking a stab at punk rock. This time, however, it worked.

There are interesting parallels between indie rock and the folk movement of the early Sixties. Both hinged on purism and authenticity, as well as idealism about the power of music within culture and society; both were a reaction to shallow, complacent times and their correspondingly shallow, complacent entertainment; both had populist roots but were eventually commandeered by white middle-class college kids. But while folk music had an outspokenly ideological bent, indie rock's political message was often more implicit. In both cases, the music's own eventual popularity derailed its crucial authenticity: the folk movement came to a symbolic end with Bob Dylan's heretical electric performance at the 1965 Newport Folk Festival; the indie movement was changed forever when *Nevermind* hit number one on the *Billboard* charts.

And both kinds of music came out of similar times. "The Eighties were a little like the Fifties — it was sort of a conservative era, money conscious, politically nasty, and Republican," says former Mission of Burma drummer Peter Prescott. "And usually that means there's going to be a good underground," he adds with a laugh. "There's something to get pissed off with communally." So it's no coincidence that the glory years of the American indie movement overlap so neatly with the Reagan-Bush era.

As usual, music was the first art form to register discontent. Underground rock protested not just with its sound but in the way it was recorded, marketed, and distributed. And since the music business is one of the most familiar manifestations of cultural power that American youth recognizes, in a larger sense rebelling against the major labels was a metaphor for rebelling against the system in general.

In D.C. kids rebelled against the bland, stifling atmosphere of official Washington, exacerbated by the conservative inhabitants of the White House; in Minneapolis it was the oppressive winters and the equally oppressive Scandinavian stoicism; in Seattle it was yuppies, rain, and that good ol' Scandinavian stoicism again; in Los Angeles it was inane California mellowness, the excruciating vapidity of suburbia, and the false glamour being propagated on soundstages all over town; in New York it was those darn yuppies and the overall difficulty of living in what was then America's hardest city; and throughout the country, anyone with the slightest bit of suss was disgruntled by the pervasive know-nothingism Ronald Reagan fobbed off as "Morning in America."

Radio was one key arena for this rebellion. Tightly controlled FM formats, mostly programmed by a small group of consulting firms, kept new music off the radio. College radio jumped into the breach, providing a valuable conduit. Now indie shows could be well promoted; records could be adequately showcased. The corporate exploitation of new wave had proved the majors could co-opt punk's musical style, but they couldn't co-opt punk's infrastructure — the local underground scenes, labels, radio stations, fanzines, and stores. They, perhaps more so than in any particular musical style, are punk's most enduring legacy.

The remarkable thing is the audience was as much a part of the do-it-yourself conspiracy as the bands and the labels. Sure, the bands were taking a big chance by going with tiny, underpowered labels, and the labels constantly flirted with bankruptcy, but the biggest leap of faith might well have been by the audience. They were falling for bands who weren't on commercial radio and would never be on the cover of *Rolling Stone*.

They had to overcome a lifetime of training in order to get to the point where they could feel like a scruffy, bibulous indie band from Minneapolis with an album called *Let It Be* was just as valid as the band that first used the title. What they realized was that the great band down the street was just as worthy as the superstar acts (and maybe even *more* worthy). And what's more, seeing the great indie bands play live didn't require $25 and a pair of binoculars. This was positively revolutionary.

The underground's musical diversity meant there was no stylistic bandwagon for the media to latch on to, so the record-buying public had to find things there on a band-by-band basis, rather than buying into a bunch of talk about a "new sound." This investigative aspect tended to attract a certain type of person — someone who would seek out the little radio stations to the left of the dial that didn't have such great reception, who would track down the little photocopied fanzine, who would walk past the sprawling chain record store with the lighted sign and go across town to the little mom-and-pop that stocked the new Camper van Beethoven record.

The American underground in the Eighties embraced the radical notion that maybe, just maybe, the stuff that was shoved in our faces by the all-pervasive mainstream media wasn't necessarily the *best* stuff. This independence of mind, the determination to see past surface flash and think for oneself, flew in the face of the burgeoning complacency, ignorance, and conformism that engulfed the nation like a spreading stain throughout the Eighties.

**T**he indie movement was a reclamation of what rock was always about. Rock & roll hinged on a strong, personal connection to favorite bands, but that connection had been stretched to the limit by pop's lowest common denominator approach, not to mention things like impersonal stadium concerts and the unreality of MTV. Indie bands proved you didn't need those things to make a connection with an audience. In fact, you could make a *better* connection with your audience without them.

Corporate rock was about living large; indie was about living realistically and being proud of it. Indie bands didn't need million-dollar promotional budgets and multiple costume changes. All they needed was to believe in themselves and for a few other people to believe in them, too. You didn't need some big corporation to fund you, or even verify that you were any good. It was about viewing as a virtue what most saw as a limitation.

The Minutemen called it "jamming econo." And not only could you jam econo with your rock group — you could jam econo on your job, in your buying habits, in your whole way of living. You could take this particular approach to music and apply it to just about anything else you wanted to. You could be beholden only to yourself and the values and people you respected. You could take charge of your own existence. Or as the Minutemen put it in a song, "Our band could be your life."

# CHAPTER 1

# BLACK FLAG

*FLIPSIDE* INTERVIEWER: DO YOU MAKE A PROFIT?
GREG GINN: WE TRY TO EAT.

It's not surprising that the indie movement largely started in Southern California — after all, it had the infrastructure: *Slash* and *Flipside* fanzines started in 1977, and indie labels like Frontier and Posh Boy and Dangerhouse started soon afterward. KROQ DJ Rodney Bingenheimer played the region's punk music on his show; listeners could buy what they heard thanks to various area distributors and record shops and see the bands at places like the Masque, the Starwood, the Whisky, the Fleetwood, and various impromptu venues. And there were great bands like the Germs, Fear, the Dickies, the Dils, X, and countless others. No other region in the country had quite as good a setup.

But by 1979 the original punk scene had almost completely died out. Hipsters had moved on to arty post-punk bands like the Fall, Gang of Four, and Joy Division. They were replaced by a bunch of toughs coming in from outlying suburbs who were only beginning to discover punk's speed, power, and aggression. They didn't care that punk rock was already being dismissed as a spent force, kid bands playing at being the Ramones a few years too late. Dispensing with all pretension, these kids boiled the music down to its essence, then revved up the tempos to the speed of a pencil impatiently tapping on a school desk, and called the result "hardcore." As writer Barney Hoskyns put it, this new music was "younger, faster and angrier, full of the pent-up rage of dysfunctional Orange County adolescents who'd had enough of living in a bland Republican paradise."

Fairly quickly, hardcore spread around the country and coalesced into a small but robust community. Just as "hip-hop" was an umbrella term for the music, art, fashion, and dance of a then nascent urban subculture, so was "hardcore." Hardcore artwork was all stark, cartoonish imagery, rough-hewn photocopied collage, and violently scrawled lettering; fashion was basically typical suburban attire but ripped and dingy, topped with militarily short haircuts; the preferred mode of terpsichorean expression was a new thing called slam dancing, in which participants simply bashed into one another like human bumper cars.

Hardcore punk drew a line in the sand between older avant-rock fans and a new bunch of kids who were coming up. On one side were those who considered the music (and its fans) loud, ugly, and incoherent; to the folks on the other side, hardcore was the only music that mattered. A rare generational divide in rock music had arisen. And that's when exciting things happen.

Black Flag was more than just the flagship band of the Southern California hardcore scene. It was more than even the flagship band of American hardcore itself. They were required listening for anyone who was interested in underground music. And by virtue of their relentless touring, the band did more than any other to blaze a trail through America that all kinds of bands could follow. Not only did they establish punk rock beachheads in literally every corner of the country; they inspired countless other bands to form and start doing it for themselves. The band's selfless work ethic was a model for the decade ahead, overcoming indifference, lack of venues, poverty, even police harassment.

Black Flag was among the first bands to suggest that if you didn't like "the system," you should simply create one of your own. And indeed, Black Flag guitarist Greg Ginn also founded and ran Black Flag's label, SST Records. Ginn took his label from a cash-strapped, cop-hassled storefront operation to easily the most influential and popular underground indie of the Eighties, releasing classics by the likes of Bad Brains, the Minutemen, the Meat Puppets, Hüsker Dü, Sonic Youth, Dinosaur Jr, and many more.

SST and Black Flag in particular hit a deep and molten vein in American culture. Their fans were just as disaffected from the mainstream as the bands were. "Black Flag, like a lot of these bands, were playing for the people who maybe felt jilted by things or left out by things," says the band's fourth lead singer, Henry Rollins. "When you say, 'Be all you can be,' I know you're not talking to me, motherfucker. I know I'm not joining the navy and I know your laws don't mean shit to me because the hypocrisy that welds them all together, I cannot abide. There's a lot of people with a lot of fury in this country — America is seething at all times. It's like a Gaza Strip that's three thousand miles long."

Greg Ginn never really liked rock music as a kid. "I considered it kind of stupid," he says. "I considered it just trying to interject some kind of legitimacy into making three-minute pop commercials, basically." Ginn didn't even own any records until he was eighteen and received David Ackles's 1972 art-folk masterpiece *American Gothic* as a premium for subscribing to a local public radio station. The record opened a new world for Ginn; a year later he began playing acoustic guitar as a "tension release" after studying economics all day at UCLA.

Ginn had spent his early childhood with his parents and four brothers and sisters in a small farming community outside Bakersfield, California. His father earned a meager schoolteacher's salary, so Ginn got used to cramped surroundings and living on limited means. "I never had new clothes," says Ginn. "My dad would go to Salvation Army, Goodwill, and he would consider those *expensive* thrift stores — 'Salvation Army, that's expensive!' He would find the cheaper places."

In 1962, when Ginn was eight, the family moved to Hermosa Beach, California, in the solidly white middle-class South Bay area a couple of dozen miles south of Los Angeles. Hermosa Beach had been a beatnik mecca in the Fifties, but by the time Ginn got there, it was a haven for surfers (and inspired Jan & Dean's 1963 classic "Surf City").

But while his peers were into hanging ten, Ginn disdained the conformity and materialism of surfing; a very tall, very quiet kid, he preferred to write poetry and do ham radio. A generation later he would have been a computer nerd. At the age of twelve, he published an amateur radio fanzine called *The Novice* and founded Solid State Tuners (SST), a mail-order business selling modified World War II surplus radio equipment; it became a small but thriving business that Ginn ran well into his twenties.

After learning to play an acoustic, Ginn picked up an electric guitar and began writing aggressive, vaguely blues-based songs, but only for himself. "I was never the stereotypical teenager," Ginn said, "sitting in his room and dreaming of becoming a rock star, so I just played what I liked and thought was good." Ginn's music had nothing to do with the musical climate of the mid-Seventies, especially in Hermosa Beach, where everybody seemed to be into the British pomp-rock band Genesis. "The general perception was that rock was technical and clean and 'We can't do it like we did it in the Sixties,'" he said. "I wished it was more like the Sixties!"

It's no wonder Ginn got excited when he began reading in the *Village Voice* about a new music called "punk rock" that was coming out of New York clubs like Max's Kansas City and CBGB. Even before he heard a note, he was sure punk was what he was looking for. "I looked at punk rock as a break in the conformity that was going on," says Ginn. "There wasn't a specific sound in early punk rock and there wasn't a specific look or anything like that — it seemed to be a place where anybody could go who didn't fit into the conventional rock mode."

Ginn sent away for the classic "Little Johnny Jewel" single by the New York band Television on tiny Ork Records. The music was powerful, brilliant, and it had nothing to do with Genesis or the slick corporate rock that dominated the music industry in the mid-Seventies; this music was organic in the way it was played, recorded, and, just as important, how it was popularized. It was hardly "three-minute pop commercials."

Ginn was hooked.

By then Ginn had developed extraordinarily wide-ranging musical tastes. He dug Motown, disco, country artists like Merle Haggard and Buck Owens, and adored all kinds of jazz, from big band to early fusion; in the Seventies he was a regular at Hermosa Beach's fabled jazz club the Lighthouse, where he witnessed legends like Yusef Lateef and Mose Allison. But besides his beloved B.B. King, there was only one group that Ginn adored more than any other. "The Grateful Dead — if there's one favorite band I have, it's probably that," says Ginn. "I saw them maybe seventy-five times."

But because Ginn was only a novice guitarist, none of those influences came through in his playing; he was simply making music to work off energy and frustration, and as generations of beginners before him had discovered, the quickest shortcut to a cool guitar sound was nasty, brutish distortion. Then, when he saw the Ramones play, Ginn "got a speed rush," he said, "and decided to turn it up a notch." The next logical step was to form a band.

In late '76 a mutual friend introduced Ginn to a hard-partying loud-mouth named Keith Morris; the two hit it off and decided to start a band. Morris wanted to play drums, but Ginn was convinced Morris should sing. Morris protested that he didn't write lyrics and, besides, he was no Freddie Mercury. But punk had showed Ginn you didn't need gold-plated tonsils to rock, and Morris eventually agreed. They drafted a few of Morris's friends — "scruffy beach rat types who were more interested in getting laid and finding drugs than really playing," Morris said — and began rehearsing in Ginn's tiny house by the beach. In honor of their hectic tempos, they called the band Panic.

There was precious little punk rock to emulate at the time, so the band picked up the aggressive sounds they heard in Black Sabbath, the Stooges, and the MC5, only faster. "Our statement was that we were going to be loud and abrasive," said Morris. "We were going to have fun and we weren't going to be like anything you've heard before. We might look like Deadheads — at that point we had long hair, but the Ramones did, too — but we meant business." They played parties to nearly universal disdain.

They soon moved their practices to Ginn's space at the Church, a dilapidated house of worship in Hermosa Beach that had been converted into workshops for artists but was in effect a hangout for runaways and misfits. They got kicked out for making too much noise and found a new rehearsal space in the spring of '77. They practiced every day, but since their bass player usually flaked out on rehearsals, Ginn had to carry much of the rhythm on his own and began developing a simple, heavily rhythmic style that never outpaced his limited technique.

A band called Wurm also practiced in the Church, and the two bands began playing parties together. Wurm's bassist, an intense, sharp-witted guy named Gary McDaniel, liked Panic's aggressive, cathartic approach and began sitting in with them. McDaniel and Ginn connected immediately. "He would always have a lot of theories on life, on this and that — he was a thinking person," says Ginn. "He didn't want to fit into the regular society thing, but not the hippie thing, either."

Like Ginn, McDaniel, who went by the stage name Chuck Dukowski, was repulsed by mellow folkies like James Taylor and effete art-rockers. He was a student at UC Santa Barbara when he saw the Ramones. "I had never seen a band play so fast," he said. "Suddenly you could point to a band and say, 'If they can do it, why can't we?'"

For their first couple of years, Panic played exclusively at parties and youth centers around the South Bay because the Masque, the key L.A. punk club, refused to book them. "They said it wasn't cool to live in Hermosa Beach," Ginn claimed, which is a way of saying that the band's suburban T-shirt, sneakers, and jeans look flew in the face of the consumptive safety-pin and leather jacket pose of the Anglophilic L.A. punks. By necessity, Panic developed a knack for finding offbeat places to stage their explosive, anarchic performances, often sharing bills with Orange County punk bands, relatively affluent suburbanites who could afford things like renting halls and PA systems.

The party circuit had a very tangible effect on the band's music. "That's where we really developed the idea of playing as many songs in as little time as possible," says Ginn, "because it was always almost like clockwork — you could play for twenty minutes before the police would show up. So we knew that we had a certain amount of time: don't make any noise until you start playing and then just go hard and long until they show up."

Their first proper show was at a Moose Lodge in nearby Redondo Beach. During the first set, Morris began swinging an American flag around, much to the displeasure of the assembled Moose. He was ejected from the building, but he donned a longhaired wig and sneaked back in to sing the second set. Eventually the band progressed to playing shows at the Fleetwood in Redondo Beach, where they built up such a substantial following that the Hollywood clubs couldn't ignore them anymore, effecting a sea change in L.A. punk.

Early on Ginn met a cheery fellow known as Spot, who wrote record reviews for a Hermosa Beach paper. Ginn would sometimes stop by the vegetarian restaurant where Spot worked and shoot the breeze about music. "He was a nerd," Spot recalls. "He was just an awkward nerd who was very opinionated. Couldn't imagine him ever being in a band." Later Spot became assistant engineer at local studio Media Art, which boasted cheap hourly rates and sixteen-track recording. When Ginn asked him to record his band, Spot agreed, figuring it would be a nice break from the usual watery pop-folk. "They only had six songs," Spot recalls. "They could play their entire set in ten minutes."

"They were just goons and geeks," he adds. "Definitely not the beautiful people."

In January '78 Panic recorded eight songs at Media Art, with Spot assistant engineering. But nobody wanted to touch the band's raging slab of aggro-punk except L.A.'s garage-pop revivalists Bomp Records, who had already released singles by L.A. punk bands like the Weirdos and the Zeros. But by late 1978 Bomp still hadn't formally agreed to release the record. So Ginn, figuring he had enough business expertise from SST Electronics and his UCLA economics studies, simply did it himself.

"I just looked in the phone book under record pressing plants and there was one there," says Ginn, "and so I just took it in to them and I knew about printing because I had always done catalogs and [*The Novice*] so we just did a sleeve that was folded in a plastic bag. And then got the singles made and put in there." Ginn got his younger brother, who went by the name Raymond Pettibon, to do the cover, an unsettling pen-and-ink illustration of a teacher keeping a student at bay with a chair, like a lion tamer.

A few months earlier they had discovered that another band already had the name Panic. Pettibon suggested "Black Flag" and designed a logo for the band, a stylized rippling flag made up of four vertical black rectangles. If a white flag means surrender, it was plain what a black flag meant; a black flag is also a recognized symbol for anarchy, not to mention the traditional emblem of pirates; it sounded a bit like their heroes Black Sabbath as well. Of course, the fact that Black Flag was also a popular insecticide didn't hurt either. "We were comfortable with *all* the implications of the name," says Ginn, "as well as it just sounded, you know, heavy."

In January '79 Ginn released the four-song *Nervous Breakdown* EP, SST Records catalog #001. It could well be their best recording; it was definitely the one by which everything after it would be measured. "It set the template — this is what it is," Ginn said. "After that, people couldn't argue with me as to what Black Flag was or wasn't."

With music and lyrics by Ginn, the record is rude, scuzzy, and totally exhilarating. With his sardonic, Johnny Rottenesque delivery, Morris inflates the torment of teen angst into full-blown insanity: "I'm crazy and I'm hurt / Head on my shoulders goin' berserk," he whines on the title track; same for the desperate "Fix Me" ("Fix me, fix my head / Fix me please, I don't want to be dead").

Drummer Brian Migdol left the band and was replaced by Roberto Valverde, better known as Robo, who originally hailed from Colombia. "A real sweet guy and super enigmatic," recalls future Black Flag singer Henry Rollins. "He had a very shady past which he would not talk about." The rumor that made the rounds was that Valverde had been a soldier in the notoriously corrupt Colombian army.

In July '79 the band played an infamous show at a spring family outing at Manhattan Beach's Polliwog Park, having told town officials they were a regular rock band. It didn't take very long for the assembled moms and dads to figure differently. "People threw everything from insults to watermelons, beer cans, ice, and sandwiches at us," wrote Dukowski in the liner notes to the *Everything Went Black* compilation. "Parents emptied their ice chests so that their families could throw their lunches. . . . Afterwards I enjoyed a lunch of delicatessen sandwiches which I found still in their wrappers."

**W**hile the Hollywood punks tended to be spindly, druggy, and older, the suburban kids who followed Black Flag and other bands tended to be disaffected jocks and surfers, strapping young lads who rarely touched anything stronger than beer. And when they all gathered in one place, fights would break out and things would get broken. The most thuggish of the suburban punks were a crew from Huntington Beach, better known as the HB'ers. "The HB'ers were all leather jackets, chains, macho, bloodlust, and bravado, and exhibited blatantly stupid military behavior," wrote Spot in his *Everything Went Black* liner notes. "It was never a dull moment."

This new kind of punk rocker perplexed the local authorities. "All of a sudden you're dealing with thick-necked guys who were drunk and could go toe to toe with some cops, guys who will get in a cop's face," says Henry Rollins. "They're white and they're from Huntington Beach and you can't shoot 'em because they're not black or Hispanic so you have to deal with them on a semihuman level. The sheer force of the numbers at the shows totally freaked the cops out to where they just said, 'Don't try to understand it, we'll just squelch it. And how will we squelch it? We'll just smash the hell out of 'em — arrest 'em for no reason, smack 'em on the head, intimidate the shit out of them.' And boy it was intense."

Police harassment blighted the early days of South Bay hardcore, and Black Flag was the lightning rod for most of it. It all started when Black Flag threw a party at the Church in June '80. In the name of property values, Hermosa Beach was then in the midst of clearing out the last remnants of its hippie culture, and the town fathers were apparently intent on preventing bohemian youth culture from ever blighting their fair city again. The police showed up at the party and almost literally told Black Flag to get out of town by sundown. Conveniently, the band had scheduled the show for the eve of a West Coast tour, so they piled in the van, took off for San Francisco, and later returned to Redondo Beach. After a year or so they came back to Hermosa Beach and were promptly given the bum's rush once again.

Between 1980 and 1981, at least a dozen Black Flag concerts ended in violent clashes between the police and the kids. And the more the band complained to the press about the police, the more the police hassled them and their fans. Not helping matters was the fact that the Black Flag logo was spray-painted on countless highway overpasses in and around Los Angeles. Then there was the flyer that got plastered all over town featuring a Pettibon drawing of a hand jamming a pistol in the mouth of a terrified cop. The caption read "Make me come, faggot!"

Ginn claims SST's phone lines were being tapped, cops sat in vans across the street and monitored SST headquarters, and undercover police posing as homeless people sat on the curb in front of SST's front door. Hiring a lawyer simply wasn't an option — they couldn't afford one. "I mean, we were thinking about skimping on our meals," Ginn explains, adding, "It's not like you're part of society. There was no place to go. That's what people just don't get that haven't been in that place. Because you don't have any rights. If you don't have that support, then the law is just the cop out there and what he tells you to do." But the band never backed down, fueling even more ire from L.A.'s finest.

Starting in 1980, L.A. clubs began to ban hardcore bands. "That's the last thing I thought would happen," Ginn says. "I thought we're pretty mild-mannered people and we don't write songs about some sort of social rebellion; it's basically blues to me. It's personal, my way of writing blues."

Rollins, who admittedly was not yet in the band when most of the harassment went down, believes much of the controversy was a Dukowskian plot. "Looking back at it, I think it was some press manipulation," he says. "And to rouse some rabble." If so, the plan backfired — what good was police harassment if you couldn't get a gig?

**B**lack Flag had booked their first tour, a summer of '79 trip up the West Coast, hitting San Francisco, Portland, Seattle, and up to Vancouver, British Columbia, when Morris, an admitted "alcoholic and a cokehead," left the band to found the pioneering South Bay punk band the Circle Jerks. He was quickly replaced by a rabid Black Flag fan named Ron Reyes, aka Chavo Pederast. "He'd go real crazy at the gigs and we just thought he'd make a really good singer," Ginn explains.

But Reyes quit two songs into a show at the Fleetwood in March '80, and the band proceeded to play "Louie, Louie" for an hour, joined by a long succession of guest vocalists. "A guy named 'Snikers' . . . jumped up and began singing 'Louie, Louie' and then proceeded to perform a most disgustingly drunken striptease during which cans, bottles, spit, sweat, and bodies began flying with a vengeance," wrote Spot. "It was the finest rock & roll show I had ever seen." For several shows afterward, the band played without an official lead singer — anyone who wanted to would come up and sing a song or two before getting yanked back into the crowd.

They convinced Reyes to come back and record the five-song, six-and-a-half-minute *Jealous Again* EP (released in the summer of '80), a nasty nugget of low-rent nihilism, with Ginn's guitar slashing all over the music like a ghoul in a splatter flick, the rhythm section pounding out boneheaded riffs at hectic speed, Reyes conjuring up a different species of temper tantrum for each track. Ginn's lyrics were laced with satire, but it wasn't very pretty — on "Jealous Again" the singer rails against his girl-friend, "I won't beat you up and I won't push you around / 'Cause if I do then the cops will get me for doing it." And it was easy to miss the sarcasm of "White Minority" — "Gonna be a white minority / They're gonna be the majority / Gonna feel inferiority." The record was a harsh wake-up call for the California dream: for all the perfect weather and affluent lifestyles, there was something gnawing at its youth. Los Angeles wasn't a sun-splashed utopia anymore — it was an alienated, smog-choked sprawl rife with racial and class tensions, recession, and stifling boredom.

**B**lack Flag became more and more of a focal point for violence and condemnation. "The Black Flag Violence Must Stop!" proclaimed the title of one editorial. All the media hype was now attracting a crowd that was actually *looking* for violence — not that Black Flag did much to stop it. "Black Flag never said, 'Peace, love, and under-standing,'" says Rollins. "If it got crazy, we'd say, 'Guess what, it gets crazy.' We were the band that didn't go, 'Go gently into that night.' One of the main rallying war cries for us was 'What the fuck, fuck shit up!' Literally, that was one of our slogans."

Refusing to give up, the band made a hilariously provocative series of radio ads to promote their shows, twitting the LAPD mercilessly. In one ad, a mobster tells the owner of the Starwood club that booking Black Flag was a big mistake. "Chief Gates says this is going to cost the whole organization plenty," says the hoodlum. "We don't need this." An ad for a February '81 show with Fear, Circle Jerks, China White, and the Minute-men at the Stardust Ballroom opens with a voice that says, "Attention all units, we have a major disturbance at the Stardust Ballroom . . ." "Chief Gates is in a real uproar," says one cop, and his partner replies, "What the hell are we waiting for then, let's go over there and beat up some of them damn punk rockers!"

Eventually the violence became too much for the police and the community. If Black Flag was to keep playing shows, they'd have to play them out of town. But back then literally only a handful of American indie punk bands undertook national tours; lower-tier major label bands did them as promotional loss leaders, something independent label bands couldn't afford. Besides, there were few cities besides New York, L.A., and Chicago that had clubs that would even book punk rock bands. The solution was to tour as cheaply as possible and play anywhere they could — anything from a union hall to someone's rec room. They didn't demand a guarantee or accommodations or any of the usual perquisites, and they could survive that way — barely, anyway.

Ginn and Dukowski began collecting the phone numbers printed on various punk records and made calls to set up shows in far-flung towns. People were eager to help; after all, it was in everybody's interest to do so. In particular, North American punk pioneers like Vancouver, B.C.'s D.O.A. and San Francisco's Dead Kennedys shared what they'd learned on the road. "With those bands, we did a lot of networking, sharing information," says Ginn. "We'd find a new place to play, then we'd let them know because they were interested in going wherever they could and playing. Then we would help each other in our own towns."

Black Flag began making sorties up the California coast to play the Mabuhay Gardens in San Francisco, doing seven in all before venturing out as far as Chicago and Texas in the winter of '79–'80. Spot went along as soundman and tour manager, a job he would do, along with acting as SST's unofficial house engineer, for several years. His assessment of the situation: "Smelly. It was everyone in a Ford van with the laundry and the equipment. It was uncomfortable."

Wherever they went, they tried to play all-ages shows, even if it meant playing two sets, one for kids and one for drinkers. It was simply a way of making sure no one was excluded from their shows. But no matter how good their intentions, Black Flag's reputation preceded them. "In some towns it was like people expected us to pull up with a hundred L.A. punks and try to destroy their club," Ginn said. "We're not out to destroy anybody's club. We're just trying to play music."

By stringing together itineraries of adventurous venues who would host their virulent new brand of punk rock, bands like Black Flag,

D.O.A., and Dead Kennedys became the Lewis and Clarks of the punk touring circuit, blazing a trail across America that bands still follow today. But Black Flag was the most aggressive and adventurous of them all. "Black Flag, back then, was the one that was opening up these places to these audiences," says Mission of Burma's manager, Jim Coffman. "It was because of their diligence — Chuck's diligence. A lot of times you'd hear 'Black Flag played there.' And you'd say, 'OK, we'll play there then.'"

In June '80, months after Reyes quit, the band still hadn't found a replacement — and their West Coast tour was a week away. Then Dukowski bumped into Dez Cadena (whose father happened to be Ozzie Cadena, the legendary producer/A&R man who worked with virtually every major figure in jazz from the Forties through the Sixties). The rail-thin Cadena went to plenty of Black Flag shows, knew the words to all the songs, and got along fine with the band. Cadena protested that he'd never sung before, but in typical Black Flag fashion, Dukowski said it didn't matter. Cadena agreed to give it a try. "This was my favorite band and these guys were my friends," Cadena said, "so I didn't want to let them down."

Cadena worked like a charm, and his sincere, anguished bark — more hollering than singing — was a big change from the Johnny Rotten–inspired yowling of Morris and Reyes, and swiftly became a template for hardcore bands all around the South Bay and beyond. The band arguably reached the peak of its popularity with Cadena as lead singer. On the eve of a two-month U.S. tour, the band headlined a sold-out June 19, 1981, show with the Adolescents, D.O.A., and the Minutemen at the 3,500-seat Santa Monica Civic Auditorium, a feat they never again achieved. Noting the rowdiness and chaos, an *L.A. Times* piece on the show wondered, "Is the whole thing a healthy release of tension or yet another disturbing sign of the escalating violence in society?" And of course it was both.

On the other hand, not everybody thought slam dancing was such a great idea. "To me, they're just like the guys who try to bully you at school," fifteen-year-old Tommy Maloney of Canoga Park told the *L.A. Times*. "Who needs 'em? The shows would be a lot more fun if they found some other place to fool around."

Cadena's arrival coincided with the onset of the band's heavy touring. Unfortunately his inexperience as a singer — coupled with his heavy smoking and some woefully underpowered PA systems — meant his voice crumpled under the constant strain. Eventually everyone realized it would be best if he moved to guitar and the band got a new singer.

**H**enry Garfield grew up in the affluent Glover Park neighborhood of Washington, D.C., same as another future indie rock powerhouse, Ian MacKaye. "Word spread around that there was a kid with a BB gun down on W Street," MacKaye recalls. "So we went down to visit this kid and he was kind of a nerdy guy with glasses." But MacKaye soon realized Garfield's appearance was deceptive — his new acquaintance attended Bullis Academy, a hard-ass military-style school for problem kids. Garfield, MacKaye concluded, "was a toughie." Moreover, Garfield had a makeshift shooting gallery in his basement, and soon MacKaye and his friends were coming over and firing BB guns, listening to Cheech and Chong records, and admiring Garfield's pet snakes.

Garfield, an only child, didn't come from as affluent a home as most of his friends and didn't have a very positive self-image; not surprisingly, he often did whatever it took to fit in. "If it was the thing to do," he says, "I would be the first person to be Peer Pressure Boy and go be part of the throng without thinking."

Garfield's parents had divorced when he was a toddler; he had a short attention span and was put on Ritalin. Thanks to "bad grades, bad attitude, poor conduct," he got sent to Bullis, which favored corporal punishment. But instead of a disrespect for authority, the experience instilled in Garfield a very rigorous self-discipline. "It was very good for me," he says. "I really benefited from somebody going, 'No. No means no and you really *are* going to sit here until you get this right.'"

Despite Glover Park's comfortable environs, "it was a very rough upbringing in a lot of other ways," he says. "I accumulated a lot of rage by the time I was seventeen or eighteen." Some of that rage stemmed from intense racial tensions in Washington at the time; Garfield, like many white D.C. kids of his generation, got beaten up regularly by black kids simply because of his race.

But much of that rage came from problems at home. "A lot of things about my parents made me very angry," he says. He told *Rolling Stone* in 1992 that he had been sexually molested several times as a child; many of his spoken word monologues refer to a mentally abusive father. "Going to school in an all-boys school and never meeting any girls, that was very hard. I hardly met any women in high school and I really resented the fact that I was so socially inept because of being separated from girls in those years. There's a lot of that stuff.

"Also," he adds, "I'm just a freak."

Garfield and his buddy MacKaye were big fans of hard rockers like Ted Nugent and Van Halen, but they hungered for music that could top the aggression of even those bands. "We wanted something that just *kicked ass*," he says. "Then one of us, probably Ian, got the Sex Pistols record. I remember hearing that and thinking, 'Well, *that's* something. This guy is pissed *off*, those guitars are *rude*.' What a revelation!"

By the spring of '79 Garfield, MacKaye, and most of their friends had picked up instruments. Except Garfield *literally* picked up instruments. "I was everybody's roadie," he says. "I basically did that just to be able to hang out with all of my friends who were now playing. I was always picking up Ian's bass amp and putting it in his car. Not that he couldn't — he's the man and I'm going to carry the bass amp for the man."

But sometimes when Teen Idles singer Nathan Strejcek wouldn't show up for practice, Garfield would convince the band to let him on the mike. Then as word got around that Garfield could sing — or, rather, emit a compelling, raspy howl — H.R., singer of legendary D.C. hardcore band the Bad Brains, would sometimes pull him up to the mike and make him bark out a number.

In the fall of '80, D.C. punk band the Extorts lost singer Lyle Preslar to a new band that was being formed by MacKaye called Minor Threat. Garfield joined what was left of the Extorts to form S.O.A., short for State of Alert. Garfield put words to the five songs they already had, they wrote a few new ones, and these made up S.O.A.'s first and only record, the *No Policy* EP, released a few months after the band formed. In little over eight minutes, the ten songs took aim at things like drug users, people who dared ask Garfield what he was thinking, the way girls make you do dumb things, and the futility of existence, all in the bluntest of terms; the rest of the songs had titles like "Warzone," "Gang Fight," and "Gonna Hafta Fight."

After releasing the EP on Dischord Records, which MacKaye and some friends had founded, they rehearsed at drummer Ivor Hanson's house — and since Hanson's father was a top-ranking admiral, his house happened to be the Naval Observatory, the official residence of the vice president and the top brass of the navy. Every time they practiced, they'd have to drive past armed Secret Service agents.

S.O.A. played a grand total of nine gigs. "All of them were eleven to fourteen minutes each in duration because the songs were all like forty seconds," says Rollins, "and the rest of the time we were going, 'Are you ready? Are you ready?' Those gigs were poorly played songs in between 'Are you ready?'s."

Garfield spat out the lyrics like a bellicose auctioneer while the band banged out an absurdly fast oompah beat. Along with a few other D.C. bands, S.O.A. was inventing East Coast hardcore. "The reason we played short and so fast was because [original drummer Simon Jacobsen] never really played drums — he was just a really talented kid who picked it up," Rollins says. "So we didn't have much besides *dunt-dun-dunt-dun-dunt-dun* as far as a beat. And there wasn't enough to sing about that you couldn't knock out in a couple of words, like, 'I'm mad and you suck.' There wasn't a need for a lead [guitar] section — you never even thought of that."

Garfield had found his calling. Indeed, he was a classic frontman. "All I had was attitude," he says, "and a very intense need to be seen, a real I-need-attention thing."

Garfield quickly earned a reputation as a fighter at shows. "I was like nineteen and a young man all full of steam and getting in a lot of fights at shows, willingly, gratefully," he says. "*Loved* to get in the dust-ups. It was like rams on the side of the mountain. I wasn't very good but I enjoyed it very much."

He eventually worked his way up to manager of the Häagen-Dazs shop in Georgetown and was making enough money to have his own apartment, a stereo, and plenty of records. It was a pretty cushy life for a twenty-year-old. But that was all about to change.

One day a friend handed Garfield and MacKaye Black Flag's *Nervous Breakdown* EP, the one they'd read about in the L.A. punk fanzine *Slash*. It was a revelation. A few months later, in December '80 MacKaye heard that Black Flag was going to be playing D.C.'s 9:30 Club, so he called SST, got Chuck Dukowski on the phone, and offered the band a place to stay — his parents' house. They took him up on it. Garfield and all his punk buddies jumped at the chance to meet the band in person. "We're like, 'Whoa, you can go over there and touch the mighty Black Flag,'" he says. "We got to spend time with them. Here's a band whose set blew you away, whose record blew you away, and they're really cool people and you're talking to a real live rock band who tours, who you admire. And that was a big deal."

Dukowski took a shine to Garfield and gave him a tape of music the band had been working on. The songs connected heavily with Garfield, yet he couldn't help feeling he could sing them better than Cadena did. Dukowski kept in touch with Garfield, writing letters, hipping him to bands like Black Sabbath and the Stooges, calling from the road and shooting the breeze about music and what was happening in the D.C. scene.

Black Flag returned to the East Coast later that spring, and Garfield drove up to New York to catch their show. Arriving hours early, he hung out with Ginn and Dukowski all day, caught their Irving Plaza show, then accompanied them to an unannounced late-night gig at hardcore mecca 7A. It was now the wee hours of the morning and Garfield, realizing he had to get back to D.C. in time to open the ice-cream store at 9 A.M., requested the I-hate-my-job screed "Clocked In."

"And right before they went to play, I thought, 'Well, I know how to sing this song,' and went, 'Dez!' — gesturing toward the mike — 'Can I sing?'" he says. "And he went, 'Fuck yeah!' So I kind of jumped up on-stage and everyone else in Black Flag was like, 'All right, Henry's going to sing. Cool!' And they launch into the song and I sang the song like I thought it should be sung. I went for it with extreme aggression. And everyone in the crowd was like, 'Whoaaaa.' I got an immediate reaction. I watched people in the crowd go, 'Fuck yeah!' I remember looking over at Dukowski, who's looking over at me, going, 'Yeah. This is *happening*.'" Dukowski had just recognized that Garfield might be the lead singer they'd been looking for.

The song finished, Garfield dashed offstage, hopped into his beat-up old Volkswagen, and drove straight back to Washington.

A couple of days later, Garfield got a call at the ice-cream store: it was Dez Cadena, inviting him to come up to New York and jam. They'd cover the train fare. Garfield was a little puzzled. "I thought they were still up there and bored and wanted one of their buddies to come hang out with them," he says. Cadena said he was switching to guitar and the band needed a new singer.

Garfield was staggered. "I'm like, 'Holy shit. Am I being asked to au-dition for Black Flag?'" he says. "What a huge, monstrous proposition to a barely twenty-year-old guy with an extremely normal background. So I went, 'I'm on my way.'"

Garfield knew about Ginn's and Dukowski's wide-ranging musical tastes and had ingratiated himself by introducing them to exotica like Washington, D.C.'s unique go-go music. In doing so, Garfield had shown he had the stylistic range to develop with the band and move on from hardcore's already stifling loud-fast equation. "Henry," says Ginn, "was somebody who we felt could break out of that narrow mode."

Garfield made a 6 A.M. train the following morning and was soon standing in a dingy East Village rehearsal room with a microphone in his hand. "They said, 'OK, what do you want to play?'" he says. "And I remember looking at Greg Ginn and saying, 'Police Story.'" Then they ran through virtually every song in their set, with Garfield simply improvising to songs he didn't know. Then they did it all over again.

"OK, time for a band meeting," Dukowski announced. "You sit here," he ordered Garfield. When they came back after a few minutes, Dukowski said simply, "OK." "OK what?" Garfield replied. "OK, YOU WANT TO JOIN THIS BAND OR WHAT?" Dukowski thundered.

Garfield was stunned. Then he accepted. They sent him back to D.C. with a folder full of lyrics that he was to learn by the time they hooked up on tour in Detroit.

When he got home, he called his trusted friend Ian MacKaye and asked his advice. "Ian, should I do this?" Garfield asked.

"Henry," MacKaye simply replied, "*go.*"

Garfield quit his job, left his apartment, sold his records and his car, and bought a bus ticket to Detroit.

Cadena wanted to finish out the tour as vocalist, so Garfield hauled equipment, watched the band at work, and sang at sound check and during the encores all the way back to Los Angeles. Much to Garfield's relief, Cadena liked his singing. "It was my favorite band, and all of a sudden I'm the singer," he says. "It was like winning the lottery."

But being in Black Flag was not always a day at the beach. The third day of the tour, at Tut's in Chicago, Dukowski picked up his bass and brained a bouncer who was beating up a girl. Garfield was shocked. "That was a very bad time," he remembers. "The bouncer got stitched up and made it back to the set while we were still playing, wanting to throw down. We barely got out of there. . . . I'd been in Black Flag forty-eight hours at that time. 'OK, so this is what it's going to be.' And it was."

Garfield set out doing what so many come to California to do: reinvent himself. One of the first things he did upon arrival in L.A. was to get the Black Flag bars tattooed on his shoulder; and as a way of distancing himself from his troubled family life, he now called himself Henry Rollins, after a fake name he and MacKaye used to use.

Rollins was now in a much different world. For instance, there was Mugger, who worked at SST and roadied for the band. Mugger was a

HENRY ROLLINS, GREG
GINN, AND CHUCK
DUKOWSKI AT AN AUGUST
1981 SHOW AT THE
NOTORIOUS CUCKOO'S
NEST IN COSTA MESA —
ONE OF ROLLINS'S FIRST
BLACK FLAG SHOWS EVER.

© 1981 GLEN E. FRIEDMAN.
REPRINTED WITH PERMISSION FROM
THE BURNING FLAGS PRESS BOOK,
*FUCK YOU HEROES*

tough teenage runaway who was often so broke he'd have to eat dog food and bread, wadded up into a ball and downed very fast. This was not the type of fellow Rollins grew up with in Glover Park. "I stupidly asked Mugger — we were going to go out in the fall on tour — I go, 'Mugger, how are you going to go on the road with us?'" Rollins says. "He's like, 'What do you mean?' 'Well, you'll be in school.' And he started laughing. He says, 'Henry, I dropped out of school in sixth grade.'"

Band practices were attended by teenage runaways and other young people living on the fringe. "These people I started meeting, these punk rock kids, were dope-smoking, heroin-checking-out, 'lude-dropping people who didn't go to school," says Rollins. "They lived on the street or scammed here or there."

The new experiences continued for Rollins after his inaugural tour with Black Flag, a short trip up the California coast that autumn, when they came home to find that they'd been kicked out of their Torrance offices and had to stay with some "lazy slacker hippie punks" at an over-crowded crash pad in Hollywood. And once the police figured out Rollins was in Black Flag, he got the full treatment. "I got hassled three nights a week," Rollins says. "And it was scary. They'd come out of the car and twist your arm behind your back and say things like, 'Did you just call me a faggot?' I'd go, 'No, sir, I didn't say anything.' 'Did you call me a motherfucker?' 'No.' 'You want to fight me?' 'No, sir.'

"That really scared me," Rollins adds. "It freaked me out that an adult would do that. Then I learned that cops do all kinds of shit. My little eyes were opened big time."

Rollins also had to get used to the powerful, diverse personalities within the band. Ginn, a slow, deliberate speaker some seven years Rollins's senior, was "the introspective, quieter guy with immense power, but not showing his cards," Rollins says. "You have no idea how he thinks, what he thinks, what occurs to him. He's a super enigmatic guy to me."

Ginn was also a hard worker, "very principled, with the most monster work ethic of any single human being I've ever encountered in my life to this day," says Rollins. "If it took twenty hours, he did twenty hours. You'd say, 'Greg, aren't you tired?' And he go, 'Yeah.' He would never, ever complain."

Ginn's strong, silent temperament was attractive and inspiring, especially to Rollins, who had learned to idolize such types back at Bullis. Those around Ginn would feel honored if he spoke even a few words to them, but the flip side to that distance was Ginn's ability to dispense a devastatingly cold shoulder. "The silent treatment was the worst," Rollins recalls. "You never got yelled at; you just kind of got scowled at." In Black Flag, adds SST's Joe Carducci, "everything was withheld and communicated sort of telepathically in bad vibes."

Chuck Dukowski was something else altogether. Dukowski was "super charismatic — this guy had lightning bolts of ideas and rhetoric and hot air just coming off him," Rollins says. "I don't mean hot air like he was just talking, but always throwing out ideas, always asking questions, wanting to know everything — 'What are you reading?' 'Why did you like that book?' 'What would you do if someone tried to kill you?' Really intense shit. 'Would you eat raw meat to survive?' 'Would you fuck naked outside in public if you had to, to live?' He was this bass-wielding Nietzschean, just an explosive character.

"One of Dukowski's things was give everybody guns and a lot of people are going to die and after a while it will all get sorted out," says Rollins. "That's the kind of rhetoric Dukowski would spew in interviews.

It was like, 'Chuck, *whoa* . . .' And he would start laughing hysterically, like in this weird high-pitched laughter. I think he was more just abstracting his rage."

Dukowski, although not a technically gifted bassist, played with unbelievable intensity, throwing every molecule of his being into every note; he had simply willed himself into becoming a compelling musician. While Ginn was the band's fearless leader, Dukowski, with his restless intellect and 24-7 dedication to the band, was its revolutionary theoretician and spiritual mainspring — a regular mohawked Mephistopheles. Dukowski set about indoctrinating Rollins into the Black Flag mind-set, goading him to the same intensity. Dukowski recognized that with some discipline and intellectual underpinning, his protégé was capable of some dizzying heights.

At a 1982 show in Tulsa, two people showed up. Rollins was downhearted, but Dukowski straightened him out, telling him that although there might be only a couple of people there, they came to see Black Flag and it's not their fault nobody else came — you should play your guts out anytime anywhere and it doesn't matter how many people are there. That night Rollins dutifully gave it everything he had.

At one point Dukowski urged Rollins to try LSD. "It will help you not be such an asshole," Rollins recalls Dukowski telling him. Rollins was opposed to drugs, but his desire to fit into the band and please Dukowski and Ginn overruled his principles. As Rollins puts it, Dukowski "was such a big influence on me. If he said to jump off a roof, I would say, 'Which roof?'" Rollins eventually began taking large quantities of acid on later Black Flag tours, using it to skin-dive into the deepest, darkest depths of his soul and bring some disturbing discoveries back to the surface.

**B**lack Flag had tried recording material for their first album with Ron Reyes, who turned out to be studio-shy, then tried again with Cadena, but it didn't come out to their satisfaction. The third time, with Rollins, proved to be a charm.

Ginn disdained most hardcore because it didn't swing — the rhythms were straight up and down, with no lateral hip shake. To preserve the subtle but all-important swinging quality, he'd start the band playing new songs at a slow tempo, establishing a groove, and then gradually speeding it up at each practice, making sure to maintain that groove even at escape-velocity tempos. Very quickly Rollins abandoned the spitfire bark he'd used with S.O.A. and began to swing with the rest of the band. Just a few months after he'd joined, he'd already begun to redefine the sound not only of Black Flag but of hardcore itself.

Released in January '82, *Damaged* is a key hardcore document, perhaps *the* key hardcore document. It boiled over with rage on several fronts: police harassment, materialism, alcohol abuse, the stultifying effects of consumer culture, and, on just about every track on the album, a particularly virulent strain of self-lacerating angst — all against a savage, brutal backdrop that welded apoplectic punk rock to the anomie of dark Seventies metal like Black Sabbath.

The songs took fleeting but intense feelings and impulses and exploded them into entire all-consuming realities. So when Ginn wrote a chorus like "Depression's got a hold of me / Depression's gonna kill me," it sounded like the whole world was going to end. "That was Black Flag: when you lose your shit," says Rollins. The music was the same way — blitzkrieg assaults so completely overwhelming, so consuming and intense that for the duration of the song, it's hard to imagine ever listening to anything else.

Hardcore's distinctive mix of persecution and bravado crystallized perfectly in the refrain of the opening "Rise Above," as definitive a hardcore anthem as will ever be penned: "We are tired of your abuse! / Try to stop us, it's no use!" goes the rabble-rousing chorus. But most songs are avowals of suicidal alienation, first-person portraits of confused, desperate characters just about to explode — "I want to live! I wish I was dead!" Rollins rants on "What I See." Occasional humor made the anguish both more believable and more horrific, as in the sarcastic "TV Party" — "We've got nothing better to do / Than watch TV and have a couple of brews," sings a charmingly off-key guy chorus over a goofy quasi-surf backing track.

Musically, the six-minute "Damaged I" is an anomaly — loud but not fast, it is based on a slowly trudging guitar riff with Rollins ad-libbing a psychodrama about being ordered around and abused, then retreating into a protective mental shell. The last sounds of the song — and the record — are Rollins barking, "No one comes in! STAY OUT!" It's hard not to read it as straight autobiography.

Today *Damaged* is easily assimilated as hardcore, but at the time there was little precedent for music of such scathing violence. Yet Ginn's explanation was typically matter-of-fact: "People work all day and they want a release," he told the *L.A. Times.* "They want a way to deal with all the frustrations that build up. We try to provide that in our music."

The album — and Rollins in particular — introduced an unforgiving

introspection and a downright militaristic self-discipline. Perhaps because he was trying to make sense of his childhood traumas, Rollins
threw himself headlong into Ginn's psychological pain research. Rollins
harbored huge amounts of anger and resentment, and Black Flag's violent music unleashed his pent-up aggressions in a raging torrent.

Ginn and Dukowski had finally found their boy. "What I was doing
kind of matched the vibe of the music," Rollins explains. "The music was
intense and, well, I was as intense as you needed."

With his tattoos, skinhead, square jaw, and hoarse, martial bellow,
Rollins became a poster boy for hardcore — unlike the older Dukowski
and Ginn, Rollins looked like he could have been an HB'er. And like so
many punks, parental and societal neglect had left him angry and alienated as hell. As the band plugged in and tuned up, Rollins would stalk the
stage like a caged animal, dressed only in black athletic shorts, glowering
and grinding his teeth (to get pumped up before a show, he'd squeeze a
treasured number thirteen pool ball he'd taken from a club in San Antonio). Then the band would throw down the hammer, and the entire room
would turn into a chaotic whirlpool of human flesh, its chance collisions
oblivious to the rhythm of the music. Rollins's copious sheen of sweat
would rain down on the first few rows in a continuous shower while his
anguished howling tore through Ginn's electric assault like a blowtorch
through a steel fence.

Robo played as if he were fending off attacks from his drums and
cymbals. Dukowski tore sounds from his bass with utmost vengeance,
doubling over and grimacing with the effort, banging his head and
screaming at the audience, far from any microphone, while his fingers
pummeled the strings like pistons. Ginn played in a spread-legged
stance, making occasional lunges like a fencer, shaking his head from
side to side as if in disbelief of his own ecstacy while his guitar barked like
a junkyard dog, utterly unencumbered by anything that would make it
sound melodious.

Opening for the Ramones at the Hollywood Palladium in the fall of
'82, Black Flag suffered from bad sound, but as one reviewer put it,
"Rollins still carried the show with his truly menacing persona. He spit
out the lyrics, convulsing to the beat, grinding his hips blatantly. Such a
gruesome and intimidating display of rock aggression and frustration was
hardly endearing, but like a high-speed car crash, you couldn't keep your
eyes — or ears — off them." Another writer observed that Rollins was "a
cross between Jim Morrison and Ted Nugent. No wonder the kids eat
him up." A larger-than-usual contingent of L.A.'s finest guarded the

venue, blocking off some surrounding streets, as helicopters hovered overhead. The show went off without incident.

The media, from local fanzines all the way up to the *Los Angeles Times*, had the field day with the band's notoriety. One skateboard magazine claimed the band had "detonated explosive riots at numerous gigs," which was an exaggeration, although a show at the Polish Hall in Hollywood resulted in a bout of bottle and chair throwing that caused $4,000 in damage to the building as well as one arrest and two injured cops.

*Boston Rock* interviewer Gerard Cosloy asked why they didn't try to stop violence at their shows. Dukowski responded with a succinct summation of the punk principle of anarchy. "Do we have a right to act as leaders, to tell people how to act?" Dukowski replied. "The easy solution isn't a solution, it's the fucking problem. It's too easy to have someone tell you what to do. It is harder to make your own decision. We put a certain amount of trust into the people that come to see us."

"Through interviews like this," Ginn added, "maybe we can let people know what we do stand for, that we're against beating people up, that we're against putting people down because they have longer hair. We've made our statement, but we won't prevent people from listening to something else, dressing some other way, or doing what they want. We aren't policemen."

Still, anyone who looked remotely like a hippie stood a good chance of getting roughed up at a Black Flag show. Maybe that's part of the reason Ginn started growing his hair after *Damaged*, with Rollins and the rest of the band soon following suit — it was yet another way to twit their increasingly conformist audience. "We're trying to always make a statement that it doesn't matter what you're wearing," said Ginn. "It's how you feel and how you think."

**D**amaged made a fairly big impact in Europe and England, especially with the press, who were fascinated by the revelation that there was a really radical punk rock scene developing in the beach communities of Southern California, which they had previously looked on as an idyllic promised land, seemingly the last place where kids would flip a musical middle finger at society. "And it caused certain people to think, 'Well, is this legitimate?'" says Ginn. "There's that element of 'This is wrong, coming from this place. People like that should be coming from Birmingham, England. You guys have it good.' But when you're surrounded by Genesis fans, I don't know how idyllic that is. When you're surrounded by that materialistic kind of a thing and you're looking for something deeper than that, then that's not an ideal environment."

A December '81 tour of the U.K. was a nightmare: freezing cold conditions, regular physical attacks from skinheads and rival English punk bands, and all manner of bloodshed onstage — at one show Ginn bled profusely after someone threw a bullet at his head; he staggered offstage, but not before angrily heaving a metal folding chair into the crowd. They even missed their first flight home.

Once the *Damaged* album was out, the band toured from early May all the way through mid-September '82, a long, grueling trek. But their headlong momentum was about to come to a grinding halt.

SST had been selling its releases to small distributors at a deliberately low list price. But because those distributors usually sold import records, their releases usually wound up in specialty shops, unthinkingly stuck in the import section and at top-dollar import prices. Being a punk rock band on an independent label, Black Flag would never appear in the rock sections of ordinary record stores, alphabetized between Bad Company and Black Sabbath, where Ginn felt they belonged. So he decided to take Black Flag's next record to a mainstream distributor. Many larger independent distributors wouldn't even return SST's phone calls, but one major did — MCA.

As part of the bargain, Ginn agreed to corelease the Black Flag album with Unicorn, a small label distributed by MCA. But in 1982, just as the album was to go out to stores, complete with the MCA logo on it, someone from *Rolling Stone* allegedly bad-mouthed Black Flag to MCA distribution chief Al Bergamo. Bergamo abruptly announced it would be "immoral" to release *Damaged*, claiming the album was "anti-parent, past the point of good taste." "It certainly wasn't like Bob Dylan or Simon and Garfunkel and the things they were trying to say," he added.

Black Flag claimed they'd warned MCA of the record's content, but that MCA, convinced the band would sell a lot of records, looked the other way. In his book *Rock and the Pop Narcotic*, Joe Carducci, who began overseeing sales, promotion, and marketing for SST in 1981, claimed MCA's disapproval of the content was a red herring — the real reason was that Unicorn was so deeply in debt to MCA that it made no fiscal sense for MCA to continue the relationship; Black Flag's "anti-parent" lyrics were just an excuse to sever ties with Unicorn.

So the band went to the pressing plant and put stickers with Bergamo's "anti-parent" quote over the MCA logo on twenty thousand copies of the record. Then a tangle of lawsuits erupted when SST claimed that Unicorn didn't pay SST's rightful royalties and expenses for the album.

Unicorn countersued and got an injunction preventing Black Flag from releasing any further recordings until the matter was settled. When SST issued the retrospective compilation of unreleased Black Flag material called *Everything Went Black* with no band credit on it, Unicorn hauled SST into court in July '83 and painted the band as, in Ginn's words, "some kind of threat to society." The judge found Ginn and Dukowski, as co-owners of SST, to have violated the injunction and sent them both to L.A. County Jail for five days on a contempt of court citation.

Upon his release, Ginn was ever the stoic. "He wouldn't even discuss it," Rollins says. "He just said, 'Practice is at seven.' He didn't discuss it. I'm not kidding — not a word. I have no idea what it was like for Greg Ginn in jail. He said nothing except he got on the bus to go to County, he had a sandwich or some kind of food in his front pocket, and a guy reached over the seat and took it from him."

Ginn still won't say much about his experience in jail, deferring to people who have spent much longer periods of time in far worse prisons. "It's not something I would recommend" is all he'll say. "It's a very demeaning thing. And I'd recommend to anybody that they try to stay out of there."

Finally, Unicorn went bankrupt in late 1983 and Black Flag was free to release records again.

But the ordeal had taken a heavy toll on Black Flag. *Damaged* had gone out of print and the legal fight had drastically curtailed touring — a heavy blow to the band's popularity, not to mention their income. And all the strife, tension, and poverty was causing considerable turnover in the band. "People would get worn out," says Ginn. "Seven guys living in the same room and touring for six months and then still having debts hanging over our head."

By this point Robo was long gone. A Colombian national, he'd encountered visa problems at the end of the December '81 U.K. tour and couldn't come back into the country. (The band had flown in the Descendents' Bill Stevenson to finish the tour with a week of East Coast shows. Stevenson lived down the street from Ginn; the Descendents — a smart, jumpy, pop-punky quartet given to titles like "I Like Food" and "My Dad Sucks" — was Black Flag's brother band and shared their practice space.)

In the first half of '82, a slight, corkscrew-haired sixteen-year-old known only as Emil began drumming with the band. He didn't last long. The story goes that Emil's girlfriend was pressuring him to quit the band and spend more time with her and that when Ginn got wind of this, he convinced Mugger to turn Emil against his girlfriend by claiming he'd slept with her. The strategy backfired, prompting a brawl with Mugger. Emil left in the middle of the marathon 1982 U.S. tour and was replaced by D.O.A.'s incredible Chuck Biscuits.

On a West Coast tour, that lineup played a grange hall in the tiny northern Washington town of Anacortes. "Henry was incredible," raved writer Calvin Johnson, reviewing the show for the fanzine *Sub Pop*, "pacing back and forth, lunging, lurching, growling; it was all real, the most intense emotional experiences I have ever seen."

Unfortunately, Biscuits lasted only several months. Biscuits, Ginn says, would not agree to Black Flag's rigorous rehearsal schedule, which was six days a week and up to eight hours a day. "Greg Ginn practices were like the long march to the sea," Rollins says. "Talk about a work ethic, he is like Patton on steroids.

"Black Flag was a bunch of very disciplined people," Rollins continues. "Very ambitious, super disciplined. Being in that band was like getting drilled all the time. You practiced the set once, twice a night. We had band practice six, seven days a week. On the weekends I had to rest my voice. I'd go, 'Greg, I'm going to a friend's house this weekend because she's going to feed me. And I will be back on Monday and I'm not going to sing Saturday and Sunday because I'm going to give my voice a rest.' And Greg would be kind of pissed. Greg would be in there seven days a week. That's how Black Flag was. There was never any anarchy in our lifestyle."

Rollins's desire to occasionally rest his voice wasn't the only thing that alienated him from the rest of the band. "I never talked a lot to Henry," Ginn says. "Henry was always kind of the loner type of person." Another part of Rollins's isolation stemmed from the fact that he didn't smoke pot and instead drank vast quantities of coffee, meaning he was amped up on caffeine while others were stoned.

"Understand another thing: Black Flag was never a group of friends," says Rollins, "never a big camaraderie." Dukowski did become Rollins's sardonic guru, but Rollins never really befriended the enigmatic Ginn. "You never knew where you stood with Greg," says Rollins. "Newer recruits would come to me and say, 'Does Greg like me? How am I doing with Greg?' And I'd go, 'You're doing fine, just don't worry about it, play your song, play like Greg says, it's cool.'"

**B**ill Stevenson rejoined Black Flag in the winter of '82–'83, in the depths of the Unicorn fracas. Stevenson was a bright guy and knew about songwriting and production, which was both good and bad — although he could assist Ginn on both those fronts, it sometimes meant he would butt heads with him, too.

They set off on a U.S. tour that January, then went over to Europe for a tour with the Minutemen, in the midst of the coldest winter the Continent had seen in years. The way Rollins tells it, the whole tour was an unending succession of unheated clubs and punk rock squats, starvation, misery, and pain; to top it off, their van got repossessed. Very early in the tour, Rollins had already grown disenchanted with at least one of his tourmates. "Mike Watt never stops talking," Rollins wrote in his tour diary, later published as *Get in the Van*. "I think I'm going to punch Mike Watt's lights out before this is all over."

But he held far more contempt for the people in the audience. At a German show, "I bit a skinhead on the mouth and he started to bleed real bad," wrote Rollins. "His blood was all over my face." In Vienna a member of the audience bashed Rollins in the mouth with the microphone; people spat on his face; someone burned his legs with a cigar; he tried to protect a stage diver from some overzealous bouncers and got punched in the jaw — *by the stage diver* — for his trouble. When the police came, the crowd beat them up, took their uniforms, and allegedly killed their police dog.

When a rowdy punk pestered Ginn during a show in England, Rollins cleaned his clock. "His mohawk," wrote Rollins, "made a good handle to hold on to when I beat his face into the floor." Later Ginn berated Rollins for the beating, calling him a "macho asshole." Rollins felt Ginn would feel differently if *he'd* been attacked. "I don't bother talking to him about it because you can't talk to Greg," Rollins wrote. "You just take it and keep playing. Whatever."

When they pulled up to one Italian club, there was a crowd of menacing-looking punks waiting for them. The Italian punks circled the van and started rocking it and pounding on the windows. The band was getting scared, trying to figure out how to get into the club without sustaining grievous bodily harm. At last they burst out of the van and made a run for it. The rabid mob immediately surrounded them — and began hugging and kissing the band and thrusting presents into their hands.

**W**hile Black Flag was sorting out its legal situation, leading hard-core bands like Minor Threat had broken up, the Bad Brains went on indefinite hiatus, and the hardcore scene had become absurdly regimented and inbred, both socially and musically. Raymond Pettibon's illustration for Black Flag's 1981 *Six Pack* EP had been uncannily prescient: a punk who had literally painted himself into a corner. Black Flag's post-*Damaged* music was devoted to charting a course out of that stylistic cul-de-sac. This meant going back to bands like the Stooges, the MC5, and especially Black Sabbath for ways to convey aggression and power without resorting to the cheap trick of velocity (although the band stuck with the even cheaper trick of volume). So Ginn slowed down the new Black Flag music, reasoning that although a speeding bullet can pierce a wall, a slow-rolling tank does more damage.

But, shrewdly realizing that plenty of other bands, bands he had plenty of contempt for, would take his ideas, turn them into a formula, and sell more tickets and records than Black Flag did, Ginn withheld the new approach from outsiders. "They didn't want to play the new songs because there were too many bands ready to steal the ideas that they were working on," says Joe Carducci. "A lot of people were looking to them for 'What do you do with this after you speed it up to the breaking point, *then* what do you do, Greg?' So Greg would keep that stuff. . . . He didn't play it in front of other people."

But Ginn would have to make changes in the band if he was to realize his new musical vision. As a guitarist, Dez Cadena was conservative, leaning toward generic classic rock like Humble Pie and ZZ Top, which Ginn just could not countenance any longer. Cadena left the group in August '83 to form his own band, DC3, which recorded several classic rock–inspired albums for SST.

And by the fall Chuck Dukowski left the group, too. Ginn was a hard man to work for, but by this point Dukowski was getting the brunt of his ambivalence. "Greg was not going to be pleased with anybody, no matter who they were, on whatever level," says Joe Carducci. "There's that sense with Greg that it's never good enough."

"I felt that we had reached a dead end in terms of the music that we were playing together," Ginn says, adding that his musical chemistry with Dukowski was more a product of endless practicing than natural affinity. "In a way, I always felt that it was kind of glued together in a certain respect, instead of a real natural groove." Ginn had felt this for a long time, but Dukowski was so fully dedicated to the band, such an integral part of its esprit de corps, that letting him go was difficult.

Ginn couldn't bring himself to criticize Dukowski outright and instead made life difficult for him in the hopes that Dukowski would quit on his own accord. But Dukowski had pinned too much of his self-image and energies on the band to just leave, and the stalemate lingered for many agonizing months. Finally, without consulting anyone else in the band, Rollins simply took it upon himself to end the standoff and fire Dukowski.

Even though Dukowski didn't play on the band's next album, *My War*, it includes two songs he wrote — one of them the title track — so the feelings couldn't have been that hard on either side. Dukowski also went on to become the band's de facto manager and the hardworking head of SST's booking arm, Global Booking. This was a masterstroke, as relentless touring would literally put the label's bands on the map and help establish SST's dominance of the indie market in the coming decade.

But the departure of his partner in crime took its toll on Ginn. For the first five years, Ginn felt no need to rule the band with an iron hand — he actually seemed to enjoy the chaos. "But then by '83, he'd taken total control of the band," says Carducci. "And he didn't seem to be enjoying himself at all."

The band's work ethic only intensified. "Greg was a fanatic and most people are not," says Carducci. "He took the business down to a level that was beneath the level lightweights could handle: they couldn't handle sleeping in the van, they couldn't handle not knowing where they were going to stay, they couldn't handle the clubs." On the road the band got $5 a day. Toward the end they made ten, and on the final tour, twenty. "If we got a flat tire, we would get an old tire that was discarded in the back of a gas station that they'd given up on and put that on," says Ginn. "It was real bare bones."

On the early tours, audiences could vary anywhere between twenty-five and two hundred. As their popularity climbed, they eventually found themselves playing six months of the year or more. But when the tours began lasting that long, it also meant that the band members couldn't hold down significant day jobs once they got home, and that's when things got really tough.

Ginn's parents would often help out with food and even clothing; Mr. Ginn would buy used clothing for pennies a pound, and the band would take a big sack of it on tour, pulling whatever they liked out of the grab bag. So much for punk fashion.

"Without the Ginn family," says Rollins, "there would not have been a Black Flag." Mr. Ginn would rent vans and Ryder trucks for the band and was so proud of his son that when he'd teach classes at Harbor College, he'd often have the Black Flag insignia painted on the pocket of his button-down shirts. Often Mr. Ginn would make a mess of grilled cheese sandwiches, buy a few gallons of apple juice and some fruit at a farm stand, and bring it to SST. "We would eat cheese sandwiches, avocados that were five for a dollar, and apple juice for days," says Rollins. "Those things would get moldy, you'd just scrape the mold off and keep eating."

It sounds pretty rough, but Ginn, ever the stoic, downplays the hardship. "I think people would consider it rough but that's all relative — there's things I would consider rough, like war," says Ginn. "I never considered it rough. I considered it not having money, but I always think, if you're asleep on a floor, how can you tell the difference anyway — you're asleep."

Perhaps because Rollins had grown up relatively affluent and an only child, he sought as much comfort and privacy as possible. When the band came back to L.A., he'd find a friend with an extra bedroom or sleep at the Ginn family's house rather than live in communal squalor with the band. "Even though he really tried, he was never comfortable with that kind of existence," says Ginn. "Which isn't a bad thing — I think that may be more typical of the average person. Obviously, I guess it is."

Rollins was over at the Ginns' house so often that they finally invited him to live there. They offered him a bedroom, but Rollins chose what he called "the shed," a small, furnished outbuilding that had been Mr. Ginn's study. Rollins's insinuation into his family annoyed Greg Ginn to no end; he got even more annoyed when Mrs. Ginn asked if her son smoked marijuana and Rollins said yes.

The rest of the band lived where they rehearsed. "Even at the end, we lived with seven people in one room," says Ginn. "And we always lived in those kind of situations — living where we practiced, or whatever, living in vans and that kind of stuff. Pretty early on, materially we didn't fit in at all."

"There were some droughts there where you were eating a Snickers bar and you'd walk in and someone would say, 'Where'd you get that?'" Rollins recalls. "You go, 'Well, I bought it.' 'Where'd you get the money to get that?' 'Uh, OK, I took a dollar out of a cash order.' That's how broke we were." Rollins's mother would occasionally send him a twenty-dollar bill and he'd splurge on a pint of milk and a cookie from the 7-Eleven. "I'd say, 'Well, I'm going out for a walk,'" says Rollins, "go over there and find a place to hide and eat it and make sure the crumbs were off my face. That's how up against it we were at certain times."

Sometimes they'd saunter into a local Mexican restaurant and buy a soda. "Then you'd wait for a family to get up and just grab the little kid's tostada that he couldn't finish and take it back to your plate before any-one noticed, because if anyone saw you, you would really bum them out and you'd get thrown out," says Rollins. "That's not the way I was raised. I was raised [with] clean white underwear, three square meals, a bed with Charlie Brown blankets, total middle-class upbringing. So all this was new. Scamming on chicks for a hamburger — we would go to Oki Dogs, hit on punker chicks, and say, 'Hey, we're poor, feed us.' We'd get Valley Girl punkers to feed us. And you'd hang out all night waiting for that plate of french fries.

"The thing that kept everyone living this pretty torturous lifestyle is the music was *that good*," says Rollins, "and we knew it. At the end of the day, we had no money, we were scruffy, we stunk, the van stunk, everyone was against us. But you'd hear that music and know, oh yeah, we fuckin' *rule*."

Even though they hadn't yet found a replacement for Dukowski, they were anxious to record their next album — the new slow, metallic Black Flag just couldn't wait to be born any longer. So Ginn, as "Dale Nixon," played bass on *My War* himself, often practicing with the hyperactive Stevenson for eight hours a day, just to teach him how to play slowly and let the rhythm, as Ginn puts it, "ooze out." "He wasn't used to playing that slow," says Ginn. "I guess nobody was."

*My War* inverts the punk-to–Black Sabbath ratio of *Damaged* — this time Sabbath's leaden gloom and doom predominates, albeit pumped up with a powerful shot of punk vitriol and testosterone. The sound got much more metallic and sludgy, with Ginn anchoring the music with bottom-heavy bass-and-guitar formations. Topped off with some serious jazz fusion influences, *My War* sometimes comes off like the Maha-vishnu Orchestra after a bad day on the chain gang.

Much of the material was strong, but because the band was solely a studio entity, there's a frustrating lack of ensemble feeling to the tracks; in particular, Rollins's vocals and Ginn's leads sound disconnected from everything else. Then there was Ginn's relentless perfectionism in the studio, which may well be what drained the spark out of many of Black Flag's later recordings. "He was never willing to just let the performance be," says Spot, who coproduced the album. "And frankly, I think that's where he screwed up." Accordingly, the band's best recordings from the later period are the live ones, *Live '84* and 1985's *Who's Got the 10½?*

*My War* boiled hardcore angst down to a wall of self-hatred so densely constructed that it could never fall; on "Three Nights" Rollins compares his life to a piece of shit stuck to his shoe, railing, "And I've been grinding that stink into the dirt / For a long time now." But sometimes the lyrics were beside the point — on the title track, Rollins's bloodcurdling screams and disturbingly animalistic roars speak volumes.

To most listeners, the music had lost the energy and wit of before — Rollins bellows anguished speeches, not the searing, direct poetry of the past. The labored chord progressions and clunky verbiage seem like shackles purposely attached to the band in order to see if they can still run with the weight. For the most part, they could — the playing is ferocious and the band often builds up quite a head of steam only to hit the brick wall of an awkward chord or tempo change. But any momentum *My War* achieves is stopped cold by a trio of unbearably slow six-minute-plus songs on side two. Although Ginn wrote the lyrics, "Scream" sums up Rollins's artistic raison d'être in a mere four lines: "I might be a big baby / But I'll scream in your ear / 'Til I find out / Just what it is I am doing here." The song ends with Rollins howling like someone being flayed alive.

Ponderous and dire, the sludgefest flew directly in the face of the ever-escalating velocity of hardcore — within the hardcore scene, side two of *My War* was as heretical as Bob Dylan playing electric guitar on one side of *Bringing It All Back Home*. "It was definitely a line in the sand," says Mudhoney's Mark Arm, who had been seeing Black Flag shows in Seattle since 1981. "It was sort of an intelligence test — if you could handle the changes of Black Flag, you weren't an idiot. And if you thought they were just selling out, then you were an idiot."

Black Flag's hardcore-metal alloy proved to be far ahead of its time. But while the bravery and vision of such a move was admirable, it also lost the band a lot of fans. Even *Maximumrocknroll* publisher Tim Yohannon, one of the band's most ardent early supporters, didn't like the record. While Yohannon acknowledged the band had labored long and hard to break ground for punk and endured crippling legal harassment in the process, those trials and tribulations couldn't redeem the record. "To me," wrote Yohannon, "it sounds like Black Flag doing an imitation of Iron Maiden imitating Black Flag on a bad day. The shorter songs are rarely exciting and the three tracks on the b-side are sheer torture. I know depression and pain are hallmarks of Black Flag's delivery, but boredom, too?"

Black Flag eventually released four albums in 1984. Ginn was unsure whether the effort and money expended in promoting albums was cost-effective so he simply decided to put out four albums in quick succession and promote them on the strength of solid touring. College radio, bewildered by the glut of releases, didn't know what to do with any of them.

**B**y the time of the *Slip It In* tour later in '84, the band was opening with an overtly metal-influenced instrumental while Rollins waited in the wings. A couple of years earlier, such a move would have prompted a hail of booing from hardcore purists, but now it only prompted furious moshing from a crowd that now mixed longhairs, punks, and metalheads. In the middle of the set, Rollins would catch his breath while they uncorked another instrumental, then come back and descend into the mire of the sludgy new material.

Both Black Flag and its audience had begun with frenzied two- and three-chord punk rock and progressed into more challenging realms. Ginn was taking a band and a following that had started at ground zero, musically speaking, and slowly lifting it up. "There weren't many people that had the status to ask something of all of these fuckin' misfits — and get them to do it," says Carducci. "Greg is one of the few people."

The problem was much of the audience wasn't always interested in going along for the ride. "We didn't pander to the audience; we didn't cater to them," says Ginn. "My attitude was always give the audience what they need, not what they want." Both band and audience thrived on the tension. As *Puncture*'s Patti Stirling wrote in a review of the *Live '84* album, "Black Flag's music creates itself best when the band has an audience; they unleash emotions at each other. It's violently sensual at best and irritatingly childish fighting at worst."

Then there was the fact that the band never explicitly allied themselves with the punk scene — their songs were introspective, never about "punk unity" or bashing Reagan; their opening bands were either not classically punk (Minutemen, Saccharine Trust) or completely obnoxious (Nig-Heist); except for Dukowski's mohawk, they didn't even go in for stereotypical punk fashion.

"People can get real nasty if you don't do what they think you should do," Ginn observes. And the nastier segments of Black Flag's audience focused their wrath on Rollins. People were not content merely to spit on Rollins — they would put out cigarettes on him, douse him with cups of urine, punch him in the mouth, stab him with pens, heave beer mugs at him, scratch him with their nails, hit him in the groin with water balloons. On tour, his chest often looked like a disaster area.

And Rollins was not shy about fighting back. At one early show in Philadelphia, a guy in the audience constantly taunted and pushed Rollins, who did nothing but grin demonically, looking just like Jack Nicholson in *The Shining*. After several long minutes, Rollins finally snapped, dragging the man onstage and holding him down as he repeatedly punched him in the face. Eventually the man escaped back into the crowd. The band, clearly used to this sort of thing, never missed a beat. Judging by Rollins's tour memoir *Get in the Van*, Rollins continued this sort of thing almost nightly for the duration of his tenure in Black Flag.

Yet none of the other band members either attracted or dispensed such violence. "I think Henry, his ego, in a way, brought some of that stuff across," says Ginn. "At some times he had a condescending attitude toward the audience, and people pick up on that." Rollins maintained a masochistic tough-guy act onstage, slithering like a snake through the crowd and biting people's ankles along the way, rolling in broken glass, daring audience members to fight with him, and yet taking extreme umbrage when people took him up on it. "When they spit at me, when they grab at me, they aren't hurting me," Rollins wrote. "When I push out and mangle the flesh of another, it's falling so short of what I really want to do to them."

**G**inn didn't want exact substitutes for departed band members — that way, old material got a fresh treatment; new material came from a different direction. Better musicianship was one of his prime goals, which is why he hired Kira Roessler shortly after recording *My War*. Roessler, who had been kicking around the L.A. punk scene since she was sixteen, was jamming with Dez Cadena's DC3 at Black Flag's practice space when Ginn overheard her and asked her to join Black Flag. "They were the coolest band I knew — my favorite," said Roessler, "so of course I said yes."

Roessler could play heavily and aggressively like Dukowski did, but she also played with more fluidity and musicality. And to seal the deal, Roessler and Ginn shared a similar work ethic: "Whatever you do, do it all the way," as Roessler put it. "It was agreed that it wasn't going to be half-assed. This is what it is — less is not an option."

**T**he Minutemen's Mike Watt recalls stopping by the studio when Black Flag was mixing 1984's *Slip It In* ("A bunch of hands fighting on the control board; it was hilarious," he recalls), and there on the console was an LP by the commercial metal band Dio. Not surpisingly, *Slip It In* often emulates the worst aspects of its sources. As critic Ira Robbins wrote, *Slip It In* "blurs the line between moronic punk and moronic metal." The Neanderthal sexuality of the title track ("Say you don't want it / But you slip it in") and the simplistic doominess of so many other songs from this era amply bear out the comment. Plenty of *Slip It In* is absolutely dreadful — "Rat's Eyes" ("If you look through rat's eyes / You will talk about shit real good") is an object lesson in plodding; the ponderous instrumental "Obliteration" isn't much better. And yet occasional stretches of music were the most powerful the band had ever done, largely because they now had a killer bassist. Speed, they proved, wasn't the only path to power — even the Sex Pistols rarely exceeded midtempo — it just took musicianship to pull it off.

After recording *Slip It In*, Ginn, Rollins, Stevenson, and Roessler woodshedded all through the winter of '83, practicing up to five hours a day, six days a week in a dank, stinking, windowless basement space below the SST offices, with floor, walls, and ceiling covered in layers of cheap shag carpet. They emerged as a powerful and cohesive unit for an eleven-week early '84 U.S. tour for *My War*. They were eager to hit the road and work their first proper album in two years — "Kill Everyone Now" was the tour motto. They toured virtually the entire year, coming home for a couple of weeks here and there to record.

On the downtime during the Unicorn fiasco, Rollins had started a demanding weight-lifting program; by the time the band hit the road in 1984, he had developed a rippling carapace of muscle. Not just a way of intimidating would-be attackers, his powerful physique was a metaphor for the impregnable emotional shield he was developing around himself.

The song "My War" rails against some vague "you" as being "one of them." Although it was Dukowski's lyric, Rollins seemed to take the concept to heart: during the *Slip It In* tour, he spotted Derrick Bostrom of tourmates the Meat Puppets carrying a copy of the Jacksons' *Triumph* album. "I always knew you were one of *them*," Rollins sneered. In fact, Rollins seemed to be living out many of Ginn's and Dukowski's lyrics to a profound degree. "I conceal my feelings so I won't have to explain / What I can't explain anyway," Rollins hollers on "Can't Decide." Ginn's lyrics certainly applied to their aloof author, but it was Rollins who was acting them out with a vengeance.

By now the band was quite longhaired, fueling even more ire among the audience. How could they be punk *and* have hippie hair? The band readily worked their lengthy coiffures into the show. "Black Flag was actually an intense hair-tossing contest between guitarist Greg Ginn and singer Henry Rollins," wrote *Puncture*'s Patti Stirling. "The suspense of whether they would knock heads, causing dual concussions, was chilling."

The band was now playing some of its most blazing shows. Unfortunately, the whole thing was beginning to unravel.

Early on, Rollins gladly deferred to Ginn and Dukowski during interviews — after all, they'd been the only constant members of the band, and the press naturally gravitated toward them as spokesmen. But then Dukowski left and gradually Ginn ceded the media spotlight to the charismatic, quotable Rollins. "I *liked* the fact that somebody was actually into hanging out with these people and doing these interviews and photo sessions," Ginn says. "There's nothing that I find more aggravating than sitting and doing a photo session. There's nothing that makes me feel more stupid. And Henry would enjoy that stuff, so I thought that was ideal. . . . He would do certain functions and I would do certain functions in terms of managing the band and this and that. It split up the work."

Ginn feels Rollins saw increased media exposure as a way to get out from under his shadow. "I think he competed, in a sense, with that kind of respect, as [someone who was] masterminding this thing," says Ginn, "so he tried to paint himself into that type of situation." And so Rollins did countless interviews despite his outspoken complaints about interviews throughout his tour diaries.

The fact was Rollins was now in his early twenties and swiftly outgrowing the subservient, self-denying side of himself — "Peer Pressure Boy," the guy who carried amps for his friend because he was "the man," the starstruck kid who couldn't believe he was in a band with his heroes, the guy who took acid because Chuck Dukowski told him to. And besides, he was the band's frontman. "I have to think that Henry was kind of suppressing himself at first with the band and then maybe the true Henry came out or something," says Ginn. "That's the only way I can understand it."

Now Rollins began to assert himself as forcefully as possible, and Ginn began to regret his decision to give the singer the limelight. In his own subtle ways, Ginn let his displeasure be known. "It just got to be this [fear that] Greg's going to get mad," says Rollins. "'We want to interview you for our fanzine.' 'Well, can you interview me *and* Greg? Or me and Bill? If you just interview me, I'm afraid I'm going to get yelled at.'"

But Rollins's self-denying side made sure he crucified himself for his move into the spotlight. In his diary, lyrics, and performance, Rollins would flagellate himself for being an ogre, then revel in being an ogre seemingly so he could flagellate himself some more. Prowling the stage in his little black shorts and Jim Morrison hairdo, Rollins strutted a narcissism disguised as self-hatred (or was it vice versa?). Instead of lashing out, it was lashing in.

Those around him began to notice a shift in Rollins's personality around 1984, when he became increasingly difficult to deal with — an insular, malevolent character straight out of a Dostoyevsky novel. "At one point he suddenly just *changed*," says Spot, "and he was no longer a friendly guy that I considered my friend but just somebody who seemed to feel like it was mandatory to be antagonistic toward everybody. I just didn't have time for it."

"I saw Henry's attitudes keep getting more extreme," says Ginn, "and him always just disliking everybody in the band, saying mean stuff about them onstage, making demeaning comments about them." ("Ask a lot of the members why they left," Rollins retorts. "They'll say two words. The first one will be 'Greg.' The other one would be 'Ginn.'")

Rollins had become quite an intimidating individual, especially to the mainstream music press. "Get close to him — it's downright scary," wrote *Rolling Stone* reporter Michael Goldberg. "Eyes that bore right through you. Hair, a tangled mess that falls past his shoulders, down his back. Ragged, ripped clothing. Lots of tattoos: Skulls and snakes, ghouls, a spider, a bat. And etched across his upper back in inch-high letters, Henry Rollins' philosophy of life: SEARCH AND DESTROY."

Sadly, as it is with so many children of abuse, masochism was an essential part of Rollins's psyche. "I hope I get bashed up soon," Rollins wrote on one early tour. "I need the pain to play. I need to play for my life or it's not worth it." Before a show in a small town in Northern California, Rollins found a piece of broken glass and tore up his chest with it. "Blood started flying all over the place," he wrote. "It felt good to feel pure pain. Helped me get perspective." Even Ginn's antipathy toward him got converted into some sort of macho toughness test, a twisted validation of Rollins's resolve.

By '84 Rollins preferred to eat apart from the rest of the band on tour. "There's just no way that I'm going to sit and listen to all that conversation when I don't have to," he explained in his tour diary. Later, instead of traveling in the band van, he preferred the back of the equipment truck, where he lay in total darkness for hours on end, alone with the PA equipment and amplifiers.

Not surprisingly, friction began to develop between Rollins and the rest of the band. Rollins first noted it in the spring of '84, during a European tour. "Bill and Kira are hard to take," Rollins wrote in his diary. "It's none of my business. They are the way they are." Apparently Rollins wouldn't deal with the problems with his bandmates head-on, preferring instead to add them to the formidable arsenal of slings and arrows that beset his tortured soul.

**B**lack Flag played every town that would have them, and many others, too, doing nearly two hundred shows in 1984. "They played every single city there ever was," says Naked Raygun's Jeff Pezzati. "Every time we'd go to a city I'd never heard of, some crappy little town, they'd say, 'Well, Black Flag was just here two weeks ago.'"

Every punk band in town would try to get on the bill when Black Flag played, so to eliminate arguments, they usually toured with an entire bill: Black Flag headlined and SST bands supported them. This arrangement ensured they'd tour with bands they liked, and it made sound business sense for SST. Since the early Eighties, a band called Nig-Heist often opened. Nig-Heist's rotating membership included Black Flag roadies Mugger on lead vocals and Davo on bass, guitarist Dez Cadena (as "Theotis Gumbo"), Stevenson on drums, and Dukowski on guitar, all wearing long wigs. This was a band whose stage presence one fanzine admiringly described as "comparable to an epileptic boy scout molesting a bag lady" and possessing "all the humor of a muscular dystrophy telethon."

Black Flag fans might have thought they'd cornered the market on outrageousness, but Nig-Heist was perfectly happy to burst their bubble. Nig-Heist was the band people loved to hate. Night after night on the spring '84 Black Flag/Meat Puppets tour, the biggest cheer Nig-Heist got was when Mugger announced they'd play only one more song. The long hair was a big part of the band's repugnance, and with songs like "Hot Muff" and "Whore Pleaser," what was there not to hate?

And Nig-Heist wasn't the only band on the bill that was blowing minds — besides Black Flag and their confrontational sludge-metal, the Meat Puppets were whipping off mind-roasting guitar solos, acid-fried renditions of songs from *The Wizard of Oz*, and transcendent country rock during their sets. The Black Flag/Meat Puppets/Nig-Heist tours gave a powerful reminder that punk rock could be anything anyone wanted it to be.

Nig-Heist, though, may also have been some sort of manifestation of Black Flag's collective id. Although they were few and far between, overtly raunchy songs like "Slip It In" and "Loose Nut" ("I'll be back in a little while / But first I gotta get some vertical smile") were a good indication of Black Flag's reputation as groupie hounds. "We wanted to fuck your women," Rollins boasts. "Big time. If we could, we would. Anytime, anywhere, we would try and get laid."

Sex was a respite from the stresses and deprivations of life in Black Flag, particularly on the road. "In those days you didn't get much else in the way of niceness or fun in your life," Rollins explains. "The gigs were fun but they were always tension filled. But meeting a nice girl who would be nice to you and fuck you? Oh my god, it was just like an oasis."

The messy, stinking van often became a steel-plated honeymoon suite after shows. "Many nights I had sex in that van, sometimes next to another guy having sex in the van," says Rollins. "And you have to have a very understanding or very enthusiastic partner to get together with you in such close proximity."

Every Black Flag release except *Damaged* featured artwork by Raymond Pettibon and SST sold pamphlet books of Pettibon's work, with titles like *Tripping Corpse, New Wave of Violence,* and *The Bible, the Bottle and the Bomb.* Like the San Francisco–style psychedelic art of the Sixties, Pettibon's pen-and-ink artwork was a perfect visual analogue to the music it promoted — gritty, stark, violent, smart, provocative, and utterly American.

Pettibon typically worked in only one panel, so the message had to be direct and powerful. One poster depicted an execution victim dead against a tree while a man with a shovel stood in the background; the text reads "THE MEEK INHERIT EARTH." A flyer for a show to benefit the legal defense against Unicorn was of a well-dressed young man being led away in chains as an admiring group of women looks on. "Everyone loves a handsome killer" the caption reads.

The fact that Black Flag, caricatured as a mindlessly aggressive punk band, could ally themselves with high-concept artwork was a tip-off that there was a greater intelligence at work here than most outsiders suspected. "Some people think that anything as physical as our shows must mean there's no thinking involved, but that's not true," Ginn told the *L.A. Times'* Robert Hilburn. "We do want to provide a physical and emotional release, but we also want to create an atmosphere where people are encouraged to think for themselves rather than accept what they've been told." Even the media's reaction to the shows worked in the band's

favor — when kids who were actually there saw how news reports sensationalized what had really happened, it made them think about how the media might be exaggerating and distorting other news as well.

Under the aegis of legendary L.A. scenester Harvey Kubernik, Rollins had started doing "spoken word" (a new term at the time) performances of his poetry and journal entries in November '83. *Family Man* — released in late September '84, making it the fourth album the band had released that year — broke Black Flag down to its increasingly distinct component parts — the band and Rollins — with one instrumental side and one spoken word side. By the following summer, Rollins had published two volumes of his prose poems, *End to End* and 2.13.61., penning lines like "NOW I UNDERSTAND THE STRENGTH OF SUCCUMBING TO THE STORM, JOINING THE MAELSTROM, FINDING POWER IN ITS TURMOIL, PULLING TOGETHER END TO END LIKE A SNAKE CONSUMING ITS TAIL . . ." Or "THE DAYS / PASS LIKE / PASSING YOUR / HANDS THRU / BROKEN / GLASS. / A LITTLE / BLOOD / SEEPS OUT. / I FEEL SOME / PAIN HERE / AND THERE . . ."

By 1986 Rollins was doing more and more stuff on his own, be it spoken word performances or freelance writing, including a much-noticed piece about 7-Eleven stores for *Spin* magazine. This flew in the face of Ginn's one-for-all, all-for-one ethos. And with the rhythm section changing so often, Ginn had no strong allies within the band. Black Flag had lapsed into the archetype of dinosaur bands like the Rolling Stones and Led Zeppelin: a charismatic frontman and an enigmatic guitarist mastermind supported by a relatively faceless rhythm section. And while Rollins's self-punishment seemed to invert metal's egotistical posturing, its self-absorption was merely the flip side of the same coin.

Perhaps as an antidote to Rollins's bardic aspirations, 1985's all-instrumental *The Process of Weeding Out* EP found the band stretching out on four longish set pieces (including some sterling playing by Roessler). The title has a triple meaning. Besides weeding out Rollins and the obvious pot reference, it refers to the way the challenging music weeds out the band's less insightful fans.

In his liner notes, Ginn decried the rise of the Parents' Music Resource Center, a group led by Tennessee Senator Al Gore's wife Tipper, who sought to censor rock lyrics they personally found offensive. "I have faith that cop-types," Ginn wrote, "with their strictly linear minds and stick to the rules mentality don't have the ability to decipher the intuitive contents of this record."

The torturous music was meant to signify the band members' intense engagement — most tattooed the Black Flag bars on their bodies — and the frustration of toiling in the face of poverty and indifference. Black Flag's work ethic — the constant touring, the fully committed performances, the relentless rehearsals — was a way of working through the pain, drowning it out in wave after wave of noise and adrenaline. As the old joke goes, Black Flag was suffering for their art, and now the audience had to suffer for it, too — Ginn even had a name for the approach: "the blasting concept," or a sonic assault on the audience. Joe Carducci recalls one show when the band played for over two hours. "By the end," he says, "people were just straggling away, like from a battlefield."

The band had become as alienated from its own audience as it was from society in general. "We were trying to play through the audience rather than to the audience," Stevenson said. "We would put our heads down, play as hard as we could, and didn't acknowledge their existence." "I was trying with my bass to slam [the audience] against the back wall," said Roessler. "We were forcing the crowd to submit to the will of the band — for longer than they could stand it."

Performances became agonizing torture tests for band as well as audience. Roessler injured her hand from playing bass and has played in pain ever since. Ginn's sweat and blood would seep into the guitar and cause short circuits. Finally, he just set the instrument's tone control where he liked it, turned the volume knob up to ten, soldered it all into place, and installed a waterproof switch. From then on, when Greg Ginn's guitar was on, it was on *all the way*.

"Everyone on stage was writhing and moaning," wrote Patti Stirling of a July 26, 1984, show. "I wanted to say, 'It's OK — you don't have to do this. Go home, have a beer, watch something funny on TV, or visit a friend.' Well, were I surrounded by this music much of the time, I would suffer too. The beat dragged so much it seemed to be going backwards."

Released in early May '85, *Loose Nut* contains some of Black Flag's most conventional hard rock ever, albeit matched up with Rollins's usual histrionic self-hatred. But the original SST gang was starting to unravel. Ginn's brother Raymond Pettibon didn't care so much that SST never paid him for his artwork, but he was getting increasingly frustrated that although he was a worthy artist in his own right, he was still best known as "the Black Flag guy."

The final straw came with the cover of *Loose Nut*. As it happens, it's a self-portrait: a man winks as two scantily clad women sit on his lap — the caption reads "Women are capable of making great artists." The artwork had originally been used in a flyer several years before and Ginn resurrected it without telling his brother. Then Stevenson, thrust into the role of layout person, cut up Pettibon's original artwork and used the pieces as elements for the lyric sheet. Pettibon became irate at the desecration of his work, and that year he and Ginn stopped speaking.

This was around the time that Spot left the SST family as well. "The band was taking itself too seriously," says Spot. "And some of the people in the band were taking themselves too seriously. It just kind of turned into people that were unlikable. I just couldn't be around them anymore."

Ginn fixes the blame squarely on Rollins. Although Rollins's spoken word performances were fairly funny, Rollins was "increasingly cutting out anything with a sense of humor" in Black Flag's music, Ginn says. "He became negative about those type of things or the songs that kind of

**HENRY ROLLINS DOING SOME DEEP THROAT AT THE 9:30 CLUB IN D.C., 1983.**

JIM SAAH

bring people together." Although he'd sing songs like "Six Pack" and "TV Party" in concert, Rollins would not countenance new songs that smacked of fun. Humor did not fit the persona Rollins was crafting for himself. "He started getting into more Jim Morrison than Iggy Pop," says Ginn, "that kind of serious 'I'm a poet' thing." A little levity would have made the darker aspects of the band more believable and thus more powerful, as it had so memorably on *Damaged*. Instead, Rollins seesawed indulgently between self-pity and macho excess. "That's what he was left with, which is just the same themes — 'I kill you, I hurt myself,'" Ginn says. "I didn't want to be a part of that."

**B**ill Stevenson left the band in late April '85. "There was a whole lot of vibing going on and the band proceeded to fall apart after that," he said. "There was a whole lot of personality things going on, which none of us cared to sort out, so Greg just started replacing people." Ginn explains this somewhat vague statement by claiming that Stevenson, who was once close with Rollins, had grown increasingly alienated from Rollins and wanted Ginn to get a new singer. Clearly, one of them had to go. Ginn edged out Stevenson.

But Stevenson hadn't really liked the direction the band took when he joined anyway. "Black Flag doing contorted heavy metal wasn't as good as Black Flag doing contorted versions of punk rock," he said. "I don't think we sounded as good slow." As it happened, the Descendents were starting up again, so it was a natural time to leave — and yet Stevenson was reportedly very upset when Ginn fired him.

With new drummer Anthony Martinez, they began a long tour in May '85, traveling through the Southwest, the South, the Northeast, over to Michigan, up to Canada, cutting south to the Northwest, down to California — ninety-three shows in 105 punishing summer days.

By that tour Rollins was drinking coffee literally by the pot and, not surprisingly, suffering from crushing headaches. He broke his wrist on an audience member's head at an August 6 show in Lincoln, Nebraska, and was constantly getting bashed by fans and foes alike. The audiences seemed to be smaller than the last time they'd toured the States, and to make matters worse, promoters were constantly underpaying the band. The ceaseless touring and nightly abuse was taking a terrible toll on Rollins physically and mentally. He got a serious infection of the vocal cords and seemed to be at the end of his psychological tether. "I am no longer human," he wrote. "I am no longer a sane person. I can't identify anymore."

**B**lack Flag was turning into the Greg 'n' Henry Show. "Henry was increasingly not wanting it to be a band," says Ginn. "He thought, 'Greg, you do the band thing and I'll do the vocal and frontman thing and we'll just get people that kind of go along with things.'"

So when Roessler — an intelligent, self-assured woman and a strong musician — tried to assert herself, Rollins (and Martinez) bridled, causing an escalating tension. Roessler had begun a master's program at UCLA, and Ginn believes Rollins may have resented the way the band accommodated Roessler's academic schedule. Also, the band had got it in their heads that it would be provocative for Roessler to exchange her tomboyish T-shirt and jeans for a coquettish punk rock Madonna look; some say this raised sexual tensions within the band to an uncomfortable degree.

For whatever reasons, by mid-August in Vancouver, things had come to a head: Rollins wrote in his diary that Roessler "has a hard time handling reality" and that she "must be out of her weak little unbathed mind." He and Ginn secretly decided to replace her once they got back home. "I never want to see her lying, rancid, fake self ever again," Rollins wrote.

And yet in Rollins's own estimation, the band was playing the best it ever had, and the proof is on the live *Who's Got the 10½?* recorded at the Starry Night club in Portland on August 23, 1985. Although Rollins's voice is clearly in shreds, the band goes at the material like trained attack dogs.

L.A. was the last stop of the tour; but despite free admission, only about six hundred people showed up. It was Roessler's final appearance with Black Flag, and Rollins took the opportunity to insult her at length during the closing "Louie, Louie," making remarks about "getting rid of cancer and what a rancid bitch she was."

They had recorded the *In My Head* album that spring. "Henry was getting narrower and narrower in what he was willing to do," Ginn recalls, which may account for the album's stultifying sameness of tone. Ginn was getting more and more upset at Rollins's growing prominence and retaliated by keeping Rollins's vocals so far down in the mix that he's almost inaudible. Other than that, the production is far more radio-ready than anything they'd ever done. While the band is tighter and better than ever — Rollins even broaches something resembling traditional singing — the material is distinctly unmemorable, and even at four minutes several songs seem interminable.

By the band's final tour, the rhythm section was Martinez on drums and C'el (pronounced "Sal") Revuelta on bass. According to Rollins, they played the same set for nine months. Ginn started the tour by telling Rollins to his face that he didn't like him. Things went downhill from there. Ginn's enthusiasm was clearly with the opening act on the tour, his arty instrumental band Gone. Meanwhile, Rollins was hobbling on his bad right knee, which had been operated on in 1982; then he rebroke his wrist yet again when he hit an audience member on the head.

Crowds were often sparse, and when they weren't, it was because they were playing small venues, mostly cramped redneck bars along anonymous stretches of highway. The police broke up several shows, just like the old days, and Rollins and members of the crew got in some scary punchups with bellicose locals. And they were still sleeping on people's floors.

Even the crew was kind of loopy. After he and roadie Joe Cole drove a hundred miles in the wrong direction, chief roadie Ratman had to surrender the wheel to Cole because he was too upset to drive. "Then he spray-painted his face white and took all the garbage on the floor of the cab and lit it on fire," wrote Cole in his tour diary, later published as *Planet Joe*. "We drove down the highway with a fire on the floor of the cab and when it became too big to control he opened the door and kicked it out. He shouted and slobbered for about 50 miles."

Rollins withdrew further from the rest of the band and most of the crew. "It is becoming very important that I keep to myself around the others," he wrote in his diary. "I'm a jerk when I enter into their conversations."

In Louisville Cole detained a mohawked punk who had spat on Rollins. After the show Rollins escorted the punk backstage, slammed his head against the wall, punched him in the chest, slapped his face, then asked why he had spat on him. "The punker answered that he thought Rollins liked to be spat on, so Rollins spat on his face as hard as he could until the guy started to cry," Cole wrote in his diary. "He was crying and apologizing and Rollins told him to leave before he really got mad. The punker left the room in tears and everybody just stood there shaking their heads."

Then again, Ginn apparently wasn't helping matters either. For years the band didn't even smoke pot, partly so the police wouldn't have anything to pin on them. But in 1985 Ginn had "resumed with a vengeance," says Rollins. "By '86 it was 'Cannot separate the man from his Anvil case with a big-ass stash.'" Rollins says Ginn began carrying a road case with him on tour that usually held about a half pound of pot. "That's when he went away and you couldn't talk to him anymore," Rollins said.

There were outside forces cleaving the band, too. By 1986 the underground scene had changed profoundly, mainly due to R.E.M. and U2, who had started in the post-punk underground and were now conquering commercial radio. As a touring musician and label head, Ginn had a ringside seat to the effect this had on many underground bands. "They started out with the ambition 'If we could just be a touring band and go around and do this, that would be cool,'" Ginn says. "Then R.E.M. came into it and it was like, 'Wow, we can make a career out of this.' There was a sharp turn." Many bands, sensing success was just a hit record away, toned down their sound and made records that would ap-

peal to radio and the press. The transition from underground to "alternative" was under way.

And Ginn saw that that mentality was about to infect Black Flag. Although the band had prided itself on being one or two steps ahead of their
peers, Rollins was beginning to have second thoughts about that approach. According to Ginn, one day Rollins just blurted out, "Why don't
we make a record that was like the last one so people won't always be trying to catch up with what we're doing?"

"And he had never said that before," Ginn says. "He had always
trusted me to go in directions musicwise that he might not understand at
first, but then in the long run they made sense with him. But he understood that that was against the grain commercially."

They could have used the money, too — they still owed a small fortune, about $200,000, to their lawyer for the Unicorn debacle and were
still living in communal squalor. But Ginn wasn't about to sell out, not after ten years of fighting to do it his way.

The alternative was simply to fire Rollins and get a new lead singer,
but Ginn decided against it for two reasons. One was that Rollins had
long since become synonymous with Black Flag and had made himself
into an underground star in the process, hobnobbing with the likes
of Michael Stipe, Lydia Lunch, and Nick Cave; corresponding with
Charles Manson; writing magazine articles and publishing books of poetry; and, of course, doing most of the band's press. Besides, Ginn, having
seen how Rollins could make life so miserable for people he didn't like,
feared the inevitable reprisals if he fired Rollins.

After returning from the 1986 tour, Ginn contemplated the situation.
And he decided to pull the plug on Black Flag. "It wasn't like a pissed-off
kind of thing; I wasn't mad at anything," says Ginn. "It just took a couple
of months and I thought about it, and I thought it's not going to be the
same anymore."

"So I was in Washington, D.C.," Rollins recalls, "and Greg called me
and said, 'I quit Black Flag.' So I said OK . . . OK . . . and since me and
Greg *were* Black Flag toward the end, that was it.

"My only regret," Rollins says, "is that I didn't join them earlier, so we
could have done it more years. I had a great time and it was an honor
playing with someone like Greg Ginn. I mean, they don't make them like
that anymore."

Just a few weeks later, Rollins was in the studio with a new band that
just happened to include Andrew Weiss and Sim Cain of Ginn's side project Gone.

**G**inn says he's glad he pulled the plug when he did. "I was real proud of what Black Flag had done from the beginning to the end," he says, "and I thought, 'I have been fortunate enough to never have played a note of music that I didn't really want to play at the time,' and I wasn't going to change that.

"The songs," Ginn continues, "are more what the band is about, rather than riots and police and tough-guy attitudes of lead singers and this and that. It's lyrics and the feeling of the music. . . . That's the main thing. In terms of the peripherals, the attitude of do-it-yourself, that kind of thing, not being a remote rock star and having layers of management and record labels and all that — instead, booking your own shows, doing your own publicity if necessary. Not everything has to be so home industry, but being willing to do whatever is necessary and not considering one's self remote, dealing with the guy at the distributor and respecting people for the job that they're doing, not thinking they should conform to some narrow aspect.

"I think," Ginn concludes, "Black Flag promoted the idea of just jumping off the ledge and doing it."

# CHAPTER 2

# THE MINUTEMEN

**I AM THE TIDE, THE RISE AND THE FALL
THE REALITY SOLDIER, THE LAUGH CHILD, THE
ONE OF THE MANY, THE FLAME CHILD**

**— THE MINUTEMEN, "THE GLORY OF MAN"**

The Minutemen of San Pedro, California, were paragons of the subversive idea that you didn't have to be a star to be a success. Their hard work and relentless, uncompromising pursuit of their unique artistic vision have inspired countless bands. "We didn't want to be just a rock band," says singer-bassist Mike Watt. "We wanted to be *us — our* band." In the process D. Boon, George Hurley, and Watt proved that regular Joes could make great art, a concept that reverberated throughout indie rock ever after. They also helped to originate the idea that a punk rock band could be worthy of respect.

In their music the Minutemen told stories, postulated theories, held debates, aired grievances, and celebrated victories — and did it in a direct, intimate way that flattered the intelligence as well as the soul. Music journalist Chris Nelson once wrote, "Their friendship formed the living core of the Minutemen, while their loyalty to each other and San Pedro informed the overarching theme of brotherhood that permeates the band's catalog."

Although they were certainly capable of byzantine riffing and spine-tingling runs down the fretboard, the Minutemen's brilliance lay not in their songwriting or chops but in their radical approach to their medium. They worked up a concept that encompassed the yin of popular/populist bands such as Creedence Clearwater Revival and Van Halen, and the yang of the intellectual wing of the English punk rock explosion. Daringly incorporating such genres as funk and jazz, the Minutemen struck a blow for originality, a perennially endangered quality in punk rock.

Their songs were jarring jolts that barely cracked the one-minute mark, but the ideas and the emotions that were conveyed in those songs were anything but fleeting. Often they were profound. Like Gang of Four, many of their songs are about the way private thoughts are affected by political systems — "Pure Joy," for instance, is about how capitalism depends on the nuclear family and, ultimately, on everyone's sense of their own mortality. Not bad for a tune that lasts less than a minute and a half.

If you're working class, you don't start a band to just scrape by; you start a band to get rich. So art bands, with their inherently limited commercial prospects, were mainly the province of the affluent. Which makes the Minutemen all the braver — they had no hope of commercial success, and yet they soldiered on through twelve records in five years, an amazing seventy-five songs in 1984 alone.

Outspokenly working class, they demonstrated that political consciousness was a social necessity, introducing a cerebral element to the nascent Southern California hardcore scene. They were the band that was *good* for you, like dietary fiber. The only thing was most people wanted a cheeseburger instead. "I think one of our problems with radio is that we don't write songs, we write rivers," Watt once said.

**S**an Pedro, California, is a blue-collar tendril of Los Angeles thirty long miles from Tinseltown. Touting itself as "Gateway to the World!" San Pedro once hosted a major army base and is now the biggest cruise ship port in the country and one of the busiest ports of any kind on the Pacific. Its ethnic working-class population is installed in the flats at the bottom of the town, below the downright alien affluence of the rambling houses up in the hills. On one side of San Pedro, cliffs at the edge of the Palos Verdes Peninsula command sweeping views of the ocean, suggesting endless possibility; from the other side of town, a sweeping view of the town's towering cranes and loading docks, not to mention the notorious Terminal Island federal prison, reveals suffocating realities.

Mike Watt and his family moved to San Pedro from Newport News, Virginia, in 1967, when he was ten; his dad was a career navy man and had gotten a transfer to San Pedro's naval station. They moved into navy housing, a small neighborhood of tract homes across the street from Green Hills Memorial Park cemetery.

One day in his fourteenth year, Watt went looking for some kids to hang out with in nearby Peck Park, a sprawling, leafy oasis that was a popular after-school destination. Watt was walking around the park when, out of nowhere, a chubby kid jumped out of a tree and landed with a thump right in front of him. The kid looked at him, surprised, and said, "You're not Eskimo." "No, I'm not Eskimo," Watt replied, a bit puzzled. But the two hit it off and strode around the park, talking.

The chubby kid introduced himself as Dennes Boon and soon began to reel off lengthy monologues that astounded Watt with their wit and intelligence. "He'd say these little bits over and over," Watt says. "The way they were set up, they had punch lines and everything. I couldn't believe it.

"I was such a fuckin' idiot," Watt continues. "I didn't know until we went to his house and he started playing them that it was George Carlin routines."

Boon had virtually no rock & roll records — "D. Boon's daddy," Watt explains, "brought him up country" — and had never heard of the Who or Cream. Watt was flabbergasted. Boon did have some albums by Creedence Clearwater Revival, though, and the band was to have a powerful influence on Boon and Watt.

Boon's dad, a navy veteran, worked putting radios into Buicks. The Boons lived in former World War II navy barracks that had been converted into a public housing project for, as Watt puts it, "econo people." Guns had not yet entered the picture, but it was still a rough neighborhood and Boon's mom didn't want the boys on the streets after school; within weeks of their meeting, she encouraged them to start a rock band. Watt wasn't sure he could play an instrument but was ready to give it a try for the sake of his friend.

They didn't know bass guitars were different from regular ones, so Watt just put four strings on a regular guitar; he didn't even know it was supposed to be tuned lower. In fact, they didn't even know about tuning at all. "We thought tightness of the strings was a personal thing — like, 'I like my strings loose,'" Watt says. "We didn't know it had to do with pitch." As Watt puts it, "It must have made your asshole pucker from a mile away."

Eventually they got the hang of the finer points of musical technique and started a cover band of hard rock staples like Alice Cooper, Blue Öyster Cult, and Black Sabbath.

Music wasn't their only outlet. Boon began painting in his early teens and signed his work "D. Boon," partly for the joke about Daniel Boone, partly because "D" was his slang for pot, but mostly because it sounded like "E. Bloom," Blue Öyster Cult's singer-guitarist. But for all their music and art, Boon and Watt were serious nerds. Boon was a history buff and both were big fans of geopolitical board games like Risk. Watt graduated near the top of his class. Boon was quite heavyset; Watt resembled Jerry Lewis, and his mom was so worried about his lack of coordination that she gave him clay to squeeze in his hands.

The two became interested in politics very early. Although Watt's interests lay in fiction, he'd keep up with Boon's historical explorations. "D. Boon would talk about the English civil war or something," Watt says, "so I would read up on Cromwell, just to know what he was fuckin' talking about." Pretty soon they started comparing the events of the past with the present, especially as seen through the eyes of their working-man dads.

**W**att's first rock concert, the legendary T. Rex at Long Beach Auditorium in 1971, was very daunting. "They were ethereal," Watt recalls. "They were a different class of people or something, like Martians." Rock musicians seemed unapproachable, otherworldly; like T. Rex's Marc Bolan, they were often fey little British men who wore spangled outfits and pranced around the stages of cavernous arenas. The lesson was clear: "Being famous was for other people," Watt says. "I thought it was something like the navy. It's something you're born into — they got it all set up for you, they tell you where to live, they tell you where to chow."

In San Pedro everyone played in cover bands, without any thought of writing their own songs or getting signed because, of course, those were things that other people did. The best band was simply the one that could play "Black Dog" just like the original, and that was the peak of their ambition — when all you know is painting by numbers, you're not thinking about getting into the Museum of Modern Art. So Watt and Boon would happily play "American Woman" over and over again, never thinking they could write their own songs or make their own records. "We didn't have the idea that you could go get signed; we didn't have the idea that you could write your own song," Watt says, shaking his head. "We didn't have that. Just did not have it."

Boon and Watt had the bad — or perhaps good — fortune to come of age during one of rock's most abject periods. "That Seventies stuff, the Journey, Boston, Foreigner stuff, it was lame," Watt says. "If it weren't for those type of bands we never would have had the nerve to be a band. But I guess you need bad things to make good things. It's like with farming — if you want to grow a good crop, you need a lot of manure."

And both young men yearned to learn of the world beyond San Pedro. Despite being technically part of Los Angeles, San Pedro was very provincial; Watt knew plenty of people who had never even been out of state and even some who'd never been out of town. Boon and Watt were not very worldly either. On a whim, Watt answered a classified ad for a bassist and drove down L.A.'s Santa Monica Boulevard, then a popular gay cruising strip. "There's a thousand guys 'hitchhiking' up there," Watt says. "And I was like, where are all these guys going? And they were all whores, you see. I didn't know! I was like, why don't these guys charter a bus? They look like they're all going to the same place. That's how out of touch I was in Pedro. I just did not know."

But Boon and Watt began to get a sense of the outside world from the great early rock magazines *Creem* and *Crawdaddy*. "The journalists had a big effect on us," Watts says. "It was a world of ideas." Through music magazines they discovered the original wave of punk rock bands, like the Ramones and the Clash. "There was pictures of these guys for a few months before we heard the records," Watt recalls, "and they had these modern haircuts and everything. And it blew our minds when we first heard the actual music. We thought it was going to be synthesizers and modern shit. But it wasn't modern. It turned out to be guitar music like the Who! That's what blew our minds. When we heard that, we said, '*We can do this!*'"

Fired up by the punk explosion, they wrote their first song — "Storming Tarragona." Named after the down-at-heel housing development where Boon lived, the song was about tearing down the projects and building real houses for people to live in. Boon and Watt, it turned out, had a powerful populist streak. "D. Boon didn't think our dads got a fair shake," Watt says, "and I think he was kind of railing against that ever since."

**B**oon and Watt began hitting the punk clubs in Hollywood in the winter of '77–'78, when they were nineteen. At first Boon thought the bands were "lame," breaking strings and playing out of tune.

"Yeah, they *were* lame," Watt concedes. "But that wasn't the main point that I saw — I saw hey, these guys are actually playing gigs. And some of them made records! People didn't do that in Pedro."

Unlike the arena rock they'd been raised on, punk placed no premium on technique or production values. Boon and Watt fit right in with the outcasts who were forming punk rock bands. "See, me and D. Boon were the guys who were not supposed to be in bands," Watt says. "We *looked* like bozos, so if we're going to be bozos, then let's go with it. And then going to Hollywood and finding out there's other cats like this, it wasn't so lonely."

George Hurley's dad worked on the San Pedro docks as a machinist. Boon and Watt knew of Hurley in high school, but only from afar — "He was," Watt explains, "a happening guy." Hurley had been a surfer and even went to Hawaii and, says Watt, "lived on the beach eating coconuts." Then, after nearly drowning in the gargantuan Hawaiian surf, Hurley, nineteen, came back to San Pedro and traded his surfboards for drums. He also had a practice space — a shed behind his house — not something Boon and Watt could take lightly. That shed was the site of many a keg party; Watt recalls that the grass outside turned preternaturally green because so many guys peed on it. It was a perfect place to practice — Hurley's mom was rarely home, since she had remarried to a man in a neighboring town and spent most of her time there. The house had descended into such anarchy that there was a sticker on the front door that read "U.S. Olympic Bong team."

Boon and Watt bravely asked Hurley to join their punk rock band the Reactionaries. "Georgie was not afraid — *liked* this punk stuff, in fact," says Watt. "For a Pedro guy, that was one in a million. And for Georgie, a *popular guy*, to like punk was incredible. Everybody knew me and D. Boon were weirdos — when punk came, of course *those* assholes would be into it. But Georgie, he took blows for that." But those blows were only verbal ("comments about fags and shit," says Watt), since Hurley's pugilistic talents were legendary.

Boon, Watt, and Reactionaries singer Martin Tamburovich had been at a local punk show when they met a tall, intense-looking guy handing out flyers for a San Pedro gig by his band, Black Flag. It was Greg Ginn, and he invited the Reactionaries onto the bill. The show — the Reactionaries' first and Black Flag's second — almost erupted into a riot when kids began vandalizing the youth center where the show took place.

The Reactionaries lasted only seven months — Boon and Watt decided that having a traditional frontman was too "rock & roll" and "bourgeois" and in early 1980 brainstormed a new band called the Minutemen. Boon picked "the Minutemen" from a long list of names Watt had made. The name appealed to Boon not only because of the fabled Revolutionary War militia, but because it had also been used by a right-wing reactionary group of the Sixties. "They'd send these notes to Angela Davis like they were going to bomb her but they never did," Watt says. "Mao had this quote which said all reactionaries are paper tigers — they're phonies. And he thought the [Sixties] Minutemen were big phonies." Contrary to legend, the band was not named for the brevity of their songs.

They started writing songs in early 1980 at Boon's tiny San Pedro apartment. As it happened, Joe Baiza of future SST band Saccharine Trust lived directly downstairs. ("He and his roommate lived like giant hamsters," Watt says. "They'd take all this newspaper and wad it up on their floor. Their pad was a gigantic hamster cage, man.") Baiza was baffled by what they were doing up there — he'd hear them playing and tapping their feet, but it would never last for more than thirty or forty seconds. "He didn't know *what* the hell we were doing up there," Watt says, chuckling.

The eye-blink brevity of their new material came from English art-punks Wire, whose classic debut *Pink Flag* featured twenty-one songs in thirty-five minutes. The approach also compensated for the Minutemen's musical shortcomings. "With the short rhythms you'd be out faster; you wouldn't have to groove on it," Watt says. "We were trying to find our sound. We weren't comfortable with saying, here's our groove. So we just said let's go the other way and just stop 'em up really big time."

The other main ingredient in the Minutemen sound was the Pop Group. The English post-punk band's caustic guitars and elemental dance rhythms supported explicit harangues about racial prejudice, repression, and corporate greed in the most didactic terms — one album was titled *For How Much Longer Do We Tolerate Mass Murder?* The iconoclasm of Wire and the Pop Group taught Watt and Boon a powerful lesson: "You didn't have to have choruses, you didn't have to have lead guitar solos, you didn't have to have *anything*," said Watt.

The lyrics were basically rants by both Watt and Boon that they dubbed "spiels." "We just say what we say," D. Boon once explained to *Flipside*. Other inside lingo began creeping into their vocabulary. "Boozh" was short for bourgeois — a no-no. "Mersh" meant commercial. "Econo" meant thrifty, efficient; it became a way of life for the Minutemen.

Unfortunately, Hurley had joined another band after the Reactionar-

A SERIES OF PORTRAITS TAKEN IN 1980, IN FRONT OF THE SST OFFICES IN TORRANCE AFTER PRACTICE. LEFT TO RIGHT: **D. BOON, MIKE WATT, GEORGE HURLEY.**

MARTIN LYON

ies split, so they enlisted local welder Frank Tonche and played their first gig in March '80, opening for Black Flag in L.A. At their second gig, in May, Greg Ginn asked if they'd like to record for his new label, SST. But then Tonche, in Watt's words, "got scared of punk rock" — actually, he walked offstage at the band's second gig after punks spat on him. Hurley soon reunited with Boon and Watt.

On July 20, 1980, they recorded the seven-song EP *Paranoid Time*. It was SST's second release, all six minutes and forty-one seconds of it. Although the agile, skittering drums, trebly guitar, and twanky bass had nothing to do with hardcore punk, the relatively straight-up rhythms and hyper tempos did. Already the band's left-wing political consciousness was at the fore. At the time, nuclear dread was making a sweeping comeback: the hawkish Reagan was to take office exactly six months later, and it was hard to forget that his shaky finger could press The Button at any time. Boon defined the moment on "Paranoid Chant" when he hollers, "I try to talk to girls and I keep thinking of World War III!"

By November '80, when they played their first club show at L.A.'s Starwood, they'd become a different band. They'd lost the use of Hurley's shed and moved into Black Flag's practice space in nearby Torrance. Sharing a space with Black Flag profoundly affected their music in unexpected ways. "When you play with a band like that, you don't want to sound like them," Watt told *Flipside*. "If they were going to play that fast heavy metal, then we couldn't do it. So we got this other stuff going."

In those days it was particularly hip to appropriate African American dance musics like funk and disco, à la Talking Heads. And that's how the Minutemen defied Black Flag's metallism. As Watt explains, "They were going for Dio and Black Sabbath and that stuff. But we'd already been there! We *grew up* on copying records. They hadn't."

Boon studied art in college and dropped out because he didn't want to end up using his art for commercial purposes. Watt studied electronics and never did it for a living because the only electronics jobs were in the defense industry. Punk rock was a godsend for their ethics. Maybe even a reward. "Sometimes you have to act out your dreams, because circumstances can get you crammed down," says Watt. "And instead of getting angry and jealous of what they got, why not get artistic about it and create a little work site, a little fiefdom. As long as it don't oppress anybody or something, I think it's kind of healthy."

Watt felt tainted by the experience of learning cover tunes and envied the younger punks for their purity. The Minutemen spent much artistic energy trying to unlearn the stifling archetypes that had been foisted on them in the Seventies; to their credit, they celebrated that process and the exciting discoveries they made along the way.

Ginn gave them all menial jobs at SST's ham radio operation; later they worked for the label itself. Watt's job, for instance, was liaison to record stores, pestering them to buy and sell SST product. It wouldn't do to have the label's artists doing such work, so Watt adopted the name Spaceman, and his indefatigable energy and gift for gab suited the job perfectly.

*Paranoid Time* sold out its 300-copy pressing, so Ginn invited them to make another record. That fall they recorded *Punch Line* — eighteen songs in fifteen minutes. On the face of it, the music was skeletal, but with Boon's skronk guitar, Watt's chordal bass, Hurley's busy percussing, it was more than the sum of its parts. While the music was eccentrically funky, like a highly caffeinated Captain Beefheart running down James Brown tunes, the songs railed against injustice, materialism, ignorance, and war; the lyrics could have been written by an idealistic young intern at *The Nation*. And this is while most forward-thinking youths were listening to English mopemasters like Echo & the Bunnymen and the Cure.

*Punch Line* attracted much more critical comment, notably from Craig Lee at the *L.A. Times*. College radio was beginning to notice the band and Rodney Bingenheimer was playing them on his influential *Rodney on the ROQ* show. They were soon playing out of town, mostly touring with Black Flag and other SST compadres like Hüsker Dü or the Meat Puppets. They often borrowed Black Flag's van, which had been dubbed "the Prayer." "The door wouldn't even open all the way," Watt says. "It had a big old gap, so the driver would have to wear all these scarves and sunglasses because this big gale force wind would be blowing in on you. The dash didn't work, the clutch was all burned out, smelling, it was terrible, it was a nightmare. One time the catalytic converter clogged up and all the fumes came into the van — it was us and Saccharine [Trust]; there was ten of us in that van — and these guys started tearing big ol' holes in the dash with screwdrivers just to let some air in."

They also began to learn other harsh realities of touring. "D. Boon had to take a shit twenty minutes after we ate — I mean, to the *minute,*" Watt says. "We'd be on the freeway and he'd be, 'PULL OVER!' And just go *pfffft!* Right out there, he didn't care. D. Boon did not have shame. He was eating a lot of spirulina and shit like that. And the mule would be kicking down the door every time. He told me he had a theory about how you knew if you were going to be artistic as a kid. You're either going to be packin' it in or spreadin' it out. He said that determined you, how you dealt with your shit. He said, 'Man, I smeared it all over the place.' And I said, 'You still do!' "

B y 1982 they'd built a modest local following, headlining small L.A. clubs on off nights. L.A.'s premier hardcore venue was the Whiskey, but the Minutemen couldn't play the Whiskey because the SST bands' violent reputation had gotten them banned there. (Eventually the band Fear got the Minutemen booked at the club — "You know, the nonviolent band Fear," Watt jokes. Right afterward they rushed home to San Pedro for what they thought would be a triumphant hometown gig later that night, only to get egged and fire-extinguished off the stage.)

The band was now a formidable, if idiosyncratic, live act. "They were just one of the oddest bands you ever could have seen," Spot says, still marveling. "Here's these three goofy-looking guys playing — in this totally stripped-down manner — these really, really short songs. So maybe at first you're not really sure if they're playing them well. Because it's not like you have a few verses and choruses and solos — they were doing stuff completely outside of normal structure. Then the way they looked — D.

Boon would just get up onstage and he would just *shake*. You wondered if he had some kind of congenital nerve disease. The only one in the band that looked as if he had anything to do with punk rock was D. Boon — the first time I ever saw him, he had a mohawk. He was this big guy wearing mechanic's coveralls and he looked like a football with a mohawk. You looked at him the first time and you were like, 'Huh? What the hell is this?'

"But after about four or five songs," Spot continues, "you were like, 'Yeah, this is cool! This is really neat! Why didn't I think of that?'"

The band's sense of indie altruism was so strong that they would donate songs to seemingly any of the myriad cassette fanzines that had begun to spring up in the early Eighties. SST's Joe Carducci finally had to step in and tell Watt he thought the band was being used. But since SST couldn't accommodate all of the band's prodigious output, Carducci released the *Bean Spill* EP, a collection of odds and ends, on his Thermidor label; SST released a similar collection, *The Politics of Time*, a couple of years later.

The Minutemen began to hit their stride with the Spot-produced *What Makes a Man Start Fires?*, recorded in July '82. The ensemble playing is crisp and utterly unique, firmly establishing what Watt once called the band's "devices" — "little songs, high-end guitar, melodic bass, lots of toms." Boon's pins-and-needles guitar tone opened up plenty of sonic real estate for Watt's bass, and Watt seized the opportunity, plunking out busy melodic figures or dense chords with a playful but assertive twang; Hurley bashed out wholly original mutated funk riffs that seemed to splash out in all directions at once and yet still propelled the music with a headlong rush.

The band's irregular rhythms emulated their idol Captain Beefheart on a very deep level. "Rock & roll is a fixation on that bom-bom-bom mother heartbeat," Beefheart once said. "I don't want to hypnotize, I'm doing a non-hypnotic music to break up the catatonic state." America was in nothing if not a catatonic state through the Eighties, and the Minutemen's music — all angular stops and starts, challenging lyrics, and blink-and-you-missed-'em songs — was a metaphor for the kind of alertness required to fight back against the encroaching mediocrity. Short songs not only reflect a state of dissatisfaction and noncomplacency; they simulate it. The band's very name suggests vigilance.

"Music can inspire people to wake up and say, 'Somebody's lying.'

This is the point I'd like to make with my music," Watt told *Rolling Stone* in 1985. "Make you think about what's expected of you, of your friends. What's expected of you by your boss. Challenge those expectations. And your own expectations. Man, you should challenge your own ideas about the world every day."

The lyrics integrate the personal and the political, asserting that the two are inseparable. And for Boon and Watt, who debated political points endlessly, the two realms were truly inseparable. "The stuff we thought about and the stuff we sang about was the same thing," Watt says. "It just became part of your tunes. We decided to sing about what we know."

A lot of what they knew was the oppression of the working man. "They own the land / We work the land / We fight their wars / They think we're whores," Boon spits out in the frantic funk sprint "The Only Minority." In the Watt-penned "Fake Contest," Boon announces, "Industry, industry / We're tools for the industry."

The album occasioned the band's first major tour, opening for Black Flag in Europe and America in the winter of '83. "It was ten of us in one van, the equipment in the trailer," Watt recalls. "It was head-to-toe slaveship action. It was hilarious. At least we were getting to tour and going to other towns. It was amazing."

European punks turned out to be far more disgusting than their

American counterparts. In Austria the Minutemen were pelted with used condoms, cups of piss, bags of shit, bags of vomit, even a toilet seat. "It was kind of funny," Watt says. "We couldn't believe it." They didn't take it personally, however, figuring that anyone who would throw a bag of vomit at a band probably wasn't listening to the music anyway. There was only one downside, really. "The spitting was really gross because when you're playing an instrument, you can't put your hands in front of your mouth when you have to holler," Watt says, "so you take all these fuckin' loogies in the mouth. It was really nasty."

Even the band's tourmates turned against them. Black Flag would take particular delight in egging Boon and Watt into one of their epic arguments. When one would make a statement, any kind of statement at all, someone in Black Flag would invariably say to the other, "Are you going to let him get away with that? Or are you that scared of him? I guess I see who *really* wears the pants in this band!" And that would be enough to set Boon and Watt to fighting like cats and dogs.

But eventually it was things like the toilet seat that really got to the Minutemen. "When I think back on it, I wonder what that shit was about," says Watt. "But it was a small price to pay for getting out there and playing; it really was."

Unlike most SST bands, the Minutemen did only one tour with Black Flag before moving on. "You've got to do more than just be an opening band for a big band," Watt says. "We liked them very much, but no man's a hero to his valet."

The Minutemen toured incessantly on their own, becoming as legendary for their relentless itineraries and thrifty modus operandi as they were for their live shows. They'd usually sleep at someone's house, lugged their own equipment, and learned how to maintain their own van. Everything was done "econo"; despite meager pay, Minutemen tours always turned a profit.

Setting up and breaking down their equipment quickly and efficiently appealed to Watt's military mind-set, but like he says, "It was a respect thing, too. You wanted to look like you knew what you were doing. Because guys were always giving you shit like you were assholes. It was a way of getting respect, especially if you were playing with a mersh band that had a crew and stuff. Then we'd really put it on."

Sometimes the Minutemen got grief for being their own road crew. "But I never thought that you should play up to 'the princeling,'" says Watt, referring to the prototypical pampered rock star. "So what if nobody sees you playing the fuckin' hero or the star. I never fancied myself like that."

There was another good reason to set up their own stuff — with his 220-plus-pound bulk and nonchalant attitude toward personal grooming, D. Boon did not look like a rock musician, especially in those days of Spandex and poofy hair. Security often tried to pull him off the stage before the band began playing. "They figured he was some goon," Watt says, "just getting up there and bum rushing." It also used to happen to Watt — he'd be getting onstage and suddenly some side of beef in a black T-shirt was tugging on his arm. That's partly why the band would remain onstage after they'd set up their own equipment, a chore they did for their entire existence.

"We just could never see mass acceptance of our music," Watt says. "But that didn't make it little to us — it still was important. But if we were going to do it, we had to make sure the dream fit the tent. A massive bourgeois tent would be too much deadweight. Let's just carry enough to get us there, and on top of that, we'll be playing songs and ideas."

But back then, in the greedy, materialistic Reagan era, making the most of meager resources was positively rebellious. For the Minutemen, "jamming econo" meant parsimonious recording budgets, short songs, and being their own crew. Overdubs were limited to occasional lead guitar lines, studio time was booked for the graveyard shift, and they avoided doing multiple takes, recorded on used tape, and played the songs in the order they were to appear on the album so they didn't have to spend money on editing the songs into the right sequence.

In the best sense of the word, the Minutemen were conservative, a time-honored concept in American thought going back at least to Thoreau. "Econo *is* an old concept," Watt agrees. "The punk rockers picked up on that, the idea of scarcity and just using what you got. And maybe more of you comes through because there's less outside stuff you're sticking on — all you got is you, so you have to make something out of it."

Watt acknowledges that the band's econo approach was based not only on the limited commercial appeal of their music or ideological grounds, but also had roots in their humble backgrounds — coming from working-class stock, they simply weren't comfortable with extravagance. And they'd never known anyone who made a living off of art. "It's bizarre to think that people live like that, so you're always thinking about what if everything goes to shit," Watt says. "You have to be econo so maybe when the hard times hit, you can weather them." The band members held on to their day jobs: Watt worked as a paralegal, Hurley was a machinist like his dad, and Boon got a general teaching degree.

And they backed it all up with a thrilling live show. At peak moments — which was most of the set — Boon's face would go beet red; he'd grin widely and start jumping up and down, a big, heavy man hopping around like a bunny rabbit. It was part confrontation and part celebration, daring you to laugh at his intensity, part caring and part not caring. "He was *trying*, like some guy trying to stock the shelves or something," Watt recalls. "You wanted to root for him. *I* wanted to root for him. It was intense, the way he played." In the early days, that was precisely what the stage-shy Watt needed. "I was petrified," Watt says. "But D. Boon was the guy who *brought you on board.*"

Boon's intense conviction won him and the Minutemen the respect and affection of the other SST bands, and eventually the indie community in general. "The guy would give you half of anything he had," recalls Henry Rollins. "He was just a big, burly, big-hearted, jolly guy. Everyone loved him." "There is not one piece of rock star," says Watt, "not one bit of phony pose in this guy."

Yet Black Flag, the Meat Puppets, the Descendents, and Hüsker Dü all outsold the Minutemen. The Minutemen's effect was more like the old metaphor of throwing a pebble into a pond and watching the ripples widen and widen. While the Minutemen's ripple never did come close to reaching the shore, they did make those influential first few rings, where the real sophisticates and musicians were. The Minutemen were a band's band.

**H**ardcore attracted a very young audience, so instead of bars, hardcore shows took place at Elks Lodges and VFW halls and even bingo halls. "Those were *teenagers* at those gigs — little kids on skateboards," Watt says. "They had a real vigor and energy in them. It wasn't you, but hey, that's the way it was." The hardcore kids hadn't been as scarred by the scourge of corporate arena rock, and they were a lot more nihilistic, jocky, and aggressive than Boon, Watt, and even Hurley. "They were going fast," Watt says. "You wanted to go fast with them."

Consequently, the Minutemen kicked the tempo up a notch. Their speed had something to do with hardcore, but after that, the comparisons cease. While politically oriented hardcore bands relied on shallow, sloganeering lyrics about Reagan — the neutron bomb was a particular favorite topic — the Minutemen mustered an informed, passionate, and poetic reply to the conservatism that had swept the country. And while hardcore bands favored traditional song structures and sing-along vocal melodies, the Minutemen's music was wordy and gnarled, their music full of confounding breaks and leaps. And then there were those uncool funk and jazz influences. "It had an intensity like hardcore," Watt says. "But if you ask the hardcore kids, they didn't think we were hardcore. They didn't know *what* the fuck we were."

The funk, jazz, and Captain Beefheart sounds set them up for no small amount of grief from the doctrinaire hardcore community. "They wanted one song — very fast, quick," Watt says. "A lot of these cats, they were teenagers, it was very social for them — it was not musical. We were music punk; they were social punk. We were punk against rock & roll and restrictive categories — it was natural that we would want to make music that was a little different because that, for us, *made* a punk band."

So the Minutemen challenged punk rockers as much as they challenged the bourgeoisie. "One of the reasons we play all these different kinds of musics is for them — to see how seriously they take 'No Rules' and 'Anarchy,'" said Watt. "We throw all this soft music, folk music, jazz, et cetera, not only to avoid getting caught in just one style, but also to show them that 'See, you didn't want any rules . . . this is what you wanted. You didn't want to be told what to listen to.'"

While Watt didn't think most of the young hardcore audience was getting their political message, he hoped they were getting another, deeper message. "We hope to shake up the young guys because punk rock doesn't have to mean hardcore or one style of music or just singing the same lyrics," he said. "It can mean freedom and going crazy and being personal with your art."

The hardcore scene was the only place the Minutemen could thrive. L.A.'s Paisley Underground scene was beginning, but not only was it typified by naked careerism, but its rigid Sixties genre exercises were precisely the kind of orthodoxy the Minutemen abhorred. The band's outspoken politics and bargain-basement production values meant they couldn't thrive in the progressive rock scene, either. "Put yourself in our place and what else could you be but a punk band?" Watt says. "There was nothing else. No other scene was like that. We would have explored it if there was."

The Minutemen felt DIY was intrinsic to the punk ethos. And yet the key punk bands — the Ramones, Television, the Sex Pistols, the Clash, Wire, et al. — had been on major labels and did little themselves besides make the music. So why did the Minutemen equate DIY with punk? "Because that was *our* version of punk," Watt says simply. For the Minutemen, punk was a fluid concept — it was things like noticing an ad in *Creem* for a record by Richard Hell and the Voidoids on the tiny New York indie label Ork Records and calling the number listed. "I called him," says Watt. "I said, 'Is this Hell?' And he said, 'Yeah.' And I got scared and I hung up.

"That, to me, was punk."

And an underground music network was starting up: record stores that championed independent labels were beginning to appear in major cities and college towns, college radio was noticing the music, fanzines were flourishing, and an underground railroad of venues was assembling. "The scene was like a big boat," Watt says, summoning up a favorite analogy. "It's really strange what held it together. There was no commander; there was no sound you had to follow. You had to play fast — I think that was the only requirement. Fast and loud. Beyond that, you could do almost anything you wanted."

The band's first published interview appeared in *Flipside* #32, just before the release of the *Bean Spill* EP. Calling them "L.A.'s best kept secret weapon," Al Flipside bubbled, "We just had to give them the cover!"

Watt used the interview to dispense classic Minutemen wisdom: "We don't have a leader in our band — no leader, no laggers"; "Politics is guns if you really get down to it"; "Music can bind people in weird ways — socially, information — a lot of people get everything they know from songs and groups."

Asked point-blank whether they were a punk rock band, Watt recalled their cover band days. "Then Johnny Rotten came," he said, "and woooo, and we wrote our own songs. In that way we're a punk rock band because it gave us the spark to write our own damn songs!" (Soon afterward, though, their Rotten bubble was burst when the Minutemen opened for Public Image, Ltd. "We were on our second song and the motherfucker is on the side of the stage, *tapping on his watch*," Watt says. "And we were like, c'mon, guy! Because we were not dawdlers at all." Tellingly, the liner notes of 1987's *Ballot Result* thank "John Rotten or our idea of him.")

Watt felt the Minutemen were a punk band by default. "Where were the gigs happening?" he explains. "Where were the records coming out? It was all the punk scene." But weren't they punk because of their ideas? "Well, the scene is where we *learned* a lot of the ideas," he replies. "Now, we weren't like a lot of punk bands, but we were a punk band because we were in the punk scene. I don't know what else to call it. I'm not ashamed of it. I mean, it was silly in some parts and in some parts it was really good, it was very empowering. We got to make our dream real. And in those days, punk could do that for the Minutemen."

With inspirational lines like "I live sweat but I dream light-years," the Minutemen felt their music was by, for, and about the working person. "The first thing is to give workers confidence," Watt said. "That's what we try to do with our songs. It's not to show them 'the way' but to say, 'Look at us, we're working guys and we write songs and play in a band.' It's not like that's the only thing to do in life, but at least we're doing something — confidence. You can hear some song that the guy next to you at the plant wrote."

The working-person idea ran deep. Between 1982 and 1984, Boon published a fanzine called the *Prole*, which lasted for six issues. Boon wrote politically oriented articles and cartoons; Watt did record reviews. And on select nights, Boon booked local underground bands at San Pedro's 300-capacity Star Theatre, renaming it the Union Theatre. Shows started early so working people could get home at a reasonable hour. "D. Boon believed that working men should have culture in their life — music and art — and not have it make you adopt a rock & roll lifestyle lie," Watt says. "See, that's punk. Having a set-up paradigm and then coming along and saying, 'I'm going to change this with my art.'"

Boon's political philosophy, as outlined in an interview at the time, was simple. "It always comes down to 'Thou shalt not kill.' And I'm not religious — you can ask him," Boon said, nodding toward Watt. "I just think killing people is the wrong thing to do."

"You're not religious about God," Watt added.

"I'm not religious about God," Boon agreed, "I'm religious about Man."

"We believe in average guys," said Watt. "What happens is, the system makes them all fuckheads."

"And I want to try to snap them out of that," said Boon. "That's why I write these songs, OK?"

But Hurley was the only guy in the band whose dad actually belonged to a union. Watt and Boon wrestled with the problem all the time, and one fanzine interviewer managed to catch a typically contentious exchange on tape.

**BOON** [proudly]: I'm just the average Joe, the guy who has been a janitor, a restaurant manager —

**WATT** [impatient]: But the average Joe doesn't write songs. He . . . doesn't . . . write . . . *songs*.

**BOON:** Well, this one did.

**WATT:** You're *not* an average Joe.

**BOON:** This one did.

**WATT:** You're a *special* Joe.

**BOON:** I was borne out of being average because of my rock band.

**WATT:** No, no, because of these tunes. D. Boon, you're special and you've got to cop to it. You've *got* to cop to it, you're *special*.

**BOON** [exasperated]: All right! Ever since I was five years old, people said I could draw! Let him draw!

**WATT** [triumphant]: That's right. That's why I'm in a band with him — he's special.

Besides the *Prole* and the Union Theatre, the band had established their own label, New Alliance, in the fall of '80. Early releases included various compilations, records by local underground bands, and the 1981 Minutemen EP *Joy*. The *Mighty Feeble* compilation included the Seattle new wave band Mr. Epp and the Calculations, which featured future Mudhoney singer Mark Arm.

When asked what had inspired the label, Boon had replied simply, "Black Flag." "Part of being a punk band was also making a label," Watt explains. "We never thought the label would get bigger; we just wanted to have it so if you saw the band you could get the record." New Alliance soon began paying for itself, with all the profits going right back into the label.

One early New Alliance release was *Land Speed Record* by Hüsker Dü, a burly threesome from Minneapolis whose music lived up to the album title. The two trios hit it off at once. "They were on the same wavelength as us, totally," Watt says. "It seemed like the same thing — make a band, try to get your own sound, and then play it all over the place and keep making records as fast as you could." They wound up doing a couple of short tours together, and the Minutemen also released their *Tour Spiel* EP on Reflex, the Hüskers' label.

Another early New Alliance release was *Milo Goes to College* by the Descendents. Again, there was an instant affinity. "Billy and Frank were fishermen, Tony was a mailman, Milo went to college," Watt says. "[They were] very hands-on, knuckles to the ground, salt of the earth — same thing, same paradigm. Anybody who was in that scene with Flag was kind of like that. Not too many bourgeois bands. Everybody was into the van, very close to the earth."

The Minutemen's themes of imperialism, exploitation of cheap labor, and the horror of the battlefield were "totally from Creedence," Watt says. "Creedence, for the Minutemen, was a political band." Creedence Clearwater Revival's 1969 hit "Bad Moon Rising" was an allegorical condemnation of the Vietnam War, as was "Who'll Stop the Rain," while "Fortunate Son" pulled even less punches, explicitly pointing out class inequities in the draft. CCR's populist influence on the Minutemen was sartorial as well — Creedence favored plaid flannel shirts, which became Watt's trademark. A few years later, the look would be called "grunge."

Another early political influence was Bob Dylan. "Bob Dylan was probably the only person who I listened to the words in the Seventies," Watt told *Flipside*. "My dad was a sailor and he was always away and Dylan seemed like a surrogate dad to me." Boon and Watt later picked up crucial ideas from KPFK, a radio station on the left-leaning Pacifica network that hosted everybody from Noam Chomsky to pioneering rock critic and Blue Öyster Cult lyricist Richard Meltzer.

But their political thinking was also profoundly influenced by punk rock's egalitarian ethos, in which they found a very powerful metaphor for the world at large. Ideas about redistribution of artistic power were a powerful analogy for redistribution of political power. "When you talk about the people who are disenfranchised, and then you look at the guys who can't get in bands . . . I mean, it's kind of close," Watt says. "The thing about having a say in your workplace, having a say in your economics, is the same idea as having a say in your music. The way we jammed econo was the same way we talked about issues. I don't want to separate them so much. We didn't have the political rap and the band rap. They *were* the rap."

So instead of spending their entire working lives as pawns in a bureaucracy that most benefited those at the top, Boon, Watt, and Hurley found a way of being their own boss. "Getting to make decisions about our own band, at least we were in charge of *something*," says Watt. "Everywhere else in our lives, we were the little tiny men, but this one, this could be us."

Still, the Minutemen realized there was no way they were going to realign the politics of even their own limited audience. The best they could hope for was dialogue — thinking about the issues was better than apathy and ignorance. "What we could do onstage is kick up a little crisis, a little ballyhoo in your mind," Watt says. "And maybe then they can articulate their own ideas about it. Maybe they'll find out they're more right wing after hearing us, I don't know. D. Boon was into that — just trying to flesh them out, see if they know what they're about."

Recorded in January and May '83, *Buzz or Howl under the Influence of Heat* boasts some genuinely catchy rock songs, like Boon's amped-up sea chanty "The Product" and Watt's "Cut," with Boon's stuttering chicken-squawk guitar accenting a bold foursquare rhythm. The EP's title is a collage of two lines from *Scientific American* articles, reflecting the dual nature of the record itself: all but three songs were recorded on a humble two-track recorder for the princely sum of $50; the rest were recorded for free. The cover was going to be a *Scientific American* photo of tree frogs but color separations cost $1,000, so their SST labelmate Joe Baiza of Saccharine Trust did a pen-and-ink drawing of Boon and Watt locked in one of their epic arguments while, behind them, hell spews forth material objects like watches, shoes, and calculators.

They did a full album's worth of recording in November '83, but then Hüsker Dü blew into town and recorded the *double* album *Zen Arcade* in three days. The Minutemen took this as a challenge and furiously wrote and recorded almost two dozen more songs within a month. "See how healthy the competition was, the community of it?" Watt says. "That's where it *was* a movement. And not a scene. It was a healthy, thriving thing."

*Zen Arcade* had been an ambitious concept album. "We didn't have a concept to unite it all like they did," Watt admits. "We didn't sound like them. But trying to stretch like they did, we came out with something that wasn't like anything we ever did again. Best record I ever played on." The Minutemen's unifying concept was simply their cars — the album started with the sound of an engine turning over and ended with "Three Car Jam," which is about thirty seconds of all three Minutemen casually revving their car engines.

The two-record, forty-five-song *Double Nickels on the Dime* stands as one of the greatest achievements of the indie era — an inspired Whitman's sampler of left-wing politics, moving autobiographical vignettes, and twisted Beefheartian twang. The album cost a mere $1,100 to record; they mixed it all on an eight-track machine in one night with producer/engineer Ethan James. The album sold fifteen thousand copies in its first year and is the band's best seller to this day.

Watt says the title is a poke at mainstream rocker Sammy Hagar, who had recently proclaimed his incredible rebelliousness with the Top 40 hit "Can't Drive 55." "You're such a wild guy, you'll break the speed limit," Watt says, chortling. "How about your tunes, though, buddy? We were making fun of him. The title means fifty-five miles an hour on the button, like we were Johnny Conservative.

"No one knew what the fuck we were talking about," Watt continues. "We'd explain it to people and they'd say, 'I don't get it, what's so funny about that?' And we couldn't tell them because it was our whole angle on rock & roll, our worldview on the music scene."

Watt knew exactly what he needed to do for the cover shot. He drove out onto the Harbor Freeway in his '63 Volkswagen bug with his buddy and upstairs neighbor Dirk Vandenberg, who sat with a camera in the backseat. It took four passes before they successfully lined up a shot with Watt's smiling eyes in the rearview mirror, the sign for Route 10 to San Pedro in the windshield, and the speedometer exactly at 55.

Watt also says that *Double Nickels* is a takeoff on Pink Floyd's 1969 double album *Ummagumma*, where each band member had their own featured side. Each Minuteman programmed one side of the album, with the rejects going on the fourth side, labeled "chaff."

Watt and Boon yearned to purge themselves of all the bad music in their past, like the jazz fusion they endured in high school (although vestiges of fusion remained in the Minutemen's gnarled rhythms and jazzy chords). So they chased out those demons with ideas from folk music, specifically the realistic, autobiographical nature of it.

Perhaps the ultimate expression of that idea was the oddly moving "Take 5, D." Boon felt Watt's original lyrics were "too spacey," and Watt agreed. "There ain't nothing going to be more real," Watt promised him, and found a new set of lyrics — an actual note from a friend's landlady that begins, "Hope we can rely on you not to use shower / You're not keeping tub caulked . . ." It doesn't get realer than that.

Loosely based on the riff from the Velvet Underground's "Here She Comes Now," "History Lesson (Part II)" is both sweetly nostalgic and delivered with the understated fervency of a pledge of allegiance: "Me and Mike Watt played for years / but punk rock changed our lives / we learned punk rock in Hollywood / drove up from Pedro / we were fuckin' corndogs / we'd go drink and pogo." The song also includes the immortal line "Our band could be your life," a rallying call that has reverberated in underground music circles ever since. The line crystallized it better than anything — the Minutemen's sense of musical liberation, their political engagement, and even their frugality were metaphors for a whole mode of living. Punk rock was an *idea*, not a musical style.

Plenty of punks thought the Minutemen were mocking them and their scene (and sometimes they were). But as "History Lesson (Part II)" made clear, they were just three guys who had grown up together and were making music they thought was good. "I wrote that song to try to humanize us," says Watt. "People thought we were spacemen, but we were just Pedro corndogs — our band could be your life! You could be us, this could be you. We're not that much different from you cats."

The album also included a song called "Untitled Song for Latin America." Boon had become a member of CISPES, or the Committee in Solidarity with the People of El Salvador, an activist group dedicated to helping Marxist rebels overthrow the country's repressive U.S.-installed puppet government. It was not a hip issue to get behind at the time — most rockers were then dedicated to smashing apartheid in South Africa.

Although Watt wrote more songs, Boon tended to write the band's "hits." "He could write these songs that spoke to people," Watt says. "And those are the words that people are always going to remember us for. D. Boon didn't have the greatest vocabulary, but he could put things together that took a lot of courage." Boon wrote "This Ain't No Picnic," which swiftly became one of the band's most popular numbers, when he was working at an auto parts outlet and a supervisor wouldn't let him play jazz and soul music on the radio, claiming it was "nigger shit." ("I think he also got caught chowin'," Watt confides.) Boon couldn't quit because he needed the income, and his bitterness and frustration fueled a Minutemen classic.

While Watt preferred a fairly complex lyrical approach, Boon tended toward slogans, which worked better in a rock context: plenty of their fans didn't know that "This Ain't No Picnic" is about racism, but they sure sang along on the chorus. But the differing approaches were a constant source of friction between the two young men, and Watt would often scold Boon for being simplistic. "You know how Nixon destroyed the hippie movement?" Watt asked Boon during a fanzine interview. "He just ended the war. Because that's all it was — 'End the war, end the war!' So he ends the war and everything falls apart. Because it was so simple-minded, they never had any goals — [it was just] some rock dude saying 'Get out of Vietnam.'"

But later, when Boon left to get a soda, Watt confided to the interviewer, "I'm really afraid — he's got a lot of really important things to say and I wouldn't want him to get reduced to Jack Shit, know what I mean?"

The ravings of Jack Shit or not, "This Ain't No Picnic" was the band's first video. Made for $440, it was nominated for an award by MTV, which had begun to air low-budget videos from indie labels. The Minutemen lost to fey English fop-poppers Kajagoogoo.

Most indie bands at that time didn't make videos. "We did," Watt says. "That was the whole idea — so people can know about the gigs. That's where we had the most control was at the gigs. So the idea was to get people to the gig. We had divided the whole world into two categories: there was flyers and there was the gig. You're either doing the gig, which is like one hour of your life, or everything else to get people *to* the gig. Interviews were flyers, videos were flyers, even records were flyers. We didn't tour to promote records, we made records to promote the tours, because the gig was where you could make the money."

Except for dinosaur acts like the Rolling Stones and Pink Floyd, major label bands usually lost money on the road in order to promote their records. But in indie rock, the reverse is true — if a band keeps its expenses low. "That's the reality, why be in denial?" Watt says. "We didn't have to live up to any rock paradigm. If it would get people to the gig, we would do it. If it wouldn't, it was boozh, an adornment, spangle, accoutrement, accessory, ballast."

The band toured relentlessly after *Double Nickels* — one 1984 tour had the band playing fifty-seven dates in sixty-three days.

**T**he loquacious Watt tended to dominate interviews; Boon would usually just noodle on his guitar and interject only when he felt he had to, usually to spar with Watt or denounce fascism. Hurley, a man of few words, was rarely even present. Not being book-learned, Hurley was a bit reluctant to try to express his thoughts in words, but he was still a Pedro boy, with much in common with Boon and Watt. "He was very much into exploring art, pushing it, expression," Watt says.

With Watt and Boon as boyhood friends, Hurley must have felt like the odd man out; since he'd been out surfing while Boon and Watt were studying Bismarck and Napoleon, he couldn't participate in the political back-and-forth. But besides being a powerful, deeply inventive drummer, he did have some invaluable political instincts, albeit not political in the usual sense. "Georgie could size shit up," Watt says. "Georgie was a guy you would want in a day-to-day situation that might be scary or dangerous. To me, that's a very political person — they're seeing where the power is stacked up. Georgie is very aware of this. He knew how to take care of things, watching your shit, CYA. To me, that's politics in a way. You can do it on a big national level, but you can do it with your van and your equipment."

But the intellectual core of the band was Boon and Watt, and the two challenged each other constantly. In a 1985 interview with an unknown fanzine writer in Minneapolis, the two argued constantly, not in a hostile way, but as if they were sparring, testing each other's conviction.

**WATT:** You listen to [Boon's] songs, it sounds like he's singing about the same thing in every fucking song.
**BOON:** I have something to say.
**WATT:** I guess. I don't think you have that much to say. Some other dude said it.
**BOON:** Well, it's got to *keep* being said until it's done.

Earlier, they argued — at length — whether there was a guitar solo in "Boiling" from *Punch Line* (there isn't). Then Watt took Boon to task for reducing the situations in El Salvador and Nicaragua to a simplistic slogan that was then popular in left-wing politics: "U.S. Out of Central America," which Boon often wrote out on a signboard and propped up onstage.

**WATT:** I can't see just saying that — "Get the United States out of Central America," just that simple. That's being simpleminded about something that's very complicated — people dying, trying to make their own destiny.
**BOON:** Can't you see why the people are dying there?
**WATT:** People who are using this as just a slogan so they can enhance their rock career.
**BOON:** Can't you see why people are dying there?
**WATT:** There's many, many reasons.
**INTERVIEWER:** Because our government is sending aid?
**BOON:** No, because of imperialism. And it's always existed there.

**WATT:** That's one of the reasons. No, there's many reasons.

**BOON:** Like what?

**WATT:** Racism.

**BOON:** There's racism against the imperialist powers?

**WATT:** No, there's racism. When the Spanish went over there.

**INTERVIEWER:** Yeah —

**WATT:** They were racist against the Indians.

**BOON:** That's not true though! They weren't very racist against the Indians.

**WATT:** Bullshit.

**BOON:** It was the whites who were very —

**WATT:** In fact, the indigenous populations of Guatemala are being murdered off by the Spanish-surnamed people.

**BOON:** By the people in power.

**WATT:** Racism.

**BOON:** But they weren't the Spanish. The Spanish married all the women and had all the children. They just killed all the braves and married the women.

**WATT:** That's not racism, huh?

**BOON:** Well, the English did it a lot better. They just murdered everybody in front of them.

This sort of debate went on all the time. "The Minutemen would just rank on each other all the time — they didn't harbor *anything*," says Joe Carducci, chuckling. "They had two perspectives, but usually they'd be arguing about the Civil War." Boon and Watt's arguments sometimes got so heated that they alarmed the people around them. Mostly they kept the squabbling on a verbal level, but inevitably tensions sometimes exploded, especially in the cramped crucible of the tour van. "You know how we handled it?" Watt says. "We'd fight. We'd roll around and wrestle. We'd pull that van over in the middle of the road."

Sometimes the fisticuffs radiated outward, like when Boon had some stickers made that said "Get Out of Central America" and was handing them out at a show at Tulane College when some jocks started picking a fight with the Minutemen about it. "They had just gone through some basketball point-shaving scandal and they were all pissed off and they were ready to fight us," Watt says. "And we were ready. 'C'mon, assholes!' And it got really, really heavy."

The double album put the Minutemen on the map. But what next? Joe Carducci had noticed how college radio had taken to *Buzz or Howl*, both for its accessibility and its brevity, which allowed listeners to grasp the whole record fairly easily, to get to know five or six songs instead of forty-five. So he suggested another EP, but with more mainstream production values and standard song lengths, in order to win more airplay and sales. "And Watt's instinct to cover his ass is then to ridicule it as 'Project: Mersh,'" says Carducci.

Carducci suggested that since he knew exactly what he wanted, he produce with engineer Mike Lardie at his side and Ethan James kicking in some "technical advice." The Minutemen agreed and they recorded the album in February '85.

The studio bill came to $2,400, a king's ransom by Minutemen standards, especially for a mere six songs. The tracks featured ornate trumpet parts on three tracks, relatively slick production values, and even fade-outs.

By this point the Minutemen could afford such a move both financially and professionally — they'd amassed such integrity and respect that anyone the slightest bit familiar with the band would see *Project: Mersh* for the experiment it was. "We wanted to see if it would fuck with people's, critics' heads, our fans' heads, the radio people's heads, yeah, because they pigeonhole you and then they'll leave you there forever," Watt said. "We think we should be competing with *all* the bands and not be relegated to any area, so we'll show 'em, you want choruses and fade-outs, huh?" And besides, it was their tenth record. It was time to mix things up a little.

It was also part of the band's continuing effort to bridge the gulf between performer and audience. After all, their roots were in proletarian rock, not obscure art-song. "We're trying to show people, hey, we're not cosmonauts from Planet Jazz, we're just like you," Watt said.

But they were not intent only on demystifying themselves; they were intent on demystifying the mainstream music business. By mimicking the "mersh" form and yet clearly destined to sell few records, they were making a point about music biz chicanery: *Any* band could sound like this if they had enough money, but that wouldn't mean they were any good. And of course, consciously setting themselves up to fail held a strong underdog charm.

And while the music was slicker, the lyrics remained pure Minutemen. The guitar on "The Cheerleaders" might recall Hendrix's "Foxy Lady," but Boon is singing lines like "Can you count the lives they take / Do you have to see the body bags before you make a stand?" "Tour Spiel"

was another part of the gag. "We wanted to be like the 'rock band' and write the 'road song,'" Watt says, chuckling at the absurdity. "It was like something a guy in a boardroom would dream up, not the guy in the van. But the whole thing about SST was the guy in the boardroom *was* the guy in the van!"

If the point was that a commercial sound doesn't mean commercial success, *Project: Mersh* succeeded admirably: it sold only half what *Double Nickels* did.

Sometime in '84 they had done an interview in Georgia with, in Watt's words, "some longhaired guy" who did his own fanzine. They eventually found out the longhaired guy was Michael Stipe, the singer of a hot new band called R.E.M. It's remarkable that the Minutemen hadn't heard R.E.M. by 1985. "Ostriches," Watt concedes. "I only knew bands by playing with them." The Stipe interview must have gone fairly well, because R.E.M. invited the Minutemen on their U.S. tour of 2,000- to 3,000-seat venues in December of the following year. "And we didn't even know who R.E.M. was," Watt says. "We went and bought their record — it was folk music; it was like a vocal band. They turned out to be really educated music guys. They'd worked in record stores."

But the tour was no picnic for the Minutemen. "The whole crew

hated us, didn't want us on the tour, the record company — I.R.S. — wouldn't put us on the posters," Watt says. "The only four guys who liked us was the band."

According to Watt, R.E.M.'s crew wanted them off the tour after the very first gig. (Perhaps they were put off by the fact that Watt often dressed up like Fidel Castro, a getup that had gotten him a thorough frisking at Newark Airport earlier that year.) "They didn't know what we were," says Watt. "They gave us a half hour and we played forty songs. They didn't know what the fuck was hittin' 'em. Plus, the music was made for little clubs so the echo was longer than the tunes!"

The tour also provided the Minutemen with solid affirmation of their econo approach, for R.E.M. had already met with one of the pitfalls of graduating from cult status to nascent fame — they had to put up with professional tour crews. "These guys were *assholes*," Watt recalls. "They'd put a line of gaffing tape on the floor of the stage that said 'Geek line' and we weren't allowed to cross. They would switch our rooms, fuck with us constantly." After the band played an entire set of Creedence songs at the Fox Theatre in Atlanta, the tour's production manager demanded they clear all cover songs with him first.

No doubt about it, it was a tough tour. In Florida Watt got food poisoning and suffered from chronic diarrhea for days afterward. "It got useless to keep changing my pants," Watt wrote in the tour story anthology *Hell on Wheels*, "so I tied a shirt around my waist and rags around the bottoms of my pant legs and just said fuck it. After three days my pants were full to the knees. Luckily, my condition improved."

On the last show of the tour, R.E.M. playfully hurled corn dogs at the Minutemen during "History Lesson." For the encores, the Minutemen joined R.E.M. for a version of Television's "See No Evil," with Watt playing one of Peter Buck's Rickenbacker guitars, Hurley pounding a tom-tom, and Boon on guitar. It was a fitting number: Television had been one of the pioneering indie punk bands who fired up Boon and Watt; the New York band had done the same for R.E.M. The jam also symbolized a passing of the torch from the hardcore-associated pioneers of the indie scene to what Watt calls "college rock," a less desperate strain of music for a whole new group of kids.

**W**att had been making noises that after *Project: Mersh* they were going to come out with a very uncompromising album with the working title "No Mysteries." They recorded in late August and early September '85 at L.A.'s Radio Tokyo ("now 16 track at $25/hour!" the liner notes proudly note) with Ethan James.

But in the meantime, Boon, like many members of the original SST bands, had become smitten with the incomparable Meat Puppets and their loose, trippy, neo–Neil Young style. Boon wanted to emulate their slack approach, but it couldn't have been further from Watt's rigorous work ethic. And on the resulting album, now titled *3-Way Tie (for Last)*, Boon won out. (Boon even sings a perfunctory version of the Meat Puppets' "Lost" on the album, while the album notes thank the Meat Puppets for "obvious inspiration.")

Even worse, the Minutemen's busy tour schedule hadn't allowed them to write and properly prepare the new material. While *3-Way Tie* was a lot mellower than anything the Minutemen had done before, it was also underrehearsed and overprocessed. "I was really surprised when *3-Way Tie* came out," says Carducci. "There just seemed to be nothing there. They hadn't really done much work on it."

And five of the sixteen songs were covers. Besides the Meat Puppets number, there's a version of Blue Öyster Cult's "The Red and the Black" (featuring a bass duel between Watt and . . . Watt) close on the heels of a reverent cover of Creedence's "Have You Ever Seen the Rain?"; "Ack Ack Ack" by key early L.A. punks the Urinals and Roky Erickson's "Bermuda" also get the Minutemen treatment.

The album had been recorded during a down period for Boon. "He got pretty lazy and didn't put as much into the music as he should because he had been partying a little too much," says Spot. "So I think Watt had to pick up the slack. And I think somehow he kept D. going. There was a show I saw one time when D. had gotten to be kind of partymeister, and I was worried whether he was going to make it through the show. He had put on more weight and was drinking a lot, and I could tell he was having a hard time singing — he didn't have the air. I was real concerned about that. . . . And a number of other people had noticed it, too. And I think a lot of people took him aside and said, 'D., you're falling behind. You're starting to get bad. Don't do that to yourself.' And he snapped back and really became himself again."

The music on 3-*Way Tie* is more eclectic than ever: there are odd psychedelic interludes, tidbits of Spanish guitar, visionary rap & roll, a spoken word piece, Latin rhythms, a literally telephoned-in track, and a great straightforward rocker ("Courage"). The politics are clear, the tips of the hat copious, the band chemistry obvious.

But 3-*Way Tie* suffers from a split personality. Boon's numbers are strongly political: "The Price of Paradise," besides featuring some of Boon's best singing, is a stinging indictment of the Vietnam War and the eerie similarities with the way the U.S. seemed to be backing into confrontations in Latin America. On "The Big Stick" he rails, "This is what I'm singing about / The race war that America supports," singing over the song's jaunty acoustic swing. But the lyrics for Watt's songs, written by his girlfriend, Black Flag's Kira Roessler, largely avoided politics in favor of more abstract realms.

The whole project is a bit sluggish and underdeveloped. "But you know what?" Watt says. "We were doing the windup to come back." They were just starting to make enough money to quit their day jobs, which meant they could concentrate on their music more than ever. "I think we were on to a new style," Watt says. "The next album was going to be very adventurous."

Sadly, they never got the chance to deliver it.

In late December, a few days after returning from the R.E.M. tour, the Minutemen were on the verge of a great personal triumph. Their hero Richard Meltzer was set to record with them and had given Watt ten lyrics to write music to. Watt came over to Boon's house to discuss the record and found his friend sitting in a beanbag chair, bright red with fever. Boon said he was heading to Arizona that night to visit his girlfriend's folks for the holidays. Watt said he looked too sick to go. Boon said not to worry — his girlfriend would drive the van and he'd lie in the back.

That same night Watt was giving a friend a ride home after a show in Hollywood when he passed a street called Willoughby. "And it was really weird — there's this *Twilight Zone* where [the key phrase is] 'Next stop, Willoughby!' And the guy jumps off the train [and dies] — Willoughby's no real town. I think it's an undertaker's service. . . . Well, when I passed that street Willoughby, I got this huge old chill."

Watt's phone rang early the following morning: December 23, 1985. It was D. Boon's dad. Boon's girlfriend had been driving the band's tour van, her sister in the passenger seat and a feverish Boon sleeping in the back. At around four in the morning, Boon's girlfriend fell asleep at the wheel. The van crashed and flipped; Boon was thrown out the back door and broke his neck. He died instantly. It was at about the same time Watt had passed Willoughby, back in California, and shuddered. Years later he would still wonder if he hadn't somehow felt D. Boon die.

All that Watt could think was, *how?* He flashed back to an image of his childhood friend, strong as an ox, playing football back in Peck Park. D. Boon wasn't quick, but it took two or three guys to tackle him. "He just seemed unkillable," Watt says, shaking his head in disbelief. "He just did."

"That was the worst, that was the worst," Watt says. "No more of him. No more Minutemen. I had really come to lean on him. I was numb. I was weirded out. It was hard for me. Boy, that was hard. I miss him."

D. Boon was buried in Green Hills Memorial Park in San Pedro, right across the street from where Watt grew up.

The next night Watt had a dream about Boon, the most vivid he'd ever had about his friend. The two were alone in a bank lobby covered floor to ceiling in orange carpet. "I'm ten feet away from him and he's studying this big rectangular painting and it's got like six or seven Abe Lincolns in it and they're like Peter Max Abe Lincoln heads with the big stovepipe hat and the beard, but in psychedelic colors," says Watt. "And I'm standing back there and I'm thinking, 'This is so fucked up, I have to tell him he's dead and he can't be here anymore.' And there was this horrible dilemma. And I wake up."

"I've never been able to figure that dream out. But I do know why I had to tell him he was dead — because D. Boon was such a fucking fierce dude, I don't think he knew he was dead. In a weird way, he did not know. I don't think you know you're dead; I think it's like the equator — somebody has to tell you you've crossed it."

The indie community was staggered by the tragedy, too. For many, it was one of those things where you remember where you were when you heard the news.

D. Boon's death broke up one of the last major indie bands who harbored the idealism of earlier times and carried it into the new music. The new crop of musicians was younger and had essentially never known a world without punk rock; maybe they detested their ex-hippie parents' hypocrisy and had grown cynical. After a friend called Big Black leader Steve Albini to break the news, Albini opened up his diary. "So there's nobody left who's been doing it since the beginning and doing it all the way

**D. BOON HANDING OUT BALLOTS FOR THEIR UPCOMING LIVE ALBUM AT A SHOW IN CHICAGO, 1985.**

GAIL BUTENSKY

right," he wrote. "Fuck. It's like Buddy Holly or something. Sure it's kind of pathetic to get all worked up over it but hell, they meant it, and that means something to me. . . . Man, what do we do now?"

**3**-*Way Tie (for Last)* had included a mail-in ballot for fans to vote on which live tracks they wanted on an upcoming album, tentatively titled "Three Dudes, Six Sides, Half Studio, Half Live." So while the nation reeled in horror from the explosion of the *Challenger* shuttle, Watt grieved for his friend and cobbled together *Ballot Result* from soundboard tapes, radio shows, rehearsal tapes, studio outtakes, and even fans' live bootlegs.

**I**n early 1985, when Sonic Youth played their first L.A. show, the band's Thurston Moore introduced himself to Watt. "He knew about Richard Hell and New York Dolls and Johnny Thunders," Watt says, "and I just listened to him spieling." Moore remembers it differently: "He approached us and he was this really vociferous kind of guy," he says. "He had brought the album covers of [Sonic Youth's] *Confusion Is Sex* and the first album, and he was throwing them in front of us and having us sign them and stuff. I was like, 'This is *insane* — Mike Watt [is asking us for our autographs].'" (Watt later wrote a song about the eventful meeting, "Me and You, Rememberin'" for the fIREHOSE album *If'n*.)

Moore and the rest of Sonic Youth were intensely interested in networking. "That's totally what it was about," Watt says. "And Thurston knew that. It was all about communications."

About a year later Watt found himself on the East Coast, still distraught over Boon's death, and Moore and Sonic Youth bassist Kim Gordon had him stay at their place on the Lower East Side. Although Watt hadn't picked up a bass since his friend died, they persuaded him to play on a track they were recording, Sonic Youth guitarist Lee Ranaldo's cataclysmic "In the Kingdom #19" (which was, ironically, about a car crash). "It was so weird," Watt says of the experience. "But then I started figuring out that *everything* they do is weird — they have the weird tunings, the guitars. I thought we were very outrageous and adventurous, but we were like ol' Chuck Berry compared to their stuff."

After D. Boon died, Watt found it difficult to run New Alliance by himself and finally sold it to Greg Ginn in 1986. He and Hurley formed a new band called fIREHOSE with guitarist Ed Crawford, a Minutemen fan who traveled all the way from Ohio to convince Watt to start playing again. Their SST debut did well on college radio and the band eventually signed with Columbia Records. George Hurley kicked around in various bands after the demise of fIREHOSE; in the Nineties he drummed with the legendary experimental band Red Krayola. Watt, still a beloved, respected, and hardworking figure on the underground scene, is currently at work on his third solo album for Columbia. He still jams econo.

Although Watt doesn't think they changed very many minds politically, he's sure the Minutemen were successful at whatever they tried. They never compromised their music (well, maybe once . . .) and exposed a lot of people to a fairly difficult vision. They rocked in a way that no one else had done before (or since). They inspired countless bands. "We weren't a lot of hot air — we almost did everything we set out to do," Watt says. "And in some ways it's because we kept our sights small. We're not going to be the biggest band — we're going to put on little shows, put out a little magazine, have a little label. We made it small enough that we could do it. *And* we held down jobs, paid our rent, and made a living.

"I just hope that maybe some people will read about us and see how we weren't manufactured," Watt says, "that we were just three dudes from Pedro and that maybe they could do the same thing themselves."

# CHAPTER 3

# MISSION OF BURMA

**"MISSION OF BURMA PLAYED A NOISILY AGGRESSIVE BRAND OF GUITAR POP THAT WAS ALWAYS REAL FUCKIN' CLOSE TO JUST-WHAT-THE-DOCTOR-ORDERED, BUT MOST OF THE TIME IT SEEMED LIKE NOBODY CARED. WHY? WELL, PEOPLE ARE ASSHOLES, I GUESS."**

**— BYRON COLEY AND JIMMY JOHNSON,**
***FORCED EXPOSURE*, 1985**

Mission of Burma's only sin was bad timing — the support system that would spring up for underground bands later in the decade largely didn't exist yet. No matter how brilliant Mission of Burma was, nationally there were relatively few clubs they could play, few radio stations to air their music, few magazines to write about it, and few stores to sell it. And yet what little network that existed was able to sustain the band for several years, until their bittersweet end.

Mission of Burma's determination against the odds was not lost on the generations of indie bands who followed. Nor was their music. Mission of Burma took elements of free jazz, psychedelia, and experimental music and injected them into often anthemic punk rock. It was, in the words of one critic, "avant-garde music you could shake your fist to," a concept Sonic Youth would take to greater commercial heights a few short years later. And in the meantime, bands like Hüsker Dü and R.E.M. were also listening to the band's bracing amalgam of power, brains, and mystery.

In fact, mystery was a great deal of Burma's strange allure. "Reading between the lines, there's something there that's unsettling," says drummer Peter Prescott. "You couldn't put your finger on us sometimes. I think there's nothing that galls people more than when they say, 'Just entertain me, don't make me work for this.' Our intent, I don't think, was to make people work, but that's the way it came out."

Incorporating the avant-rock of underground Cleveland bands like Pere Ubu, the angular slash-and-burn of the English post-punks, the trancey repetition of German bands like Can and Neu, and the aggressive propulsion of the Ramones, Mission of Burma "invented a new way to snarl," wrote critic Rob Sheffield, "the sound that American indie bands have been tinkering with ever since."

**C**lint Conley grew up in tony Darien, Connecticut. An avid music hound, he explored everything from the cutting-edge jazz of Ornette Coleman to the proto-punk New York Dolls. He moved to Boston in the fall of '77 to found a quirky, cerebral art-rock band called Moving Parts.

Roger Miller was born and raised in Ann Arbor, Michigan, just in time to see local bands like the Stooges and the MC5. He began playing rock music not long after the British Invasion peaked — he was fourteen — and with his two brothers soon formed Sproton Layer, an amazing band that sounded like Syd Barrett fronting Cream. (SST later released a Sproton Layer album.) Miller later explored free jazz, then pursued a music degree, studying piano and composition, but never got his diploma.

Miller had begun experiencing tinnitus, a persistent ringing in his ears due to excessive noise exposure, back in Ann Arbor. He moved to Boston in early 1978 and, realizing he'd injured his ears, planned on avoiding rock entirely by making music with prepared piano and tape loops. But when he saw Moving Parts' ad for someone who could play rock *and* read music, he couldn't resist.

At the time anything seemed possible; simplistic but powerful punk groups like the Ramones, Dead Boys, and Sex Pistols had cleared away rock's deadwood, opening a path for countless new bands. "I knew this would be my last chance to be part of a revolution," Miller says. "In the Seventies, you couldn't do anything because there was no revolution. But in the immediate post-punk era, all of a sudden everything was wide open."

Miller joined Moving Parts that March, but the band would not last much longer. Keyboardist Eric Lindgren wrote complex music, while Miller and Conley, although accomplished musicians, noticed they both preferred the simple pleasure of banging on a basic E chord at top volume. They had also hit it off personally, starting the moment Miller arrived for the Moving Parts audition and, hearing the Ramones on the stereo, started doing a punky dance. "And then Clint came out of the kitchen and he was doing the same dance," says Miller. "Right then, I knew, 'This is cool, I'm tight with this guy.'"

With his long hair, beret, clove cigarettes, and trademark bottle green velvet coat straight out of early Pink Floyd, Miller clung to his Sixties roots, so much so that Conley nicknamed him "Lovebead." "He was a very 'everything's groovy' kind of guy, just open to any and all ideas," Conley says of Miller.

Miller and Conley left Moving Parts later that year and began auditioning drummers. Often they'd screen applicants by blasting records of "out" music like Sun Ra, the *No New York* no wave compilation, and James Brown until, Miller says, "finally the guy left."

Eventually Peter Prescott asked for an audition. He'd cut his musical teeth on Seventies dinosaurs like Black Sabbath, Led Zeppelin, and Pink Floyd but eventually saw the light with Eno, Television, and the Ramones. Prescott had played in a band called the Molls, which emulated genteel Seventies English art bands like King Crimson and Roxy Music; the lead singer played bassoon. Then Prescott saw Moving Parts. "I liked them," Prescott says. "But I *loved* Clint and Roger. Something about them was, like, pretty compelling."

The feeling was mutual. "He played unusually," Conley says of Prescott. "He played upside-down beats." They tried out the ex-Molls drummer three times before asking him to join in February '79.

The trio went nameless until one day Conley was walking around New York's diplomatic district and saw a plaque on a building that read "Mission of Burma." Conley liked it — "It was sort of murky and disturbing," he says. Mission of Burma's first show was on April Fools' Day 1979 at the Modern Theatre in Boston, a funky, decrepit old movie house. The show featured only bands making their debut; Boston hipsters wholeheartedly supported local music and the show was respectably filled.

Some time that summer, Martin Swope began his association with the band. Swope, a self-described "retiring guy," was a very cerebral person, slight of build and studious of appearance. "It would always be very hard to picture him being very physical with an instrument on a stage," Prescott says. "But he enjoyed doing sound."

Swope had known Miller back in Ann Arbor; influenced by avant-garde composers such as John Cage and Karlheinz Stockhausen, they'd cowritten some compositions for piano and tape loops. Swope had come out to Boston and moved in with Miller and Conley around the time Mission of Burma was forming. One day Miller came up with a song called "New Disco" that seemed to demand a tape loop. "And that," Miller says, "was kind of the start of it."

Swope began playing tape loops over a few songs in the band's set. And once he started doing that, it made sense for him to do the band's live sound, too. He began working loops into more and more songs until they became a distinctive element of the band's sound. "Then," says Conley with mock indignance, "he started showing up on our album covers!"

During the show, from his spot at the mixing board out in the club, Swope would record a few seconds of sound from a particular instrument onto a tape loop, manipulate it, and send the signal out into the PA. Nothing was prerecorded; he did it all on the fly. This was particularly difficult with tape and not a sampler, which hadn't been invented yet. On "Mica," for instance, Swope recorded the vocal and overdubbed it onto itself several times, then manually spun the tape very fast so it sounded like a demonic munchkin. A lot of people never knew about Swope's contribution and were mystified by how the musicians onstage could wring such amazing phantom sounds from their instruments.

The band also took great inspiration from pointy-headed punks Pere Ubu, and Swope's noises and tape effects also had a direct lineage to Ubu synthesizer player Allen Ravenstine's atonal, arhythmic sonic commentary. Swope's tapes also had intellectual appeal — they recalled the cut-up approach of avant-garde literature; it was also a modernist idea to emphasize that what was coming out of the PA was not a direct representation of what was actually happening onstage. Indeed, even Conley, Miller, and Prescott had little idea what they sounded like to the audience as they played.

Swope didn't go to rehearsals since the band didn't have a proper PA system; besides, he didn't like going down to the basement because of the exposed fiberglass on the walls. So he was a different kind of member, but a member all the same. "We split our money four ways," says Conley. "It was kind of novel, looking back. I can't remember us thinking, 'Oh, this is kind of neat having somebody who's not onstage.' It's just sort of the way it mutated."

Punk's idea of maximizing minimalism ran deep in Burma. There was no second guitar to carry on the chords while someone else played a melody line, so everyone, even Prescott, had to be inventive. The idea was "strip it down as far as you can go, then do as much as you can possibly do with it," according to Miller. "In fact, do *more* than you can possibly do with it." Even Miller's guitar was a statement: a lowly, one-pickup Fender Lead One. Unlike the Les Paul or the Stratocaster, the Lead One had no rock legend enshrouding it. "They were like Chevrolets," says Miller. "Get rid of one Chevrolet, you get another one."

Locals loved the band from the start. "We were obviously destined for something," says Miller. "People knew that right away." The hip local music paper *Boston Rock* did a lengthy interview with the band even before they had a record out and mentioned Burma in practically every other issue; since *Boston Rock* was published by Newbury Comics, Boston's leading alternative record store, the synergy was fairly powerful.

Boston college radio was far ahead of the rest of the country in terms of supporting its local independent bands. The town had a unique tradition of "radio tapes," recordings made exclusively for local college stations. Some of those tapes became very popular, becoming hit singles you couldn't buy. Burma scored a major coup when Peter Dayton of Boston's reigning kings of cool La Peste produced a radio tape of Conley's "Peking Spring" and Miller's "This Is Not a Photograph." There were so few bands that when something good came along, especially something local, it received copious airplay. MIT's WMBR loved "Peking Spring" and it became the station's most played song in 1979.

Had Burma started a few years later, the song might have been the band's first single, but in 1979 the possibilities for manufacturing, distributing, and marketing independently released singles were dauntingly limited. By the time the band found a label, they felt "Peking Spring" was too old — "It was already a hit," says Miller. "It had already lived its life, at least in Boston."

Rick Harte had started Ace of Hearts Records in 1978. He tooled around town in a spiffy little Volvo sports car, living beyond the means of his modest job at a hi-fi store. "Rick had money," explains Jim Coffman, who later managed Mission of Burma. "He didn't have to worry about a lot of things." Harte didn't have cutting-edge taste, but he could read people's reactions to bands very well. He was a familiar figure in the clubs and had the money, the talent, and the inclination to record bands. And on top of it, people just liked him. "He's just a really good guy," says Prescott. "I couldn't say a bad word about him if someone had a knife to my throat."

Harte's specialty was well-produced, tightly played recordings, with great stereo separation and a walloping bottom end; Harte's covers, printed on expensive heavy stock, were strikingly attractive — everything was done with meticulous care. "No other bands at the time approached it like that," Harte says. "It was rehearsed and discussed and planned and then we'd go to the studio to the recording session and then another night to do the overdubs and then only one mix a night, never any more. It was the way to achieve the ultimate result."

"Rick Harte had a real aesthetic as far as the music, the packaging, the way the records were recorded — he was meticulous," says Gerard Cosloy, then a Boston area teen with a fanzine and a talent for talking his way into nightclubs. "Those records sound amazing, they look amazing. He set a standard that we're still trying to live up to today."

Harte was by no means prolific — his painstaking approach precluded that — but Ace of Hearts had released a glittering string of singles by Boston bands, including the Neighborhoods, the Infliktors, and Classic Ruins, all of whom played fairly conventional rock music, even though it was considered "new wave."

After hearing the buzz about Burma, Harte went to check them out. At first he didn't understand what the fuss was about. "The first time that I saw them," he says, "I was going, 'Gee, most of that didn't make much sense to me.'" But he did like two songs and, figuring two songs make a single, he approached Burma about recording.

Harte had just released the Neighborhoods' "Prettiest Girl" single, which went on to become a huge local hit, selling a still astounding ten thousand copies. The single was Harte's very persuasive calling card. "If you want to do that with us," Harte offered Burma, "we'll do it." It was an offer Burma couldn't refuse. In Boston, unless you could imagine being signed to a major label, Harte was virtually the only game in town. "People say, 'How do you get a recording contract?' and I don't know," says Miller. "This guy came, said he'll record us. That's how you do it. That's one of the reasons we went along with him — here's the only guy in town who has a label and he wants to do a record. That sounds great. As simple as that."

They worked slavishly, recording late at night, when studio rates went down, until daylight. Harte's method was utterly painstaking, layering electric guitars, acoustic guitars, and feedback. Unaccustomed to the rigors of recording, various band members would occasionally have "psycho-moods" and storm out of the studio. At one point they trekked up to a studio on a Vermont mountainside and mixed the song "Max Ernst" for two stressful days, completing the mix only in the last of the twenty-eight hours of studio time they'd rented. To top it off, they wound up scrapping that mix and using one they'd done earlier.

Like so many first-time-recording bands, Burma succumbed to studio rapture, where insecurity, the allure of technical tricks, and obsessive fussing can make a recording far from what the band originally intended. "It was sort of ironic for the first single of this noisy, furious machine," Prescott says. "What came out was probably a lot more polite than we approved of. But Rick's input may have made it palatable enough that people did get into it."

"It didn't sound anything like the band," Miller says, adding with a chuckle, "And if it sounded like the band, you know, we might not have been so popular."

But even though Harte's recording shaved down many of Burma's sharp edges, it was still a raw blast of noise at a time when synth-pop bands like Martha and the Muffins, the Cure, and Orchestral Maneuvers in the Dark were considered edgy. One reviewer called the arty new wave pulse of "Max Ernst" "raw power played to the edge of control. You expect the song to explode or collapse." Asked why he chose to write a song about the painter Max Ernst, Miller replied, "He got accepted eventually, but when he started he was involved with Dada, which is about as against the grain as you can get. After years of bashing his head against the wall, something happened." The interviewer wondered aloud if this was a theme song for Burma. "Maybe," Miller said. "Everything's a theme song." In fact, it would turn out to be quite an apt theme song.

Another theme song for many who heard the record was Conley's "Academy Fight Song" — the kind of song one plays three times a day for weeks on end (as a Minneapolis kid named Paul Westerberg did). "And I'm not-not-not-not your academy," Conley sings to a needy friend over the song's huge, anthemic chorus. Conley never liked to talk about lyrics and was typically evasive when asked if the song was angry. "Yeah, pretty angry," Conley said. "It's just a big conceit. A metaphor." He still won't elaborate on the song's basis. "I find the whole notion of talking about lyrics very embarrassing," Conley explains.

The Boston radio scene was then fairly open — local bands got played on even the large commercial stations, mostly because many of the DJs had come from the area's numerous free-form college stations. In fact, the program director of Boston rock stalwart WBCN, Oedipus, had hosted what many consider the first all-punk radio show in the U.S. during his days at MIT's station. "Academy" won WBCN's Juke Box Jury competition three weeks in a row, beating out bands like the Who and the Rolling Stones. As a result, the classic "Academy Fight Song" / "Max Ernst" single, released in June '80, sold out its 7,500-copy initial pressing in weeks, something very few independent punk singles had done before.

Still, Conley was working for the Census Bureau, Prescott was moving cars around a Pontiac dealership, Miller was tuning pianos and busking on the Boston subway, and Swope, as he told *Boston Rock* in typically enigmatic fashion, found "money on the ground."

But Burma had a lot of things going for them. They won *Boston Rock* magazine's awards for best local band and best local single. They'd already opened for Gang of Four, the Cure, and the Buzzcocks and struck up friendships and artistic affinities with all of them. Prescott even bragged that the Fall told them Burma was "the only band they could stand."

And the underground field wasn't as crowded as it would later become. Back in 1981 the same faces would show up at indie rock shows, even by widely differing bands — that April the Dead Kennedys' Jello Biafra sang encores with Burma on two successive nights — so attending a show wasn't just being in a room with a bunch of other people; it was more like the latest meeting of a tiny club. A very tight community developed, and enthusiasm about a band could spread like wildfire, albeit within a small forest. That's how "Academy," a record on a tiny regional independent label, got named one of the ten best singles of 1980 by the influential *New York Rocker*, along with songs by the likes of the Clash, Elvis Costello, and the Pretenders.

**H**arte wasn't just the record label — he worked closely with his bands, putting in endless hours choosing material, working out arrangements, doing extensive preproduction, even tweaking amplifiers. He was manager, mentor, number one fan, and more. And he was definitely ambitious. "A band should only think national," he told *Boston Rock*. "Selling records to a local market is a hobby, like making records for your friends. It doesn't justify the cost and effort." But because he spent so much time on the music itself, Harte didn't have much time for the business end, and his distribution and promotion left a lot to be desired, even by the standards of the time.

There just wasn't a lot Harte could do about sales anyway. Being one of the relatively few indie labels in the country, Ace of Hearts didn't have the clout to make sure manufacturing, distribution, and retail kept up with demand. Simply getting the records into stores was difficult. In Boston Harte simply brought them to the shops himself. There were some national distributors, but the chain stores didn't carry this type of music; business was confined to a small number of individually owned (or "mom-and-pop") stores, and even they didn't buy much American indie music because there was little support from college radio, never mind commercial radio, at the time.

Harte says his distributors were very good about paying him as long as he had another hot release upcoming. "You can get paid," he explains, "if you have something they want." But often distributors didn't pay Harte for the records they had sold. Harte would threaten not to send them anything else, but it was an empty threat — the fact was Ace of Hearts needed to get its records out there more than the distributor did.

Mission of Burma's saving grace was its unfailing appeal to the press, who found the music easy to write about; an added bonus was that the band members, all articulate and very genial, were good interviews. But there was very little national press about the underground: *Spin* didn't exist yet; *Rolling Stone* covered the music only sporadically. *New York Rocker's* circulation was limited at best, *Trouser Press* didn't last, and *Creem* was vainly struggling to stay afloat. Fanzines weren't nearly as plentiful as they would become in a few years — the home computer was still in its infancy, and even photocopiers weren't as accessible as they soon would be. Pretty much all American indie bands had going for them was word of mouth and touring, and even those things were hard to mobilize.

Compounding Mission of Burma's problem was the fact that their music was difficult to grasp on first listen — there was a lot of chaos to get through before the pop elements emerged. Plenty of people didn't bother to give the band a second chance, but others were won over by the band's determination. "People would hear us and it wouldn't make much sense," says Conley, "but we were doing it with such conviction that they would give it another shot."

Many people who liked the band's relatively well-groomed records were often in for a rude shock when they saw the band live, where they were another beast altogether. For instance, in the typical buildup into a chorus, most bands would play in rhythmic unison, but not Mission of Burma — typically, Miller's guitar would be squealing, Prescott would be playing what amounted to a four-bar drum solo, Conley would be playing some melodic figure, and Swope would be making some freakish noise. What ordinarily would be a straightforward moment of tension was instead a few seconds of bracing chaos.

But what really stuck out was the volume — huge, body-shaking mountains of it that made the band's sound literally palpable. Despite his ear problems, Miller had his guitar cranked up so high that all kinds of phantom harmonics ricocheted around the room, wringing jaw-dropping

textures from his instrument. Conley's bass also assumed gargantuan proportions, while Prescott's booming drums made a sound like the hammer
of the gods. Combined with Swope's unearthly tape loop sounds, the effect was simply overwhelming.

"Why is there so much faith in this band?" an interviewer asked in
July '80. "I think we're real original," Conley replied. Punk had largely
been modeled on older styles of rock — even the Ramones recalled the
Beach Boys and Phil Spector. Burma was more modern — they played
fractured, discordant music with no clear reference points. And rather
than girls and cars, they sang about surrealist painters. It may have been a
northeastern thing — older, and more urban, artsy, and affluent than
what was going on in California at the same time, though the band's similarities to even other Boston bands were few. Their volume and speed
connected them to some bands, their occasional pop hooks tied them to
others. But no one else combined the two.

The tug-of-war between art and pop sensibilities was symbolized by
Conley's and Miller's disparate writing styles. "Clint wrote these real anthemic songs, but kind of wounded sounding, too, in a deeper way than a
punk rock song often was," Prescott says. "And Roger's stuff was much
more sort of analytical — angular parts and quick changes, that sort of
thing. It was almost, not John Cage, but almost that kind of a look at
rock."

MISSION OF BURMA
AT BOSTON'S PUNK
BASTION THE
RATHSKELLAR, CIRCA
1981.

DIANE BERGAMASCO

While Conley's songs were more melodic, more conventionally structured, more pop, Miller's compositions were arty and iconoclastic, often incorporating as many as half a dozen distinct sections. Typically, his songs got over on things like guitar textures rather than melody. "He was more a hardcore modernist — always exploring, always making things sound new," Conley says.

In fact, making things sound new was the whole idea. The band members were outspoken about their distaste for conformism, especially within the postpunk scene, where bands were already tailoring their music to contrived images, threatening to reverse punk's hardwon gains. "It's so much style over content," Prescott grumbled in an interview in the *Boston Phoenix*. "It's gone full circle into crap again."

The band was furiously idiosyncratic not only collectively but individually: the usual snipe at Mission of Burma was that they'd be really good — if only they all played the same song at the same time. In an interview in *Boston Rock*, Prescott declared, "My idea of this band is to fuck up whatever anybody thinks we're going to do. I don't want to satisfy expectations. If they think we're a dance band — we're not. If they think we're an art band — then we're not."

"See," Conley chimed in, "we're nothing!"

Miller in particular expressed his disdain for the ordinary with his zest for the Dada movement, whose downright aggressive absurdism was also an attack on the complacency of its day (not to mention a key tributary of punk rock). Even Miller's lyrics, often alienated ruminations, seemed less like personal commentary than metaphors for an aversion to the mundane. With song titles like "Max Ernst" and the Magritte-like "This Is Not a Photograph," Miller's lyrics reflected what was in the air around college campuses at the time, when surrealism and dadaism were very much in vogue and even band posters tended toward kitschy dadaesque collage.

The band's love of spontaneity even ran to their set list — they never used one.

Jim Coffman ran the Underground, which for a time was Boston's hippest club, an odd shoe box of a place small enough that it could feel crowded with even a handful of people. The hip British bands liked the Underground and often gave up shows at larger venues to play there; Burma was often their opening band. It was a natural step for Coffman to manage them. With his connections to promoters in other cities, Coffman would get the band out-of-town gigs with bands like the Fall, Human Switchboard, Sonic Youth, Johnny Thunders, Dead Kennedys, Black Flag, and Circle Jerks. As a result, the band members were able to quit their day jobs, although they lived just above poverty level. Even at Burma's peak, the band members only got a $500 a month payout, but it was then possible to pay $120 a month in rent and buy cool clothes from thrift stores. "And we were hip, so we'd go into clubs and get in for free," Miller says. "They'd give us free beer. You had a girlfriend and if there's food in her house . . ."

At the time the cool thing for Boston bands to do was have official colors, as if they were a sports team, and Burma took primer gray and fluorescent orange, the color scheme for the "Academy" single. It seemed to embody the band's contradictions — the gray, machinelike aspects and the sensational Day-Glo side as well.

Burma was founded on just such opposing elements. "There's always been this idea that if you put brains in rock & roll, you'll poison it or something," Prescott says. "But it doesn't have to be." In concert Mission of Burma was no stoic art unit; it was all high energy, Miller and Conley bouncing and lunging around the stage, Prescott flailing viciously, often screaming like a traumatized drill sergeant as he rolled around the drums. But live, Burma was like the little girl with the curl in the middle of her forehead: When they were good, they were very good. And when they were bad, they were horrid. "But that was the nature of the beast," says Tristram Lozaw, a longtime Boston rock critic and musician. "Because they took chances, you never knew whether you were going to get one of the most spectacular experiences of your life or if it was going to be a ball of incomprehensible noise."

Yet Conley did not exactly live for performing. "I'm not sure why I'm in this business," Conley revealed to *Matter* in 1983. "I don't like making albums and I've never felt very comfortable on stage. The idea of being an entertainer has never been my thing."

"I think I struggled more with self-consciousness than anyone else in the band — I always felt sort of awkward onstage; it wasn't a natural thing

for me," Conley admits. "I never said anything in the microphone. I just
felt uncomfortable having people look at me." Conley's belief in the band
kept him going through the band's numerous tours, but it never got any
easier. He took to drinking to dull the anxiety, a move that would eventually take its toll.

The late Seventies saw the advent of the "rock disco" phenomenon.
Clubs preferred the ease, predictability, and economy of DJs while
seemingly every critic paid lip service to the new buzzword "danceable." All this made it even harder for bands, especially not particularly
danceable bands like Burma, to get gigs. So it wasn't easy to set up their
first national tour: a 22-day, 15-show, 11-city engagement in the winter of
'80. Such a tour was unprecedented for a Boston underground band —
and all they had on vinyl was a single.

Incredibly, the tour was done by jet. Eastern Airlines offered a $300
flat rate for unlimited travel within the United States for a month. The
catch was you always had to fly out of Atlanta. So even if they were traveling from San Francisco to Seattle, they had to go back through Atlanta.
And because they would hopscotch all around the four corners of the
country, they'd endure all sorts of extremes in weather — a blizzard in
Milwaukee, blistering heat in Austin. "Sheer insanity," says Miller, still
marveling at the folly of it all.

They got to know the boys in Mission of Burma very well at Eastern's
lounge in the Atlanta airport. Virtually every day the band would straggle
in with their instrument cases, looking more and more haggard, com-
mandeer an empty patch of floor, and try to get some sleep. "The whole
thing seems like some fever dream," Conley says.

Distribution was weak at best. "When we got to the cities," Conley
said, "everybody was saying, 'We've heard about your single. . . . Where is
it?'" There was no way to find out essential marketing information like
whether enough records would be in stores when the band came to town
or whether their appearance generated sales — the apparatus simply
wasn't in place yet. "It was like a new frontier," Coffman says. "Indie music, it was do whatever you can, call whoever you know." Coffman relied
on local promoters to help the band get to the right local record store, the
right radio station, the right critic. "Everybody was just figuring it out for
themselves," Coffman says, adding that sharing information was the key
to survival. "There weren't too many secrets back then — everybody was
just kind of helping everybody out."

They played clubs that could hold about two hundred patrons. Sometimes little bits of national press about the band had reached those towns, sometimes local sophisticates had managed to score copies of hip New York papers like *New York Rocker* or the *Village Voice*. When that happened, the place was respectably filled. When it didn't, one of America's greatest rock bands would sometimes find themselves outnumbering the audience. "If it had gone along that way all the time, I think we wouldn't have done it even as long as we did," Prescott says. "But there were moments when you knew it was connecting." In Minneapolis they played two nights and drew enough people to make the then astronomical sum of $800. The opener was an unpopular local band called Hüsker Dü. ("The most amazing thing I remember about them," says Hüsker Dü guitarist Bob Mould, "was hanging around at sound check and watching Clint Conley plug his electric razor in the back of his SVT [amplifier] and shave. I was like, 'These guys are so square, they're cool!'")

They opened for Black Flag in New York. Today the bill would be considered an odd pairing, but in the then tiny world of indie rock, nobody batted an eyelash — Burma and Black Flag were stylistic compadres, just two bands who both played hard, loud, and noisy.

The band got "money gigs" in major cities and college towns, but then there were all the shows on the long stretches in between. Usually no one there had heard of the band except for the poor sap who booked the show, which inevitably attracted no more than a handful of people. Like the time they played Montgomery, Alabama. "Oh god," says Prescott, somehow grinning and grimacing simultaneously at the memory.

"There were about ten people in the crowd and it was clown night — people were wearing clown suits," Miller says. "After about the third song, this girl in a clown suit came up and put a note in front of me onstage and it said 'Do you know any Loverboy?' I went, 'Ha-ha-ha' and put it down. We played the next song and someone slipped us a note that said 'Do you know any Devo?' 'Ha-ha-ha.' And after the next song, there was a note that said 'Would you please stop?'"

As they were getting ready to play their second set, the owner of the club came backstage and approached the band. "You guys sounded good," he said, "but everyone's having such a good time. . . . Why don't we just call it a night — no sense goin' back out, is there?"

"There were moments where you realize," says Prescott, "that certain kinds of music will never be accepted by certain people."

On tour they slept on friends' floors and splurged on the occasional motel — except during their frequent trips down to New York. The company Conley's father worked for kept suites at a couple of midtown hotels, so sometimes the band would stay at the posh Waldorf Towers. "We'd be living the life of real rock stars with open liquor cabinets and all that stuff up in the big suites," Conley recalls, shaking his head. "Ironic."

**A**fter touring they recorded the *Signals, Calls and Marches* EP from January through March '81, concentrating on their most crowd-pleasing material. As usual, Harte and the band slaved over the recordings. "We loved it, we were way into it," says Prescott. "We didn't do it in a punk rock way. We really wanted to get the fire in it, but we were very serious about making good recordings."

*Signals* began with Conley's anthemic "That's When I Reach for My Revolver," which swiftly became one of the band's most popular songs. Conley had first seen the phrase in the title of a Henry Miller essay, not knowing it was a reference to an infamous line often attributed to Nazi leader Hermann Göring, "When I hear the word culture, that's when I reach for my revolver." "I wasn't too happy to hear about that because I don't want to be linked to that sort of thing," Conley says. "But it was a phrase, it had power, I had this riff. To me, that's just sort of the alchemy of writing songs."

The song was instantly catchy, with quiet but tension-filled verses that exploded into a gigantic chorus; the formula would be replicated with vastly greater commercial success ten years later. But from there, *Signals* get increasingly unconventional, as if easing the listener into uncharted realms: "Outlaw" recalls Gang of Four; "Fame and Fortune" begins as a triumphant rocker then wanders into a placid pool of reverie; "Red" attains a cool propulsion, then Swope's almost operatic two-note loop, Miller's harmonics and counterrhythms, and Prescott's odd flourishes put it over the top. The extended, droning instrumental "All World Cowboy Romance" closes the EP on a grand note.

Despite its diversity, *Signals* was of a piece, and it was all good. Burma hadn't yet captured all the physicality and sonic free-for-all of their live shows, but the anthemic streak that came barreling through seemed to say that, true to their name, these guys really were on a mission.

Swope did the lyric sheet for *Signals, Calls and Marches*, taking all the words and then alphabetizing them. You had to piece the lyrics together yourself, which, as Burma expert Eric Van has said, was a metaphor for listening to the band's music. But it was also a metaphor for even finding out about the band in the first place. Nothing was easy. "For people who are around now, it's hard to convey just how marginal this music was," Conley says. "We alienated about five-sixths of the people that we played in front of because we were just loud and blurred and fast and painful, punishing. But the people that liked us were very intense and kept coming back."

When *Signals* was finally released on, fittingly, the Fourth of July of that year, Burma's local popularity was such that the six-song EP entered local FM powerhouse WBCN's charts at number six, even though the band was largely unknown in the rest of the country. But because the EP was released in the dead of summer, when college radio went into hibernation, it didn't get even the modest exposure it could have if they'd waited until fall. Still, *Signals* went top five on Rockpool's progressive charts, right up there with Siouxsie and the Banshees and the Pretenders, and sold out its first run of ten thousand copies within the year.

**M**ission of Burma had no careerist goals whatsoever. "I don't think any of us wanted to be rock stars," says Miller. "That was what I thought punk had set out to do — to get *rid* of rock stars." At the time, rock was still considered to be exclusively popular music — if you played rock music, you *wanted* to be a star ipso facto. Burma's rejection of that was extraordinary. "Exactly," says Prescott. "Everyone said, 'You don't want to be popular, you don't want to be famous? What's wrong with you?'"

But when X signed to Elektra in 1982, the mood changed . . . for a minute. "It did occur to us that, wow, there are other bands getting signed to major labels — maybe it's possible," Prescott says. "And then we'd look at each other and go, 'Naaaah.'"

Coffman knew some people at PolyGram, but the label was then struggling to establish even the Jam, who were massive in their native England and boasted tuneful, well-recorded songs with clear roots in classic rock. "If we can't get the Jam on the radio," they told Coffman, "we're not going to get Mission of Burma on the radio."

Reasoning that the label was cool enough to sign the Gang of Four, they sent a copy of *Signals* to Warner Brothers and got a note back saying they only liked "That's When I Reach for My Revolver." "So we said fuck them," says Miller. "Of course, they'd said fuck us first. If we'd had six 'Revolver's, they would have taken us. And then we would have been dropped the next year."

Artistically (and in many other ways), the band was liberated by the fact that they'd never sign to a major label. "In a way, we were cheating because we didn't have that light at the end of the tunnel," Prescott says. "And who knows? We were human — if the light had been there, maybe we would have turned crappy quicker. It's a really hard thing to say. Now I'm glad that it was like it was."

In 1981 three-week tours of the Midwest, South, and West drummed up a buzz for the band. That fall they played a big show in Hollywood with the Circle Jerks and Dead Kennedys, but the hardcore punks in the audience were unimpressed. "We got out there and we were like little lambs to slaughter," says Conley. "We were art-punk weenies out there." All the audience did was murmur and spit at the band. "Not the most enlightened audience, is it?" Jello Biafra asked them after their set. (After the show the crowd erupted into a huge riot.)

Back at home Burma had been enjoying continuing support from WBCN. But 1982 saw the debut of WCOZ, one of the early radio consultant stations, whose playlist was determined not by the DJs, but by a central office hot on the trail of the lowest common denominator. In response, WBCN shifted to a more commercial format. The area's abundant college stations stepped in to fill the gap, but WBCN's defection dealt Burma and the entire Boston scene a devastating blow.

After the relatively studied recordings of the single and *Signals*, the band wanted their next release — their first album — to sound more like their live show. Having played out a lot — and playing very loudly at that — they had been discovering different ways to warp and harness noise through various types of distortion, feedback, and tonal phenomena; noise became a more central part of the arrangements. To simulate that, they decided to record the instruments in the same room simultaneously, instead of overdubbing separately. The large room at Rhode Island's Normandy Studios would allow the band to crank the amps up to peak volume and take advantage of the space's massive acoustics. Incorporating Swope's loops more often was another part of the strategy, and his contributions, which vary from up-front to nearly subliminal, make the sound all the denser.

Sure enough, the band's sonic phenomena and furious onstage energy are much more vividly captured on *Vs*. The first vocal on *Vs*. is Prescott screaming his head off after two minutes of blistering one-chord

MISSION OF BURMA
SIT FOR A PORTRAIT
BACKSTAGE AT CBGB
ON THE LAST TOUR.
LEFT TO RIGHT: PETER
PRESCOTT, ROGER
MILLER, CLINT
CONLEY. THE HAND AT
UPPER LEFT BELONGS
TO THE EVER-
ENIGMATIC MARTIN
SWOPE.

LAURA LEVINE

rock. The music became more deeply bipolar, going from eerie medita-
tions like "Trem Two" and the grandeur of "Einstein's Day" to more aggro workouts. Prescott's rhythms both skitter and pound, Conley and
Miller crash their hulking chord clusters against each other like wrecking
balls, accumulating a huge mass of ringing tone. Even in the fairly subdued "Trem Two," the tensions they set up were cataclysmic — the song
dwells on one percolating note, and when it finally changes, everything
starts rushing out on a par with their loudest, most cacophonous cli-
maxes.

In "The Ballad of Johnny Burma," Miller hollers, "I said my mother's
dead, well I don't care about it / I say my father's dead, I don't care about
it." At the time both his parents were very much alive. "It was more like
cutting loose from all that stuff — they're all dead and now I'm free to be
me," Miller says. "At that point in Burma, it was like, here I'm finally doing this thing that I've known I should be doing since I was in eleventh
grade. I was certain, like all of us were, that we were doing the right
thing."

Vs. appeared that October and won glowing reviews in places as
prominent as the New York Times and the English music weekly Sounds.
"Vs. is by far our best recording," Miller says. "If that's all we did, then
that's enough. It's one of the fifteen hundred greatest rock & roll albums
of all time."

**W**hen Burma started, the possibilities seemed limitless, at least in terms of the exploding post-punk scene. "There always seemed to be mechanisms for expanding your audience," says Tristram Lozaw. "You'd play at [Boston's tiny] Cantone's, then you'd play a bigger club, then a bigger one. Then you'd go on tour and you'd be on BCN." It was the route Talking Heads had taken, along with plenty of other bands.

But then the door shut. "It was the conservatism of the country and also the onset of a lot of the hardcore stuff — it excluded a whole artier side of rock and it narrowed the underground," Lozaw says. To celebrate the April '82 release of "Trem Two" — the new single by an important, critically acclaimed band — Mission of Burma played a club in New York to a grand total of seven people. At a Cleveland show, the club owner requested that the jukebox replace the band for the second set.

Even worse, WBCN, not hearing a "hit," gave scant airplay to Vs. "It was very disturbing to me because I thought that we built this whole thing and that it was really going to just take off," says Harte, his disappointment still plain. "And they simply didn't play it." The "us against the world" stance of the album title was becoming all too true.

Boston's nightclubs also abandoned the band. In October '82, after the band played the Paradise, the club's manager told Burma they could never play there again because not enough people came. (This may well have been because the band played their hometown perhaps too frequently, as much as twice a month, seriously hurting their draw.)

At one point they played a sparsely attended show in Atlanta the same night R.E.M. had sold out a big college theater. R.E.M. had quickly become college darlings while Burma, who had started before them, still toiled in obscurity. Conley says it might have been a dream, but he thinks that late that night, long after the gig, the two bands' vans passed each other in a parking lot. He saw R.E.M. bassist Mike Mills looking out the window. "He was just peering out, looking at us from another world," says Conley, still wistful after all these years, "a world of privilege and packed houses and upward mobility . . . and nice vans."

There were good cities, too — Washington, San Francisco, Lawrence, and Ann Arbor — but eventually the boredom of the road got to even this brainy band. They became fixated on a game that involved bouncing a large plastic soda bottle back and forth, hacky-sack style, at rest stops and backstage. "It was quite amazing," Conley deadpans. "You could make sport of it." On one dark night somewhere in Oklahoma, the band pulled off the road and shot off fireworks, a small but spectacular show seen only by a precious few.

**M**iller knew when he joined Mission of Burma that it was probably just a matter of time until he'd have to quit. He ignored his tinnitus until after the deafening Vs. sessions, when the condition became too pronounced to ignore.

Onstage Miller began wearing earplugs *and* headphone-style protection designed for people who fire shotguns, and that still didn't prevent the ringing. Sound, it turns out, doesn't just enter through the ear canal but also through the bones of the face and skull. On tour, late at night when it was very quiet, he could hear what was happening. "The tones would come in by beeping until they became stable," says Miller. "And there would be this new tone. And by the end of this tour, it would be a constant beep. For the rest of my life. And it just freaked me out."

Miller first broached the subject to the band in the fall of '82 after a show in Washington, D.C. "It was a pretty awkward thing to talk about," he says. "I was fucking with four or five people's lives. And then eventually I just had to say c'est la vie."

In early January '83 Miller announced he would be leaving Mission of Burma because of his worsening tinnitus. In an interview with *Boston Rock*, Miller, ever the composition major, specifically identified the pitches of his tinnitus. "In September a middle E appeared in my left ear," he said. "And in December a C-sharp below E formed. In my right ear, a slightly sharp E began in October. They're forming fairly interesting chords that never leave. When it's quiet at night, the notes are screaming."

Amazingly, neither Conley, Prescott, Swope, or Harte was particularly devastated. In fact, Harte says they all felt what he calls "a twisted sense of relief." The band had made amazing records, enjoyed plenty of college radio and press support, and yet no one was coming to their shows or buying their records. "It just seemed like it wasn't working," says Harte.

At first, though, Prescott felt differently. "It was probably more of a bummer for me because I felt it was a really good working situation," says Prescott. "I liked playing with them, I loved what they wrote, I thought we could do some more. Then shortly after that I was kind of glad — I knew it was a thing that Roger had to do for his own hearing, and it was a good time for Clint to remove himself from music."

Tinnitus was not the only hazard of rock & roll life to which Burma had fallen prey. Stage anxiety, strange hours, long stretches of boredom, and ready availability all made alcohol an attractive drug. And it nearly got the better of Conley. "Things were going great and we were having a blast and there was never any reason to turn it off," Conley says. "But after a while I realized it was becoming a problem."

Conley was not, as they say in recovery-speak, a "jackpot drinker," prone to big, messy binges that leave disasters in their wake. "It was more of a controlled, low-level draining of my energies and output," he says. "I could feel my songwriting falling off. I was just having a harder time finishing things, really getting a little stuck."

During the mixing of Vs., Conley "had to take a little vacation" and did a brief stay in a rehab center. The claustrophobic "Mica" seems to be about that experience.

Conley spent the last year of the band's existence clean and sober. "And very happy to be," he says brightly. "It was not a grueling, white-knuckle experience for me even though I was in clubs, which is a strange way to get sober. I felt completely free and exhilarated that I was not in the grips. It was a very happy year, actually. It was challenging. I felt very lucky."

So when Miller announced that the band would have to end, Conley wasn't as crestfallen as one might think. "In a lot of ways, I felt my life changing," he says. "I wasn't attached to Burma forever. I was going through enormous changes in my own life, so I thought, 'Well, maybe it's time for something new here.' At that time I definitely was thinking it was going to be more music. As it turns out, it just didn't work out that way. But it worked out very well.

"I remember Roger saying [he was going to quit] and thinking, well, maybe this has run its course," Conley says. "The band had accomplished what we set out to do and I felt really good about what we'd done, so it wasn't a sense of incompletion or that sort of gnawing to it. I thought, 'Hey, we did pretty good.'"

Still, it all might have worked out better if Ace of Hearts and Coffman had been a better team. "We weren't in sync always," Coffman admits. "It was like, he would do what he would do, and we would do what we would do. We would hope that we would all get it done, but it wasn't that coordinated. We were just inexperienced."

In January '83 Harte hired twenty-two-year-old Mark Kates to work the press and radio for Ace of Hearts. Coffman claims that "they smoked way too much weed to get anything done," but Harte vigorously disagrees. Kates, Harte says, was a godsend. "He had this way of just making things happen," says Harte. "There'd be things in the paper and there'd be people at the gigs. He just had it, he made shit happen."

Still, no matter how industrious Kates was, promoting Mission of

Burma was an uphill struggle. "Although Mission of Burma and some of the other great Boston bands at the time were truly world class, the indie rock scene in Boston was pretty small and generally unknown to the populace at large," says Kates. "In a city where money and education and insurance and things like that dominate the workforce, what we did wasn't understood by the average person."

When the band announced two farewell shows in the former ballroom of Boston's old Bradford Hotel on March 13, Kates phoned up every media outlet he could think of and plied them with the intriguing news that Mission of Burma's guitarist might be going deaf and drummed up some local TV coverage. One Boston newscast closed with a quick profile of the band and some cacophonous performance footage after which a stuffy anchorman quipped, "Some of our audience may be saying it's *about time* they quit!"

Thanks to all the media attention, the Bradford shows were filled with curiosity seekers eager to catch a glimpse of the highly touted local heroes before they broke up. Although neither the all-ages matinee nor the regular evening show sold out, they were packed. But the shows weren't very sentimental, perhaps because the reality of it was just not sinking in. "It didn't register with people," says Coffman. "People were like, 'Yeah, they'll get over it. They'll come back. His ears will be fine.' I think there was a lot of denial." About the only nod to the finality of the occasion was the fact that Martin Swope made his one and only appearance onstage with Burma, playing guitar on the Kinks classic "See My Friends."

As the band left the stage, Conley yelled out, "Stop going to discos, they're bad for your health! Support live music!"

But that wasn't the end. Coffman had lined up some high-paying shows after that, so they played Detroit, Chicago, and Washington, D.C., with Harte in tow, recording every show. In D.C. the hostile audience of hardcore punks chanted, "Oi! Oi! Oi!" throughout the set and heartily urged Conley to cut his hair. The audience at the Detroit show was far more friendly, probably because it mostly consisted of Miller's family. The band always gave it their best — as documented on the live *The Horrible Truth about Burma*, the band tore off a positively explosive version of Pere Ubu's "Heart of Darkness" in Chicago. But there were only six people in the audience to hear it. "It was horrifying, it was sad," says Harte. "And I don't understand it."

Mission of Burma's final show was at the Paramount Theatre in Staten Island, opening for Public Image, Ltd. The show was a disaster —

"the Altamont to the Bradford's Woodstock," Conley cracks. At first PiL's management wouldn't allow Mission of Burma to use the PA, so the vocals came out the onstage monitors for the first half of the set. One of PiL's roadies patrolled the front row with a bullwhip, menacing anyone who got too close, until Miller demanded he go away. To top it off, many of the die-hard Burma fans who had come down from Boston on two specially chartered buses had taken some bad acid.

Still, the band was in ferocious form, particularly on the final number, a version of "The Ballad of Johnny Burma" that sent the band into an incendiary state of abandon.

"That was a nightmare," Prescott says of the show. "It should have been a really cool thing, but we had sort of played the last show in Boston. So this was bound to be a mess because we had to go one more. Yeah, that was sort of a bummer. It wasn't very good. And [Public Image, Ltd. was] a band I admired a lot at the time. It was just kind of not a fun night."

In typical self-deprecating fashion, the band jokes that "the horrible truth about Burma" was that their live shows were nowhere near as cohesive and coherent as their records, but *The Horrible Truth* was finally the raw, cacophonous document the band had been striving for from the start. Yet Harte still managed to make it an exercise in studio trickery. Although the various live performances were recorded on an old Crown two-track recorder, Harte split them up into twenty-four tracks, equalized each one, and then put them back together. *The Horrible Truth* was engineered in no less than seven different studios.

Although the band seemed like it was going nowhere, Coffman insists things were just about to turn around. "Things were starting to happen, whether it was the *Rolling Stone* [article] or whatever, you could just tell," says Coffman. "Things were catching up to them. And all the groundwork that had been laid, whether it was touring or college radio or whatever, would have paid off.

"They were just about to break," Coffman adds. "A lot of people were like, 'What the fuck is wrong with these guys? They're *breaking*! People love them now and they're breaking up!' So it was kind of a drag."

**M**ission of Burma conducted their career in the most exemplary way. From the start, they insisted that Boston bands appear on the bill at local shows, a tradition they upheld until the very end. "We felt real strongly about supporting the local scene," Miller says. "I'm not nationalistic, but if you're in the area, you should work where you are.

You have to support that which is growing around you." Later on, when hardcore created a younger audience for punk, they also went out of their way to play all-ages shows, often hurting their draw by playing two sets a night.

Those practices were soon emulated by many bands across the country, but musically speaking, Burma wasn't a group that a lot of bands copied directly. That's because the bands that Burma truly influenced understood what Burma was about, which was to be original and true to one's vision — and damn the commercial torpedoes. On their 1988 *Green* tour, R.E.M. covered "Academy Fight Song," helping to touch off a comprehensive set of reissues of the Burma catalog.

Having mixed aggressive, noisy guitars, pounding drums, and positively heroic pop melodies way back at the dawn of the Eighties, Burma will forever be called "ahead of their time." "I suppose it's an honor, in a way, to be ahead of your time," said Conley wearily. "But on the other hand, it would be nice to be right *with* your time."

Mission of Burma helped lay the groundwork for the many, many bands that followed in their wake. "They helped to create a *commercial* environment where anyone would give a fuck about those bands," says Gerard Cosloy. "And they helped to create a *creative* environment where those bands could do what they did." So the minuscule record sales and attendance figures were not in vain. "Because of what they did, other bands, like Yo La Tengo or Unwound, bands like that, are able to do what they want, when they want," says Cosloy. "*That's* the legacy."

But perhaps Mission of Burma's greatest accomplishment is this, as Prescott puts it: "We never sucked."

# CHAPTER 4

# MINOR THREAT

"A LOT OF PEOPLE I KNOW — EVERYONE, MAYBE —
JUST FEEL A GREAT USELESSNESS. YOU'RE A HUMAN
BEING AND THE WORLD IS SO BIG; EVERYTHING IS JUST
SO UNTOUCHABLE AND UNREACHABLE. THEY JUST WANT
TO DO SOMETHING THAT THEY CAN BE A PART OF
AND THEY CAN MOLD AND THEY CAN MAKE."

— IAN MacKAYE, 1983

Black Flag may have been its godfathers and the Bad Brains may have revved up its tempo to light speed, but hardcore has no more definitive band than Minor Threat. The band's adrenalized rhythms, fierce attack, and surprisingly tuneful songs set them apart from anybody before or since. The music couldn't have made more perfect sense to the shirtless teenaged boys who crammed their shows — it was an impeccable show of precision violence, awe inspiring in the economy of its aggression. And yet the band combined such bracing vehemence with an infectious bonhomie.

Minor Threat epitomized one of hardcore's major strengths: It was underground music by, for, and about independent-minded kids. These kids weren't on the hipster-bohemian wavelength, either because they *weren't* hip or bohemian or because they simply felt the whole trip was needlessly exclusive and elitist. So it figures that hardcore would become popular in a definitively uncool city like Washington, D.C. Hardcore wasn't some druggy pose copped from Rimbaud, it was about things its audience encountered every day, and it certainly wasn't some lowest common denominator corporate marketing ploy; hardcore kids knew the consequences of the former and grasped the larger implications of participating in the latter. And it had a beat they could dance to.

Even as early as 1981, the underground was becoming balkanized.

You had to be an insider to even know of Minor Threat's existence, never mind actually hear their music. They were superstars of a subset (D.C. hardcore) of a subset (the national hardcore scene that Black Flag had created) of a subset (punk). And they made no effort whatsoever to cross over into anything larger — although at the end, the very possibility tore the band apart.

Inspired in no small way by the intensely spiritual Bad Brains, the band, particularly singer Ian MacKaye, brought a sense of righteousness to the American underground. For all the intimidating noise they generated, the band was actually composed of four nice boys from Washington, D.C., who worked hard, played fair, and were always happy to provide a leg up for anyone else who wanted to follow the path they had chosen.

But besides formal innovations, a social movement that lives on to this day, and some incredible records and heart-stopping shows, Minor Threat's Ian MacKaye and Jeff Nelson also fostered Dischord Records, the label that has set ethical standards, indie style, since its inception. The label made a mythos out of the D.C. scene, inspiring like-minded souls in cities across the nation to start their own scenes — after all, if it could be done in sterile Washington, D.C., it could be done anywhere.

**W**hen he was thirteen, Ian MacKaye and his family moved to Palo Alto, California, for nine months in 1974 — his father had won a fellowship at Stanford University. While he was away, some of his friends began smoking pot and drinking. "I missed that little transition," says MacKaye. "And if I had been there, I don't know — I don't think I would have gone with them, but I've always wondered. But what it did afford me was an opportunity to come home to see the results of this transition."

The results, among other things, were that his friends had begun committing petty crimes and getting wasted. "I thought, 'This is fuckin' gross, man,'" he says. "'These kids are twelve, thirteen years old and this is it? This is what they're going to do for the rest of their lives?' Because that's what it felt like. This is the eternal quest to get fucked up. That's entertainment? Fuck that. I was not interested."

While MacKaye was away in California, somebody broke into the home of the new kid in the neighborhood, Henry Garfield, and stole some things. Garfield accused MacKaye's friends and beat them up at every opportunity. And when MacKaye returned from California, Garfield would even try to beat him up, too. "Every time I saw Henry, I had to run," says MacKaye. "Because he would beat the crap out of us."

Then one day, just before MacKaye turned fourteen, he and his friends were skateboarding when Garfield walked by. "He saw us and we said, 'Come on!'" says MacKaye. Garfield dropped his grudge and joined them. After that Garfield and MacKaye were inseparable until they were in their early twenties, when Garfield joined Black Flag and became Henry Rollins; they remain close friends to this day.

MacKaye and Garfield got into hard rock, especially gonzo Seventies guitar god Ted Nugent. "We would read about the Nuge and the thing that really rubbed off on us was the fact that he didn't drink or smoke or do drugs," says Rollins. "It was the craziest thing we'd ever seen onstage and here's this guy saying, 'I don't get high.' We thought that was so impressive."

They also learned a powerful lesson when they saw Led Zeppelin play. "My god, that was one of the gigs of all time," says Rollins. "And we saw people passed out in their chairs. There's guys drooling on their leg, asleep, because they're 'luded out. We both said, 'Well, that will never be us.' We were on our bikes or skateboards until three in the morning, we were up in the attic listening to 45s until three in the morning. We were not interested in getting bombed or passing out."

Rollins recalls that MacKaye would never blindly go along with the crowd. "Ian would go, 'Well, let's see: *Why?*'" says Rollins. "By the time we were all seniors in high school, every day of the summer was, 'Well, it's Monday morning, what's Ian doing?' Because that was going to make what we were doing that day."

**M**acKaye had wanted to be a rock musician since he was twelve. "I saw *Woodstock* so many times, I listened to rock & roll records all the time, I wanted to be in a band," he says. "All I wanted to do was break guitars. We would just go shoplift plastic guitars and practice breaking them for our concerts. I didn't even learn how to play the motherfucker, I just broke the thing.

"But it was just so clear to me," MacKaye continues, "that I would never be in a band because I wasn't talented — I had no idea how to play guitar. There was no hope for me because I wasn't part of the industry-sponsored, don't-try-this-at-home nature of rock. You look at rock & roll at that time — Nugent or Queen or whatever — they're *gods*. So I knew that I could never be like that. And I gave up — I just started skateboarding."

In eighth grade MacKaye discovered a band called White Boy, a bizarre local father-and-son act who played proto-punk songs with titles like "Sagittarius Bumpersticker" and "I Could Puke." The records were clearly handmade; the label's mailing address was obviously just their home. "I thought that was the coolest thing in the world," MacKaye says. "That was my first inkling of an underground independent music thing."

Then MacKaye discovered punk rock through hip friends and a hip local radio station — in this case, Georgetown University's WGTB. He delved further into the music at Yesterday and Today, a record store in the humdrum Washington suburb of Rockville, Maryland. MacKaye and his buddies would stop by there once a week and stock up on the latest punk singles while owner Skip Groff happily lectured them on rock history.

**M**acKaye's classmate Jeff Nelson was a bespectacled, preternaturally lanky State Department brat who "lost tenth grade and half of eleventh grade to pot," as he puts it, "and then lost half of eleventh and twelfth grade to punk." He and MacKaye first met when Nelson set off a pipe bomb outside their school and MacKaye went to investigate; they quickly became friends.

MacKaye and Nelson saw their first punk show in January 1979 — a benefit concert by the Cramps for WGTB, which had run afoul of the school's dean by running an ad for Planned Parenthood and lost its funding. "It blew my mind because I saw for the first time this *huge*, totally invisible community that gathered together for this tribal event," MacKaye says. "And it was so dangerous, so scary for me — I mean, Lux Interior was *vomiting* onstage. Totally crazy scene. Every given was really challenged at this gig. At that moment I realized here was a community that was politically confrontational, that was theologically confrontational, that was artistically confrontational, that was sexually confrontational, physically confrontational, musically confrontational. There was all kinds of craziness. Everything was in the room.

"I thought, 'This appeals to me. This is the world I think I can breathe in. This is what I need.'"

MacKaye was working at a pet shop with Garfield, and a few days after the Cramps show, he shaved off all his hair with a dog trimmer, a major statement in the age of designer jeans. And then a week or so after that, he saw the Clash. Ian MacKaye had become a punk.

In the midst of the chaos of the Cramps show, some guys were hanging out flyers for their band. They called themselves the Bad Brains. "And they were *the* coolest-looking, most heavy-looking dudes in the joint," says MacKaye. "They were so awesome."

The Bad Brains had begun as a jazz-rock fusion band but, having discovered punk, used their chops to play punk rock at faster speeds than anyone had previously attempted, with more precision than anyone had previously been capable of, and with more explosive passion than anyone had previously imagined. They released the epochal "Pay to Cum" in 1980, a blistering minute and a half of pure punk fury. "The Bad Brains," says MacKaye, "were really one of the great bands that existed of any time." Just as important as the music, the Bad Brains' Rastafarian spirituality and righteous politics struck a chord in D.C. punks; it made them realize punk was something you could hang an ethos on.

Bad Brains' lightning chops aside, punk rock's rudimentary musical requirements convinced MacKaye that anybody could do it, and soon he and Nelson were playing in a high school punk band called the Slinkees with their school friends Geordie Grindle, who played guitar, and vocalist Mark Sullivan. They played precisely one show before Sullivan went off to college, then drafted singer Nathan Strejcek after Garfield turned down the gig and renamed themselves the Teen Idles.

The Teen Idles, MacKaye said, were "trying to get away from a really corrupted music, you know, basically your heavy metal bands that were into heroin, cocaine, just a lot of drinking. We just drank a lot of Coke and ate a lot of Twinkies."

The band played proto-hardcore tunes that skewered their social milieu. "When I became a punk, my main fight was against the people who were around me — friends," said MacKaye in the essential 1983 hardcore documentary *Another State of Mind*. "I said, 'God, I don't want to be like these people, man. I don't fit in at all with them.' So it was an alternative."

At the time the major labels were in the midst of co-opting punk rock by dressing it in skinny ties and modish haircuts, virtually willing a trend called "new wave" into existence. Many fans bought in, as did plenty of bands, pushing punk back to the margins. Vanguard punks like the Clash and the Damned were losing their edge so quickly that by 1980 Strejcek would holler in the Teen Idles' "Fleeting Fury," "The clothes you wear have lost their sting / So's the fury in the songs you sing."

To resuscitate that precious fury, the Teen Idles tried to look as daunting as possible, sporting shaved heads, mohawks, and various other punk gear. Nelson and MacKaye would even pound nails and tacks into the soles of their boots so they'd make an ominous clacking sound. "I remember going to the dentist at one point, and I had these round upholstery tacks on the bottoms of my boots," Nelson recalls with a chuckle, "and there was a marble lobby in the office building and a big door at the end, and I couldn't even pull it open because when I'd pull on it I'd just slide toward the door. I couldn't get in!"

They also took to wearing chains on their boots so they'd rattle as they walked down the street — the idea was to intimidate the jocks and rednecks who had started to hassle them for looking different. But the tough-guy look couldn't have been further from the truth. "In our shows and within our own community, we were totally goofy guys," says MacKaye now. "We were painfully honest — we didn't shoplift, we didn't vandalize, we didn't spray-paint. We were just good kids. That was our whole joke: We don't *do* anything — everybody hates us just because of the way we look."

But the tough look backfired, drawing even more altercations than before. "It was a great way to learn about how much hatred really exists in this world," says MacKaye. "If you do something so dumb as spray-paint your hair, then next thing you know you have grits from southern Maryland chasing you down the fuckin' street just because you chose to do something a little different. You realize just how fucked up our society is."

The Teen Idles did two demo sessions at a local studio in February and April '80 and remained unbowed even after the engineer and a visiting band openly laughed at them as they recorded. They began playing shows at pizza joints, house parties, an art gallery/Yippie commune called Madam's Organ in D.C.'s racially diverse Adams Morgan neighborhood, and the Wilson Center, a Latin American youth center in nearby Mount Pleasant. After playing a dozen or so gigs, opening for local bands like the Bad Brains or MacKaye's brother Alec's band the Untouchables, they decided to light out for the Coast.

MacKaye and his circle took their inspiration from West Coast punk rock rather than from the older and more debauched New York punks. They resented the fact that everybody said you couldn't be a punk if you didn't live in New York — what did being punk have to do with geography? Besides, no one was more punk than California bands like the Dead Kennedys. By that time New York bands such as Mars and DNA had developed their own powerful reaction against new wave, called no wave, and the music was far more radical than the jacked-up punk rock of the West Coast bands. But after going up to New York to check out the scene, MacKaye and his crew weren't having any of it — no wave, says MacKaye, was "artier and druggier and didn't really speak to us. Plus, they were snobby to us because we were just little kids."

So MacKaye and his buddies devoured West Coast zines like *Damage*, *Slash* and *Search & Destroy*, eager for any shred of information about California punk. They grew to love the Germs, the bands on the Dangerhouse label, and especially Black Flag. "That Black Flag single was life-changing for us," MacKaye says. "*Nervous Breakdown* — one of the greatest records ever released, in my opinion."

And in early August '80 the Teen Idles, along with roadies Mark Sullivan and Henry Garfield, took a bus out to California to play some shows. Very quickly they learned the difference between being a punk in D.C. and being a punk in Los Angeles. When they arrived at the L.A. bus station, a cop, wary of violence-prone punks, hassled the Teen Idles, calling them "faggot" and "clown." In retaliation, Nelson grabbed his ass at the cop, who promptly handcuffed him for an hour.

They were supposed to open for the Dead Kennedys and the Circle Jerks at L.A.'s Hong Kong Cafe, but the club owner dropped them from the bill when he saw how young they were. They had to settle for playing the next night, opening for the notorious Mentors and an outfit known as Puke, Spit and Guts. The Teen Idles made quite an impression. "People were freaked out how fast we were," MacKaye says. "They could not believe it." On the other hand, the band could not believe their paycheck: $15.

When they played San Francisco's fabled punk bastion Mabuhay Gardens (making a grand total of $11), they met up with a bunch of bad-ass L.A. punks with names like Mugger (of the SST posse), Drew Blood, and Critter. "They were terrifying and they just beat up anybody who crossed them," MacKaye recalls, still a bit awed. For the Teen Idles, who were constantly harassed for being punks back home, it was an empowering encounter. "We brought that home," Sullivan says. "I don't think we'd been home three days before we were walking down M Street or something and somebody says, 'Hey, fag!' And six lightbulbs went on over six little heads and six little guys trounced somebody. And it was a very powerful feeling."

"I don't know if you've experienced a carload of hillbillies going by and yelling, 'Faggot!' at you or getting beat up by marines in Georgetown," says MacKaye, "but there's something so satisfying about someone yelling something at you as they go by and then racing after the car and dragging them out of the car at a red light. And seeing those guys do that stuff made us feel like we need to defend, we need to circle the wagons. We need to fight back." Fighting also proved to be an effective way of separating the wheat from the chaff, punkwise. "We were trying to stand out, and the one way it seemed at the time was violence," says MacKaye. "Violence was one way to ratchet it up, to make it too unpleasant to people who weren't really down.

"I had intellectualized violence quite a bit," MacKaye continues. "I had a philosophy of violence, which was that I bruise the ego. That was my theory. I fought a lot, but I never maimed people. I was not a cruel fighter. My concept was that I would never back down from a fight. I would just come at people. The idea was to break their will — I didn't want to hurt nobody, I really didn't want to hurt nobody. All I really wanted to do was tell them not to hurt me and not let them have the sense that they were going to dominate us."

When Black Flag first played D.C. at a club called the Bayou, the owner installed three extra stage bouncers for the occasion. "That made the night so fun for us, man!" MacKaye bragged to *Forced Exposure*. "I'm talking those motherfuckers were leaving blood pouring! 'Cause it's good, to me, that's justified aggression. I believe in that, I'm an aggressive person."

I n the fall of '80 Yesterday and Today's Skip Groff had taken the Teen Idles to Inner Ear, a small studio just across the Potomac in Arlington, Virginia, and recorded them with owner Don Zientara engineering. It was the beginning of a key relationship.

Inner Ear was just Zientara's house — he had a reel-to-reel four-track recorder and some homemade gear; the mixing board was on the porch, connected by a bunch of wires to the basement, where the band played. "Everything was held together with clothespins," Zientara says, chuckling. Back then, before the advent of the home four-track machine, there were very few options between recording on a boom box and in a full-blown professional studio. Inner Ear was a godsend.

Although Zientara was about fourteen years older than the members of the Teen Idles and more accustomed to recording things like harp music and Celtic folk tunes, he was a former folkie and appreciated what they were doing. "They were teenagers," Zientara says, "and they had everything that came with teenage years — the slight bit of arrogance, distrust of elders and organizations and companies, they brought all that in. It was reinforced by the fact that they were punks at the time and everybody held their nose up as they passed by. That made them more cliquish in many ways — it was them against the world, and they played music with that in mind.

"This music, it was 'Let's give it 100 percent for a minute and a half, and then drop down out of sheer exhaustion, then shove it out of the way and get on to the next one,'" Zientara continues. "It wasn't like we were taking the time to archive this for posterity. There was no posterity, there was no future. There was just the present."

The band had not thought about what they'd do with the tapes and simply shelved them.

The Teen Idles played their last show on November 6, 1980, opening for former Jefferson Airplane bassist Jack Casady's new wavish band SVT at the newly opened 9:30 Club. It was a key event, and not just because it was the Teen Idles' swan song. They had also struck a key blow for all-ages shows.

Washington had a law that excluded minors from bars. Yet there was another law that stated that any establishment that sold alcohol must also sell food. This technically made it a restaurant, and minors could not be barred from restaurants. Still, the risk of being prosecuted for barring a minor from a restaurant was far smaller than the risk of being fined for serving alcohol to a minor, so minors didn't get into rock shows. MacKaye and his friends would stand outside clubs and try to hear now-legendary punk bands like the Damned and Stiff Little Fingers as they played inside, a frustrating experience they would never forgive or forget.

But at the Mabuhay Gardens in San Francisco, the Teen Idles were allowed in once they got big Xs drawn on their hands, signaling they were underage. They suggested this to the 9:30 management, vowing that if any underage punks were caught drinking, the club could just ban them all forever. The 9:30 Club opened its doors.

Right after the final Teen Idles show, MacKaye and Nelson brainstormed ideas for their next band on a long drive up to Colgate University in upstate New York, where Mark Sullivan was enrolled. By the time they got back, it was decided: the band was going to be called Minor Threat. The name was disingenuous. "We were minors — underage — and also just diminutive," says the 5′7″ MacKaye. "Just a small threat, nothing to worry about." They also agreed that MacKaye would be the singer. "I just had an idea of how one might sing," he says. "I watched *Woodstock* sixteen times, watched Joe Cocker, and I wanted to be the singer."

When they got back, they recruited guitarist Lyle Preslar, a pupil at the upscale private Georgetown Day School, whose band the Extorts had recently broken up. (Henry Garfield began singing with some former Extorts and they became S.O.A.) Preslar brought in his

towheaded schoolmate Brian Baker on bass. Baker had been something of a guitar prodigy — as a child in Detroit, he had jammed with Santana at the city's rock palace Cobo Hall. At first both Baker and Preslar were a bit scared of Nelson, with his mohawk and a German army officer's uniform he'd found in the trash and stitched back together. "I was such a tough, scary-looking crazy guy," says Nelson. "But basically that was me being shy."

Very quickly, though, the music fell into place. It was delivered with the speed, power, and precision of a jackhammer, a series of violent starts and stops interspersed with flat-out sprints that had the band playing as fast as they humanly could. The rhythms dealt almost exclusively in what would become hardcore's signature, a hyperactive one-two beat. Nelson played like a machine — with his wiry arms moving at a blur, they looked like piston rods on a locomotive; his stamina was mind-boggling. He and Baker formed a fearsome rhythm team. Using the classic combination of the chunky attack of a Gibson Les Paul guitar and the crunch of a Marshall amplifier, Preslar played barre chords, rock's bread and butter, with a strength, speed, and accuracy that are extremely difficult to duplicate.

On top of it all, MacKaye spouted his lyrics like a frantic drill sergeant, halfway between a holler and a bark. Considering he was essentially shouting, and within a very narrow range, MacKaye's vocals were very tuneful. As the band hammered out their strict rhythms, MacKaye phrased against them, as if he were fighting the conformity of the beat. Yet his offbeat phrasing was carefully devised; he sang it virtually the same way every time, even live.

Guy Picciotto was a friend of the band and was invited one day to attend a Minor Threat practice at Baker's mother's house. "Just being in the room and watching them practice, the force of [MacKaye's] delivery and the way that those guys worked, it was really pretty intense," Picciotto remembers. "They were writing 'Screaming at a Wall' and it was just such an incredible song. It had this breakdown in the middle that was so incredible, and I remember them piecing it together and arranging it, and it just felt like I was at a Beatles practice or something."

The band's first show was on December 17, 1980, opening for the Bad Brains. And people were blown away. "They were an incredible band," says Mark Jenkins, then the editor of the alternative biweekly *Washington Tribune*. "They were powerful, they were charismatic, they were passionate, they just demanded your attention."

"So many things went on in such a short time," says Nelson. "All of a sudden, we were a well-oiled machine. It was just weird."

**T**he band seemed fueled by an unquenchable rage. "I was very angry," says MacKaye. "I was nineteen and about to leave the ranks of the teenagers and I was furious — the evolution of punk rock had grown from these silly kids to being embattled silly kids to being embittered silly kids, then embittered kids and then *violent*, embittered kids. It just kept getting ratcheted up." Even though their look was deliberately provocative, MacKaye and his friends still were outraged at getting hassled; not only that, they were all in late adolescence, a turbulent time for anyone.

And to top it off, the older D.C. hipsters dismissed them as "teeny-punks." "No one took us seriously," says MacKaye, his frustration still evident. "And it drove us *crazy* — how much more real could we be? We were kids! We picked up guitars! We taught ourselves how to play! We wrote our own songs!"

Garfield got MacKaye a job taking tickets at the Georgetown Theatre, right on the neighborhood's main drag, Wisconsin Avenue. The street was a promenade for yuppies, preppies, college kids, and other straitlaced, affluent young Washingtonians — in other words, a place MacKaye and his punk friends loved to hate. MacKaye worked there three nights a week for five years, sitting behind the glass and glaring out at the straights. "Every Friday night," says MacKaye, "I just sat there and I just watched a parade of fucking idiots going by. It was party night, it was Georgetown, and it just turned my stomach." It's no coincidence that most Minor Threat songs were written in that window.

By now the punk rock movement had been well tamed by the major labels and willing accomplices like Ultravox, Joe Jackson, and Spandau Ballet. A pioneering few began devising an ultra-punk — undiluted, unglamorous, and uncompromising — that no corporation would ever touch. "We were a new kind of punk rock," says MacKaye. "We were *hardcore* punk rockers."

Hardcore was the latest volley in a transatlantic tennis game, with punk rock as the ball. The British had received the first wave of American punk bands — Richard Hell and the Voidoids, Television, Talking Heads, Blondie, the Ramones, et al. — and fired back with the Sex Pistols, the Damned, Buzzcocks, and countless others.

"When the ball came back this way, there was an intense spin that Americans put on it when they sent it back over," MacKaye says. "That's why it became so amped — it was just so much more intense, it was a lot less of a fashion thing. The kids were younger and they just went to town with it." So while the first wave of punks abandoned the music and moved into post-punk, a younger crowd took their place and developed hardcore, a combustible mixture of white teenage male angst and frustrated energy.

There was a quantum difference between early punk and hardcore — it was something like the difference between bebop and hard bop in jazz, or the leap from Chuck Berry's affable rock & roll to Jimi Hendrix's freaky electrocution of the blues. It was all about the intensity of your delivery.

Because many kids on the scene came from just two high schools (Wilson and Georgetown Day) the D.C. punk scene was very inbred, socially and aesthetically. They all listened to the same music, went to the same schools, played parties at each other's houses. "In a sense, it was a small town scene even though it was a city," says Mark Jenkins. "If virtually everyone had a Wire song in their repertoire, it was because they were kids, they didn't have that many records, they all listened to each other's records, they reinforced themselves."

A case in point is the "Stepping Stone" phenomenon. MacKaye says Minor Threat didn't even know "Stepping Stone" was originally a Monkees song and only knew the Sex Pistols' version. A latter-day "Louie, Louie," "Stepping Stone" enjoyed a tremendous renaissance in the early Eighties underground; Minor Threat was just one of many D.C. bands to cover the song (at Minor Threat's second show, each of the seven bands on the bill covered the tune).

Their light-speed take on the song is indicative, the extreme velocity tracing directly to the Bad Brains. "They were so fast and so good," MacKaye recalls. "And that was an aesthetic. And that's what we danced to. So we started to play fast, too. We also knew that, as an aesthetic, it was our own — for a few moments there."

Having one's own aesthetic was a rarity for many Washingtonians. "If you grew up white in this city and you're not part of the political establishment," says MacKaye, "or you're not part of the true culture, which is a black culture, then you have no culture. There is nothing here." So they decided to make their own culture, and it couldn't have been more different from black culture. "Hardcore in general seemed the least funky music ever played on guitar," says Mark Jenkins. "To a certain extent I think it's the effect of streamlining — just taking all the syncopation out of it, turning it into this blur."

In their one-year existence, the Teen Idles had amassed $900, all of which went into a band kitty kept in a cigar box. When the band dissolved, they had to decide whether to split the money four ways or press up the recordings they'd done with Don Zientara. The choice was obvious. "We just said, 'Let's document ourselves,'" says MacKaye. "We figured that having a record would be pretty cool."

"I don't remember thinking it was going to be anything more than just one record," adds Nelson. "We didn't have any grandiose plans."

With Groff's help, MacKaye and Nelson, still in their late teens, commenced work on their debut release, the Teen Idles' eight-song *Minor Disturbance* seven-inch EP, released in January '81. MacKaye dubbed their new label Dischord Records.

Nelson designed the sleeve, which featured a punk rocker's hands with the telltale underage Xs drawn on them. They arranged the pressing and printing, ordering an initial run of a thousand copies. Everything had to be cut, folded, and glued by hand; MacKaye, Nelson, Strejcek, and their friends spent much of their waking hours assembling the covers.

Drawn by the cover shot of punk heartthrob Penelope Houston of the Avengers, they discovered an obscure fanzine called *Touch & Go*, published out of the unlikely punk outpost of Lansing, Michigan, and edited by Dave Stimson and one Tesco Vee. Impressed, they sent *Touch & Go* a Teen Idles single. Although the record got broken in the mail, the *Touch & Go* folks liked the cover art so much that they taped the record together just to see what it sounded like. They managed to hear a few seconds at a time, enough that they immediately wrote back and asked for another copy.

*Touch & Go* wrote up a glowing review and soon orders began trickling in from readers. Dischord sent copies to other fanzines, as well as radio stations like KPFA and KUSF in San Francisco. Reviews and some airplay followed — the Bay Area's *Maximumrocknroll* radio show had "Get Up and Go" at number one for weeks — and more orders rolled in. "We couldn't believe it," says MacKaye. "First of all, it was an eight-song single. Nobody had ever *heard* of an eight-song single. They were freaked out. But nobody could tell us why we shouldn't do it. No one could explain why a punk would ever follow any mainstream rule about how many songs you could put on a single."

They had decided that if *Minor Disturbance* sold, they'd simply put all the money into releasing another record. Dischord was short on cash, so Henry Garfield put up money he'd earned from managing an ice-cream store to record his band, S.O.A., and their ten-song seven-inch became Dischord's second release. When the money came back from those first two seven-inches, they had the funds to make more records. In the four months after the Teen Idles record came out, key D.C. punk bands including Youth Brigade and Government Issue — friends of Nelson and MacKaye — formed, and Dischord released seven-inch records by both of them. "We were all working our asses off," says MacKaye. "I was working all the time trying to pay for everything. But it was all about documentation."

I n March '81 Black Flag came to the East Coast for the first time, playing the Peppermint Lounge in New York. The whole D.C. crew drove up for the gig. "And we also raised hell," MacKaye says. "We got in a lot of fights. Everybody hated us."

The cool, older, more intoxicant-friendly New York crowd did not appreciate the rambunctious kids from D.C. who knocked into anyone with long hair ("hippies") or those who weren't slamming with them. Writing in his fanzine *The Big Takeover* (ironically, the title of a Bad Brains song), Jack Rabid assailed the D.C. punks' behavior as "a stupid, macho, phoney trip," adding, "If you insist on this bullshit attitude than [sic] we may as well forget all the positive aspects of our scene and chuck the whole thing out the window. And may a hippie beat the living shit out of you."

Two weeks later the D.C. crew headed up to the Dead Kennedys show at Irving Plaza and even more fighting broke out. "It was the most crazy brawl," MacKaye says. "I can remember one fight at that show that started in front of the stage and rolled — it was four or five of us fighting — across the floor to the top of the stairs and then rolled down the stairs fighting. It was incredible! It was like a Western or something."

Critic Lester Bangs, in a review of the Black Flag show, called MacKaye and his cohorts "muscleheads from Washington," which irritated the D.C. crew even more than being called "teeny-punks." "When he called us muscleheads, we were like, 'Fuck you!'" says MacKaye. "We were so mad." Not long afterward a review of a Dead Kennedys show also called the boisterous D.C. crew "muscleheads," so in typical punk fashion they turned insult into asset: a musclehead, they reasoned, must be someone with a very strong brain. Not long afterward Dischord issued the landmark D.C. hardcore compilation *Flex Your Head*. It sold a remarkable four thousand copies in the first week of its release.

M inor Threat debuted with Dischord's third release, an untitled seven-inch EP recorded in early May '81. In a mere eleven minutes, the eight songs inveigh against blowhards ("I Don't Wanna Hear It"), stubborn friends ("Screaming at a Wall"), Bible freaks ("Filler"). The songs were all about very specific aspects of their lives: "Bottled Violence" rails at those who got drunk at shows and beat up people; "Minor Threat" warns of growing up too soon; "Seeing Red" is about getting taunted for looking like a punk. All of it packed a powerful gut-punch power, delivered at extreme velocity; the amazing thing was you could also sing along with it. Minor Threat had delivered a quintessential hardcore document.

The natural teenage revulsion toward adults and authority figures was only magnified by the unique environment of Washington, D.C. "When you live in Washington and you see these people downtown, it's like, 'Who are these people?'" says MacKaye. "'Who are these starched motherfuckers?' It is such a falsehood. It is so gross to me and so weird, so much the antithesis of anything natural. I just hate it, I have always hated it. When I was a kid, I hated the mask of adulthood. And I was threatened by it."

But despite their hometown, Minor Threat songs rarely aimed at larger political issues, concentrating instead on interpersonal conflicts. "We were pretty much middle class, upper middle class, whatever," Nelson says. "Maybe that had something to do with it. I think it would have been false bravado and swaggering if we had been much more vicious and more bitching about 'the system' oppressing us."

Countless hardcore bands sang variations on the "Reagan sucks" theme, but MacKaye pointedly avoided taking any potshots at the doddering hawk in the White House. It took far more nerve to call your own people to task than to deplore things like the situation in El Salvador, which MacKaye feels most bands didn't even understand anyway. "I fuckin' hated Reagan," says MacKaye. "I've always hated the government. I guess what I felt like was it wasn't my domain. I didn't know enough about politics to really sing about them. And I didn't know enough about the world to really sing about it. But I knew enough about *my* world to sing about it."

"The whole point is if you deal with yourself and people you can exert influence upon," said Preslar, "then maybe you can put those people in a mentality that will be beneficial to everybody else later on. And that's the only hope you can possibly have."

Like the music itself, the lyrics were very concise and unambiguous, an approach that MacKaye eventually discarded. "That really direct, clear thing leaves no wiggle room for anybody," he says. "It comes off way too much like I know every fuckin' thing in the world." Literally every one of MacKaye's lyrics was addressed to some unidentified second person. So the effect on the listener was simultaneously to feel accused (the singer is hollering at "you" all the time) and righteous (the "you" is easily transferred to someone in the listener's own life). The lyrics set up such a well-defined value system that people bonded tightly with MacKaye as an arbiter, a moral compass, particularly for the inordinate number of abused and neglected kids who had embraced the hardcore subculture.

"There was definitely a point early in Minor Threat where he was a preaching motherfucker," says Nelson. "It definitely was 'holier than thou' sometimes. And how could it not be when you're presenting, so vehemently and so stridently, such an antiestablishment approach. My approach would have been more conciliatory. It would not have had quite the same impact, I don't think. I don't think it was a conscious thing — that's the way he is. He is very direct, very unabashed."

MacKaye and his brothers and sister were raised in a family environment that exemplified the best of what the Sixties counterculture was about. MacKaye's parents, says Rollins, "raised their kids in a tolerant, super intellectual, open-minded atmosphere. I think they're both real hippies — real-deal, microbus, be-in, dropout hippies. So they didn't whack the kids around and there wasn't 'Go do this and be all you can be rah-rah-rah'; it was like, 'Well, son, let's listen to what you're listening to.' During Ian's teenage years, the house is filled with all of Ian's crazy dyed-hair friends who were very wonderful people who I know to this day and Ian's parents never batted an eye. You come in with a mohawk and [his mother] Ginger would go, 'Oh wow, that's really wild! Do you want something to eat?' It was never a double take ever."

MacKaye's father, a former White House correspondent for the *Washington Post* and later the religion editor there, was also a noted theologian and very active in St. Stephen's Episcopal Church in Washington, a highly progressive church that held rock services, ordained female priests, and sanctioned same-sex marriages as early as the Sixties. The church was involved with all kinds of protests in the Vietnam era, and the MacKayes would often put up visiting demonstrators, mostly hippie kids. His upbringing may be why although MacKaye held a staunch antiestablishment stance, his most deeply held ideas had strong connections to the best aspects of Christian morality. "Ian's not a religious person," says Mark Sullivan, "but he behaves like one."

Nelson remembers MacKaye getting very angry at him when he got stoned before the Damned's first show in D.C. "I was supposed to go to Ian's house to meet his parents for the first time," Nelson recalls. "And he was really pissed off. He felt sort of betrayed as a friend that I had done that.

"His thing was 'I don't need drugs, I'm not going to take them,'" says Nelson. "A very unusual strength of will. A very tiny percentage of the population has anything like that kind of willpower and determination and self-control and resistance to peer pressure. It's a whole host of things which make him the pretty amazing person that he is."

Even before MacKaye thought of a name for his brand of sobriety, the Teen Idles had had a song called "Milk and Coke," which pointedly championed their two favorite beverages. But by the time of Minor Threat, MacKaye had written a forty-six-second outburst called "Straight Edge."

"OK, fine, you take drugs, you drink, whatever," MacKaye explained when asked about the song's title. "But obviously I have the edge on you because I'm sober, I'm in control of what I'm doing."

Alcohol was a major target of MacKaye's ire, and in a 1983 interview he got particularly vehement on the subject. "There's nothing I hate more than hearing people use that shit as an excuse," he said. "Too many times it's 'I'm sorry what happened last night, I was fucked up.' Well, fuck that shit, man. I don't like getting hit by some drunk motherfucker just because he's drunk. I don't buy it. Can you imagine what drinking has done to people's conscience, just in what they've done under the influence and allowed themselves to do under the influence and then when they sober up, realizing what they'd done? It's sad to me, it's sad."

Although Minor Threat's music came across with brutal force, it was carefully composed and precisely played, a compelling metaphor for the sober, righteous lifestyle advocated in the lyrics. It was also a compelling advertisement for it as well — you couldn't play this incredible music if you were fucked up; you certainly didn't play it to get laid.

"Straight edge" soon became more than a song; it became a way of life among the Dischord crowd. In a very punk way, they made a virtue out of what they weren't allowed to do: since they were underage, they were forced out of the clubs. So they simply declared it cool not to drink. Besides, teen drinking laws were practically set up in order to entrap kids; straight edge leapfrogged out of that dynamic. "Since we weren't allowed to legally drink," said Nathan Strejcek, "we said, 'Fine, we don't want to,' just to piss the lawmakers off. This is where we established a new place in modern society for ourselves . . . clear-minded thinking against the most evil of all, the adults!"

"What would punks be doing now?" said MacKaye in 1983. "Sitting around and getting fucked up and being rowdy. I don't want to be that. I want to beat that and I know that we can. The merchants of Georgetown want nothing more than to have punks smashing out windows, spray-painting the walls, drink in the streets and beat up people. And the reason we fuck them so good is we went to Georgetown and we're honest as shit, we never steal, we go to the store, we pay our money, we're just totally nice, and best of all, we got our heads shaved and we're totally punk rockers and we're totally going against what they want."

Renouncing sex, drugs, and drink was renouncing the unattainable rock & roll myth, making music relevant for real people — you couldn't pursue the rock & roll lifestyle and then get up in the morning and go to school or work. But you could if you went to sober all-ages matinees. Ethics aside, straight edge was a way of rescuing rock music from being simply a vehicle for selling drinks. (The band didn't sell T-shirts and other merchandise for the same reason: the music was not a vehicle for generating revenue; it was an end in itself.)

MacKaye railed against alcohol as an emotional crutch, but he also felt it was symptomatic of a larger laziness and uncreativity, a function of a mindless consumer culture that stifled individual thinking. "The bar thing cripples people," MacKaye said. "I'm not saying, 'Don't go to bars.' I'm not saying, 'Don't drink alcohol.' I'm merely saying, 'Try to find a little more entertainment from your own resources.' As opposed to going out and buying it."

MacKaye's reasoning about straight edge was sound and persuasive, but no one is that vehement on a particular issue without having a personal stake in it. As it turns out, a member of MacKaye's immediate family was an alcoholic, and at a very early age he'd seen the damage done; by the time he was eleven he'd resolved never to drink, long before he was in a band. It may also be why the concept of moderate drinking is barely even part of the discussion.

Straight edge caught on throughout the hardcore community, but MacKaye has always steadfastly denied he wanted to start a movement. "I was trying to defend myself against the idea that I was a freak for not drinking," MacKaye says. "I'm not a freak, I didn't feel like a freak. What I felt like was somebody who had made a choice in my life." Free choice and independent thinking — *flex your head!* — were the real point of straight edge.

"At least," MacKaye said, "it's not a *bad* set of rules."

Although there were few places for bands like Minor Threat to perform, Dischord already had a strong mail-order business, so they just called customers, record stores, and radio stations and asked where to play. Eventually MacKaye lined up an ambitious cross-country jaunt that stretched all the way to San Diego, and they set out in August

'81. Nathan Strejcek's new band, Youth Brigade, was also along for the ride; there were fourteen or fifteen guys on the trip, a few of them not even yet sixteen.

MacKaye's pen pal Corey Rusk of the Necros arranged for the band to stay at his parents' house in Ohio, then they continued on to Chicago, where they had a gig at the seminal punk club O'Banion's. O'Banion's management almost canceled the show when they realized the band was under twenty-one, but MacKaye talked them into it, agreeing to make their young pals stay outside. "We're all set up and right next to me was the exit to the street," MacKaye recalls. "We had already made a plan with everybody. We set up and I said, 'Good evening, we're Minor Threat from Washington, D.C.' And then I kicked the door open and everyone just ran in."

Local punk mainstay Santiago Durango did sound for that show. "They played and there were about five people there, but, boy, they blew the roof off that club," says Durango, who later joined Big Black. "I thought, 'Whoa, what energy, what . . . *everything.*' I thought, 'Holy shit, what am I doing playing music — these guys are just awesome!' They were very tight-knit — they brought their own little fans. At one point they thought that somebody had said something to them, so they all banded together and started chasing some phantoms down the street."

Then it was on to Wisconsin, where they stayed with a band called the Bloody Mattresses, a bunch of punk rock kids who were living in a former dental office building; each resident lived in a former dentist's office and the waiting room was their living room. The bands stayed there for a few days, subsisting on that masterstroke of the Reagan regime, government cheese.

They had just played at a club called Merlyn's — "That was a tremendous night of fighting, people got thrown down the stairs," MacKaye recalls — when the parents of the guitar player in Youth Brigade called and said to bring their van home or they wouldn't pay for college.

While Youth Brigade went home, Minor Threat stayed on, sneaked across the Canadian border, and played a show in Windsor, Ontario, with the Necros, then went home dejected, having canceled the rest of the tour.

**T**hey recorded the *In My Eyes* four-song EP in August '81, again at Inner Ear with Don Zientara engineering; Skip Groff supervised the recording.

The title track had a regulation hardcore chorus, but the verses were an innovation — they slowed down to a mere Sex Pistolsian velocity. In the already heterodox world of hardcore, something like that was, as MacKaye puts it, "a real break." In the song MacKaye restates the straight edge ethos, alternating his delivery from line to line, mockingly stating, "You tell me you like the taste," then screaming, "You just need an excuse!" The band is right behind him every step of the way, dropping out only as MacKaye angrily demands, "What the fuck have *you* done?" More than just an accusation leveled at the object of the song's wrath, it was a challenge to anyone within earshot.

"Out of Step" is an excellent example of the way MacKaye would sing against the beat — as he bellows the chorus line "Out of step with the world!" he's singing in a different meter than the band, making him literally out of step with the music. But the song was far more important for its lyrics, in which MacKaye refined the ideas first brought up in "Straight Edge." The reason he's out of step with the world: "Don't smoke / Don't drink / Don't fuck."

It was a moral universe that seemed to have an uncomfortably puritanical ring to it. "Of course, what it all boils down to is sex," MacKaye opined in a 1983 interview. "It's all a social thing and for people to loosen up, to drink a little alcohol to loosen up their sexual organs or whatever, to get the nerve to do what everyone wants to do anyway. It seems pretty stupid. You've opened a Pandora's box of talk. I could go on all day about it."

The puritanical tag stuck to the band, which one reviewer called "the Stooges fronted by a Zen monk," getting to the point where MacKaye felt obliged to pronounce himself "not asexual" in an early *Maximumrocknroll* interview. The "don't fuck" line, he stated, referred to uncaring, "conquestual" sex. It was, MacKaye says now, about people whose "whole being is just about getting laid, so all other issues, everything else that's important, like friendships or other people's feelings, are secondary." He felt the whole mentality was promoted by the media. "On television kids see people every night going off with different people. And these characters never have any of the real-life problems that occur, like pregnancy, VD, et cetera. It's always clean. It is a myth. It's wrong. And a lot of people get caught up in the fantasy." So renouncing casual sex was just like renouncing alcohol — it was just another self-destructive behavior that society foisted on young people, ultimately for commercial purposes. And Ian MacKaye, for one, was having none of it.

But straight edge was not as hard-and-fast as others interpreted it to be. MacKaye summarized straight edge as "controlling things and not letting them control you," which gave both Nelson and Preslar the leeway to acknowledge in interviews that they were occasional drinkers and yet still considered themselves solidly straight edge. "There's a difference between alcohol as a beverage and alcohol as an abusive drug," Preslar explained.

But the other members of Minor Threat were less concerned with accusations of puritanism than the idea that the band was telling people what to do. The prime culprits were the "Don't smoke / Don't drink / Don't fuck" lines in "Out of Step." The "I" ("*I* don't smoke . . .") was only implied, mainly because the extra syllable didn't fit the line. But Nelson, who was laying out the lyric sheet, insisted on inserting the first-person singular before each line to make clear that it was a statement about MacKaye himself, not an imperative. MacKaye, a stubborn fellow, refused. The argument got more and more heated, until Nelson finally shouted, "*You* don't do these things. But *I* might want to!" And with that, MacKaye bounded upstairs and kicked a hole in Nelson's door.

"And that's when it dawned on me what the argument was really about," says MacKaye. "It wasn't so much about what other people were thinking, it was because the people in the band were starting to feel hemmed in by my aesthetic." MacKaye understood their position and yet he also felt a little betrayed. "I really wanted to feel we were all together on things," he says. "But I understood their point." In a rare show of compromise, MacKaye relented and allowed an "I" in parentheses in front of the first line.

But the straight edge controversy would not go away, and they felt obliged to rerecord the song in 1983 with a brief explanatory speech by MacKaye that began: "Listen, this is no set of rules. I'm not telling you what to do. . . ." But it was too late. Bands like Boston's SS Decontrol and Reno's 7 Seconds took up the straight edge call and began broadcasting it to their communities as doctrine, something that disappointed MacKaye — instead of thinking for themselves, they seemed to be parroting what they'd been told, which was precisely not the point. Eventually, hardcore kids across the country were walking around with Xs on their hands to show they were "straight edge." (The phrase now appears in several dictionaries.)

Still, it wasn't as if the whole D.C. hardcore scene abstained from drugs and alcohol; far from it. "The straight edge thing was maybe cool for six months when you were sixteen," says Mark Jenkins, "but by the time you got a little older and had some more options and you started ex-perimenting, it sort of slipped away." But straight edge was attractive to a whole new crop of kids repulsed by the cocaine-fueled yuppie excesses of the Eighties. "That's why I really was into Minor Threat," says Dinosaur Jr's J Mascis. "It really amazed me somehow, because I was totally not into drugs at all by fifteen, it was passé to me. To hear that, I could relate to it so much more — wow, punk rockers that aren't junkies! This is a step closer to my reality. It was pretty cool."

Most Minor Threat songs brilliantly, concisely got their points across. But then there was "Guilty of Being White." MacKaye had meant well — the song was inspired by his experiences at D.C.'s Wilson High, which was about 70 percent black, where he and his friends had gotten picked on by black kids on a regular basis, getting punished for everything from black poverty to the death of Martin Luther King. But the song was widely misinterpreted. "To me, at the time and now, it seemed clear that it's an antiracist song," says MacKaye. "Of course, it didn't occur to me at the time that I wrote it that anybody outside of my twenty or thirty friends who I was singing to would ever have to actually ponder the lyrics or even consider them."

The suspicions of racism, although unfounded, were only bolstered by MacKaye's shaved head, which duplicated the look of the skinheads. (The original skinheads began in England in the mid-Sixties and were multiracial, working-class, hippie haters. But within a decade, racist orga-nizations such as England's National Front had co-opted the look; reac-tionary nationalist punk rock bands exported it to the U.S., where it took hold among the more benighted strata of white American youth.) But MacKaye says his coif had everything to do with the fact that he had curly hair and so couldn't spike it properly. He envied his brother and his friends who could go to Georgetown and instantly attract abuse simply by virtue of their vertical hairdos.

MacKaye had been drawn to punk partly because it provided a community framework for his outsider thinking. "I've always been enthralled by gangs and communes, any collection of people where it's a family kind of thing," MacKaye says. He already had a gang, so the next logical step was to have a commune.

On the first of October '81, MacKaye, Nelson, Sab Grey of Iron Cross, and former Untouchables Eddie Janney and Rich Moore moved into a dowdy four-bedroom house just off a main road in Arlington. The house was unattached, so they could rehearse in the basement without bothering anyone, and it was in a neighborhood just safe enough that they wouldn't have to worry about getting ripped off. At $525 a month, the rent was cheap, yet everyone was so broke that they often dined on whatever MacKaye could bring home from his job at an ice-cream store — "I would bring home anything with nuts in it on the premise that maybe it was a little more foodlike than, say, chocolate," MacKaye recalls.

They named their new home Dischord House. "It was about having a place to practice," says MacKaye, "a place to do the records, and just an epicenter for this community." The place became just that, as well as a famed way station for hardcore bands coming through town.

"It was about trying to cohere, bring us all together," MacKaye continues, "and give us a project to work on and something to create an energy, something we could build with." Minor Threat's "Stand Up" celebrated the security of that community: "You came to fight / But if I do fight / Nothing to fear / 'Cause I know / My friends are here." It was an awful lot like the tribal family of Mods the Who's Pete Townshend had celebrated in the early Sixties. In both cases, these were people fresh out of their teens, realizing the vast amount of freedom that was suddenly at their disposal and yet yearning for some structure to cope with it all.

"Basically, we were misfits, we were people who were looking for a tribe — we didn't feel comfortable in society, so we were looking for our own society," says MacKaye. And MacKaye resolved not to make the same mistakes the Sixties hippies had. "The hippies failed," MacKaye said. "They struck out against that shit, but then they just settled down and got their careers happening."

In fact, the Sixties counterculture was a far greater model for MacKaye than his haircut suggested. "I came from the Sixties, I grew up in the Sixties," he says, "and I felt like there were higher goals, there were more important things — normal life is something to fight against, not for. And I couldn't understand what happened to this whole notion that people should live alternative lives. I was wrapped up with it as a kid. I never understood what happened to these people who were starting their own farm, these people who were fighting the government. What happened? Everyone was just getting high. That was it, all anybody wanted to do. The late Seventies, all everybody wanted to do was get high. So what's up? I wanted to be part of some vocal, active, revolutionary gang/ tribe/family/community. I wanted to be a part of something, I wanted to have parameters of some sort that made me feel like I had a culture. And

if I wasn't going to be raised with a culture that went beyond my immediate family, then I damn sure was going to create one."

Initially, Dischord Records was run by MacKaye, Nelson, and Strejcek
at Strejcek's house. But according to MacKaye, Strejcek wasn't tend-
ing the business well enough, perhaps distracted by his girlfriend.
"So," MacKaye says, "we decided to take it back." Strejcek is still bitter
about it, but there's no doubt that in the ensuing years Nelson and
MacKaye worked extremely hard to make Dischord a success.

During Minor Threat's existence, Dischord was a very small-scale operation, dealing exclusively in small runs of seven-inch records. The label's principals lived hand-to-mouth; Nelson worked at a 7-Eleven, and
MacKaye worked virtually around the clock, at the ice-cream store
by day, taking tickets at the movie theater by night, and driving a newspaper delivery truck in the wee hours of weekend mornings, somehow
also managing to run the label and rehearse with the band in his free
time.

Even though it was a fairly small operation, there were still plenty of
things to do. Cutting, folding, and gluing the seven-inch covers, then inserting the photocopied lyric sheets, was a lot of work, so they'd have folding parties and invite their friends. "You'd just watch TV," Nelson recalls,
"and get blisters and burn your nails from folding over the paper and gluing those down." Some copies would get a special touch: "Folding all the
lyric sheets and sealing them with a kiss or a fart," says Nelson. "That's
what we'd do on some of them, we'd write 'S.W.A.K.' or 'S.W.A.F.' on a
few of them."

Filling mail orders meant hauling cardboard boxes out of the Dump-
ster of the 7-Eleven and cutting them down to size. Nelson would then
neatly hand-letter the address, draw a decorative box around the recipi-
ent's name, and stamp each package. "They would want to kill us at the
post office," he says.

On behalf of the label, Nelson and MacKaye made good friends with
store owners across the country. This was before fax machines and e-mail,
so it was strictly by phone and regular mail; Dischord would send records
and trust the stores to send money back. "Those friendships and contacts
made and kept were crucial for a label being taken seriously and building
up credibility," says Nelson. "It's not just the kids who are buying the
records, it's the store owners who know to watch Dischord Records or
Touch & Go and then are passing on their feelings about that to the

kids. When something is so small and so underground, it involves everybody — not just record store owners but club owners, magazines, bands. It was in everybody's interest to cooperate."

Then there was the job of contacting distributors such as Systematic in San Francisco, who, says Nelson, "were really, really nice people, always behind in paying but they trusted us and loved us and we trusted them and loved them." MacKaye and Nelson would call radio stations — mostly college — and follow up. But college radio airplay was scant — back in the early Eighties being into hardcore punk and going to college were two different things.

Although Dischord House was in Arlington, they put MacKaye's parents' Glover Park address on the records, figuring they might not be at Dischord House very long (in fact, MacKaye still lives there) and wanting to preserve their beloved D.C. connection. All correspondence went to the Georgetown address, and very soon so did kids who wanted to see MacKaye.

T hat summer, after the abortive national tour, Preslar decided he wanted to go to college. Minor Threat played a farewell gig around Christmas 1981 and then Preslar went off to Northwestern University, where he wound up rooming with future Urge Overkill singer Nate Kato and also befriended Kato's buddy Steve Albini. Meanwhile, Nelson and MacKaye pursued a one-off project, and Baker joined Government Issue.

But Preslar soon grew to dislike college life and began having second thoughts about quitting the band. And in the meantime, the *In My Eyes* EP was winning rave reviews in fanzines across the country, while Black Flag and the Dead Kennedys had been talking up the D.C. hardcore scene and Minor Threat in particular.

Then MacKaye's hero H.R. from the Bad Brains took MacKaye aside at a show. "They had come back from the West Coast," MacKaye says, "and he said, 'Ian, man, there's kids from all over the country who want to know. You can't just come out with these songs like "Straight Edge" and then not follow up. You have to get it together because they want to see you. They want to know.' And so I was like, 'Then let's do it.'" There was little standing in the way, since Baker wasn't very happy in Government Issue and Preslar had quit Northwestern after one semester. The reformed Minor Threat played their first show in April '82.

But they hadn't counted on a painful backlash from their friends and fans. Within the D.C. scene, people believed that if a band broke up, it was simply mercenary to re-form. Of course, there was absolutely nothing to be mercenary about in the low-stakes world of D.C. hardcore, but that's the degree of youthful purism that existed. Sharon Cheslow, a D.C. musician and fanzine publisher, wrote in the local zine *If This Goes On*, "Playing old songs just to please an audience seems far away from Ian's original attitudes. If Minor Threat had just thought up a new name, discarded some of the old songs and created a whole new set, they would've been D.C.'s best hardcore band."

In response, they wrote a song called "Cashing In" that rails against the disloyalty of their own community. "There's no place like home / So where am I?" MacKaye sings with undisguised bitterness. "I just felt so betrayed by my friends," MacKaye says, "for doing what I wanted to do, for doing what I thought was the right thing." They performed the song only once, at their first show after reuniting. Afterward Baker and Preslar heaved handfuls of change at the audience.

**W**hen Minor Threat got asked to open for PiL at a Halloween show that year at Maryland University, MacKaye was dubious about the steep ticket price (about $8), but the rest of the band was adamant that they do it. Unfortunately, Public Image had demanded such a high fee that the promoters couldn't afford to pay the opening band. "So I really put my foot down," says MacKaye. "I said, 'I want to be fed and I want soda.'" But when they arrived, the college students who were working the show had eaten all the food and there was nothing left but some supermarket brand of soda. "For us, we were connoisseurs of soda," MacKaye says, "and it was such a slap in the face."

They eventually got pizzas and Coca-Cola, then played an intense show. "We rocked the fucking house," MacKaye recalls. "Everybody was singing along. We had a huge following at the time and people were just really going off."

Earlier that day MacKaye had spotted PiL singer John Lydon, and when Minor Threat left the stage, MacKaye was excited that one of his early heroes had witnessed what he had wrought. "And we came offstage and just as we walked to the back doors, which were flung open, I saw this limousine pull up and Lydon got out of this limousine!" MacKaye says. "They weren't even at the fuckin' show! Those fuckin' assholes!"

Which is why, to this day, MacKaye does his best to catch the opening bands. "I'll just never forget how insulted I was," he says, "by the fact that they weren't even there."

In late '82 Brian Baker announced that either he was going to move from bass to guitar or he was going to quit. Conveniently, he'd already found a successor, Steve Hansgen. The rest of the band was dubious about the switch, but when Hansgen showed up to his audition, sang along word for word to every song, and not only knew all the bass parts but also played them even better than Baker, he was in.

Taking their cue from the drastic stylistic evolutions of the Damned ("the Beatles of punk," says Nelson), Minor Threat vowed to modify their sound with each new release. With the *Out of Step* album (Dischord #10), recorded in January '83, once again at Inner Ear with Zientara and Groff, "Now we had two guitar players," says MacKaye, "and that's metal." That was fine with Baker, who was a metal fan to begin with, but truth be told, the transformation is subtle at best — *Out of Step* is a hardcore album through and through.

Some songs took aim at the hardcore scene itself — the backbiting, disillusionment, and false nostalgia that had set in within just a few short years. By virtue of being among the first to point out hardcore's nascent decline, MacKaye once again became its conscience. "It Follows" notes that a lot of the things MacKaye was fleeing by being a punk — herd behavior, bullying, gossip — had infiltrated the punk scene.

On the other side of the continent, in his "Sub Pop" column in the *Seattle Rocket*, Bruce Pavitt said of *Out of Step*: "Honest, introspective, this release focuses on pride, honor and friendship." Actually, several songs were about the disintegration of MacKaye and Nelson's friendship. It didn't help that the two old friends lived in the same house, played in the same band, and ran the same record label. "There was," says Nelson, "no space at all." "Sit in the same room / We look the other way," MacKaye sings on "No Reason." "Fuck conversation / We've got nothing to say."

But elsewhere, the lyrical themes broadened considerably. When the band first started playing in the D.C. punk rock community, MacKaye was simply addressing his small circle, many of whom could readily recognize the specific people the songs were about. But then the band's music began to reach more and more people outside the Dischord scene. "It's getting more complicated because I'm dealing with a larger crowd," recalls MacKaye, "and I'm realizing that now I'm dealing with, like, the fold — not punk rockers but normal people." And in the process, MacKaye became more and more unsure — things were not so cut-and-dried anymore. By *Out of Step*, he'd written a song called "Little Friend" in which there was "No description for what I feel / It's a non-emotion, it's something gray / Way down inside of me" — quite a leap from the black-and-white world of the first EP.

The big dilemma for Dischord had always been whether to re-press a catalog item or sink the money into a new release. *Out of Step* sold thirty-five hundred copies in one week, but because the distributors would take months to pay up and Dischord couldn't get credit terms with any pressing plants, they couldn't afford to get another few thousand copies manufactured. They wrote letters to the pressing plants pointing out that they'd worked with them for several years already, and included financial statements, reviews, and radio station playlists to bolster their case, but no plants were forthcoming. With *Out of Step*, the situation was made awkward by the fact that they had to decide whether to use their limited funds to re-press the album or release the debut by the Faith. And just to make things more complicated, the Faith's singer was none other than MacKaye's younger brother Alec. In the end, they simply borrowed money from friends and pressed both.

Alternative Tentacles had released the *Flex Your Head* D.C. hardcore sampler in England and now several labels wanted to release *Out of Step* in Europe. Ruth Schwartz, a DJ at the *Maximumrocknroll* radio show in Berkeley, told her friend John Loder about the band. Loder recorded the English anarcho-punk group Crass and ran their label as well as Southern Studios in London. When Loder caught a Minor Threat show in New York and offered to press and distribute Dischord records, MacKaye and Nelson accepted. Southern Studios had credit terms with their plant so they could press new releases as well as keep the back catalog in print. And, even better, they had European distribution. Almost everything Dischord released has been pressed and distributed through Southern since 1984. Not only were the days of folding parties over, but the label could boast professional-looking records and MacKaye and Nelson now had more time for other projects.

In spring of '83 Minor Threat played a forty-nine-day, thirty-three-show U.S. and Canadian tour. By now the hardcore scene was flourishing and there were far more places to play. "The first time we toured, there were five or six places that we could call," MacKaye says. "Second time we toured there was thirty places and the third time we toured there was fifty places. If you visualize a map of the United States, you could visualize little spots appearing — there's a scene in L.A., Washington, San Francisco, Detroit, Boston, New York, things started to appear. Reno, Madison, Seattle, Salt Lake City, Austin, Gainesville. Then you could go there — your people existed. There was no reason to go to a town unless you knew some punk rockers. You didn't want to play in a rock club — you only wanted to play with punk rockers."

Still, during the southern leg, the crowds could number as few as a couple of dozen, and never topped 150. They made $863 at a San Francisco show, the most they'd ever made. MacKaye had set up the tour using no written contracts, which was a sore subject among the rest of the band, who felt some promoters had taken advantage of the practice and ripped them off. MacKaye argued that promoters were going to rip them off anyway, contract or not.

A big part of Minor Threat shows was the dance floor and the interaction between the audience and the band. MacKaye always made a point of passing the mike into the crowd so people could sing along (and amazingly, the mike always came back). If the PA conked out, he'd just conduct the crowd, who would bellow along over the roar of the amps. It was a powerful expression of community. "I love hearing people sing along with bands — I think it's incredible," says MacKaye. "There's few things that affect me more powerfully than a room full of people singing with a band."

MacKaye never told anyone to get off the stage. Sometimes this encouraged a rapid and irreversible descent into chaos, but usually it just meant a steady stream of stage divers and kids who just wanted a few seconds of attention while they did some silly dance for their buddies. Anarchy, it seemed, could work.

And yet for all the camaraderie, Minor Threat seemed to invite confrontation every step of the way. "When Minor Threat was on tour, I would get into fights *every* night," MacKaye recalls. At one show in Dallas, a kid jumped up onstage and tore MacKaye's shirt right off his back. "And I just dropped the mike and ran after him," he says. "He couldn't believe I came after him — I'd left the cage. And I jumped into the crowd and I grabbed him by the shirt, ripped his fuckin' shirt off, and I just grabbed him by the pants and tried to pull his pants off, too." That was right about the time the police showed up and shut down the gig.

In San Francisco MacKaye again got attacked onstage. San Francisco was home to a hardcore gang called the Fuckups, who were led by one Bob Noxious. The Fuckups specialized in beating up singers from bands;

Noxious had tackled 45 Grave singer Dinah Cancer onstage and the gang's women's auxiliary, the Fuckettes, vowed to get MacKaye. The Fuckettes were all skinheads, so when they blindsided MacKaye, he didn't know they were women. "All I know is I'm singing at the On Broadway in San Francisco and these two kids tackle me," he recalls. "And I just started fighting them. Because I'm in the middle of a song and I'm being violently tackled. They blindsided me. I landed on one of them and they were between my legs. So I started punching them. Then Bob Noxious comes up and I punched him out. . . ."

Crossing into Canada, their van was stopped by the border patrol. Spotting a punk rock band, the guards thought they'd hit pay dirt and searched the van closely. After much snooping around, one of the guards found a secret door Nelson had built into the wooden frame holding the bed and equipment in back. "And what's in *here*?" the guard said expectantly. And he opened the door to find . . . eight hundred pieces of bubble gum.

The band's straight edge stance earned them a fair amount of taunting, especially from a band like Hüsker Dü, who were far from straight edge. The two bands played on the same bill in San Diego in January '83. "They were fucking pricks to us," MacKaye recalls. The first thing Bob Mould said to MacKaye was "Straight edge *sucks*."

"Fuck you," MacKaye shot back.

Then the Hüskers decided to have a little fun. "We got a bottle of aspirin and just started spreading them all over the stage," says Mould, "just fucking with them. It was good-hearted, we meant no malice, it was just our way of being sometimes — being the pranksters, the fucks."

On an earlier tour, the band arrived to stay at Jello Biafra's house, only to encounter a fellow in the living room who apparently began vomiting and then passed out as soon as the band walked in the room. In another room they found an impressive collection of bongs; next they came across a bunch of people smoking pot; finally there was a room with giant syringes scattered around. It was all a joke for their benefit. Bands would do things like dedicate a song called "I Was Drunk" to Minor Threat; even Black Flag changed the chorus line of "Six Pack" to "Straight Edge" at one D.C. show, precipitating a major falling out between MacKaye and Rollins.

Even the rest of the band chafed at the chaste image MacKaye lent Minor Threat. "It was a little like being on tour with one of your parents," says Nelson. "It wasn't like there were that many girls hanging around with which you could have had fun, but you would definitely be embarrassed to do something like that even though he never said it. It was just a sensed thing."

But the band clung to their all-ages policy no matter what. Just before an L.A. show, the club's manager announced he would admit only those twenty-one and over. So Minor Threat simply moved the show — and the entire crowd — to a local rehearsal studio.

It was the longest tour any of them had been on, and road fever got the best of even the mild-mannered Nelson. In San Francisco they stayed at the Vats, a former brewery that the politico-punk band MDC had converted into living and rehearsal space. Nelson was going to the store for sandwiches and asked if anybody wanted one. "No, I don't want anything," Baker said, a bit brusquely. When Nelson came back and began making his sandwich, Baker grabbed a slice of Nelson's bread and started eating. Nelson snapped. "I said something to him and he said something back," says Nelson, "and I leaped across the table at him and I was throttling him over a piece of bread!"

When they got back, Preslar and Baker took up dreary day jobs while MacKaye and Nelson devoted themselves to running the label full-time.

**H**ardcore was made by a bunch of bellowing, crew-cut, shirtless young men playing loud, fast, aggressive music. But MacKaye takes strong issue with the idea that the music was macho. "See, to me, Lynyrd Skynyrd was macho," he says. "It's contextual. It didn't seem macho to me at all. It seemed like spaz." But to begin with, many of MacKaye's lyrics involve fighting, and what is more definitively macho than fisticuffs? "It was very testosterone laden," agrees Sharon Cheslow, "a test of how much abuse you could take in dancing and how intense and aggressive the music could be."

There were no women in any of the key D.C. hardcore bands, even though women like X's Exene, Patti Smith, the Germs' Lorna Doom, and many others were in punk's greatest bands. MacKaye chalks it up to social conditioning: "There's a certain kind of aggressiveness that leads the boys to pick up the instruments," he says. "Another aspect was that hardcore's aggression came from a need to express years of pent-up anger at society and family," says Cheslow. "Although many of the females had just as much anger, it wasn't as easy or socially acceptable for us to release. The angry young boy thing was very romanticized. Angry young girls were a threat."

Even as recently as the early Eighties, most girls weren't encouraged to play anything besides classical piano or acoustic guitar — they just didn't have any way of learning how to rock. "And the guys either didn't want to take the time to show their female friends," says Cheslow, "or didn't want to come across as condescending, and a lot of the girls didn't want to ask for help."

Cheslow recalls that when her band Chalk Circle started playing out, a lot of guys teased them. "There was constant ridicule by a lot of the guys of female musicians who they felt were 'lame,'" says Cheslow, "not loud enough, not fast enough, not distorted enough." So women assumed an auxiliary role, taking photographs, helping to run Dischord, publishing fanzines, hosting shows in their parents' basements.

"Some people say the early punk rock was corrupted by the fact that it was all boys," says MacKaye. "But I say that's bullshit. Whether we were boys or not, we were breaking ground. It made what's happening now totally possible."

In 1981, if you were going to try to explain what was going on in Washington, you would say [major label new wavers] the Urban Verbs, not Minor Threat," says Mark Jenkins. "There was plenty of other stuff happening. It was only in retrospect that people saw the hardcore scene was maybe the most important thing — hardcore and go-go — to happen in Washington in the early Eighties." Thus no record company scouts ventured to D.C., and with the entertainment industry so far away, bands didn't think too much about signing major label record deals, leaving the scene free to flourish and its sound to develop unmolested.

Unlike first-wave English punks like the Sex Pistols, the Clash, and the Damned, who clearly sought a wider audience through media hucksterism, hardcore punks were happy, even determined, to limit their appeal. The music was resolutely unmelodic, humbly recorded, and vastly unsexy. It was a point of honor not to reach out beyond their own nationwide tribe. It was not only a way to cement a fledgling community, but like slam dancing itself, it was also a way to feel powerful at a time in life when one can feel particularly powerless: the Man would never take this music away.

Ironically, though, slam dancing was a significant factor in the decline of the hardcore scene. When it started, hardcore dancing was only *stylized* violence, an expression of the clamor and aggression of the music, and of the participants' adolescent inner tumult. "It was a lot of fun," said Dischord stalwart Cynthia Connolly of a typical early Minor Threat show. "It was a group of people having a real good rowdy time. It wasn't violent like L.A." But as time went on, the difference between fighting and dancing became extremely hard to discern. Hardcore dancing became like sumo wrestling, with beefy contestants marching into the ring, defying all comers to knock them out. A whole new crop of kids had come in, attracted by the music, media hype about punk aggression, even the misleading term "slam dancing." They neither knew nor cared about the style's basis — "It was completely a reaction to the Bump, the Hustle, all these fuckin' dances," MacKaye explains — they only saw an opportunity to bash heads. By the summer of '83, MacKaye had quit slam dancing — "I'm tired of being run into by fucking marines," he grumbled.

"Whereas before I used to get in a lot of altercations with outsider people — jocks or hippies who were hittin' people," MacKaye said in 1983, "I now get in many more altercations with punks on the inside, which is a testament to maybe what the problem is." As a result, many of the original faces began disappearing from the scene. "If *they* stop going to shows," MacKaye warned, "then it's the idiots' domain."

By the summer of '83, the idiots were taking over. Hardcore's regional pride gave way to mere territoriality and escalating competitions as to who was the toughest, who controlled the hardcore turf of their town. "Nobody knows each other anymore, so it's not going to be nearly as fun and unifying and family-like anymore," MacKaye said. "If people knew each other, it would just be more relaxed and it would be a lot better. But unfortunately, there's new kids and pretty much the core dropped out of the scene here. The more idiots who came in and the more new people — although they're not necessarily the same — the more the core dropped out. And you wind up with a hollow scene."

One of the signal moments in the decline of the original D.C. hardcore scene came when MacKaye's brother Alec's beloved band the Faith broke up in August '83. At the band's last show, people wept. "Then it was like, 'What is this?'" says MacKaye. "'What do we have?'" Hardcore became hopelessly played out. "We realized it was done," says MacKaye. "The cake was made. You can't cook it anymore."

Out in Seattle, young Mark McLaughlin was thinking the same thing. "That was what killed hardcore off for me, was how quickly people decided what was hardcore and exactly how to do it," says McLaughlin, later known as Mark Arm. "It became this by-the-numbers, follow-the-rules sort of thing. By '83 I was bored out of my mind with most of it. I was still listening to Minor Threat and a few bands, but you'd hear this new band like Stalag 13 or something that was just this fake Minor Threat band, what the fuck's the point of this?"

**M**inor Threat itself was not immune to the forces tearing hardcore apart. All the kids jumping onstage and thrashing around were really starting to bother the band, especially Preslar and Baker, whose guitars were constantly getting knocked out of tune. "They just could not fucking stand being run into all the time," says Nelson. "They wanted to be a bit more professional and just be able to play their stuff and not have to tune up all the time."

Eventually they got fed up. "I remember them saying, 'Fuck it man, that's it! I can't stand that shit anymore!'" says Nelson. "But sometimes they'd be jerks about it to the kids. They'd overreact or whatever. Their reaction to the kids — wanting to hit them or kick them offstage — maybe it rankled me, but I think it really pissed off Ian. It was just embarrassing for them to be so mean to somebody who was, in a way, just dancing to our music or appreciating it."

Hansgen seemed to join in the disdain for the audience a little bit too much for a new boy, and this rankled MacKaye. Fortunately, Baker decided he wanted to play bass again, so Hansgen left, the band played a few well-received shows as a four-piece, and started writing new songs.

The only problem was Preslar, Nelson, and Baker had become big fans of U2. And MacKaye hadn't. U2's sound was even starting to creep into their music, but MacKaye simply didn't have the ability to sing songs that were so melodic. "I didn't know what to do with them," he says. "I couldn't sing to it. I hated it. And we just argued and argued about style. They're like, 'We have to evolve!' And I'm like, 'We *are* evolving! Don't force evolution. It's a big mistake — let it come, just play music. Let's write but don't try to sound like somebody else. We don't *need* to sound like somebody else.'"

"A lot of the songs we wrote at the end were the best songs we'd ever had," claims Nelson. "But some of them were way too much like U2."

Things got to the point where MacKaye wouldn't go down to the basement for practice. He'd just sit upstairs and work on the label while the rest of the band practiced songs he couldn't possibly sing. Significantly, Preslar had traded his distortion-friendly Marshall amp, the backbone of the band's sound, for a slick Roland Jazz Chorus amp, a favorite of new wave bands . . . like U2. To make matters worse, Preslar and Baker were unhappy that MacKaye and Nelson owned the label they recorded for, a potential conflict of interest. The issue was moot since there were no profits to speak of, but what if they got big? It was an increasingly valid question.

MacKaye had never been particularly close to Preslar and Baker, and now even his friendship with Nelson was disintegrating. "I really wanted to continue to move more subversively," MacKaye says. "And he wanted to go more mainstream. I couldn't understand." The friendship hit a low point at a 1983 show in Calgary, when MacKaye sang all of "Betray" directly at Nelson.

And MacKaye was growing increasingly uncomfortable with his own celebrity. "Before, I knew everyone on the floor — I knew everyone, if not by name, at least by sight," said MacKaye, "and have the same amount of respect for them that they had for me. Now I walk into a show and I'm 'Ian MacKaye,' which is not an easy thing for me to deal with."

When Minor Threat opened for the Damned in D.C., MacKaye was disgusted by the steep $13.50 admission and voluntarily cut the band's pay in half, just to drop the ticket price by fifty cents. Preslar was outraged.

The band was growing intensely fractious. Rehearsals often consisted of playing a song and then arguing for twenty minutes, playing another song and then arguing another twenty minutes. Sometimes the music would start back up again, or sometimes someone would fly up the basement steps and out onto the porch and get in his car and leave. MacKaye and the volatile Preslar got into more than a few screaming matches. "I

OPPOSITE: **IAN MACKAYE AND FRIENDS ONSTAGE AT A MINOR THREAT SHOW AT THE WILSON CENTER IN D.C., 1983.** LEFT: **IAN MACKAYE AND BRIAN BAKER AT THE 9:30 CLUB, 1983.**

JIM SAAH

hated arguing with those guys," says MacKaye. "That's effectively what ended the band — we just didn't like each other by the end of it. It fuckin' *sucked.*"

Then one day in October, there was a note from Nelson on Mac-Kaye's door that read "The band has decided to break up, so just split the money up." MacKaye wasn't going to let the band go without a discussion, so he called a meeting in the dining room of Dischord House. The other three had some demands: They wanted to get a manager. They wanted to consider signing to a major label. And they wanted a two-tiered stage: "One tier would be for them," MacKaye explains, "another would be for me, me and all the kids."

MacKaye considered all of it. And he concluded that the band had gone in irrevocably separate directions. The band members had probably always harbored profound philosophical differences, but they'd only surfaced because of the band's success. "Up until that point, our aspirations were to be in a band and to tour and do a record," says MacKaye. "But all of a sudden we were in a position where [commercial success] could be had. And what they wanted and what I wanted were two different things."

They all agreed that Minor Threat had been a good band and an important part of their lives. And rather than sully the band's name by continuing, they decided to break up.

**B**ut there was still an opportunity for one last argument. Nelson wanted to document "Salad Days," a song they had played publicly for the first and only time at their final show — September 23, 1983, opening for D.C. go-go legends Trouble Funk at Washington's Lansburgh Center. MacKaye bitterly refused and the two roommates quarreled until MacKaye finally agreed to record the song. They recorded their final release, the "Salad Days" single, on December 14, 1983. MacKaye came in, did his vocals, then left. The flip, a cover of the Standells' Sixties garage classic "Good Guys Don't Wear White," was a nostalgic look back at their origins — in Minor Threat's hands, the song was a pointed reminder that punks, for all their intimidating affect, weren't necessarily thugs.

But the A-side delivered the most powerful punch. The song is incredibly poignant — a pensive bass intro launches into a brief propulsive new wavy section, then into a standard hardcore beat, albeit with an almost Motown-like lilt to it. "Look at us today / We've gotten soft and fat / Waiting for the moment / It's just not coming back," MacKaye hollers. For D.C. hardcore, the dream was over.

The song wasn't released until a full year later. "The saddest time was when 'Salad Days' came out," recalled Marginal Man's Kenny Inouye. "At the time, everyone was bummed out at how stagnant and separated and elitist everything had become. Here it is, on vinyl, everything I was thinking then. When that part came in that says, 'Do you remember when? / Yeah, well so do I,' I just lost it."

**M**inor Threat has a comparatively small legacy — two years and twenty-five songs, but it's a powerful and enduring one. It has everything to do with the decision to stop before the band went downhill, not to mention the simple fact that those twenty-five songs are never less than very good; many are even great.

"I guess it's the song 'Straight Edge' and 'Out of Step' and the philosophy and the unyielding way it's presented which makes it still seem fresh," Nelson says. "If you took away that particular message, maybe it would have faded more into oblivion."

The hardcore bands that sprang up in the ensuing years played music that somewhat resembled Minor Threat and the other original hardcore bands, but there was a crucial difference. "We were trying to up the ante — we were hearing something, interpreting it, and throwing it back," says MacKaye. "But then I started hearing bands who were just playing the same thing, they weren't putting their own spin on it, they were just emulating it. And that's when it lost its soul for me."

There were vast numbers of bands still playing the music, and a self-sustaining subculture had sprung up worldwide, but as far as MacKaye was concerned, hardcore was played out by 1983. "You think about an explosion, there's the thrust of the actual explosion, the heat of that is intense," says MacKaye. "But the farther away you get, the colder it gets, until eventually it's just shit drifting down to the ground. That's the way I felt. I would never take credit for being at the initial blast. But I was pretty fuckin' close to it."

# CHAPTER 5

# HÜSKER DÜ

**TAKING INSPIRATION FROM HÜSKER DÜ
IT'S A NEW GENERATION OF ELECTRIC
WHITE BOY BLUES!**

**— SEBADOH, "GIMME INDIE ROCK!"**

On many levels Hüsker Dü never let anyone catch their breath. The band's songs were unbroken walls of speed and noise; in concert they played number after number without any breaks in between; they recorded new albums just as the previous one was coming out. The band was in a headlong rush toward a lofty peak, and it was hard not to get swept up in the quest.

Hüsker Dü's metamorphosis from fast 'n' bilious hardcore band to nonpareil buzz saw tunesmiths did seem nothing short of miraculous, but truth be told, they were just one more indie band who made their first records before they figured out exactly who they were. It wasn't until their 1983 EP *Metal Circus* that they took on the unmistakably magical sound of a group becoming themselves.

For all the speed and clamor of their music, Hüsker Dü was perhaps the first post-hardcore band of its generation to write songs that could withstand the classic acid test of getting played on an acoustic guitar. Widely hailed albums like *Zen Arcade*, *New Day Rising*, and *Flip Your Wig* injected other rock traditions into hardcore, crucially advancing the music, widening its audience, and placing Hüsker Dü at center stage in American indie rock.

Hüsker Dü played a huge role in convincing the underground that melody and punk rock weren't antithetical. Over in Boston, for instance, Charles Thompson was listening closely to Hüsker Dü's aggro-pop (as well as Hüsker Dü's Scottish cousins the Jesus and Mary Chain) and would later use many of their ideas in his own band, the Pixies. In turn, a scruffy misfit from rural Aberdeen, Washington, named Kurt Cobain would hear Thompson's band and transfer those ideas to his band Nirvana. Countless other key bands of the alternative era, from Soul Asylum to Superchunk, owe a huge debt to Hüsker Dü.

Among other things, they became the key link between hardcore and the more melodic, accessible music that would eventually be termed "college rock." SST's first signing outside of Southern California, Hüsker Dü quickly became the label's star attraction, providing the struggling SST with a crucial financial leg up. Hüsker Dü shared the pragmatism (and the stage) of peers like the Minutemen, Black Flag, and Minor Threat, but just as their music was more pop, so were their ambitions. Their eventual move to a major label sent shock waves through the indie community. R.E.M. and U2 had paved the way, but no one from *the community* had ever made the leap. From then on, indie labels were perceived in a new light — not as a miniature parallel universe to the majors, but as farm teams for the mainstream. "College rock" was now a viable commercial enterprise.

But even this mighty band could not withstand the withering white glare of the major label spotlight and went down amidst tragedy, recrimination, and despair, still stubbornly clinging to their hard-won artistic freedom. Such is the fate of the pioneer.

**B**ob Mould grew up in Malone, New York, a sleepy farm town wedged between the massive Adirondack State Park and the Canadian border. His parents ran a grocery store. A Beatles fan, Mould delved further into Sixties pop when his dad found a source of used singles for a penny apiece. Mould grew up on bedrock classics by the Byrds and the Who, followed by a long, dark night when he got into metal in his early teens.

But then, when he was seventeen, the Ramones came into his life. "I thought, 'Aha, this is the Beatles,'" says Mould, who quickly picked up the guitar. "I figured if they could do it, anybody could."

In 1978 Mould began attending prestigious Macalester College in St. Paul, Minnesota, on an underprivileged student scholarship. He'd chosen Macalester because in the Sixties the school had supported the left-wing Students for a Democratic Society; legendary liberal politicians like Hubert Humphrey and Walter Mondale had taught there, too.

But Mould was disillusioned as soon as he arrived — the Sixties counterculture had long ago vacated Macalester. In its place was a group of kids who called themselves Young Republicans. "I remember watching these kids getting up in the morning on my dorm floor, putting on a suit and tie and a briefcase, talking about this guy from California named Ronald Reagan and how he was going to be the next president," says Mould. "And I'd be sitting there arguing with those fucks in speech class and poli sci and just *hating* that, thinking, 'This is not acceptable behavior. This is not what we're supposed to be doing with our late teens.'"

The experience galvanized Mould. "It wasn't so much about 'smash the system' but 'make our *own* system,'" he says. "We had to make our own system to live inside of, that doesn't go along with this, because it's going to be ugly. . . . Seeing that scary times were coming. That was my particular awakening — watching the kids on my floor wanting to grow up and exploit the lower class."

He quickly became a cog in the nascent Midwest punk network, a group of like-minded souls who worked hard, with little reward besides seeing the coolest bands of the day play their town. When a punk band visited Minneapolis, Mould was part of the welcoming committee, carrying their gear and even bringing sandwiches or beer or perhaps something stronger. Mould also "helped out" bigger names, like Johnny Thunders and Nico. ("John was a demanding person," Mould recalls. "You'd think Dilaudids would be it, and he'd just throw them away and say, 'You got anything better?'")

**F**reshman year Mould started buying pot from a record store clerk, a plumpish kid with heavy sideburns and a black leather motorcycle jacket, named Grant Hart. The last of five children and the son of a credit union employee and a shop teacher, Hart came from a "typical American dysfunctional family," he says. "Not very abusive, though. Nothing really to complain about." But when he was ten, his older brother was killed in a car accident. Hart inherited his brother's records as well as his drum set and soon began playing in everything from wedding bands to garage-rock combos. He largely avoided contemporary rock, opting instead for soundtracks and fifty-seven-cent compilations of Fifties and Sixties pop hits.

Hart and Mould hit it off, and Hart would often visit Mould's dorm room, where they'd play records for hours. Hart sized up his new friend as "an upstater pretending to be a Manhattanite," but Mould was an impressive guitarist. "He would pull a record out of the bag and put it on the turntable," recalls Hart, "and by the second verse, be playing along with it."

One night in March '79, Hart was hanging out with his pal Greg Norton and a keyboardist named Charlie Pine at Ron's Randolph Inn, a little tavern where bands sometimes played. Pine walked up to the club's owner, mentioned he had a band, and received a gig on the spot. Only one problem: Pine didn't actually have a band. So he asked Hart to form one. Norton had a bass, so he was in, then Mould signed on, too.

The quartet began intensive rehearsals in Norton's mom's basement in suburban Mendota Heights. "Bob was this dorky kid in a leather jacket with long hair and a Flying V like the Ramones," Norton recalls, but he sure could whip up a big noise on his guitar. They quickly worked up a bunch of covers — everything from Fifties rocker (and fellow Minnesotan) Eddie Cochran to the Buzzcocks, trendy oldies like "Sea Cruise" and "I Fought the Law" — and plenty of Ramones.

They had been jamming on Talking Heads' "Psycho Killer" when someone started babbling all the foreign phrases they could think of, parodying the song's French verse. At one point someone hollered, "Hüsker Dü" — the name of a popular Sixties board game "where the child can outwit the adult." (The phrase is Norwegian for "Do you remember?") The name stuck.

Hüsker Dü played their first gig on March 30, 1979. Then Pine got another gig a week later, a lucrative Spring Fest show at Macalester. Pine didn't know that Hart, Mould, and Norton had secretly been practicing without him and had developed a couple of original tunes. They played them as the encore of the Spring Fest show, and when Pine tried to play along, Hart's buddy "Balls" Mikutowski yanked the plug out of Pine's keyboard, pointed at Pine, and gave him the finger, then pointed at the rest of the band and gave them a vigorous thumbs-up. With that benediction, Hüsker Dü was born.

The band had lofty ambitions from the start; to them, a deal with punk-centric Sire Records seemed practically inevitable. "I think we kind of felt that what we were doing was good, that it was *really* good," says Norton. "It was, 'OK, we're not from L.A. and we're not from New York and we're not from London,' but we felt that we were good and we could play with the best of 'em." But the problem was not that they weren't from L.A., New York, or London — they weren't even from Minneapolis. "We were St. Paul people, which was like East Germans," Hart explains. "So we had to live that down."

At their first Minneapolis club show that summer, they were asked to stop playing because they were too loud. "We just sort of came out of nowhere, playing this real, real fast punk stuff, and people hated it," said Mould. "We just kept playing faster and faster to get people to hate us more [laughs]."

It was an awkward time to start a punk band in Minneapolis — the city's leading punk outfit, the pioneering Suicide Commandos, had just broken up after their major label debut bombed; hipsters around town had soured on punk and began embracing new wavy bands like the Suburbs. "We just didn't fit in," said Mould. "People said, 'We've seen it all, blah, blah, blah.' We weren't cool, because we were the only punk band around, and punk was going out [of style]. But we stuck to our guns." The band did have a small but rabid following dubbed the Veggies, who never missed a show and turned even the smallest turnout into a slam-dance fest.

And they had some help starting the band — Hart's mother let him use the credit union's photocopier to make flyers; Mould's father got a van and drove it out to Minneapolis, caught a nap, and drove a cheap used car back to upstate New York; Norton's mom let the band use the basement of her house as a rehearsal space and clubhouse.

An enigmatic name like Hüsker Dü, they hoped, meant they wouldn't be pigeonholed as a hardcore band. "It's not like Social Red Youth Dynasty Brigade Distortion," Mould explained. "When you see a name like that you can pretty much guess that the band has been listening to music for a year, and playing instruments for six months, been in a band for two months and they wrote all their lyrics the night of the show. That's all well and good. I don't have any qualms with that, but we don't want to be lumped in with them."

But they immediately got lumped in with the hardcore bands anyway.

Luckily they were able to put hardcore to work for them, playing the northern Midwest hardcore circuit — Madison, Milwaukee, and Chicago, mostly. Local hardcore kids would go to Hüsker Dü's shows and put up the band that night; when their bands played Minneapolis, Hüsker Dü would reciprocate. Shunned by the arty hipsters, Hüsker Dü had found a community that would support them. "You're in this very meager thing and you learn lessons and you take them home with you," says Mould, "and then when the Effigies or the Meat Puppets or the Minutemen come through, we give up our floor, we give up our food. You give. You give back."

And then they won some key out-of-town fans. In March '80 they arranged to play a Chicago show the same night as Black Flag was playing, billing it as a Black Flag afterparty. Sure enough, Greg Ginn, Chuck Dukowski, Dez Cadena, and Spot showed up at the tiny club and were blown away by Hüsker Dü. "We were on fire," says Mould. "We were way too jacked up on everything, amphetamines in particular. I just remember bouncing from wall to wall to wall, just throwing myself off the walls. And I had this hammer and I was smashing stuff. We were just going nuts."

"We were on a mission," Hart explains, "to impress the hell out of Black Flag."

By the end of the set, Hart had knocked over his kit, drums and cymbals spread over the floor. The band retreated to a utility closet, where they found a paint bucket that Mould heaved out onto the floor, splattering blue paint everywhere. A woman who worked for the club got angry at this and began scooping up the paint with a cymbal and flinging it onto Hart's drums. "Not a smart move," says Mould. "So he went flying out there, and he grabbed her and threw her down in the paint and then picked her up and started bouncing her off the wall. She was leaving these blue butt prints.'"

The Black Flag guys looked on in astonishment. "They were sort of scared to come back, but they were just like, 'Uh . . . What *are* you guys?'" says Mould. "We're like, 'We're Hüsker Dü, who the hell are you?'"

D espite the warm reception from the reigning kings of American punk rock, when they recorded their first single in November '80, Hüsker Dü's morale was low. "We were really confused," Mould says. "We were getting shit from all sides." Maybe that's why they chose two of their slowest songs. Hart's dirgey "Statues," with its trancey bass line, skeletal guitar, and buried, yowling vocal, sounded a whole lot like Mould's favorites, Public Image, Ltd.; so did Mould's "Amusement," for that matter. The single aimed for the robotic, alienated pose considered sophisticated at the time, and fell flat because of it.

A new independent label in town called Twin/Tone had expressed interest in the band, then pulled out, reportedly because one of the co-owners quite understandably felt the single sounded too much like Public Image, Ltd. To make matters worse, Mould, Hart, and Norton were already indignant that Twin/Tone had signed the Replacements, a young, loud, and snotty Minneapolis band who had played only one or two gigs, while Hüsker Dü already had a modest regional following.

"I don't know if it was resentment," says Mould, "but it sure can be a motivator to make you realize that, well, some people get it handed to them and some of us gotta work. I don't think it was ever resenting, it was more like, 'Well, that's one way to do it.' So we just thought, well, 'We'll just make our own label and make our own scene.'"

So they added $2,000 to an existing loan at Hart's mom's credit union and founded Reflex Records (so named because it was a reflex against Twin/Tone) so they could release two thousand copies of the "Statues"/"Amusement" single in January '81.

Derivative as it was, the single won praise in *New York Rocker*, Boston's *Take It*, and Minneapolis's *City Pages*, then got picked up by Systematic Distribution, which dealt with the West Coast and got the single written up in fanzines all around the country.

They made their first trip out of the region in June '81, touring for seven weeks in Canada and on the West Coast on the "Children's Crusade '81" tour. First stop was Calgary, then a rollicking oil boomtown. "It was the Wild West," recalls Mould. "A lot of cowboys, a lot of Indians. Not many punks." They played four sets a night for six nights at the roughneck Calgarian Hotel. "You'd walk in and do sound check, and there'd be a couple Native Americans shooting pool," says Mould. "And maybe an hour later some cowboys walk in, they pick up some pool cues and start laying into each other. Come eight o'clock when the two guys in town with mohawks walk in, guess what happens — they stop hitting each other and start on the punks."

They'd made solid connections with Vancouver bands like D.O.A. and the Subhumans and stayed there for a week, playing shows and hanging out. D.O.A. also hooked up Hüsker Dü with some Seattle punkers who were starting up a paper called *The Rocket*, which later became Seattle's preeminent music paper. The band stayed in Seattle for a week or so and managed to score a few gigs on short notice. "It was easy at the time," says Mould, "because you either played New Wave Monday at the disco or you just found the other kids hanging out on the strip in the U-District and said, 'Hey, do you have a place we can stay? Is there punk rock here?'

And they say, 'Oh yeah, the Fartz are playing at [the club] WREX, down [in the neighborhood] where the junkies shoot up, down on the water. Go down there!' Then you just go down there and you just pick up a gig. And you play more gigs. That's how it went."

The hardcore grapevine had already spread word of the Hüskers, but hardly anybody had heard their music. Remarkably, the band exceeded the hype. "Wow" went a review from the key Seattle zine *Desperate Times*. "I had heard that this was a great band, but of course that can never prepare one when a band is this great. . . . [O]nly idiots would want to sit down during their sets. . . . They come on with such force and energy, energy that builds with each song, that I felt as though the bar would explode at any moment." Word got around town fast, and a local promoter put them on the bill with the Dead Kennedys at the Showbox club before nine hundred people, by far the Hüskers' biggest crowd to date.

After the success in Seattle, it was down to Portland. About twelve people showed up. "Usually, what we would do was be as antagonistic as possible and try to clear the room at that point," Norton says. "There wasn't anybody there, we might as well see if we can piss everybody off and make 'em leave. You do what you have to do to entertain yourself." The band made noise and feedback until everyone went away.

Fortunately, the Dead Kennedys' Jello Biafra had really enjoyed the Seattle show and invited them not just to stay at his house in San Francisco, but to open for the Dead Kennedys at the Mabuhay Gardens, where they played a tornadic twenty-minute set at the overpacked club. "It was really cool at first. The kids were having fun diving off the stage. Then they started thrashing into us," said Mould. "It was so packed, the bouncers couldn't get them out the back, so they had to drag them across the stage during our songs. We didn't stop, and the tension just kept on building."

Biafra was a very helpful host, even forging rent receipts for the band so they could get food stamps, which was crucial since they'd long since run out of money. Next stop was Southern California, where Mike Watt was trying to line up some gigs for them, but it was the height of L.A.'s unofficial ban on hardcore shows, so Hart, Mould, and Norton went straight back to Minneapolis.

They arrived to find that Minneapolis was a different place. While Hüsker Dü was away, the Replacements had created a stir. Not only was there competition for the Minneapolis punk crown, but the competition was now the pet project of their nemesis Twin/Tone. "That year they were proving themselves at all costs," says Terry Katzman, then a local soundman and journalist. "They knew when they came back to Minneapolis that the Replacements were going and the ante had gone up."

The 7th Street Entry was the small ground floor annex to the recently opened First Avenue club, a place for developing local bands to play while big national acts played the big room upstairs. It was there that Hüsker Dü played an August 15 homecoming show to record what would become their first album.

Engineer Terry Katzman was at sound check and thus was the first local to hear them after they got back. Katzman was stunned by what he heard. "I was about to have heart failure — I couldn't believe how *fast* they were," Katzman recalls. "They came back a different band." Writing about the performance in the Twin Cities column of the zine *Discords*, Katzman exclaimed, "It's hard to believe but the only Mpls hardcore band have gotten even faster during their stay away."

The band had plenty of slower material, but only the fast stuff got played on the Children's Crusade tour. When they opened for another band, they usually had a short time to make their point, so they always came out with both guns blazing. And when they headlined, there was usually almost nobody there, so they'd retaliate and try to drive out the few adventurous souls who'd come to see them by playing even faster, louder, and noisier than ever.

Besides, they'd been playing constantly for months and had become far better musicians. "And there was a point there where we were like, 'Let's see how fast we can play it,'" says Norton. "I guess we were just trying to blow people away." Along the way they'd witnessed speedy bands like D.O.A., the Fartz, and the Dead Kennedys and realized that playing fast was the cool thing to do. As a result, "the fast stuff got meteoric," says Hart, "and the slower stuff became less important." They were also taking plenty of cheap trucker's speed, but Norton insists amphetamines weren't responsible for the breakneck tempos — they took speed mostly as an appetite suppressant because they had no money for food.

Even Mould admitted the resulting record was "speed for speed's sake." Recorded for $350, the pointedly titled *Land Speed Record* almost completely dispensed with structure, sounding less like guitar, bass, drums, and vocals than a sustained explosion, an almost formless mass that owed much to the squalling, teeming free jazz Hart, Mould, and Norton were listening to at the time. "It sounds just like when you go to a gig and your ears are blown off," explained Mould.

Seventeen songs in twenty-six minutes, *Land Speed Record* is a fiery admixture of adrenaline and bile, a 200-proof distillation of rage; if you listen closely, you can almost hear the sound of blood boiling. Any melody was obliterated in the cacophony, and except for occasional phrases like "It's all lies anyway," the lyrics were incomprehensible; titles like "All Tensed Up," "Guns at My School," "Let's Go Die," and "Don't Have a Life" tell the story. *Land Speed Record*, Mould once noted, is "like the bad part of the acid."

But a style was forming. Oddly enough, the key was their takeoff on the *Gilligan's Island* theme. If you could find the tune, regrettably familiar to just about anybody on the planet, buried in the band's dense attack, you could start to pick up the structures and melodies deeply inscribed in the originals, too.

Yet the band felt compelled to be as noisy as possible. "We could sound slick and have no feedback and be pleasant," Mould explained at the time, "but our lyric matter is not; therefore, why should we sound like the dB's? We are not singing about JoAnne and Shirley and Sally, we're singing about starving people, military-industrial complexes, and messed-up city transit." And indeed, the cover of *Land Speed Record* is a photo of the coffins of the first eight soldiers killed in Vietnam; like many punks, the members of Hüsker Dü actually agreed with Sixties counterculture values but despised the hippies for selling out those values. "We're doing the same thing that the peace movement did in the Sixties," Mould said, "but the way they did it didn't work. They sat in the park and sang with acoustic guitars. We take electric guitars and blast the shit out of them over and over again until the message sinks in. We're saying the same thing they did, that you're not going to screw us around, you're not sending me to war to fight for Dow Chemical, or some outrageous reason. We're not going to be passive. We'll fight back our own way."

The Hüskers had gotten cast as a hardcore band when what they were really doing was playing folk rock played at light speed, encased in an almost palpable cloak of swarming electronic distortion, car accident drumming, and extreme volume. "We were really surprised when we found out there were other bands doing something similar, with the speed and everything," Mould told *Matter* writer Steve Albini in 1983. "We just do what each song requires, we don't try to play slow or fast or anything." But Mould was just being canny — despite their un-hardcore name, the band looked like hardcore, sounded like hardcore, and smelled like hardcore. They just knew the pitfalls of being pigeonholed.

By 1982 Norton was working as a waiter, Mould was still at Macalester, and Hart was unemployed, dependent on the kindness of friends and family. When they realized they didn't have the money to put out *Land Speed Record* themselves, Hüsker Dü called Joe Carducci at SST. Carducci said they were interested, but they'd have to wait until SST had enough money to put it out. Carducci then tipped off Mike Watt that Hüsker Dü was looking for a label, and Watt offered to release the record on New Alliance. They sent him the tape, and the album sold out its initial pressing of a thousand copies in days.

That February, while they recorded the *In a Free Land* three-song EP in Minneapolis, Hart and Norton got a poisonous taste of Mould's formidable dark side. "Bob was such a bastard at that time," Hart recalled. "Literally the meanest person that I have ever met. You know, the silent psychic intimidation routine, where somebody just fumes for, like, four days? Bob can fume like nobody I know. He's intimidating you without saying a word."

Even in a genre founded on rage, Hüsker Dü was already known for being a particularly angry band. "People have misconstrued the pessimism and anger in our songs," Mould protested. "We're really the opposite of all that; we're not callous, insensitive people. But we're frustrated by the fact that most people seem to end up that way — hopeless, defeated. We're afraid of ending up that way ourselves, and that fear comes out in our songs."

Released on April 1, 1982, on New Alliance, *In a Free Land* was the best expression of Hüsker Dü's cyclonic intensity to date — "This band is one of the hottest, most awesome bands ever to walk a stage," raved *Maximumrocknroll*. Plenty of bands played as fast and angry as they could while remaining within punk's simple parameters; the Hüskers were now revealing elements of pop and psychedelia in their sound and standing out from the pack in the process.

They were also beginning to disavow the preachy aspects of hardcore. "What we try to do in our music is pose questions, not answers," said Mould shortly after *In a Free Land* came out. "We have our own answers, but they're good for us and not necessarily good for everyone else." They were also beginning to abandon the sound, but not the intensity, of hardcore. The heroic title track sounded as if Mould were singing to a classic Clash tune played at 78 RPM.

After *In a Free Land*, the band arranged to tour all the way to Los Angeles and then record twelve songs in two days in June with Spot at Total Access Studios. Thanks to the pre-*Thriller* record industry slump, there was a recording studio glut in Los Angeles. For as little as $400, a band could get a studio all to itself for three days, just enough to record and mix an entire album if they had their parts down. To save time and therefore money, they rarely did a second pass at a song. "In our whole ouevre," notes Hart, "there's probably not five second takes." The quality of the performances sometimes suffered, but they really didn't have a choice. Like so many other underground bands, the rough-and-ready nature of Hüsker Dü's recordings was originally a necessity, not an aesthetic. And then it became an aesthetic out of necessity.

The resulting *Everything Falls Apart* EP was released on Reflex in January '83. While *Land Speed Record* sold mainly on the West Coast (and in England, through a deal with their friend Jello Biafra's label, Alternative Tentacles), thanks to endless touring and good press, *Everything Falls Apart* sold all over the country. The initial pressing of five thousand copies sold out in a few weeks; another five thousand were pressed that summer.

Mould wrote or cowrote ten of the twelve songs on *Everything Falls Apart*; one of the few he didn't write was a frantic cover of Donovan's benignly druggy Sixties hit "Sunshine Superman." Unlike virtually every hardcore band, Hüsker Dü proudly stuck up for classic rock. "You know the whole deal with tearing down the old to make room for the new?" Hart said. "Well, music isn't city planning."

The title track is fairly catchy and melodic yet sacrifices remarkably little of the band's signature rage. "Blah, Blah, Blah," "Punch Drunk," and "From the Gut" hark back to the high-velocity thrashing of *Land Speed Record*, but as the record wears on, more and more noticeable melodies begin emanating from deep within, like someone whistling in a steel mill. The band was gradually beginning to ditch their more thrashy material, alienating much of the hardcore segment of their audience. "We'd been talking about the set," Norton recalled. "And someone said, 'Do we really have to do this?' And we all said, 'Oh, I thought you wanted to do this.' 'No, I thought *you* wanted to do this. . . .'"

They were starting to get a sense of themselves, gaining the self-confidence to drop the social and artistic crutch of the hardcore scene, which had grown stiflingly doctrinaire. "What I remember hardcore as being is, like, any band that just got up there and is real aggressive instead of 'We have to sound a certain way and this is, like, the formula for it,'" Mould said. "And the new bands are just locked in[to] the formula. Afraid to do anything else because they think it's such a pure form. Which is just a bunch of shit. It's just a bunch of rules, that's why we don't play along with that game anymore."

**M**inneapolis has got a lot of talent for such a relatively small city," Terry Katzman, now the Twin Cities correspondent for *Boston Rock*, wrote in November '82. "And someone is bound to take notice."

At the time, it had been four years since the ill-fated Suicide Commandos had signed to a major label, and it would be a couple more before the majors took any notice of Minneapolis. "I think they're probably scared of people who have a good idea of what they really want to do," Mould theorized, "as opposed to people who are completely malleable jelly tofu bands who can say, 'Make us big, we'll do everything you want.'"

But popularity was not something Hüsker Dü wanted to avoid. Shortly after *Everything Falls Apart*, an interviewer opined that Hüsker Dü would never have a hit record. "I don't know," said Mould. "I wouldn't write it out of the question." Hart added that the band had always had a "serious pop edge." Mould even went so far as to claim that had they slowed down *In a Free Land* a tad, sent ten thousand promo copies to all the key stations in the big cities and college towns, and backed it up with a big publicity push, the band could have broken nationally. Although none of those things were possible, the band made no secret of grand ambitions.

**N**ot only did the band run their own label; they also did their own driving and equipment hauling. But for Hüsker Dü, DIY wasn't an ethical decision or even a point of pride. It was a necessity. "We didn't have anybody banging down our door, offering to do it all for us," says Norton. "It just gets back to that do-it-yourself attitude like the Minutemen had and [Black] Flag had and the Meat Puppets had — we learned from [Mission of] Burma and D.O.A. and the Subhumans and Minor Threat."

"We just enjoy doing it that way," Mould said. "When you start giving up parts of your independence, when you start hiring road people and publicists and let others do your booking, it gives off an impression, an illusion for people. We're not that hard to find, we're a fairly accessible band, we don't hide from people."

In retrospect, Hart believes that taking on so many responsibilities may have hurt the band in the long run. "The DIY thing, I don't know, it's like we handicapped ourselves in a lot of situations to maintain that," he says. "There were things that, by all rights, we should have been able to let go of and oversee."

In fact, Hüsker Dü's popularity meant they couldn't release their own records: the band's releases now called for initial pressings of ten thousand, which they couldn't afford. SST had the organizational wherewithal, the financial credit, and the enthusiasm for the larger pressings, and so Hüsker Dü became the label's first non–West Coast artist.

In December '82 Hüsker Dü took off on a five-week tour that wound through the Midwest, Southwest, and on into California, where they intended to record and mix their next album with Spot — in one day. Making a whole album in one day was trying enough, but it became impossible when the power got cut off because the studio hadn't paid the electric bill. "We were trying to jump power from other parts of the building," Mould recalls. "Stuff like that freaks everybody out." The album wound up being a seven-song EP.

The new material was more fully realized and diverse than anything they'd previously done. It was still very fast and very loud, but the EP, titled *Metal Circus*, also got even more overtly melodic; compared to *Land Speed Record*, it was like Rodgers and Hammerstein. As Norton told the *New Musical Express*: "I don't tend to walk down the street whistling hardcore."

Not only were Hart and Mould singing more tunefully, but Hart's busy drumming, all singsong beats and light-speed snare rolls, rushed the music along more precisely than ever; Norton's bass lines often carried much of the tune while Mould's guitar swathed it all in a crackling blanket of electronic distortion.

Although *Metal Circus* did have a song about nuclear annihilation (and what self-respecting underground rock album of the time didn't?), the lyrics became more personal, less political. "Politics will come and go, but we're still people, that will never change and that's just what we're gonna sing about," Mould said. "It's a personal thing this time — how we're fucked or you're fucked or everybody's fucked at one time or another."

The band rationalized their new introspective approach with high-minded statements like "The revolution begins at home" and "We're into personal politics," but Hart says it was just a way of justifying the change in direction. "Any time somebody has a new idea, they are rectifying that new idea with the entire body of their work," he says. "It's hard for somebody to say, 'I did a 180 in my work.' You usually try to put it on something."

Mould in particular was growing well tired of the hardcore scene, beginning with its hypocritical embrace of anarchy, which had long since become an empty buzzword, while the anarchy symbol, a circled letter A emblazoned on countless black leather jackets, had become the peace symbol of the Eighties — an important concept drained of all meaning. "There's an attitude, whether people like to say that or not, you know, 'The first rule is no rules,'" Mould said. "That's a bunch of shit, there are rules, there always have been."

"Basically, they were going, 'Be different, be different. Be like us or we'll kill you,'" Norton says of the hardcore crowd. "Everybody had the shaved head, and at that point that's when we said, 'Fuck this shit, man — we're not doing this to be fashion icons, we're not doing this to front anything, we're doing this because the music is the most important thing. We're doing this because we're into what we're doing, and at that point we quit shaving and quit cutting our hair and started wearing whatever the hell we felt like."

(A case in point was Norton's signature handlebar mustache. He had forgotten to pack a razor on a 1982 tour, and as his mustache grew longer and longer, it started to get in his mouth when he played. Norton had groused about it to Black Flag's Dez Cadena, who replied, "Man, if it's getting in your mouth, you should just curl it up!" "So I thought, 'Yeah, right!'" says Norton. "It was like, 'Punk rocker with a handlebar mustache, OK!'")

The scene was flooded with poseurs and violent thugs who knew and cared little for the music's original impulses. "You can't tell the people who are into it from people who are coming in from [the dull Minneapolis suburb of] Edina with chains on their boots," Mould said. "A year or two ago you could walk into a club and you'd know somebody and what kind of music they were into just by talking for ten seconds. Now you've got kids coming in from all over the place and they go out and punch people on the floor." Even the music itself was getting stale. "There's more to life than that same beat, over and over," Mould said.

The members of Hüsker Dü weren't alone in their feelings — in his *Matter* column that same year, Steve Albini wrote, "Wanna be the big new teen in hardcore circles? Get some other dillheads together, call yourselves Antagonistic Decline or Vicious Tendencies or Unrepentant Youth or some such thing, copy every lick from the Dischord collection and write songs about military intervention, whether you know anything about it or not, and you're guaranteed a good review in *Maximumrocknroll*."

"A lot of these bands are pretty idealistic, and that's all well and good, for them. They think they can really do something," Mould said. "But I'm not out rioting in the streets. I'm not throwing firebombs. I'm not spray-painting the Capitol. So why should I sing about it? It's not right to lie to people like that."

So it was no accident that *Metal Circus* opened with "Real World," a pointed tirade not just against hardcore orthodoxy but an outburst of middle American pragmatism — "You want to change the world / By breaking rules and laws / People don't do things like that / in the real world at all," Mould screams. "Reading the fanzines and stuff, you'll see a lot of kids write in and sign their letters 'anarchy and peace,'" Mould explained to *Conflict* publisher Gerard Cosloy. "I don't think that many of them live what that means; I mean, they all live at home with their parents, they all value greatly their possessions, I'm sure."

Hart contributed two songs, including "Diane," a chilling account of the rape and murder of a local waitress told from the killer's point of view; the song was a fairly direct descendant of Fifties teen tragedy songs and folk murder ballads. While the lyrics to Hart's "It's Not Funny Anymore" also indicted the conformism of the hardcore scene, the fact that it was also a sweet, impassioned speed-pop gem sure to irritate the mohawk crowd meant even more.

When *Metal Circus* came out in October '83, various tracks — particularly the perversely sing-along "Diane" — got picked up by dozens of radio stations around the country, mostly college. College students largely shied away from hardcore, but Hüsker Dü's more tuneful take was striking a chord.

They'd done three West Coast tours and a couple of smaller Midwest jaunts before making it out to the East Coast for a two-week headlining tour in April '83. They went east with a little trepidation, since it was unknown territory and they had no idea what the turnouts would be. But the Philadelphia show miraculously sold out, and so did Boston, and so did Washington. "The thing that we didn't realize," Norton says, "was college radio was playing the hell out of Hüsker Dü."

Surprisingly, the turnout for the first New York show was lackluster, although the band turned in a blazing performance, "a titanic show, one so fraught and locomotive even the band looked surprised," wrote the *Village Voice*'s R. J. Smith. At the end of their set, Mould immediately threw down his guitar and pressed his fists to his temples in agony. "I usually have a good headache by the time we're done playing," Mould explained. "I scream myself to the point where my head is bursting."

The second-billed Replacements got paid only $100, less than the opener, "a pretty shitty punk band" (Norton's words) called the Young and the Useless. Norton complained that the Replacements were getting the shaft, but to no avail. "The guy who booked the gig was like, 'Yeah, well, your friends from Minneapolis are just lucky to be on this bill,'" says Norton. "'They should pay *me* a hundred bucks.'" (The Young and the Useless later evolved into the Beastie Boys and continued to command at least $100 per show for the rest of their careers.)

The tour had been pegged on an appearance at the punk-friendly Music for Dozens night at Folk City, the fabled Greenwich Village hole-in-the-wall where Bob Dylan often performed in the early Sixties. The band knew their initial splash in New York was crucial. "And when the Folk City show presented itself, it was tailor-made for our manipulations," Hart says. "I think it was a good way for us to demonstrate that we were part of a greater thing — we were today's manifestation of a type of freedom of thought that we had by no means originated."

So Hüsker Dü cannily covered the Byrds' "Eight Miles High" in homage to the Vietnam era folk-rock scene. Except they tore the song up into a million screaming pieces. "We thought we were playing it just like the Byrds," Mould said. "That's been my personal problem for all these years: I always thought I was making pop records."

"Eight Miles High," of course, is a preeminent classic of Sixties psychedelia. At the time there was a slew of American bands — the Three O'Clock, the Bangles, Rain Parade, et al. — who were copping superficial aspects of the Byrds and other trippy Sixties bands but weren't actually psychedelic at all. This disgusted Hart, Mould, and Norton just as much as the conformity of the avowedly nonconformist hardcore scene did. So they took psychedelia's most sacred cow and gave it a good thrashing.

Quite simply, it's one of the most powerful pieces of rock music ever recorded. The Hüsker Dü version takes the song's original themes of disillusionment and foreboding and turns them into a death shriek for the collapse of the Sixties counterculture, something Mould had been ruing ever since his encounters with the Young Republicans back at Macalester. Mould's almost wordless vocals were a direct descendant of John Lennon's primal scream approach, only ten times as horrific; cathartic, ultimately life-affirming, his bloodcurdling howls were as direct, honest, and arresting as an infant's wail.

Starting with *Metal Circus* and most powerfully evident with "Eight Miles High" (released as a single in May '84), Hüsker Dü was doing something that virtually no punk band had done before: making music that could make you cry. Songs like "Diane" and "Everything Falls Apart" were powerfully moving, not just bilious statements of alienation, but music you could hang your heart on.

**A**lthough the band toured frequently, it was for relatively short periods of time, usually two or three weeks at a clip — because of their Minneapolis base, it was easy to hit virtually any part of the country and come back in a couple of weeks. Spring through fall of '84 marked the beginning of the band's most extensive touring, hitting the Midwest, East, and Southwest in May and June, then going back and covering pretty much the same ground in September and October.

The band had developed an unrelenting attack for their live shows, playing song after song in quick succession, a continuous wall of sound with no breaks — no sooner would the last shrieking notes of guitar feedback fade away than the band was hurtling off into a new song. (Quips Hart, "It gave everybody who was up in the air a chance to touch the ground again.") Hart would just count off the first number, and the band would plow through an hour's worth of material with barely a break, save a testy gripe from Mould about the stage divers, usually on the order of "Stay the fuck away from the microphone."

The effect was relentless and disorienting. "We play so fast and rattle so many songs off in a row, it doesn't give people a chance to turn to their friend and say, 'What do you think of it?'" said Mould. "People have to think about it in their own mind. They can't listen to their friends and get that acceptance."

The band was changing and improving drastically with each new release, and anyone who saw a Hüsker Dü show was seldom disappointed. While Norton took care of the heroic leaps and lunges, Hart would flail wildly with his hair in his face, a cartoonish parody of a rock drummer. Mould mostly stayed anchored to the mike, occasionally lurching about the stage as if the trusty Flying V guitar dangling around his knees was pulling him against his will.

In concert the band inspired nothing short of awe. The sheets of sound were so dense and enveloping that it was mesmerizing; they played so fast that it seemed like time stood still. The crowd would become a swarming mass of energy — people would run around in circles at the back of the room out of sheer ecstasy, bouncing up and down or slamming around the room like errant subatomic particles, completely caught up in the swirl of the music. Hüsker Dü tapped into levels of visceral and psychic power that few bands have before or since, and the effect was extraordinary.

The band did make a motley crew. The strapping, mustachioed Norton was a far cry from the chubby Hart, with his lank, stoner-length hair and hippie necklaces; the burly Mould, as Steve Albini put it in a *Matter* profile, looked like "a St. Paul gas station attendant after a hard day's work." "The sum of the parts was a pretty bizarre mix," agrees Mould. "That's sort of an off-putting thing — when you see that for the first time, you think, 'What's *this* shit?'"

With his long hair and barefooted stage attire, the eccentric Hart got tagged as the hippie of the band. He protests that the long hair was only to make his face look a little slimmer and that he played barefooted simply so he could work the bass drum pedal faster, but the wide-eyed sincerity of his songs was far more San Francisco '67 than New York '77. Mould, on the other hand, generally wrote more incisively bitter songs. His melodies did not go down as easily, and his voice ranged from an apoplectic scream to a cutting, sardonic sneer like some sort of punk rock W. C. Fields.

Mould and Hart had differing natures, to put it mildly. In a jokey teenzine-style survey in *Matter*, Hart said his favorite vice was "smoking pot"; his perfect afternoon would be spent "hanging around somewhere where there's flowers and birds and stuff." Mould's favorite color: "Gray." His favorite food: "Beef."

They professed to have no leader, but gradually Mould came to the fore, partly because he played guitar and wrote and sang most of the songs, but mostly because of his gruff, uncompromising nature. "It always seemed like Bob's way or the highway," says Hart. "He was a guy who could stink up an entire room with his bad vibes."

Despite the friction, Hart and Mould did their best to accommodate each other so the one thing they agreed on — the band — could continue to exist. Their logo (and every hardcore band had a logo) was a circle enclosing three parallel lines with another line going through them perpendicularly. "The circle is the band," Mould explained, "the three lines across are the members, and the intersection is the common train of thought."

"There was definitely an intense dynamic between the three of them," says the Butthole Surfers' King Coffey, who wrote the band's first out-of-state fan letter and briefly roadied for Hüsker Dü on an early Eighties tour of Texas. "There didn't seem to be much humor involved with how they approached their music. But as guys, they were cool, they'd hang out. They just took what they were doing very seriously."

Although whoever wrote a song sang it, songwriting credits didn't appear until the band's fourth record. And once Hart began to get some songs on the band's records, an increasingly tense rivalry began to erupt. "I think Grant may have been threatened by the fact that Bob was writing so many songs," says Norton. "And maybe Bob was threatened by the fact that Grant was writing so many songs. And so they both were writing a *shitload* of songs."

Although Mould was much more prolific, the band's albums gradually contained more Hart compositions. "I was learning to have the confidence to not be intimidated," Hart explains. Nonetheless, it wasn't until the band's final album that at least one of the prime spots on an LP — the first and last tracks of each side — was occupied by a Grant Hart song.

As the third man, Norton was in a position to decide a lot of controversies but instead elected to stay out of the fray. "I don't think I was the swing vote, I think I was the neutral — I was Switzerland," says Norton. "I didn't want to jump into the middle of that because I looked at it like it was the punk Lennon and McCartney. Grant was the McCartney, the pop love songs, and Bob was the dark side, Lennon. I just said, 'Great, keep it up, boys!'

"Which kind of reminds me of watching *Spinal Tap*," Norton jokes, "where the bass player is going, 'Well, Nigel's like fire and David's like ice. That makes me tepid water.' I guess that was my role. I was the luke-warm guy."

P erhaps because Hart, Mould, and Norton didn't socialize much outside the band, they treated each other with deference on the road. "We were always a pretty clean band," Hart reveals. "There was never puke or a bunch of spilled stuff in the van." By late '83 they had grown tired of sleeping on floors and made the big leap to staying in mo-tels, albeit three to a room.

But it's not like they were living the easy life at home. By the end of '83 Mould was giving guitar lessons and renting an unheated basement room for $70 a month. Hart, who had no fixed address, was on food stamps. "We were on the road so much," Mould says, "we'd just have a box of possessions that we'd leave in somebody's basement and take the sleeping bag and sleep there for a month under the stairs until you go on tour again." When they got to Southern California, they'd sleep under the desks at SST along with everyone else. "We'd stay there while we were making the records," says Mould, "and play basketball and drink and eat once a day, get a couple of bucks and buy a big package of cheese and some bread and that would be about it."

Whenever they played Vancouver, B.C., they'd stay at the infamous Abandoned House, a punk rock squat where guests would climb through a hole in the ceiling and sleep in the attic; for food, someone would go to the nearby Chinatown, steal a fifty-pound box of ribs, and everybody back at the house would eat them and throw the bones out the window.

"Hopefully we were going to just make enough money from the gig to get some food, maybe some beer, be able to buy smokes, and have enough gas to make it to the next gig," says Norton. "That's all that was important to us."

"That was the difference between the SST stuff and a lot of the other bands — with SST, it was almost like, who can have it worse?" says Mould. "Not consciously that way, but in some weird way that was part of paying your dues. People getting into it now have no idea what work is really like."

**B**y the mid-Eighties rumors had begun to circulate that someone in the band was gay. Most thought it must be Norton — after all, he had the handlebar mustache. "I have never encountered anybody in my life," Hart says, "who was so patient with that kind of bullshit." But both Hart and Mould had male lovers, although never, as was later commonly believed, were they ever involved with each other. "It would have been fuckin' bullshit," Hart says.

According to Hart, both men took lovers on tour and their orientation was an open secret in the indie community. But most people who knew cared very little. Part of the reason it was never a big deal was that the band never emphasized sexuality — theirs or anyone else's — in their music or their performance. "It was very workmanlike," says their friend Julie Panebianco. "This is what we do — we come and we play and our sexuality has nothing to do with anything. And no one really did think it had anything to do with anything. It was just not an issue and consequently no one cared."

"It just served to be even one more thing that we were bad-ass about," says Hart. "It was not ever any kind of a weakness, it was a superiority type of thing, like the Spartans of ancient days or something."

**H**üsker Dü spent the entire summer of '83 preparing material for the next album, rehearsing in a former church in St. Paul where Hart lived, along with a bunch of young drifters, runaways, and musicians. Everyone at the church was enjoying the particularly pure LSD that was going around. "I tripped probably twenty-eight times [that summer]," Hart admitted. "It was the acid bender of my life." Mould stuck with his usual speed and alcohol, although amphetamines eventually began to get the better of the band. "It was a way of life," says Mould. "After about six months of doing it nonstop, you just sort of lose track of it. You start doing it and you don't stop for years."

Now approaching peak form, the band would jam for hours, brainstorming music and lyrics. It may have seemed like more Hüsker Dü bravado, but the band sensed the next album was going to be a milestone. "It was a coming-of-age work and we knew it when we were writing it," says Mould. "It was like, this is going to change everything because it's that good."

This was happening against the backdrop of an underground scene rebounding from an utter rejection of anything resembling conventional

rock music and beginning to revisit the music everyone had actually listened to growing up. Besides, change was inevitable — bands were getting older and were getting better at playing their instruments and writing
their songs. Hardcore's limited chordal and rhythmic palette fostered a
sameness of sound, and the punk ethos had made a virtue of this short-
coming. But Hüsker Dü knew more was possible.

"Right now we're at a stage where we have to think things through in
a big way," Mould had told Steve Albini in *Matter* shortly before the band
recorded their next album. "We're going to try to do something bigger
than anything like rock & roll and the whole puny touring band idea. I
don't know what it's going to be, we have to work that out, but it's going
to go beyond the whole idea of 'punk rock' or whatever."

The stage was certainly set for Hüsker Dü to make some sort of
grandiose move. By 1984 Minneapolis was pop music's "it" city, thanks to
the Midas touch of R&B production team Jimmy Jam and Terry Lewis
and a diminutive virtuoso named Prince, who was going supernova with
his album and movie *Purple Rain*. And the city also boasted several critically lauded underground bands, including Soul Asylum, the Magnolias,
and the Replacements. Minneapolis happily embraced the attention — it
was novel for this white-bread, snowbound town to be considered hip,
and for a city that had long strived to be cosmopolitan, something of a
vindication. "The music scene is so good for Minnesota," Mould exclaimed at the time. "It's probably the biggest export the state's ever had!"

**M**ould and Hart were writing songs at a prodigious pace and had a
plentiful supply of unreleased music. Consequently, their live sets
skimped on the album they'd just released and instead concen-
trated on the one they were about to record. "We're always progressing,"
Mould said. "We're not trying to show people where we were eight months
ago. I would think that if people like the band and they have the records,
that they would really be excited about hearing new stuff. If people want to
hear us play a bunch of old hits, they pick the wrong band to follow."

Playing unrecorded material also had a practical advantage — because the songs were worked out on the road, they were in polished form
once the band entered the studio, which also made them quick, and
therefore economical, to record. "They knew what they wanted to do,
knew how they wanted it to sound, and that was that," says Spot. "In the
studio, you *worked*. We didn't have much time. We had ten hours to do a
whole lot of stuff, and everybody was there and everybody did a whole lot
of stuff in ten hours. They were very serious, very driven."

They were getting ready to tour their way to California for the recording of their double album, now titled *Zen Arcade*, when Mould saw Hart's artwork for the new Man Sized Action album on Reflex. "Bob was going, 'I can't believe this — Grant did the artwork for this, and there's not a single songwriter credit on the record. He didn't credit the songs anywhere. I tell you, when we record *Zen Arcade*, we're having individual songwriter credits,'" Norton recalls. It was a blow to the band's precarious unity and the rivalry between Hart and Mould, which had been on a low simmer, went up a notch.

"And I didn't think anything of it," Norton says. "Of course, Bob was and is a savvy businessman, and I didn't realize that if I just rolled over on that one, I wouldn't be making as much money as these guys were. Later on, I said, 'Hey, wait a second!'"

**A**nd so in October '83, just as *Metal Circus* was hitting the stores, the band recorded twenty-five tracks — at least twenty-one of them first takes — with Spot in California at Total Access in a remarkable forty-five hours, then mixed it all in one marathon forty-hour session, bringing the whole thing in for $3,200.

*Zen Arcade* was Hüsker Dü's most strenuous refutation of hardcore orthodoxy. While most of the songs are loud and fast, even the most violent passages give way to overtly musical chord changes and melodies that no hidebound hardcore zealot would tolerate. Many tracks are just speedy, heavily distorted pop songs. A couple are piano solos, others just voice and acoustic guitar; "Hare Krsna" proudly borrowed from the Bo Diddley–fied 1965 Top 40 hit "I Want Candy," and "Turn on the News" has nearly the same chord progression as the solo section of Lynyrd Skynyrd's "Freebird." The closing instrumental lasts fourteen unpunk minutes. The album's variegated styles prompted a typical Hartism. "It's geodesic shaped," Hart said. "The idea is that everyone will have to get a new stereo."

*Zen Arcade* is a concept album — and a double album at that — the very epitome of dinosaur rock excess, and yet the loose story line could have been about any of thousands of hardcore kids: A young man runs away from his feuding parents and worthless friends, wanders the streets of a big city trying to figure himself out, is tempted to join a cult, hooks up with a girl, who soon OD's. Eventually, after plenty of harsh introspection, he comes back home but returns withdrawn, enveloped in a protective emotional shell. "I'm not the son you wanted," the character sings, "but what could you expect / I've made my world of happiness to combat your neglect." As the zine *Hard Times* put it, the story encapsulates "the wreckage of our era: betrayal, alienation, pain, egotism, emotional suffocation, and isolation."

Unfortunately, the story ends with the lamest of narrative cop-outs — it was only a nightmare. The finale, the fourteen-minute instrumental epic "Reoccurring Dreams," might be a summation of the rest of the protagonist's life — like all lives, it's a tumultuous improvisation, full of exhilarating highs and static lows. Hart compares the minute of high-pitched feedback that closes the track to the sound of a flatlining EKG.

The theme shouldn't have come as any surprise — in their song lyrics and interviews, the band had been discussing personal evolution and self-discovery for over a year. *Zen Arcade* both described that change and embodied it by experimenting so boldly — and succeeded spectacularly. The story obviously reflected the band's own self-discovery, but it may also have been somewhat autobiographical on Mould's part — as an angry kid stuck in an unhappy family situation and trying to figure out his sexuality ("His parents, they can't understand why their son he turned out wrong," he sings in "Whatever"), all in a claustrophobically small, conservative town, he must have had his own fantasies of running away to the big city. Unlike the character in *Zen Arcade*, though, Mould actually did it.

Up until *Zen Arcade* their best seller had been *Land Speed Record*, which had sold over ten thousand copies. The band had warned SST that the new record was going to be big. "It was so much better than anything else that was out there at the time," says Mould. "We just knew it was going to sell more than three thousand."

SST erred on the side of caution and in July '84 did an initial pressing of somewhere between thirty-five hundred and five thousand copies, which sold out just a couple of weeks into the band's tour to promote the album. The album was often out of stock for months afterward, considerably denting sales and frustrating the band. "That was sort of the beginning of us knowing that things were a little askew," says Mould, "when we're out promoting the record and doing in-stores, and the best we could do was make special flyers to give to people because we had sold all thirty-five hundred copies that got pressed."

Joe Carducci says SST realized they had a big seller on their hands, but they had to be particularly cautious about financial expenditures because Black Flag had a slew of albums coming out that year and the Minutemen had decided to make their next one a double as well (in fact, *Zen Arcade* was held up so SST could release *Double Nickels on the Dime* on the same day). So even though SST had some cash by that point, the label's resources were already stretched. Besides, pressings of more than five thousand copies were mysterious territory for SST. No one could be sure how many records Hüsker Dü would sell, and if SST printed up too many copies, they'd eat the cost.

But those who managed to get the record, loved it. *Zen Arcade* wound up on countless year-end best-of lists — the *L.A. Times'*, the *Boston Phoenix's*, and the influential *Village Voice* poll; the *L.A. Herald's* Mikal Gilmore went so far as to place *Zen Arcade* in a league with the Rolling Stones' *Exile on Main Street*, the Clash's *London Calling*, and Bob Dylan's *Highway 61 Revisited*. "All of a sudden," says Mould, "we went from being this band that was making our own posters for the instores in Columbus because they couldn't sell the record, to sitting up there with that. All of a sudden you get a little self-conscious because you realize that everybody's looking at you. And it's not this innocent and pure secret anymore. It's now 'critically acclaimed' and 'trendsetting' and 'attention-grabbing.'

"I don't think it's about selling out, it's just that all of a sudden, your world becomes invaded by other people, by the mainstream, by *Rolling Stone*, by *Musician* wanting to go on the road with you for three days — all these things that we railed against, and we were sort of getting sucked into it and it starts to move faster and you become a willing accomplice without knowing it. To me, you think, 'Finally, we're changing things.' But you're being changed *by* things as much as you're changing things. It's a two-way street. I only know this years later. At the time you have no idea — the tornado spins and if you can grab your shoes as they go by, you're doing well."

*Zen Arcade* not only made Hüsker Dü a nationally known, critically respected band; it also expanded the music's audience beyond the punk underground. "That was the beginning, for us, of the college-educated, 'less prone to black leather motorcycle jacket' crowd," Hart says. "More women were coming to the shows. People were getting more interested in the lyrics and reading between the lines."

With *Zen Arcade* there was a thrilling feeling that American postpunk had finally arrived because it could sustain something as ambitious as a double concept album. *Zen Arcade* had stretched the hardcore format to its most extreme limits; it was the final word on the genre, a scorching of musical earth — any hardcore after *Zen Arcade* would be derivative, retrograde, formulaic. The album wasn't only about a character coming of age, nor was it merely about Hüsker Dü coming of age, or the

unmistakable sound of a band leaving its musical adolescence behind —
it was about an entire musical movement coming of age.

**A**t this time Hart, drummer of one of underground rock's hippest,
most celebrated bands, was living at his folks' house in suburban
South St. Paul. One day, on a manila envelope that Hart was using to sketch out the track sequence of the next Hüsker Dü album, he
found a note: "Grant: Would appreciate it if you didn't have a party while
we were gone — we'll be back Monday. Food in freezer. Love, Mom."

**T**he liner notes for *Zen Arcade* mention that "Carducci wants another album already, but not another double LP," and they obliged,
recording *New Day Rising* just as *Zen Arcade* came out in July '84,
releasing it a scant six months later.

Hüsker Dü were hardly resting on their laurels: from the summer
of '84 to the summer of '85, they released eight LP sides of consistently
excellent music. And SST had absolutely no complaints about the deluge — after all, a steady stream of albums by its top band helped SST with
everything from cash flow to having the leverage to get paid by its distributors for other releases.

Even better for SST, Hüsker Dü had deferred taking royalties on
their albums so the label could stay solvent. Most of their income came
from touring anyway, so record royalties seemed like gravy. "We were being real nice guys," says Norton. "Which may not have been a good thing
in hindsight." But with the success of *Zen Arcade*, record royalties weren't
just gravy anymore — they were the whole turkey. Hart says that by 1987
SST owed Hüsker Dü something like $150,000, which the label was still
paying off years later.

Hüsker Dü didn't even have a contract with SST until the very end
of their association with the label. "It was all based," says Hart with a sigh,
"on peace, love, and anarchy."

**H**aving dispensed with adolescence with *Zen Arcade*, the band approached more adult situations on *New Day Rising*. "You grow up,
you change your perspective," Mould explained. "You're not always eighteen years old, drunk, with a mohawk, driving around screaming and hollering about anarchy — you don't *do that* all your life."

As Hart, Mould, and Norton became better musicians, they discovered they were increasingly able to play at slower tempos and still have the rhythms hang together, allowing for more extended melodies. And as usual they were writing better songs. The band was still coalescing, still forming out of the big bang of *Land Speed Record*, into something focused.

*New Day Rising*, with its alternating currents of radiant fury, caustic introspection, and urgent desire for redemption, made for an exhilarating ride, starting with the incantatory "New Day Rising," where Mould and Hart sing the title phrase over and over as the track builds with an almost gospel fervor. Hart's torrential "The Girl Who Lives on Heaven Hill" typifies the band's unique blend of catchiness and intensity; Hart's piano-driven "Books about UFO's" achieves an irresistibly jaunty, jazzy swing the band had never attempted before. Mould's "Celebrated Summer," perhaps his best song to date, manages to be teeming, fast, and wistful all at the same time, as does the jackhammer folk of another Mould classic, "I Apologize."

Hüsker Dü occupied an unexplored no-man's-land between hardcore noise and pure pop, reclaiming melody from the domain of mass-produced mainstream pap, but furiously smudging it over with distortion, a sort of smoke screen to deter the straights. "They had tuneful material," says Spot. "They were kind of working from within a classic pop structure. And doing something else with it. Kind of like they broke into it with a coat hanger and got the keys out and went on a joy ride. And then wore the tires out."

Upon its release in January '85, *New Day Rising* won widespread critical praise — U.K. tabloid *Sounds* called Hüsker Dü "the most exciting and important American rock group since the Ramones," adding that the band's mission was to "breach and expose the gap between modern American youth and their image."

**B**ut the band was starting to have its fill of SST. At first Hüsker Dü worked with Spot because he was the hip producer at the time — and he was cheap, too. But after a couple of records, "We had no other choice but to work with him," says Hart. "SST *made* us work with him." They had wanted to self-produce *New Day Rising*, but SST, perhaps wary of a self-indulgent financial quagmire, insisted on flying Spot to Minneapolis to supervise.

Spot, surely aware of the power struggle, arrived in Minneapolis and promptly asserted his authority by ordering that the entire recording console be moved two inches. "There was a lot of tension between everybody," says Spot. "They wanted to produce it themselves and then I was there. I had to do what the record company wanted. And it was one of those situations where I knew my territory and I did my job, whether it was popular or not. So it came out of that era where maybe everybody was starting to take it too seriously." *New Day Rising* would be one of the last recordings Spot did for SST.

The album does have some sonic problems; on "Heaven Hill" it sounds like Hart is singing inside a giant oil drum. Elsewhere, the vocals are smothered in a heavy mist of amplifier fuzz and cymbal wash. Hart and Mould vowed to produce themselves next time. It wasn't such a bad idea — Mould had already produced various bands, including Soul Asylum, and knew his way around a recording studio.

The more zealous precincts of the underground community seemed to believe that *New Day Rising*, with its modestly improved production values and musicianship, better-crafted arrangements, and more prominent melodies, was a "commercial" album, an accusation the band had to defend against constantly. But in the absolutist logic of the underground, anything that was popular was bad, ipso facto. In 1985 a fanzine interviewer asked Norton: "If you were signed to a major label, your music would have a much greater possibility of breaking mainstream listening venues and becoming what most people would consider commercial. How do you respond to that?" Norton replied that becoming popular is not necessarily the same thing as selling out, but the response surely fell on deaf ears.

**T**hat spring the members of Hüsker Dü were publicly stating their allegiance to SST, even as three major labels pursued the band after the critical swoon over *Zen Arcade*, not to mention twenty thousand copies sold of a double album and thirty thousand of *New Day Rising* (and this was before they'd even toured *New Day Rising* on the crucial East Coast). And yet Mould strongly hinted that jumping to a major wasn't out of the question. "If a band is responsible and level-headed about things, you can make that jump," Mould told *Rockpool* in April '85.

But years later Mould admitted they were thinking much more seriously about a jump than they had let on at the time. "We knew there was a much bigger audience that we could at least have a shot at," Mould said in 1999. "And we were five or six years into our career at that point, knowing unconsciously at least that it couldn't last forever. You want to try to make a run for it."

SST tried to help Hüsker Dü play ball with radio, but the way Hüsker Dü perceived it, SST's real allegiances lay elsewhere. "I think there's a little reluctance on their part to let anything get a little more attention than Black Flag," Hart said once they were safely off the label. "SST is a lot like some kind of commune, and that's perfectly fine and good, but a lot of times there's the syndrome of the head of the commune."

Hart said the band was annoyed at SST's insensitivity — the label allegedly refused to allow them to debut the "Makes No Sense at All" video at the Museum of Modern Art and irked the band by including a Hüsker Dü track on the *Blasting Concept* compilation, with what they felt was a misogynistic Raymond Pettibon cover illustration. "With SST there was nothing that was ours," Hart said. "There was nothing that we could be proud of without them trying to take that away from us."

Hart went on to hint that SST thought the Hüskers might be a little "soft" because they stayed in motels and occasionally wrote happy songs. "We don't have to convince the world that we're suffering to convince them that we're artists," Hart said, jabbing at Black Flag's angst-ridden style. "There are those that choose to take that course. There's nothing wrong with being happy."

All the while, Mould was still running Reflex Records with the band's stalwart supporter, Terry Katzman. "It was really important to showcase other talent from your same town," Norton explains, "to let other people in the rest of the country know that, hey, we've got a little burgeoning scene going on here and there's some good music and entice people to come to Minneapolis to tour or make it easier for Minneapolis bands to tour."

Reflex released a few regional compilations, as well as area post-punk bands such as Rifle Sport, Man Sized Action, Otto's Chemical Lounge, and Articles of Faith, with Mould and/or Minneapolis studio mainstay Steve Fjelstad usually producing; they got the bands a fair amount of press in fanzines nationwide. The label was run as a co-op: the bands paid for recording and the label paid for pressing, with profits split fifty-fifty. By 1984 the label had a distribution deal with Dutch East India Trading. The Minutemen released their 1985 *Tour Spiel* EP on Reflex. But by May 1985 the band was now too busy to deal with Reflex, even with Katzman's assistance. "It would really have had to have been organized, and they

weren't that organized," says Katzman. "Totally *unorganized* is what we were."

**A**n SST press release at the time described Hüsker Dü as "three guys from the twin cities with one desire: to set people hümming their tünes and then to kick their ass." The band's next album did just that, in spades.

As the label's best-selling band by far, Hüsker Dü finally had enough clout to produce their own record. Instead of cramming the recording and mixing into a hectic, amphetamine-fueled few days, they recorded over several months, from March through June (although May was spent touring *New Day Rising*). This time the sound was crisp and the vocals distinct, more a considered studio creation than just three guys cranking it out as fast as they could. And the songs were stronger than ever.

The result was their best, most consistent album. *Flip Your Wig* delved even further into pop melody, but the approach remained quintessentially Hüsker Dü — even on Mould's sublime "Makes No Sense at

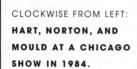

CLOCKWISE FROM LEFT:
**HART, NORTON, AND MOULD AT A CHICAGO SHOW IN 1984.**

GAIL BUTENSKY

All," Hart's drums roll and tumble as frantically as ever, Norton's bass gamely keeps pace, and Mould's guitars still strafe the changes with overwhelming volleys of distortion and speed. Six years, six records, and hundreds of gigs into their career, Hüsker Dü was at the top of their game.

The two songwriters were trying their level best to outdo each other, and with spectacular results: Hart countered Mould's infectiously swinging "Hate Paper Doll" with the expansive Sixties pop sounds of "Green Eyes"; Mould answered Hart's hectic soul wipeout "Every Everything" with the towering complacency-buster "Games." The cacophonous raga of Mould's "Divide and Conquer" blows through eight verses before a righteous chorus finally puts the song through the roof; the song's whirling dervish intensity is matched only by Hart's passionate rave-up "Keep Hanging On." Except for the two instrumentals tacked on to the end, every song sounds like a hit in some alternate world where the rivers run with an equal mixture of battery acid and honey.

*Flip Your Wig*, released that September, won the band even more airplay, debuting at number five and soon becoming the first independent release to top the charts of the top college radio tip sheet *College Music Journal*, going on to spend nearly half a year on the charts. The band got major stories in national rock magazines *Creem* and *Spin* while both *New Day Rising* and *Flip Your Wig* made the top ten of the 1985 *Village Voice* Pazz & Jop critics poll, an unprecedented feat. Mould was understandably optimistic about the band's future. "Hüsker Dü's a kind of diamond in the rough right now," he said. "We're just starting."

Although the Hüskers had already enjoyed some commercial radio airplay, "Makes No Sense at All" made modest inroads into radio's AOR (album-oriented rock) format, traditionally the preserve of mainstream rockers like Bryan Adams and ZZ Top. This fueled speculation that the band would soon succumb to a major label. "A lot of majors have been calling," Mould told *Boston Rock* in the fall of '85, "and they're all really interested in the band, but I don't really know if we're all that interested in them." The band members also told several other magazines that they were not interested in signing to a major label.

But that didn't mean it was the truth. "We were elusive for half a year," Hart admitted. Added Mould, "It saves a lot of questions by doing that."

At that point the band was touring constantly and usually selling out the house. But their audience was growing incrementally, not by leaps and bounds. The band felt they'd hit a sales ceiling that only a major label could break through. There were also outside forces at work. One of the biggest indie distributors, JEM, had gone bankrupt by 1985. "When that happened, that changed everything," Mould explains. "It wasn't many months after that everybody *had* to go to a major, because when JEM couldn't pay on the indie stuff, a lot of indie labels got shoved out right at that point."

Then a quite prestigious label renowned for its artist-friendly attitude and long-term dedication to its bands, Warner Brothers had been in touch with Hüsker Dü since *Zen Arcade*. During the *Flip Your Wig* sessions, the label made an offer that Hüsker Dü agreed to sign.

The clincher was the promise of complete creative control of their records, from the cover to the music, something no other major was prepared to grant. Hüsker Dü's contract soon became a model for many indie bands seeking to jump to a major.

It was a momentous move. Hüsker Dü was the first key American indie band to defect to a major; the event marked the end of an era within the American indie community. "It was definitely a parallel universe, is the way to describe it; it was definitely a subculture that had no mainstream intentions at all," says King Coffey. "There was no radio besides college radio. People had to learn about this music by reading underground publications and listening to college radio. There weren't any A&R people hanging out and trying to befriend you in L.A. — who the fuck cared? That's why it was really shocking and revolutionary when Hüsker Dü got their deal."

Some insiders were shocked and others outraged, and many were excited to see their favorite band graduate to the big leagues. And still others had apparently seen it coming a mile away. When Ian MacKaye heard the news about Hüsker Dü, he flashed back to 1981. "I heard about them — Hüsker Dü, they're from Minneapolis," MacKaye recalls. "When you heard them, the walls fall down, people are dancing, no one

can stop. It just sounded so incredible." But MacKaye was disappointed
by the slow, arty "Statues"/"Amusement" single and later asked Mould
about it. "And [he] said, 'Well, we were just trying to get on college radio,'" MacKaye recalls. "It kind of tipped their hand from the very get-go
for me. So when they signed to Warner Brothers [five] years later, I wasn't
surprised. *Of course* they'd be the first to go!"

**W**arner did acknowledge Hüsker Dü's grassroots appeal and
worked the band through roughly the same channels they had
come up in, albeit with far more financial and organizational
firepower. "Warner was the most reasonable of the labels about listening
to our concerns about not wanting to be packaged," said Mould. "Don't
make a big stir, just let us put out records. Don't try to make us something
we're not."

Warner knew the band had toured relentlessly for five years and built
up a large, loyal fan base, the kind that money just can't buy. The band
might not score any blockbuster hits, but if they kept overhead low and
hit a modest sales target, they'd make a profit. And it never hurts to have
a hip band on one's label.

At the Warner's alternative marketing department, Hüsker Dü had
staunch, sympathetic allies in Jo Lenardi and their old friend Julie
Panebianco, both former indie scene stalwarts. "We had our little spot
that they let us work in and we had distribution," says Mould. "It all
looked good."

But despite all this, the band's sense of independence was not a natural fit with a major label. "I can engineer our records," Mould said
around the time of the signing, "since I know exactly what it should
sound like. I'd also like to still be able to work with booking the band. I've
booked Hüsker Dü for quite some time now and I don't think we need a
manager to tell us what we're worth. Most importantly, we don't want
someone to work on our image, since we'll never have one." For all
Warner's good intentions, these could not have been completely welcome words.

**W**ith no contractual commitment to SST, they could have given
*Flip Your Wig* to Warner Brothers but decided it would have
been unreasonably short notice for SST, for whom they still felt
deep loyalty and respect — as Mould later put it, "We just kind of owed

them one." Warner thought they were crazy — the album was the band's most accessible ever. Hart and Norton say they followed Mould's lead on the decision; Hart hints that Mould unsuccessfully tried to use *Flip Your Wig* as a bargaining chip to pry an even better deal out of Warner.

They started recording their major label debut *Candy Apple Grey* four months after completing *Flip Your Wig*. Warner was not happy that they had lost the brilliant *Flip Your Wig* and gotten *Candy Apple Grey* instead, a record that was not a patch on the previous three albums. Even the cover art was weak.

Hüsker Dü's major label signing was swiftly followed by the Replacements', and indie-style rock enjoyed a short-lived mainstream heyday: for a brief while you could see Hüsker Dü on the *Joan Rivers Show* and the *Today* show, and the Replacements on *Saturday Night Live*. "We thought, and rightfully so, I think, that we could change things if we could have a higher platform to speak from. It was with the best of intentions," says Mould. "We were hyperaware of what we were trading off."

U nfortunately, Hart began using heroin during a long break after the *Candy Apple Grey* tour and eventually became a full-blown addict. Mould went completely sober right around the same time. "I was a really bad drinker and really bad with speed," Mould admitted. "I said, 'It's just time to stop this shit because I'm not going to make it to thirty if I keep it up at this rate.'" Sobriety cast a wedge between him and Hart, but Mould also had his beefs with Norton. "Some people got less interested in the band as a means of expression and more interested in the band as a paycheck," Mould said, apparently referring to Norton, then taking aim at Hart: "Some people had to go off and follow their muse and follow their vices a little farther down the road."

Hart had turned to heroin as a respite from the stress of being in such a stormy band, but soon after he started, he'd found another reason to escape: in mid-1986 he'd taken an HIV test and come up positive. He didn't tell anyone in the band.

Despite all the strife, Warner gave Hüsker Dü its enthusiastic promotion and support — even Bob Merlis, the label's courtly VP of publicity, was once spotted in the mosh pit.

By the time of 1987's *Warehouse: Songs and Stories*, Hart and Mould were feuding openly. Hart accused Mould of making sure Hart never had more than 45 percent of the songs on an album. Since Mould had eleven songs he wanted to include on the next release, Hart insisted on contributing as many as possible, which meant releasing a twenty-song double album. Although not happy about it, Warner honored their commitment to the band's creative freedom but also insisted that the band's mechanical royalties would be paid as if *Warehouse* were a single album.

The band had hired Mould's close friend David Savoy to run their office, and when Warner insisted the band hire a proper manager, the twenty-four-year-old Savoy got thrust into mediating between an increasingly conflicted band and its label. In the spring of '87, on the eve of their first tour to promote *Warehouse*, Savoy jumped off a Minneapolis bridge to his death. The devastated band went ahead with the tour anyway, but Hüsker Dü never got over the blow.

After Savoy's death, Mould, who had been calling the shots through Savoy anyway, assumed the managerial role. Even though an established manager would have given the band more clout at the label, Mould was unwilling to relinquish control; the band even turned down the advances of Cliff Burnstein, an already successful manager who soon copiloted Metallica and many other bands to platinum Valhalla. One can only wonder what would have happened had the band taken up Burnstein's offer.

*Warehouse* sold about 125,000 copies in the U.S. — it hit the label's sales target, and yet with various promotional expenses, the band made little more than they would have with less sales on SST. The major label gambit had failed. "As it turned out, it didn't make that big of a difference in the long run," Mould admitted years later. "The sales went up, but not enough to justify, you know, to say it was the smartest move ever made."

The problem was not with the label or even the band's feuding; it was with the music. "They wrote pop songs that were very dense and very layered and very loud and very compressed," says Panebianco. "They *still* sound different. It just sounded different from anything anybody played on the radio then or before or since. It was too aggressive for regular radio."

So Hüsker Dü became sacrificial victims of the industry's unfamiliarity with this "new music." They were like the first pancake that always gets thrown away. "[We were] truly thinking we're changing things when in fact we're on Warner Brothers and the AOR guy still doesn't know what track to lead with," says Mould. "And doesn't that sound like REO Speedwagon? What's the difference, really? That's usually a good time to fold up your tent and start over."

t all came down to one sad episode before a show in Columbia, Missouri, on December 11, 1987. Hart was trying to beat his heroin addiction with methadone and was keeping a bottle of the drug on ice in a dressing room sink. Unfortunately, the bottle leaked and its entire contents spilled down the drain. Hart played the show, but it didn't look good for the next night, the last show of the tour, by which time he would be going through withdrawal. The next day Mould and Norton told Hart they'd understand if he wanted to cancel that night's show. Hart said he felt fairly good and wanted to play. But Mould had already canceled the show, as well as the band's appearance at an AIDS benefit Hart had helped put together at New York's Beacon Theatre.

Hart quit the band four days later, followed shortly thereafter by Mould.

Hart has asserted it wasn't his drug addiction that broke up Hüsker Dü, claiming that Mould had grown weary of the compromises required in a band of equals and was increasingly taking charge. "It just became that it was easier to be around Bob," Hart said, "if you were playing a part of Bob's game." Besides, Hart felt that Mould's songs were getting increasingly "square."

Norton agrees that the realities of the band's own success, more than Hart's drug problem, were its undoing: "Being together for nine years, the amount of touring that we did, the pressures of being on a major label, the more demand for your time, the less time you have for yourself," he says. "Then definitely maybe some of the steam started going out. Because the energy was being sucked from different places, whereas before it was just the three of us, let's get in the van and go blow the doors off this town."

The bottom line was that Hüsker Dü had become what the band had never wanted it to be: out of control. "The band was like a train speeding uphill and downhill, and nobody could get near it or they'd get run over," said Mould, who claimed it was he who quit the band first. "Certain people would try to be the conductor and certain people would pull the brakes. And nobody could get on or off. When it finally hit down in that valley and slowed down, Bob jumped off. Bob got off the train . . . and it's the best thing I ever did."

Hart has no regrets either. "No matter what bitter kind of monster it turned into, there were some very satisfying moments," he said. "I can't think of anything else I would have been better off doing for that amount of time."

Six months after the breakup, Hart learned that his HIV test had been incorrect. He was fine.

In the end, Mould felt Hüsker Dü had been done in by their own greatest success: *Zen Arcade*. Looking back on the band's career in 1990, Mould said the landmark album was "the beginning of the end." "It was the best record we ever made, but it was the one that we emulated. And when we went to Warner Brothers we couldn't change because we would have sold out," Mould told *The Bob* zine. "God, that was a weird situation. People really wanted to hold on to the past. And in a way I think it made us want to, too. It's weird. I'm certainly not ashamed of anything the band did, but, boy, looking back it's like, we could have done more. Something else should have been done."

# CHAPTER 6

# THE REPLACEMENTS

**I GUESS YOU COULD SAY WE'RE A SLOPPY ROCK & ROLL
BAND THAT TRIES TO STRADDLE THE LINE BETWEEN
COMEDY AND TRAGEDY.**

**— PAUL WESTERBERG**

Within the Eighties indie scene, the Replacements upended a lot of perceptions about what was OK. While their crosstown rivals Hüsker Dü toed the line in terms of left-wing politics and SST-style pragmatism, the Replacements couldn't give a hoot about any of that — they never booked their own shows or drove their own van, and the closest they got to a political song was . . . well, they never even got close to a political song. Instead, the band's leader Paul Westerberg wrote the kind of heart-on-the-sleeve rock songs, not to mention witty wordplay, that were almost totally absent from the underground.

Southern California punk rock bands like the Descendents and Circle Jerks had already done the young, loud, and snotty thing, but the Replacements did it in a way that folks from outside the community could understand; along with R.E.M., they were one of the few underground bands that mainstream people liked. It was anarchy without the rage; not only did they lack pesky political baggage, but their music was catchy and had obvious roots in classic rock bands like the Faces and the Stones. And, hey, a couple of them were even kinda cute.

The Replacements made a career out of a prolonged adolescence, although it was an awkward adolescence. Along the way, they magically metamorphosed from a raucous bunch of post-teens into the band that produced the landmark *Let It Be*, one of the best rock records ever made.

And if indie rock was becoming predictable even by the early Eighties, this band was nothing if not spontaneous. They'd screw up a gig at the drop of a beer can; they'd toss their instruments around the stage, hand them to members of the audience to play, or stumble through an hour and a half of cheesy covers. Sometimes they demanded that unless the audience threw money onto the stage, they'd keep playing badly. With their self-deprecating, even self-destructive style, they pioneered the "loser" sensibility that has been imitated in various ways ever since. Even their name implied they were second best. And yet on a good night, they were one of the best rock & roll bands one could ever hope to hear. The Replacements rocked hard.

The son of a Minneapolis Cadillac salesman, Paul Westerberg had attended a Catholic school for problem kids, but because he skipped graduation (he refused to wear a cap and gown), he never got his diploma. "The years thirteen to eighteen were pretty much hell," Westerberg said in a 1983 interview. "I was nervous, paranoid, and frustrated. I did my share of drugs. I didn't know what I wanted in life."

Luckily for Westerberg, his life began to take direction after he experienced a rock & roll epiphany in 1974, when he was fourteen. He'd just gotten a guitar and learned the three basic chords G, C, and D. And on his TV were power-poppers the Raspberries, playing their hit "Go All the Way," whose chords were . . . G, C, and D. Westerberg was floored. It was not, as it turned out, hard to rock.

Westerberg eventually joined a cover band, but he really wanted to play the songs he'd been writing. "I knew I was on my way," Westerberg said. "I could tell this . . . magic." Inspired by the Ramones, the New York Dolls, and the Sex Pistols, he formed a band as soon as he got out of high school. He got a job at a steel mill, then worked as a janitor in the office of Senator David Durenberger. He'd write out set lists for his band on Durenberger's stationery. "There'd be songs like 'We're Gonna Get Drunk Tonight,'" Westerberg said, "and at the top it would say 'From the desk of U.S. Senator . . .'"

In 1978 nineteen-year-old Yes fan and onetime juvenile-home escapee Bob Stinson saw his eleven-year-old half-brother Tommy starting down the same bad road he had traveled. So he gave him a bass and an amp just to keep him off the street, and they started jamming together. That year Bob met Chris Mars, seventeen, a soft-spoken high school dropout with a dark peach fuzz mustache. "We were all kind of long-haired dope-smoking teens," says Mars. "We'd light a joint and if the wind blew, your hair would singe."

With Mars on guitar and then drums, they started playing songs by Ted Nugent, Aerosmith, and a high-speed instrumental version of the Yes warhorse "Roundabout" in the Stinsons' mom's basement. They called themselves Dogbreath and they were driven by an imperative as old as rock & roll itself: "What do you do to keep yourself out of trouble and away from the factories?" said Mars.

One day Westerberg was walking home from work when he heard a band blasting in the Stinsons' house; they were so loud they rattled the windows. They sounded pretty good — a bit rough around the edges perhaps, but not bad at all. Almost every day after work, Westerberg would walk by the house, hide in some bushes and listen. Westerberg didn't know that the drummer was in fact his recent acquaintance Chris Mars. Mars knew Westerberg played guitar and by coincidence got the rest of the band to go see him play one night. Dogbreath didn't care for Westerberg's Tom Petty and Bad Company covers, but they invited him over to jam anyway. He was delighted to realize that this was the band he'd been listening to in the bushes.

When Westerberg arrived, he asked, "Where's the bass player?"

"He's sitting right there," Bob replied, gesturing toward the twelve-year-old boy across the room. "Tommy was so little," Westerberg said. "He came up to like half the size of his amp. I'll never forget it."

The Dogbreath guys had never heard punk, but that didn't prevent them from dismissing two Westerberg originals as "fuckin' punk rock." Then they tried to get Westerberg to sing "Roundabout." Being a young man of refinement and taste, he refused.

Dogbreath soon got a singer who "was really shit," according to Westerberg, "a hippie who had, like, a lyric sheet, sat down, and read the lyrics." Then they fired the hippie and Westerberg started, in his words, "yelling into the mike and stuff," but Bob didn't like that either, so they got another singer. But Westerberg really wanted to be the singer and, as legend has it, took the new guy aside one day and said, "The band doesn't like you. I think you're great, but they think you suck." The singer soon quit and Westerberg took his place.

Basically, the Stinsons' band was a good excuse to get drunk and party. "Rehearsals" consisted of taking a little speed and drinking and then maybe playing some songs as an afterthought. They'd play until Mrs. Stinson stomped on the floor.

Still, they balanced out each other well — the volatile, raucous band and the relatively disciplined, focused Westerberg, who showed up to practice in neat, clean clothes and insisted on playing songs until they got them right.

The rest of the band soon discovered first-generation English punk rock like the Clash, the Sex Pistols, and the Damned and cut their hair, leaving their suburban stoner identity behind, if only in appearance. "[Punk] was the perfect new sound vehicle by which to express our mentally ill, late adolescent attitude," Mars wrote in an unpublished memoir. "With the unbridled instability of the band already in place, punk — or something like it — proved the most logical direction to take ourselves."

The band realized they needed a better name than Dogbreath. Westerberg felt they should think in terms of taking the place of something — "Like maybe the main act doesn't show," Mars wrote, "and instead the crowd has to settle for an earful of us dirtbags." Mars came up with "the Substitutes," which lasted the few minutes it took Westerberg to come up with something better: "the Replacements." Everybody liked the name. "It seemed to sit just right with us," Mars wrote, "accurately describing our collective 'secondary' social esteem."

A commercial FM radio DJ and a fabulously nice guy, Peter Jesperson was also the manager of the only hip record store in town, Oarfolkjokeopus, the locus of Minneapolis's rock community since the mid-Seventies. A noted music connoisseur around town, Jesperson also spun records at the Minneapolis new wave/punk club the Longhorn and had cofounded Twin/Tone Records with local recording engineer Paul Stark, who owned a twenty-four-track mobile unit, and sportswriter and sometime rock critic Charley Hallman in January of '78.

When Westerberg handed Jesperson a four-song demo tape in May of '80, it was only to see if the band could get a show at the Longhorn. As it happened, Westerberg was eavesdropping on Jesperson's office just as he put in the tape, only to run away as soon as he heard the opening notes of the first song, "Raised in the City." Had he stayed, he would have heard Jesperson play the whole song through and then rewind it and play it again. And again. And again. Jesperson was blown away. "If I've ever had a magic moment in my life, it was popping that tape in," says Jesperson. "I didn't even get through the first song before I thought my head was going to explode."

He called Westerberg the next day and asked, "So do you want to do a single or an album?" Westerberg was astonished. "You mean you think this stuff is worth recording?" he asked. The Replacements had barely played out yet and they already had a record deal.

The classically oriented Stark trusted Jesperson's opinions about rock music completely, but, being an immensely practical man, he wanted to know more about the band. "It wasn't a question of whether they were good," says Stark. "The question from my point of view was are they going to be able to travel, are they going to be able to record, can they write songs in a timely manner?"

The Replacements' first gig was in June '80 at an alcohol-free coffeehouse in the basement of a Minneapolis church. Tommy had recently injured himself falling out of a tree, so the remaining three members played the show. They were so nervous that they got drunk on whiskey-and-Cokes — and maybe took a few pills, too — and when someone smelled the alcohol on their breath, they were thrown out of the building and told they'd never play in Minneapolis again. Jesperson arrived to find a dejected Mars sitting on the church steps, his head in his hands.

By their second show, they had asked Jesperson to be their manager because, as Westerberg once put it, "we didn't want to talk to the asshole at the bar." Jesperson happily accepted. Jesperson could calm down the band, talk sense to them, occasionally buy them lunch when they were broke, and simply cheerlead when things got discouraging. Later that summer they played a few local club gigs to sparse crowds. When they'd finish a song, the only noise they'd hear was the low hum of conversation at the bar, tinkling glasses, and Jesperson's loud whistle and fast, nervous clapping.

No doubt about it, Jesperson was a believer. "His enthusiasm kept us going at times, definitely," Mars says. "His vision, his faith in the band was a binding force."

Jesperson, a huge Beatles fan, had big plans for the band and made sure they were aware of only the finest musical influences, from David Bowie to an obscure Seventies power-pop band from Memphis called Big Star. "He gave us culture," says Mars. "Peter was the kind of guy where you'd go to his apartment and it was hours and hours of stuff, whether it was Moby Grape or Badfinger," recalls Bob Mould, "trying to fill your head with all this stuff. And I think with Paul, he found a cooperative subject for his dissertations on pop history."

Bob Stinson was another eager student — he'd never really listened to the Beatles until Jesperson made him listen to *Revolver*. After that Bob would go down to the basement and play one channel of the album through Tommy's bass amp and the other through his guitar amp, playing it loud and distorted — almost as if he were trying to make the Beatles sound like punk rock.

Westerberg felt his first truly good song was a number called "I'm in Trouble." "It was an actual song with a beginning, a middle, an end, and a bridge," he said. "Also, it was melodic and it rocked. It was everything I wanted and it was easy to write." After that a whole slew of songs came, and mere weeks after their live debut, it somehow seemed time to record an album.

Jesperson chose a modest eight-track home studio in town called Blackberry Way. Recording commenced in the fall of '8o. The Replacements had no clout at even modest Blackberry Way, so their studio access was catch-as-catch-can. It took about six months to record the album.

"The sessions were a gas," Jesperson recalls. "The band was exploding right before my very eyes. [It was recorded] mostly live, very few overdubs. I really could never tell you how exciting it was. And they were 100 percent unaware of how great they were."

One day was the occasion for a saliva war. "It all started when Bob, by accident, with his intended destination being the floor, spat out a loogie which landed on my neatly pressed denim cuff," Mars wrote. "In retaliation I shot a phlegm ball hitting my mark at the sideburn area. He then caught me with a goober on the pant leg. So I then hung a juicy one on his guitar. Back and forth the saliva flew when just then Paul, oblivious to the war inside, walks right in through the isolation door, catching the cross fire. Now he's in on the fray, launching his own arsenal of snot. On and on it went for the remainder of the session and beyond as we dodged each other's hawking slobber all the way to the bus stop."

Although this was punk rock, most of the songs hit on themes (not to mention chord progressions) that dated as far back as Chuck Berry, but updated for the Eighties. "Westerberg," wrote *Option*'s Blake Gumprecht, "has the ability to make you feel like you're right in the car with him, alongside him at the door, drinking from the same bottle."

"And I ain't got no idols, I ain't got much taste / I'm shiftless when I'm idle and I got time to waste" goes the chorus to "Shiftless When Idle," one of many Westerberg songs that detailed the inglorious facts of adolescent life in the late Seventies and early Eighties — getting wasted and driving around ("Takin' a Ride"), buying lousy pot at an arena show ("I Bought a Headache"), getting a crush on the girl at the convenience store ("Customer"), playing rock music to counteract boredom ("Something to Dü"), loitering ("Hanging Downtown"), and feeling just plain alienated (virtually every other song on the album). The lyrics detailed the dullness and complacency of middle American life while the music railed against it. But more remarkably, the songs took the adult stereotype of teenagers as lazy, maladjusted human beings and gleefully ran with it, nullifying the insult by celebrating it. You couldn't get much more punk rock.

And there was far more poetry than virtually any American punk rocker had yet dared — when Westerberg refers to marijuana as "a long-haired girl shakin' way past her years," it's a reference to getting tired of pot just as much as it's a beautiful metaphor for the obsolescence of hippie culture.

With his perfect raw-throated adolescent howl, Westerberg was cool but self-effacing, singing about chasing girls and getting wasted, yet quite ready to admit failure at the former, and sometimes even the latter. His words didn't take stands, just described feelings that a lot of his audience felt, too. There were no strident political exhortations, no hipper-than-thou posturing.

In fact, you could cut the self-deprecation with a knife. In the lyrics to "Shutup," Westerberg hollers, "Well, Tommy's too young / Bobby's too drunk / I can only shout one note / Chris needs a watch to keep time." The joke even extended to Westerberg's handwritten liner notes: "Kick Your Door Down" was "written 20 mins after we recorded it"; of the throwaway "Otto," he wrote, "We ain't crazy about it either"; on "Careless," he scrawled, "Don't worry, we're thinking about taking lessons." Westerberg considered calling the album "Power Trash," a phrase that stuck to the band for years afterward. He wound up with *Sorry Ma, Forgot to Take Out the Trash*.

Twin/Tone couldn't afford to release the album until September '81. It hardly seemed important at the time, but the Replacements hadn't signed a contract with Twin/Tone. "They were much more innocent times," says Jesperson. "There wasn't any precedent for mistrust in our close-knit little circle." A few short years later, when major labels started chasing the Replacements, Paul Stark suggested that they "get this on paper." "And they were like, 'Oh, *now* you want to sign us?'" says Jesperson. "Whereas in the early days, *they* would have been interested in signing and we would have been, 'Hey, don't worry about it.'"

"From the moment you start expending any energy or certainly finance on a band, you should get something signed on paper," Jesperson says, with the hard-earned wisdom of hindsight. "It's just too messy to do later on when tables have turned. When you first sign somebody, you have the upper hand usually, so it's a better time to sign an agreement right then, rather than having the artist rise and the record company goes, 'C'mon, you guys, you have to sign a contract.' That's what happened with the Replacements. It got really creepy."

Cover bands had been the rule in Minneapolis, so for a local band that played originals to get signed — even to a local indie — was a rarity. And the bands that did get signed tended to harbor art-rock pretensions. So when the Replacements showed up at gigs in their street clothes, got sloshed onstage, played their sloppy songs with a bass player who was still in junior high, and liked to yell swear words into the microphone just to hear them come booming out of the PA, it annoyed a lot of bands around Minneapolis.

"A lot of musicians in town wanted that Holy Grail of a major label contract with lots of money," says Stark, "and the Replacements were just kind of pissing on that, saying, 'That isn't what we want, we're just going to do what we want to do. If we want to get drunk, we're going to get drunk. If we want to sound like shit, we're going to sound like shit.'

"But most local musicians who were jealous of them had no idea the amount of work this band put in," adds Stark. "For being an antibusiness band, this band worked hard. They worked it harder than any of our bands."

From the start the Replacements were deeply suspicious of the music business, and Stark and Jesperson felt there was only one way to deal with that. "We kept them isolated from it," Stark says. "They had nothing to do with the business end at all. They didn't inquire and didn't want to." Stark has some regrets about that now, thinking they might have gotten over their distrust had they learned how everything really worked. "But at the same time, Paul developed more of a character," Stark says, "because of the isolation, because he wasn't influenced by the outside as much."

The isolation came at a cost. "They also had a somewhat inflated sense that they'd made a splash," says Jesperson. "And if they'd made a splash, then they'd sold a chunk of records and they should have had a bunch of money coming." Which often put Stark in the uncomfortable position of denying the band's requests for cash. "Is it going to be used for beers or is it going to be used for gas? I had to make a lot of decisions

along those lines," he says. "You wire them $400, and $200 went to the van and $200 went to booze and drugs."

Stark says Twin/Tone's attitude about the drinking and drugging was pretty much laissez-faire. "But when it starts affecting the band's business or our business, then there's something wrong," he says. "In the Replacements' case, they were able to define a wide-enough spot where drugs and alcohol were so much a part of the thing, it didn't get in the way. As long as they had someone like Peter who would get them to show up on time."

Against the backdrop of straight edge and the new puritanism then being advocated by the Reagan regime, getting wasted was once again a rebellious act. "The alcohol and the drug use back in the early Eighties," agrees Paul Stark, "is almost a statement."

Their first out-of-town gig was in December '80, opening for Twin/Tone's top band at the time, the Suburbs, at a skating rink in Duluth. They were very nervous. During the second song, Westerberg tried to be punk and bang the mike stand into his guitar but instead bashed the microphone into his forehead, sending blood streaming down his face. Of course, there was nothing to do but smash his guitar. "Kids were skating around as we played," Westerberg recalled. "I think they were more puzzled by us than anything else."

They were also trying to land a coveted opening slot for Johnny

DRINKING WAS A BIG PART OF THE REPLACEMENTS' IMAGE. THE BAND IN A TWIN/TONE PUBLICITY PHOTO FOR *HOOTENANNY*, TAKEN NEAR THE STINSONS' HOME. LEFT TO RIGHT: CHRIS MARS, PAUL WESTERBERG, BOB STINSON, TOMMY STINSON.

Thunders at First Avenue. Thunders had been the guitarist for the Heartbreakers, one of the earliest New York punk bands, and a particular hero of Westerberg's. Unfortunately, a band Westerberg had never heard of called Hüsker Dü got the gig. (Despite the two bands' ensuing rivalry, things were always pretty friendly on a personal level — eventually Westerberg even collaborated with Bob Mould on some songs; although the tapes they made were stolen from Hüsker Dü's van, Mould says it was no great loss. "It wasn't like you're going to find 'Your Cheatin' Heart' in there," he says reassuringly. "Nobody should worry about those.")

Hüsker Dü had already established a small following of local hardcore kids by the time the Replacements came along, but it was the Replacements who got the deal with the big local label. And to this day, there's still some bitterness about it. "The Replacements, they played one [sic] gig and they made their album," says Mould. "They were sort of blessed, I guess. As opposed to the rest of us who just had to play lots of gigs and save our money."

Still, the Hüskers took the Replacements under their wing. In the nascent Minneapolis punk scene, there weren't too many shows to go around, and Hüsker Dü often got the Replacements on the bill for out-of-town gigs. And the Replacements began to play faster and faster. "I think the speed came from doing gigs with Hüsker Dü, I really do," says Mars, recalling his first Hüskers show. "They took the stage and I'd never seen or heard that kind of speed or energy. I thought, 'Whoa, this is cool.' I liked it."

But despite the 200-mile-per-hour tempos, the Replacements were not, at heart, a hardcore band. "We were confused about what we were," says Mars. "There was the hardcore scene that was bubbling up. We knew Bob Mould — did we fit in there? We weren't quite sure. There was some uncertainty." "They were never part of the punk thing," says Mould. "They were like a fast bar band to me. They wrote original songs and stuff but . . . It was a different thing."

And Westerberg just never cottoned to the hardcore milieu. "I never really liked being part of a group or a team or anything," he said in 1984.

"I want no part of it. I get a kick out of hardcore sometimes — it's fast, aggressive. But I don't like all the shit that surrounds it, the *group*, the *idea*. I like to be alone and have my own idea."


I n January '82 Hüsker Dü took the band to O'Banion's in Chicago. "Now, Minneapolis was a little tamer than Chicago in terms of that heavy punk look," says Bob Mould. "Chicago was a lot more of a leather scene, and I just remember their eyes bugging out when they saw that."

At the show the Replacements debuted a song called "Kids Don't Follow." With its breakneck pace and big sing-along chorus, it sounded like a revved-up arena-rock anthem. And to Jesperson, it sure sounded like a hit. Listening to a tape of the show on the ride back to Minneapolis, he decided Twin/Tone should release the song with all due speed. "I will do anything to get this out," Jesperson pleaded to Stark and Hallman. "I will hand-stamp jackets if I have to." His partners OK'd the money for the recording but took him up on his offer — to save money, Jesperson and virtually everyone he knew eventually had to hand-stamp ten thousand white record jackets for The Replacements *Stink* EP.

They recorded and mixed eight songs within the week. "Paul [Westerberg] and I produced them, for better or worse," says Jesperson. "We'd give suggestions, but we really didn't know what we were doing. We just did it because we didn't know anybody else who would." It was released in June '82, just five months after the O'Banion's show.

"*Stink* was our balls-to-the-wall hardcore punk attempt, obviously," Mars says. The music certainly echoes the sound of hardcore on some cuts, but it's nowhere near as ferocious as the actual hardcore of the time. "I couldn't write hardcore worth a shit, but I certainly tried to sound as tough as I could," Westerberg later admitted. The loud-fast sub-two-minute blasts "Fuck School," "God Damn Job," and "Stuck in the Middle" were about as hardcore as Westerberg could manage, but they were still far more melodic than even the most tuneful skinhead band. And there was nothing hardcore at all about the wistful, majestic "Go."

With themes like school and kids, Westerberg remained fascinated with youth. "Stuck in the Middle" is about the limbo of adolescence, but it's also about the geographical problem of being neither here (L.A.) nor there (New York). On "God Damn Job," Westerberg yowls, "I need a god-damn job" — a distinctly unpunk sentiment. The subject of "Dope Smokin' Moron" was all too familiar to most high schoolers. His surprisingly thoughtful lyrics made it clear that Westerberg was making a strong bid to become poet laureate of the American teenage wasteland, where suburban kids grew up in the stunning cultural silence following the baby boom, going to vapid arena rock shows, drinking cheap beer, watching too much television, driving nowhere.

Although more precisely and aggressively played than *Sorry Ma*, the more hardcore-oriented numbers on *Stink* (original title: "Too Poor to Tour") still ring slightly false. "I think it might have been a little more calculated because of maybe not being true to ourselves and trying to fit in somewhere," Mars admits. "I liked the stuff that we did, but attitudewise and productionwise, I think we were trying to go for something that might have been a little contrived."

(One of the best moments on *Stink* is one of its most spontaneous: the EP opens with a recording of an actual Minneapolis policeman closing down a rent party the Replacements played. The loudmouth who boldly yells, "Hey, fuck you, man!" in the background is Dave Pirner of Soul Asylum.)

By the time of *Stink*, the band was fairly popular in Minneapolis, although they still couldn't quite sell out the 300-capacity 7th Street Entry. The band began playing occasional gigs around the Midwest, where they drew sparse crowds. "It was like, well, 'There's four people here tonight,'" says Mars, "'let's get drunk and go ahead.'" They'd occasionally warm up for popular bands like the Dead Kennedys, but people rarely came to see the opening band. "It was a slow, slow struggle," Mars recalls. "Still, at that point, it was a good way of staying out of trouble." Of course, many club managers they encountered would disagree.

After a show at Minneapolis's Walker Art Center, a young security guard there named Bill Sullivan decided he wanted to join the Replacements' road crew and see the world. "I approached Paul after a show and told him that I was an experienced tech, which I wasn't," says Sullivan, "and I told him that I drank less than Jesperson, which I didn't." Westerberg took a shine to the puckish Sullivan, and they took him along on their first full-fledged tour, their first trip out east, in April '83.

Although Sullivan's parents were upset with his career choice, his mother still packed him and the band a cooler full of turkey, ham, sandwich bread, and cookies as well as a garbage bag full of socks and underwear. "Of course, by the time we got to Detroit, that cooler was just trashed," says Sullivan. "The turkey was swimming in beer." Thankfully, none of the band ever drove the tour van — that was left to the roadies or Jesperson (in fact, none of the band members had driver's licenses).

Tommy dropped out of tenth grade to go on the tour; Mrs. Stinson appointed Jesperson Tommy's legal guardian while he was on the road. Before that, when the band would play clubs, they'd have to hide Tommy until just before show time. "They wouldn't let him play the pinball machines or nothin'," Bob recalled. "And you know, he'd cry."

**W**hile they were preparing to record their next album, Westerberg brought in a powerful acoustic ballad called "You're Getting Married One Night." But when he played the song for the band, it was met with a resounding silence. "Save that for your solo album, Paul," Bob said finally. "That ain't the Replacements."

It was never released, but they did eventually play the song on the road, including one tense night at City Gardens in Trenton, New Jersey, where a gauntlet of bad-ass mohawked punks lined the edge of the stage, giving the band a massive hairy eyeball. Westerberg responded by playing this most unpunk of songs as Jesperson looked on in horror. "I thought, 'Oh shit, they're going to just *kill* him!'" says Jesperson. But by the end of the tune, Westerberg had even the most hardened punkers in the palm of his hand. "At least you fuckers ain't enemies," he said after the song ended. "That's nice to know."

"That's still, to me," says Jesperson, "a very moving moment."

The band was now disavowing the hardcore aspects of *Stink*. "We're not a hardcore band," Westerberg said. "We write songs rather than riffs with statements." "That was maybe the beginning of thinking, 'Aw, I don't know if we fit into this,'" says Mars. "So let's have a hootenanny here, let's settle down and have a hoedown and loosen it up and have some fun."

Besides, the new material Westerberg was coming up with was all over the map, maybe because Westerberg had to write for a tough, diverse audience: his own band. "If it doesn't rock enough, Bob will scoff at it," Westerberg said, "and if it isn't catchy enough, Chris won't like it, and if it isn't modern enough, Tommy won't like it."

So they decided to try a fresh approach on their next record. Stark engineered the album himself, partly because he had the twenty-four-track mobile unit and partly because Jesperson and Westerberg wanted to try somewhere else besides the modest Blackberry Way. First they tried to record on the Longhorn stage and then the stage at First Avenue, but neither worked out. They ended up recording at the Suburbs' rehearsal space in a warehouse in Roseville, just outside downtown Minneapolis.

Stark worked from the mobile truck parked elsewhere in the building; neither could see the other, so they communicated via intercom.

Very soon Stark began to learn the secrets of working with the band. Bob, for instance, couldn't play worth a damn until he'd had a couple of beers. "But by the time he's had *five or six* beers," says Stark, "it's too late." Westerberg wrote in fits and starts, so the album was recorded over several sessions, starting in October '82 and finishing up the following January.

"At that point, the band and I were playing games — I don't think they liked me a whole lot," says Stark, whose no-nonsense demeanor some describe as "Spocklike." "Unfortunately I had to have a love/hate relationship with the Replacements where I was more on the hate end, being the president of the label, which is everything evil. Then when I was in the studio having to be the boss saying, 'No, you've done enough here,' or, 'Let's try it again . . .'"

At one session the band got annoyed at Stark's meticulous recording style, so Mars and Westerberg switched instruments and they all improvised a bluesy shuffle — less a shuffle than a stumble, really — with Westerberg howling, "It's a hootenanny" over the primordial changes. At the end of the take, Stark, who of course couldn't see the band, asked them, "Do you want to come in and listen to that or do you want to try it again?" Westerberg simply declared, "No, first song, side one." And that's what it became.

"*Hootenanny* was a complete joke from their point of view — they did not care what they delivered," says Stark. "'The label wants an album, we don't care' — *that* attitude. And that was fine." But *Hootenanny* wasn't just a goof — in many songs Westerberg revealed a sadder, more sensitive side that suddenly pushed his songwriting persona into three dimensions. Underneath the bravado was candid self-doubt and melancholy. Westerberg had injected a classic singer-songwriter sensibility into punk rock, which made *Hootenanny* a revelation. It wasn't just power-trash anymore.

Right after "Hootenanny," the record explodes into a hardcore-style ode to running red lights ("Run It"), then an anthemic midtempo rocker ("Color Me Impressed"), then the eerie "Willpower"; with its desolate echoed vocal, dark melody, and sparse arrangement, it could almost have been a Cure song. "Buck Hill" is a surf/B-52's homage to a local ski slope; Westerberg reads the personals right out of the *Minneapolis City Pages* above the cheesy lounge jazz of "Lovelines," while the Beatles/Chubby Checker pastiche "Mr. Whirly" is a salute to the bed spins; Westerberg even managed to turn a recent bout with pleurisy into the jaunty boogie "Take Me Down to the Hospital." All the while, Westerberg was coming out with memorable lines: "Times ain't tough, they're tedious," he sings in "Heyday."

Like the rest of the band, Westerberg was still living with his parents because he couldn't afford his own place. He'd write songs in the basement while his folks were away at work. "And of course, being alone you tend to get a bit . . . introspective," Westerberg says. But when he brought his more sensitive material to the band, they'd inevitably turn it into a spoof, and those songs largely fell by the wayside. Westerberg got around that dynamic on *Hootenanny*'s striking "Within Your Reach" by simply playing all the instruments himself. With a synth, heavily processed guitar, and a drum machine (but since this was a Replacements track, the machine somehow manages to drop a beat at one point), it sounds like a cross between a Stones ballad and the electro-pop then ruling the alternative charts.

Jesperson was crazy about the song, but Bob, ever the hard rocker, originally objected to including it on the album, claiming it wasn't representative of the band. Even Westerberg wasn't sure about including the most emotionally vulnerable song he had yet recorded. "That's a little embarrassing for me," Westerberg said of the song. "I can listen to it alone and kinda enjoy it, but I still cringe a little."

In fact, Westerberg had trouble sharing his feelings in general. "I remember Westerberg in a complete despairing moment in Ohio and I kind of tried to give him a hug and it was just like, 'Don't even go there,'" Bill Sullivan recalls. "Close, with Westerberg, is quite a few paces away.

"Minnesota boys are famous for that," Sullivan adds. "Ask the chicks."

Closing the album, the folky acoustic shuffle "Treatment Bound" is an extended complaint about their lack of success. "We're gettin' no place fast as we can / Get a noseful from our so-called friends / We're gettin' nowhere quick as we know how."

But that was soon to change. Tracks off *Hootenanny* got played on over two hundred radio stations across the country, mostly college. And critics loved the album. "This one captures all the do-it-yourself-with-lots-of-rough-edges-who-cares-we-tried spirit that is the essence of all great independent American rock 'n' roll," wrote Elizabeth Phillip in *Matter*; a slew of critics placed *Hootenanny* in their year-end top tens, leading *Village Voice* critic Robert Christgau to deem it "the most critically acclaimed independent album of 1983."

The musical chairs of the title track, the frequent studio banter, and the home-recorded in-joke of "Treatment Bound" were all charmingly self-effacing, but it had more than a whiff of self-sabotage. Westerberg carefully constructed the music and lyrics, then he and the band nearly obliterated most of it in a shit storm of distortion, speed, and drunken slobber. *Minnesota Daily* critic David Ayers rated the album highly but made the insightful observation that "it's as if [Westerberg] can't bear to be taken seriously, so he subverts his art with artifice."

And yet on some level Westerberg must have burned to be taken seriously — the man had never shied away from making overt generational statements in his music and clearly recognized his own talent. But when you've grown up with low expectations and then the world tells you you're great, how do you cope with it?

Says Sullivan, "Those guys used to get together in the van and put their hands all together and then Paul would say, 'Where are we going?' And the band would go, 'To the middle!' And he'd go, 'Which middle?' And they'd go, 'The *very* middle!'" But it was all false modesty. The Replacements, it seemed, secretly believed in themselves and yet adopted a loser persona to insulate themselves against failure.

And despite their considerable gifts, failure was easily within reach. The problem was the Replacements didn't just represent youthful aggression, energy, and confusion — they embodied it. "Without Peter, there's nothing they could have done," says Stark. "There's no way that band could have held together or amounted to anything if Peter hadn't baby-sat them during those early years." The band's shambolic performances were the true outcome of a living-on-the-edge lifestyle. This was a double-edged sword — sometimes they'd be exhilaratingly fierce and reckless, and sometimes things would swiftly devolve into a musical train wreck, the band drunkenly staggering halfway through the songs, trading instruments midsong, bickering, joking.

At times it seemed as if Westerberg and his merry crew were consciously emulating the notoriously sloppy, dissipated performances of Johnny Thunders, who was in turn acting out some fantasy version of Keith Richards. Westerberg, Mars, and the Stinsons were testing the bounds of the old truism about rock & roll being at its best when it's teetering on the edge of disaster. It *was* riveting sometimes. And sometimes it was just frustrating. "Unprofessional?" wrote David Ayers of the band. "Sure. Thrilling? You bet. There isn't another band going that you could see 20 nights in a row and be moved every time for a different reason."

Alcohol was key to the Replacements' erratic performance style, and the band was consuming it in ever-larger quantities. "If it's a small crowd, it helps sometimes because you see double," Westerberg cracked, "and then you can fill the joint." But levity like that only sought to avoid the real reasons the band drank so much.

"Maybe the people who feel the need to create and express themselves also need to cloud that over sometimes," Westerberg explained in a more candid moment. "Sometimes you don't want to be creative. You just want to be normal and not have to worry, or think, or write. People will then turn to distractions like drugs, liquor, or whatever."

And then there were the endless, boring miles spent in the van, the countless hours to kill between sound check and show, the presence of booze anywhere a touring band goes. "First thing we do when we finally pull up," Westerberg drawled in "Treatment Bound," "Get shitfaced drunk, try to sober up," and it wasn't too far from the truth. And besides, getting fucked up was what rock bands did, right?

It was also a backlash against the structure Westerberg had brought to the band. "I distinctly remember me and Bob looking at each other and wanting to just let loose like we used to," says Mars. "I remember purposely changing tempos and Bob would wail off on some lead that had nothing to do with the song and we'd be grinning at each other and there'd be that little ghost of the past coming up. We'd not only buck the system as the band, we'd also buck the system *of* the band."

For a group that worried about losing control of its own destiny, getting drunk for a show was a good way to ensure they'd never be successful enough to be co-opted. "We were very afraid that it got to the point where things seemed to be out of our control," Westerberg said. "We were afraid some guy would sign us up and make us do this and that. We never really stopped long enough to sit down and realize we can do anything we want. No one can tell us what to do. We were afraid of becoming what we hated, which at the time was a self-important and arrogant band."

The Replacements were one of the first bands to openly and directly acknowledge the confusion and uncertainty of being a professional musician. "We definitely had a fear of success," Westerberg said in 1987. "We had a fear of everything. We were all very paranoid, and I think that goes hand in hand with the excessive drinking thing. We'd get drunk because we were basically scared shitless, and that snowballed into an image."

Eventually the Replacements would become a sort of cartoon, typecast as a bunch of idiot savant boozers. Through the Replacements' music and the band's well-documented besotted pratfalls, fans could get the vicarious thrill of being a melancholic slob, a lovable asshole, a soulful drunk, a free spirit. But for the band itself, booze and drugs would exact a heavy toll.

**W**hen Westerberg pulled a disappearing act, it was usually to a bar. Bob also disappeared occasionally, but he was easy to find, too. All someone had to do was find the nearest railroad tracks. And there would be Bob, kicked back with a six-pack of beer on the embankment overlooking the tracks, watching the trains go by.

Bob Stinson was given to saying "ain't" and using double negatives ("I'm not taking no credit or anything like that . . .") but was nonetheless a bright man. "You would take for granted he was an idiot, but he was far from an idiot," says Stark. "He probably had the greatest potential of anyone [in the band] and yet spent so much time polluting it with drugs and alcohol that you would just think he was dumb. But he wasn't at all." As Westerberg once said, "I don't know if he's the stupidest genius or the smartest idiot I've ever known."

"That was the thing about Bobby — you could never tell if he knew the future or if he was unsure of the past," says Sullivan. "Or if he even knew what time it was. He would always say, 'Relax, it's Tuesday.' And everybody would look at him. Because he would never say it on a Tuesday. No one knew what the fuck he was talking about."

"If we couldn't find something, Bob would just go, 'Hey, if it was up your ass, you'd know where it was!' And we'd be like, '*What???*'" recalls Jesperson. "Whenever we'd be stuck in traffic, he'd say, 'Close your eyes and floor it.'" The latter was an apt motto for Bob's guitar playing, not to mention his lifestyle. Bob had a formidable dark side, especially after he'd had a few, that the band, even Bob himself, openly referred to as "Mr. Hyde." "He was just a weird guy — he was as uncommon an individual as I have ever known in my life," Jesperson says. "He was just unlike anybody." "He could be really exasperating and tough to deal with, and he could be just as sweet and lovable as he was," says Sullivan.

Sullivan kept guitar strings in a couple of World War II ammo cases, and one day while Bob was sleeping in the van, he tied the boxes to the guitarist's shoes. "And we stopped at a truck stop," says Sullivan, "and he got out of the van and walked into the truck stop, got a soda pop and some chips, went to the bathroom, walked back and got into the van, dragging these things the entire way, without any recognition of the joke. Would not even give you the satisfaction of going, 'Fuck you.'"

And although Bob Stinson was a fantastic guitarist, capable of putting a song over the top with a thrillingly melodic solo, in some ways he remained a rank amateur. At one show Westerberg added extra dots to the fretboard on Bob's guitar just before the band hit the stage. "And when Bob looked down to play his solo, he was completely lost," says Sullivan, chuckling. "No idea where to go."

Although Sullivan was almost as much of a prankster and reprobate as the band was, it was still his responsibility to wrangle them from show to show, a trying task at best — the joke within the band was that Sullivan always carried a one-way plane ticket to Minneapolis in his shirt pocket. And sometimes the craziness really did get to him. At one point Sullivan told Bob that he wanted to quit. "I remember Bob saying to me, 'You don't want to quit. Think of the Who's roadies — those guys are probably making *lots* of money,'" says Sullivan. "All of us thought something was going to happen here. Because when it was good, it was really, really good."

But when it was bad, it was really, really bad.

"They were contrary," says Sullivan. "We were in Nashville and the whole place was packed with country music executives. They played all their punk rock — just as loud and fast as they could until they virtually cleared the room until there was nothing left but punks. And then they played country music the rest of the night." Later that tour they played in L.A. and resolutely refused to play anything anybody could slam-dance to. "They would just *torture* them," says Sullivan. "We played in Dayton, Ohio — or something like that — and these people weren't just throwing vegetables at us, they were throwing *canned* vegetables at us.

"The more welcome we were, the more they pissed on the people that welcomed us," says Sullivan. "The more unwelcome they were, the better they played, which was cool. Frustrating at times, but in hindsight it was really cool when they would play a better show at a clothing store for twenty bucks and five quaaludes than they would play at the big club in town, opening for R.E.M., because they weren't supposed to."

**B**y 1983 the hipper rock bands started to understand there was a history to the music. And as a way of legitimizing themselves and aligning themselves with their roots, they'd do covers, chosen with the utmost care. The Replacements were one of the first bands to do this, only sometimes they took the idea to its logical conclusion and did entire sets of covers — and not always the coolest songs, either. And they usually played them pretty badly.

Through all of it was the unstated knowledge that the golden age of rock & roll had passed by the Replacements and their peers. They'd grown up on arena-rock junk like Kiss and Aerosmith. So, their defiance bolstered by punk rock, they decided to celebrate their fucked-up heritage. They'd do stuff like T. Rex's "20th Century Boy," Bachman-Turner Overdrive's "Takin' Care of Business," and Motörhead's "Ace of Spades," not to mention more hallowed material like Tony Joe White's "Polk Salad Annie" and Johnny Cash's "Folsom Prison Blues." Sullivan would sometimes come up onstage and sing his version of "If I Only Had a Brain" from *The Wizard of Oz*. "If I would not be just a roadie," Sullivan would warble, "Working for these loadies . . ."

(In fact, Sullivan was a frequent visitor to the Replacements' stage. At a show at the Channel in Boston, a bouncer started beating up a kid in front of the stage and Tommy jumped on the bouncer. Then Tommy was jumped by another bouncer, who was in turn jumped on by Westerberg. Then Sullivan ran out onto the stage, surely to rescue his charges from danger. No such luck — instead he just grabbed the microphone and finished the song.)

They'd also cover lightweight pop tunes like the DeFranco Family's "Heartbeat — It's a Lovebeat" as well as various country standards in their "pussy set," a result of playing the hardcore circuit, opening for bands like the Effigies, Black Flag, and Social Distortion before hundreds of identical skinheads who all felt they were being nonconformists. "They thought that's what they were supposed to be standing for, like, 'Anybody does what they want' and 'There are no rules,'" Westerberg said. "But there *were* rules and you *couldn't* do that, and you *had* to be fast, and you *had* to wear black, and you *couldn't* wear a plaid shirt with flares. . . . So we'd play the DeFranco Family, that kind of shit, just to piss 'em off."

But few hardcore kids got the point of the "pussy set"; after a show in Virginia, a horde of them retaliated by knocking over the band's microphone stands, then went outside and bashed up their van.

That particular night also marked the debut of Mars's rarely seen alter ego, "Pappy the Clown." Every once in a while, even the relatively steady Mars would lose it. He'd get lit to the gills, sneak off somewhere, and put on whiteface and his loudest, silliest clothes, maybe don a goofy hat and tie balloons around his neck, and reappear only minutes before showtime. "I remember one time when Pappy showed up," says Sullivan.

"Chris — I mean *Pappy* — looked over at me and he held out the drumsticks and I was like, 'New sticks?' He shakes his head. '*More* sticks?' He shakes his head. I'm, like, '*What?!*' He goes, 'New drummer.'"

After *Hootenanny* the Replacements began to attract a bigger out-of-town following, and in the spring of '83 they kicked off their first trip to the East Coast. The tour wound through Detroit, Columbus, Cleveland, and Philadelphia, but the real destination was New York, where they had dates booked at Folk City and Maxwell's in Hoboken.

They went back the following June and played the hallowed punk bastion CBGB. Although they came out of the punk scene, the Replacements didn't *look* punk — when they showed up at CBGB, "the punk rock guy was not going to let us in — we were in flannel and long hair and the punk rock guy was like, 'What do you guys want?'" recalls Sullivan. "And we're like, 'We're the Replacements.' And he says, 'The fuck you are.'"

Things went downhill from there — Bob got eighty-sixed from the CBGB bar almost from the moment he walked in the door, setting the tone for the rest of the night. The Replacements were the last of five bands, which meant they went on in the wee hours of the morning — on a Monday night. The Folk City show had also been a bomb. Promoters Ira Kaplan and Michael Hill had done the band a big favor by placing them on a plum bill that also included the Del Fuegos and the Del Lords, but the band successfully snatched defeat from the jaws of victory. "The Replacements were so loud and obnoxious that the people just cleared right out," says Sullivan. "It was pretty uncomfortable." Even the woman doing sound walked out, so Jesperson did his best to handle the board.

The band's self-image as misfit/loser/yokels had gotten the better of them at two of the most storied clubs in the world's most intimidating city. "CBGB was punk; we weren't punk," Sullivan says. "Folk City was legendary; we weren't legendary."

Things went a little better when they returned to Folk City a few months later. They had stayed the night before at the home of some well-to-do punk kid outside of Washington, D.C. "Of course, Bobby, being ever resourceful, found the medicine cabinet," says Sullivan. "The guy had a typical mom who had a lot of problems dealing with life, so there was Valiums and Percodans and the whole nine yards. By the time we pulled up in front of Folk City, Paul was like, 'Oh, let's just bring half the

stuff in.' So they played with half stacks, and they were just so mellow that
night. They played all the songs nice and mellow, and they just put them
out. That night was a huge success. All due to mixing Valium and beer."
(Don't try this at home, kids.)

The tour ended in a dive bar in Worcester, Massachusetts. One person paid. "And he didn't like it," Sullivan quips. "We had to buy him beer
to keep him around."

D espite being the biggest offender, Bob was also the first to realize
that the drinking was getting out of hand and was the first to try to
do something about it. The *Hootenanny* tour included the band's
first big show in L.A., a headlining spot at the Palace. With great difficulty, Bob had gone on the wagon for the show. He showed up ready to
play — and the others didn't. "Bobby was really, really pissed off," Sullivan recalls. "The next morning the door of my hotel room got kicked
right off the hinges. Bobby was standing there in a tutu and a top hat with
a case of Budweiser and a bottle of Jack." According to Sullivan, Bob
never went on the wagon again as long as he was a Replacement.

The night after that, Bob played his most infamous show, at the University of San Diego. Dressed only in his underwear, Bob wandered into
the school theater and tore down a sixty-foot curtain. "And as he's walking
onto the stage, anything he walked by — a table, a chair, a telephone — it
would gather up into it," says Sullivan. "And he gets up onstage in that
thing and he drops the curtain and the underwear and played the show
naked except for his guitar. He was hammered, but he was *rockin'*. I think
he was kind of pissing the other guys off because he was really taking the
spotlight that night. And the crowd was going nuts for it.

"Somebody threw a shoe at him," Sullivan continues, "and he's playing and this shoe is coming at him and he catches it and he spins the guitar around, pisses in the shoe, throws the shoe back, spins the guitar back
around, and finishes the solo." When Sullivan came onstage to sing
Roger Miller's "Kansas City Star," Bob suddenly took his guitar off and
jumped Sullivan from behind. "I will never forget the look on Bill's face,"
says Jesperson, chuckling, "when he realized he had a naked Bob Stinson
wrapped around him."

"At the end of the night, it was just, 'Bob! Bob! Bob! Bob! Bob!'" says
Sullivan. "For years, whenever I've come back to San Diego, it's all any
stage crew guy in the entire city can ever talk about."

The indie touring circuit was still in its infancy, and the band didn't always have the luxury of playing lucrative college gigs; they simply weren't cool enough to play many of the larger clubs, either. "When we played Seattle, there was no club — there was the Central Tavern, a blues bar," says Sullivan. "There were VFW's, Mexican restaurants — we played a Mexican restaurant in Indianapolis — we played clothing stores."

In Davis, California, they were booked to play a place called 617 Anderson, which turned out to be someone's house. "And I pull into the driveway of this house and I'm like, 'This *can't* be the gig,'" says Sullivan. "And then four girls in little black miniskirts walk out and I'm like, 'This *better* be the gig!'"

That night the band played in the living room, which was covered floor to ceiling in plastic; the keg was in the kitchen. "It was a pretty fun gig, actually," Sullivan recalls.

The band's lowest ebb probably came during an eight-date tour with R.E.M. in the summer of '83. Audiences are not always receptive to opening bands, but then again, the Replacements were not good at playing second fiddle, either. So Westerberg decided that every night they should go out and alienate the crowd to the best of their ability. Unsurprisingly, this goal was handily achieved. The band was drinking heavily; although R.E.M. wisely gave them a minimum of alcohol, the Replacements would wait until R.E.M. was onstage and then barge into their dressing room and take all their booze.

Soon R.E.M.'s management wanted the Replacements off the tour. The rest of the band just wanted to play, while Westerberg, as he put it, was "just content to go up there and pull fruit out of my pocket or something." It all led up to one gigantic argument somewhere in Kentucky or Ohio, with crying and threats by various Replacements to fly home or even quit the band entirely. "We just didn't realize that we should never *ever* open up for another band and play to people who aren't equipped to deal with who we are," said Westerberg. "We'd much rather play for fifty people who know us than a thousand who don't care."

The Replacements somehow managed to last out the tour and even managed to rub off on R.E.M., too. "[R.E.M.] benefited a lot from it — they were really stiff onstage," says Sullivan. "By the time we were done playing with them, they all of a sudden had covers in their set. They were doing all kinds of things that they had never done before."

In the fall of '84, *Village Voice* writer R. J. Smith traveled with the band for a week through the Midwest and Canada, playing Scrabble with them in the van and making a creditable attempt to keep up with their high jinks. They played a series of dismal gigs, including a college cafeteria in Illinois, which all descended into dissolute anarchy. Conditions were bad: exhaust was leaking into the van, the rail-thin Westerberg suffered a relapse of his pleurisy, and everyone, except for Mars, was drinking heavily. "The Replacements," Smith wrote, "are balled-up boluses of high hopes and low feelings, wildcat growls and boredom, longings they try to beat down with a stick but never quite can."

Despite all the critical hosannas, the Replacements had not exactly hit the big time. They usually made just enough money to get to the next gig. Fortunately, an informal network of band-related floors had sprung up; the Replacements would stay with the Del Fuegos in Boston, for example, or with Naked Raygun in Chicago, and they'd return the favor when those bands were in town. Every once in a while, they'd treat themselves and all pile into the same fleabag motel room, although one guy had to sleep in the van and guard the equipment. "Actually, that was kind of nice," Mars recalls, "because you were alone and you could sleep with nobody snoring in your face."

Sleep was a rare and sometimes dangerous commodity. On one early tour, they traveled in an electric-company van that carried the band, three other people, and all their equipment. It was summer and they kept the sliding side door open for some air. When Mars went in back for a cat-nap, he'd tie his belt to the biggest amp he could find so he wouldn't roll out onto the freeway.

"Sometimes it's great fun, but you spend a lot of time broken down on the side of highways, sleeping on people's floors," says Sullivan. "You wake up and your eyes kind of focus and there's a pile of dog shit right there. And you don't know if it was there when you lay down or if it got dropped there while you were sleeping, but that's what you wake up to. All these people had pets and first thing in the morning their bird was squawking or their dog was barking, there's hair all over the floor . . ."

It couldn't have helped matters that the band had a "tradition" of never cleaning out the van while they were on tour. After a few weeks they'd be knee-deep in stinking garbage.

Westerberg made up road names for everybody. Tommy was "the Brat," Jesperson was "the Wimp," Sullivan was "the Drunk," and Mars was "the Chince," so named because of his habit of squirreling away all his per diem money. Bob was "the Dunce," although for a while after he shaved his head except for a small clump of hair, they called him Patch. Westerberg's nickname was "the Louse," although Bob called him Fall Downstairberg.

Tommy was called the Brat for good reason; he could be petulant and spoiled, capable of all sorts of petty cruelty. On one early tour, the band intersected with the dB's at a show at Duke University. The band's guitarist Peter Holsapple knew Jesperson was a big fan and gave him a copy of the brand-new dB's single. As they pulled out of the parking lot of the auditorium, Jesperson couldn't wait to get home and throw the disk on the turntable. "I had the single up on the dashboard of the van," Jesperson says, "and Tommy actually knew how much that meant to me and broke it in half and threw it out the window."

And there were times when Tommy just disappeared. During a show at CBGB in the summer of '83, he got so annoyed at the band that he walked offstage and went AWOL for two days. The band went up to Boston without him, played a show using the Del Fuegos' bass player Tom Lloyd, then went back down to New York to pick him up after a friend of a friend tracked him down.

Ironically, Tommy originally disdained the rest of the band's drinking regimen. "I even remember him saying, 'Ewww, why would I ever want to do that? Look at you guys, you look disgusting and you act stupid!'" says Jesperson. "And suddenly, it was like, boom, he just jumped in headfirst. He started [playing in the band] when he was twelve, and I don't think he started [drinking] for a couple of years — he was probably fourteen before he started slamming whiskeys. He could even have been fifteen."

Since Bob was quite eccentric and at times a scary drunk, Tommy looked elsewhere for guidance. Eventually he and Westerberg became very close, so much so that they even began to look alike. "Paul was almost like the role model for Tommy more than anybody," says Jesperson. "He learned some really good things from Paul as well as how to get stinkin' drunk all the time. But I'd also have to say that Paul and I had a lot to do with fathering, or big brothering, Tommy."

Consequently, Tommy would do almost anything to win Westerberg's approval. "If Paul broke something, Tommy would have to break something bigger," says Jesperson. "If Paul did something bad, Tommy would have to do something worse. That was problematic, as you can imagine. Because Paul didn't need to be egged on."

**T**he last line of the last song on *Hootenanny* is "We're gettin' nowhere, what will we do now?" What they did was to come out with the best album of their career.

What had made the band great was its musical approximation of the

THE REPLACEMENTS
AROUND THE TIME OF
*LET IT BE.* LEFT TO
RIGHT: **PAUL
WESTERBERG, CHRIS
MARS, BOB STINSON,
TOMMY STINSON. NOTE
BOB'S SHINER.**

LAURA LEVINE

adolescent disregard for danger. But as they got older, that recklessness began to fade, if only slightly. And on the next album, *Let It Be*, something even better began to take its place. The band was actually growing up. "We used to tune for an hour onstage and drink two quarts of whiskey," Westerberg joked at the time. "Now we're down to one quart and tuning for half an hour."

The band had finally grown tired of playing loud and fast exclusively. "We're losing our inhibitions," he proclaimed early in '84. "When we started, we were afraid; we thought we'd hide behind sort of a wall of aggression. Now we're softening a little where we can do something that's a little more sincere without being afraid that someone's not going to like it or the punks aren't going to be able to dance to it."

The band released the "I Will Dare"/"20th Century Boy"/"Hey, Good Lookin'" single in July '84. With its sunny rockabilly swing, "I Will Dare" was a nigh-perfect pop song, complete with Westerberg's jaunty mandolin and a nifty guitar solo courtesy of their number one fan and booster, R.E.M.'s Peter Buck. Later Westerberg noted that the title was a good slogan for the Replacements. "We'll dare to flop," he said. "We'll dare to do anything."

The version of the Hank Williams classic "Hey, Good Lookin'" was recorded live at a club in Madison, Wisconsin. Afterward Bob claimed his solo was deliberately off-key, but after the show, as the band was driving home in the van and listening to the tape, he repeatedly tried to snatch the tape out of the machine while Westerberg replayed the gloriously tone-deaf solo over and over again as the rest of the band roared with laughter.

**W**esterberg was acutely conscious of the fact that their new album *Let It Be* placed much more of a focus on songwriting than ever before. "To the Replacements fan who liked us in the beginning, it may not really please," he said, "but there's certainly some good stuff on there."

There certainly was. Right off the bat, there was "I Will Dare." And "Sixteen Blue" is as accurate and affecting a portrait of the woes of adolescence as has ever been committed to vinyl — topped off by a towering solo from Bob, the song is a classic. "Androgynous" is just voice, piano, and a brushed snare, a poignant profile of "Dick," who wears a skirt, and "Jane," who wears a chain. "And they love each other so, androgynous," Westerberg croons, "Closer than you know, love each other so." But "Unsatisfied" might have been the album's (and the band's) high point: a soaring hymn to restlessness, frustration, and ennui, Westerberg had hit upon a moving new way to declare that he can't get no satisfaction.

All the drama was perfectly leavened by raucous numbers with titles like "Tommy Gets His Tonsils Out" and "Gary's Got a Boner," as well as a stomping cover of Kiss's "Black Diamond." Even an ostensibly slight song like the anti-MTV tirade "Seen Your Video," which is just an anthemic chord sequence climaxed by the words "Seen your video / That phony rock & roll / We don't wanna know," is delivered with enough passion and conviction to raise the hairs on one's neck.

While there are strong elements of metal, hardcore, and arena rock, it's tempered and given some sort of classic resonance by undeniable strains of honky-tonk country and Chicago blues. The arrangements are sophisticated, a quantum leap past anything they'd ever done before — the songs have several distinct sections and dramatic dynamic shifts, and instruments like piano, lap steel, twelve-string guitar, and mandolin are all over the record.

They considered titles like "Get a Soft On" and "Kind of a Sewer" before settling on *Let It Be*. Copping the Beatles album title was the height of cheekiness, but it was also a poke at Beatles freak Jesperson. That mixture of self-deprecation and bravado — tacitly acknowledging they'd never be like the Fab Four and yet daring to cop their album title — was pure Replacements.

And if not quite fab, they certainly were four distinct characters: Paul, the romantic loser; Tommy, the bratty pretty-boy; Bob, the classic rock & roll wildman; Chris, the quiet one. The cover of *Let It Be* highlights this perfectly. There they are, sitting out on the slanted roof of the Stinsons' mom's house — a silly place to have your picture taken — Tommy, the waifish rock imp wiping some hungover sleep from his eyes, Mars looking good-naturedly at the camera while Bob squints at it like maybe he just got caught doing something bad; Westerberg is too cool to even acknowledge the camera and looks away, studying something in the middle distance. They're all in jeans and canvas basketball sneakers. It was a great little piece of mythmaking.

"Vocalist Paul Westerberg sings from the heart and he knows how to break it," wrote *Seattle Rocket* critic Bruce Pavitt. "This is mature, diverse rock that could well shoot these regional boys into the national mainstream."

How right Pavitt was. The dividing line between the indie and major worlds was between punk-derived music and the blues-rooted fare of the bloated, indulgent, aged superstars who had attained seemingly eternal life on classic rock radio. The Replacements were a bridge between the two. At long last here was some indie music the mainstream rock press and public could love. A 1985 issue of the indie-phobic *Rolling Stone* actually picked the Replacements as one of "The New Stars in Your Future." *Let It Be* was highly decorated by the press corps, winning effusive praise and high standings in year-end polls. Robert Christgau gave it an A+ in his capsule reviews in the *Village Voice*, and his *Voice* colleague John Piccarella proclaimed, "The Replacements are the best rock and roll band of our time." *Let It Be* placed number four in the 1984 *Village Voice* Pazz & Jop poll and number six in the *L.A. Times'* top fifteen of 1984. All of this brought the band a sizable following from outside the indie nation.

And what's more, girls liked them. Indie rock was primarily a boys' club, but the Replacements were one of the first indie bands who drew almost as many girls as boys to their shows. In a fairly unsensuous rock scene, they provided a noticeable jolt of sexuality.

The drunk and sloppy act had been amusing at first, but it was getting tired fast. What with all the adoring press, things were rapidly getting more serious and the Replacements obliged by kicking out intense, much more focused, and well-behaved shows. Audiences reciprocated, and instead of the usual friendly heckling, it was now more respectful listening. The Replacements were swiftly becoming a band to be reckoned with.

Well, sometimes. When they played the University of California at

Davis, they were given a fancy oak-lined conference room as a dressing room. While waiting to go on, they decided to play baseball in there — with full beer bottles as bat and ball. But they'd miss a lot, which meant the bottles would hit the wall, ripping huge dents in the wood. The damage totaled some $1,900.

Then they decided to force-feed Mars with beer, which meant that Pappy the Clown took over on drums that night. Halfway through the show, Pappy fell off his drum stool and wedged himself between the stage and the back wall. The show came to a grinding halt; then the soundman shut off the PA. Westerberg soldiered on, stumbling through a string of Frank Sinatra covers, much to the displeasure of the crowd, which had begun to trash the place. "It was real, real ugly," says Sullivan.

Afterward an old acquaintance of Sullivan's — "a crazy kid from my high school who was famous for biting somebody's ear off," says Sullivan — said he heard on his police scanner that the cops were coming to arrest the band. They frantically loaded up the van and followed Sullivan's friend's complicated directions for a back route to the highway to make their escape, cutting through side roads, fields, and dirt paths. After a bumpy, stressful ride, they finally made it to the highway, and everybody breathed a big sigh of relief.

Then Westerberg leaned over to Sullivan and said he wanted to go to a party back in Davis. "Eventually he convinced me to turn around and go back," says Sullivan. "And nothing ever happened."

The last gig of a long 1984 tour was scheduled for the Bowery club, a converted church in Oklahoma City. When the van pulled up to the address listed, all they found was a church. There weren't even any cars in the parking lot. The exhausted band wanted to cancel the show and go straight home. But then when Jesperson knocked on the door, the club owner bounded out and and shouted, "The Replacements are here! My favorite band in the whole world! *Let It Be*'s the best album of 1984!" They proceeded to play a particularly shambling and yet playful, upbeat show: a few of the best songs from *Let It Be*, some impromptu blues jams, and a long string of tossed-off, fragmentary covers that pretty much define the parameters of their music — Black Sabbath's "Iron Man," Thin Lizzy's "Jailbreak," Tom Petty's "Break Down," the Rolling Stones' "Jumping Jack Flash," plus a blistering version of Bad Company's "Can't Get Enough of Your Love," no doubt first honed back in Mrs. Stinson's basement.

Soundman Bill Mack had discovered a tape recorder hidden in the balcony; apparently some fan was hoping to make a bootleg. On the ride home Mack popped the tape in the deck — the sound quality was surprisingly good and the show was a classic mess. Westerberg joked that Twin/Tone should release the tape, and the label took him up on it, releasing the cassette-only *The Shit Hits the Fans* in 1985. Reviewing the cassette in *Puncture,* one A. Korn wrote, "THIS CASSETTE IS TOTAL TRASH — but the fan's instinct to invest his idols with supernatural power overwhelms me." It was just that instinct that the tape aimed to demolish — or was it to perpetuate?

"If this isn't their worst release," wrote Byron Coley in a *Forced Exposure* review, "I guess it's their best."


**O**verall the band was winning favorable reviews everywhere they went, and *Let It Be* was already looking like a classic. Although many bands would have welcomed the acclaim with open arms, the members of the Replacements were more than a little wary. "It starts to sink in that, hey, maybe you're on to something," says Mars. "And then you start getting a little bit uneasy because it's starting to go a little further than you ever anticipated." So although the band could easily have sold out the main room at Minneapolis's First Avenue, they elected to play multiple dates at the club's smaller annex, 7th Street Entry.

"Probably part of that is our stiff Minnesota attitude of not calling attention to yourself," says Mars. "I definitely shied away from the adulation." (It's probably not a coincidence that in many of the Replacements' photo sessions, Mars is somehow covering his face.) "Part of it was maybe a little guilt — 'Now what, are people going to look at our little pocket-sized band and look at it differently?'" says Mars. "There was a little fear in that, too. Lots of mixed emotions. You kind of want to hang on to the ideals of where you started — already."

Bob Stinson had the most difficulty handling all the attention, drowning himself in drugs and alcohol. "Bob sort of went off and became a little erratic; I'm not sure what was going on in his head," Mars says. "Bob just went off like a rocket. Took advantage of the perks. You can never really say what came first, the chicken or the egg — is the band responsible or not? I don't know why Bob chose to adopt some of the things that he did."

Another complication was the yawning gap between critical acclaim and financial reward. Even as late as *Let It Be,* the band insisted they'd never seen any money from record sales. In fact, Twin/Tone wasn't getting paid reliably by distributors, but even if they had, the band wasn't selling enough records to recoup their expenses (something they would have realized if they had paid attention to their own business). On one of the *Let It Be* tours, shows could pay as much as $1,250 and as little as $200, but virtually all of it went toward reimbursing recording costs, hotels, gas and van, and instrument repairs. They collected a per diem (daily spending money) of between $10 and $15, and their pay basically amounted to whatever they could save from that. What booze didn't come free, they'd mooch; they didn't eat much.

"Selling records isn't what we're all about," Westerberg said in early '84. "But we'd like to make enough money to get us from gig to gig and not have a van that's always breaking down." Yet that was simply not in the cards for a band of the Replacements' commercial stature. At that time, Bob Stinson worked a day job as a pizza chef.

It would be years before the Replacements made any money from their Twin/Tone sales (1989 or so). "Being in the Midwest, there was nothing we could do to develop a band past a certain point," Stark says. "Unless you were on one of the two coasts, unless you have connections to major label distribution, there's nothing we can do from here. We didn't have the expertise here, nor did we have the clout and the go-out-to-lunch power that you need to have. You need to go out to lunch and spend face time with people that are going to influence, whether it be press or radio or distribution, stuff like that. I just never really cared to play that game. I came into the business from a producer/engineer point of view. I was more interested in developing groups." Twin/Tone was still essentially a hobby. "The intention was to develop more and more back catalog," Stark continues, "so at some point if we stopped putting out new records, we could coast on our catalog."

So while the Replacements and *Let It Be* were Twin/Tone's top priority, there was only so much the now five-person label could do. "All we did for six months was *Let It Be*," says Stark. "Sales on *Let It Be* weren't high enough to do the next level up, which would be to hire some independent [radio promoters] to work markets. It was time for a major label to take over."

The Replacements knew what they had to do to win a major label deal. "You have to be pretty good every night, and not do stupid things and not break a lot of stuff," Westerberg said at the time. "Maybe we'll learn, maybe we won't. I guess they're going to have to take us like this or let us slowly rot away." Yet by 1984 several major labels had checked out the Replacements but were reluctant to risk large amounts of money on such a notoriously wayward band.

By fall, however, the buzz was so strong that several record companies had overcome their reservations and were actively pursuing the band; at the same time, the Replacements were growing increasingly dissatisfied with Twin/Tone. Still, their appetite for self-destruction wasn't going to make it easy for any major label. In New York they played a show at CBGB packed with music industry types interested in signing the band. They got up onstage and played nothing but shambling covers for the assembled execs. After destroying the Rolling Stones' "Start Me Up," Westerberg leaned into the mike and said, "Do we get a record contract now?"

"They wanted us to play our best songs as best we could," Westerberg said later. "And we didn't feel like it. And so they figure, 'They're a small-time bunch of amateurs.' That's one way to look at it, and that's partly true. But I think it's also the spirit that makes rock so immediate." Or maybe they simply didn't grasp the importance of the moment. "It's big business, it's not something you know about or understand," says Mars. "I remember thinking, 'So what, they're a company? Why are they so big?' It just didn't register. I could care less."

Eventually one major label — Warner Brothers — did decide to take them on, but it's telling that Mars is unsure of why the band agreed to the deal. "I don't know if we decided," he says, "or *they* decided." Perhaps the fact that their longtime rivals Hüsker Dü had recently signed to a major label helped prompt the Replacements to do the same. "When the Hüskers headlined CB's, *we* had to headline CB's," says Sullivan. "When Hüskers got guaranteed $1,000 somewhere, we had to get guaranteed $1,500 the next time. When the Hüskers did three nights at 7th Street Entry, we had to do *five.*"

But their feelings about the signing were ambivalent at best. "For me, it was a lot of mixed feelings — 'Are we leaving something behind that we shouldn't?'" says Mars. "'Or is it a good thing to move on?' Not having the mentality of a career musician, maybe you don't welcome it like someone else might."

They all went to their lawyer's house in south Minneapolis to do the signing. The lawyer tried to get the band members to read the contract before they signed it, but none of them cared to. "It's so funny, knowing more about the business and looking at the contract we signed and how horrible it was," says Mars. "We had no business sense. We didn't think in those terms." After they signed, the cocaine was broken out, and then the band members went their separate ways to contemplate (or not to contemplate) what they had just done.

"I remember being a little unsure, and I think all of us were a little unsure because we didn't really know how things were going to change," Mars says. "And then, to our surprise, it didn't really change that much. We thought we had the run of the show with the indie and maybe it wouldn't be so easy with a major, that there would be more demands or something. I guess there was, but we didn't play the game. So that hurt us."

Did they regret signing to a major? "Oh, no, it was good," says Mars. "It was instantly more tour support. Traveling got more comfortable. Those things were definitely perks. And better distribution. That was a good thing." But even after they signed to a major label, Westerberg was still writing songs in his parents' basement while they were away at work.

B ut if the major label signing didn't hurt, the slow invasion of drugs into the Replacements camp did. Even though they couldn't afford the stuff, some of the band members had begun delving into cocaine — there's even a powdery sniff at the beginning of "Lovelines," back on *Hootenanny*. "The thing was you didn't have to afford it because it was handed to you," says Mars. "That was the atmosphere. It was all around.

"Making a marriage work with two people who are relatively sober is very difficult," continues Mars. "Now you get four people that are with each other more than a married couple would be, because you're traveling, you're playing, you're stuck in the same van, and then you add cocaine and booze into the mix. To get it to be able to last for any length of time is really a feat. You do have to give up a certain part of yourself in order to make it work."

And in order for the Replacements to continue to work, Westerberg felt he had to make some major changes. In 1986 the band fired Bob Stinson, partly for being unwilling (or unable) to play the band's less rocked-out material and partly for being too drunk and drugged up to even try.

That year they also fired Peter Jesperson. "I couldn't believe that it happened and I still can't believe it happened," says Jesperson. "It was like being thrown out of a club that you helped start." Unfortunately, it was for an age-old rock & roll reason. "Everybody was drinking and doing more drugs than they needed to," says Jesperson, very much including himself. Apparently, the band needed a scapegoat for it all and Jesperson fit the bill — "It probably looked worse for the manager to be fucked up than for the band members to be fucked up," Jesperson admits. "But it was kind of like the pot calling the kettle black."

It was even more ironic, because it seemed like the hellions in the Replacements had driven their fastidious, nice-guy manager to drink. "They certainly did," says Jesperson. "They didn't like it if everybody wasn't drinking with them. Had I tried to be more of a sober manager, I don't know that I necessarily would have lasted so long. But then, on the other hand, I did drink more than I probably should have and that was part of the reason that I got the boot. It was a classic catch-22."

No one knew that catch-22 better than Bob Stinson. He had gone through a court-ordered thirty-day rehab program and had been dry for three weeks when the Replacements played the last gig of a five-night stand at 7th Street Entry in the summer of '86. "Paul came over with a bottle of Champagne," recalled Stinson's then-wife, Carleen, "and he said to Bob, and I'll never forget this, he said, 'Either take a drink, moth-erfucker, or get off my stage.' It was the first time I'd seen Bob cry." West-erberg fired him a couple of weeks later.

Getting fired was just as devastating to Jesperson, who had plucked the band from obscurity and worked with them when no one else would. "My favorite thing in the whole world was music," he says, "and then I find a band that I think is amazing and I get involved with them as much as you possibly can get involved with an artist — I would have lay down in the road for them — and suddenly they just said, 'You're fired, you're gone,' and they didn't talk to me anymore."

Perhaps predictably, the Replacements' substance abuse actually peaked after Stinson and Jesperson left. "It got worse with Tommy and Paul," Mars told *Spin* magazine, "and it was to the point where I was afraid that they wouldn't wake up the next day." By early '87, around the time of their second Warner's album, *Pleased to Meet Me*, the band had sunk into a drug-induced paranoia. That paranoia could be extreme.

The band thought Twin/Tone was licensing Replacements records in Europe and not reporting the income to the band; they were owed, by their estimate, about $30,000. Then there was the fact that without con-ferring with the band, Twin/Tone had decided to release their albums on CD, a format the band abhorred. They decided to take matters into their own hands and went to the Minneapolis recording studio where their Twin/Tone masters were kept. "We got this notion — we'll just walk in there and say, 'We're thinking of recording here,'" says Mars. "We didn't even have to do that because people knew who we were, and we got into where they kept the tapes and looked for the Replacements and grabbed whatever we could." And then they threw the tapes — *Sorry Ma*, *Stink*, *Hootenanny*, *Let It Be*, the whole thing — into the Mississippi River. Luckily, as it turned out, the tapes were only safety masters.

Although *Pleased to Meet Me* wound up selling about 300,000 copies, the Replacements were never the same without Bob Stinson. "When I left," Bob told *Spin*'s Charles Aaron, "the Replacements were like a body without a face." The band never did break through to the big time and sputtered to a close in 1991 after two subpar albums, with only Westerberg and Tommy Stinson remaining from the original lineup. The fawnings of a whole raft of Johnny-come-lately mainstream critics notwithstanding, the band never completely fulfilled its formidable promise. "You could list a hundred reasons," Westerberg said in 1993, "but the bottom line is we didn't go for it hard enough."

But there was no taking away the glory of the Replacements' indie years. "Could it have been the last bastion of true pockets of uncontaminated stuff from anything major?" says Mars. "Maybe that was the last instance of where that was true, but what do I know — the attitude of doing something fun and doing something creative and keeping yourselves out of trouble took precedence over any sort of career opportunity."

Tragically, Mars is exactly right — once Bob Stinson was fired from the Replacements, he found it impossible to stay out of trouble. His problems with drinking and drugs worsened dramatically; he was clinically depressed, unemployed, and virtually homeless; and on February 18, 1995, he was found in his girlfriend's apartment, dead of an apparent overdose at age thirty-five.

# CHAPTER 7

# SONIC YOUTH

**"A LOT OF BANDS OUT THERE ARE TAKING PEOPLE
FOR A RIDE BY PRETENDING THAT THEY ARE DOING
SOMETHING VALID, WHEN IN FACT THEY ARE JUST
REHASHING THINGS THAT HAVE BEEN DONE A MILLION
TIMES BEFORE. AT LEAST WE ARE STICKING OUR
NECKS OUT AND HAVING SOME FUN. THAT'S WHAT
MUSIC IS ABOUT; NOT FOLLOWING THE RULES."**

**— STEVE SHELLEY, *CUT*, MARCH 1989**

By the late Seventies, just about all the original New York punk bands were either out of touch, out of gas, out of town, or out of existence, leaving the hordes of aesthetic pilgrims who had migrated to New York on the heels of the punk explosion to create a new scene of their own. The city became a petri dish for all kinds of musical experiments, from the ultra-minimalist dance beats of Liquid Liquid to Klaus Nomi's warped techno-opera, from the Lounge Lizards' noirish jazz to Polyrock's pointy-headed future-pop.

A precious few, annoyed by how quickly the music industry had chewed up punk and spit it out as "new wave," formed a small and insular movement defiantly dubbed "no wave." The music was spare but precipitously jagged and dissonant, with little regard for conventions of any sort; the basic idea seemed to be to make music that could never be co-opted. Although shows by no wave bands were very sparsely attended, a tight-knit little community developed. But when Brian Eno recorded four no wave bands — Teenage Jesus and the Jerks, DNA, Mars, and the Contortions — for 1978's *No New York* compilation, he unwittingly fomented the scene's demise, as jealousies were sparked by the fact that some bands were picked to record and others weren't.

Despite the fracturing of the no wave scene, it was a heady time —

the New York art scene was beginning to explode and the city's underground rock community got swept up in its coattails. By 1980 downtown New York City rock clubs resembled art spaces and art spaces resembled rock clubs. As more and more artists started playing in bands, the music began to take on a noticeably sculptural quality, as if the musicians were shaping shards of sound. Graffiti by music-friendly artists such as Keith Haring and Jean-Michel Basquiat was all over the East Village and SoHo; musicians like Laurie Anderson and Talking Heads were bridging the "high" art world and the "low" rock world; eminent downtown New York composers such as Rhys Chatham, Steve Reich, Glenn Branca, and Philip Glass were all making music that, like rock, dared to place a premium on timbre, harmonic texture, and rhythm.

Sonic Youth took those ideas and transplanted them to rock music. Few American bands were asking to be taken seriously as art, but Sonic Youth did, and they got enthusiastic affirmation from the hipper precincts of the music press; that, coupled with the band's strong connections to the art world and a rabid European following, gave them a unique prestige. Some accused the band of being charlatans borrowing promotional ideas from the art world to browbeat the underground into building a consensus of cool around them, but however finely calculated Sonic Youth's astute promotional tactics, the power of their best music is undeniable.

And the indie rock and art scenes have a lot in common: in both, talent is one thing, but otherwise it's all about making the right connections and orchestrating one's own creations into discernible and desirable movements. Relationships are currency, something Sonic Youth had picked up on not only from the art world but from the camaraderie of the SST bands. It was a survival tool: empowerment through grassroots maneuvering, as opposed to the way things were done in the mainstream — basically marketing them into existence. This was very autonomous, very self-sufficient. This was punk.

The band members' voracious appetites for all kinds of music and their enthusiasm for spreading the word about it was a big part of the networking process. "We were, on the one hand, trying to take it all in," says guitarist Lee Ranaldo, "and on the other hand, using whatever position we had to reflect people back out to see a larger world." That kind of advocacy, given credence by their prescient taste in opening bands, immeasurably boosted the band's stature. And as the decade wore on and indie rock became more and more codified, Sonic Youth was a vivid reminder of the original impulses behind the movement.

The members of Sonic Youth well remembered the Beatles and the Sixties, when there was a glorious interplay between the avant-garde, progressive politics, and popular culture, and they carried it on, perhaps more than any other band in the Eighties indie community. In doing so, they dignified the scene, but they also heralded the end of what former SST label manager Joe Carducci once called SST's "New Redneck" sensibility, marking indie rock's transition from the working-class side of suburbia to the world of urban aesthetes. Yet for all the artsiness, Sonic Youth's appeal boiled down to one very basic thing: the perennial charms of whaling on a very loud electric guitar.

Within four years of existence, Sonic Youth emerged as an indie archetype, perhaps *the* indie archetype, the yardstick by which independence and hipness (the very equation is in no small part due to them) were measured. They made records that were not only artistically respected but popular; they helpfully provided at least the illusion that rock still had some fresh tricks up its sleeve. Sonic Youth was more an inspiration than an influence, which may be why, despite their renown, so few of the bands who have cited them as mentors and heroes have directly copied their sound.

And despite their status as indie royalty, the band's stature was actually enhanced, not diminished, by signing to a major label. Famously, the band retained their artistic control, but in retrospect, that wasn't much of an issue since there was no pressure on them to sell records anyway. The real coup was the unspoken understanding that they were so cool that their chief function was as a magnet band, an act that would serve mostly to attract other, more successful bands. This move paid off beyond anyone's wildest dreams when Sonic Youth brought a hot young band called Nirvana to Geffen/DGC Records.

Thurston Moore grew up in Florida and small-town Bethel, Connecticut, and was weaned on the standard hard rock fare of the day: Aerosmith, Kiss, Alice Cooper, and the like. He'd just started at Western Connecticut State College, where his late father had taught music and philosophy, when he suddenly decided to move to New York, arriving in early 1977.

Punk was in first bloom, a heady time, especially for an artistic kid fresh from the suburbs. "It was David Johansen to Patti Smith to John Cale to the Ramones to the Dictators to *Punk* magazine to *New York Rocker* to *Rock Scene* to St. Mark's Place to Bleecker Bob's to Manic Panic to Gem Spa to Max's to CBGB, etc.," Moore wrote. He joined the Coachmen, a guitar-based quartet heavily in the vein of the hippest bands in New York at the time, Television and Talking Heads. Art student Lee Ranaldo soon became a fan, and he and Moore struck up a friendship.

Ranaldo was in a band called the Flucts (a reference to the Fluxus art movement), who mined similar musical territory to the Coachmen. He was a Deadhead from the suburban wasteland of Long Island who had gone on to study art and filmmaking at the State University of New York at Binghamton, where, by his own admission, he spent more time taking drugs and playing music than attending class. After moving to New York, he joined Glenn Branca's guitar sextet, touring the U.S and Europe several times. Branca felt Ranaldo understood his musical sensibility better than anyone in the ensemble and made Ranaldo his trusted musical lieutenant.

The ensemble's six electric guitarists played Branca's compositions — a kind of minimalist heavy metal — at astoundingly high volumes. In order to achieve the sonic phenomena that were his trademark, Branca would string guitars with the same gauge strings, all tuned to the same note, producing a fascinating chorus effect, or devise unique tunings that produced massive, complex chords. Branca also used volume as a compositional element, actually calculating the overtones produced by the cacophony and incorporating them into the total effect of the music, which was staggering.

After the Coachmen broke up, Moore jammed with Stanton Miranda, whose band CKM also included an artist named Kim Gordon. Miranda soon introduced Moore to Gordon, and the two hit it off.

The daughter of a UCLA sociology professor father and a homemaker mother, Gordon had been born early enough to witness the late Sixties California rock scene firsthand, and by high school was a devotee of challenging jazz musicians like Don Cherry, Archie Shepp, and the Art Ensemble of Chicago. Gordon moved to New York after getting an art degree and began curating gallery shows. She also immersed herself in the no wave scene and befriended Glenn Branca. Gordon wasn't a musician but got the bug after she played in a one-gig band with members of Branca's and Rhys Chatham's ensembles. "I was sort of raised all my life to do art," Gordon later explained. "I just felt like I should be doing music. It seemed to me that this was really the next step after pop art, you see, entering directly into a popular form of culture instead of commenting on it."

Moore took to Gordon instantly. "She had beautiful eyes and the most beautiful smile," he wrote, "and was very intelligent and seemed to have a sensitive/spiritual intellect." The feeling was mutual — "There was something special about him, like he exuded this air of boyish wildness but incredible goodness," Gordon said. "I guess it was love at first sight." Gordon began to introduce Moore, five years her junior, to the finer things in life, like jazz and modern art. A generation earlier Gordon might have been a cool beatnik hipster; Moore, on the other hand, boiled over with punk rock energy. "He was definitely a wild kid," Gordon recalls. "'Wild' was his main description."

**W**hen Moore saw Branca's ensemble, he was blown away. "It was the most ferocious guitar band that I had ever seen in my life," he exclaimed, "even more so than the Ramones or Teenage Jesus and the Jerks."

Moore and Gordon formed a band that went through names like Male Bonding (then a new term) and Red Milk before settling on the Arcadians in late 1980. The Arcadians played their first show at the June '81 Noise Festival at New York's White Columns gallery — nine consecutive nights of three to five bands each — curated by Moore. Early in the festival, right after Branca's set, Moore asked Ranaldo if he wanted to join the band. Ranaldo accepted and the lineup played three songs at the Noise Festival later that week sans drummer, Ranaldo having rehearsed with them for the first time only the night before. They played three gigs with Moore and Ranaldo taking turns whacking a couple of drums, before meeting drummer Richard Edson.

Moore's intensity was evident to Edson from the first time they played together. They were jamming at Edson's East Village practice space, getting into it so intensely that they were playing with their eyes closed. "And I open my eyes and I see these red spots on my drums!" Edson recalled. "Even though my drum set was a piece of shit anyway, I had a priority interest — I wanted to make sure that they stayed *nice*. I was like, 'WHERE THE FUCK ARE THESE RED SPOTS COMING FROM??!' I looked at his guitar and I noticed one of the knobs was missing. It was just a piece of metal sticking up and he was playing and hitting his hand against this metal and I looked at his hand — he was bleeding from his hand! I was like, that's pretty cool that he's so committed that he'll play right through any kind of pain and bodily injury BUT THE MOTHERFUCKER WAS BLEEDING ON MY DRUMS AND

I DIDN'T APPRECIATE THAT! So I was like, 'HEY . . . WHOA! WHOAA!!! STOP! STOP! *STOP!*' He was like, 'Oh yeah? Hey, man, I'm sorry! No problem.' That was my introduction. . . ."

Edson wiped off the blood and joined the band, which Moore rechristened Sonic Youth. Part of the name came from MC5 guitarist Fred "Sonic" Smith and part came from the reggae music then in vogue, much of which came from bands with the word "youth" in their name. "It's a state of mind," Ranaldo says of the name. "It was never about being twenty, because we weren't even twenty when we started. We had more experiences than just making rock music in a garage."

"It was odd," said Gordon. "As soon as Thurston came up with the name Sonic Youth, a certain sound that was more of what we wanted to do came about." That sound took the heady, transcendent discord that Branca had extracted so purely from rock and injected it back into a bracing stew of the Stooges, MC5, Television, noise-jazz guitarist Sonny Sharrock, Public Image, Ltd., and no wave.

The result was a particularly New Yorky strain of rock experimentalism that recalled the hypnotic steel-gray drones of the Velvet Underground, another band with close ties to the art world. The music was avowedly forward-thinking, thoroughly cloaked in teeming layers of distortion and dissonance. It was intellectual but also bracingly physical, right down to the often violent contortions Moore and Ranaldo went through to wrench the right sounds from their instruments.

**E**dson had been aboard only a few weeks when Branca invited Sonic Youth to be the first artist on Neutral Records, a label he was starting with financial help from White Columns owner Josh Baer. Underground labels were few and far between, even in New York, so it was a major break for a band as obscure and challenging as Sonic Youth to make a record. As it turned out, most of their contemporaries went undocumented.

That December they recorded five songs in one late night session at the cavernous Plaza Sound studios in Radio City Music Hall, where punk icons like the Ramones, Richard Hell and the Voidoids, and Blondie had all recorded their debuts. It was an intimidating place for a young band. "We thought, 'Where are we?'" said Moore. "So we just let the engineer take care of it." Like so many first-time recording bands, they played very cautiously and conservatively, omitting what Moore calls their "loose, just crazy, noisy stuff."

Not that the material they recorded was very conventional. "It was a lot more wide open as to what a song was," Ranaldo says. "A song was a lot more about sound and structure than it was about chords and progressions and stuff like that." On "The Burning Spear," Moore's guitar makes a sound like Chinese gongs and Ranaldo plays a power drill put through a wah-wah pedal. (Unfortunately, the drill broke soon afterward and the song was apparently never the same. "We could never find a drill with the same tone as that one," Gordon said regretfully.)

Despite the band's looser tendencies, Edson laid down strict, danceable syncopations in the funky "street beat" style then favored by hip New York bands like the Bush Tetras and ESG. "He had a desire for discipline," Moore said of Edson. "Whereas we were just an anarchy band, and really into being loose, anything goes."

The fact was the band wasn't sure what they wanted to sound like yet. "Our first album was just a bunch of songs we wrote because we had the chance to record them," said Ranaldo. "After that we understood better and better what we wanted to do."

Neutral released the mini-LP in March '82 to very little notice — no surprise, since the tiny label had no track record, no connections, and no real plans. Besides, Neutral's staff — namely, Moore — didn't know too much about the music business. "I didn't know what a distributor was," Moore admits. "I remember Glenn saying, 'I think this is how it works: Call these distributors, see how many copies they'll take, and write down how many they'll take, and I think they should pay you within six months.' We didn't know." Much to Moore's relief, Branca eventually replaced him with Peter Wright, a savvy Englishman who had worked for the Buzzcocks' label New Hormones.

But Moore had wisely sent promo kits to the U.S. press, and what little reviews the mini-LP got were at least uniformly favorable, very encouraging to such an obscure band. And when word got back that the Bush Tetras had liked the bass sound on the mini-LP, "I was like, 'Wow, we kind of impressed the Bush Tetras,'" says Moore. "'Maybe we should take this seriously!'"

The band began a serious rethink of their music after Moore saw his first Minor Threat show in May '82. "I just thought, 'My god! The greatest live band I have ever seen,'" Moore said. "Sonically, they were just so stimulating." Immediately the band — and Moore in particular — began to listen to whatever hardcore they could get their hands on.

"We were so fascinated by it, especially Thurston, but we knew we weren't *of* it," says Ranaldo. "We were apart from it in a lot of ways —

older, more art-schooly kind of music, not straight edge. But we were totally fascinated by it." Despite their distance from hardcore, the members of Sonic Youth realized they could incorporate elements of it into their music. "I wanted to play high-energy music and I wanted to destroy, you know," said Moore, "but at the same time work on sound and whatever."

Hardcore's organizational energy was just as important as its musical energy — it showed how Sonic Youth could thrive outside the usual New York art world system of grants and patronage. "The way those kids networked was a marvel to us," says Ranaldo. "You had these little pockets in all these cities, and all of a sudden you were hearing about — it wasn't just Boston and L.A. and New York and San Francisco — it was Louisville and Athens, all these weird little towns that you'd never even heard of before."

Unlike most hardcore kids, the members of Sonic Youth had firsthand experience of virtually the entire history of rock music, with the exception of the early rock & rollers. "We had real ties to Sixties music in a firsthand way, both British Invasion and San Francisco psychedelia — that stuff made a big impression on us," says Ranaldo. "Which set us apart from young kids who were seventeen in 1980 that had really only heard about it from their parents' record collection, if at all."

But no wave was just as resolutely antihistorical as hardcore, which meant that Sonic Youth didn't speak up about their Sixties roots. "You didn't want to be associated with the excesses of hippie music or any of the spiritual yearning side of it," says Ranaldo. "The fact that it was involved with drugs and the questing that went hand in hand with the music at that point, people, didn't want to be associated with that — and yet so many of the parallels are obvious. I would assume that with a lot of those people, it was only later that they were able to admit being really involved in a lot of that music. I know in the early days of our group, when I would admit to having a thing for the Grateful Dead at one period, it almost felt like a blasphemous thing to say."

The band also had no strong connections to either hardcore or the New York art rock establishment. "We were," Moore said, "a part of nothing.

"We just said fuck it," he continued, "and got cheap guitars and screwdrivers and turned the amps up to ten."

E dson left the band in the summer of '82. (He continued playing with the hip art-funk band Konk and soon became an actor, appearing in *Desperately Seeking Susan, Stranger than Paradise, Pla-*

*toon,* and even an episode of *Miami Vice.*) The band made a flyer that said simply "Sonic Youth needs drummer" and stuck it on the wall at SoHo's Rocks in Your Head, one of the city's few underground record shops.

Bob Bert had drummed in a noise band called Drunk Driving and studied painting at the School of Visual Arts. A familiar face on the New York punk scene almost from the beginning, Bert was a big Branca fan, so when he heard the maestro had started a label, he picked up its first release, the Sonic Youth mini-LP. "I loved it," says Bert. "It was like PiL's *Second Edition* — only better, more extreme." When he saw their flyer, he called Moore right away and got the gig. Bert traded Edson's busy little syncopations for an explosive tribal stomp — it wasn't the manic hardcore style Moore had envisioned, but it merged with Gordon's simple bass lines for a much more visceral impact.

I n the mainstream world of the early Eighties, it was still novel for a woman to play a leading role in a band. But not in punk rock.

Both Moore and Ranaldo had been playing guitar since high school, but Gordon was just learning how to play bass and it took a bit of a leap for her to get onstage. "I thought of it more emotionally, not in terms of trying to play *music,*" says Gordon. "I couldn't do anything if I thought in terms like that — I always have to make a different picture for myself.

"As a woman I felt kind of invisible in the middle of it anyway," Gordon continues. "I was there as a voyeur, pretty much," she adds with a little laugh. Not entirely comfortable with the spotlight, Gordon preferred having a key role that wasn't obviously key, which precisely describes the bass guitar. "It's so important — it's supporting but it's . . . ," she says, trailing off. "I like things like that. It fits my personality." Gordon preferred being a subtle but decisive force offstage as well, so while Moore often instigated everything from songwriting to record deals and Ranaldo was the musical maestro, Gordon was often the band's aesthetic (and business) conscience.

Early on Moore taught her simple bass parts; he'd play reggae records for her, to show how effective even just a few notes could be. The simple approach worked in their favor anyway — busy bass lines would have cluttered up the already teeming music.

While Moore and Ranaldo didn't possess tremendous technique either, that didn't prevent them from tossing off dense torrents of sound.

"And she never plays like that," Ranaldo says of Gordon. "Her stuff is all very spare and minimal and yet it's very intricate. There's something about the way she thinks harmonically, rhythmically, that's really amazing to me." As a vocalist, Gordon developed a sort of insouciant holler, like a kid calling to her friends about something great she'd found but trying not to seem too excited about it.

Gordon was an artist who simply transferred her highly refined aesthetic skills to rock music, a genre that, as punk proved, required a sensibility more than chops anyway. "She was totally coming from an art school background," says Bert. "That's what made the band."

Sonic Youth's small hipster following was very much in force when Bert debuted with the band at CBGB in the fall of '82. "I was on cloud nine," Bert says. "Just seeing Arto Lindsay and Lydia Lunch in the audience, that, to me, was like, 'I can die tomorrow and my life will have been wonderful.'"

Sonic Youth had also struck up a friendship with the Swans, a dire, noisy East Village band that was as brutally slow as it was slowly brutal. "We connected with them because it was safety in numbers almost," says Moore. "And it just became who could be more intense." Soon they were rehearsing in the Swans' rehearsal space — singer Michael Gira's dank, windowless basement apartment in the drug-infested no-man's-land of Sixth Street and Avenue B.

A month after Bert joined, they embarked on a two-week tour of the South with the Swans. In retrospect, the idea seems preposterous — both bands were barely known even in New York. "It was just an adventure," Moore explains. "We just wanted to see what would happen. What do bands do? They go on tour." The only underground booking agent in town wasn't interested in the still obscure Sonic Youth, so Ranaldo simply called up clubs and got the shows himself.

The Savage Blunder tour kicked off in November '82, with the Swans headlining — "Next to our friends the Swans, who were very loud and had a percussionist who pounded metal," Gordon explained, "we were total wimps."

Unsurprisingly, the tour was less than a resounding success — they usually played to around a dozen people. At a show at the Cat's Cradle in Chapel Hill, the Swans played their set to, as Gordon put it, "six jeering cowboys" who kept chanting, "'Freebird . . . Freebird . . . Freebird. . . .'"

All ten members of the touring party shared the same van, which

prompted the title of Gordon's tour memoir, a 1988 *Village Voice* piece called "Boys Are Smelly." Tensions ran high, mostly within the volatile Swans. At one point the tempestuous Gira and the band's drummer got into a huge fight in the crowded van and after some preliminary name-calling ("Dickhead!" "Asshole!") began strangling each other. "Meanwhile," wrote Gordon, "everyone else is crammed around them trying to mind his or her own business, being really cool."

They did another tour with the Swans in December, this time through the Midwest, and it was just as miserable, perhaps more so. "I don't think we should have done it," Moore said. "Because we were still kind of filthy at the time." Low turnouts, no pay, little food, constant cold, and cramped conditions put everybody in a foul mood. Moore vented his frustrations by continually castigating Bert about his drumming, which he felt was not, as Moore puts it, "in the pocket."

As soon as they got back, Moore decided Bert should go. Gordon got the unenviable job of delivering the news. New drummer Jim Sclavunos had gained substantial downtown cred playing in the no wave bands Teenage Jesus and the Jerks and Eight-Eyed Spy. While Bert was an inspired pounder, Sclavunos was a lighter but technically better player.

Meanwhile they were all holding down subsistence-level day jobs; at various points Moore sold Chipwiches on the streets of New York, peddled fruit from a sidewalk cart, sold furniture, and was a janitor at a record mastering studio, never holding down any job for very long. In order to pay for their next recording, they borrowed money from a wealthy, some-what eccentric Swiss couple named Catherine and Nicholas Ceresole, who held a weekly salon for downtown artists and musicians. The Ceresoles went on to help bankroll several more Sonic Youth albums and frequently put up the band in their luxurious home on Lake Geneva, just down the street from Jean-Luc Godard.

In early '83 they arranged to record a single with Branca alumnus Wharton Tiers, who had a primitive studio, Fun City, in the basement of a Gramercy Park brownstone. But the band had so much material that the single was eventually bumped up to a whole album. Things got off to a bad start when the temperamental Sclavunos walked in, saw Fun City's rudimentary setup, learned that Tiers had never made a record before, and walked out, only to return after much coaxing.

As Sclavunos had no doubt predicted, the sessions were a comedy of technical errors. Someone inadvertently erased the instrumental tracks of "Shaking Hell" so they used a cassette tape that had the music on it; when the tape machine munched another track, Tiers repaired it with cellophane tape. Entire sessions were wiped out by what Moore once described as "accidents with magnets"; one tape was nearly lost when someone accidentally poured cola on it.

It took three months to complete, but *Confusion Is Sex* was profoundly original, with few touchstones of conventional rock music other than volume, distortion, and bludgeoning syncopation. The songs, wrote critic Greil Marcus, "resembled nothing so much as the sort of chants little kids come up with when they've been sent to their rooms without supper." Practically a concept album about urban dread, *Confusion* was difficult listening, especially in early 1983, and much more violent than the mini-LP.

With its rattletrap drumming, ominous bass drone, profoundly dissonant guitars that sound like they're strung with chicken wire, and Moore's dire, caterwauling vocals, "(She's in a) Bad Mood" typifies the album's desolate sense of menace, with long, bleak, droning sections interrupted by convulsive outbursts of guitar. Gordon sings a few genuinely disturbing songs: "Protect Me You" is a child's prayer to "demons" whose whispering "sends the night away"; the lengthy introduction to "Shaking Hell" is the embodiment of anxiety, the song rife with eerie but elliptical images of abuse: "I'll take off your dress / Shake off your flesh." Even with no real verse or chorus, the song is an indelible experience.

Except for a couple of favorable reviews, *Confusion* received scant notice. But Sonic Youth was forming a new language for the electric guitar. Throughout the record the guitars make uncannily unique sounds and chords; on the drumless instrumental "Lee Is Free," the guitars resemble the tuned gongs of Balinese gamelan music. "Our feeling is that the guitar is an unlimited instrument and for the most part people have not taken it to full advantage," Ranaldo said.

In order to obtain unusual effects, Moore and Ranaldo stuck drumsticks and screwdrivers under the guitar strings, an approach that dated from at least the forties, when John Cage used metal screws, rubber erasers, and strips of paper to attain new sounds for his "prepared piano" compositions. But the main weapon in Sonic Youth's arsenal was alternative guitar tunings, departing from the standard E-A-D-G-B-E for whatever sounded good. "It's just that when you're playing in standard tuning all the time," Moore explained, "you're sounding pretty . . . standard."

Glenn Branca had also based his music on unique tunings, but Moore and Ranaldo both say they'd been investigating the technique before they even arrived in New York, trying to replicate music by the likes of Crosby, Stills & Nash, Hot Tuna, and Joni Mitchell. Blues, folk, and country musicians had been using alternative tunings for decades. Still, although there is a practically infinite number of tunings, Sonic Youth's clanging, metallic chords bore more than a passing resemblance to Branca's.

Much to the band's chagrin, it would be years before an article about Sonic Youth didn't mention Glenn Branca's name. Moore protested, but the connection was obvious — Moore had joined Branca's guitar orchestra in the summer of '81, and he and Ranaldo both appear on the recordings of the maestro's first three symphonies; after that they released their first recordings on his label. "It was just an obvious influence," says Bert. "'Hey, we can take this approach that Glenn and Rhys Chatham are doing and blend it with the MC5 and have a whole new thing.' Which is what they did. Which is why they're great."

With Sonic Youth, the approach to tuning stemmed partly from lack of technique — it's easy to get cool sounds out of an open-tuned guitar — and lack of funds. They could only afford cheap guitars, and cheap guitars *sounded* like cheap guitars. But with weird new tunings or something jammed under a particular fret, then those humble instruments could sound rather amazing — bang a drumstick on a cheap Japanese Stratocaster copy in the right tuning, crank the amplifier to within an inch of its life, and it will sound like church bells.

Not only did the radical approach make Sonic Youth sound like no other band; it also provided a bottomless wellspring of compositional ideas. "When you tuned a guitar a new way, you were a beginner all over again and you could discover all sorts of new things," says Ranaldo. "It allowed us to throw out a whole broad body of knowledge about how to play the guitar."

"Their vocabulary in the beginning was really wide," says Steve Albini, an early fan of the band. "When you'd see them live around that time, it was borderline psychedelic, that's how weird it was."

At first Moore and Ranaldo played in identical tunings, but later on they started to tune their guitars differently from each other in order to achieve even wilder effects. "I'd be strumming something and he'd be listening to it and if there was something that didn't sound right, [we'd adjust] it until they sounded harmonically pleasing," says Ranaldo. "Whatever 'harmonic' meant to you at that time."

Each song was based on a particular tuning, which in turn was based on the unique properties of the particular guitar it was being played on. Finding those tunings was not just a painstaking process of trial and error for the unschooled Moore and Ranaldo, but an exercise in patience for the rest of the band, who would wait while the guitarists retuned, restrung, and sometimes even rewired their guitars.

Rather than individual members bringing in complete ideas for the rest to flesh out, songs were jammed into existence during lengthy rehearsals. Then they'd take the best bits of their improvisations and knit them together. "It wasn't just a one singer-songwriter type of thing," Gordon says. "You get a different kind of music that way." It certainly made for music that relied less on melody and conventional song structure and more on mood and texture. It was also an arduous process, especially since every member of the band had to like every part or it would be discarded. "We really had a much stronger work ethic from the beginning than a lot of people we knew," says Ranaldo. "We rehearsed diligently and regularly."

Another problem was that most of those cheap guitars sounded good only in a certain tuning or with a drumstick jammed under the strings at a certain fret — so Sonic Youth needed a lot of guitars. Fortunately, it was easy to get a used cheapo guitar for $50, and often people would just give the band guitars, knowing they'd make good use of them. Soon the band was toting around upward of a dozen guitars to every gig.

At first Ranaldo and Moore tuned their instruments backstage like everyone else, but after a while there were too many guitars, so after the previous band played, they'd start tuning onstage. A cheer would inevitably go up as the crowd thought the set was starting. But it soon subsided as Moore and Ranaldo did nothing but methodically tune one instrument after another for fifteen minutes or more, then leave the stage. In a way, the band considered it all part of the act. "It opened up to the audience this notion of what we were all about," says Ranaldo. "They'd see all the guitars and the fact that . . . they were all differently tuned. I always thought it was a cool prelude to the beginning of the set — it was like a briefing."

When Moore and Ranaldo played a two-week European tour with Branca's ensemble in May '83, performing Branca's *Symphony No. 3*, they figured out a scam to help their own band. "Every venue we played with Glenn," says Ranaldo, "we sidled up to the promoter at some point and said, 'Hey, we've got a band, too, we're going to come to Europe next month — can we get a gig?'" Pretty soon they'd booked a whole two-week tour.

There was only one problem: Sclavunos had quit. So they asked Bert back. (Once again Gordon was given the difficult task.) Luckily, the affable Bert had remained cordial with the band and had even kept going to their shows. Even better, his drumming had considerably sharpened in the six months he'd been away. But now that the shoe was on the other foot, he had some demands, namely that (a) the tour wouldn't cost him anything and (b) they wouldn't fire him again when they got back.

The first show of the tour was June 11, 1983, in Lausanne, Switzerland. Bert flew six hours to Paris, waited another six hours for the train, then rode eight hours to Lausanne (Gordon had already flown to Europe for the last few dates of the Branca tour) and went straight from the train station to the stage (via a quick stop at McDonald's). The band was wildly received by the drunken crowd. "The kids were just *freaked*," Bert recalls. "They had never heard anything like this before." At the end of the set, Moore and Ranaldo's extended feedback duel sparked a minor riot. "There were fires and people screaming and fighting," says Bert. "It was just total pandemonium." Sonic Youth obligingly encored with a twenty-minute rendition of the Stooges' "I Wanna Be Your Dog."

They traveled not by van but the excellent Eurail train system, often having to cram guitars through train windows when they were late to the station. The band often played government-sponsored youth centers, a common institution in Europe, and attracting a crowd was easy: "You could say 'underground from New York' and the place would be crowded no matter who's playing," Bert said. Everywhere they played, they were a smashing success — even if the band played badly, the music was so radical that everyone had their minds blown. Still, the best record deal the band could line up was with the tiny German label Zensor, which released their first two records.

Back home they all went back to their day jobs; Gordon worked at the legendary Todd's Copy Shop near the Bowery, a perennial employer of New York underground musicians and artists. And yet morale was high — until they played an off gig in New York that September. In a stroke of bad luck, a *Village Voice* critic was there and panned it. The *Voice*, the only hip paper left in New York, had not been kind or even attentive to Sonic Youth or any of the other arty "noise" bands who were making galvanizing music right in the paper's own backyard. "[Robert] Christgau was the editor and he wasn't interested in supporting anything that wasn't Hoboken pop," claims Gordon. "Anything that was weird was self-indulgent."

In retaliation, Moore wrote a scathing letter to the *Voice*, complaining that the paper didn't respect its local scene. Christgau replied that the paper was in the business of criticism, not advocacy; Moore fired back by renaming the song "Kill Yr. Idols" "I Killed Christgau with My Big Fucking Dick." (The feud has long since ended.)

But the band received some crucial and very prestigious national press when respected critic Greil Marcus wrote a ringing, full-page appreciation in *Artforum*. "It's as if Sonic Youth has gone back to the very beginnings of the process by which the world reveals itself as something other than its advertisement, as if the band has discovered the most marginal no," Marcus wrote. "The power of Sonic Youth's no will be negligible; few will hear this music. That the spirit of the act is still at work may not be."

Later that year they returned to Europe for two more tours. "At that point we just thought the band was so special," says Ranaldo. "And we'd go to Europe and it would be verified for us, because after shows people would just be like, 'We've never seen anything like this.' They'd never experienced any of that New York stuff that we were coming out of, so we were like this apparition that came out of nowhere. They didn't know the Contortions or DNA or any of the stuff that had inspired us."

It wasn't only the adulation that attracted Sonic Youth to Europe — there, musicians got far more money and respect. Besides, Europe was a more practical place to play. "America was almost impossible to deal with," says Moore. "It's almost ten times the size of Europe. There's way more vast wastelands of space here where we didn't have that much information about where to play. There were no offers that we could get."

hortly after Bert rejoined the band, they played Manhattan's trendy Danceteria club on a bill with the Swans and Lydia Lunch. The show's promoter, Ruth Polsky, who had been instrumental in establishing New York's underground rock scene, was a bit tipsy that night and mistakenly paid Lunch for all three bands twice. Nobody said anything and Sonic Youth used their share to record the *Kill Yr. Idols* EP at Fun City for Zensor in October '83.

The band was excited about the new material. "There was just something about it that consolidated what we'd done up to that point," says Ranaldo. For one thing, they were now playing exclusively in alternative tunings and beginning to master their limitless possibilities — their guitars sounded like anything from angelic dulcimers to a swarm of killer bees, and the music ranged from apoplectic violence ("Kill Yr. Idols") to an almost catatonic beauty ("Early American"). *Village Voice* critic Tom Carson later called *Kill Yr. Idols* "cut-and-dried howls of impeccably discordant anguish."

Thanks to the October '83 European release of *Kill Yr. Idols*, awareness of the band on the Continent reached new heights. "Berlin was incredible," recalled Moore. "It was like we were the Monkees or something. It was great — screaming girls. Too much." And live, the band was on a roll. "Every gig was just me and Lee running through the audience, getting on people's shoulders, and Lee playing his guitar with other people's teeth," Moore said. "We were totally nutzoid at this point."

But their crucial London debut was a nightmare. They were set to open for industrial dance unit SPK at the ultra-trendy Venue club, but it was at the end of a grueling six-week tour — "We're totally dirty and ragged and everybody there looks right out of *The Face* magazine," said Moore. "We're just greasy people in ripped jeans." Moore's hands were so ravaged by a month and a half of abuse that he could barely move them. Then, after telling the entire U.K. music press they'd play at 9:00, the club made them start at 8:00. On top of that, they weren't allowed to sound check and even had to move SPK's equipment themselves so they'd have room to play. By show time they were so furious they refused to get onstage.

But by 8:30 a respectable crowd had gathered, so they figured, why not play a few songs. Two songs in, Ranaldo's amplifier started smoking, then Moore's guitar started sputtering out, and Gordon broke a string; even Bert's drums started collapsing. In frustration, Moore started smashing bottles on the stage with his guitar and even heaved a monitor at a bouncer. Moore kept smashing things even after the curtain closed, screaming, "I hate the English!" and "Bomb London!" at the crowd.

It was a critical show and it had been a colossal disaster. "That's it," Bert thought. "We're fucked." Or so they thought — two weeks later the reviews came in, and *Sounds* and *NME* both raved about the performance. The next time they played CBGB in New York, the line went around the block.

**D**uring the summer of '84, they played practically once a week in New York. They were playing by rote, but as Moore told *Matter*, "It was getting to the point where it was much more physical, too, and much more violent, because that seemed like one way to take it, and so the music was getting really crazed, and we were getting totally insane, and it was getting to the point of overkill."

The band started to realize there was nowhere left to go with that approach. Besides, after all the touring, they'd grown tired of playing the same songs over and over. So they retreated to the rehearsal room, where they changed everything about their guitars, from the tuning to the pickups, so they couldn't play their old songs anymore even if they wanted to. "We killed those songs," Moore said. And they began working on a whole new batch of music that wasn't quite so violent.

**M**oore and Ranaldo changed or tuned guitars constantly during the live show, sometimes taking up to five minutes between songs and killing the momentum. The solution was little transitional pieces played by whichever guitarist wasn't changing instruments; either that or they'd play prerecorded sound collages through an amplifier, using source material like church bells, their own rehearsal tapes, the Stooges' "Not Right," Lou Reed's transcendent *Metal Machine Music*. The between-song sounds solved another problem, too — they drowned out all the heckling the band regularly endured.

They decided to incorporate those transitional pieces into the next album, with the aid of producer Martin Bisi, who had recorded downtown avantists like Material and Elliott Sharp, as well as many early rappers. It worked like a charm — with no spaces between songs, the album's two sides went by like a daisy chain of dreams.

The album leads off with a brief instrumental for several guitars, with a melancholic, meowing slide line playing off a delicate stack of crystalline arpeggios. Then "Brave Men Run" (the title comes from a painting by noted American artist Edward Ruscha) attains a majesty the band had never before reached. "Brave men run in my family," Gordon murmurs, "Brave men run away from me." Moore moans through "Society Is a Hole," a one-chord hymn to big-city anomie, and, like so much of the album, a chant swathed in harsh, intriguing guitar textures and drumming straight from the heart of the urban jungle. Even the album's bona fide love song, "I Love Her All the Time," has but one chord, with a noise section in the middle.

America was a very fashionable subject at the time. The country, plagued by fears of Japan's overpowering economic rise and terrorism from various Arab nations, suddenly turned very nationalistic. The music world was experiencing similar feelings, spurred by the dominance of precious, synthetic, and oh-so-English pop like the Thompson Twins and Culture Club. There was a sudden profusion of "roots-rock" bands like the Blasters, the Del Fuegos, and Jason & the Nashville Scorchers; even X and R.E.M. qualified as Americana, while SST's Meat Puppets came up with their countrified masterpiece *Meat Puppets II*. Bands like Tom Petty and the Heartbreakers, John Cougar Mellencamp, and Bruce Springsteen brought Americana to the mainstream.

It was against this backdrop that Sonic Youth named their new album *Bad Moon Rising*, after the 1969 hit by Creedence Clearwater Revival, one of the first and best Americana bands. Taking its title from an old blues term for an ominous situation ahead, Creedence's "Bad Moon Rising" was a deceptively upbeat song that was really an oblique comment on the war, assassinations, and unrest then ripping the country apart, even as phony flower power and saccharine pop hits attempted to smooth over the maelstrom. That refusal to ignore harsh realities was a sentiment shared and explored much further by Creedence's more radical contemporaries the MC5, the Stooges, and the Velvet Underground. Sonic Youth tapped into that same refusal.

Greil Marcus limned the idea in his 1983 *Artforum* piece on Sonic Youth, calling it "negation." "Negation is the act that would make it self-evident to everyone that the world is not as it seems," Marcus wrote, adding that negation had all but disappeared from rock until Sonic Youth. But now the concept was spreading through the American indie underground — bands like Big Black, Killdozer, and the Butthole Surfers were delving into the dark underside of American culture and coming back with some forbidding prizes. It's no coincidence that all these bands soon forged strong aesthetic and social relationships.

Creedence's "Bad Moon Rising" proved to be a very prescient song: the year 1969 saw the Los Angeles–based killings by Charles Manson and his "family"; later in the year the Rolling Stones held their disastrous, era-ending concert at California's Altamont Speedway. And of course, the Vietnam War was in full swing.

And 1984 had a lot in common with 1969. The U.S. was intervening in two suspiciously Vietnam-like civil wars (in El Salvador and Nicaragua); banks were failing at a rate not seen since the Depression; homeless people were flooding the streets; a new drug called crack was ravaging America's cities.

And so Ronald Reagan's 1984 campaign slogan that it was "morning in America" rang false to the members of Sonic Youth, who saw the effects of Reagan's regressive social policies on the streets of New York every day. "That was one of the reasons we wanted to do this Americana-themed record," Moore says. "In a way, it was a reaction to that." While many hardcore bands were simplistically hollering, "Reagan sucks!" Sonic Youth came up with a more sophisticated, more thought-provoking, more effective way of saying the same thing.

The album's cover shot, by noted art photographer James Welling, features a scarecrow with a flaming jack-o'-lantern for a head, set against a twilit urban skyline. One could not hope for a more foreboding and thoroughly American image. But the band saved their most startling statement about American culture for the album's finale.

At rehearsal one day, someone had started banging out a huge, almost heraldic guitar riff. The band had come up with plenty of killer parts like that one but usually discarded them because, Bert says, "they'd rather try to come up with something totally out of this world." But this one stuck, and Moore wrote the lyrics with Lydia Lunch after he bumped into her on the uptown bus. They called it "Death Valley '69."

The title came from *The Family*, Ed Sanders's book about the Charles Manson case. The band had been passing that book and Manson prosecutor Vincent Bugliosi's *Helter Skelter* around for months, discussing them at length in the tour van and the rehearsal space. Ostensibly, the lyrics to "Death Valley '69" are an elliptical but harrowing account of one of the Manson family's killing sprees, but, as Gordon said, "for us, the song really talks about an entire era of our society."

Manson symbolized exactly the ominous side of American smiley-face culture that Sonic Youth wanted to expose. "In a lot of ways, what America is ultimately about is death," Gordon told Craig Lee of the *Los Angeles Times*. "California is supposed to be the last frontier, this paradise, so it's symbolic that the whole Manson thing happened here."

The song was later released as a single, with cover art by Savage Pencil, the nom de plume of U.K. music journalist Edwin Pouncey, and it was a watershed for the band. It had started out as a riff that made them laugh because it sounded so much like Sixties biker-rock kings Steppenwolf. But it sounded like Steppenwolf only in the context of everything else the band did — in the real world, it still sounded like Sonic Youth, but it was straightforward enough for newcomers to get a handle on the band. As Hüsker Dü had done with "Eight Miles High," Sonic Youth had presented a key to their code. And just like "Eight Miles High," it wound up as one of the most hair-raisingly intense slabs of rock music ever committed to magnetic tape, a masterpiece of murderous, exultant clangor, or as *NME's* Mat Snow put it, "a 'Whole Lotta Love' for the einsturzende slam-dance generation."

But when they completed *Bad Moon Rising*, they had no idea who was going to release it. It was a very discouraging time for Sonic Youth. They'd enjoyed so much early success — getting written up in hip New York art magazines, making records, touring Europe — "And then all of a sudden it just kind of stopped," says Ranaldo. "We were moving ahead so fast and yet the world wasn't caught up enough." Moore and Ranaldo had a falling out with Branca and were also convinced that Neutral was not paying them proper royalties. So the band now had no label, they were unknown in their own country, and they still needed day jobs. "It was a very poor point," said Ranaldo. "If there was ever a time when I thought we were gonna break up or something, that was it, because nothing was happening for us."

But soon that would all change.

**B**ack in 1982 Boston-area high school senior Gerard Cosloy read about Sonic Youth in *New York Rocker* and bought their mini-LP. Reviewing the record in *Boston Rock*, Cosloy wrote, "Glenn Branca pals who, from the sound of this excellent debut, do some pretty capable puttering around on their own. Metal, noise and ping pong ball rhythms make for a truly mesmerizing mixture. *No New York Pt. II* swings into full gear and I couldn't be happier."

Down from Boston, Cosloy bumped into Moore at 99 Records, a small but influential Greenwich Village shop (and home of the label that released Branca's earliest recordings), and they chatted about hardcore. Cosloy sent Moore a pile of copies of his zine *Conflict* to distribute in New York, and in return Cosloy arranged Sonic Youth's first Boston show in August '82.

Not many people attended that show besides Cosloy, *Forced Exposure* editor Jimmy Johnson, members of the Boston hardcore band the

Proletariat, and legendary Boston scenester Billy Ruane. "Absolutely nobody knew who we were," says Moore. "There was no scene then."

Still, Cosloy had been blown away by their performance. "My response was, 'Wow, this is totally awesome, this is one of the most exciting rock bands I've ever seen,'" Cosloy says. "I didn't get to see Led Zeppelin when they first played, I didn't get to see the Rolling Stones when they first played, but I kind of doubt they would have affected me the same way even if I had.

"To me," Cosloy continues, "it was like, 'They could be huge *right now* doing exactly what they're doing because that's how good they are.' And I really believed that." Cosloy pauses a moment and adds, "I was probably a little naive."

After the Boston show, Cosloy and the band became fast friends, with Cosloy crashing at various Sonic Youth apartments whenever he was in New York.

Then, at age nineteen, Cosloy dropped out of U. Mass. and in the summer of '84 landed a job at Homestead Records, the newly created label division of the Long Island based distributor Dutch East India Trading, one of many distributors who were eager for a little vertical integration. Cosloy's responsibilities ranged from "sanitation engineer" to college rep to A&R person. He quickly signed Sonic Youth.

But the band still had no label in the U.K. and Europe, where they were far more popular. So Moore made a press kit and sent it to every hip English label he could think of. No one bit except Paul Smith, who ran Doublevision, a new London-based label co-owned by Stephen Mallinder and Richard Kirk of the pioneering English synth-noise duo Cabaret Voltaire. Smith loved the Sonic Youth tape but couldn't manage to interest Mallinder and Kirk, so he shopped it around to a number of U.K. indies. After meeting with total indifference, Smith started a new label called Blast First just so he could release the new Sonic Youth album.

*Bad Moon Rising* came out in March '85 to little fanfare in the States. Everyone from *CMJ* to *Rolling Stone* ignored it. The New York press — who initially liked the band — now criticized Sonic Youth as pretentious, too arty, and intellectual. To some extent, the controversy, far from diminishing the band's stature, actually raised it by making Sonic Youth a group considered worthy of debate. The band was learning about the power of the press.

An October '84 gig at New York's Pyramid Club had paid only $10. The band could only manage to attract about two dozen people to a Friday night show at Maxwell's in nearby Hoboken. Gordon and Moore were now making their living as housepainters.

It was a different story in the U.K, a much smaller country in which a buzz could spread almost instantly. After a few good reviews in the three British music weeklies, *Bad Moon Rising* sold an impressive five thousand copies there in six months.

Although the band was fascinated with California, they didn't play a West Coast show until the Gila Monster Jamboree, a mini-festival in the Mojave Desert outside L.A. on January 5, 1985. Topping the bill were the Meat Puppets, along with Redd Kross and Psi Com. The band borrowed some comically oversize drums and amps from Psi Com, which they picked up at the home of their singer, a guy named Perry Farrell. "He was just this gothy guy with all these lizards all over the house," recalls Bert.

It turned out to be a wild gig: someone associated with the festival also dealt LSD and sold about three hundred hits that night — and there were only about 350 people there. "All these people were out there and they were all taking acid," says Moore. "I had not expected that to happen — I had forgotten acid even existed, let alone people taking it."

They played Seattle a week or so later, and a very blown-away Seattle DJ, rock critic, and indie entrepreneur named Bruce Pavitt paid them $100 for the right to include "Kill Yr. Idols" on a compilation record he was putting together called *Sub Pop 100*.

They began a long European tour in March '85, beginning and ending in England, where the populace was convinced that the synthesizer was the future of rock music. Sonic Youth proceeded to change a lot of influential minds. By this time Sonic Youth was refining its approach — instead of gales of noise and aggression, both the songs and the way they were arranged became more considered or, as writer Guido Chiesa put it, "a gem of textures on the edge of atonality." Sometimes the band made downright pretty sounds, and sometimes they'd go off into lengthy instrumental sections packed with tension and drama, like a Grand Prix car race through narrow city streets.

The first show of the tour was at London's ICA, and it was packed with press. All too aware of the show's importance, Moore was so nervous that he was nearly incapacitated by stomach cramps and chills; he lay on a couch, shivering in a parka until show time. Miraculously, the pain disappeared midway through their first song. Some of the assembled British music press liked the show; most hated it. But few had seen anything so intense.

Sonic Youth helped get other noisy American guitar bands like Big Black and the Butthole Surfers over to the U.K. as well; those visits helped further the revolution. Both Big Black and the Butthole Surfers soon signed with Blast First, making the label the preeminent booster of this dark, loud new music from America. "Once Sonic Youth became stars over there, everybody wanted to do it," says Craig Marks, who co-managed Homestead Records at the time, "because you got your picture in color on the cover of a big music paper. It was like playing rock star within a small circle. It was very, very 'fab.'"

The American bands were quite different from the foppish prima donnas many of the premier English bands had become. "What it reinforced was the work ethic that American bands had," says Ranaldo. "You'd play fifty shows in forty days, and it was really like punching a clock every day in terms of how much time and energy you were putting into it. You'd go to Europe and meet the Mary Chain and they'd play like once every two months and there'd be a big riot and they'd play for fifteen minutes and they'd make a big deal out of how hard it was. And you'd just be like, 'You've got to be kidding!' Musicians here weren't afraid to go out and work really hard for satisfaction more than for success. That's what it came down to — you were working for some other notion of glory than financial."

Bert, Moore, and Ranaldo in particular were all avid consumers of rock magazines, books, and documentaries. They'd studied the mistakes everyone from Chuck Berry to Neil Young had made and weren't about to repeat them if they could help it. But Moore was deeply uninterested in the business end, leaving it to Gordon and Ranaldo. Ranaldo was the de facto tour manager, holding the cash, advancing the shows, and arranging places to stay. But no one in the band was expert in music business negotiations. "The business aspect was really hairball back then," says Bert. "They would sign anything." Bert says the band got in a legal hassle after signing the contract for *Kill Yr. Idols* with Zensor, only to get a call from Rough Trade's lawyers, pointing out that they had already signed another contract giving Rough Trade the same rights.

Fortunately, the band was savvy about a lot of other extramusical matters. Moore had begun publishing a fanzine called *Killer* in 1983, interviewing Ian MacKaye in the first issue; *Killer* #2 featured Gordon on the cover and pieces on Black Flag, Minutemen, DNA, and Flipper. It was an excellent way to network and to plug his friends' bands: connections were made, small IOU's accumulated; it was a way in to the flourishing post-hardcore community. Moore sent a copy of *Killer* to Jimmy Johnson, who had just started a hardcore fanzine called *Forced Exposure*, and struck up a correspondence with Johnson and his outspoken, musically omnivorous partner Byron Coley. It would prove to be an invaluable connection.

Sonic Youth recognized two things: One, that without substantial radio airplay, press was the main promotional outlet for underground bands, and two, that underground music fans paid particular attention to music criticism. The band also knew a thing or two about critics. "One thing Sonic Youth always did, almost to a gross point, was that they always knew who the hot journalists were and they always became really close," says Bert. "You'd go to a party and Kim would know who the *Village Voice* writer was in the corner of the room and she'd make sure she went over there. They were really good at schmoozing in every respect. They always made sure they met as many popular, famous people as they could, whether it be the art world or the music world. They were always really good at that — they always knew who to meet, who to know."

Bert recalls when former Branca musician Tim Sommer began to make a name for himself with the legendary WNYU hardcore radio program *Noise the Show*. "He was starting to be a big deal and they were best friends with him," Bert says, "and all of a sudden two years later they wouldn't give him the time of day." Bert also points to Moore's connection to *Forced Exposure*, which soon became perhaps the most influential zine in America. "He totally got himself in there," says Bert, "and we got on the cover."

The *Forced Exposure* connection later paid off even more handsomely for Sonic Youth, as they, the Butthole Surfers, and Big Black all appeared there regularly, forming an aesthetic cabal of sorts that got dubbed "pigfuck" by the *Village Voice*'s Robert Christgau (New York's nonpareil Pussy Galore also belonged to the club). While Ranaldo detests the term, he does acknowledge that those bands had things in common. "I think all of us were of a generation slightly older than the kids making hardcore music, old enough to have seen a little bit more of the Sixties music in a sort of firsthand way," he says. "It was just people trying to figure out how to do a life involving music at a time when there was no infrastructure at that level to do it."

The other thing they had in common was their fierce dedication to sculpting a kind of ugly beauty, and that notion of "negation" that Greil Marcus had identified a couple of years earlier. These were the qualities that tied together so many of the bands Sonic Youth respected, from the Velvets to the Pistols. This was also a time when relatively conventional bands like R.E.M. and the Replacements were taking the avant edge off the underground. Someone had to come in and do something weird before things got too normal.

The members of Sonic Youth realized that "a life involving music" depended on cooperation — if bands worked for each other, everybody would benefit. They became dedicated networkers, corresponding not just with press and fellow bands but labels and promoters as well. "They made themselves available to help people out," says former Big Black leader Steve Albini. "When we'd go to New York, if they couldn't set up a show, they would give us advice about where to go." Sonic Youth became respected gurus of the indie scene, the band that everybody else went to for advice, information, and inspiration. They were a little older and they were from New York City, which gave them an air of authority, and the fact that they were one of the few indie bands with a woman playing a prominent role signaled that they were perhaps a bit more cultured than the rest. And Gordon and Moore being a couple lent the feeling that Sonic Youth was in some sense a family — steady, grounded, and wise. By coming to the aid of promising new bands like Dinosaur Jr, Die Kreuzen, Mudhoney, and Nirvana among countless others, Sonic Youth made itself a linchpin of the indie community — and as the scene's premier tastemakers, they also became its kingmakers.

Although all the schmoozing surely helped advance the band's career, Ranaldo insists it was mostly done to sate the band members' inquisitive natures. "You figured if you met the right people, it would be helpful to get the band gigs and all that stuff, but more than that, you felt like you were part of something that was happening and you wanted to know other people that were part of it and what they were doing and what their little piece in the puzzle was," says Ranaldo. "It's part of just a natural curiosity and enthusiasm that we have and a lot of people have. . . . We're all voracious acquirers of information, whether it be books or movies or whatever, we're just really vastly into what's going on in culture and trying to synthesize what's going on. I think that was just a natural impetus, a natural tendency."

The band would never waste an opportunity to plug musicians past and present: over the course of a rambling 1985 *Forced Exposure* interview, the band name-checked Bachman-Turner Overdrive, Alice Cooper, the Swans, John Fogerty, William Burroughs, Steppenwolf, the Meat Puppets, Minor Threat, Chuck Berry, and an extremely obscure album track by Sixties one-hit wonders Shocking Blue called "Love Buzz," which, by some strange coincidence, Nirvana would cover as the A-side of their first single.

"To me, their 'strategy' of always staying in touch with the very new was possibly motivated by a pure desire to constantly learn," says Sub Pop cofounder Bruce Pavitt, "and perhaps also, instinctively, as a solid marketing approach. By staying so close to their roots at all times, they managed to get through the Eighties — and Nineties — with barely a scratch. I can't think of any other group that garnered such ubiquitous political support. They somehow managed to never burn any bridges — which, for rock & roll, is a minor miracle."

**M**oore and Gordon had no problem hitting the road — unlike the other two, they got to be with their spouse on tour; but Bert and Ranaldo, who had both married in 1984, the same year Gordon and Moore did, didn't have that luxury. It was especially hard on Bert, who worked a day job making fine art silk screens on top of rehearsing three times a week and touring. Since the best they'd ever done on a European tour was break even, Bert was just barely eking out a living. The rest of the band wasn't as worried about making the rent because Ranaldo had a well-paying job assisting a metal sculptor; Gordon and Moore of course split their expenses.

At the end of the spring '85 tour, they returned to London, where they had become the toast of the English hipster set; members of important U.K. bands like the Fall and the Jesus and Mary Chain attended their shows, and the band responded with a pair of legendary performances.

Afterward, they met with Paul Smith to plan the year ahead. But Bert already knew what his plans were — he announced his resignation to his stunned bandmates. "I was getting kind of bored," Bert explained to *Flipside*. "I was really broke and I just wanted to change the scene."

The boredom mostly stemmed from the fact that they'd been playing the same set — *Bad Moon Rising* in its entirety — for over a year. Bert may well have also been frustrated by second-class-citizen status. The balance of power always lay in the original trio of Gordon, Moore, and Ranaldo. "We just drove the group a lot more," Ranaldo says of those days. "The drummers have always sort of brought up the rear in a certain sense."

In retrospect, Moore completely understood Bert's exit. "We were still unknown," Moore said in a 1994 interview. "I mean, people were coming to see us and we were freaking 'em out, having a great time, but we were sleeping on floors covered with cat piss every night. So he split."

**F**ortunately, a new drummer couldn't have appeared more readily. Steve Shelley played in the Crucifucks, who had an album on Alternative Tentacles and some touring under their belt. The Michigan band played a lurching variation on hardcore and specialized in the usual mix of alienation and blunt political ranting. One lyric rails against religious fundamentalists: "I wanna take the president / Chop off his head, and mail it to them in a garbage bag" goes a song called "Hinkley Had a Vision."

Moore and Ranaldo were impressed when they saw Shelley with the Crucifucks at a 1985 CBGB Rock Against Reagan benefit. When Shelley left the Crucifucks, he asked Ranaldo about living in Manhattan; this led to Shelley's subletting Moore and Gordon's apartment while they were off in Europe. When Sonic Youth returned, they hired their house sitter without so much as an audition.

Besides being a fantastic drummer (the fact that he owned a van didn't hurt, either), Shelley represented a direct link to hardcore. The mild-mannered drummer, several years younger than the rest of the band, did make for an unlikely punk veteran — he wore studious-looking wire-rim glasses, bowl-cut hair, and attire that tended toward the wholesomely preppy, leading *Matter* writer Glenn Kenny to declare Shelley "positively cute, in a 'My Three Sons' kind of way." But looks were deceiving — Shelley played with shuddering force, a very musical wallop that propelled the band more intensely than ever before.

Shelley also had a somewhat more conservative attitude than Moore — once they began touring, Shelley would always want to get to sound check promptly; Moore preferred to go thrift shopping. "Steve is super responsible and only would drive fifty-five," recalls Gordon. "Thurston would speed and then stop, like, five times."

**T**he "Death Valley '69" single was doing so well that they decided to make a video. Although Shelley was now their drummer, Bert had played on the song, so they simply included them both in the video. Director Richard Kern made wildly brutal low-budget art films, and "Death Valley '69" was no different. The video intercuts decidedly phallic-looking nuclear missiles, the feral dancing of avant actress Lung Leg, and intense live footage, but the most memorable scenes are of the band lying around a house brutally slaughtered, apparently by Mansonesque killers.

Ranaldo's wife was about to give birth at the time; the call came that she was going into labor just as Ranaldo was getting ready for his scene. "As soon as Richard got the shot," Bert recalls, "Lee swipped all these cow guts off himself, jumped up, and took a taxi to the hospital, totally covered in blood."

As before, Bert remained on cordial terms with the band and played a show with them that June at tiny Folk City (Moore's poster offered "free admission if you're naked") as part of the Music for Dozens series, along with Butthole Surfers drummers King Coffey and Teresa Taylor. One drummer pounded in each corner of the room while film projectors and strobe lights went off all over the place — just like a Butthole Surfers show.

Flexing her art school muscles, Gordon had begun writing trenchant articles about rock and related subjects for the prestigious *Artforum*. "People pay to see others believe in themselves," Gordon wrote in one 1983 essay. "As a performer you sacrifice yourself, you go through the motions and emotions of sexuality for all the people who pay to see it, to believe that it exists. The better and more convincing the performance, the more an audience can identify with the exterior involved in such an expenditure of energy."

Sonic Youth's demonstrative performance style amply bore out that statement, and yet it's easy to imagine the self-consciousness of a band with that level of objective insight into their own craft. They could well have been paralyzed at the thought of going onstage, but Sonic Youth never let a little knowledge get in the way of a good catharsis. "[Performing] was always the high point of the day," Ranaldo says. "We'd go through long drives and no sleep and bad food just in order to get to that moment where you can release. Rock in general is about that emotional release, so we never let the knowledge on the one hand contradict the idea of release on the other."

But for all the band's physical intensity, they could also seem emotionally aloof. Even their intensity functioned as a shield. "If you put out a certain amount of energy while you're doing something," says Gordon, "it's almost like a buffer so nothing else can come in." Even the lyrics are guarded — often, they are opaque, even nonsensical; when they are personal, they are heavily veiled.

Their self-consciousness came out most in interviews, where the band knew mystiques are made (and unmade). Moore could be profoundly goofy and quick with absurdist wisecracks, almost fundamentally incapable of giving a straight answer to anything. The glacially cool Gordon would not suffer fools gladly — one writer said Gordon's "deadpan, icy stare could stop stampeding buffalo"; those closer to her recognized it as the defense mechanism of a shy person. Ranaldo, on the other hand, was deeply earnest and as the most candid member of the band didn't qualify his enthusiasm for anything.

But if no one could decide exactly how detached the band's approach was, it may have been because the band couldn't decide either. In a 1985 interview, they recalled an *NME* writer who didn't believe that their infernal version of "I Wanna Be Your Dog" was "sincere." "They thought that was totally tongue-in-cheek," said Ranaldo.

"But it was," Gordon protested.

"Not totally," Ranaldo replied.

"It was *tongue*," Moore said, settling it.

By 1985, thanks to SST, R.E.M., and countless local bands, there was finally some sort of underground club circuit, making it possible for Sonic Youth to play throughout their native country, and Gerard Cosloy booked their first U.S. tour for that summer.

All the European roadwork paid off. The band had toured the Continent five times and worked up their live show before wildly appreciative audiences. By the time of the first U.S. tour, the band was a fearsome live force, phantom harmonics and stunning riff volleys ricocheting around the room in a breathtaking cross fire of sound. At peak moments Gordon, Moore, and Ranaldo would all be lunging and swooping and jerking in completely different rhythms, like some grungy version of a *Peanuts* dance scene.

And yet turnouts were disappointing. "We thought we were going to be greeted by cheering crowds everywhere," Ranaldo says, "but there were plenty of shows where there was just a handful of people." American bands, they realized, got a much better reception in Europe. "It was far more difficult to impress an American audience than a European audience, just because of the wealth of great stuff that happens here compared to over there and also because audiences are far more critical here than they are over there," says Ranaldo. "We were going out west and trying to make it in the land of SST, where they didn't need another good band — they had amazing bands all around their home turf."

Sonic Youth began to realize that it might be a good idea to find a new label, even a major to help broaden their audience. "At that time, there was no such thing as 'Be proud to be indie,'" Moore says. "Being indie was just sort of like, there was nothing else you could be — major labels had no interest." Sometimes a feeler would go out, though — Warner Brothers had once asked for a copy of *Bad Moon Rising.* "And they called back," Moore recalls, "and they said, 'Are you sure this is the one we asked for, because this is just a bunch of noise — it's just crap.' So there was still this complete chasm there of aesthetics and values."

The band was fascinated with SST and felt it would be for them. In fact, they seemed to be actively campaigning to get signed to the indie powerhouse. All along the tour, Moore scrawled graffiti on dressing room walls that said "Hello to Black Flag from Sonic Youth," knowing Ginn and company would soon be coming through town; Gordon pointedly praised Raymond Pettibon's work at length in the April '85 *Artforum.*

In retrospect, even the whole Creedence/1969/Americana concept seems like a calculated attempt to ingratiate themselves with SST: Manson had been a frequent subject of SST illustrator Raymond Pettibon for years; SST's beloved Minutemen outspokenly championed Creedence Clearwater Revival. "Raymond Pettibon and John Fogerty are our heroes," Moore proclaimed in a *Forced Exposure* interview. "They're our life's blood."

And the feeling was mutual — almost. Although SST partners Greg Ginn, Chuck Dukowski, and Mugger were interested in Sonic Youth, Joe Carducci wasn't. "Record collectors shouldn't be in bands" Carducci is said to have grumbled, and since SST signing decisions had to be unanimous, that was that. But shortly after Carducci left the label in early 1986 — and legend has it that it was *minutes* after he left — Ginn called Moore and Gordon and offered to sign Sonic Youth. They quickly accepted.

"It was the first real record company we were on that we really would have given anything to be on," says Ranaldo. "Homestead picked us up and did great things for us, but they were just some really little start-up company. SST was like nirvana."

Moore broke the news to a very shocked and saddened Cosloy. "He wasn't too happy about it," Moore says, "but he dealt with it."

Now Sonic Youth was on the same label as Black Flag and the Meat Puppets. "We got into the whole SST family," says Moore. "And that was great because we were really into their whole enterprise. They were involved with the American youth music movement, which we really saw as being really credible and contemporary."

After intensive rehearsals that winter, they began recording their SST debut in March '86.

They called the album *EVOL*, after a piece by video artist Tony Oursler. The reverse spelling represented the flip side of the same vapid, failed, hippie ethos they had pilloried in *Bad Moon Rising*. That "evol" is also short for "evolution" was only fitting, since with Shelley's arrival the band began the dramatic ascent to their artistic peak. Shelley was a big part of this rise — precise, powerful, and inventive, his playing both nailed down the beat and suggested all kinds of possibilities the music didn't seem to have before. The music was now suffused with ragalike crescendos, and an Eastern feeling pervaded many of the new songs.

At the same time, the band's music was starting to acknowledge, ever so slightly, more conventional music. This was the mid-Eighties, when the likes of Bruce Springsteen and Prince were making mainstream music interesting again. "All of a sudden there was a lot of songs you didn't mind getting caught humming on the street again," Ranaldo says. "And we were in a position where it didn't go against our set of morals as underground hardcore avantists to like a Madonna song."

The members of Sonic Youth were fans of pop art and the fertile juxtapositions of postmodernism, then all the rage in intellectual and art circles, and their iconoclastic embrace of Madonna did have ironic and academic aspects, but for all their artistic pretensions, they were also just like anyone else who had grown up in America in the Sixties and Seventies and grooved to AM pop radio. "We were just pulling influences from wherever we found them and not worrying about the way in which they clashed together," says Ranaldo, "because something about that kind of juxtaposition was as interesting to us as anything else." And besides, turnabout is fair play: mainstream culture was avidly assimilating the underground at the time, with MTV and even Madison Avenue appropriating avant-garde film innovations, the federal government making grants to provocative performance artists, major corporations investing in painters like Julian Schnabel and David Salle.

In the spirit of dancing with the mainstream, *EVOL* marked the public beginning of Sonic Youth's long fascination with celebrity, something that had kicked into a yet higher gear in America with the rise of MTV and Reagan's telecentric presidency — the album has a song called "Madonna, Sean and Me," another called "Marilyn Moore"; "Starpower" posits the idea of lover as celebrity (or vice versa). But *EVOL* also extracted a grimy beauty from the grit and menace of mid-Eighties New York, a city that encompassed almost dizzying extremes of splendor and squalor. The songs were far more melodious than ever before; the arrangements ranged from huge and dramatic to hushed and intimate, the recording far better than anything they'd previously attempted. *EVOL* served notice that Sonic Youth was not just a "noise band"— there were actual songs; even the rave-ups were orchestrated.

The band was now in such control of its power that it could rein it in to produce music that was refined and often quite beautiful, especially in two showcases for Gordon's new breathy, dreamy delivery. On "Secret Girls," she recites enigmatic poetry, sighing softly after each line while a forlorn piano plays as if in the next room, guitar noise even farther in the distance. Loosely based on Hitchcock's *Strangers on a Train*, "Shadow of a Doubt" comes off as a tightly constructed dream. A guitar plinks like an underwater koto; "Kiss me in the shadow / kiss me in the shadow of doubt," Gordon whispers between sensual crescendos.

Perhaps inspired by Madonna, Gordon had cut her hair, begun dressing more stylishly, and dispensed with the oversize glasses she used to wear — and in the process became something of an indie rock heartthrob. "I definitely know I'm a woman and what that means," said Gordon at the time. "Now I might be more conscious of it than in the past. Sexuality is something I'm deeply interested in."

"Expressway to Yr. Skull" was the album's finale, its magnum opus. "We're gonna kill the California girls. . . ." Moore sings the first line, dreamily, like some homicidal twist on a Beach Boys lyric. The song builds to a cataclysm, Moore's slide guitar wailing like an air raid siren, then back down to a meditative, after-the-storm feeling, the whole roller-coaster ride ending with a good three minutes of Moore and Ranaldo drawing sounds from their guitars like the music of the spheres, or maybe the sonorous decay of the closing piano chord of the Beatles' "A Day in the Life."

The move to SST instantly catapulted Sonic Youth out of the New York art ghetto and onto a national stage. None of their New York peers ever made a comparable leap. It helped that at the same time, Sonic Youth had come up with an artistic breakthrough of an album. Released in May '86, *EVOL* made the band more accessible and strengthened their alloy of the physical (Stooges) and the cerebral (John Cage), not only embodying the debate then beginning to peak in the art world about "high" and "low" art, but perpetuating a hybrid that rock music had been exploring since the Beatles' *Revolver* and on through the Velvets, Roxy Music, Mission of Burma, and beyond.

**B**ack before the term got too specified, Sonic Youth often got tagged as "industrial," but that wasn't quite it. Particularly in the mid-Eighties, New York was a veritable symphony of clangs, clanks, booms, thuds, buzzes, and hums; any resident whose ears had been opened by John Cage and Karlheinz Stockhausen (not to mention the frenzied free jazz of Ornette Coleman, John Coltrane, and Eric Dolphy) became a connoisseur of noises. "That stuff can't be discounted, how important an idea those cityscape sounds are," Ranaldo says. "The early periods of this band couldn't have happened anywhere but New York."

The band also took ideas from conceptual art and media-savvy, urban angst-ridden artists like Robert Longo and Cindy Sherman. They were also big Warhol fans, especially for the way Warhol, like Sonic Youth, mixed high art and popular culture. The music itself was the sonic analogue of the monumental, rough-hewn, and yet thoroughly premeditated and marketed neo-expressionist art that was the height of New York hip, but that was probably unconscious. Far more conscious were the band's use of avant-garde movements like cut-up art, which they adapted for their lyrics, and "appropriation art," which they adapted for their album covers.

Even the bands that Sonic Youth made sure to champion were, in a way, appropriated art, things that were recontextualized and made to shed new light on Sonic Youth itself. Sonic Youth no doubt loved these bands, but the association with groups like Dinosaur Jr, Mudhoney, and Nirvana also served to take the arty edge off Sonic Youth and emphasize their rock side (conversely, the other bands gained an artsy association they might not otherwise have gotten). "A lot of bands," says Ranaldo, "are trying to present themselves as a singular entity in the center of it all. And I think we've always been the exact opposite, trying to present ourselves amidst a universe or a society of stuff going on."

**T**he band set out on a six-week U.S. tour in June '86 with their beloved European booking agent Carlos van Hijfte as tour manager. Van Hijfte had never been in the U.S. or even road-managed a tour, but the band didn't care — he was their friend and they wanted to show him America. Also along for the ride were soundman Terry Pearson and a preposterously gigantic silver boom box that spewed anything from Black Sabbath to their beloved Madonna on the endless drives down the interstates.

There was a good crowd in Raleigh, where they'd played four distant years before on the Savage Blunder tour to approximately ten people. But elsewhere in the South it was a different story: desolate gigs in New Orleans, Houston, Dallas, and Austin with perhaps fifty people in the audience. Shelley estimates the crowd never exceeded 350 on the whole tour. They hooked up for several dates with fellow SST band Saccharine Trust, starting in Tucson, where the club billed the show as a hardcore night, hoping to draw the music's built-in audience. But the hardcore kids of Tucson, no fools, stayed away in droves and the show was a bust. A confrontation ensued when the club allegedly refused to pay the bands their guarantee. "The club owners are sub-moronic with very low IQ's, cheeze business suits and pistols packed neath their vests," wrote Moore in a tour diary for *Forced Exposure*. "They ripped us and Saccharine off for big bux."

Then it was over to Southern California, up the coast to Seattle, a long haul to Denver, and a punishing twelve-hour drive in the July heat to Kansas City. "All day in the van roof melting drops of corrugated scuzz on our 100 degree parched skin," wrote Moore in his tour diary. "Sweating and shitty and irritable. Living hell." In Michigan they picked up Dinosaur Jr, who had recently released their debut album on Homestead. The Dinosaur guys were awed by their heroes. "They were so good and their shows were different every night and they were angry as shit on stage," Dinosaur bassist Lou Barlow recalls. "Kim's bass was fucking up and she'd be like, 'Urgh,' all uptight about it."

Now that the band was on SST, the mainstream music industry was beginning to take notice: music biz house organ *Billboard* praised a show at L.A.'s Roxy. "Although the band may be too raw and uncompromisingly experimental for many listeners," wrote reviewer Chris Morris, "Sonic Youth is unmistakably rewriting the vocabulary of the electric guitar in the '80s." Even *People* acknowledged the band, albeit in a backhanded way: "Meanwhile, out on the lunatic fringe . . ." the *EVOL* review began, going on to term the album the "aural equivalent of a toxic waste dump." And that was a positive review.

Respected *New York Times* critic Robert Palmer decreed that Sonic Youth was "making the most startlingly original guitar-based music since Jimi Hendrix" while a *Melody Maker* year-end roundup of 1986's best albums (*EVOL* was number twenty-two), said, "*EVOL* is a murderous crush of perversity, paranoia and naked, twisted visions of blind rage, soli-

tary insanity and silent, thoughtful violence. With truly modern psychedelia, erotic sex and pounding, mindless brutality, it is a cruising, career-
ing mix of variety and movement." "Starpower," released as a single with
the noisiest parts edited out, vastly raised the band's profile on college radio; at number twelve, *EVOL* was the highest indie entry on *CMJ*'s 1986
year-end chart.

Each Sonic Youth record was selling more than the last; each was getting more praise and airplay than the last. And musically, the band was
progressing by leaps and bounds. They were perfectly poised to capitalize
on all the hard work.

They recorded the follow-up to *EVOL* in the spring of '87 at Sear
Sound in midtown Manhattan; the studio boasted a vintage
sixteen-track, vacuum-tube board — technologically it was outdated, but the band wanted the unique "warmth" of the tube sound. "You
can hear, actually, the sound of the tubes on the record," Moore claimed.
"You can hear the coils kind of, like, relating to each other, in a way."

But perhaps the band was emulating the working method of one of
their favorite new writers, William Gibson, who wrote his pioneering "cy-
berpunk" novels not on a computer but on an ancient manual typewriter.
Or maybe they hoped the "dirty" sound of tubes would compensate for
their musicianship and songwriting, which were cleaner than ever.

Unlike any of their previous records, *Sister* is mostly up-tempo, with
the band rocking out often, clearly for the sheer joy of it — they even
cover the garagey "Hotwire My Heart" by the early San Francisco punk
band Crime, which was the indie equivalent of the Stones covering a
Slim Harpo tune. The tunings were not as harsh and dissonant as before,
the changes less arty — many numbers are downright sleek by comparison to their previous material. But this was still Sonic Youth, and despite
all the catchy hooks, no song except for "Hotwire My Heart" has anything
resembling pop music's standard verse-chorus-verse structure.

With *Sister* the band reached its fullest realization — for a long time
afterward, anything else would be perfecting a formula. "Between *EVOL*
and *Sister*, they basically defined Sonic Youth, in sonic terms," says Steve
Albini, "and they have stayed within those parameters ever since."

Some of the lyrics weaved in themes from visionary science fiction
writer Philip K. Dick, who had replaced Charles Manson as the band's
obsession. Dick had written *Do Androids Dream of Electric Sheep?* — the
basis of the film *Blade Runner* — and his dark vision of a beat-up, glitch-

SONIC YOUTH IN A PHOTO
SESSION FOR *DAYDREAM
NATION*, 1988, STANDING
IN FRONT OF THE
APARTMENT BUILDING OF
THE LEGENDARY AVANT-
GARDE COMPOSER LA
MONTE YOUNG.

MICHAEL LAVINE

laden high-tech future fit well with Sonic Youth's approach, from their
fascination with dystopia to their embrace of outdated electronics. Like
Dick, Sonic Youth found beauty and genuineness in the messed-up and
broken — like a bloodied hand bashing down on the groaning strings of a
banged-up Japanese Telecaster copy.

The album title refers to Dick's twin sister, who died shortly after
birth, while the song title "Schizophrenia" refers to a Dick story and ultimately to the author himself, whose mental health began to fail in his
later years. But only a couple of *Sister* songs actually have anything directly to do with Dick's writings. More prevalent is Christian imagery,
which appears in nearly all of Moore's songs, notably "Catholic Block,"
"Cotton Crown," "White Cross," and even "Schizophrenia," where a
character proclaims that "Jesus had a twin who knew nothing about sin."

As in *Confusion Is Sex*, Gordon's songs often deal in images of abuse
by speaking in the voice of the persecutor — in "Beauty Lies in the Eye,"

she murmurs, "Hey fox, come here / Hey beautiful, come here, sugar"; "Let's go for a ride somewhere / I won't hurt you," she says in the creepy "Pacific Coast Highway." Out in America, a lot of young women were listening, especially those who later made up the Riot Grrrl movement, which particularly decried sexual abuse, harassment, and assault, and Gordon became an influential and highly visible role model for a generation of young women about to form their own bands.

Although it didn't quite equal *EVOL*, *Sister* had the bigger impact on the indie world when it was released in June '87. Years of hard touring, plenty of glowing press, the powerful SST cachet, a decent showing on college radio, and the most inviting music the band had yet made all conspired to sell sixty thousand copies of *Sister*. The album reached number twelve in that year's *Village Voice* Pazz & Jop poll — the first Sonic Youth album to crack the top twenty of that influential list.

**B**y the summer of '88, as it became increasingly apparent that the patrician Republican candidate for president, George Bush, would trounce his feckless Democratic opponent, Michael Dukakis, ensuring yet four more years of Reaganism, the band entered SoHo's Greene Street Studios to record by far their most ambitious album yet, the classic *Daydream Nation*.

Despite the success of *Sister*, Sonic Youth had grown disenchanted with SST. "SST's accounting was a bit suspect to us," Moore says, an alarmingly common complaint of SST bands. The band was also disturbed that the label had also been firing employees. "We didn't like what was going on over there — it seemed sort of odd," says Moore. "People we liked were being let go."

"We felt like there was a little too much of a stoner administrative quality going on out there," adds Ranaldo. "For as fuzzy-headed a group as we sometimes come across as, that's really what it came down to — we wanted the business side of what we did to be serious and so the people that dealt with the business, we wanted them to know what was going on when it came time to ask those questions. We just felt like it wasn't really happening."

By then Sonic Youth's sales chart was definitely pointed up, and yet the band felt SST couldn't, as they say in the music industry, take it to the next level. "SST is growing, but not fast enough for us," Gordon said.

And they felt SST wasn't musically what it used to be, perhaps due to the stoner quality Ranaldo had detected. "[Greg Ginn] was signing, like, these bands from North Carolina, bands that he liked, but they were kind of boring compared to what was already there," Moore says. "He had this thing that a lot of distributors won't take you seriously unless you have a lot of product. So you become less specialized and you become validated as a label. It was all very uninvolving for me."

By 1987 SST had started to show unmistakable signs of hubris, such as releasing over eighty titles that year, a ridiculous amount even by major label standards. "Toward the end," Ranaldo says, "we felt like whatever money was coming in from whatever records were making money was being used to fund a bunch of lame-ass records."

Unlike bands such as the Minutemen or Saccharine Trust, Sonic Youth had no particular allegiance to SST — it was a business relationship, no more, no less. "They completely respected us," says Moore, "but we did tell them that we didn't want to do the next record with them." Ranaldo describes the split with SST as "very unamicable." (They eventually resorted to legal recourse to get their master tapes back from the label.) Sonic Youth had replaced the late, great Minutemen as the label's heart and soul, and the band's defection hit SST hard, starting off the label's fairly rapid descent back into obscurity.

Blast First's Paul Smith had long suggested that Sonic Youth could sell more records than SST was capable of selling. Of course, Smith had his own motives — he wanted Sonic Youth on the upcoming American branch of Blast First, not just because he loved the band, but because it would attract funding to the venture. In 1987 Smith set up a New York office and began trying to lure all the U.K. Blast First artists, including Dinosaur Jr (SST), Big Black (Touch & Go), the Butthole Surfers (Touch & Go), and Sonic Youth. But despite Sonic Youth's enthusiastic lobbying, none of the other bands made the move. Even worse, Big Black's Steve Albini was annoyed at them for trying to spirit away the best-selling artists on his good friend Corey Rusk's Touch & Go label; Sonic Youth's relationship with Albini was never the same.

Smith struck up a relationship with West Coast–based Enigma Records, which in turn was distributed by Capitol Records and half-owned by EMI, similar to the relationship R.E.M.'s label I.R.S. Records had with the music biz behemoth MCA Records. Smith convinced the band to go along for the ride. And so Sonic Youth did the seemingly unthinkable and edged ever so gradually into the major label world.

Indie paragons like *Maximumrocknroll*, the Dead Kennedys' Jello Biafra, and the band MDC all preached strongly against dealing with corporate America. But at the same time, many alumni of the indie scene, from college radio DJs to people who had gotten their start packing boxes at indie distributors, were starting to get substantial positions at major labels. Naturally, they were looking to work with bands they knew and liked.

Moore felt independent labels had lost what made them good in the first place, which was that they didn't try to compete on any level with the majors. But, noting the steady growth in their sales, indie labels had lately begun to aim higher. "The whole thing of becoming bigger and bigger to me was wrong," Moore said. "You should find a great neutrality and just stay there and maintain that force."

Unfortunately, capitalism doesn't work that way — the indie scene wasn't an alternative network of dedicated music fans anymore; it was now just another industry looking for increased market share — and not doing it very well. If that was the case, Sonic Youth figured, why not work with people who knew what they were doing? "I didn't feel any allegiance for the independent scene anymore, that's for sure," said Moore, "because it was in disarray as far as I was concerned."

There had been the possibility of going straight to a major label, but Moore shrewdly decided against that just yet — going with a major would delay the release date of the new album, and he wanted it to come out at the end of the year, boosting its chances for a strong finish in the important *Village Voice* Pazz & Jop poll. Sure enough, *Daydream Nation*, recorded for a mere $30,000, finished second behind Public Enemy's landmark *It Takes a Nation of Millions to Hold Us Back. Rolling Stone* also piled on the hosannas, not only placing the album second in its critics' poll, but naming Sonic Youth "Hot Band" in its "Hot" issue and placing the album at number forty-five on its list of the hundred best albums of the Eighties. The album was number one on *CMJ*'s year-end chart; in the U.K. it topped the independent charts of both the *NME* and *Melody Maker*.

And with reason: the album mixed the streamlined propulsion of *Sister* and the jagged high drama of *EVOL*, all executed by a band at the peak of their powers. The music is shot through with all kinds of strikingly vivid feelings: joy, ennui, sensuality, cynicism, frenzy, poignancy. Laden with guitar hooks, well recorded, and meticulously structured, it flows, like *Bad Moon Rising*, in one long blurt, with many passages so dense and ingeniously arranged, they border on the orchestral. The cover art, a photo-realist painting of a burning candle by distinguished German painter Gerhard Richter, seemed to speak of faith, illumination, and a righteous constancy that would eventually overwhelm the blithe ignorance of the "daydream nation" the U.S. had become.

Unfortunately, Capitol had no idea what to do with Enigma's releases; consequently, it was difficult to find *Daydream Nation* in stores. "Enigma was basically a cheap-jack Mafioso outfit, I guess," Moore concluded. "You can quote me on that, but I'm not quite sure how truthful that is. That was the impression we were given."

The band placed much of the blame on Paul Smith, who was already on thin ice with them ever since Blast First's 1986 double-LP live set, *Walls Have Ears*. The album documents two incredible Sonic Youth performances, one with Bert on drums and one with Shelley; although the sound was not so good, the packaging was done with care. The problem was the band knew nothing about it until Smith presented them with finished copies. "[Smith] really thought we were going to be so pleased with it, that it was going to be like opening a surprise package at Christmas," says Ranaldo. "He was totally flabbergasted when we were horrified by it." Sonic Youth took swift legal action and forced Smith to halt production of *Walls Have Ears* at about two thousand copies. And yet two thousand copies was all it took for the album to make the U.K. indie charts, where it resided for several weeks.

The band parted ways with a crestfallen Smith after the Enigma debacle and began shopping for a major label deal. Several labels were interested, but the band was most interested in Geffen. Among other people, they consulted Bob Mould on how to negotiate a major label contract, and Mould counseled them to retain creative control, among other points. Sonic Youth wound up with a unique deal that, among other things, gave the band members the ability to sign other bands. By letting such things be known, and talking a good game, the band preserved their underground credibility through the transition.

Their 1990 major label debut, *Goo*, continued the streamlining of their sound and songs, going in for a far more conventional rock approach. The album debuted at number one on the *CMJ* charts and even made the *Billboard* Top 100. Then Neil Young invited them on a tour for his latest comeback album, *Ragged Glory*. Although Sonic Youth was met by massive indifference by Young's audience, it was a significant toe-dip into the mainstream; conversely, Young benefited from a massive hipness infusion from Sonic Youth and repeatedly called "Expressway to Yr. Skull" "the greatest guitar song of all time."

Yet being on a major label was not always so glorious. "It's not really very exciting," Ranaldo revealed. "It's frightening." Still, the band continued with Geffen throughout the Nineties, sustaining its large cult following with a long string of albums that were by turns intriguing, visceral, dark, puzzling, joyous, cerebral, and moving.


**W**hy did Sonic Youth succeed when all of their peers — bands like Live Skull, Rat At Rat R, and the Swans — eventually fell by the wayside? "In a lot of ways, Sonic Youth are trailblazers but in a lot of ways they're followers," Bob Bert observes. "A lot of times they were jumping on bandwagons and stuff. They were really good at that."

That may be so, but there's no taking away the fact that they were (and remain) a great band. Another, more practical reason is that unlike their peers, Sonic Youth simply managed to stay together; their personal and collective longevity was vastly helped by the fact that they never got stuck in the quagmire of heavy drugs. And although it would be easy to assume that Gordon and Moore would side together on most issues, it was in fact as likely for the two of them to disagree with each other as with anyone else in the band. Gordon and Moore rarely seemed to discuss band issues among themselves, which was surely as good for their relationship as it was for the band's.

But all that meant nothing without the band's relentless determination. "We were very focused on what we wanted," Moore says, "even though we never knew what was going to happen from one month to the next. But we were focused on how we wanted to exist." So when the band wanted to tour Europe, they made that happen; when they wanted to sign to SST, they made that happen; when they went to a proper major label, they did so on their own terms.

According to Moore, squabbling within the band was remarkably minimal. "We always got along fairly well through those indie years," Moore says, then struggles to recall an instance of band disharmony. "I remember Lee being in Phoenix and coming out of a rest stop with an ice cream," he says, "and I remember getting really bitter toward him because I couldn't afford to have one."

Many bands begin to fragment when one member starts to take control. The members of Sonic Youth had read enough rock history to know not to repeat that mistake. But perhaps more important, that same sense of history — as well as each member's formidable cool — had made them each too self-conscious to, as Ranaldo puts it, "start wearing silk scarves and prance in front of the other three onstage."

And best of all, Sonic Youth inhabited a charmed zone where they were successful enough to keep going and yet low profile enough to elude the compromises of success. Although each record sold more than the last, there were no spikes in their sales graph that would have prematurely attracted the attentions of the mainstream music business. "Luckily, we were smart enough in the early days to work it out so we were making enough money to subsist off it," says Ranaldo. "We never went for the stupid route that might have given us a lot of cash in the short term but also would have been the death knell."

But no one ever believed the band would last as long as it has. "When I was in the band, there was never even a *thought* that we'd even be around five years later," says Bert. "There was no thought of it ever being much beyond a tiny little footnote in Lower East Side history."

By the early Nineties, the band had become more famous for being influential than for their music. "Interviewers would say, 'Why are you significant?' Or, 'How does it feel to be influential?'" says Gordon. "And it became this catchphrase, whereas nobody actually talked about *why* we were influential.

"We were influential," Gordon concludes, "in showing people that you can make any kind of music you want."

# CHAPTER 8

# BUTTHOLE SURFERS

*MELODY MAKER* INTERVIEWER: ARE THE BUTT-
HOLES CLOSER TO GOD OR SATAN?
GIBBY HAYNES: GOD, DEFINITELY. WHY TAKE
A CHANCE?

The Butthole Surfers really seemed like they were from another planet. Upon first hearing, their music inspired the nearly universal reaction, "What the hell *is* this?" It was creepy and dark and ugly and weird. Admitting you liked it would probably lose you some friends. And that was *nothing* compared to their live shows, depraved acid hallucinations of transgression and horror that were often physically dangerous to band and audience alike.

And in a way, the Buttholes really *were* from another planet: Texas, to be exact. The Lone Star State was largely out of the cultural loop, even the underground loop. But that didn't mean it didn't have its fair share of artists, misfits, and rebels; more than most places in the country, bands made their own fun there, and thanks to the vast quantities of sunshine, both liquid and otherwise, the fun wound up being pretty bizarre. By the time the rest of the country found out about what was going on there, the underground scene in Texas had become a weird, inbred mutation.

Although they were galvanized by bands like Black Flag and Public Image, Ltd., the Butthole Surfers weren't punk rock in the generally accepted sense of the term. Their music was too eclectic and acid-fried for that, largely free of the rage and angst that typified the genre. In fact, it had a lot to do with the newly coined genre of performance art that had begun to sweep the art world in the early Eighties. But in terms of doing-it-yourself, being confrontational, and assuming an overall damn-the-torpedoes attitude, they were punk rock 100 percent. It was a completely self-invented, self-willed band — they produced their own records, booked their own tours, designed their own album covers, and staged their own increasingly ornate stage shows.

And yet this enigmatic band would never reveal their motives. Were they out to frighten? Insult? Seduce? Repel? Rebel? Or merely to entertain? It was hard to tell, which may have been precisely the point: the underground had noted the fate of painfully sincere, classically oriented bands like Hüsker Dü and the Replacements and begun championing bands who favored sensationalism over emotion, experimentation over classicism. The Buttholes, always up for a good submersion in the fetid cesspools of the psyche, were a reminder that the underground was still the rightful preserve of some of the culture's most bizarre manifestations.

With vocals hollered incomprehensibly through bullhorns, wild jungle drumming summoning up an unholy blend of violence and lust, gory films, dry-ice foggers, strobes, and a naked dancer short-circuiting every last brain cell of every last member of the audience, the Butthole Surfers were the real deal: while many underground bands tried to express insanity by making meticulously insane music, the Butthole Surfers allowed their genuine perversity to dismantle their music completely.

When the Butthole Surfers played, it was like a twisted circus had come to town. It was a low-budget performance art spectacle that *Spin*'s Dean Kuipers once called "a gypsy commune of killer clowns reveling in their own morbid fascinations." And yet, Kuipers went on to point out, the band was disgusting but not offensive. This was probably because their grotesquerie was at once so inward-looking and yet universal — everyone appreciates a good doody joke.

In 1982 Jeffrey "King" Coffey was "a friendly, goofy, sixteen-year-old kid" playing in a Fort Worth hardcore band called the Hugh Beaumont Experience and publishing a fanzine called *Throbbing Cattle*. In the midst of the infernal Texas summer, he and a buddy took a Greyhound bus down to Austin to check out a crazy band they'd been hearing about.

When they walked into the Ritz club on Austin's rowdy Sixth Street, they were blown away. It wasn't just the fact that the place was packed with punk rockers, which was an amazing thing to see in Texas in 1982 — it was the people onstage. "Here was this band that didn't really look like a punk rock band — they just looked *weird*," says Coffey. "It was more of a performance art kind of thing. And they were playing this weird, hideous music."

The singer had dozens of clothespins stuck in his hair and was wearing nothing but underpants and occasionally making unspeakable noises with a saxophone. The guitarist was rocking back and forth, glaring psychotically at a wall of the club like he was going to kill it. The bass player had his hair in a pompadour the shape of the Alamo. "They just looked like dweebs," Coffey recalls, "but really fuckin' *scary* dweebs."

The singer was Gibson "Gibby" Haynes and he was no stranger to show biz. He happened to be the son of Jerry Haynes, better known as Mr. Peppermint, longtime host of a popular kiddie TV show in the Dallas–Fort Worth area. Although he was a "freak" in high school, the six-foot-four Haynes had also been a top student and star basketball player; on an athletic scholarship to San Antonio's Trinity University, he studied economics, was named "Accountant of the Year," was captain of the basketball team, and graduated with honors. After graduating in 1981, he got a job with the prestigious accounting firm Peat, Marwick and Mitchell and was on track for a lucrative career.

But by then he had hooked up with Trinity art and business student and Frank Zappa fan Paul Leary Walthall, who soon shortened his name to Paul Leary. Leary had grown up on proletarian rock like Creedence Clearwater Revival and his beloved Grand Funk Railroad, but his tastes broadened once he got to art school. Besides punk rock, one of his favorite discoveries was Sixties conceptual artist Yves Klein, who once put on a performance that involved a ten-piece orchestra playing a C-major chord for twenty minutes while three naked women, covered in blue paint, rolled around on a canvas under his direction.

So when Leary saw a tall, crazed-looking guy walking around campus with spiked hair and a black leather jacket, he knew he'd found a kindred spirit. "Gibby was the weirdest guy at school, so we fell in real well," said Leary. "We both liked horrible music."

Leary and Haynes published a fanzine called *Strange V.D.*, which featured the most horrendous medical photographs they could find accompanied by captions describing fictitious diseases like "taco leg" and "pine cone butt." Haynes surreptitiously printed the zine on the photocopier at work but got caught by one of Peat, Marwick's partners after he accidentally left a photograph of some mutilated genitalia in the machine. Shortly thereafter he left the firm.

Haynes headed to Southern California in the summer of '81; having dropped out a semester short of an MBA, Leary joined him in Venice and together they eked out a living making Lee Harvey Oswald T-shirts, pillowcases, and bedspreads and selling them on the beach. "Then we just decided that was too much work and thought maybe music would be easier," said Leary. "So we started a band."

They returned to San Antonio and began playing dire art noise in various underground venues, including their debut at an art gallery. "It was more of a performance piece than a musical piece," Leary said. "It involved lots of stuffed dummies and toasters and Big Mac hamburgers and things. We played music while Gibby ran around with a piece of meat hanging out of his mouth."

The band changed its name for every show — at various times they were called: Ashtray Babyheads, Nine Inch Worm Makes Own Food, Vodka Family Winstons, and the Inalienable Right to Eat Fred Astaire's Asshole — until one fateful night. "We had a song called 'Butthole Surfers,'" says Leary, "and the guy who was introducing us that night forgot what we were called and so he just called us the Butthole Surfers." Since that was their first paying show, they decided to let the name stick. At the time — and for years afterward — one could barely utter the band's name in public, and their name was often abbreviated in advertisements as "B.H. Surfers."

San Antonio didn't exactly warm to the Butthole Surfers. "They hated us there" was Haynes's succinct assessment, and besides, the town was not exactly a rock mecca, so they sold all their possessions, bought a cranky old van, and went back out to California in the summer of '82 with drummer Quinn Matthews and his bassist brother Scott. Almost immediately they got on a bill with the Minutemen, the Descendents, and fellow Texans the Big Boys at the Grandia Room and cut a short demo tape with Spot. But L.A. was crawling with musicians trying to make it, and though most of them were far from well-off, they still had more money than the Butthole Surfers — according to Leary, the penurious band was reduced to scavenging from garbage cans for their dinner.

Still, Leary and Haynes somehow managed to land a show at the Tool and Die in San Francisco. But on the way up from L.A. their van began breaking down; by the time they reached the Bay Bridge into San Francisco, the engine was about to die. They barely made it up the slight incline to the crest of the bridge, coasted down the rest, took the first exit simply to get out of traffic, then limped into town until the engine finally gave out completely — right in front of the Tool and Die. They had just begun unloading their equipment when a woman came out of the club and asked what they were doing. "We told her and she said we weren't playing," Leary says. "And we cried."

It's hard to imagine this band of reprobates weeping, but the situation was desperate. "We were hoping to get like twenty-five bucks or something," Leary says. "We didn't even have gas money to get out or anything." The club eventually took pity on the band and let them play three songs. Luckily, Jello Biafra happened to catch the set and invited the Butthole Surfers to open for the Dead Kennedys at the Whiskey in L.A. on the Fourth of July.

It was a crucial break. The Buttholes schmoozed Biafra assiduously, with Leary's and Haynes's formidable sweet-talking skills very much in play. Knowing Biafra's fascination with obscure regional scenes, they enthusiastically bent his ear about countless Texas bands — none of which really existed. The Buttholes fit in perfectly with Alternative Tentacles' cavalcade of punky weirdos, and Biafra offered to release a record by the band.

They found a place in a grimy, industrial neighborhood at the south end of downtown L.A. Leary's job at a lumberyard lasted only a couple of weeks — "Everybody I was working with was missing hands and fingers and stuff," he says. "I just didn't want to do that." Desperate to avoid a day job, Scott Matthews decided he would try to get on the game show *The Joker's Wild* instead, but after trying for a week or so, he gave up and headed back to Texas along with his brother.

Haynes and Leary soon retreated back to San Antonio ("with our legs between our tails," quips Leary). The band almost immediately re-formed in order to open for the Dead Kennedys in Dallas, but later that night Haynes broke his hand punching Scott Matthews's face. The Matthews brothers soon elected to leave the Butthole Surfers.

King Coffey's band the Hugh Beaumont Experience had been on the bill that night, and he and the Buttholes hit it off. "We kind of shared a similar aesthetic," says Coffey, "as far as being punk rockers but also being into drugs and arty kind of aspects of music."

As it happened, the Hugh Beaumont Experience was about to break up. According to Coffey, a couple of the members found themselves in legal difficulty and left town. So the Buttholes needed a drummer and Coffey needed a band. Neither situation lasted long.

Haynes and Leary liked Coffey's style — he used just two drums and a cymbal and played standing up. "I would just be jumping up and flailing at the drums like this trained monkey," says Coffey. "I guess it was hysterical to look at." In turn, Coffey looked up to the slightly older Haynes and Leary. "They had gone to college and studied art," says Coffey, "and they obviously were *really* intelligent." He joined in the spring of '83.

The band had already started recording their first EP at a San Antonio studio called the Boss. Haynes and Leary knew the owner, who not only let them sleep there at night, but also let them record at bargain-basement rates.

Coffey was the last of several drummers on the recordings and appears on "Barbecue Pope" and the Beefheartian rockabilly of "Wichita Cathedral." The opening number is "The Shah Sleeps in Lee Harvey's Grave," basically frenetic bursts of hardcore noise alternating with Haynes shouting, in his best Yosemite Sam voice, couplets such as "There's a time to shit and a time for God / The last shit I took was pretty fuckin' odd!" Elsewhere are walloping, almost mechanistic grooves topped by Haynes's hysterical shrieking; songs like "The Revenge of Anus Presley" are a somehow blissful wallow in an absurdist, scatological mire.

In fact, the absurdist, scatological part was a major aspect of the band's aesthetic, especially Haynes's, as a 1986 interview in *Brave Ear* fanzine so clearly revealed:

**GIBBY**: Remember the perfect pencil?

**PAUL**: One time he took a shit in the ladies room and he wanted someone to go look at it. He tells me someone drew a pencil in the toilet and I had to check it out.

**GIBBY**: I told him it had to be seen to be believed. A perfectly drawn pencil in the toilet. I mean, how do you get someone to look in the toilet? You got to tell them there's a drawing of a perfect pencil on the bottom.

The resulting *Brown Reason to Live* EP was released on Alternative Tentacles. The notes listed no musicians, and all the band's bio contained were enigmatic jokes like "As their sound developed, so did their ability to judge between right and wrong."

All their recording had been done on credit and the band had run up quite a bill, but Alternative Tentacles didn't have enough money to pay to get the tapes for the band's first album out of hock. So as a stopgap they released the cheaply recorded *Live PCPPEP* EP (a classic Butthole Surfers title: part potty joke and part drug reference) — mostly concert versions of material on the first EP — on Alternative Tentacles. Although they weren't very pleased with the record, the band lived off the exceedingly modest royalties for the better part of a year.

The band now included bassist Bill Jolly and soon added another member. Figuring they could beef up the sound with another drummer, they drafted Austin art-punk musician Teresa Taylor (aka Teresa Nervosa) that fall. She and Coffey bore a strong resemblance, and they often told interviewers they were brother and sister. Visually and sonically, the effect was striking. "It did sound a world better to have communal drums playing," Coffey says, "like a tribe."

In the early Eighties, a sprawling underground tape-swapping network had sprung up as home-duplicated tapes of hardcore bands crisscrossed the country through the mails. The Butthole Surfers' demo was a popular item. After a Dead Kennedys/Necros show in Detroit, Jello Biafra had stayed at the home of Necros bassist Corey Rusk and given him a Butthole Surfers tape. Rusk loved the tape, but it soon got stolen. Some time later, Rusk's friend Ian MacKaye stayed over while on tour with Minor Threat. MacKaye had a tape of some weird new band called . . . the Butthole Surfers. Rusk eagerly made a copy.

The Necros were probably the only punk band in Toledo, Ohio, in the late Seventies. They had hooked up with Tesco Vee and Dave Stimson, who published *Touch & Go* fanzine in Lansing, Michigan. Stimson and Vee liked the band so much that they created Touch & Go Rekords just to release a Necros four-song 45 in the spring of '81. "We didn't even know what a record label was," says Rusk. "It was just something you put on the piece of paper on the vinyl."

They pressed a hundred copies of the Necros record (titles included "Sex Drive" and "Police Brutality") and sold fifty, mostly to friends, when Systematic Distribution in California called. They wanted seventy-five copies. "It blew our mind, like, who are these people that would want seventy-five of these and we don't even know who they are?" says Rusk. The Necros began touring the country, opening for bands like D.O.A., the Misfits, and Black Flag.

Rusk was so excited about the prospect of recording that he started working at a lumberyard his senior year of high school, loading boards on trucks to finance a Necros EP produced by MacKaye later in '81. Touch & Go started releasing records by tasteless provocateurs the Meatmen and noisy hardcore outfit Negative Approach, with Rusk doing sales and distribution while the more outgoing Vee did the promotional work.

Then Vee moved to D.C. in late 1982, leaving the operation to Rusk and Lisa Pfahler, Rusk's girlfriend. The couple ran a strictly bare-bones operation, doing everything themselves just to save money. Rusk even saved up for a reel-to-reel four-track recorder and installed it in his grandmother's basement so he could record bands himself. "We worked just nonstop," says Rusk. "You couldn't have done it if you didn't love it. It was a twenty-four-hour-a-day job."

In January '84 Pfahler and Rusk moved into a house in a down-at-heel neighborhood of Detroit, next door to a Chrysler factory. They ran the label there until the fall of '85, when they moved to an apartment above an all-ages club on Detroit's bustling Michigan Avenue called the Graystone, which they ran.

The Graystone was a logical step: since he was seventeen, Rusk had been promoting all-ages shows by countless bands, including the Minutemen, Black Flag, and the Misfits, and even though he delivered pizzas for a living, he never took a penny for his efforts — all he asked was to get reimbursed for expenses. It was a great deal for the bands — where the local rock club might have paid the bands about $300, they might walk away with nearly triple that at one of Rusk's shows.

P artly because they worked without contracts and partly because they felt the low-powered label couldn't do bigger bands justice, Touch & Go had released only records by friends. But in 1984, after various key distributors picked up several releases, Rusk and Pfahler started to think about approaching bands they didn't know personally. The first was explosive Milwaukee band Die Kreuzen. "We got to know them a little bit at a time from playing with them and talking to them and felt comfortable that they were people we could be friends with," says Rusk. Rusk and Pfahler also dreamed that someday maybe they would put out a record by the Butthole Surfers. And then it happened.

"One day, it was the summer of '84, they called us out of the blue," says Rusk. "I remember being in bed, it was in the morning and Lisa and I were still in bed and the phone rang and it was Gibby from the Buttholes and we were both peeing our pants."

Alternative Tentacles didn't have enough money to release the band's first album, so the Buttholes were interested in talking with Touch & Go even though the label was far from established. But Pfahler and Rusk, who were now married, wanted to meet the band first and see them play so that, as they had with Die Kreuzen, they could see if they could become friends before they became business partners. The Rusks soon set up a show for the Butthole Surfers at a tiny club in nearby Hamtramck and invited the band to stay at their home.

At the time, Haynes and Leary were crashing at friends' places or at the Boss. The whole band was washing dishes for a living. Then they all decided they were better musicians than dishwashers, so why not make Rusk's show the first stop of a national tour?

But their only vehicle was their new bassist (Bill Jolly had left, having "forgotten he was in the band," says Leary) Terence Smart's compact '71 Chevy Nova. Even pulling a U-Haul trailer, how to fit five people, two drum sets, two amps, two guitars, two Radio Shack strobe lights, and a female pit bull named Mark Farner of Grand Funk Railroad? "Well, you saw out the barrier between the trunk and backseat," Leary explains. "You take out the backseat. And you cut a shape out of a piece of plywood to fit in so that three people can lay down horizontally with the dog. It was two people in the front seat and three people and the dog in the trunk."

They stowed their few possessions in a friend's garage, painted the Nova in wild fluorescent colors, with "Ladykiller" scrawled on the sides and "69" on the hood and trunk, installed a roll of barbed wire on the front bumper, painted teeth onto the front grille, and took off for Detroit. "Screw you, Texas," Coffey remembers thinking, "we're never coming home again." It was the beginning of a two-year odyssey.

For five freaks traveling through deepest, darkest redneck country, the trip up to Michigan, as Coffey puts it with some understatement, "was a real eye-opener."

On the way, Taylor and Coffey walked into a fast-food joint outside Dallas. Coffey had a nose ring and an outgrown purple mohawk that was lapsing into dreads; these were the days before MTV had spread the punk look far and wide, and virtually everyone in the restaurant stared at the pair like they were from Mars.

No sooner had they placed their orders than two rednecks walked up to Coffey. One of them said simply, "I don't like it," and punched Coffey in the head, knocking him to the floor. The two men laughed as they walked away. "And everybody in the restaurant was just looking at me like, 'Yeah, you got what you deserved,'" says Coffey. "All I did was order a filet of fish and fries."

After that they made sure to travel in a group if possible. Still, the band started looking freakier and freakier — Leary began sporting a sideways mohawk done in cornrows and dyed hot pink; Taylor let her hair grow into dreads, although she eventually shaved off all the dreads except for three that popped out of her head at random spots, and those were dyed brilliant red. "Our bass player then basically did his hair like Bozo the Clown," says Coffey. "And Gibby had a fucked-up geometric haircut that was just . . . fucked up."

At the Hamtramck show, Rusk decided the Butthole Surfers were one of the most amazing bands he'd ever seen. "They were just outrageous," Rusk recalls. "They were just so over the top. With the two stand-up drummers, they all just seemed like they were out of their minds." Rusk even took a shine to Mark Farner, and the Butthole Surfers had a new label.

For the Butthole Surfers, Touch & Go wasn't only a label. "If we needed a loan, [they] would wire it to us," said Coffey. "If we needed to go into a studio, Touch & Go would write us a check. It was all recoupable, but Corey and Lisa were always there for us." On one tour the state police confiscated the band's van in Massachusetts and deposited the band, their equipment, and Mark Farner in a parking lot by the side of the highway. They called the Rusks, who happened to be in New York, and the couple drove all the way up to Boston to pick up the band and take them to the next show.

And as they spent the next couple of years roaming the country in search of sex, drugs, and shows, the Rusks' place was home base, where they'd sometimes stay for weeks while Haynes plotted the next leg of the tour.

The best Haynes could do was line up perhaps a week of shows, a month in advance. So the band was never sure what the next few months would hold. They'd simply aim for parts of the country where they hadn't been and hope for the best. "We'd pull into a town," Haynes said, "and we didn't know where the clubs were. We'd literally pull over somebody and say, 'Hey, where do the queers hang out? Where's the college area?'"

They lived like gypsies, blowing into town, taking up residence, and (barely) scratching out an existence. "When I think about it now, it's so laughable because we were literally living from hand to mouth," says Coffey. "We had this really cocky attitude, like, 'We're the best band in the world and every other band is so inferior so ha-ha-ha, fuck you, world.' But looking back on it, we were punks living out of a van."

The band usually found places to play, but sometimes their outrageous stage show would burn some bridges. "It seems like everywhere we play we insult people and make them regret having us there," Haynes told *Forced Exposure*.

"Takes 'em about six months to forget about it," Leary chipped in. "Then we come back."

"Where do they get most pissed off?" the interviewer asked.

"Between the ears," replied Haynes.

On their first trip to New York, they played the East Village's notorious Pyramid club. The club's gender-bending regulars stayed out of the small performance space in the back, but a small crowd of underground cognoscenti who gathered for the show saw something they'll never forget. Once the band had cranked up a surging, demonic whirlwind, a scantily clad Haynes skulked onto the stage with his back to the audience, then slowly turned around to reveal his face, which was distorted by a transparent plastic mask of a woman's face. It was an unbelievably simple trick, but the effect was horrific. His hair was full of clothespins, which he shook off in an impressive spray.

"Gibby had star status," says photographer Michael Macioce, who saw that show and soon befriended the band. "All of us that were around him were aware that this was a person who unfolded like a flower — but in his case, the flower that unfolded turned into this . . . *creature*."

In New York they met kindred spirits like Sonic Youth and Live Skull — arty bands who played the punk circuit because there was nowhere else to go. "We kind of understood each other," said Thurston Moore, "because we were doing something apart from the two-second hardcore song."

The few years they had on the hardcore kids made all the difference, and it was tremendously exciting to come across a band that was on the same wavelength. "The Butthole Surfers were the hugest band in the world to us and a lot of people," says Moore. "When the Butthole Surfers came to town, it was this huge event. People don't realize that — a lot of what was going on in the indie scene, a lot of it's been dissipated just by the way things have developed. You don't really remember how heavy certain things were."

But there was a big difference between the cool, self-possessed New Yorkers and the wild-eyed Texans. "Whatever insanities we had, we tried to get out onstage," says Lee Ranaldo. "When we came offstage, we weren't drug-addled freaks. And those guys were. Onstage or offstage, there was no dividing line between the two."

The previous year the band had made a very important New York connection via Mark Kramer, bassist for the mega-bizarro East Village band Shockabilly. Kramer had been on tour with Shockabilly when he happened to use the dressing room toilet in a Dallas nightclub and began to laugh out loud.

"What the fuck is so funny in there?" demanded the club's manager, who had dropped by to leave the band some beer and pretzels.

"Well, there's some graffiti in here that says BUTTHOLE SURFERS: WE SHIT WHERE WE WANT," Kramer replied. (The Buttholes knew their rock history: the graffito was a paraphrase of something Mick Jagger had said when the Stones were busted in the mid-Sixties for urinating behind a gas station.)

The Butthole Surfers, the manager explained, were a bunch of assholes who were a rock band.

Kramer was intrigued. A few nights later Shockabilly played Austin. "And, sure enough, I'm introduced to a guy named Paul, who I'm told is the guitarist for this band of assholes," Kramer recalls. Leary was clearly in sweet-talking mode: "He says he washes dishes at some foul dive in a bad part of town," Kramer continues, "and that the only decent thing

about it is that he can listen to anything he wants to listen to in the
kitchen, and he always listens to Shockabilly."

Early the next year Shockabilly did a brief tour of Texas. The opening
act arrived in a desecrated little Nova, "a car that seemed to have just
been dragged ass-first out of some junkyard," in Kramer's words, contain-
ing "five acid-drenched band members" and a pit bull. "In the eyes of this
dog," Kramer says, "rests all the peace and serenity I would be deprived of
while crossing Texas with these psychopaths."

The next time Kramer met up with the Buttholes, they were all
crashing at the East Village apartment of inveterate indie scenester
and former Touch & Go employee Terry Tolkin. "They had no
money whatsoever, not a single penny amongst them," Kramer recalls.
"Gibby was a wholly unmanageable drunk twenty-four hours a day,
awake or asleep. Coupled with the enormous amounts of acid he was taking, I was constantly in fear for *my* life, *his* life, and the life of anyone we
passed on the street who was unlucky enough to cast him a sidelong
glance. I imagined myself his champion — his protector in the big city. I
imagined that he couldn't possibly get out alive without my stewardship.
But these kinds of people never get a scratch. He'd have walked away
from a fifty-car pileup, I'm sure. He was untouchable. Communicating
with him was not unlike being trapped in a very small cage with a gorilla.

"'What???!!! What the FUCK did you just say to me? You fucking ho-
mosexual!!! You goddamned dick smoker!!! I heard you!!!! I heard what
you said!!! I will fucking cut your throat!!!! Speak, asshole! SPEAK NOW
or be dead in ten seconds!!!!'

"'I didn't say anything, Gibby. I swear it. I mean, I *did* say something
maybe five or ten minutes ago, but you didn't seem to hear me, so I —'

"'What???!!! Don't you ever fucking call me that again or I'll skull-
fuck you with my tiny Texas cock!!! OK??? OK!!!??? Do you fucking understand me now, you little New York City motherfucker?!!! Or do you
wanna die right here and now with your fucking face nailed to my
lap??!!'"

The rest of the band was no less curious. "Looking into King's eyes, I
spied what seemed like a streak of intelligence, but somehow, for some
reason, he could barely speak," Kramer recalls. "Teresa was equally mute
in both words and facial expressions. Yet these two came alive onstage,
side by side, drumming on their feet with a musical precision that, for me,
redefined the term 'reckless.'

"I was constantly in awe of what was happening around me," Kramer says. "I loved these people. They were, well, family."

Every night they parked the Nova, now covered in graffiti, on a dingy street on the Lower East Side, where it acquired a fresh layer of graffiti by morning. Eventually they got rid of it and bought a van from what Leary calls "a gypsy" for a very hard-earned $900. Naturally, it was a lemon — the engine ran on only two cylinders and gobbled gallons of oil.

Now almost penniless, the band practically starved between gigs. Coffey recalls Smart reaching the breaking point one day and suddenly screaming, "I NEED MILK! MY BODY NEEDS MILK!" They explained to him that they only had $5, which had to last for another couple of days — milk for one person was out of the question. "And then he said — quite sanely — 'Why are you doing this? This is insane!'" says Coffey, who replied, "I'm doing it, Terence, because I'd much rather be in New York, playing in a kick-ass band full-time than washing somebody's dishes for a living. This is what I want to do. This is *it*."

But it wasn't easy. "I remember Gibby getting the flu, and six months later he's *still* got the flu," Leary says. "That kind of stuff. It was bad.

"I can't believe we lived through that," Leary continues. "Man, I'll tell you what, I'm glad to be alive — it kind of seemed like we were in a constant state of suicide the whole time. It wasn't like, 'Gee, we're going to become successful and make a lot of money.' It was more like, 'Man, we're going to have a lot of fun before the end comes and we all hit the can.' I didn't think there was any way out."

They were eventually reduced to scavenging for cans and bottles so they could turn them in for the nickel deposit. It was quite a comedown for Haynes, who was all set to be a successful accountant just a couple of years before. One day some prankster ran up and kicked all the bottles out of Haynes's bag. "Gibby and the rest of us were on our knees, scurrying to collect the bottles again," says Coffey. "And I looked in Gibby's eyes, and he was about to cry. It was just so pitiful — this big, strong guy like Gibby being reduced to tears because here he was on the streets of New York, groveling for bottles. But good god, we needed those bottles."

**T**ouch & Go released the band's debut album the final week of 1984. Haynes had wanted to call it *Psychic . . . Powerless* and Leary had wanted *Another Man's Sac.* So they compromised and simply put the two phrases together: *Psychic . . . Powerless . . . Another Man's Sac.* The title is nonsensical, and yet it does conjure up something. "Yeah," Leary agrees in his Texas drawl, "and it's kind of bad."

Like the best Butthole Surfers albums, *Psychic . . . Powerless . . .* makes it impossible to concentrate on anything else while the record is playing. The troglodytic rhythms crowned with tortured guitar, various rude noises, and Haynes's horrific vocals are a grotesque echo of the mediocre music of the Seventies and early Eighties. "We . . . come from the same place of just hating what we heard, and wanting to make something that was even worse that people would hate even more and somehow get paid for it," said Leary. "That's what we were trying to do; make the worst records possible."

This approach extended even to the album cover: a pair of photos from an old book about skin diseases overlaid with crude fluorescent pink, orange, and green doodling courtesy of Haynes and Leary; one horribly disfigured face is made to throw a skeleton-handed peace sign.

The influences were clear: the cacophonous jungle howl of the Birthday Party; the Fall's caustic chants; Pere Ubu's art-punk; the synthetic mystique of the Residents; the eerie, bleak side of Public Image, Ltd.; and the turgid, rambling assault of Flipper. But *Psychic . . . Powerless . . .* found the band synthesizing it all into a singular, relentlessly squalid vision. On the lumbering "Lady Sniff," Leary's elemental twang momentarily parts for the sounds of farting, vomiting, bird calls, belching, Japanese television, and hawking up phlegm. "Pass me some of that dumb-ass over there, hey boy, I tell ya," Haynes hollers, redneck-style.

**H**aynes had taken to making his stage entrance with a dummy duct-taped to his body so it looked like he was dancing with it — then he'd tear it off and start attacking it. He'd sing through a megaphone, an idea that was stolen ad infinitum over the next ten years. Often he'd wear several layers of dresses and peel them off one by one until by the end of the show he was down to his skivvies. He'd stuff his clothes with condoms filled with fake blood so that when he'd fall on the floor, he'd turn into a gory mess; he'd hurl reams of photocopied pictures of cockroaches into the crowd; he'd pour a flammable liquid into an inverted cymbal, then whack it, sending up a geyser of flame; he'd usually set his hands on fire, too. There was the time he made his entrance through a hole he'd cut in a mattress covered in fake blood. Often the whole band would rip apart stuffed animals onstage, like a frenzied pack of psychotic cannibals. "It was just madness," says Coffey. "It was just the more the merrier."

Once the band began to make a little more money, the special effects began to get fancier. It all began when Coffey joined the band — he had put a strobe light under his clear plastic drum, lighting it up brilliantly. A few months later the band met a guy with a bunch of stolen strobes, and they got several thousand dollars' worth of lights for a few hundred bucks. The show snowballed from there. "It just seemed like what we wanted out of a rock show ourselves, so we were willing to try to deliver it," says Leary.

The visual chatter and tandem thunder of two stand-up drummers flailing at their instruments added yet more to the chaos, and the strobe lights flashed almost constantly, giving the proceedings the air of a traumatic nightmare. "It was just a mind-fuck of a show," says Coffey. "In some ways it was like the Mickey Rooney–Judy Garland movies, like, 'Hey, kids, let's put on a show!' But that got horribly confused in the land of psychedelics and punk rock."

The Buttholes were hardcore, but in the original sense — being hardcore wasn't necessarily about playing really fast or having militant lyrics. It was about being extreme. "We'd try anything to get attention," says Coffey. "But it wasn't attention for attention's sake; we were trying anything that would be as much of a spectacle as humanly possible." The stage show grew gradually until one day they realized that all the props and special effects took up more space in the van than the instruments.


**T**hey had recorded most of a second album in San Antonio before they set off for Detroit and parts unknown, then carried the tapes around the country for months, recording and mixing tracks whenever they could scrape up enough money.

The back cover was a photograph of the straining crotch of a female bodybuilder in a thong bikini, her inner thighs bulging with veins. As usual, the artwork bore no credits or pictures of the band, which they felt would only distract from the purity of the package. The album's title — *Rembrandt Pussyhorse* — stemmed from Haynes's and Leary's penchant for stringing together three-word nonsense phrases (a device they'd use on at least two more records). Even the rest of the band didn't understand what it meant. "It's a Gib thing," Coffey says with a shrug.

The opening dirge "Creep in the Cellar" is seemingly a paean from

Haynes to his own darkest impulses. "There's a creep in the cellar that I'm gonna let in," Haynes intones in slow-motion singsong, "and he really freaks me out when he peels off his skin." During playback of the song's rough tracks, the sound of a backward fiddle appeared out of nowhere. It turned out that a country band hadn't paid their bill, so the studio simply recorded over their multitrack tape. Amazingly, the manic sawing fit the Buttholes track perfectly. "By the time we figured out how to turn it off," says Leary, "we didn't *want* to turn it off."

With goth, industrial, and even techno overtones, the music was not punk in the already established sense; several songs eschewed punk's typical 4/4 time and were in 6/8, like sea chanteys from hell. The tracks were crammed with nearly subliminal sounds and low-rent versions of the high-tech digital effects — stuttering quasi-scratch tricks; huge, booming drums; pitch shifting — then ruling the Top 40 and dance charts. A prime example was the bizarre, almost cubist deconstruction of the Guess Who's 1970 hit "American Woman," a song that managed to be both misogynistic and antiwar.

Haynes barely sang at all, preferring instead to wail, mutter, howl, and shriek, funneling it through various electronic devices. When an interviewer asked why Haynes electronically manipulated his voice so much, Leary explained, "It's just because, y'know, he's got knobs and he can do it. It's like, why does a dog lick its balls?" Haynes added, with alarming plausibility, "It's probably just my need to express my multiple personalities."

There was a very creepy Gibby on "Perry" — the *Perry Mason* theme recast as nightmarish carnival music while Haynes, ad-libbing in a repulsively haughty English accent, encapsulates the band's raison d'être: "It's about coming of age, it's about learning how to do it, it's about learning how to experience things the way they ought to be experienced, it's about growing up, it's about licking the shit off the floors, it's about doing the things that you ought to do. It's about being a Butthole Surfer."

In a *Playboy* review of the album, ex-Monkee Mickey Dolenz said he'd love to direct a Butthole Surfers video. Sadly, they failed to call his bluff. In his *Seattle Rocket* "Sub Pop" column, Bruce Pavitt called *Rembrandt Pussyhorse* "the coolest record ever made. This unbridled, surreal burst of imagination is enough to erase years of indoctrination by schools and television viewing. It's finally OK to do whatever the fuck you want. We can only go up from here."

**T**he band wandered all over the country — Chicago, Detroit (where "people would throw animal parts at us," Leary says. "It was a real cool town for us"), Seattle (where they stayed for a month and made a big impact on local musicians such as future Soundgarden guitarist Kim Thayil), Atlanta, New Orleans — winding up in San Francisco in the summer of '85.

Once they'd grown tired of San Francisco, the band wondered, Where to next? They were all tripping one day when someone jokingly suggested moving to R.E.M.'s home base of Athens, Georgia (which also happened to have been a notorious drug mecca). "We thought it would be a trip to, for no apparent reason other than it seemed funny, move to Athens," says Coffey. "And stalk R.E.M."

They wound up a few miles outside of Athens, in tiny Winterville, where they stayed about seven months, working up new material and playing gigs. And stalking R.E.M.

Their first night there, Coffey spotted R.E.M.'s Mike Mills at a club and invited him to a barbecue in Winterville. Mills smoothly put him off by suggesting that Coffey contact R.E.M.'s management with the particulars, which Coffey dutifully did. "And of course the next day was spent waiting for Mike Mills to show up," says Coffey. Not surprisingly, Mills never came.

The Butthole Surfers' obsession with a pop band like R.E.M. is a bit surprising. "I think we were fascinated by the amount of fame they were getting," says Coffey. "And they were easy subjects for ridicule. But by the same token, we also had a certain fondness for some of their songs, like their radio hit songs. We'd say, 'Aw, this is horrible!' And then of course it would be in our heads for two weeks." (By 1987 they often ended shows with a demonic version of R.E.M.'s hit "One I Love.")

And of course, R.E.M. were already wealthy men by this time, unlike the Butthole Surfers. "I think we were jealous of them," Coffey says. "Hell *yeah*," Leary agrees. "Jealous as shit."

In Georgia their rickety van called it quits in spectacular fashion — as Haynes and Leary were pulling into a parking lot, the engine started smoking and quickly burst into flame. The two men bailed out of the van, Mark Farner in hand, and watched it burn.

**A**fter an Atlanta show that August, they stayed at the home of a friend whose younger sibling knew Amy Carter, daughter of ex-President Jimmy Carter. Amy happened to be over at the house that night, but she avoided the unsavory activities in the living room and stayed in her friend's bedroom, waiting for her parents, who were due to pick her up at 4:00 A.M. Naturally, the Buttholes were excited to witness the arrival of the former president. At about 3:30 Amy came out and deposited her suitcase in the living room, briefly introduced herself, smiled, and retreated back to the bedroom.

Haynes then took the opportunity to touch his penis to the suitcase.

At 3:45 the house was quickly surrounded by Secret Service cars, almost as if a raid were about to occur. Naturally, the Buttholes, high as kites, got a bit nervous. But then at 4 A.M. sharp, a black limousine pulled up, and Amy emerged from the bedroom and went out the door carrying her desecrated suitcase. Her parents lingered in the carport area as some excited and very stoned Butthole Surfers peeked out from the curtains, trying not to scream in disbelief.

And then it happened: former United States president James Earl Carter picked up the suitcase to which Butthole Surfers singer Gibson Jerome Haynes had applied his genitals. The president then put the suitcase in the trunk, got in the car, and they sped off into the humid Georgia night.


I t was time to hit the road again, and by the time the tour reached New Orleans, Terence Smart had fallen in love with the Buttholes' old friend Michiko Sakai and wanted to leave the band and be with her instead. "Poor Terence," says Leary. "One night we were sleeping on some wretched floor of a punk rock dive in Atlanta, Georgia, and he woke up and he just couldn't take it anymore. He was screaming, 'WHY? WHY ARE YOU DOING THIS?' We were like, 'Well, it's fun [laughs].' He was out of there within five minutes. We never saw him for a long time." (Smart and Sakai eventually married and had a son named Maxwell.)

Touch & Go recommended a nineteen-year-old Canadian named Trevor Malcolm to replace Smart. Malcolm came down to Winterville to join the band, sight unseen, carrying a tuba stolen from his former high school. The instrument took up a lot of space in the van, but Malcolm insisted on carrying it everywhere; but, while the Buttholes were on a Canadian tour, a local paper ran a picture of him playing the tuba. No one was happier than Leary when Malcolm's old school waited for the band to get to Windsor and confiscated the instrument.

**T**he band was beginning to see the results of all the touring. Word was spreading through fanzines and word of mouth that the Butthole Surfers were a great live band. And although the band's original following consisted of punks and freaks, a more chin-stroking, collegiate crowd began to filter in. "While our records might have been weak," says Coffey, "we had a reputation of being a good freak show to check out."

By now the Buttholes' show featured a grotesque assortment of films projected on a backdrop behind the band. Among the filmic arsenal: autopsies, atomic explosions, accident scenes, facial plastic surgery, meat-processing procedures, people having epileptic seizures, scare-tactic driver's education films, etc. "We tried to get *Operation Dry Pants*," says Leary, still ruing the missed opportunity, "which is about toilet training of Down's syndrome [kids]."

At first Taylor, a media major at the University of Texas, borrowed films from the school's vast visual library; later, as their cinematic appetites grew more specialized, a certain "Dr. Haynes from the University of Texas" would order films from medical catalogs. And very soon, just as people would offer drugs to the famously pixilated band, others would offer films. The most infamous depicted a man undergoing penile reconstruction after a farm accident. "I recall the day that arrived in the mail," says Coffey. "We screened it for the first time and we were just screaming in complete horror." Sometimes they ran it backwards.

"It just seemed funny," Leary says of the more ghastly aspects of the band's stage show. "And fun. I mean, rock music's got to be something that your mom would hate — if you want it to be really satisfying. We made music that moms would really hate, shows included — like nudity and violence and belching flames and smoke and hideous, loud, damaging music."

The Butthole Surfers' shows seemed almost intentionally designed to freak out not just moms but the many audience members who were tripping. The music was nightmarish and violent; the films were horrific. "I always thought we'd be a *terrible* band to take acid to," says Coffey, "just a really bad, bad idea." If the projectionist was really on top of it, he or she could focus the heinous imagery on the periodic walls of smoke that would come spilling off the stage. "And it makes this cool effect," says Leary, "where you can see this image come blasting out at you — *in focus.*"

"The full-on shows would make people puke and scream and run out, that kind of thing," Taylor said. "It was what we'd always wanted."

Actually, not all the films were so shocking — they'd often do a split screen with undersea footage, nature scenes, or even a treasured color negative of a *Charlie's Angels* episode. The contrast was Haynes's idea. "It was a total mixture of good and bad images coming at you, so it was more of an assault that way, your mind can't quite digest it," says Coffey. "It's not completely good *or* bad — it's *both*."

Still, the gross-out footage is what really embodied the band's aesthetic. "Listen, man, one has no choice but to laugh in the face of terror," Haynes explained. "I think probably most airline pilots, when they see the ground coming at them, just before they hit, go, 'Oh my god, we're in trouble! Ha-ha-ha!'"

The hardworking Leary taught himself how to use an old vacuum-tube eight-track recorder and started in on their next album. "They were kitchen recordings," Coffey said, "done right next to the fryer and the bacon grease." Leary acted as his own apprentice, learning from his mistakes, although the beauty of Butthole Surfers records was that the mistakes often became the keepers.

They recorded half of the four-song *Cream Corn from the Socket of Davis* EP in Winterville. "Comb" opens with some all too realistic vomiting sounds, followed by Haynes's heavily distorted voice, like a short-circuiting fifty-foot robot, splattering a sonic wasteland of nuclear guitar noise and Godzilla-stomp drums. The EP also features "Moving to Florida," in which Haynes plays a crazy old coot intent on nuking the Sunshine State. "I'm going to hold time hostage down in Florida, child," Haynes drawls in an extended monologue. "I'm going to explode the whole town of Tampa Bay."

Leary explains the EP's enigmatic title by revealing that originally the cover art was to feature a depiction of Sammy Davis Jr., who had a glass eye, with creamed corn spilling out of his eyeball socket. "But it was just too brutal," Leary says.

With *Cream Corn* and beyond, the Butthole Surfers were kicking over a rock and were looking at all the stuff that squirmed around underneath: incest and bad trips and corrupt businessmen and schizo rednecks and Bible thumpers and all kinds of bad American craziness. It was on very much the same wavelength as David Lynch's masterpiece *Blue Velvet*, which came out the following year. But in exploring that dark, forbidden territory, they were also welcoming it and even partaking in it. And the pressure was always on to up the ante, to bring some-

thing even more unpleasant into the circus, if only to keep things interesting.

**M**alcolm quit the band in Winterville. He was miserable, partly
since when the band drew lots for which room they'd get, he
drew the worst lot and wound up in the basement with the washing machine. At night he would watch in horror as blue bolts of electric-
ity shot across the room. "It was stressful — he didn't know anybody there
and he was in this tiny, tiny room that's emitting sparks and playing with
the Butthole Surfers," says Coffey. "You know, I'd split, too."

A temporary bassist played a Midwest tour, but he didn't want to go
on the upcoming European tour, so the band had to think fast. They
called Kramer, their New York friend. "Kramer, you better not have been
lying when you said you wanted to play with us worse than you wanted to
fuck your little sister," Leary said on the phone, " 'cause we need you
bad."

Kramer was on his way.

**O**nce, they had pulled up to the City Gardens club in Trenton,
New Jersey, and were told their show had been canceled in favor
of the Replacements. ("We were replaced by the Replacements!"
Coffey notes.) But the Buttholes pleaded poverty and successfully lob-
bied to open the show as Playtex Butt Agamemnons. The Buttholes'
chemical excesses unnerved even the bibulous Replacements. "I remember them showing up and asking me if I knew where they could find
some acid," recalls Replacements roadie Bill Sullivan. "They were really
insane then. They actually scared *us*. They scared the *hell* out of us."

Most people were sure the band tripped for every show. "Not *every*
show," Coffey clarifies. "Personally, I can't play drums on acid. The one
time I did, I got a little too lost in the ride cymbal."

But pot was a necessity for most of the band. And when they couldn't
get it, which often happened in Europe, there was hell to pay. "We would
just drink more to compensate and [the band] would get pissed off because there was no pot around and we would have literally violent shows
where people would get punched out," Coffey says. "We would piss on
and punch out anybody else in our path."

For a bunch of Texans who had never been out of the country, Europe was "like going to the moon," Leary says. "Those people are differ-

ent over there. It really inspires you to kick it up extra hard. It's an alien environment and they start to piss you off after a while." It's an unusual comment considering that Europe is renowned for paying bands better, putting them up in hotels, and even feeding them. "They feed you a load of crap is what they do," Leary scoffs. "They get you a cake and they smile and they're sticking something else up your ass at the same time. I'm telling you, you don't want to get involved with those Germans over there. They'll take you to town."

The night of their appearance at the huge Pandora's Box festival in the Netherlands, Kramer went to fetch Haynes for sound check. "It is firstly most important to state that, on this night, Gibby had eaten an entire handful of four-way acid tabs and drank an entire bottle of Jim Beam before the sound check had even begun," Kramer notes.

Leary was furious at Haynes for getting wasted for such an important show. "Fuck that stupid-ass motherfucker," he snarled to Kramer. "I hate this fucking band. I swear to fucking Christ on a stick, I hate this fucking band more than I hate myself. And that's a lot. I don't even care if we ever play again. If you can't find him, fuck it. FUCK IT!!!!" With that, he began smashing a couple of guitars with his bare fists.

The festival featured several stages, and Kramer eventually found Haynes at a Nick Cave and the Bad Seeds show. As Kramer tells it, Haynes was completely naked, repeatedly fighting his way onto the stage and charging at Cave as hulking security guards punched and kicked him off the ten-foot-high stage and back into the audience, where he would remain for a few seconds before trying to claw his way back onstage again. Finally, guitarist Blixa Bargeld came forward and kicked Haynes in the groin with a pointed German boot. This time Haynes did not get up.

Kramer pushed his way through the crowd to come to the aid of his bandmate, only to find him lying unconscious. "I bend over to see if he is still alive, but he seems not to be breathing," Kramer says. "I poke him in the shoulder. Suddenly, like a volcano, he bursts to life and swirls his fists in every direction, clipping me but good, along with a few innocent girls, and drawing the ire of their boyfriends and the enraged security guards, who are now motivated to leave Mr. Cave to his own devices, descend the stage, and join the boyfriends in administering a thorough and none-too-subtle beating upon Gibby's face, head, and shoulders, until he is once again unconscious on the floor."

Or so it seemed. Actually, Haynes was only pretending he'd been knocked out, and as the hired thugs walked away, he rose to his feet and began screaming at them, "DUTCH FAGGOTS!!! GODDAMN

FUCKING DUTCH FAGGOTS!!! A WHOLE FUCKING COUN-
TRY FILLED WITH NOTHING BUT FUCKING TURD BUR-
GLING FAGGOTS!!!! I FUCK YOUR ASS IN HEAVEN AND
HELL!!!!! FUUUUUUUCK YOOOOOOOOU!!"

"The ensuing chase and capture was the stuff dreams are made of,"
Kramer says. "Stark naked like the day he was born, beaten, bruised,
bloody, and tripping, this icon of modern music ran like Jesse Owens
through the entire complex, down the halls, up the stairs, grabbing beer
bottles from people's hands as he went and throwing them down on the
concertgoers below. A hail of beer cans, bottles, and miscellaneous
garbage rained down upon the Dutch persons as I finally caught up with
Gibby just as a throng of the biggest security guards I had ever seen
caught up with him, too.

"At this time there were perhaps twenty hands upon him, holding
him down, and although Gibby *is* completely crazy, he is *not* stupid. 'I'M
SORRY!!!! I'M FUCKING SORRY!!!! PLEASE DON'T BEAT ME
ANYMORE! I HAVE A BRAIN TUMOR!!! I CAN'T HELP THE WAY
I AM!!!! PLEASE DON'T HIT ME AGAIN!!! IT'S AGAINST MY RE-
LIGION!!!!'"

Haynes then made a successful run for the dressing room and
slammed the door behind him. Kramer could hear Leary and Haynes
screaming at each other inside, and when he finally worked up the courage
to open the door, he found the two of them smashing guitars, bottles, and
chairs in what Kramer calls "the most potent example of bad behavior I
have ever seen. To this day, more than fifteen years later, I have no more
vivid memory of the effect a life in music can have on a human being."

Moments later a man entered the dressing room and asked if he
could borrow a guitar. "BORROW A GUITAR??!!! WELL, WHO THE
FUCK ARE YOU???!!!" Haynes screamed, eyes flashing in delirious an-
ticipation of forthcoming violence. But the man was totally unfazed.

"I'm Alex Chilton," the man answered calmly.

Haynes was flabbergasted. After a long pause, he methodically
opened the remaining guitar cases one by one and gestured at them as if
to say, "Take anything you want."

Just before they went onstage, Haynes chugged an entire bottle of red
wine; moments into the set he dived straight into the horrified crowd,
which parted like the Red Sea. Haynes knocked himself unconscious on
the floor, to warm applause from the theater's security team. "I look down
at Gibby," recalls Kramer. "He tries to move, but then collapses as vomit
begins pouring from his mouth."

After the gig Haynes was irate about having been unconscious for most of the show and insisted on getting paid within five minutes or he'd be "taking it out on your Dutch testicles!" Haynes snatched up the fistfuls of guilders and stuffed them in a pair of pants in his guitar case, but almost immediately forgot that he had been paid and went on yet another rampage, streaking naked through the festival complex and screaming that he had been ripped off.

"FUCKING DUTCH FAGGOTS!!! A WHOLE FUCKING COUNTRY OF COCK-SUCKING QUEENS!!!! YOU FUCKING BEAT ME UP AND THEN YOU RIP US OFF!!!! WHICH ONE OF YOU FAGGOTS STOLE OUR MONEY??!!!! FUCKING DUTCH FAGGOTS!!!!"

Yet another chase scene ensued, and yet another pack of Dutch goons wrestled Haynes to the ground, and yet again he profusely apologized. "After which he is released once again," Kramer says, "and once again dashes through the halls screaming obscenities while grabbing beer bottles from people's hands as he runs and hurling them against the brick wall."

"Those fuckin' Dutch," Leary explains, "they kind of get you pissed off after a while, man."

"We thought we had just ruined our careers by botching this show," Coffey says. "Of course, the Dutch loved it — 'The mayhem it is beautiful, it is wonderful, every song erupted into chaos!'" The next day the local paper ran an article about how the Butthole Surfers were the sensation of the festival. "So of course, every time when we came back after that and just played music, people would be horribly disappointed," says Coffey. "'[In Dutch accent] How come you do not beat up people?'"


Kramer's now defunct band Shockabilly was far more popular in Europe than the Butthole Surfers, and several unscrupulous promoters simply billed the band as Shockabilly, angering audiences who had paid their money to see another band. One such show was a graduation party for engineering students in Stavanger, Norway. In protest, Leary walked onstage with his pants around his ankles. The promoter nervously asked Kramer if he would mind asking Leary to pull up his pants, but Kramer pretended to misunderstand. "Get up and dance now?" he hollered back. "Of course you can get up and dance! Come on up!"

This little game went on until the police showed up, at which time Leary gingerly pulled up his pants and ran into the dressing room, locking the door behind him. "As I tried to jimmy the door open, I could hear Paul on the other side piling what sounded like guitar cases against the door," says Kramer. Haynes managed to talk the police into leaving the scene, and after much coaxing, Leary emerged.

Meanwhile, "the crowd of all these Aha-looking types were staring at us with crossed arms," says Coffey. "When it became obvious that the crowd were just assholes, Gibby rightfully snapped, 'Fuck you, guys,' and insisted that everybody leave the room."

Haynes proceeded to verbally and physically abuse the audience, heaving beer bottles at the walls until he forced literally everybody but the band out of the club. The band resumed playing to the now empty house. People started to creep back into the room, but Haynes bullied them right back out again. And then the band played some more. "That was pretty fun," Coffey says, smiling at the fond memory, "literally forcing people out of the room during a show."

T hey then began a U.S. tour in November, but Kramer quickly fell very ill from food poisoning, perhaps exacerbated by the stress of knowing that the driver of the van they all crammed into on those late night after-show drives was invariably tripping his brains out. Jeff Pinkus replaced him in early '86.

Finally bored with the claustrophobic Athens scene, they left Winterville and resumed their peripatetic existence.

Taylor quit in December, done in by the stresses of being in the band, and they drafted a new drummer, a woman named Cabbage, "who really couldn't play the drums at all," says Leary. "She had a place to practice, though." They rehearsed in Cabbage's warehouse space in a section of downtown Atlanta that resembled a war zone; the band stayed at her house, too.

Cabbage introduced the band to her friend Kathleen Lynch, who made her debut at one of the Butthole Surfers' most infamous shows.

In early '86 they drove from Los Angeles all the way to New York just to play two lucrative weekend shows at the Danceteria club, only to arrive to find that the second night had been canceled. The band was livid; Haynes got quite drunk just before show time. "During that show it was just complete bedlam," says Leary, a man who knows from bedlam.

After only a song or two, Haynes picked up a beer bottle and viciously smashed Leary over the head with it. Leary's eyes rolled back in his head as he crumpled to the floor. Then he quickly got up and resumed playing. It was a stunt bottle, made out of sugar. Then Haynes picked up a real bottle and heaved it the length of the room, where it exploded above the exit sign. Soon Haynes had set fire to a pile of trash in the middle of the stage. "And you're really thinking, 'Should I get out of here?'" says Michael Macioce. "That was the type of feeling you had — you were *in danger* at one of their shows."

Then Lynch jumped onto the stage from the audience and began dancing. Macioce then left — it was about three in the morning by this point — but he called his friend Kramer the next day to see how the rest of the gig had gone. "That girl, she pulled down her pants and Gibby started sticking his thumb up her ass!" Kramer told Macioce. He was fucking her with his thumb just back and forth and this went on for like a half hour or forty-five minutes, just like that!"

And that was only the beginning. The band had played only five shambolic songs before Leary leaned his guitar against his amplifier, producing ear-splitting feedback; the strobes were flickering, sirens were flashing, the films were rolling, and through the dry-ice fog a couple of open fires burned brightly.

"Gibby filled up a plastic whiffleball bat full of urine — he managed to pee in the little hole in the end of the bat," says Leary, "and made this 'piss wand.'" Haynes then began swinging the bat, spraying urine all over the crowd. But it didn't stop there — Lynch, now completely naked, lay down on the stage and Haynes, in Leary's words, started "mounting" her. Later Leary saw video footage of the scene. "Her legs are up in the air and there's Gibby's pumping butt in the strobe lights and the smoke," says Leary, chuckling. "It's really fuckin' hideous, man."

In the midst of the chaos, Leary went around discreetly poking screwdriver holes in every PA and monitor speaker in the place.

After the show there was a tense confrontation between the Danceteria management and the band. The Buttholes got paid, but they literally walked out of the place backward as the club's hired goons not so subtly showed them the door. "You'll never play New York again!" the club's manager screamed after them. "And we were playing at CBGB within two weeks," Leary crows, *"for more money!"*

Afterward the band invited Lynch to become a part of the stage show; she wound up dancing with the Butthole Surfers for years. By the Buttholes' next New York visit, she'd become an integral part of the show. "She had a shaved head . . . her body was painted, the show was just wild," remembers Kim Gordon. "Gibby was swinging her between his legs and blowing fire. It was, like, the most insane thing."

Gordon had attended the show with her bandmate Steve Shelley. "I remember standing kind of toward the back with Steve, and somehow he ended up getting his glasses broken," says Gordon. "I don't know exactly what happened. . . ."

Lynch quickly became nicknamed "Tah-dah, the Shit Lady." According to Leary, the story around was: "She got a job in New York City at some sort of Sex World place, and the first night on the job they were telling her the routine, like, 'OK, if a guy looks at you, you take off your clothes and you do this and do that.' So she gets in there and the first thing she does is bend over and sprays a wall of diarrhea. And then she stands up and goes, 'Tah-dah!' So everybody is running out screaming. Of course, they didn't fire her — the next night they were out there advertising, 'We got black pussy, we got white pussy, and we got the Shit Lady!' She became a featured attraction."

Lynch was never a formal member of the Butthole Surfers, though. "We would begin a tour and out of nowhere Kathleen would show up," says Coffey. "And then kind of disappear again. She was like the wind."

Nobody in the band really had a conversation with Lynch until years after she left — in fact, she didn't speak for an entire year, a practice Coffey believes had a spiritual basis, like fasting. The silence posed constant practical problems, however, like the time they stopped at a roadside restaurant in Louisiana. "Kathleen jumps out of the van and is the first one to rush into the restaurant," Coffey recalls, "and greets the hostess by kind of half squatting and making gesturing motions toward her crotch and somehow getting across, 'I need to pee, where is the bathroom?'" The hostess waved vaguely toward the bathrooms, with one eye on the band of freaks who had just walked in the door.

"She loved the human body, smells of the human body, dirty socks, urine, things of the body were really beautiful to her, BO was beautiful, and we had a hard time making her bathe," Taylor recalled. "I remember once we pretty much had to hold her down and do her laundry and she was yelling, 'No, no!'"

The live show was reaching new heights. That March at San Francisco's I-Beam, Leary stripped naked and dived into the crowd while Haynes leaped on Lynch and the two rolled around the stage like fighting cats, knocking equipment and mike stands around the stage like bowling pins. The audience looked on, aghast. By the end Haynes was alone onstage howling, "No! No! No!" like a wounded animal through

the megaphone and bashing a flaming cymbal, sending up towering mushroom clouds of fire. Then a stuffed lion dropped onto the stage, and the rest of the band madly tore it to bits, hurling the stuffing into the crowd.

That fall Rusk booked the Butthole Surfers for Halloween weekend at the Graystone, with Big Black and Scratch Acid opening one night and Die Kreuzen and Killdozer opening the next. All five bands stayed at the Rusks' apartment, and after both shows they went up to the building's big, flat roof and barbecued and set off fireworks all night, as was the Graystone tradition. Another tradition was watching the nightlife on the street below. There was a redneck bar on one corner and a lesbian bar on the other. "And when the bars would let out at night," says Rusk, "we'd all get up on the roof and watch the lesbians beat up the rednecks."

The second night of the Butthole Surfers' visit, the bands partied on the roof as usual. Then they all watched as a convenience store across the street went up in flames. "And as soon as the fire trucks pulled away, Gibby and Paul said, 'Let's go!'" says Steve Albini, then of Big Black. "And they bolted down the stairs, out the front door, ran across the street, and looted this liquor store. They came back with six smoky, damp cases of beer."

nfortunately, Cabbage never improved her percussive skills. "We figured she'd catch on eventually — just a little bit of rhythm is all it takes," says Leary. "And she just got worse and worse. We finally reduced her to one drum and then with no microphone at all." The band knew she came from Tennessee, so when they passed through there in April '86, "We kind of dropped her at her family's place," says Coffey, "and said, 'See ya!'"

In the fall of '86, they settled in Austin. In the Sixties Austin hosted a thriving hippie scene and became known as a home for renegade music of all kinds: psychedelic pioneers the 13th Floor Elevators, Janis Joplin and the Crazy World of Arthur Brown, whose titular singer sported Day-Glo robes and face paint and highlighted performances by shooting flames from his headpiece. Thanks to locals like Waylon Jennings and Willie Nelson, the town was also the headquarters for country music's famed "outlaw" movement. It was a fitting home base for the Butthole Surfers.

The Buttholes moved into a rental home in a no-man's-land just off the highway at what was then the northern edge of Austin. They painted the walls silver and slept on pieces of plywood suspended from the ceiling. They'd also gotten hold of a device that shot foam insulation between walls, and the house was filled with sculptures they'd made with the machine. Much of the house became a recording studio; when the parts for a new mixing board came, everyone smoked lots of pot and sat around soldering hundreds of connections.

The band missed Taylor and asked her back. Since the band was determined not to tour so much anymore, she accepted and moved into the house; they finished their third album there.

According to Pinkus, one of the advantages of recording the album at home was that "we could take hour-long breaks to do bong hits," and there was more than just a bit of stoner humor in the statement — not paying for recording time meant they could work at a more relaxed pace and really explore the possibilities of the studio. This was something most bands on indie labels couldn't afford to do.

Unlimited studio access allowed the Butthole Surfers to confront an interesting problem — how to replicate the polymorphous perversity of their performances on record. They couldn't include a strobe light and a smoke machine with every record, so they threw in all the studio tricks they could muster in a vain but admirable effort to make a sonic analogue of their live show.

But Leary has a low opinion of the music. "I always thought we were the band without talent at all — it's just all a bunch of schlock," he says. "God, it's music to drool into a bucket to." So perhaps the overwhelming studio gimmickry and the riotous showmanship were just a way of making up for lackluster music? "Yeah," Leary says with a little laugh. "That's probably one reason." Another reason for the outrageous shows was to justify the band's large performance fee. "We wanted to be able to charge a lot of money for the tickets," Leary says, "so we felt obliged to kind of give something back."

Despite the nearly universal disapproval of the indie community, the Buttholes resolutely refused to feel bad about wanting to make money. "Whatever weed we were smoking, we wanted it to be more plentiful and of better quality," says Leary. "And we wanted better-quality food, we wanted better quality accommodations, we wanted better-quality vehicles to travel around in, we wanted better equipment to play on, and all those wants far outstripped what we were bringing in."

The individual members didn't directly make any money from the band. Instead, Haynes, the former accountant, controlled the funds and disbursed them as necessary. "There was so little resources that all the money was in one pocket and we all stuck together," says Leary. "If one person bought sunglasses, all five of us bought sunglasses; if one person bought shoes, we all bought shoes. We were just never apart, not for any meals, not anything. We were just always together. If we got a motel room, we all stayed in the same room."

Many shows ended with Haynes walking offstage with the petite Taylor tucked under his arm, while she continued banging a drum. It almost looked like something a dad would do. And perhaps the Butthole Surfers were like a family — or maybe more like a cult — with Leary and Haynes as the dysfunctional parents, Taylor and Coffey as the quiet, odd twins, and whoever was playing bass as the sullen teen who inevitably ran away.

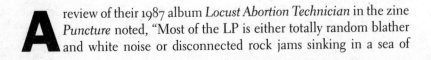 review of their 1987 album *Locust Abortion Technician* in the zine *Puncture* noted, "Most of the LP is either totally random blather and white noise or disconnected rock jams sinking in a sea of

blood and puke." And yet, the review continued, "they manage to exude brilliance."

"Sweat Loaf" was a rewrite of Black Sabbath's ganja anthem "Sweet Leaf" and contains yet another potential band motto: "It's better to regret something you *have* done than to regret something you *haven't* done." "U.S.S.A." surely features some of the most hideous sounds ever recorded — the rhythm track sounds like an idling garbage truck as Leary's guitar imitates a dying cow, while Haynes desperately shrieks "U.S.S.A." over and over . . . and over and over. "The O-Men," with its relentless, hyperactive pounding and satanic vocal prefigures the advent of industrial speed-metal by several years; on "Kuntz" the band electronically manipulates a Thai pop recording so that the singer repeatedly says a certain naughty word.

"Twenty Two, Going on Twenty Three" features a tape of an actual radio call-in show in which a woman described being sexually assaulted — it's a terrifying listen, although as it turns out, the woman was a pathological liar who called the show every night.

**A**fter two albums and three EPs, by early '87 the band was earning a decent living from royalties and touring, but they continually reinvested the money in their studio and toys for the live show. They could now command up to $6,000 a show, an astronomical amount for a band on an indie label. But for many months the road-weary Buttholes restricted their live shows to Texas, with occasional trips to other cities if the offers included round-trip airfare.

Then the highway department told them they'd have to move because they were widening the road and offered them $600 for their trouble. The silver-tongued Leary, arguing that he was running a business out of the home, wrangled them up to $15,000.

They used the money to put a down payment on a home in Driftwood, in the hill country outside Austin. Surrounded by miles of scrubby ranch land, the place provided a welcome respite from the hurly-burly of the road, as well as from the constant stream of friends and admirers who would otherwise be dropping by their place with a bag of pot or a case of beer, expecting to get wasted with the band.

But Coffey, who didn't have a driver's license, recalled the way he had always wound up stranded back in Winterville and asked for his share of the band fund so he could get a place in town. The band's communal lifestyle was coming to an end.

After recording *Rembrandt Pussyhorse* in a hodgepodge of cheap studios and doing *Locust Abortion Technician* on an obsolete eight-track machine at home, the band wanted to record their next album in a real studio, and wound up at one of the first digital facilities in Texas. They had been playing most of the material on the road for some time, so recording went quickly, finished in about a week.

*Hairway to Steven* was more sparse, but just as strange as ever. There were no song titles, just crude little pictograms for each track, forcing radio programmers to identify songs by phrases like "Defecating Deer" and "Two Naked Women Bending Over." The album's heightened production values are hardly evident in the surging, distorted nightmare of "Defecating Pitcher Throws to Urinating Batter," but things tend more toward the folk rock of "Syringe" or the downright pastoral instrumental "Urinating Horse," with its acoustic guitar and nature sounds or the jumpin' jive of "Rabbit Defecates on Fish."

The anarchic presentation of the band had very little to do with its business dealings. "As a band they were grossly manipulative and demanding," says Steve Albini. "If it was possible to take advantage of someone, they would — gladly — and they would feel justified in it because they saw it as their livelihood." Even their former benefactor had a similar take: "As far as business goes, 'sharp' is one way of putting it," said Jello Biafra. "I've heard the term 'cutthroat' bandied about quite a bit. Let's put it this way: They've definitely got the Texas wildcatter mentality down."

"We always fought for ourselves — that's why we have such a trail of enemies behind us," Leary counters bitterly. "I have no vast memories of cool people from my indie days. That's where I learned how to get ripped off." But that attitude sometimes left even their friends feeling a bit ripped off. Michael Macioce recalls the band choosing one of his photographs for the cover of *Rembrandt Pussyhorse* and then getting rebuked by Haynes and Leary when he dared to ask $300 for it.

Even as the band was committing mayhem, they kept one eye on the bottom line. When Macioce caught a Butthole Surfers show in Leeds, England, he stopped by the dressing room afterward, proudly displaying a show poster he'd torn off the wall. Coffey thought that was a great idea and ran out and brought back as many posters as he could find. Naturally, Haynes set them on fire, creating a roaring blaze right there in the dressing room. Leary looked on impassively as he kicked back on the couch, practicing scales on the guitar, pausing only to drawl, "Hey, somebody put out that fire before they decide not to pay us."

"And then he goes back to playing his guitar," says Macioce. "That was so Paul."

Although they were the flagship band of Touch & Go, the Butthole Surfers were not part of the interconnected indie tribe that had sprung up around SST, Dischord, Touch & Go, and other labels. "We never did feel like a part of that community, really, not at all," says Leary. "We played to their crowd, but we were not really a part of the scene or anything." Part of the reason they weren't part of "the scene" was the simple fact that they moved around too much to get settled anywhere, but their political incorrectness was a much bigger alienating factor.

The band was thoroughly do-it-yourself, but not for the political ends professed by indie culture — empowering the individual and staying out of the corporate loop. "Our goal was to *become* part of the corporate loop, which we eventually did," says Leary. "I just never understood any of that ethics crap — you know, being self-righteous, this way or that way is the right way to do it. Nah, fuck all that crap — if people started throwing that stuff at us, we'd just immediately do the opposite. We'd start eating meat."

A t the urging of both Steve Albini and Sonic Youth, the Buttholes had signed with Blast First for U.K. releases. Blast First had released both *Locust* and *Hairway*, and Paul Smith's hard work on the former was paying off. They did a celebrated European tour in 1988, selling out venues like London's 4,000-seat Brixton Academy and appearing on the cover of *Melody Maker* (with their eyes clearly dilated).

With a little prompting from Smith, the U.K. press perceived the connections between the American Blast First bands and pronounced that a movement was in effect. Which is precisely the kind of thing that sells papers.

The Buttholes held other charms for the British music press, too. For one, Haynes was quite the irreverent wild man. When *Melody Maker* interviewed him, Thurston Moore, and Dinosaur's J Mascis for a cover story about a Blast First compilation, Haynes teased Moore, already something of an indie-world Brahmin, relentlessly. "Hey Thurston, have you ever fucked Lydia Lunch?" he asked. The usually witty Moore could mumble only a half-baked comeback. "What did you say?" Haynes replied. "Fucking Lydia Lunch is like rubbing a dog?" The razzing didn't let up there. "Thurston Moore? Is that your real name?" Haynes drawled. "I mean, give me a break. You made that up. That's a good one. Did you have a mom and shit like that?"

Partly because of copy like that, the U.K. press was smitten with the band and conveyed its unbridled enthusiasm in their own inimitable way. "The Butthole Surfers are masturbatory in the best sense of the word," wrote one overheated *Melody Maker* scribe. "But their 'play' is not light fingered, frisky or merely mischievous — rather, it takes the form of gratuitous devastation. Plunging in at the anus and excavating, tunneling a giant point of exit at the sockets, they are one giant surge of flesh, one part holy revelation."

*Melody Maker*'s writing team the Stud Brothers breathlessly proclaimed, "The Butthole Surfers stand blood-stained, shit-caked and semen-sodden among the last unrecognizable avatars of romance, situated between the rational and the marvelous, stranded between this world and the next, this world and the last. They draw their power from those abandoned clearings across which higher and lower worlds once passed. All they desire is all you can do."

*Melody Maker* critic Simon Reynolds astutely noted that the Buttholes were "shaping up to be the post-punk equivalent of the Grateful Dead — massive success built up slowly outside the conventional networks, a cult reputation built on impressionistic, trippy shows."

And similarities to the Grateful Dead went even further than that. As the Grateful Dead were then doing for a huge second wave of new fans, the Butthole Surfers offered a glimpse of a freedom that had evaporated before their youthful audience had gotten a chance to drink from its cup. Haynes and Leary had been born in the late Fifties, too young to have participated in the Sixties counterculture but just old enough to have gotten a vivid impression of it. "Hell yes," Leary said, "I wanna sound like Hendrix, I wanna be all those motherfuckers. I grew up wanting to be those motherfuckers. I think every fan wants to pretend that he's the person that he respects and that's what we're doing, probably."

The band's sound cut a direct path to psychedelic-era freaks like the 13th Floor Elevators and Captain Beefheart. Live, they'd cover Sixties bands like Blue Cheer, Iron Butterfly, and Donovan, while the stage show recalled Sixties "happenings" like Andy Warhol's Exploding Plastic Inevitable and Pink Floyd's early multimedia freakouts. So the Butthole Surfers actually came out of a tradition — "Yeah," Leary cracks, "probably a tradition of taking LSD!"

**T**aylor quit for good in April '89, after touring *Hairway to Steven*. "It just must have gotten to be too tough for her," says Leary, clearly sympathetic. "She was a cute young girl and really sweet and here she was hanging out with the Butthole Surfers. She was a damn good trouper. I can't blame her for it being too much after a while."

After leaving the band, Taylor suffered what seemed to be an aneurysm, although it was later determined she was suffering from strobe light–induced seizures. "When the neurologist asked me if I had ever been exposed to flashing lights," said Taylor, "I had to laugh and say, 'You'll never even imagine, in your wildest dreams, the shit I've flashed.'"

**A**lthough the early shows were exciting, anything-can-happen affairs, by the end of the decade they were becoming all but routine. At various predetermined points in the show, they would do the fire cymbal or tear up a stuffed animal or Haynes would twist knobs and dials and make weird noises for twenty minutes. The band seemed to be merely going through the motions.

Same goes for all the drugs and booze the band was consuming. "It was nuts, it was fun," says Leary. "But then you think, 'What do I do if I get off the hamster wheel? What's out there? I don't know.'"

Careerwise, the band was in a tough position. As early as *Locust Abortion Technician*, they were playing the largest rock clubs in town — and then kept playing those same clubs to the same faces for three years. "We'd sold as many records as we could ever hope to sell through indie distribution, we'd been exposed as well as we could ever hope to be exposed in the indie realm," says Coffey.

Although major labels had come calling, none of them offered a satisfactory contract until Rough Trade offered a one-album deal for "some stupid-ass money," as Coffey puts it, so stupid-ass that even Rusk reportedly admitted they should probably go for it. So in 1989 they signed with Rough Trade, whom they felt had superior distribution to Touch & Go. "We needed to sell more units," says Leary, "in order to maintain a lifestyle that would be somewhat human."

The band looked at the break with Rusk, their greatest supporter, strictly as a matter of survival. "If you look at punk rock bands from 1981, their success rate is not good," Leary told the *Chicago Reader* in 1999. "It's basically poverty, misery, and death. We had to claw and fight for everything. The ones that made it are the ones that fight. That's what punk rock was about anyway. It's not about causes or right and wrong. It's about fighting."

The title track of 1990's *Hurdy Gurdy Man* EP is a cover of Donovan's hippy-dippy-trippy Sixties classic; the video got airplay on MTV's *120 Minutes*, then a crucial outlet for underground rock, and the song became a modest college radio hit. The band even did a jingle for MTV.

The parting with their old label had been amicable, but by the time of their 1991 Rough Trade album *Pioughd*, the band was beginning to snipe at Touch & Go. "Touch & Go were smart," said Pinkus. "They never showed us anything until it was too late." But if Touch & Go were smart, Rough Trade was not: after releasing *Pioughd*, Pinkus and Haynes's (as the Jack Officers) techno-house album *Digital Dump*, and Leary's solo album *The History of Dogs*, the label went under. Unlike many other Rough Trade bands, the Buttholes came out of the disaster unscathed — not only had they already collected on their advance and been paid royalties, but since they had recorded themselves, they avoided the fate of many other bands on the label, who found themselves at the bankruptcy auction, bidding on their own master tapes.

**T**he Buttholes made a small fortune playing the first Lollapalooza tour that summer. It was the first tour they'd ever done where they didn't have to drive their own van, set up their own equipment, tune their own guitars, or collect their own money at the end of the night.

The following year they signed with the major Capitol Records. "As long as we have control over the music and the packaging," Coffey says, "if the label wants to slap their label on it and distribute it better, let's give it a shot — we've done everything else at this point." Five years later the president of their label still wouldn't say their name in public.

**B**ack when Coffey was playing in the Hugh Beaumont Experience, he might have been repulsed by the idea of signing to a major label. And when he joined the Butthole Surfers, the prospect of signing to a major was so remote that it wasn't even worth thinking about. "It would be like me saying, 'I am *not* going to live on Pluto — Pluto sucks,'" says Coffey. "It's just not going to happen."

Leary had no problem being on a major label. "I *always* wanted to be on one," he says, "and especially the one that Grand Funk Railroad had been on." Still, indie purists accused the band of selling out. "If ever I got grief from those people, I would just tell them to kiss my ass," says Leary. "*You* go live in a fuckin' van, you asshole. You go home to your nice mommy-and-daddy little bed there and think about what a sellout I am. I had *lots* of good answers for those fucks."

Another answer Leary used to have was this: "Eat shit and die."

"To me, it was just a matter of, if you want to do something, the only thing that's going to keep you from doing it is giving up," Leary says. "Because we were proof of that. If you just don't quit, you *will* succeed — that is the bottom line."

# CHAPTER 9

# BIG BLACK

**HOW MANY BOYS WANT TO BE WHIPPED
BY STEVE ALBINI'S GUITAR?**

— KIM GORDON, *VILLAGE VOICE* (FALL 1988)

As early as 1983, hardcore's hyperthyroid tempos and free-flowing aggression were beginning to lose favor with punk-generation people entering their twenties. Those folks were in college or just out; they'd outgrown hardcore's slam dancing, skateboarding, and strict moralizing, but they weren't quite ready to abandon aggressive, cutting-edge music. There had to be a new way to be intense. Arty U.K. bands like the Fall and Gang of Four as well as Australia's Birthday Party showed the way, and a new music began to take shape, filtered through some of the precepts and aesthetics of hardcore. And while so many indie bands were trying to outdo each other's sincerity, this new breed substituted a seething brand of irony — or was it contempt?

No band exemplified this new approach better than Big Black. Instead of resting on emotional vulnerability and familiar rock tropes, the band's music — jagged, brutal, loud, and nasty — was original to a downright confrontational degree. Big Black distilled years of post-punk and hardcore down to a sound resembling a singing saw blade mercilessly tearing through sheet metal. No one had made records that sounded so harsh. No wonder they called one of their records *Headache*.

Like their fellow negationists Sonic Youth and the Butthole Surfers,

Big Black explored the less-than-flattering aspects of American culture, but at much further length and in far closer, far less forgiving detail than ever before. While it may not have been a direct swipe at a nation obsessed with a show like *Lifestyles of the Rich and Famous*, it sure was a turd in its silver punchbowl.

And Big Black introduced one of the indie world's foremost characters, a person who would help define not just the sound of underground music through the next two decades, but also its discourse — the irascible, outspoken, intelligent, and relentlessly ethical Steve Albini.

Virtually nothing could live up to the standards Albini so brutally outlined in his constant screeds — except Big Black. This was a band with *policies*. Their principles, outlined in the band's live album *Pigpile*, were "Treat everyone with as much respect as he deserves (and no more). Avoid people who appeal to our vanity or ambition. . . . Operate as much as possible apart from the 'music scene.' . . . Take no shit from anyone in the process." Albini put those beliefs into action literally with a vengeance. He had few sacred cows and would unhesitatingly take on the indie community itself, little of which met his stringent criteria, judging by his frequently voiced disdain for various labels, bands, producers, club owners, and so on.

Musically, Big Black's insistent drum machine rhythms, abrasive textures, and obsessively repeated riffs provided a major part of the blueprint for so-called industrial rock. Their bracingly intense music aside, the saving grace of the band's often obnoxious approach was that it was thought-provoking. Big Black set a standard for freedom of expression and forthrightness that has been emulated to varying degrees ever since.

S teve Albini's father was literally a rocket scientist, which meant moving his family all over the country before settling in Missoula, Montana, for Albini's formative years. Scrawny, bespectacled, and too smart for his own good, Albini had no luck with women in high school, and few friends. Instead, he got his kicks doing things like setting off M-80s in the bathroom of the local drive-in.

Having read about punk rock in *Rolling Stone* and *Creem*, he discovered Suicide, the Ramones, and the Stooges, whose music, as he later put it, "got me through high school." Albini saw punk rock as a haven for difficult people such as himself, and he took to it with open arms. "The status quo was about fitting in and about being allowed into a preexisting environment," says Albini. "The greatest thing about punk rock for me, as an outsider, was that the concept that you had to be allowed *in* was no longer valid. You could be operating in a vacuum, you could be as fucked up an individual as you cared to be, and if you did something of worth, all these external conditions were immaterial."

In the fall of '79, his senior year of high school, he was struck by a car while riding his motorcycle and broke his leg badly. Such was Albini's unpopularity that he got several phone calls on his hospital bed from anonymous "jocks and rednecks" expressing delight at his pain. While he recuperated, he taught himself how to play bass.

The following year he left Missoula and enrolled at Northwestern University, in the Chicago suburb of Evanston, to pursue a journalism degree. Albini arrived as "a total dillweed who didn't know jack shit," as he put it, and had trouble even locating Chicago's fledgling punk scene.

He eventually discovered the *Chicago Reader*, the fanzine *The Coolest Retard*, and the progressive station WZRD, and began catching sparsely attended shows by the Replacements, Hüsker Dü, Dead Kennedys, Flipper, and others. Then Albini found a local band he could love, Naked Raygun. "I was convinced that I had seen the best band that had ever been," says Albini. "I went to their shows religiously."

Santiago Durango and Marco Pezzati had started the post-punk powerhouse in the summer of '80, with Pezzati's brother Jeff eventually joining on lead vocals. In Naked Raygun's dawning days, "it was like a space age rockabilly band," Albini said, "with this bizarre jungle drumming going on."

At Northwestern Albini was also pursuing a minor in fine art. For a project on "process sculpture" and performance art, he planned to stand behind a Plexiglas wall and taunt people while inviting them to throw things at him; the wall and the objects would then become the sculpture. "People could be as destructive as they were inclined to be, as long as I was the object of their destruction," says Albini. "I sort of liked the idea." Unfortunately, Albini's first customer, his friend John Bohnen, threw a bowling pin right through the barrier, cutting short the performance.

Albini's confrontational streak ran deep: he'd continually get fired from his DJ spot on Northwestern's radio station for playing loud, abrasive records in his morning time slot, which the station had reserved for quieter music. "The patsies that were the student administrators of that radio station were fuckin' mainstream radio wanna-bes," Albini scoffs, adding, "I got a kick out of just being a thorn in their side."

Albini also began writing the instantly controversial monthly column "Tired of Ugly Fat?" for the excellent Chicago zine *Matter* in which he ranted about the local music scene, often singling out specific people for very harsh and graphic castigation. On the rumor that Al Jourgensen, the leader of a wimpy dance-pop unit called Ministry, might be producing a Chicago art-noise band, he wrote, "If you do, and you make them one-tenth as wimpy as Ministry, I'll cut your balls off and sew them shut in your mouth."

Just as Albini's fanzine writings were deliberately ugly in a provocative way, so was the music he championed: loud, aggressive bands like Scratch Acid, Meatmen, and the Swans. According to his friend former Killdozer singer Michael Gerald, Albini's outspoken opinions quickly divided the Chicago underground scene into two distinct camps: "people who thought he was a genius and people who just thought he was an asshole."

His confrontational aspects — his every *Matter* column implicitly screamed, "Hate me, please!" — were the preemptive instincts of someone who's been routinely picked on. *Choosing* the reason you get your ass kicked is a way of exercising at least some control over the situation. It harks back not just to the earliest inklings of punk rock, but to the origin of the term "punk" itself, which referred to someone at the bottom of the jailhouse pecking order who realized that self-abasement was his only means of survival.

One of Albini's first college bands was a short-lived "arty new wave band" called Stations, unremarkable except for the fact that it featured the novel addition of a drum machine. Albini had become enamored of the idea and got the cheapest drum machine he could find — a Roland TR-606. He'd walk around campus all day with the device pumping the same unvarying beat into his headphones. "It was a really great soundtrack to your life," says Albini. "And that's how I worked up a lot of the ideas that were on the first Big Black record."

There were big advantages to a drum machine: it could play really fast for a long time without getting tired, it would always keep a steady beat no matter what chaos was erupting around it, and it always did exactly what it was told. "Since then I've gotten an awful lot better at communicating with people," says Albini, "so I've never been tempted to use a drum machine since."

Albini had begun writing some songs but didn't know any musicians who could play them the way he wanted — or as he put it in a *Forced Exposure* piece, "I couldn't find anybody who didn't blow out of a pig's asshole." So he simply decided to do it himself, even though home recording was practically unheard of. In the spring of his sophomore year, 1981, he bought a guitar on a Wednesday, then called a friend who owned a four-track recorder and obtained its use in exchange for a case of beer. That Friday, the beginning of spring break, he began recording the *Lungs* EP in his living room while his peers were off in Florida catching rays, hangovers, and STDs. Most of it was done in a week.

It wasn't a very auspicious debut. The vocals on *Lungs* aren't aggro enough to get over; the lyrics are self-conscious and pretentious; the music is merely sketchy, mostly derivative of Albini favorites like Cabaret Voltaire, Killing Joke, and the Cure. If it sounds like a demo tape by the angry nerd down the hall of your dorm, it's because that's exactly what it was.

*Lungs* is one of Albini's few artistic regrets: "It just makes my flesh crawl," he said. "I can't listen to that record anymore." But he'd forged a unique style, using the drum machine as well as a determination to avoid the "standard rock stud guitar sound." Until then Chicago pop-punk bands like the Effigies and Naked Raygun were as far out as local rock got; the cold, dark, and resolutely unlistenable *Lungs* redefined the town's ideas about what was radical.

The lyrics are elliptical studies of creepy types like crackheads, child abusers, and even an individual who lives in a hole, sometimes including sophomorisms like "You can't ignore the beauty in the things that you love / Like you can't stand the hatred and the lies." But even if his lyrics did contain a fair amount of clinkers, Albini did come up with a great name for his one-man band: Big Black. "It was just sort of a reduction of the concept of a large, scary, ominous figure," Albini said. "All the historical images of fear and all the things that kids are afraid of are all big and black, basically. That's all there was to it."

Albini used the *Lungs* tape to enlist other musicians for the band. He really admired Naked Raygun guitarist Santiago Durango, but Durango, a local punk scene celebrity, was out of Albini's league. He did manage to get once and future Minor Threat guitarist Lyle Preslar, who was temporarily at Northwestern, but they soon found they were incompatible — "We'd end up throwing things across the room at each other after a while," said Albini.

Albini gave a tape to Jon Babbin, who was then starting his own label in order to release records by a band he managed: the Effigies, then one of Chicago's premiere punk bands. Ruthless Records wasn't much more than a logo; band members did virtually all the work themselves. But

Ruthless's association with the Effigies helped convince distributors and retailers to take at least a few copies of anything on the label.

Babbin liked the Big Black tape and released a 1,500-copy pressing on Ruthless in December '82. Many copies of the *Lungs* EP had unique inserts, including dollar bills, locks of hair, Bruce Lee photos, used condoms, old photographs, rubber animals, and blood-spattered pieces of paper courtesy of a friend of Albini's who suffered from chronic nosebleeds. Things like blasting caps, razor blades, fish hooks, and firecrackers were pulled out by the distributor, Dutch East India Trading, fearing lawsuits.

Through some mutual friends, Albini managed to meet Naked Raygun's Jeff Pezzati, who was impressed by Albini right away. "He was this wiry journalism student with this really hot girlfriend who went to Northwestern — in fact his girlfriend was in *Playboy*'s Girls of the Big Ten issue of 1985," Pezzati recalls. "He knew a heck of a lot about, right from the start, how to release a record and get the word out that you have a record." Albini convinced Pezzati to play bass with Big Black. "I do remember that he was . . . not in awe, but real happy," Pezzati recalls. "He jumped at the chance to have a band play his stuff."

They rehearsed at Pezzati's place, a former coach house in the then dicey Lincoln Park area. It is said that at one point, every punk band in the city rehearsed in the building's storied basement. Albini was not shy about telling Pezzati what he wanted. "He told me exactly what to play," says Pezzati. "He kind of had it all down. I was spoon-fed."

One day the two were practicing loudly downstairs while upstairs, vainly trying to concentrate on a football game on TV, was Santiago Durango. Durango was the soft-spoken son of a successful Colombian doctor; he was well educated — with a degree in poli sci from the University of Illinois — and yet very punk rock. "He's a complete maniac on one hand," Pezzati explains, "and this nice normal guy on the other."

Durango and his family had moved from Colombia when he was ten. He eventually went to an all-boys Catholic high school, where his small stature and Hispanic background ensured outcast status. For Durango, punk rock was salvation. "When I heard punk for the first time, I felt like a fish that had found the water he belonged in," he says. "Punk changed my life completely. It transformed me. I found a home."

Durango was soon playing in an early Chicago punk band of high school pariahs called Silver Abuse. "I was very angry and very alienated, and I just wanted to yell back because everybody had been yelling at me for so many years," says Durango. "So we went out and took it to people, insulting people, berating them severely." The first two times the band played, they incited near riots by taunting the audience.

After leaving Silver Abuse, Durango wanted to form a more serious band and cofounded Naked Raygun. Bands like Strike Under and the Effigies had established the city's punk scene, but Chicago's clubs had shunned punk rock until one night Naked Raygun packed the Cubby Bear club, opening the city's nightlife to punk rock shows.

Durango would often go intentionally haywire during Naked Raygun shows, throwing away everything they'd rehearsed, twirling his amplifier knobs at random, and just making the wildest sounds possible. This excited Albini to no end, so when Durango came downstairs to Albini and Pezzati's rehearsal and asked to play along since he couldn't hear the game anyway, Albini was delighted. "I was like, 'Sure, Mr. Durango, anything you want!'" said Albini. "And then it got really great."

Albini and Durango clicked. Although Albini had a very clear creative conception, his songs were diamonds in the rough. As it turned out, Durango was a brilliant song doctor who could rework arrangements and tweak sounds until a song shone and sparkled. "Any time he thought I was making a mistake, he would say, 'You're a stupid person.' And he was always right," said Albini. "He ended up being absolutely crucial to Big Black."

With Durango and Pezzati on board, the ideas sketched out on *Lungs* began to take almost palpable shape onstage; it was time to bring it to the studio. Albini knew the Chicago label Fever Records, which basically was two University of Chicago students with a little extra money to throw around. Albini "sorta conned" the two into financing his next project, affording a full band and a twenty-four-track studio. The trio drafted drummer Pat Byrne, on loan from Urge Overkill, to double up with the drum machine.

Albini had liked the work that transplanted Englishman Iain Burgess had done on Naked Raygun's first EP and asked him to engineer the second Big Black EP. Albini explained, "We wanted it to be more aggressive than normal. . . . We just wanted it to sound really high energy and powerful without using any of the clichéd tricks to do that." Burgess was sympathetic to Big Black's ideas, but the problem was that he fancied a drink now and then, and often during sessions he would retire to the couch and fall fast asleep. Still, the band regarded him as an invaluable guide through the recording process.

Back in 1983 punk fans with enough experience in recording studios to work as engineers were still few and far between, especially in Evanston. So Burgess and Big Black inevitably got saddled with mellow, ponytailed types who had no clue as to why or how to achieve the sulfurous sounds the band envisioned. "Half the battle was always trying to neutralize them, get them to understand what we were trying to do," recalls Durango. "They couldn't deal with it."

But through sheer force of will, Albini and the band got their way, and the leap from the first EP is startling. With a proper studio, the tracks had texture and bite; rehearsing with a band meant the songs were more fine-tuned. Albini's guitar playing had improved drastically, scything the music with a steely glint; Pezzati's bass had the demeanor of a junkyard dog; and Durango's guitar supplied a grinding propulsion. And in a proper studio Albini could now let it rip on vocals — "It's real hard to get up and scream when it's you alone, screaming in a room into this four-track," says Pezzati. "You're thinking, 'I hope I don't wake anybody up upstairs.'" Even the drum machine now kicked butt.

But best of all, the band was totally simpatico. "There wasn't that much debate about 'Is this any good?' or 'What should we do here?'" says Albini. "It just seemed like all the decisions were sort of making themselves."

The sound was, in fact, far bigger and blacker than *Lungs*. Albini got a signature clanky sound by using metal guitar picks that he would notch with sheet metal snips, creating the effect of two guitar picks at once, making the sound doubly clanky. "I always thought that our guitar playing was not so much playing guitars," says Durango, "but assembling noises *created* by guitars."

There were plenty of synth bands at the time, but virtually all of them sounded wimpy. Big Black's innovation was to use synthetic sounds as instruments of aggression. Albini saw that the best thing to do with a drum machine was to exploit its idiosyncrasies, rather than vainly try to make it sound natural. On many songs Albini made the machine accent the first and third beats of the bar, not the second and fourth as in most rock music. The effect was a monolithic pummeling, an attack. Thanks to Roland the drum machine, as the band soon dubbed their silicon-hearted fourth member, their groove, normally the most human aspect of a rock band, became its most inhuman; it only made them sound more insidious, its relentlessness downright tyrannical.

The point, Albini says, was to make "something that felt intense when we went through it, rather than something that had little encoded *indicators* of intensity." Albini was something of a connoisseur of intensity. "Heavy metal and stuff like that didn't really seem intense to me, it seemed comical to me," he says. "Hardcore punk didn't really seem intense most of the time — most of the time it just seemed childish. I guess that's how I would differentiate what we were doing from what other people were doing."

Albini's lyrics on *Bulldozer* are miniature short stories, shot through with bilious misanthropy. "It's sorta like a Ripley's *Believe It or Not,*" Albini explained. "If you have an interest in things sort of out of the ordinary, and you stumble across something like this, you think, 'This can't be!' But it turns out to be true, and that makes it even wilder."

The Gang of Four–ish "Cables" is about a bunch of guys Albini knew back in Montana who liked to sneak into the local abattoir to watch the cows get slaughtered. "They take a pressurized gun and drive a bolt through the snout of a cow," Albini explained, "and they clip a cable to either side of the bolt. And then there's this winch that hauls the cow into the stall, and then there's a compression hammer that crushes the cow's skull.

"That was like TV for them," Albini continued. "It was that or go home in the trailer park and get drunk. Sniff glue. There was nothing else to do."

"Pigeon Kill" is about a town in rural Indiana that apparently took great delight in getting rid of their pigeon population by feeding them poisoned corn; elsewhere, there is the Texan redneck (the amphetamine rockabilly of "Texas"), the despondent paraplegic ("I'm a Mess"), and "Seth," the dog trained to attack black people — the latter track opens with a harrowing snippet of a white supremacist's harangue. "Steve Albini was one of the few people writing song lyrics that were funny, but in a mean-spirited way," says Killdozer's Michael Gerald. "Kind of like laughing at old people when they fall down."

The EP was originally going to be called "Hey, Nigger," the cover a drawing by Albini of a repulsive, obese man uttering the title. "The idea being," says Albini, "that an offensive term used by an offensive person is only offensive if you allow that person's commentary to have some weight or value." Albini felt it was an antiracist statement and debated the point at length. It took the objections of virtually everyone he knew, including Pezzati and Durango, to persuade him to drop the idea. Albini insisted on packaging the first two hundred copies of *Bulldozer* in an expensive gray sheet metal sleeve in homage to PiL's *Metal Box*, making it very difficult for the tiny label to make its money back.

Like many Chicago bands, Big Black started by making trips up to Madison, Minneapolis, and Detroit. But touring was no picnic for Big Black — they made the long drives in a cramped car, not a van; they couldn't afford to stay in motels, so they slept on people's floors; bathing and decent food were rare. "It was very, very grueling," says Durango. "We used to say it was 'going into combat.' And that's what it was. You really had to prepare yourself for it. It was very hard on you physically. The best part was the playing. And even that, some club owner would try to fuck you over. Or you'd get someplace and you'd draw three people and they'd be uninterested.

"It was not," Durango concludes, "glamorous at all."

Early on they played the tiny No Bar club, located in the basement of a record store in Muncie, Indiana. The place held about a hundred people. "I think the sound system was a stereo with some microphones plugged into it," says Durango. "We went in there and they packed the little place and we had just an awesome show. It was really great, with the going back and forth between the band and the crowd. And from that day on we always went back there. It was always out of our way, but they had been so good to us that Steve never forgot. Steve is very loyal. And we always went back and packed that little club for those guys."

Albini set up the rehearsals, booked the studio time, and arranged the tours. "Steve is dangerous — he knows how to use the phone," says Durango. "He was always connected with all sorts of people." So when a buzz on Big Black erupted in New York, he was able to line up an East Coast tour, including a stop at New York's Danceteria. Albini was already a formidable frontman — "He was really intense, sweated a lot, veins bulging, he was good," says Pezzati — and the New York crowd, as well as the press, loved the band.

Before they'd gone off on that East Coast tour, their Chicago audiences consisted of "us and three flies buzzing around," according to Durango. "And all of a sudden, people started perking up and paying attention to us. And that pissed us off, because we were the same band, but now because we'd played New York and Boston and Washington, all of a sudden we were good." The situation was only magnified once the band toured Europe and won acclaim in the U.K. music press. The band was so disgusted by their own town's shallow about-face that they actually refused to play there. "We *enjoyed* not playing [Chicago]," says Durango. "For all those idiots who told us we were no good, that was a nice little comeback."

But much of the band's local unpopularity may have stemmed from Albini himself. "He was very vocal," Pezzati explains, "didn't like anything — or didn't seem to anyway — and pissed a lot of the wrong people off." By 1985 Chicago's Club Metro was the only punk-friendly hometown club large enough for Big Black. They had played one show there and drawn well, but then Albini bad-mouthed the club in a fanzine interview and was permanently banned from the club.

The feisty Albini would not roll over when promoters or record labels tried to rip him off, and he encouraged others to do the same. In 1985 the Meat Puppets played on a bill with Big Black in Boston. When the Meat Puppets got stiffed by the promoter, Albini sprang into action. "He talked me into going in and getting money out of them by pretending I had a gun," recalls the Meat Puppets' Curt Kirkwood. As instructed, Kirkwood ambled into the office with his hand thrust into his black trench coat and demanded more money. Unfazed, the club manager directed Kirkwood to sit on a bench outside the office and emerged a few minutes later with another hundred dollars.

And no one was immune from Albini's seemingly bottomless pool of bile. Even in a very informative and uncharacteristically sunny *Matter* article about how to make your own record, he couldn't resist slipping in a gratuitous dig at English producer Martin Hannett (Joy Division), calling him a "miserable little junkie."

"I don't know that he was wrong to piss people off, but it's just the way he was," Pezzati says. "There was a lot to criticize back then.

"I'll say one thing for him — he had a terrible diet, man," adds the health-conscious Pezzati. Albini consumed vast quantities of Slim Jims, preferably the ones with the gold wrapper because the ink from the label stuck to the meat. "He would always show it to me, every time," says Pezzati, "and say, 'Look!' And then he would eat it."

Although Albini lacked culinary discernment, he had worked up a very circumscribed aesthetic to guide his music: Melody meant almost nothing. Aggression, rhythm, and texture were all.

The key was noise. "I don't give two splats of an old Negro junkie's vomit for your politico-philosophical treatises, kiddies," Albini wrote in *Forced Exposure*. "I like noise. I like big-ass vicious noise that makes my head spin. I wanna feel it whipping through me like a fucking jolt. We're so dilapidated and crushed by our pathetic existence we need it like a fix." Albini went on to compare the desperate need for a jolt to the twisted cravings of grisly serial killers such as Robin Gecht, John Wayne Gacy, and Dean Corll. "Me, I'm not that desperate yet," Albini wrote. "I stick with the noise. But an *articulated* noise that hangs there in your memory and causes further damage.

"Big Black is a way to get the old blood to boiling," he continued, "without having to buttfuck and garrote little boys, or hang around slaughterhouses."

Like so many of his interviews and *Matter* columns, it was an inspired and defining piece of self-promotion, and Albini would reiterate the sentiment from time to time. "I would shoot myself in the face if I didn't have some way to blow off steam," Albini told a German interviewer. "And because I don't like sports, and because I don't like disco dancing, and because I don't take drugs, and because I don't drink, and I don't beat my head into the floor, and I don't have a wife to beat, I have Big Black."

Like Randy Newman before him, who also profiled rapists and racists without overt comment, Albini was an intelligent social misfit who liked to test the tolerance of the white liberal crowd that made up most of his audience. After all, pissing off the squares was like shooting fish in a barrel — it was a lot more interesting to piss off the hipsters.

After growing up in Montana, where race relations were relatively placid, it was a shock to come to Chicago, one of the most racially divided cities in the country. "Half the population doesn't speak, interact, eat, or hang out with the other half of the population," says Albini. "And that just seemed bizarre to me." Given his divided new hometown and his magnetic attraction to confrontation, it's no surprise he worked the racial angle heavily in his lyrics — the word "darkie" appeared in the first line of his first EP. "But also the word 'darkie' is a comical word," says Albini. "And in a way that's a play on the concept of a hateful word. Can a word that's so inherently hilarious be hateful? I don't know."

Being confrontational as an art statement was a commonplace in places like New York, but in Chicago it was still something of a novelty. "He's very sharp and biting and he said exactly what he thought — and pissed a lot of people off," says Touch & Go's Corey Rusk. "I also think sometimes he'd say something just to piss somebody off, even if it wasn't exactly what he thought, just to fuck with somebody. And if that person wasn't bright enough to catch on that they were just being fucked with, then they might go away thinking that yeah, he is a racist or he is a homophobe."

"There can be no light without generating heat," adds Durango. "And confrontation generates heat and light." And when Albini's statements went a little too far, Durango took it with a grain of salt. "It was just a matter of rolling your eyes and going, 'There he goes again,'" says Durango. "But sometimes you think it's really calculated in a way. Because it keeps him in the limelight. You have to wonder whether it's not sort of contrived and not genuine, more of a publicity stunt.

"But on the other hand, I roomed with Steve, so I knew what a putz he was," Durango continues. "I would see people getting really upset with him about stuff and taking him really seriously, and then I knew that this was the same guy who couldn't find his underwear in the morning."

Albini defended his rather un-PC creations by insisting that he knew in his heart he was not a prejudiced person. "So once that's given, once you know what you think, there's no reason to be ginger about what you

say," he said. "A lot of people, they're very careful not to say things that might offend certain people or do anything that might be misinterpreted. But what they don't realize is that the point of all this is to change the way you live your life, not the way you speak.

"I have less respect for the man who bullies his girlfriend and calls her 'Ms.,'" he added, "than a guy who treats women reasonably and respectfully and calls them 'Yo! Bitch!' The substance is what matters." Dubious reasoning like that, along with lines like "I'm God's gift to women / Except for that college girl / I'll kill her" ("Racer-X") did not exactly endear Albini to the feminist community.

Nor did the steady stream of gay jokes that spilled from the Big Black stage, but Albini defends those as well. "Given how intermingled the gay and punk subcultures were, it was assumed by anyone involved that open-mindedness, if not free-form experimentation, was the norm," Albini says. "With that assumption under your belt, joke all you like. The word 'fag' isn't just a gay term, it's funny on its own — phonetically — like the words 'hockey puck,' 'mukluks,' 'gefilte fish,' and 'Canada.'"

The problem was most people who heard Albini's lyrics and stage banter hadn't met him personally, so they didn't know where he was coming from. He gave absolutely no clue as to his real beliefs; the listener was left to guess whether he was an unabashed bigot or a merciless satirist. "Some people are uncomfortable being confronted with a notion without having that notion explained to them," said Albini. "We're much more interested in sending the information out as we perceive it, and letting people deal with it on their own terms."

Albini's lyrics provoked some eternal questions, like does the artist have a social responsibility? In the liner notes to the *Pigpile* live album, Albini made his position known in his own special way: "Anybody who thinks we overstepped the playground perimeter of lyrical decency (or that the public has a right to demand 'social responsibility' from a god-damn punk rock band)," he wrote, "is a pure mental dolt, and should step forward and put his tongue up my ass."

Many of those who heard Big Black's music couldn't grasp the idea that what Albini said in the context of a song didn't necessarily reflect what he actually felt, but rather reflected impulses that, as a rational, civilized human being, one normally suppressed in the course of social interaction — quashing the quite understandable urge to murder someone for messing around with one's tools, for instance ("Grind").

Others grasped Albini's argument yet still felt he reveled in the material a little too much for comfort — but of course comfort was exactly what he was not after. It was risky territory — it seems downright impossible to immerse oneself in something so completely and not be affected by it, like the phenomenon of undercover cops who actually become criminals. Deep down, some armchair psychoanalysts felt, Albini really did have some issues with women, gays, and minorities and covered them over with his arty justifications. Sometimes Albini did seem to be flirting with racism. In one *Matter* column he described a visit to a doctor whom he termed a "splay-toothed, thick-lipped goat herder . . . from some developing nation's sole medical school." This was several steps past an ironic character study.

But Albini was interested in an audience that thought for itself. By not explicitly spelling out his position, he felt he was dealing with his audience on an intelligent level; he was opting out of the mainstream paradigm of the preaching rock star and his unquestioning flock. And, of course, he simply got a big kick out of pissing people off.

L ooking for better nationwide distribution, Albini began negotiating a deal with Homestead Records. Albini liked Homestead's parent company, the distributor Dutch East India, because they had bought more Ruthless releases than any other distributor and because a previous Dutch East indie label, Braineater, had released records by two Albini favorites, the Wipers and Sisters of Mercy.

Gerard Cosloy had started writing for *Matter*, made friends with editor Elizabeth Phillip, and soon made Albini's acquaintance. "I had a lot of respect for him then and now," says Cosloy. "He does not suffer fools gladly. He sees through the bullshit very, very quickly." These two acerbic, highly intelligent, nerdy-looking guys with glasses got on very well; they liked to engage in verbal sparring where each would try to say something more offensive than the other could stand, the nerd version of two jocks punching each other on the arm until one begs the other to stop.

The two found they had a lot in common not just ethically and socially but aesthetically as well. "There are certain idiosyncrasies about bands that we both picked up on, things about texture, definitely things about the way guitars sound," Cosloy says, "the idea that the way the guitar is traditionally supposed to sound in the context of rock music — the whole R&B-based Keith Richards, Chuck Berry, John Fogerty guitar — that there's other directions it could go in."

When Cosloy arrived at Homestead, he picked up the negotiations with Albini. "Steve was probably a thousand times more effective than any manager or lawyer could have been," recalls Cosloy. "I'd say he was more organized and thorough than any manager or lawyer I've ever dealt with."

Their arrangement was unorthodox — Big Black merely licensed their records to Homestead for a specified length of time. They took no advance and paid for their own recordings (Albini once estimated that the band's entire recorded output cost between $2,000 and $3,000). And perhaps most unusually, they signed no contracts — the members of Big Black just didn't believe in them. "We came from a punk perspective — we did not want to get sucked into a corporate culture where basically you're signing a contract because you don't trust the other person to live up to their word," says Durango. "We had ideals, and that was one of our ideals."

Big Black figured contracts were worthless anyway — if a record company was going to screw a band, they'd do it with impunity since the band couldn't afford to retaliate. Besides, "if you don't use contracts, you don't have any contracts to worry about," says Albini. "If you don't have a tour rider, you don't have a tour rider to argue about. If you don't have a booking agent, you don't have a booking agent to argue with."

Albini and the band resolved to conduct their career on a high ethical plane. "It just seemed like you could behave like a pig or you could not," says Albini. "It never seemed like there was any advantage to being like a pig." This was especially true in the small world of indie rock.

Just before their Homestead debut, 1984's *Racer-X* EP, Big Black did a fairly extensive national tour. The close-knit indie network came in very handy. "You would call people in different cities that you'd met or were recommended to you by somebody else and ask them where you should play," says Albini. "Because nobody had any expectations of greater cultural importance, nobody had any aspirations to being a mainstream act, it was very easy and very comfortable to keep traveling in the circles that you were familiar with. . . . You'd know that if you were going through Ohio, you'd cross paths with *these* people, and *those* people have been recommended by *these* people and so on."

Unlike many of their peers, Big Black always made money on their tours — for one thing, since they didn't have a drummer, they didn't need to rent a van; they took along no roadies, and since Albini booked the tours, they didn't give up a percentage. "We just kept the scale really small," says Albini, "and didn't try to go places where we weren't welcomed."

Not only did Big Black resolutely refuse to pander to or compromise for the mainstream; they refused to do so with their own audience. "We are perfectly satisfied with the number of people who like the band," Albini declared in 1987 at the peak of the band's popularity. "It wouldn't bother us at all if half that many did. I don't think it would change anything if ten times as many came to see us. It wouldn't change the way we do anything, it wouldn't change the number of people that give a shit, it wouldn't change the effect of the band — it would just be more bodies."

In print and in interviews, again and again, Albini strongly took to task sacred cows like Public Image, Ltd., Suicide's Alan Vega, Wire's Colin Newman, the Stranglers, Hüsker Dü — all former favorites — for softening up and/or selling out. And to many people, Steve Albini gradually became "Steve Albini" — a larger-than-life cartoon of a strict indie rock zealot with dubious positions on just about any minority group you could name. "If you repeat a lie about someone often enough, that sort of becomes the truth," says Cosloy. "So it becomes Steve Albini, Evil Ogre, this very bad guy who goes to record stores and takes records on major labels and breaks them over his knee, then paints a swastika on the front of the store. In Steve's case, it's funny, because those things could not be further from the truth."

*Racer-X*, released in April '85, was a tad less frantic, less teeming than *Bulldozer*. Albini said he was going for a "big, massive, slick rock sound" but admitted that the effort fell short, ending up "too samey and monolithic."

The characters this time around, besides Speed Racer's mysterious older brother, are "The Ugly American" ("I hate what I am," growls Albini), a murderously jealous small-town loser ("Deep Six"), the masochist of "Sleep!" ("Your foot in my face is what keeps me alive"). There is even a mechanistic take on James Brown's "The Big Payback" that has Albini proclaiming, "I'll cut your throat / I'll make amends."

It was Big Black's third EP, and the band would go on to make one more record in that format. "Back then EPs carried a lot more weight," Cosloy explains. "An EP was not necessarily thought to be a precursor to an album or a promo item. An EP could exist as its own entity."

Of course, it was a lot quicker and cheaper to record six songs than ten or twelve, but Albini also figured that Big Black's abrasive music was easier to take in small doses. The lyrics in particular were growing more and more malevolent. It got so the band would play a little game of seeing how long it took a journalist to get around to using the phrase "the dark side of human nature" in interviews. But it's important to remember that Albini, Durango, and Pezzati were in their early twenties, and just about any male that age is fascinated by gruesome imagery. "That's just what was interesting to me as a postcollegiate bohemian," says Albini. "We didn't have a manifesto. Nothing was off-limits; it's just that that's what came up most of the time."

And the lyrics and even vocals weren't supposed to be the focal point anyway. "It seemed like, as instrumental music, it didn't have enough emotional intensity at times, so there would be vocals," Albini says. "But the vocals were not intended to be the center of attention — the interaction within the band and the chaotic nature of the music, that was the important part."

Eventually Pezzati, who had an increasingly demanding job, a fiancée, and two other bands (including the now nationally popular Naked Raygun) amicably left Big Black in late '84.

Dave Riley had moved to Chicago from Detroit in 1982, having worked at a recording studio that was home to both George Clinton and Sly Stone. Albini was impressed when he saw Riley play with a band called Savage Beliefs and eventually handed Riley a copy of the *Lungs* EP, saying, "Listen to this, and if you don't think it sucks, then maybe you can play with us someday."

Riley had already met Durango when the latter, drunk, was propping himself up on a sink at the Cubby Bear. "You're in Savage Beliefs, aren't you," Durango slurred. "You guys are really good. You've got real style." And then he threw up in the sink.

But Riley had never met the infamous Albini before. "For some reason, [I] expected a guy of much greater stature who was somewhat of a prick," says Riley. "I was clearly right about him being somewhat of a prick, but a benevolent and ultimately decent-kind-of-guy prick."

Like Albini and Durango, Riley was also a misfit, the perennial target of what Riley calls "insidious crap perpetrated by imperceptive emotional retards." As a teenager he'd been in a car accident that permanently damaged his face. "So he had a funny way of speaking," says Albini. "Especially when he got drunk, it was sometimes difficult to communicate with him because you could tell he was struggling just with the mechanics of speaking to you."

Riley joined the band the week *Racer-X* came out, although he kept his day job as a litigation law clerk. Once he learned the group's repertoire, they began writing songs for the band's first album.

**T**he last sentence of the liner notes for *Racer-X* read, "The next one's gonna make you shit your pants," and although the *Atomizer* LP did not quite induce spontaneous defecation, it amply delivered on the promise.

Sure, Riley was a stronger bass player than Pezzati, and he brought a bit more melodic sense to the band's music, but by this time Big Black had both refined the ideas first suggested on *Lungs* and exploded them into something much huger than anyone but Albini had ever imagined. Riley's gnarled bass sound combined explosively with the brutally insistent hammering of the drum machine while his funk background gave the music an almost danceable kick; Albini's and Durango's guitars, respectively billed as "skinng" and "vroom" in the liner notes, were reaching new heights of sonic violence. But it's not like a lot of people realized how good it was at the time. "Now, *Atomizer* sounds like a great, accessible record," says longtime Chicago music journalist Greg Kot. "But back then, you had to listen to it ten times just to get through, to penetrate the fact that there was actually music going on underneath this assault. It was that radical a statement."

Albini has a simpler explanation for the superiority of *Atomizer*: "We just had a higher-than-average percentage of really good songs." With a powerful rhythm ripped straight from Gang of Four and guitars that sound like shattering glass, "Kerosene" is probably Big Black's peak. As Riley explained it, life in small-town America is boring: "There's only two things to do. Go blow up a whole load of stuff for fun. Or have a lot of sex with the one girl in town who'll have sex with anyone. 'Kerosene' is about a guy who tries to *combine* the two pleasures."

One of the band's most controversial songs was "Jordan, Minnesota" about the rural town that stood accused of conducting a huge child sex ring; twenty-six people were indicted, a large portion of the town's adult population. "And this will stay with you until you die," Albini rails on the chorus.

The story confirmed everything Albini felt about human nature. "I felt sort of vindicated in my concept that everyone in the world was as perverse as you could imagine them being, that perversion was not restricted to TV preachers and classical perverts — *everybody* was perverted, *everybody* was strange," says Albini. "Everybody has the roots of greatness *and* evil in them." (The case began a long line of horrific child abuse and satanic ritual abuse stories that flooded the media in the late Eighties. Years later the Jordan case was dismissed after the children's testimony was found to have been coerced.)

And there lay the basic Big Black lyrical formula: Present people doing evil things that most people sometimes vaguely contemplate but never actually carry out — because they aren't sociopaths. On *Atomizer* there is the corrupt cop ("Big Money"), the shell-shocked veteran who becomes a contract killer ("Bazooka Joe"), the violent alcoholic ("Stinking Drunk"), the sadist ("Fists of Love"). The approach deflected attacks rather handily — as *Puncture* writer Terri Sutton put it, "The topics are so deliberately loaded that you can't criticize their 'art' without looking like some fucking puritan."

Big Black's audience seemed mostly to be male nerds brimming with frustration and fury — just like the band. "We were just repressed dweebs who opened the hatch where the demons come out and put them in the record bottle," says Durango. "It's a release. Just because we were puds didn't mean we didn't have this aggressiveness." Dweebs don't usually get to enjoy the kind of brute power that the bullies who torment them do. Getting up onstage and cranking up amplifiers to absolutely concussive levels of volume lets them exercise a simulacrum of power, and being experienced witnesses of that power, they wield it like connoisseurs, with all the expertise of those who have come to identify with their oppressors.

Not surprisingly, the band — and Albini in particular — attracted a

somewhat twisted following. Among the strangest fan gifts Albini was sent
were, he says, "a turd, a blood-and-hair-caked condom, photographs of
themselves and their turds."


**U**p until *Atomizer* the band wasn't a big draw. They had yet to sell
out Chicago's Cubby Bear, which held about three hundred
people. "We could play anywhere where there was an active underground music scene," says Albini, "we could find a show and we
would do OK, but we weren't really that popular." But then *Atomizer* won
a pile of positive national press and even the locals began to take notice.

Atomizer sold three thousand copies when it was released. "And we
were thrilled," says Albini. "We were *ecstatic.* That seemed like an un-
fathomable number of records to sell." It kept selling, too, to the point
where Big Black had enough clout with Homestead that Albini could call
up label head Barry Tenebaum and demand that either he pay fellow
Chicago bands like the Didjits or Big Black would leave the label. The
gambit worked, too.

The band got paid better for shows, but conditions were still pretty
much the same as ever. Every town seemed to have a ratty punk rock
house that was more than willing to put up the band, but Big Black eventually worked up a better strategy. "If it was possible to stay with a gay couple or a gay man, we always did, because their houses were always much,
much nicer," says Albini. "Generally they had cats, the places were always
clean. So 'Crib with fags' was always one of our rules for the road. You always crib with fags."

The drum machine would often befuddle the house soundperson,
who would hem and haw, complaining that it would somehow blow their
speakers, or that it wouldn't work with their sound system. Sometimes
they'd refuse to put the drum machine through the monitors and the
band would have to threaten to cancel the show. "You'd sort of have to
convince them that you knew what you were doing and that you weren't
going to hurt their stuff," says Albini. "Then it would be OK."

Sounds that aggressive didn't come lightly, and the band members
slammed their hands against the steel strings until they drew blood. "Oh,
we bled," says Durango. "We bled and bled. We used to have to put plas-
ters on our fingers." The other hazard about playing in Big Black was Albini's custom of setting off a brick of firecrackers onstage before they
played, a tradition dating from the band's earliest performances and carried on virtually ever since. "Yeah, every fuckin' show," says Durango with

**BIG BLACK IN
TRANSIT, NEW YORK,
1986.**

GAIL BUTENSKY

a resigned little laugh. "By the end, I just didn't care anymore. You get this feeling like 'When is it going to explode in front of your eye,' but it just never happened. They used to fly all over the place. I would stand off to the side at first, but by the end, it was just, 'OK, let's just do it.'"

If Big Black's live shows lacked the visual excitement of a live drummer, Albini more than made up for it. "It looked like someone had plugged Steve into the amp," recalls Cosloy. "It wasn't like he was pogoing up and down for sixty minutes, but he was pretty scary to watch onstage." Albini would yell, "One, two, fuck you!" to count in most songs and, with his guitar dangling from his specially made hip-slung guitar strap, prowl the stage like a spindly gunslinger.

The band was brutally loud, but they also knew the value of varying the attack, like during "Jordan, Minnesota." "We would get to a point in the song where we'd hit this really creepy noise, prolonged so it would just hang in the air, discordant so you would get a creepy feeling," says Durango. "And [Steve] would start pretending that he was one of the kids being raped, but I mean really intensely. And just impeccable timing. It was actually very disturbing to watch. . . . It would really get people unsettled."

A lot of fans would try to one-up the outspoken Albini by heckling him, just trying to get a reaction. And Albini or someone else in the band, usually Riley, would dismiss them with an acidic comeback or a joke so offensive it practically singed one's eyebrows. It was the perfect way to defuse — or was it heighten?— the effect of the extremely violent, intense music.

Visiting Europe was something of a reverse commute in those Anglocentric times, but Sonic Youth had already paved the way. And once in Europe, a band could expect much better treatment than they got back home. When Big Black toured Europe in 1986, promoters paid the band well, supplied hotel rooms, and even specially designed tour vans, complete with driver.

Overseas, no one knew anything about Big Black except for their music — there weren't even any pictures of the band on their records — and they apparently took Big Black songs such as "Ugly American" as straight autobiography. "Especially in Europe, people were surprised that we weren't these big, mean, ignorant people who were chemically dependent," says Riley. "We were three puds, basically."

But the response to the band's shows was very enthusiastic. "In fact, it was kind of overwhelming for a while," Riley says. "Needless to say, I got used to it really damn quick. People actually appreciated what you were doing and it was kind of cool. It was much different from America. We were treated with respect in Europe. When we toured in the States, it was like a 'Oh, use the back door with the busboys' kind of thing. Very different."

By then Big Black had gotten the all-important European label deal. And, like so many things in the indie world, it had something to do with Sonic Youth. Albini, like just about everybody else in the Chicago scene, occasionally promoted shows for out-of-town bands. Soon after he immersed himself in the Chicago punk scene, he began arranging shows for bands like Killdozer, Butthole Surfers, Rifle Sport, and Scratch Acid. And in 1983, when no one else would book Sonic Youth on their second Chicago appearance, Albini got them a show. It was a smashing success and paved the way for more out-of-town underground bands to play Chicago.

The favor came back to Albini. In 1986, when it came time to look into overseas record deals, he contacted his old friends Sonic Youth, who had just returned from England. Sonic Youth recommended Paul Smith's label Blast First and the deal went through.

At the same time, Albini had taken over operations of Ruthless Records in 1985, after the Effigies made a deal with Enigma Records. Albini helped engineer some of the records, assisted the bands with artwork, and served as liaison to distributor Dutch East India Trading. But his commitment to Big Black and his nascent engineering career (not to mention his day job as a photo retoucher) meant Albini couldn't properly promote the label's releases. "It was kind of foolish for me to get involved in it," he says, "and I feel like I didn't really do a great service to any of the bands." (Still, Albini released records that probably never would have been released otherwise: powerful, original music by bands like Minneapolis's Rifle Sport; Dark Arts from Columbus, Ohio; Madison's the Appliances SFB; and Chicago's End Result.)

To make matters worse, Dutch East India just wasn't working out, which was doubly bad since it owned Big Black's U.S. label Homestead as well. "Their accounting was always fucked," Albini claims. "They would do every sleazy, cheap trick to avoid paying you, like send you a check that wasn't signed or send you a check that had a different numeral and literal amount. Or they'd send you a statement that had all these figures on it and a total at the bottom and they'd send you a check for that total amount, but if you added up all the figures, it was actually a couple of thousand dollars off. 'Oh yeah, I guess you're right, I guess we did the math wrong. Sorry. We'll get a check out to you.' And you'd never end up getting the check."

But the final straw was when Homestead asked Big Black if they could make five hundred copies of a twelve-inch single of the song "Il Duce" for free distribution to radio stations. The band agreed on the condition that the single was not to be sold to the public. "We didn't want our audience milked for extra money by an alternate format," Albini explains.

And yet a few weeks after the single went out, Albini started seeing them in stores, although not in Big Black's hometown of Chicago. Albini then called a few stores around the country and abroad. "And sure enough, Homestead had been making and selling them at a ridiculous price — as a 'collector's item' — all over the world, except in Chicago. I called Homestead, and Barry said, 'Oh, no, we aren't selling any.' I then called one of their salespeople, posing as a record buyer, and asked if the title was available. He said, 'You're not in Chicago, are you? We're not allowed to sell this in Chicago.'"

Albini severed ties once and for all with Homestead and Dutch East India.

Despite the band's growing popularity, a major label was out of the question. "You can't find a person more concerned with the importance of remaining independent than Steve Albini," says Killdozer's Michael Gerald. "He'd receive phone calls from major labels, and his reaction was just to hang up. He wouldn't say, 'No' or 'Try to convince me.' He wouldn't say anything. He'd just hang up. He wasn't interested in anything they had to say."

"We wanted to have pointedly offensive records, and no big record company would put up with that," Albini explains. "And it was obvious if you just go to the record store and just listen to records, all the good ones were not on major labels. Why would I want to be part of that?" And with the indie label system more than well in place by 1986, there was just no reason to.

Besides, there would be commercial pressure if they signed to a major label. "Once you start putting out records because you have to make a living off of it, then you're in trouble because you're making music for the wrong reasons," Durango says. "That's OK for people who are entertainers and have no qualms about that, but for us it was a little more than that."

Another big reason the band shunned the majors was because of the clueless crowd they'd inevitably attract. "There already seemed to be a percentage of the audience that didn't get what we were on about and were just there for a party," says Albini. "I didn't see any advantage in increasing those proportions."

Not even the lure of big money could entice them. "None of us ever imagined that the band was a job," Albini continues. "The band was always a diversion. It seemed unrealistic to think that we could make a living out of it. So we didn't even entertain those notions."

"We didn't want to save the world," Riley concludes. "We just wanted to play in a punk rock band."

Fortunately, there was a very cool indie label right in town: Touch & Go. Corey Rusk and Albini had first met in the summer of '83 on a panel at the New Music Seminar in New York. It turned out to be quite an illustrious little group on the dais — also on the panel were Gerard Cosloy and Def Jam Records cofounder Rick Rubin. Rusk and Albini met again when Big Black played the Graystone in Detroit with the Butthole Surfers. When Big Black arrived at the Rusks' house, they were impressed. "He and his wife had made this amazing hospitality lifestyle," Albini recalls. "People would turn up and there was always a bong on for them, there was always beer in the fridge, there was always a barbecue running. It was great."

The house was also something of a zoo — besides dogs and cats, the Rusks kept a python, some prairie dogs, a chinchilla, and some hedgehogs. "They had some sort of African bullfrog that was about twelve inches in diameter," says Michael Gerald, "and that's the way to describe it because it was as flat as a cowpie. I do recall perhaps eight people there sitting around watching in amazement as the frog shat. Apparently it did this only about once a year. It shat a shit as big as itself. It came out so slowly that Corey had time to go and get his video camera and tape it."

As usual, Rusk threw an epic barbecue to kick off the weekend of shows. Albini immediately ingratiated himself by bringing along "a big bag of meat," and, standing around the sizzling flesh, Albini and Rusk soon discovered they shared an intense, lifelong fascination with fireworks.

"When I first met him, I felt like I was meeting another person like me," Albini says. "I sort of felt like we were the same person in different bodies. We had a lot of the same attitudes; we appreciated a lot of the same stuff. We both sort of had run-ins with some of the hardcore punk scene which we had sort of gotten disillusioned with and didn't feel like it really represented what we liked about punk. We both liked fireworks; we were both pretty committed to doing things in what we thought was the right way rather than doing it the way other people were telling us to do it. And in both cases it seemed to be working."

Albini and Rusk have been good friends ever since, gathering in Rusk's backyard nearly every Fourth of July to blow up electronic gear, plush dolls, and many of the larger fruits and vegetables.

Big Black's first Touch & Go release was the five-song *Headache* EP, issued in the spring of '87. The notorious cover of the original, limited edition — packaged in a black plastic "body bag" — featured two gruesome, truly horrific forensic photos of a man whose head had been split down the middle, perhaps in a car accident. (The imagery, Albini says, "was a good play on words.") Seeing those photographs provided the same jolt Albini often spoke of in connection with his music. Then again, maybe it was just a pointless, puerile gross-out. "At the time," he says, "it seemed like a good idea."

A sticker on the cover read "Not as good as *Atomizer*, so don't get your hopes up, cheese!" And indeed, it wasn't as good as *Atomizer*, though few bands would ever advertise the fact on their own record. "We didn't want to sit there and screw people," Durango explains. "If we felt it wasn't as good, then we should just be honest about it."

*Headache* recycled many of the same sounds, and with songs about a hard-bitten detective, a union thug, and a man so revolted by his own newborn child that he hurls it against a wall, it recycled many of the same themes as well. Albini's targets were quite distant from his or his audience's existence — had any of the geeky college boys in the audience ever tangled with a Teamster goon? So while the songs are a pointed refutation of the vapidly escapist pop and navel-gazing singer-songwriter drivel of the time, their unrelenting immersion in the dank depths of American life is just as reductive.

The band was no longer at the top of their game: one big reason, Albini claims, was that Riley was "kind of fucked up most of the time" (a charge Riley denies). Albini was a teetotaler, so Durango and Riley became drinking buddies on the road, especially since Albini was often off doing interviews or organizational work. But apparently Riley was getting a little too far into his cups. "The problem with Dave," says Durango, "was that he fucked up a number of our shows."

At a show in Milwaukee, "he couldn't even sit on the stage," says Durango. "We tried to plug him in and he fought us off. He was fucked up beyond fucked up — he was FUBAR." When they played a key show at CBGB, Riley drunkenly smashed Roland the drum machine. "I think Steve could have strangled him right then and there," Durango says. They called in Peter Prescott of the opening band the Volcano Suns to play live drums, but Prescott barely knew the songs and the show was a flop.

Riley's other offenses, Albini says, included: "always late for rehearsal, never having equipment together, needing a ride to everything, a fresh excuse for every day, generally unkempt and unreliable, impossible to communicate with when loaded, flashes of brilliance offset by flashes of belligerence." These are annoying offenses for any band, but they particularly bothered the efficient, hardworking Albini.

"It was like living in a dysfunctional family," says Durango. "It was kind of a love-hate thing. [Steve] was always mad at Dave, always threatening all kinds of things." But Albini never fired Riley, perhaps because it was too difficult to change horses in midstream. "That may have been the reason," Durango says, "or maybe on some subconscious level he understood that that was something Dave brought to the band."

Even by late '86, both Durango and Albini had to keep day jobs — Riley was now in school — which limited the amount of time they could tour. But it also gave them the economic freedom to do whatever they wanted with the band.

Albini did have to be resourceful, though. For instance, when he couldn't afford to pay his phone bill, he'd just let the phone company blacklist his name and then start a new account under a slightly different one. "So in Chicago, there were listings for Steve Albini, Albin, Albono, Albani," Durango chuckles. "The guy was amazing, sneaking all his furniture out of an apartment because he couldn't pay the rent and they were going to lock him out, packing a little apartment's worth of furniture into a little station wagon."

But Albini's diary entries in the summer '86 issue of *Forced Exposure* revealed a sensitive side that few knew existed. "I'm an abject failure at everything I try," he wrote, "partly because I can never be satisfied with doing only part of it. I want to do everything and I want it all to be perfect. As a result, I accomplish almost nothing, and what I do get done is slipshod crap."

In response to a letter condemning him as a hatemonger, he wrote, "Is it really such a fucking sin to be frank about all this shit? Christ, people go much wilder on this shit in private than I ever do in print. All I'm doing is owning up to what everybody else is saying behind each other's backs. If I've got an opinion on something or an observation about something, and somebody asks me for it, well there you go. I try to retain my integrity (the little I can) by being honest and upfront about this shit, and all I get is grief. It's as though people don't mind you thinking unkind things as much as they mind knowing about them in the first place. And a lot of the people ragging on me for being straight so much have some pretty massive skeletons in their closets. I keep mine in the foyer to greet my house guest. That's all."

**T**hen one day Durango told Albini that he had decided to enter law school, starting the fall '87 semester. They decided to keep the band going until then and then call it quits. The band members had never looked on Big Black as a full-time job, and besides, now pushing thirty, Durango wasn't getting any younger. But it might have been a good time for the band to stop anyway.

By *Headache* the band was showing signs that it had reached the end of its creative line. "I was feeling that I was tapped out ideawise," Durango concedes. "At that point I think we had tried everything that we wanted to try, musically and in the studio." They put a more righteous face on it in the *Pigpile* liner notes: "The members of Big Black have often been asked why we chose to break up (the end of the band having been announced well in advance) just when we were becoming quite popular. The best answer then and now is: To prevent us from overstaying our welcome."

In the year following the announcement of their impending demise, the band received more acclaim than it ever had. They were now enjoying substantially increased press, airplay, record sales, and concert fees, and the possibility of modest commercial success was not out of the question. "Oh yeah, we could have, had we pursued it," says Riley. "But see, Big Black was never about that. For Big Black to make any money, it wouldn't have been Big Black anymore."

Besides, being in a lame duck band wasn't so bad. "It was great," says Albini. "We didn't have to worry about anything. Who cares if we make an enemy, I'm never going to see this guy again! OK, this soundman is being a pain in the ass, let's straighten him out, what do I care? It was liberating, it was really great."

N ew York punk priestess Lydia Lunch raved about a January '87 show in *Forced Exposure*: "RAM-BATTERING WITH BRUTALLY BUTT-FUCKING GUT-BUSTERING BALLS-OUT BLITZKRIEGS OF SHEER PO-ETRY AND PAIN, I WAS PULVERIZED INTO NEAR OBLIVION AS WALL AFTER WALL OF FRUSTRATION, HEARTACHE, HATRED, DEATH, DISEASE, DIS-USE, DISGUST, MISTRUST, & MAELSTROM STORMED THE STAGE WAGING WAR WITH MILITARY PRECISION INSISTENTLY INVADING EVERY OPEN ORIFICE WITH THE STRENGTH OF TEN THOUSAND BULLS, AS JACK-HAMMERING ON THE BASE OF MY SPINE WITH A BUCK KNIFE-BURNED THE DREAM OF MY HANDS WRUNG FIRMLY AROUND HIS THROAT."

Lunch added a fantasy about her and Albini that must surely have sent the latter into paroxysms of ecstasy. "PARKED IN PITCH-BLACK OVER-LOOKING SOME STINKING, USELESS, LIFELESS HELLHOLE GARBAGEPLOT WHERE NEITHER OF US WANTED TO LIVE OR DIE, WHERE FOR 32 SECONDS OF HIS MEASLY LOUSY LIFE HE WASN'T IN TOTAL CONTROL OF HIS SKINNY, TIGHT NECK, TAUT, POWERFUL, RHYTHMIC THRASHINGS, THOSE IRRE-SISTIBLE REPETITIONS, SUCKING YOU INTO AN INCREDIBLE POUND-ING LIKE A HEAD AGAINST A WINDSHIELD OVER & OVER & OVER THE BANGING BRUTALITY, SQUEEZING, FORCE-FEEDING HIM HIS OWN LOVE/ HATE/LIFE/DEATHTRIP FLIRTATIONS IN REVERSAL. TO DO TO HIM WHAT HE DOES TO ME."

Other reviewers had quite different reactions. In a review of a show from the same tour, *Puncture*'s Terri Sutton described Big Black's brutal, frenzied audience as "marionette puppets, translating messages of violence into more violence.

"Is that it?" Sutton asked the band. "Is that what you want, guys?"

The initial pressing of the band's final album, *Songs about Fucking*, was about eight thousand records, and it went on to become Big Black's best seller. Even Robert Plant liked it.

The sarcastic album title was more than explained in Albini's notes for the song "Pavement Saw." "The male-female relationship, as a subject for song," Albini wrote, "is thoroughly bankrupt." The song "Tiny, King of the Jews" was also revealing. As the last song on the last Big Black album, it's hard not to lend it particular significance. "Man's gotta hate someone / Guess I'll do," Albini growls, "And when I'm through with myself / I start on you."

Albini booked the band's final tour to begin in early June '87. An L.A. promoter had offered the band $5,000, but the manager of the venue they were supposed to play thought Big Black was a racist band — "Why he thinks this, I have no idea," Albini wrote in his tour diary — and refused the booking. Then the promoter found them a show for $2,500 at a smaller venue. "So," wrote Albini, "I told him to eat shit." A $6,000 New York gig also fell through.

Albini turned twenty-five on July 22, the day Big Black played the Pukkul Pop Festival in Belgium. Sonic Youth's Kim Gordon presented him with a birthday present of a pair of mud-spattered panties that had been tossed onstage. Later Albini pissed on goth kingpins the Mission's amplifiers.

"I am now quite happy to be breaking up," Albini wrote. "Things getting much too big and uncontrollable. All along we've wanted to keep our hands on everything, so nothing happened that we didn't want to. With international multi-format/multi-territorial shit, that's proving elusive. I prefer to cut it off rather than have it turn into another Gross Rock Spectacle."

At a sold-out (thirteen hundred tickets) show in London, Bruce Gilbert and Graham Lewis of one of Albini's favorite bands, Wire, helped the band play an encore of Wire's "Heartbeat." "If I die right now it will all have been worth it," Albini wrote.

The tour then jumped to Australia, then back to San Francisco, Providence, Boston, and New York, and on to their final performance ever, on August 11 in Seattle, at the Georgetown Steamplant, the former generating plant for Boeing Airfield and the largest cast concrete building in the world. Much to Albini's later regret, they smashed their guitars at the end of the show.

I felt good about the way the band conducted itself," says Albini. "We treated everybody good, we never took advantage of anybody, never shit on anybody, never did anything that I wasn't proud of."

"It meant nothing to us if we were popular or not, or if we sold either a million or no records, so we were invulnerable to ploys by music scene weasels to get us to make mistakes in the name of success," Albini wrote in the liner notes of the posthumous *Pigpile* live album. "To us, every moment we remained unfettered and in control was a success. We never had a manager. We never had a booking agent. We never had a lawyer. We booked our own tours, paid our own bills, made our own mistakes and never had anybody shield us from either the truth or the consequences."

After Big Black's final tour, Albini returned to Chicago and promptly got depressed about not being in a band anymore. He tried making music, but his neighbor would call the police whenever any sound escaped from Albini's house after nightfall. Then his basement flooded, ruining lots of equipment. On top of it, he was broke and yet desperately wanted to quit his day job.

Eventually, Albini started a new band with the now defunct Scratch Acid's peerless rhythm section — bassist David Wm. Sims and drummer Rey Washam. "The two of them with him was like . . . Cream!" says Gerard Cosloy. "Actually, I can't stand Cream so it's not like Cream at all. But it was the perfect supergroup."

Albini had recently discovered a Japanese comic book called *Rapeman*. "You open up this comic book, and there's this superhero who rapes people, as his profession," said Albini. "It's pretty amazing." Washam and Albini both became fascinated with the comic and eventually came to the conclusion that Rapeman would make a great band name. And in classic Albini fashion, it was sure to annoy the hell out of people.

On their first American tour, in the summer of '88, Seattle's KCMU refused to allow the band's name to be used in on-air promos for their show; there were even picket lines and news crews at a few gigs. "It was the typical motley alliance of housewives and lesbians at the picket line — housewives offended by the concept of punk rock and lesbians offended by the concept of rape," said Albini. "The really annoying thing was that the majority of the people on the picket line were precisely the kind of people that we would have liked at the gig, people that, politically, basically think like we do. But sometimes people are so dead set on being stupid that they won't allow themselves to experience something themselves."

Jeff Pezzati recalls being on tour in Europe with Naked Raygun when Rapeman first came over. The two tours trailed each other around the Continent, and Pezzati would hear the reaction every step of the way. "The Europeans took that name so goddamn seriously, it was like someone had hit them with a brick in the head," says Pezzati. "If he had picked any other name, he would have been the king of the world in Europe."

The band released 1988's *Budd* EP, named after R. Budd Dwyer, the disgraced Pennsylvania State treasurer who shot himself to death at a 1987 press conference. The music is spacious but intense one moment, dense and intense the next; one number features probably the most virulent utterance of the word "motherfucker" on record. The band eventually released an album the following year, *Two Nuns and a Pack Mule*, but Albini disavowed it shortly afterward.

The band didn't last very long after that. Albini explained the breakup of Rapeman by saying simply, "Someone couldn't get along with someone else. That's it."

Fortunately, Albini had something to fall back on. Even before Big Black started, Albini had done some modest demos for other bands, while other bands would bring Albini along to sessions so he could explain to the engineer what the band wanted. Later he recorded Urge Overkill in their practice room on a four-track and recorded a few local punk bands in a little studio in Evanston.

Around 1985 he began to undertake more serious recordings. Albini would often record and mix an entire album in one day for about $200. "I just consider this a service that I do," Albini said in 1991. "Because, like, when I was in a band it really frustrated me that there weren't good, cheap studios out there to record in. So what I have done is built a good, cheap studio for all the bands out there."

In 1987 Albini bought a house in a nondescript neighborhood in northwest Chicago, quit his day job, and began working on building his own basement studio; it was small, but the equipment was all top-notch. Even better, Albini didn't charge for studio time, just his time, so a band could bring blank tape and a friend to do the recording and it wouldn't cost them anything.

He soon recorded a long list of fine bands: Slint, Poster Children,

Pixies, Gore, the Wedding Present, Head of David, AC Temple, Scrawl, Pussy Galore, Boss Hog, Zeni Geva, the Breeders, Tar, Shorty, Pegboy. The sheer quality of the bands he recorded and the excellent sounds and performances he extracted from them made his reputation. By 1991 Albini claimed he was getting three or four offers a day to record bands. That fall alone the prolific Albini recorded albums by the Volcano Suns, the Didjits, Urge Overkill, the Jesus Lizard, and the Wedding Present as well as literally dozens of lesser-known bands.

Albini's recording philosophy: "When you listen to something and it grabs you by the face and drags you around the room, that's great. It doesn't have to be a macho rock stud kind of loud, but it should jump out of the speakers at you."

He achieved his goal with the aid of an ever-growing collection of vintage microphones strategically placed around the room. One Albini trademark was to mix the vocals very low — on the Jesus Lizard albums Albini recorded, singer David Yow sounds like a kidnap victim trying to howl through the duct tape over his mouth; the effect is horrific. The recordings were both very basic and very exacting: Albini used few special effects; got an aggressive, often violent guitar sound; and made sure the rhythm section slammed as one.

Albini disliked getting credited at all on the records he worked on. But if there was a credit, he insisted that it say "recorded by" as opposed to "produced by" because, he says, he never forced his wishes on the band. "I will do a good job for them," he wrote in *Forced Exposure*, "but that does not include shouldering any responsibility for their lousy tastes and mistakes."

Albini claimed to be willing to record anybody who asked, although if it meant going to another studio or going out of town, they'd have to be a band he either liked very much musically and/or personally. And if it was a band on a major label, "Then I stick it to them," Albini says. "Because it's not their money, it's the big-ass record company's money who's not going to pay them anyway." Even still, Albini recorded for bargain basement rates — topping out at around $25,000 at the time. And unlike virtually all other producers, Albini refused to take royalties for his work. "It is an insult to the band to say that because I recorded this album," he said, "and not somebody else, you're selling more records and therefore I want a cut."

As Spot had done with SST and Jack Endino would do with Sub Pop, Albini worked for low rates, enabling his friend Corey Rusk's label, Touch & Go, to get off the ground. "Steve's the patron saint of Touch & Go," Rusk says.

And though a saint, he remained Albini. In 1988, he recorded the Pixies' *Surfer Rosa* album in a week and charged them only $1,500. And yet he later called the now classic album "a patchwork pinch loaf from a band who at their top-dollar best are blandly entertaining college rock." A couple of years later, when they were on a major American label (Elektra) and flush with dough, he charged them $4,000 to record one song.

Albini went on to record albums by the likes of PJ Harvey, Bush, Nirvana, and even Robert Plant and Jimmy Page. He brushed aside accusations of sellout, pointing out that he had always said he'd record anyone who asked, and besides, he was plowing the money back into the studio of his dreams, the world-class Electrical Audio Studios in Chicago. Even his fancy new studio is in keeping with his core values: "See this place?" he says, gesturing grandly toward the air-conditioning ducts, the plumbing, the walls, and the electrical wiring. "This place was built entirely by *punk rockers!*"

# CHAPTER 10

# DINOSAUR JR

STARTING BACK IN '83, STARTED SEEING
THINGS DIFFERENTLY
HARDCORE WASN'T DOING IT FOR ME NO MORE
STARTED SMOKING POT
I THOUGHT THINGS SOUNDED BETTER SLOW

— SEBADOH, "GIMME INDIE ROCK"

Dinosaur Jr was one of the first, biggest, and best bands among the second generation of indie kids, the ones who took Black Flag and Minor Threat for granted, a generation for whom the Seventies, not the Sixties, was the nostalgic ideal. Their music continued a retrograde stylistic shift in the American underground that the Replacements and other bands had begun: renouncing the antihistorical tendencies of hardcore and fully embracing the music that everyone had grown up on. In particular, Dinosaur singer-guitarist J Mascis achieved the unthinkable in underground rock — he brought back the extended guitar solo.

Dinosaur Jr had nothing to do with regionality, making a statement about indie credibility, or even speaking to a specific community. It was simply about creating good rock music. Even Mascis seemed removed from the feelings he was conveying in the music, which was ironic since he'd come up through hardcore, that most engaged of genres. But while he'd embraced the intensity, he'd abandoned the sensibility of hardcore. Throwing in the twin bogeymen of the underground, classic rock and the navel-gazing singer-songwriter sensibility, made Dinosaur Jr's music acceptable to a much broader range of people, people who were a little more complacent and less radicalized than the hardcore and post-hardcore types.

Dinosaur also represented a continuing shift on a professional level, too. By the time they came along, the indie underground didn't have to be do-it-yourself anymore — there were booking agents and road managers and publicists at a band's disposal, particularly if the band was on SST, which hit its commercial peak in the Dinosaur era.

Rare was a label like Dischord or Twin/Tone that could survive on a steady diet of local bands. Instead, indie labels that stayed alive did so by diversifying. No one had done this better than SST, which by the late Eighties dominated the indie landscape with a roster that also included bands like Screaming Trees, Volcano Suns, All (on the SST subsidiary Cruz), Soundgarden, Meat Puppets, Sonic Youth, fIREHOSE, Bad Brains, Das Damen, and Negativland.

SST would use its power and experience to break Dinosaur Jr. SST worked Dinosaur's singles to college radio just like "real" record companies, instead of encouraging stations to choose various album cuts. But in the end, if Dinosaur Jr's songs had been mediocre, SST could have done only so much. As it turned out, Dinosaur's music was awfully good; it also reached precisely the right audience. The band and college radio developed a symbiotic relationship: Dinosaur thrived on college radio and college radio thrived on making underground stars out of bands like Dinosaur.

The classic rock influences, the extreme volume, the band's so-called "slacker" style, even their quiet verse/loud catchy chorus formula would soon be imitated and finessed into a full-fledged cultural phenomenon.

J oseph Mascis Jr. grew up in affluent Amherst, Massachusetts, essentially a company town for the area's famed Five Colleges and a bastion of touchy-feely post-hippieism. Joseph, better known as J, was the son of a successful dentist and a homemaker. He says his parents were "really uptight and not very affectionate," and, consequently, young J grew up somewhat aloof and self-absorbed. All the furniture in his room was arranged to create a wall around his bed, and there he'd lie for hours, listening to music. Green plastic curtains covered the windows, suffusing the room with an emerald light, and the floor was literally covered with stuffed animals and records. "I was a weird kid," Mascis acknowledges. "It made people uncomfortable sometimes."

Mascis had taken a few guitar lessons in fifth grade but quickly switched to drums and played in the school jazz band for years. He was a voracious music listener, exploring the Beatles and the Beach Boys by age ten, then moving into standard hard rock like Deep Purple and Aerosmith. His older brother introduced Mascis to classic rock like Eric Clapton, Neil Young, Creedence, and Mountain, but by eighth grade, he says, "I was strictly Stones." Then he discovered hardcore. "I didn't listen to anything else for a while," Mascis says. "Didn't understand how anyone else could."

Lou Barlow and his family moved from a moribund auto industry town in Michigan to blue-collar Westfield, Massachusetts, when he was twelve. "It's more of a metal kind of town," Mascis says of Westfield. "It's like *Wayne's World.* I can see Lou getting beat up in high school a lot." The introverted Barlow found it difficult to make a whole new set of friends. "I retreated into my room and that was it," he says. "I never came out." Barlow caught the punk rock bug after hearing the Dead Kennedys on one of the many college radio stations in the area. After that, "I just listened to the radio all the time," Barlow says. "My grades plummeted — well, they were down there anyway — and I didn't have any friends."

Soon after picking up the guitar, Barlow met fellow punk fan Scott Helland at Westfield High; they jammed in Barlow's attic accompanied by a friend on pots and pans. Soon they put up an ad at Northampton's redoubtable Main Street Records: "Drummer wanted to play really fast. Influences: Black Flag, Minor Threat."

J Mascis answered the ad and his dad drove him down to Westfield in the family station wagon for an audition. Barlow was awed the moment Mascis walked in the door. "He had this crazy haircut," says Barlow. "He'd cut pieces of hair out of his head — there were bald spots in his hair. He had dandruff and he had sleepy stuff in his eyes. Everything 'sucked,' which was, like, amazing. I was like, 'Oh my god, he's *too cool!*'"

And best of all, "he wailed," Barlow recalls. Mascis convinced them also to induct his Amherst chum Charlie Nakajima, who sported a Sid Vicious–style lock and chain around his neck. They called the quartet Deep Wound and Mascis's mom soon knitted him a sweater with a red puddle on the chest with the band name on it. They began playing local hardcore shows at VFW halls and the like — someone would rent a PA, an established national band would headline, and a handful of local bands would pile onto the bill.

Deep Wound went on to play a few shows in Boston, opening for the F.U.'s, D.O.A., MDC, and S.S.D. (It is unknown if they ever played with a band whose name was not composed of initials.) Even though Deep Wound didn't boast much besides sheer velocity, the band managed to get some national notice in a brief (if comically generic) mention in *Maximumrocknroll* — "Deep Wound are a hardcore band who 'are mostly concerned with the struggles of youth in society.'"

Barlow and Mascis quickly became good friends. "It was almost romantic, I guess — it's got that overtone," says their mutual friend Jon Fetler, Deep Wound's "manager." "It was these two talented kids finding each other." And yet they barely knew each other. "He didn't say much so I didn't really know anything about him particularly," says Mascis. "But when he would talk, it would always be quotes from fanzines. . . . I would be like, 'Didn't I just read that in your room?'"

Mascis was hardly more communicative. He spoke very slowly, if at all; he always seemed to be in a daze. People consistently assumed he was a pothead, but he'd been straight edge since his midteens. "I think it's just my general way of being," says Mascis. "Everyone always thought I was stoned ever since I can remember. Didn't talk that much. Perma-stoned."

Class differences within the band sometimes threatened their laconic friendship. "[Mascis and Nakajima] were from Amherst, they went to school with Uma Thurman and all these professors' kids," says Barlow. When Barlow wrote a song called "Pressures," "a very 'things are all coming at me and nothing seems real' kind of song," says Barlow, they made him change the title to "Lou's Anxiety Song" just to distance themselves from the unsophisticated sentiment.

A friend pitched in some money to record an EP for Boston's short-lived Radio Beat label. "It was terrifying — total red light fever," says Barlow. "We played our songs way too fast. There wasn't really much of a cohesion in the sound, but we tried." Steve Albini, in a *Matter* review, said the EP "alternates between really cool inventive hardball and generic thrashola garbage," although he felt it was mostly the latter.

Mascis had picked up the guitar again and gradually taken over songwriting duties from Helland and Barlow on the grounds that their material wasn't "hooky" enough. Although he was still the band's drummer, he insisted on playing guitar on the EP's "Video Prick," festooning this minute and a half of standard hardcore thrash with flashy guitar licks of the "widdly-diddly" variety. Even amidst the EP's shoddy production, it was evident that J Mascis was one hotshot guitar player.

**C**onflict fanzine publisher Gerard Cosloy had become a big Deep Wound fan while promoting various hardcore shows in Boston. The evening Cosloy moved into his dorm room at the University of Massachusetts at Amherst, he went to a hardcore show in nearby Greenfield and bumped into Mascis, who was also just starting at U. Mass. The two kindred spirits became fast friends. "J was definitely a different sort of individual," remembers Cosloy. "He was sort of quiet, but when he had something to say it was usually something very, very funny and usually something very biting. He was pretty hard on people. Very hard on people. . . . Especially for people in the punk rock scene, there was this whole sense that 'Hey, we're all part of the same thing, we should all be friends! Hey brother!' J did not really give off that vibe."

Mascis cut quite a figure on campus. He wore rings on all his fingers and hippie-style necklaces and moussed up his hair into an arty thicket like his hero, Nick Cave of the Birthday Party. "He had huge fuckin' hair," Cosloy recalls, "like stick-your-finger-in-the-socket-type hair." Mascis made a particularly unusual impression during his visits to the school cafeteria. "J would walk over to the table carrying this mountainous plate of food and proceed to sit there and not even really eat it — he'd just begin to organize it in different patterns and shapes," says Cosloy. "People would be sort of staring, like, 'What the fuck?' I mean, it was hard not to be impressed. You just sort of knew you were dealing with a visionary."

Cosloy often mentioned Mascis in Conflict stories — "He was fascinated with J's whole thing and he wrote about it really well," says Barlow — and featured two Deep Wound tracks on his Western Mass.-centric Bands that Could Be God compilation. Cosloy began managing Deep Wound and started introducing Mascis to American indie bands like True West, the Neats, and the Dream Syndicate; Mascis in turn was introducing these bands to Barlow, but they also dug the hyperkinetic stomp of bands like Motörhead, Venom, and Metallica. "We loved speed metal," said Barlow, "and we loved wimpy-jangly stuff.

"Once hardcore homogenized into this scene and there's all these bands with the same kind of chunky sound," says Barlow, "that's when we all just sort of went, 'Fuck it.' " Just as important, the music was simply not a good fit with such introspective kids. "Hardcore was not a very personal music to me," Barlow admitted. "I loved hardcore, but I felt like I wasn't powerful enough and didn't have enough of an edge to really make it," he added. "I felt like a wanna-be the whole time."

Soon they were delving into the Replacements, Black Sabbath, and

Neil Young. It was still mostly aggressive music, but it was slower. "We had sex," Mascis explained. "You lose the thrashing drive after sex." And since Deep Wound was nothing *but* "the thrashing drive," they called it quits in the summer of '84, just before Mascis's sophomore year at the University of Massachusetts.

Cosloy had dropped out of U. Mass. after one semester to move to New York and run Homestead Records. The two kept in touch, and Cosloy promised that if Mascis were to make a record, he'd put it out, whatever it was. "Gerard really did give J something to shoot for," says Barlow. "That was pretty cool, because that gave J free rein to just absolutely redefine what he wanted to do with music."

Mascis had been quietly writing songs on his own and eventually played some for Barlow. "They were fucking brilliant," says Barlow. "They were so far beyond. I was still into two-chord songs and basic stuff like 'I'm so sad.' While I was really into my own little tragedy, J was operating in this whole other panorama." Mascis had somehow incorporated all the music he'd ever listened to — the melodiousness of the Beach Boys, the gnarled stomp of Black Sabbath, the folky underpinnings of Creedence and Neil Young, the Cure's catchy mope-pop. "Something just clicked with him and he did it," says Barlow, still marveling. "It was a totally genius little idea." Within a year Mascis had gone from writing standard-issue hardcore to composing music that had strong melodies, gorgeous chords, and dramatic dynamic shifts. "And he's playing all this *amazing* guitar," says Barlow. "I was like, '*Bluhhhhhhh.*'"

Barlow gladly accepted Mascis's invitation to play bass and took a job at a nursing home so he could buy equipment. He had played guitar and sung in Deep Wound, but he was now content to take any role. "I really accepted my service to his songs," he says. "Being a bass player can be a great role. I was very keenly aware of how powerful it was. I was very optimistic and very into it."

Soon Mascis enlisted frontman Nakajima and Nakajima's high school buddy Emmett Jefferson "Patrick" Murphy III, better known as Murph, on drums. Mascis had also been listening to George Jones, Hank Williams, and Dolly Parton, and the music had rubbed off on him. "Earbleeding country," says Mascis. "That was the concept behind the band."

Murph had played in a local hardcore band called All White Jury, but his roots were in prog rock and fusion bands like the Mahavishnu Orchestra, Rush, King Crimson, and especially Frank Zappa. He hailed from the well-to-do New York suburb of Greenwich, Connecticut; his father was a professor at U. Mass. Murph had some doubts about the group;

a self-described "hippie punk," he was pretty seriously into partying, something the straight edge Mascis and Barlow turned up their noses at. "They always thought I was a pot-smoking jerk," says Murph. "They totally had that righteous, fascist attitude. I used to laugh at them and say, 'Wow, you guys are really uptight to be so secular in your thinking.'" But Nakajima, also a stoner, convinced him that it was two against two and it would balance out. And all the while Barlow continued to worry that as the working-class Westfield kid, *he* was the odd man out. "Oh, they were fuckin' snotty as hell," says Barlow. "People from Amherst were assholes." "It was really tense and weird," says Murph. "But we couldn't deny that we could play together."

They called the new band Mogo, after a book in Mascis's mother's vast collection of romance novels, and played their first show on Amherst Common in the first week of September '84. The stage was within earshot of the local police station, and out of nowhere Nakajima began spouting a punk anticop rant into the microphone. Mascis was appalled. He also didn't like the fact that Nakajima regularly got stoned for practice, and the next day he broke up the band. Then a few days later he called Murph and Barlow and asked them to form a new band, a trio, without Nakajima. "I was kind of like too wimpy to kick him out, exactly," Mascis admits. "Communicating with people has been a constant problem in the band."

Mascis decided to do the singing himself, with Barlow taking the vocal on a few numbers. Barlow took the job very seriously; he would go out for a jog every day and sing the lyrics as he went, then come home and practice playing the songs on bass.

This time, they called the band Dinosaur. Dinosaurs were just beginning to enjoy one of their periodic revivals in the public imagination, and besides, the word fit their music to a T: "He was also playing tons of leads and we were listening to a lot of old Sixties and Seventies heavy rock," says Barlow, "so it just seemed really appropriate."

Locally the band wasn't noted for much besides its ear-splitting volume. "The one sort of statement that J had was, 'We're going to be really fuckin' loud,'" says Barlow. "And he was very serious about that. He was very serious about being excruciatingly loud."

According to Mascis, the reason for the volume wasn't power madness or better distortion. "After playing drums, guitar seemed so wimpy in comparison — I was trying to get more of the same feeling out of the guitar as playing drums," Mascis explains. "That's why I tried to have it get louder and quieter with pedals and stuff — it was hard to get it to have any dynamics like drumming. I was trying to get the air coming off the speakers to hit me in the back, to *feel* playing as much as hear it."

As a result, it was hard to tell exactly how the songs really sounded, even to the people in the band. "I could never really hear anything [J] was playing because he played way too loud," says Barlow. Barlow would have to wait until the band was in the studio to hear the true beauty of the songs' construction.

The band's audiences couldn't fathom the intense volume either. "We ran into a lot of problems playing early on," says Mascis, "because if you have no fans *and* you're really loud, no one wants to deal with you. The clubs are like, 'What are you doing? Get out!' We got banned from every club in Northampton." Dinosaur even had trouble when they later traveled to Boston to open for Homestead bands like Volcano Suns and Salem 66. One soundman actually threw beer bottles at the band — afterward, recalls Mascis, "we were just sitting there driving home, saying, 'Why are we in a band again?' We just were driven to do it for some reason, I don't know why. Just because we had nothing better to do."

**M**ascis took Cosloy up on his offer and the band recorded an album for about $500 with a guy who ran the PA for local hardcore shows and had an eight-track studio in his house in the woods outside of Northampton. Musically the album was all over the place, incorporating elements of the Cure, R.E.M., the Feelies, Scratch Acid, and Sonic Youth, not to mention SST bands like Hüsker Dü and the Meat Puppets and their hardcore-country fusion. "It was its own bizarre hybrid," says Cosloy. "This was definitely music that hardcore punk was the foundation for, but there were more classic influences that turned it into something completely different. It wasn't exactly pop, it wasn't exactly punk rock — it was completely its own thing."

But in a way, it was *very* punk rock, and not just in the way the rhythm section's bludgeoning force was so clearly derived from hardcore. "The most punk rock thing about J's stuff was how much he mixed all his influences," says Barlow. "He was playing new wave guitar next to heavy metal guitar next to crazy Hendrix leads next to weird PiL single note things. He threw all that stuff together. That was probably the most punk rock thing about it."

Mascis's whiny low-key drawl, the polar opposite of hardcore's boot-camp bark, provided an evocative contrast to Dinosaur's roiling music. Mascis traces his quasi-southern twang back to John Fogerty and Mick

Jagger, both of whom grew up even farther from Dixie than Mascis did. But while his vocal phrasing may have had roots in Stones songs like "Dead Flowers" and "Country Honk," Mascis's voice itself more closely resembled Neil Young's, and the comparisons came early and often and indeed never stopped. "I definitely like the Stones more than Neil Young," Mascis reveals. "That got annoying, being compared all the time."

And the comparison probably didn't help the band, either. Indie rock was becoming very circumscribed — if it didn't hang on an imaginary laundry line between R.E.M. and the Replacements, few people wanted to hear about it. "People's initial reaction to them," says Cosloy, "was, 'What the fuck is this?'"

D inosaur's self-titled debut didn't make much of a splash commercially, selling but fifteen hundred copies in its first year. The larger rock publications and influential critics completely ignored it, although not for lack of trying on Cosloy's part. He tirelessly championed the record, buttonholing press, radio, and whoever else would listen. But most people thought Dinosaur was a joke. "There were people who literally laughed at me," Cosloy says. "I remember [*Village Voice* music editor] Doug Simmons, any time he tried to bring up the fact that Homestead was a flop label, that it would never get anywhere, he'd say, 'What do you guys have? *Dinosaur?*' That was the example of the loser band on the label."

A small flock of fanzine writers and bands did recognize Dinosaur's greatness. Boston's Salem 66 gave the band some opening slots, and Cosloy got Dinosaur some New York shows, which Barlow would drive the band to in his parents' station wagon. On one such jaunt, Dinosaur opened for Big Black at a sparsely attended show at Maxwell's. After sound check soundman Ira Kaplan (guitarist in a new band called Yo La Tengo) begged them to turn down. "You guys have really good songs," said Kaplan, visibly frustrated. "You really should turn down, you can't hear anything you're doing!" It only made the band dig in their heels more.

The members of Sonic Youth caught the show but didn't much care for what they saw. But a few months later they caught Dinosaur at Folk City. The first song began quietly enough, but then the band suddenly erupted in such an overwhelming blast of volume that Thurston Moore felt himself pinned to the back wall. The set ended a few songs later when, after playing an epic solo, Mascis fell back against his amp and slid to the floor in an exhausted heap. This time Sonic Youth walked up to Mascis afterward and declared themselves Dinosaur fans.

Barlow was a little bewildered by the attentions of one of his favorite bands. "It was so weird to have Thurston and Kim showing up at shows, going, 'Oh, you guys are really great!'" says Barlow. "We're like, 'What? How could the coolest band in the world like *us?*'"

Mascis had no problem with it at all. That summer he took a bag full of canned tuna and Hi-C down to New York and house-sat Gordon and Moore's apartment on Eldridge Street while they were on tour. Barlow and Murph stayed up in Massachusetts and practiced together. "That was the only time I could hear what Murph was playing, because J played so loud," says Barlow. "So me and Murph just practiced together to lock on, which helped the band immeasurably. [J] never seemed to appreciate it, but that's what we did. Me and Murph just locked on."

**D**inosaur still had not toured, until Sonic Youth, who had just released *Evol,* invited them on a two-week stint of colleges and clubs in the Northeast and northern Midwest in September '86. Even without extensive road experience, Dinosaur was a jaw-dropping live act. "There was nothing like them at that point," says Lee Ranaldo. "They had nothing to lose and everything to gain and they were going for it every night."

The two bands became quite friendly; they'd often eat breakfast together out on the road, and Mascis would partake of his usual morning meal — Jell-O and whipped cream, cut up and stirred until it was a gelatinous slurry. On the last show of the tour, in Buffalo, Dinosaur played Neil Young's "Cortez the Killer" with Ranaldo on vocals, then followed it up with an epic jam.

Mascis, Murph, and Barlow were in great spirits on the ride home. As they were driving back into Northampton, someone slipped in a tape of *Evol.* Mascis turned to Barlow and said, "Man, this is really weird, I feel like I'm going to cry."

"Me, too!" said Barlow. "We just toured with our favorite band!"

"We were kind of naive but so happy," says Barlow. "'Wow, man, we just toured with the coolest fuckin' band in the world! They're the coolest. And they like us. And we don't even know why!'"

The band recorded three songs for their next album at a sixteen-track basement studio in Holyoke, then recorded the rest of the album with Sonic Youth engineer Wharton Tiers at Fun City Studios in New York. Murph and Barlow played as hard as they possibly could, while Mascis practically crooned over the turmoil. It was a perfect metaphor for Mascis himself — the placid eye of a storm he himself had created.

Mascis was very specific about what he wanted Murph to play. "When I write songs, the drums are always included as part of the song," Mascis says. "The melody, the drums — that's the song to me." Mascis was a powerful drummer himself, and this began to sow feelings of resentment and inadequacy in Murph. "J controlled Murph's every drumbeat," said Barlow. "And Murph could not handle that. Murph wanted to kill J for the longest time. . . . He kept saying, 'It may be your scene, but I can't deal with J. The guy's a fucking Nazi.'" Barlow tried to placate Murph by assuring him that Dinosaur was such a great band that it was worth putting up with all the unpleasantness.

Between Mascis's seeming apathy and Murph's bitterness, Barlow felt like he was the only one in the band who thought they were anything special. "Maybe because I was the only one who was getting high a lot," he says. "We played the same set a lot and the same songs the same way and that really lends itself to getting high after a while and really *feeling* it, being really into it. And just having visions during the set, like whoa, pure power — savage, raw power."

Although the music was delivered with brutality, it also harbored catchy, serene, positively life-affirming melodies that routinely attained a kind of forlorn grandeur. "J was an amazing, amazing songwriter whose songs really touched me in a way that a lot of material from that period didn't," says Lee Ranaldo. "Black Flag or a lot of the bands that were popular from that period had songs that you really loved, but they didn't touch you in a personal, emotional way the way that a lot of J's early stuff did."

Moreover, the music was crammed with absolutely incredible guitar playing. Solo after solo was rich with style, technique, and melodic invention. In the process, Mascis became the first American indie rock guitar hero. His epic soloing fell right in with the perennial tastes of his peers — children of affluent parentage, the kind who drive their parents' old BMW off to genteel party schools in New England like Hampshire College and go skiing up in Vermont or out in Vail. These folks had favored the likes of, well, dinosaur bands like the Grateful Dead and their ilk since time immemorial. They were complacent, even bored, and their musical tastes reflected that anomie (and the fact that they had a little extra money to buy pot). J Mascis was one they could finally call their own.

Mascis used pedals, and lots of them — wah-wah, distortion, flanger, volume. This was unheard of in punk rock — only hippies played wah-wah pedals! It was the next step from Hüsker Dü's wall of sound, but while Bob Mould also used distortion and pedals, he used them to create a constant sonic veil that the listener would have to penetrate; Mascis deployed them more strategically, often shifting suddenly from a pensive verse to a huge, soaringly melodic chorus. That technique would provide the blueprint for early Nineties alternative rock.

Barlow contributed two songs to the second album. Cowed by Mascis's songwriting prowess, he worked on "Lose" for months before getting up the nerve to show it to the band. His other contribution, "Poledo," is a sound collage made completely on his own with a portable recorder and a pair of cheap mikes, a hint of things to come.

Gerard Cosloy was smitten with the entire album. "I was absolutely certain that record was going to change everything for them," he says, "that that record would completely turn everything inside out, that they would go from being this maligned, hated band to being the coolest band on the planet." And this, thought Cosloy, was the record that would silence the naysayers and finally put Homestead Records on the map.

Cosloy was awaiting the master tape and artwork when Mascis called with stunning news: They had decided to release the album on SST, not Homestead. Mascis assured a dumbstruck Cosloy that it was purely a business decision and nothing personal, but Cosloy wasn't having it. "There was no *way* I couldn't take it personally," says Cosloy. "That was one of my favorite bands on earth. I felt like I worked incredibly hard for them, maybe the results weren't so visible at that particular moment, but I felt like I'd really put my ass on the line for them on many occasions, and this was a really, really shitty way of splitting up. I didn't take it very well. I was pretty fuckin' angry about it and probably still am. . . . I just wish he could have done it a little differently. Yeah, that was pretty fuckin' cold."

Mascis says he had been reluctant to sign the two-album deal Homestead owner Barry Tenebaum was insisting on — "I really was not into being bound to anything at that point," says Mascis, "like, loans and all that kind of thing freaked me out" — but Cosloy says Homestead would gladly have done the album as a one-off. "There's no way we would have not put that record out," says Cosloy.

While the two parties had been haggling, Dinosaur's fairy godparents Sonic Youth had sent a tape of the new album to Greg Ginn at SST.

SST flipped over the record. "The stoners at the label loved the guitar," Barlow explains. After all, heavy music was making a comeback, largely under the aegis of SST; Black Flag had released the sludge-metal-punk landmark *My War*, and everybody at the label was openly worshiping Black Sabbath for the first time since they were in junior high. And Dinosaur had simply always wanted to be on the label. As Mascis noted, "We wanted to be on SST since we were like fifteen years old, but it just seemed, like, totally out of reach."

Abandoning Cosloy and Homestead didn't come without a price, though. "I wasn't really friends with Gerard after that," says Mascis. "So that was a bummer, blowing off Gerard. But we wanted to be on SST anyway. It was a casualty of our ruthless record business."

And yet even Cosloy admits the choice was obvious. "SST was the label everybody wanted to be on," he says. "Everyone's favorite bands were on the label; SST was funnier and cooler and it also had the machinery. It was in the place to do a lot of damage whereas Homestead was just me and Craig [Marks], but mostly me. We were not really prepared to go after things. We didn't have the financing or the support. At SST the people who were running the company were the people in the bands that believed in it. The people who owned Homestead aren't very comfortable with musicians and think of them as weasels trying to scam money off them. There's no real way to compare."

Unfortunately for Barlow and Murph, the contract Mascis signed with SST was structured so that only he received royalty checks from the label. "I had nothing to say about it," says Barlow. "I thought he deserved it, actually. But selling records was not how we made our money at all — we were making money by being on tour. It had nothing to do with how many records we sold. That was completely foreign to us."

So it was Mascis's responsibility to dole out payment to the other two. And Barlow claims he neglected that responsibility. "J's a real prime, stinking red asshole — that guy is the cheapest bastard," Barlow says. "He does not get how Murph and I helped him get anywhere that he was. He could not have done that without us. He didn't see how we were all integral."

After recording the album, Mascis moved to New York and left his bandmates behind, and the alignments within the band began to change.

MASCIS, MURPH, AND
BARLOW IN AN EARLY
SST PROMO PHOTO.
NOTE MASCIS'S OLD
"DEEP WOUND"
SWEATER.

JENS JURGENSEN

Barlow now joined Murph in feeling profoundly alienated from Mascis. "I realized there was no way I'd know what was going on in his head," said Barlow. "It was really bad. He's a really, really, really uptight person, and the whole time he comes off as being mellow."

Barlow felt bandmates should be close friends, but Mascis was utterly uninterested in that kind of intimacy. "J was one person who just seemed to think that was absolutely nowhere in the whole realm of what was going on," says Barlow. "He just had nothing to say, yet he had everything to say. That was really quite a puzzle for a while. It really drove his music."

"It was really frustrating," Barlow says of the alienation between him and Mascis. "It was kind of weirdly heartbreaking."

Barlow had been spending more and more time at home smoking pot and recording his own songs. "That's where I started to discover that I had an ego," says Barlow. "I just became so involved with writing my own songs and really getting into my own sound of things. Just getting totally self-involved. It was pretty great. So when I played for Dinosaur, I was able to play for Dinosaur — do my thing and be quiet." In the Boston area, early pressings of *You're Living All Over Me* came with a tape by Barlow titled *Weed Forestin'*. It was under the name Sebadoh, a nonsense word Barlow sometimes sang on his home recordings.

"He put out the Sebadoh record and then it was like the door shut —

'I'm not going to contribute anything [to Dinosaur],'" says Mascis. "That was always a bummer." Mascis says he would have welcomed more participation from Barlow, but Barlow says he was both intimidated by Mascis's songwriting and frustrated by his bandmate's inscrutable demeanor. In response, Barlow suppressed his own wishes and became an almost literally silent partner in Dinosaur. "I figured out a way to be myself despite being in the band," says Barlow. "I was super passive-aggressive."

"We both did that a lot," says Murph. "But that causes tension. You can't do that without feeling a certain amount of resentment and negative energy."

Mascis's insularity was getting to Murph as well. "J's way of maybe saying thank you or acknowledging something was so subtle that I wouldn't see it," says Murph. "And so I thought he was just being a dick, he wasn't even acknowledging the effort I'm putting into trying to execute his work. That was a big thing for me."

And yet Mascis could exert a powerful effect on his bandmates. "J, just for the longest time, if he saw somebody socially having fun or doing something that he wasn't able to do, he would probably try to put a damper on you and just bum you out or say something negative to the other person so they would see you in a more negative light," says Murph. "That was the major part of it, J being such a control freak and just not letting up."

But when a show went well, Murph explains, "and you really felt like you had executed something as a band — really pulled something off — there would be those really short moments of true glory where we would all feel like, 'Wow, this is worth it.' But it was very fleeting and it would always come back down to reality. For me, that taste of euphoria would make it worthwhile."

"There were few bands that could blow people away like that," adds their friend Jon Fetler. "Dinosaur was one of the ones where people would come back after the show and say, 'Man, you blew my circuits.'"

**B**arlow and Mascis were an odd match from the start — Barlow was the type of person who needed to pick over his feelings like an archaeologist at a dig; he needed a lot of feedback and encouragement and deeply wanted Mascis's approval, whereas Mascis cruised through life unquestioningly and was maddeningly self-sufficient. Barlow was skittish, tense, insecure; Mascis didn't seem to care about anything whatsoever, and as the band's singer, guitarist, and songwriter, he called the shots.

All that pain was manifested on their second album, *You're Living All Over Me*, in the lyrics, in the music, even in the title. "All this struggling that we'd been doing since 1985," said Barlow, "bouncing off each other and having no clue, not being friends, not knowing if anybody liked our band, not knowing why we're playing really loud everywhere and being really obnoxious, and all of a sudden everything was channeled into this one record — this is the reason why, this is it."

It was amazing how Dinosaur turned one of rock's traditional equations on its head. The volume and noise didn't symbolize power; it just created huge mountains of sound around the desolate emotions outlined in the lyrics. Mascis's vocals, cool and collected amidst the chaos, suggested resignation and withdrawal. It was, as one critic put it, a powerful sound that didn't suggest power.

Song titles like "Sludgefeast" and "Tarpit" certainly bespoke a consistency of vision, and indeed *You're Living All Over Me* had an overall murkiness that lent the band a mystique. When the master tape of *You're Living All Over Me* arrived at SST, the label's production manager promptly panicked because the meter was "pinning," meaning the level on the tape was so high that it was distorting. But Mascis confirmed that that was the way he wanted it to sound. (The group reasoned that since an electric guitar sounded better with distortion on it, a whole distorted record would be even better.) On top of it, Mascis sang like he had marbles in his mouth, while his guitar effects garbled what he was playing. The music was dense and heavy; it was like a pond one could never see the bottom of, so it never grew tiresome to listen to.

Mascis insists that most of the lyrics are about people's responses to him — nobody was sure if he was oblivious, aloof, or just shy. "A lot of people had intense reactions toward me because I guess I was so blank," he says. "I was intense but not giving back anything — not normal, like other people would act. And that freaked people out sometimes." Still, it's easy to feel that Mascis was writing not about others but, scathingly, about himself: on the debut album's "Severed Lips," Mascis drawls, "I never try that much / 'Cause I'm scared of feeling"; "Got to connect with you, girl / But forget how," he whines on "Sludgefeast," from *You're Living All Over Me*. Countless other songs outline alienation and an inability to connect with another person.

Mascis's lyrics took on new meaning for Barlow when he began connecting them with his bandmate's interior life. "I started to see his songs as probably his only noble act as a human being," Barlow says, "to describe this bizarre ambivalence that was floating around."

ith their buddy Jon Fetler along for the ride, the dysfunctional band began a U.S. tour in June '87 to promote *You're Living All Over Me*. Unfortunately, SST missed the release date and the record didn't appear in stores until the band had reached California. But minuscule turnouts weren't the half of it — the band's frictions hit a hellish peak.

Right off the bat, their clunker '76 Dodge van broke down somewhere in Connecticut, about an hour and a half into the tour. And that was the least of their problems. As Fetler wrote in his diary, "Band tensions somewhat high. Murph feeling disgruntled, undervalued. Seems like it's building — he wants to quit after Europe tour or before if he hits J. He keeps saying, 'I'm gonna pop him, man.'" And it was still only the first day of the tour.

The simple fact was that these were three neurotic young men barely twenty-one years old, all cooped up in a van and living on $5 a day. Murph's genteel Greenwich upbringing didn't stand him in good stead when it came to the rigors of the road, and he grumbled often about the conditions. In such close quarters, small personal tics began to loom large. "The guy chewed like a cow," says Barlow of Mascis. "Loudly." Barlow had his own irritating quirks. "I would put things in my mouth," he says, "just random things, and chew on them." This led to the infamous Cookie Monster episode. "I bought this Cookie Monster doll on the tour, and I looked in the van once and Lou was there sucking on its eyeball," says Mascis. "Something about that disturbed me to my core. I couldn't handle it. I think I had to throw the thing out. It was weird."

Another of Barlow's schticks sprang from his insecurity about where he stood with Mascis. He'd deliberately do something obnoxious and then when someone pointed out that it was "annoying," he'd claim he didn't know what the word meant. "He's going [makes loud chewing sound] some weird annoying sound for, like, an hour and you're like, 'Lou, shut up!'" says Mascis. "And he's like, 'What?' I didn't understand how he could not know what 'annoying' meant in the first place and how that meant that we didn't like him or we're not his friends because we're annoyed by him. . . . That was one of our bizarre things on the road."

"Murph and Lou would fight a lot, too, which was hilarious," Mascis continues. "I just remember sitting in the van — the argument would just be like, 'Murph, *maaaaan!*' 'But, Lou, *maaaaan!*' 'But, Murph, *maaaaan!*' Just like that — for half an hour. Lou had no real ability to listen at that point. Murph would say something and Lou would just be saying the same thing, as if he'd never heard anything Murph said. And Murph was trying, but he's weird, too."

But Mascis was no better. "The whole close quarters thing really freaked him out, it really did," says Barlow, "far more than he even knew." Rightly or wrongly, Barlow felt Mascis's anxiety might have had something to do with homophobia. "I thought so," says Barlow. "I wrote quite a few songs about it." ("J did have a penchant for just the most disgusting, ass-raping put-downs," says Fetler. "That just peppered our banter.")

"At the time, I was twenty and basically of indeterminate sexual preference, and it was one of those weird times when people did a lot of hypothesizing about whether someone was gay or not," says Barlow. "There was that going on with Murph a bit and then with me, of course, because I had never had a girlfriend or whatever and chose to put everything in my mouth."

The band's suffocating tensions did fuel some great shows, even when hardly anybody showed up. "Some of these shows were just super because there'd be six kids that would be right up front," says Fetler. "And then about three other couples talking in the back. That was it. But for the kids that were there, that record, *You're Living All Over Me*, was such a pure thing for them."

After a show in Phoenix, Murph took the wheel for the overnight drive through the southwestern desert to L.A. while Mascis, Barlow, and Fetler slumbered in the back. Suddenly there was a huge bump as the van ran off the road. "We were all up at the same time in a flash, realizing that we almost died," says Fetler. Terrified, they asked Murph what happened. "And Murph looks around," says Fetler, "and says, 'Well, I consciously decided to fall asleep.'" According to Fetler, Murph had been "experimenting with extrasensory driving techniques," he explained. "I was trying to *feel* the road, man." (Murph denies the whole thing.)

When they finally arrived in L.A., they were welcomed by the enthusiastic SST staff. Fetler's diary records that they were "greeted by a heavyset, longhaired, wild-eyed fellow who exclaimed, 'Dinosaur! Way cool, dudes!'" *You're Living All Over Me* was playing on the office stereo; the receptionist was even wearing a Dinosaur T-shirt, the first the band had ever seen. They all went over to Chuck Dukowski's house and watched a Lydia Lunch film. It was a good morale booster after the ordeal of the past two weeks. But SST's local clout was given the lie that night when they played a show in a strip mall in Orange County and drew not one paying customer.

After San Francisco, Portland, and Seattle, they were on the home stretch of the tour when the van blew a gasket in Mountain Home, Idaho. It would take several days for replacement parts to arrive, so the band set up camp in a motel, just killing time, stewing in their own juices.

"I remember one day in Kentucky Fried Chicken just ripping Lou apart for an hour or something," says Mascis. "That was a big turning point. He was really devastated." It's not something Mascis is proud of today. "I feel bad about it," he admits. "I was an asshole a lot of the time when I was younger."

After that incident Barlow began accumulating a mental file of the slights Mascis threw his way but never actually confronted his bandmate on them. "I just totally took this martyr role," Barlow says. "'OK, you don't like me, well, I'll just try to be as inconspicuous as possible.' And I made sure that I didn't put things in my mouth, and I made sure that I just played my parts." Barlow says Murph and Mascis would barely deign to break down equipment after shows, so he began to do it. Then he says he started to do more than his fair share of driving as well. "I just totally involved myself in just being the martyr," says Barlow. "I was *totally* passive-aggressive."

Murph's own moment came one night when the four of them were in their motel room, watching TV. Barlow had been insisting on arranging their mattresses in a row on the floor; Murph wanted to stay as far away from his bandmates as possible. "I was getting really uptight about this, and I could tell those guys were all laughing at me," says Murph. "They thought, 'This is so funny, Murph is taking this so seriously.' They didn't realize I was just, like, freaking. Or they probably did realize it and thought it was funny anyway. That's when I cracked."

Mascis tossed some offhand barb at Murph. "And Murph just yells at him, 'You should be raped by a bald black man!'" says Barlow. "And J goes, 'And that would be *you*, Murph?'" With wicked precision, the remark hit on both Murph's sexual insecurities and the fact that his hairline was prematurely receding. "And Murph," says Barlow, "just had a total breakdown."

Murph hurled a table, a suitcase, and a lamp across the room and began crying and saying, "I can't take it, I just can't take it!" "And it was such a dramatic burst of violence and energy that it caused everyone to just go, 'Whoa . . . ,'" says Fetler. Hours later Murph was still weeping and pacing around, smoking a cigarette to calm his nerves; Mascis was sound asleep in bed.

Barlow had read enough of the rock & roll canon to know that some of the most powerful bands — the Who, the Kinks, the Rolling Stones — had tumultuous internal lives. Mascis was aware of the effect the tension had on the music, too. "That's why a lot of people liked us, because we were a psychodrama onstage," he says. "It's like a circus kind of show, which might be fun to watch but not necessarily fun to be in the middle of."

At times it seemed as if the assault was not just from within. Soon after the initial pressings of *You're Living All Over Me* were shipped, a band featuring former members of San Francisco acid casualty groups such as Big Brother and the Holding Company and Country Joe and the Fish laid claim to the name "the Dinosaurs." Mascis renamed his band Dinosaur Jr, no comma or period.

**B**arlow's nonexistent romantic life was decisively jump-started by one of his own songs. "'Poledo' was probably my biggest attempt at meeting a girl through music, to totally express myself in a song," Barlow says. "I believe in music in that way — if you want something to happen, you write a song about it." It worked beyond Barlow's wildest expectations.

To Kathleen Billus, music director of Smith College's radio station, "Poledo" "felt like the answer to my dreams," she wrote in a later memoir, "like what I'd been wanting in a song my whole life, something I was aching for but wouldn't be able to describe." When Barlow did an interview at the Smith radio station in September '87, she jumped at the chance to meet him. They hit it off and soon became a couple.

But the romance had to get put on hold while Dinosaur Jr did a four-week European tour in October '87. Whatever image Mascis had been cultivating, it came to fruition on that tour. The British press loved his lackadaisical manner, his tasteful mishmash of influences, his offhand wisdom. (Pushed by an English interviewer to name something he was scared of, Mascis was at a loss for words but eventually answered that he was scared of all the butter the British put on their food.)

"Who do you listen to?" asked *Melody Maker*'s David Stubbs. ". . . Uh . . . everybody," Mascis replied. "Now, this may not seem like much of an answer," wrote Stubbs. "This is not Quote of the Year and wants for the delicious aphoristic quality which we so enjoy in an Oscar Wilde or a Nietzsche. But stark print cannot do justice to its catatonic deadweight, more eloquent than any Pete Burns rant, the sprawl of the drawl, the great mental cloud which attempts to conceive of the great swathes of rock history in which Dinosaur are soaked. The pause that precedes this answer is like the death of the word."

They were flattered that these Americans liked English bands such as the Jesus and Mary Chain and the Cure. The English press, whipped to

a froth by the exotic brutishness of Blast First bands such as Sonic Youth, the Butthole Surfers, and Big Black, had found a new object for their love/hate relationship with American culture. Mascis was some sort of idiot savant worthy of equals parts reverence and condescension. To Americans, the band was readily recognizable as a typical bunch of apathetic Northeast ski bums; to the British, they were like the wildmen of Borneo.

And after Dinosaur's tour, a whole wave of English groups, dubbed "shoegazer bands," sprang up in their wake, playing folk chords through phalanxes of effects pedals to make swirling, deafening music; they uniformly adopted a nonchalant demeanor and paid lip service to Neil Young and Dinosaur Jr.

**M**eanwhile Barlow was retreating more and more. "I was afraid of stepping on anybody's toes," said Barlow. "I felt really bad about it and didn't want to perpetuate the weirdness. I just wanted to play bass." But Mascis has a different take. "Lou couldn't really have a conversation," he claims. "He could just say what was on his mind, but he couldn't process things coming back. It was just really strange."

But very little was coming back to Barlow from Mascis anyway. "We never communicated, really," says Mascis. "Didn't really know how, I guess. Too young. We hadn't learned that yet."

As Gerard Cosloy had predicted, *You're Living All Over Me* was a big hit in the indie world. Throughout the country little pockets of fans had been slowly but surely spreading the word about Dinosaur. "It built up to a critical mass of people," says Cosloy, "disaffected hardcore fans, indie rock fans who wanted something that wasn't so fuckin' bland, people who were into noisier and more experimental things who were beginning to open up to things that were a bit more melodic — this whole new consortium of bands, writers, DJs, musicians, freaks, whatever, all began to come together. Dinosaur was the band that they came together around."

But the more successful Dinosaur became, the more that success displaced their creativity. For better or worse, soundmen weren't throwing bottles at them anymore. They rarely practiced and professed to have little interest in advancing their career. "We're totally lazy," Barlow admitted. They'd realized their longtime dream of being on SST but had set no bearings beyond that.

"It's different to function without a goal than with a goal," says Mascis. "It was, like, 'Well, we're still around. Now what?'" The band never did regain that sense of purpose, although they did have a powerful incentive to keep going. "I knew I didn't want to get a job," Mascis says with a laugh. "That was always motivating me."

Success was the worst thing that could have happened to the band. "It seemed to kind of kill J's motivation," says Barlow. "Once the shows became packed, it just became another thing J had to do as opposed to what it was early on. He just made it clear that he really couldn't be bothered and he'd rather just go back to sleep — if it was all really up to him, he wouldn't be doing it."

So while Barlow was so idealistic about music that he wrote a song specifically to get himself a girlfriend, Mascis just wrote songs because that's what he was supposed to do. "And that was why his songs were so fuckin' amazing and why he had such an amazing grasp of the guitar," says Barlow. "He *wasn't* idealistic, he was just insanely pragmatic.

"Once he knew that people demanded something in particular," Barlow says, "he just sort of figured out a way he could live up to those demands but not really give too much of himself."

Mascis told *Spin*'s Erik Davis that he found the guitar to be a "wimpy instrument." "You really don't like guitar?" Davis asked.

"No," Mascis replied.

"Why do you do it?"

"Dunno."

I t's no wonder that the songs of Dinosaur's third album, *Bug*, didn't quite have the spark of *You're Living All Over Me*. The songs didn't come as easily to Mascis, and it didn't help that they were in a hurry to capitalize on all the acclaim they'd received over the previous year or so. Mascis says he had been hoping that Barlow would take up the songwriting slack, but Barlow was in full retreat and deeply immersed in his homemade Sebadoh tapes, which Cosloy was now releasing on Homestead. Despite his prolific Sebadoh output, Barlow wrote no songs for *Bug*. "I realized that if I wasn't going to be able to interact personally with the people in the band, there's no way I'm going to be able to give them songs I really care about," said Barlow. "If I had tried to interact with J and tried to write songs, the band would have broken up a lot sooner."

"I was really afraid of him," adds Barlow. "After a while my fear of him just exceeded everything else and I couldn't even play him my songs anymore. It kind of devolved to that point."

"We were just in a bad state," says Mascis. "The band was going down already."

M any of the songs on *Bug* were recorded not long after they were written. Barlow and Murph were only minimally involved in the sessions. Mascis told them exactly what to play, they'd make slight modifications, then record their parts and leave Mascis to finish the rest.

The band tried on a lot of different ideas on the first album, as if they were seeing which ones fit the best; on the second album it all jelled. By *Bug* it was starting to become a formula. "It's the album I'm least happy with of anything I've done," says Mascis.

But Mascis's appraisal of the album is probably colored by the experience of making it — despite some filler, *Bug* is a powerful record. "Freak Scene," the album's single, was classic Dinosaur, probably because it so directly encapsulated the band's roiling inner life. One passage alternates a guitar sound like a garbage disposal with bursts of glinting twang; there's a completely winning melody delivered in Mascis's trademark laconic style and not one but two memorable, molten guitar solos. On top of all that, the lyrics seem to be about Mascis and Barlow's dysfunctional relationship: "The weirdness flows between us," Mascis yowls, "anyone can tell to see us." The song was a big college radio hit and seemed to be blasting out of every dorm room in the country that year.

"Yeah We Know" finds the band in thunderingly good form — Murph's pounding, musical drumming powers one of Mascis's best songs to date. Perhaps the song draws some of its vehemence from the fact that, as Mascis now admits, it's about the band itself — "Bottled up, stored away," Mascis yowls, "Always ready to give way." But the album reserves its most harrowing psychodrama for the closing "Don't," a dirge-metal noise orgy with Barlow screaming, "Why, why don't you like me?" for five minutes straight. It was a bit ironic, to say the least, for Mascis to have Barlow sing such words. "That was kind of twisted," Mascis admits. "'All right Lou, sing this: "Why don't you like me?" over and over again.' That was kind of a demented thing."

Barlow sang the song with such violence that he began coughing up blood afterward.

In October '88 Dinosaur Jr did another European tour, once again with Fetler in tow as confidant and referee. In Holland they stayed with their European booking agent. Barlow had been annoying Murph for some reason now lost to the sands of time, but that was nothing unusual. "There were always little bitter bickerings going on," says Fetler. "That was part of the chatter — 'blah-blah-blah fuck you blah-blah-blah.'" But tensions were apparently higher than anyone realized.

That night, when Barlow went into Murph and Fetler's room to get an extra blanket, Murph started growling ferociously in his sleep, then stood up — still sleeping — and started heading for Barlow. Mascis saw the whole thing. "I just remember Murph sleepwalking, getting up like some primitive animal, this caged animal, going at Lou like he was going to kill him," says Mascis. "I was standing behind Lou watching Murph come at him in his boxer shorts. I was thinking, 'Either Murph's going to wake up or he's going to kill Lou.' And I was waiting to see what happened. And right when he got there, he woke up."

"It was very heavy," wrote Fetler in his diary, "and kind of weird."

And yet the tour was hardly a complete nightmare. In Europe the halls were huge, the audiences enthusiastic, the accommodations topnotch. But the band's internal strife was plain to see, especially as the tour culminated, in a string of U.K. dates with Rapeman. "They were near disintegration at that point, and the drag-ass depression hung over them like a bad smell," recalls Rapeman's Steve Albini. Of course, Rapeman didn't help Dinosaur's morale by stink-bombing the band's van, dressing rooms, hotel rooms, sound checks, and even meals.

T he British press had fastened itself even harder on to the idea that Dinosaur was a bunch of sleepy-headed apathetic types — Mascis's vocals were "a sculpted yawn," the band were "titans of torpor," "Numbosaurus Wrecked," "a cult of non-personality." One writer compared Mascis to the "giant three-toed sloth."

One of the few British journalists who got it right was *Sounds'* Roy Wilkinson, who actually made the journey to Amherst to see the place that had birthed Dinosaur. Said Murph, "We have to have been affected by where we came from. Around here it's the easy life. There's no harsh things — no poverty, no crime. . . . And people don't struggle that hard to live." Dinosaur, then, seemed to answer a very American question: What happens when you get everything you ever wanted?

Dinosaur came to represent "slackers," then a new term for the particularly aimless subset branded by the media as Generation X, the group of kids who had grown up in relatively comfortable, uncontroversial times, kids whose parents, as Kim Gordon once put it, "created a world they couldn't afford to live in." Slackers didn't care about much except music, which they consumed with discernment and gusto. Mascis, with his listless demeanor and guitar heroics, became something of a slacker poster boy, even though he and the band rejected the mantle wholeheartedly. After all, he and Barlow had grown up on committed, hardworking bands like Black Flag, Minor Threat, and the Minutemen. "The whole thing at that time was to be like you didn't give a shit about stuff," says Barlow. "I was always a step behind that. I never really could get into it."

**B**arlow had moved in with his girlfriend Billus in her room in the Friedman dorm complex at U. Mass. in the spring of '88. The relationship gave him confidence and self-esteem, enough to drop his subservient relationship to Mascis. "I just started speaking my mind and not giving a shit what he thought," says Barlow. "I could just see it really bugging him, but I really enjoyed it." And that's when it really started to go downhill.

"He didn't really talk until he got his girlfriend," says Mascis, "and somehow that jump-started his ego, and he went from 'I am Lou, I am nothing' to 'I am the greatest.' He just went *ffffft*, just flipped the scales. And then he started talking *a lot*. And then I was realizing from a lot of the things he was saying, 'Hmmm, maybe I don't like Lou.' I'd never heard him talk before so I didn't really know what was going on in his head. And then when you hear what's he's talking about, it was like, 'Hmmm, *interesting* — I'm not really into that.'"

Starting with the *Bug* tour, Barlow occasionally abandoned his usual parts and indulged in what Fetler calls "sonic dronings," Sonic Youth-inspired playing that wasn't anywhere near what he'd played on the record. Barlow had been playing tape collages between songs for a year or so, surely borrowing the idea straight from Sonic Youth; but now he was setting them off *during* the songs. It may well have been Barlow's way of asserting himself after being so subdued; at any rate, Mascis took the unsolicited modification of his music as a personal affront.

It had all come to a head at an early '88 show at a small club in Naugatuck, Connecticut. The place was far from packed and the band wasn't playing very well. They were halfway through "Severed Lips" when Barlow began making feedback with his bass instead of playing the usual part.

"Lou is sitting on the drum riser, just making noise through every song — this one note — and just trying to goad us, taunting us, basically," says Mascis. "And I'm playing and I'm like, 'I think Murph's going to beat up Lou.' And it goes on a little bit more and I'm thinking, 'Yup, this is going to be bad, Murph's going to beat up Lou.' And I keep playing and I keep thinking that, and finally, I think, 'Huh, I guess Murph's not going to beat up Lou. I guess I'll have to do it.'"

Mascis rushed across the stage and tried to hit Barlow with his guitar. Barlow raised his bass like a shield while Mascis bashed away at him repeatedly. ("It made a pretty good sound," Mascis recalls somewhat fondly.) After a few failed bashes, Mascis stalked offstage yelling, "I can't take it! I can't take it!" Barlow called after him, "Can't take *what*, J? Asshole!" and raised his fists in triumph. "I got really psyched, like psychotically happy, and just went, *'Yes!'*" says Barlow. "I felt like he'd proved to me that he actually had feelings. He never would react to anything at all, ever."

"I remember just sitting there at my drum set going, 'OK, this is my perfect opportunity to pummel *both* of these guys,'" says Murph. "But instead I just walked off." Barlow followed Mascis and Murph backstage and assured them that he didn't mean anything by the feedback. The band went out again, played what was surely a fearsome cover of "Minor Threat" and drove home in silence. It was the beginning of the end.

I n one fall of '88 interview, Mascis acknowledged the band's overwhelming internal strife but admitted he was just too lazy to fire anybody: "I just know I'll always be in a band," he said, "so I'd rather just have one and keep going rather than have to start another one."

But in July '89 Mascis decided Barlow had to go. He and Murph went over to Barlow's house to deliver the news. Tellingly, it was the first time either of them had ever been there. Mascis had a knack for delegating unpleasant tasks, so Murph did most of the talking while Mascis hovered in the doorway. "I would be the spokesman for J, and I would kind of present bad news or pave the way," says Murph. "He was just into having other people execute his dirty work. J is very smart that way — he gets a great network of people to suffer the blow."

But somehow, even after an hour of talking, they hadn't managed to convey the idea that they were firing Barlow. Instead, Barlow had the impression that the band was breaking up entirely. "I said, 'OK, that's cool, see you guys later,'" says Barlow. "And they left."

"We did kind of let him believe that," Murph admits. "That was the evil thing. J and I were just spineless." In fact, they had already booked a tour of Australia and arranged for Northwest punk mainstay Donna Dresch, who had played for a time with the Screaming Trees, to fly in from Washington State to replace Barlow. They were even thinking about signing with Warner Brothers.

A day or so later, Barlow heard about all this from a friend. Distraught, he called up Mascis, and Murph and Mascis dropped by Barlow's house again. "We had everything out," says Mascis. "I didn't say anything. I was just sitting there, observing. Murph was doing all the talking. We couldn't deal with each other at all."

The next day Murph and Mascis were sitting in their friend Megan

Jasper's kitchen, talking about Barlow and regretting that they hadn't been more straightforward with him when suddenly Barlow burst in the door. "You fucking assholes!" Barlow screamed. "I can't believe you didn't have the balls to tell me to my face! I have to find out on the street!"

"All of the disgust that I was holding in for all those years just came out," says Barlow. "It was pretty rough to deal with, not so much because of what they had done to me, but just the role I had chosen to play and all of the stuff that I had chosen to let build up inside of me and never really deal with. I had to sort through a lot of that and I was really extremely angry." After some more scolding, Barlow left without further incident.

Mascis served as some kind of perverse muse for a whole series of Sebadoh songs. "I got a lot of hatred out just by writing songs," Barlow says. "I just wanted to get under his skin. I wanted to wheedle my way in, in some way that was just not anything like what J was doing. So he was a real inspiration in a lot of ways."

Most of the screeds came out on singles, including one titled "Asshole"; the sleeve even has the Sebadoh name set in the same typeface as the Dinosaur logo. Barlow coyly acknowledged his target by including a snippet from the film *Say Anything*. "This song is about Joe," says a girl's voice, "and all my songs are about Joe."

Barlow insisted he was obsessed not with Mascis but with the issues of control the situation represented. The relationships within Dinosaur, he held, were a metaphor for a larger truth about the human condition. "That's a weird little kink in human nature that I couldn't figure out," Barlow says. "This idea of negative charisma and the way people tend to project things onto people and also control, the myriad ways people can control other people. Sometimes it has nothing to do with actually telling them what to do. It has to do with totally vibing people out. And there was so much of that going on."

Barlow's screeds alienated many Dinosaur fans, most of whom bought Mascis's image as a benign, gifted narcoleptic. But Mascis himself says he didn't care about Barlow's attacks. "It's just more Lou to me," he says wearily. "I've had a lot of Lou in my life."

The rift between Mascis and Barlow was enthusiastically covered by the press. "It makes me sick that I spent six or seven years putting my heart and soul into that band," Barlow told *Cut* zine in 1990. "They're sleazebag snob pigs like no one I have met in my entire life. J's always been an asshole." It was a bit of a one-sided feud, though, since Mascis rarely fired back, not out of his usual avoidance of communication, but because he'd honored a request by Barlow that he not talk about him to the press.

**W**hen Mascis was asked in a *Melody Maker* interview what the band planned to do now that Barlow had gone, his reply may have defined the slacker ethos right then and there. "We have no plans for what we want to do next," he said. "We have no plans about anything, really."

By the summer of '90, Dinosaur released a great new single, "The Wagon," which *Melody Maker* named one of two Singles of the Week. "Am I allowed two-word reviews?" asked writer Everett True. "Sheer exhilaration!" He went on, of course.

By this time Mascis had decided to move to a major label. "The thing I thought was great about it was they would just pay you on time," says Mascis. "I like Greg Ginn and stuff, but they wouldn't pay you. Homestead I didn't like and they were more just, like, dicks. They didn't pay and they didn't care. It was like all these indie labels that are ripping you off are supposed to be better than the major label who won't rip you off."

Other than that, Mascis's reasons for moving to a major are unclear. "It just seemed like the thing to do, I don't know," says Mascis. "Just because we could do it. I'm not sure."

Mascis says he got little grief from the indie cognoscenti for going major label. "It wasn't that polarized yet," he says. "It was just kind of this weird thing — 'Wow you're on a major.' There were a few bands that did it and stuff, it's just kind of odd, you're not really sure what to think of it. I can see now how it's damaging, after being through it. I didn't really have any concept."

**M**ascis solved his communication issues by playing virtually every instrument on Dinosaur's 1991 major label debut *Green Mind*, which won the attentions of commercial radio, the major music magazines, and even MTV.

Meanwhile Barlow had come back into Mascis's life — terrified that he might go broke now that he wasn't in Dinosaur, Barlow hired a lawyer and sued Mascis for $10,000 in back royalties. "But I didn't owe him anything — we hadn't gotten any money," says Mascis. "I was really flipped out about that. I thought that was just really a bummer to me. Instead of calling me up and asking me, he just assumed. I'm not sure what was going on with him at the time, but that was really . . . I don't know." But during months of legal wrangling, some money actually did come in and the two settled.

It was the beginning of a rough period for Barlow. Because he was paying a lawyer to recover the money he felt he was owed, Kathleen Billus was supporting him. "And she eventually supported me until she hated me and dumped me," says Barlow, "*for the lawyer that was getting me the money from J!* It was just nuts!" (Barlow and Billus soon reconciled and eventually married.)

**B**arlow was convinced that Dinosaur could have achieved widespread popularity if they'd only preserved their original inspiration. Mascis, he says, deliberately avoided any steps that might have brought the band greater fame. "For him it was, 'I don't know if I want to be famous,'" says Barlow. "Or 'I don't know, I have nothing to say.' I was, like, '*What?*' He just got too caught up in it or something. I mean, Jimi Hendrix wasn't asking himself all these questions, he just fucking *did it*. And they got off on it. Black Sabbath, any fucking band, they were into *music*. Why deny it? That just drives me absolutely insane. Isn't this what it's all about?"

Shortly after *Nevermind* was released and immediately began scaling the charts, Barlow bumped into Mascis on the streets of Northampton. "I was like totally high and drunk," says Barlow, "and I was like, 'They fucking beat you to it! You could have done it, you asshole, we could have fucking done it!'"

# CHAPTER 11

# FUGAZI

PEOPLE ARE LIVING IN THINGS THAT HAVE HAP-
PENED, THE 60'S HAVE HAPPENED, YOUR PARENTS
HAVE TAKEN ALL THE DRUGS THEY CAN TAKE,
YOU'VE HAD THE 70'S, YOU HAD HEAVY METAL —
GET WITH IT, IT'S OVER WITH, WAKE UP. KIDS ARE
LIVING RE-RUNS, THE SAME CRAP OVER AND OVER
AND THEIR MINDS GET CLOSED TIGHTER AND
TIGHTER, IT'S SUCH A WASTE. THE SAME POLITI-
CAL CRAP, THE RADIO IS DEAD. I THINK THE WHOLE
THING IS GONNA FALL DOWN TO THIS LOWER
LEVEL, CAUSE I KNOW KIDS ARE GETTING INTO IT,
THEY DON'T HAVE ANYTHING ELSE. WHAT WE HAVE
AT THESE SHOWS, AND WITH THESE RECORDS —
THIS IS OUR BATTLEFIELD, THIS IS WHERE WE'LL
BE FIGHTING ABOUT WHAT WE'RE FOR. WE DON'T
HAVE ACCESS TO ALL THE THINGS PEOPLE IN THE
60'S HAD, WE HAVE TO DO IT ALL OURSELVES,
WHICH MEANS WE HAVE TO GET HAPPENING, WE
HAVE TO GET WITH IT.

— GUY PICCIOTTO, *FLIPSIDE* #47 (1985)

Fugazi was a vital force in the indie scene throughout the Nineties
and beyond, but the late Eighties were when the band earned a reputation for righteousness and integrity, which are among the indie
nation's best and most distinguishing attributes.

If Dinosaur Jr represented the apathetic "slacker" style that began appearing in the late Eighties, Fugazi embodied its polar opposite. No band was more engaged with its own business, its own audience, and the outside world than Fugazi. In response not only to a corrupt music industry but to an entire economic and political system they felt was fraught with greed for money and power, the band developed a well-reasoned ethical code. In the process, Fugazi staked out the indie scene as the moral high ground of the music industry; from then on, indie wasn't just do-it-yourself, it was Do the Right Thing.

Perhaps it just came down to the fact that the band's leader, former Minor Threat frontman Ian MacKaye, had watched the movie *Woodstock* so many times, but Fugazi held dear the old idea that a rock band can be a vital, inspiring part of a community of people looking to improve society. Not only did the band accomplish this is on a local scale, but they inspired a lot of others to do the same all over the world.

Fugazi has sold nearly 2 million records to date. That's a remarkable figure for any band, even one on a major label. While indie bands were now routinely defecting to major labels, Fugazi proved that a defiantly, exclusively independent route, taken without a shred of compromise, could succeed by *anybody's* yardstick. What other people see as limitations, they hold as virtues.

The band was also a remarkable second act for MacKaye, who had already led one crucial and influential band; the continuing success of Dischord Records was yet another validation of MacKaye's approach — in an era where most prominent indie labels were signing bands from all over the country, Dischord remained a bastion of regionalism. And musically, Fugazi's Eighties output also played an important stylistic role in modern rock music, being extremely instrumental in fostering the rock-funk fusion that eventually dominated Nineties alternative rock.

Like great gospel singers, it almost seems as if moral rectitude is what fuels Fugazi's immense musical power, as if rocking that hard requires a vast reservoir of righteousness. Their live shows have always been electrifying outbursts of passion and energy punctuated by unique, thoughtful improvisation, either musical or in the form of exchanges with the crowd. And as it does for the downtrodden members of society, the band sticks up for the literally downtrodden people in their concert audiences. If any band since the Minutemen embodies the idea that "our band could be your life," it's Fugazi.

**T**hroughout 1984 Washington, D.C., punk bands were forming and
then quickly dissolving at a furious rate. The D.C. scene had always suffered a lot of turnover, partly because much of the government workforce changed over with each new administration. Besides,
most of the Dischord scene's denizens were in their late teens and early
twenties, and a lot of them were going off to college or simply felt they'd
outgrown the punk lifestyle.

But not Ian MacKaye. For MacKaye the Sixties counterculture and
the early punk underground had furnished the blueprints for a better
existence. Punk was not something to grow out of; it was something to
grow *with* — it was a valid, sustainable way to live one's life. "That's when
I started to focus on the idea of what we were doing as being *real*, of being a working model of a real community, an alternative community that
could continue to exist outside of the mainstream — and legitimately,
and self-supporting," says MacKaye. "I'm talking about working, paying
rent, eating food, having relationships, having families, whatever. I saw a
counterculture that I thought could exist."

After Minor Threat, MacKaye continued to help foster that community, doing everything from producing records to hauling amplifiers for
virtually every band on Dischord, the label he worked day and night to
sustain. A constant parade of musicians trooped through the Dischord
House living room down to the basement to rehearse.

There were still plenty of D.C. punks who shared MacKaye's dedication, who were so deeply wedded to the scene that they either skipped
college or attended a nearby school just so they could stay involved.
MacKaye obliged by releasing their bands on Dischord or giving them
jobs at the label or even a room in Dischord House. But it was such a
tight, socially inbred community that when so many bands broke up at
the same time, the ensuing strains and social awkwardnesses put the
whole scene in limbo.

Also, the skinhead phenomenon was rampant and D.C. was not
spared its mindless violence. "Every show," as MacKaye puts it, "sucked."
Fighting and other idiotic macho behavior were spoiling the entire scene.
It was particularly dispiriting for MacKaye, who had spent so much of his
young life on his bands, his label, and his community, only to see outside
forces come in and almost ruin it all.

The Dischord crowd was clearly not going to win the scene back, so
they simply decided to cede it to the skinheads and develop a whole new
scene. They would develop a new ethos for punk, what Dischord House

resident Tomas Squip described as "the heartfelt thing" as opposed to the "aggressive thing."

They set October '84 for the debut of the new movement that they dubbed "The Good Food Revival" in honor of the celebratory feast they would hold. A sign on the wall in Dischord House read "Good Food October Is Coming. Get Your Bands Together."

But October came and went and precious little happened, partly because nobody wanted to start a band that didn't include MacKaye or his former Minor Threat bandmate Jeff Nelson and partly because nobody could quite agree on what direction to take. "There was a lot of really heavy conversation," MacKaye says. "We'd get together and talk and get into fights and argue about things."

That winter they held a big meeting at Dischord House. "OK, this summer we're going to do it, summer '85, Revolution Summer," blurted out Dischord employee Amy Pickering. And the phrase stuck. Soon an anonymously posted sign began appearing around town: "Be on your toes . . . This is Revolution Summer."

One of the main spearheads of the D.C. punk renaissance was Rites of Spring, whose singer-guitarist was Guy (pronounced the French way) Picciotto. Wiry and intense, Picciotto had attended the upscale Georgetown Day School and was at the same 1979 Cramps show that had introduced MacKaye to the communal power of punk rock. As it had with MacKaye, the experience changed Picciotto's life forever. "From thirteen on," says Picciotto, "there wasn't a single fucking thing that existed that I didn't want to undercut or question in some way."

Picciotto was soon playing in a punk band that appeared at his school's annual talent show sporting shaved heads and party dresses. He'd frequently get hassled at school by older jocks, who liked to drag him down the hall by the dog chain around his neck.

A couple of years later he joined Insurrection, which also featured drummer Brendan Canty, a wild-haired problem child who had bounced from school to school around the D.C. area. The two became best friends, but Picciotto says Insurrection was "lamentably terrible, one of the worst bands in town," and a demo they did with MacKaye was so bad that only MacKaye, ever the archivist, kept a copy. Picciotto's next band, he resolved, would be "meaningful to me and to a lot of other people."

To that end, Canty, Picciotto, bassist Mike Fellows, and D.C. hardcore mainstay Eddie Janney (Faith, the Untouchables) formed Rites of

Spring in the spring of '84. The band was named after the plangent
Stravinsky masterpiece that caused a riot at its 1913 premiere; even better,
the symphony's theme of death and rebirth had special meaning for the
D.C. scene.

Picciotto told *Flipside* that what animated Rites of Spring was "a constant friction between what you see, and what you want to achieve and
things that you know are right. That rub is what creates the pain and the
emotion and then there's the hope that maybe you can overcome it, make
it happen. It's the same politically and personally — to me it's all one issue because the same problems keep coming up over and over again —
lack of commitment, lack of caring."

Rites of Spring had commitment and caring in spades, playing
deeply earnest, impassioned music that burst out of the claustrophobic
hardcore format and into a more wide-screen, epic sound; Picciotto sang
with melodramatic desperation, as if he were being martyred for every
word. Lyrically, Rites of Spring was about extreme emotion and shying
from no feeling or experience. The style was soon dubbed "emo-core," a
term everyone involved bitterly detested, although the term and the approach thrived for at least another fifteen years, spawning countless
bands.

Picciotto rarely sang at Rites of Spring practices, preferring to save up
all his feelings for shows and recordings. The outpouring of emotion was
so intense that people actually wept at their shows. "[If] it looks like we're
playing with a lot of despair or emotion or frustration," said Picciotto,
"we're at the same time joyful — it's the greatest moment of relief, our
playing time, the moving, the music, everything about it — there's so
much joy."

Modesty, though, was not the band's strong suit. "We've come to
realize that this is real and it matters," Picciotto said. "And this separates
us from everything that has gone before — total, utter commitment and
belief."

As he was for so many D.C. punk bands, Ian MacKaye was one of
Rites of Spring's earliest and most fervent supporters, attending all their
shows, spreading the word, and even roadying for them. MacKaye
recorded a Rites of Spring album in February '85 and a (typical of D.C.)
posthumously recorded seven-inch EP the following January.

Rites of Spring played only fourteen shows, partly because they simply couldn't afford to play very often — they were always smashing equipment. "We were breaking shit in *practice* — it was getting ridiculous," says
Picciotto. MacKaye once recalled seeing Rites of Spring's second show:

"They were dirt fucking poor, and Guy smashes a guitar and Eddie turns around and smashes his guitar and runs it through his speaker cabinet. Then Brendan kicks the drums, punches holes through all of them. Then they were totally out of equipment. It was kind of tragic."

As Picciotto said at the time, "To hurt yourself playing guitar while falling around onstage is far more noble than to be sitting weeping to yourself somewhere."

**B**ack in the hardcore days, MacKaye and his friends were mad about the things all teenagers are mad about. And they lashed out at the first thing they saw, which was the forces oppressing them from within and without their immediate social circle. But as they got older, their perspective naturally broadened, and by 1985 Dischord had started donating modest amounts of money to progressive organizations such as Handgun Control, Planned Parenthood, the Union of Concerned Scientists, and the American Civil Liberties Union, as well as local homeless shelters, homes for battered women, soup kitchens, and so on.

They had grown up in what is basically a company town, and the Dischord crowd's newfound activism was largely a product of the city they lived in, much as the cinematic aspirations of so many L.A. punks were a product of theirs. And, as the mostly well-educated, privileged children of dedicated civil servants and journalists, they were in a better position than most to make a difference, or at least feel like they could. After all, these were the children of dutiful, good-hearted people dedicated to making the world a better place; the fruit had not fallen far from the tree.

The antiapartheid movement was a big part of the Dischord crowd's new political consciousness. Revolution Summer began with the Punk Percussion Protests Against Apartheid on June 21, the summer solstice of 1985. Outside the South African embassy, punks banged on drums, scrap metal, bits of wood, whatever they could find, for hours on end. "We want to show that we give a fuck about something that we think is totally wrong," MacKaye said at the time. "And just like the civil rights movement in the Sixties, this is a chance for us to all band together."

Fittingly, Rites of Spring played the kickoff show of Revolution Summer that night. "Punk is about building things," Picciotto told a packed 9:30 Club, "not destroying them." The band closed with "End on End," and the audience kept singing the song's refrain and clapping in time for a long, long time after the band left the stage, which was covered in flowers and, of course, broken equipment.

Revolution Summer was off to a rousing start.

Wise, respected, and enthusiastically supportive, MacKaye was the spiritual center of his community. "He was the cheerleader, he really supported the bands," says Picciotto. And yet MacKaye himself didn't have a band.

Then MacKaye cofounded Embrace that summer of '85. After half a dozen or so membership changes, the lineup wound up being MacKaye, bassist Chris Bald, guitarist Michael Hampton, and drummer Ivor Hanson: the same as the late lamented D.C. hardcore band Faith (minus Eddie Janney), except now MacKaye was singing instead of his own brother Alec.

MacKaye's lyrical approach had changed dramatically in the two years since Minor Threat. He wasn't railing against teenage hypocrites, bullies, and poseurs anymore — the subject of his songs was often himself. MacKaye was hollering lines like "I'm a failure" and "I am the fuckup that I can't forgive" against the anthemic music, as if to counter the personality cult that had sprung up around him by showing that he was his own harshest critic.

Like Picciotto, MacKaye felt the personal was political. "Personal purifying is the beginning of everything," MacKaye said. "Once you get your own shit together, once you get your own mind together, it makes life for you and the people around you so much more agreeable and understandable as opposed to constant fucking problems." But mostly, MacKaye's Embrace lyrics were activist manifestos that were just a little too strident for their own good — "No more lying down," MacKaye hollers in "No More Pain," "We've got to speak and move."

Musically, Embrace went even further down the trail blazed by Rites of Spring; far more melodic than hardcore, Embrace borrowed from mid-Seventies hard rock and metal as well as from Empire, an extremely obscure English band whose only album caught on wildly with the Dischord crowd. "It seemed like this weird lost link between what happened with [early English punk band] Generation X," MacKaye explains, "and where punk could go."

With a new music that packed a wider palette of emotions, musical devices, and lyrical approaches than hardcore, the Dischord crowd actually accomplished what they had set out to do: establish a whole new scene. "The more thuggish kids would come and they just hated it, because it was nothing like the kind of music they wanted to hear," says MacKaye. Their strategy of musical passive resistance had worked like a charm.

Rites of Spring played only two out-of-town shows — the band members were so deeply obsessed with the local scene that it barely occurred to them to play outside of D.C. One away gig was a summer of '85 show in Detroit opening for Sonic Youth (naturally, Picciotto broke a guitar at that show). Watching Sonic Youth play, Picciotto recalls, "I kind of had my mind blown." Being in a touring band and taking your music all over the country suddenly seemed like a fantastic idea. But Rites of Spring dissolved that winter and never got the chance.

A few months after Rites of Spring's demise, Embrace broke up, having lasted only nine months and never having toured. As it turned out, the tensions that had ripped apart Bald, Hampton, and Hanson back when they were in Faith had never been resolved. "So basically I'd just formed a band that had a giant bomb strapped to its chest," MacKaye says. "But the desire to be in a band was so great that we just decided not to see the bomb."

After that experience MacKaye resolved that his next band wouldn't be so hastily convened.

In the summer of '86, the musical chairs continued when Canty, Picciotto, and Janney joined Michael Hampton to form the melodic One Last Wish, who promptly broke up that fall; the following spring Canty, Picciotto, and Janney reunited with Michael Fellows and reprised the Rites of Spring lineup as Happy Go Licky. Although the personnel was identical, the approach was not. "We barely ever practiced," says Picciotto. "We just kind of would get onstage and things would just develop."

But the D.C. punk scene — and indeed the national punk scene — was eagerly awaiting MacKaye's next band. Thankfully, Happy Go Licky was becoming popular, which took some of the pressure off MacKaye locally. But strife within Happy Go Licky was constant; the band members had never dealt with the frictions that had done in Rites of Spring, and everyone in the band knew it wouldn't last long. Canty began casting about for another band.

Quiet, good-natured Joe Lally was a metal fan from Rockville, Maryland, well outside the D.C. Beltway. Sometimes he'd visit the Yesterday and Today record store in Rockville decked out like a member of the Obsessed, a local metal band he worshiped. "The first time I saw him," Canty recalls, "he came into our record store, he had long blond hair like Iggy Pop and fishnet stockings on. He went straight to the heavy metal section."

Soon afterward Lally saw the Dead Kennedys and the Teen Idles, became hooked on hardcore, and cut his hair and changed his wardobe. His metalhead buddies didn't quite understand. "Since I was the punk amongst them," Lally recalls, "they always felt like they had to come over and punch me in the head once in a while to keep me happy while I was watching the band."

Clearly, it was time to get out of Rockville.

After seeing an early Rites of Spring/Beefeater show in D.C., Lally found his way into the Dischord community. He'd been doing various drugs since his early teens, but the Dischord bands inspired him to reconsider. "They may not have even necessarily been talking about drugs," says Lally, "but seeing those bands, it was like, 'So what are *you* going to do? What are you going to do with your life?'"

Those questions made such an impact on Lally that he quit his lucrative NASA computer job, moved out of Rockville, and went on tour with Beefeater as a roadie in the summer of '86. He was a hard worker and even went vegetarian and straight edge with the rest of the band.

Lally often stopped by the Dischord House, where Beefeater rehearsed, and he and MacKaye hit it off, talking endlessly about their favorite bands: the Obsessed, the Jimi Hendrix Experience, the MC5, James Brown and the Stooges, as well as Jamaican dub reggae.

MacKaye had been looking for musicians for a new project that would be "like the Stooges with reggae." But, mindful of his bitter experiences with both Minor Threat and Embrace, he didn't want to call it a *band*. "My interests were not necessarily to be in a band [per se]," MacKaye says, "but to be with people who wanted to play music with me."

MacKaye had been mightily impressed when he saw Lally sing a flawless version of the Bad Brains' frantic "Pay to Cum" with Beefeater at the band's homecoming show. Shortly afterward Beefeater's Tomas Squip mentioned to MacKaye that Lally wanted to play bass in a band. MacKaye reasoned that anyone who could sing "Pay to Cum" had more than enough rhythm to play bass and soon asked Lally if he was interested in playing together.

MacKaye also invited drummer Colin Sears of the D.C. hardcore band Dag Nasty, and the trio's first get-together was on September 24, 1986, in the Dischord House basement. "We practice til ten o'clock," MacKaye wrote in his journal. "It sounds pretty potentialful [*sic*]." Partly inspired by the up-front, melodic bass lines of Joy Division, Lally began writing tuneful, dub-style parts behind the thundering guitar riffs Mac-Kaye was playing. A sound was born.

**A**fter a few months, Sears left and Brendan Canty began dropping by in February '87. But Lally and MacKaye's music was far from the jammy Happy Go Licky. MacKaye knew exactly what he wanted and playing with him was a matter of hewing to that vision. Canty relished the challenge, although it was difficult at first to rein in his flashy tendencies and make the music groove.

The music was a bit unusual, but that was fine with Canty. Working at Yesterday and Today, where he had discovered countless obscure but great bands from the MC5 to Funkadelic, he'd learned a valuable lesson: "No matter what you do, you're probably going to be lost in the annals of music," says Canty, "so you might as well play what you feel like."

Guy Picciotto dropped by one day to check out his close friend Canty's new band, secretly harboring the idea that maybe he could find a place for himself in it. But he was bitterly disappointed. "I didn't see an entry, I couldn't see a point where I could play with the band," says Picciotto. "It seemed really completed already, the way Ian was playing guitar, the way it worked with Joe. They'd already written a bunch of songs. It had a completely different feel from what I'd been doing with Brendan. It seemed just solid and done."

Picciotto left the practice room despondent. His band was breaking up and his longtime friend and bandmate was playing with someone else. He and Canty even had to move out of the punk rock house they lived in. "I didn't know what the fuck to do," says Picciotto. So, after graduating from Georgetown University with a B.A. in English, he did what so many directionless people do — he hit the road, taking a bus to Texas with little besides a knapsack. He sold Halloween pumpkins in Amarillo for a few days, then met up with some friends and spent a couple of months driving all over the country in a used Cadillac, returning to D.C. thoroughly refreshed.

In the meantime, Canty also decided he wanted to figure out what he wanted to do with his life and went out west to think it over. When he returned to D.C., Lally and MacKaye asked him if he wanted to rejoin the project. Canty accepted and the new band booked its first show, at the Wilson Center in early September '87.

But the group was still unnamed, and they had to come up with something quickly. "Otherwise people would probably call it 'Ian's new band,'" MacKaye says. "And I don't think anybody wanted that."

MacKaye found the word "fugazi" in *Nam*, author Mark Baker's compilation of war stories from Vietnam veterans; the term is military slang for "a fucked-up situation." "It applies to the band," MacKaye explained in an early interview, "in the way that we view the world."

"It kind of lets you cuss without actually cussing," MacKaye says now. "It was ambiguous enough that it didn't have any particular taste or color or flavor to it. It wasn't immediately suggestive, like Jackhammer or Pussywillow. It didn't have any overtly leading connotations to it. It was left to people's imagination."

Live, the band was a fairly open entity, too. They'd always leave a space onstage for their unofficial dancer Charlie — a PETA accountant by day, Charlie would jump up onstage wearing little more than a short skirt with nothing underneath, gyrating wildly to the amusement (or disgust) of the assembled multitudes. Others would come up and play trumpet or bang a drum or dance. There were people all over the stage, dancing and carrying on like it was a gospel revival.

It was in that spirit of openness that Fugazi entertained the idea of Picciotto's contributing somehow. Also, Lally and MacKaye knew that Canty and Picciotto were best friends; they both were huge fans of Picciotto's music, too. "We didn't know how it would fit," says MacKaye, "but it seemed like it should include Guy."

So they began inviting him to practices; at first Picciotto had resisted the idea, feeling that bands should be self-contained units, but gradually warmed to the thought of being back with Canty, not to mention finding a new outlet for his demonstrative stage presence. Inspired by hip-hop's (particularly Public Enemy's) revival of the age-old showbiz concept of the foil, Picciotto began singing backup vocals. He'd found an entry after all.

After Happy Go Licky broke up, on New Year's Day 1988, Picciotto became more and more involved with Fugazi, doing everything from roadie work to singing lead on his own song "Break-in," and soon MacKaye asked him to join as a full member. He accepted.

Still, MacKaye felt the band was informal enough that he could take on some side projects. After producing the searing Rollins Band album *Life Time* in Leeds, England, in November '87, MacKaye stopped off in

London, where he was introduced to Chicago musician Al Jourgensen. MacKaye remembered selling records by Jourgensen's synthetic dance-pop band Ministry at Yesterday and Today and was a bit dubious when Jourgensen said he had recently discovered hardcore. But MacKaye agreed to listen to an instrumental track Jourgensen was working on.

MacKaye liked what he heard — an ominous, spacey groove that exploded into a repetitive, mechanistic hardcore-style riff more than a little reminiscent of Big Black — and Jourgensen invited him to do a vocal for it. MacKaye recalled a conversation they'd had about Jourgensen's wrestling with signing to a major label and wrote the elliptically anticorporate "I Will Refuse" in an hour and recorded the vocal. He later recorded five more tracks with Jourgensen, and the results were split among a 1988 single and the excellent *Trait* EP under the name Pailhead, both on Chicago's seminal Wax Trax label, helping to initiate a hardcore-industrial synthesis that lives on to this day. (Jourgensen signed to a major label within the year.)

O nce MacKaye was back, Fugazi kicked into high gear. In January '88, they did their first tour — a quick trip to benighted Michigan cities like Flint, Lansing, and Ypsilanti. The trip up was a twelve-hour drive just to play someone's basement; everyone in the van was miserable. Then Picciotto passed a Queen compilation tape up front. "We were rocking out to the Queen tape," says MacKaye. "And that's when I knew we were a band."

A one-month U.S. tour that spring inspired further bonding. A week or so in, the van's radiator conked out and the band was stranded for three days in Miles City, Montana, waiting for a replacement part to arrive. After checking into a motel, all they could do was walk around town, killing time. After a day or so the locals would even stop and ask them how the repairs were going. And the experience united the band. "We were all living in this one motel room together," says MacKaye. "That was a great galvanizer, I always thought, that experience."

But they were still getting to know each other, and conversations in the van tended toward what Canty calls "true confessional type stuff." MacKaye and Picciotto, the most outspoken members of the band, would get into heated exchanges about any number of topics. While they were both strongly principled, they also had very different temperaments — MacKaye could be maddeningly stubborn but just as maddeningly well reasoned; Picciotto was more volatile and happy to play devil's advocate.

The voluble Canty often put his two cents in, too, although Lally was usually content to let the others do the arguing.

On one seemingly interminable drive from Olympia down the coast, Canty happened to mention that he wasn't sure whether playing in a band was the right thing to do with his life. No one else could understand his indecision — he was in a great band and he was on tour — what else could he possibly want? Picciotto, who was little more than a backup singer/roadie, was particularly incensed. Things quickly escalated from an offhand remark to a discussion, to a heated discussion, to a full-blown argument.

It was a tense moment, but an essential one. "It was about commitment," MacKaye says. "And when the call for commitment comes up, that's when stuff comes on the table. If you're going to jump in with someone, then you better know about each other. And I think that was really what was going on." Canty decided to throw his chips in with the band.

But perhaps he'd already made up his mind. On that first mini-tour up north, the band made about $250 at a show in Flint. Afterward Canty did a little math. "'If I make fifty bucks out of this and we can do this five, six nights a week, *I can quit my day job,*'" Canty thought to himself. "Immediately, it was like, *'Awesome!'*"

On those long drives, they worked up some novel ideas about how they were going to conduct their business: they wouldn't do interviews with magazines they themselves wouldn't read; they would play only all-ages shows and tickets would be $5.

Five dollars, they reasoned, was cheap, and it meant the box office wouldn't have to deal with making change. It also freed them to play a lousy show and not feel bad that people had paid a lot of money to see it. It wasn't a hard-and-fast policy at first, although it soon became that way. "It just became perverse to make it five," says Picciotto. "And that's always been my attraction to it — the perversity of it, insisting on this thing. . . . The idea that we could undercut it and make it work was comic and it was also kind of a statement." That kind of thinking was the impetus behind everything the band did.

Due to poor communication, their first show in L.A. was actually $7 — "much to our horror," MacKaye says — and they never did get below $6 in Los Angeles. Still, the precise dollar amount wasn't important. "It's about putting on music for a reasonable price," MacKaye says.

But they had to be very frugal to be able to offer the $5 admission, sleeping in motels only when absolutely necessary, routing tours efficiently so they wouldn't waste gas and time, taking along one roadie at most, and, says Picciotto, "not eating a whole lot." They also observed Mike Watt's famous dictum "If you're not playin', you're payin'" and rarely took days off. Luckily, they didn't pay any percentages to middlemen — MacKaye was both the band's booking agent and its manager.

But over time Fugazi made up for the low ticket price in volume — more people came to a show that cost so little, and pretty soon Fugazi shows began to be consistent sellouts, although this wasn't necessarily due to the band's popularity so much as MacKaye's shrewd assessment of what size venue they could fill in a given town. The low ticket price didn't come without some challenges, however. "When it's five bucks, you get every jackass on the street who has five bucks and nothing to do that night," says Picciotto. "And if he wants to throw some cans at the band, it's open to him, too. But it makes it interesting, man."

The all-ages admission policy was also key. "Everyone has to be able to come in," said MacKaye. "We don't play shows that discriminate against people." The whole band had bitter memories of being underage and standing outside clubs while their favorite bands played inside. "If you were fourteen, somehow your musical taste was considered rotten and you weren't allowed to go into a place to enjoy bands," Picciotto says. "So we just vowed in blood that we would never do the same thing to other kids."

They even did their best to personally answer all their fan mail. Picciotto recalled when he was a teenager writing to obscure English punk bands like Rudimentary Peni, Dead Wretched, and Blitz. "Those fuckers wrote us back, and it blew my mind," recalls Picciotto. "It was so cool to feel that connection. I've always kept that in mind. If someone writes you, you send them a letter back. It's just a cool thing to do."

"It was all stuff that was already part of us because it was just *punk*," MacKaye says. "It was just the way we were." Of course, plenty of others had come up with different interpretations of punk, just like various Christian denominations come up with different interpretations of the Bible. Fugazi's particularly dogmatic slant emphasized pragmatism, modesty, and fair play — not the first concepts to come to mind when discussing the indisputably punk rock Sex Pistols, for example.

Far from complicating their lives, Fugazi's conditions actually simplified things. If no club in a particular city could agree to Fugazi's terms, the band would simply skip that town. Occasionally the band would pull up to a club and learn that their conditions had not been met. And they'd start packing the van back up. Sometimes the promoter would relent, sometimes not. If not, he or she would get a good, long look at the band van's taillights.

"The power of 'No,' man, that's the biggest bat we've ever wielded," says Picciotto. "If it makes you uncomfortable, just fuckin' say no. It's made life so much easier for us, man. I think bands are fragile, particularly our band — we're super fragile, we're control freaks — if things upset us, we can't deliver. . . . That's what it's about — all this shit, just setting it

up so we can go out and play without cares, man. It eliminates everything. It just slashes through all that crap."

Another unorthodox decision was not to sell things like T-shirts,
posters, or even recordings on the road. They felt it turned their music
into a mere merchandising vehicle; besides, it was a pain to lug all that
stuff around, and they'd have to pay, transport, and house someone to sell
it for them. So they just jettisoned it.

T hey also jettisoned the trappings (and traps) of hardcore. The band
strove to avoid what MacKaye called "established ritualistic patterns," which portend the imminent demise of any movement.
Hardcore's fate was particularly fresh in their minds. Insisting on all-ages
admission and $5 tickets largely kept them out of even the hardcore cir-
cuit; most Fugazi shows were promoted by punk kids at impromptu
venues — people's basements, community centers, vegetarian restaurants, even dorm rooms. "That's the thing about underground organization," says Picciotto. "You *find* the Elks Lodge, you *find* the guy who's got
a space in the back of his pizzeria, you *find* the guy who has a gallery. Kids
will do that stuff because they want to make stuff happen in their town."
In Omaha they played a show in an abandoned supermarket that local
punk kids had turned into a venue by renting a PA system and making a
stage out of plywood and milk crates.

Playing unusual venues also had a potentially big payoff — not in financial terms but in terms of how much more fun and rewarding it could
be. "There are times when it's a disaster," acknowledges MacKaye, "but
there's other times when it's the best — you can't imagine how good it is."
And not only did playing unusual places break up the monotony of touring; it also sent a clear message to the audience: "It gives them an idea,"
said Picciotto, "that this band is moving in a different kind of network and
that things can happen in a different fashion."

Operating outside the mainstream music business, and even the
now-established indie scene, afforded the band a unique amount of freedom. As MacKaye sang it in "Merchandise," "We owe you nothing / you
have no control."

The idea of avoiding established patterns also extended to the band's
music itself. Even though many of the songs built up to hearty sing-alongs
with clear roots in second-generation English punks like U.K. Subs and
Sham 69, the music's sinuous funk and reggae beats defied the notoriously inbred punk sound; the hulking but catchy riffs recalled traditional

punk rock nemeses like Led Zeppelin and Queen. Even Fugazi's trade-mark startling stops and starts kept listeners on their toes. The implicit message, as with the Minutemen, was to stay alert, keep an open mind, don't be afraid of change, question things.

Since Rites of Spring and Embrace had virtually never made it out of town, the hardcore crowd wasn't at all prepared for Fugazi. "People were baffled by it — 'What is this, reggae music? Funk? What the fuck is it?'" says MacKaye. Of course, reggae and punk had a long mutual history. "But the kids who were going to these shows were not educated about the past," MacKaye explains. "Their deep roots were Minor Threat."

Besides constant jackhammer tempos, another hardcore relic that had to go was slam dancing. For one thing, it made life miserable for any-one who didn't want to join in, but it also seemed that people were slam-ming almost sheerly out of habit, since violent dancing simply did not go with the music. Knee-jerk slamming bespoke an entire mind-set that ex-tended far past the dance floor; if people were that conditioned, it proba-bly pertained to most aspects of their lives. And Fugazi, for one, wasn't going to be a party to it.

Famously, MacKaye would single out specific members of the audi-ence and in witheringly formal terms ask them not to hurt people. "Sir, I hate to belabor the point" went one typical MacKaye rebuke, "but why don't you think about the fact that you are consistently kicking the same people in the head every time."

The politeness was key. "See, they have one form of communication: violence," MacKaye explains. "So to disorient them, you don't give them violence. I'd say, 'Excuse me, sir . . .' — I mean, *it freaks them out* — 'Ex-cuse me, sir, would you please cut that crap out?'" His admonitions seemed preachy to some, but most were deeply grateful. And by and large, people would obey — it wasn't cool to disrespect Ian MacKaye.

Of course, MacKaye's quest for audience civility was quixotic at best, which made the gesture all the more meaningful — he'd never back down, even though everyone knew he'd never completely succeed. "Built into the band very early on was not shrinking from confrontation," says Picciotto. "There was just a really open thing going on between the crowd and the band." Consequently, there were two kinds of Fugazi shows — the show where there was a delirious, transcendent uplift as the band, the music, and the crowd all seemed to surge and heave as one, and the ad-versarial show where the band and the more obnoxious element of the audience were at odds, MacKaye and Picciotto unhesitatingly killing the momentum of the set by scolding the knuckleheads in the crowd.

Often one of the band would haul an offending audience member onto the stage and ask him to apologize on mike; sometimes Picciotto would hug and kiss any man who climbed onto the stage, which proved to be a very effective deterrent. The unrepentant would be hustled out of the venue and handed an envelope with a five-dollar bill in it — the band kept a stack in an equipment box for just such occasions.

At one early gig in Spokane, Washington, a handful of merciless slam dancers were ruining the show for everybody else. "Put your hands in the air if these guys are bugging you," Picciotto told the crowd. Immediately the place was a forest of hands. So the band told everybody but the slam dancers to get up onstage, while Lally, MacKaye, and Picciotto came down to the floor and played as the slammers did a circle dance around them. "It was great," Picciotto said afterward, "the whole thing was like a celebration of life."

People in concert crowds were not used to being noticed and singled out by a band — it was as if the television set had started talking back to them. "It's almost like some kind of code has been violated that really makes people feel weird," says Picciotto. "And I'm *into* that. I'm into that kind of weirdness. Really, the ultimate concept is we are human beings just the same as anyone else. If we see something on the street that we think is fucked up, we would testify about it. If we see something going on in the room, just because we're the jukebox doesn't mean that we give up our power of speech or our power of observation — those things are still operating. And so we used them."

The fact that the people onstage spoke out against injustices in the audience not only diminished the barrier between audience and performer; it also forced people to be responsible for their actions. According to Picciotto, "It was really about the moment and seizing the moment and making it happen, not letting bullshit dictate things, which is what was happening. The violence and stuff that is attached to it and the weird misogyny of a lot of punk rock, the way the room breaks down, that stuff sucks, it's a drag and I think it's really important to work against it and try to make something different — if only because it's interesting, if only because it's not boring. But also because it will be better."

They had deliberately done the first U.S. tour without having a record out. MacKaye even asked promoters not to mention his name in flyers for the shows — he knew well that much of the interest in Fugazi would be based on the fact that the band included "the

dude from Minor Threat." They'd have to show the world — and themselves — that Fugazi wasn't just "Ian's new band." With no record out and
thus no advance hoopla, people would take Fugazi at face value.

But Minor Threat's formidable legacy still loomed large. Fugazi audiences fully expected some Minor Threat songs and heckled the band if
they didn't get them — and this went on through the band's first few years.
The sharp-witted MacKaye gave as good as he got, though. "People were
punk rock so they had a lot of smart-ass shit to say," MacKaye says. "But
I'm a punk rock kid, too, so they're tangling with the wrong guy. I'm good
with that, too — I can be a smart ass and I'll confront people, too — I'm
not worried about it. . . . A lot of this stuff is about confrontation and
there was also a lot of intimidation. There was a lot of kids who wanted to
kill me."

Fortunately, Fugazi was more than good enough to win over crowds
who were expecting Minor Threat II. "Some nights when we play, I walk
into a club and think, 'This is going to be fucking hell on earth!' " said
MacKaye early in the band's existence. "Then we go in, and at some
point we establish a rapport, it's amazing, things start happening, the
crowd is transformed, all of a sudden they look like a bunch of angels! And
they don't see Minor Threat anymore, they see Fugazi, and they love it."

The band's connection to the audience was heightened by the fact
that many of the songs were consciously written with the thought of the
crowd singing along like a congregation. "I was just really interested in
having people sing," MacKaye says. "Singing is an inclusive thing. It gives
somebody something to do at a concert — they feel like they're a part of
it. . . . When I see people singing, it makes me feel like I'm getting something back."

The members of the socially conscious Reno hardcore band 7 Seconds were inveterate networkers, and their Positive Force Records
was the impetus for a clutch of Positive Force political action
groups to form all around the country. However, none of them ultimately
survived except for the Washington, D.C., chapter, which was started
around Revolution Summer by, as Picciotto puts it, "a bunch of punk
rock kids." Although the group had no defined leader, its main organizer
was (and remains) Mark Andersen. Positive Force promoted Fugazi's local shows, found offbeat places for the band to play, and generally acted
as a liaison between the band and the organizations it was aiding. If the
band played a local show, it was a benefit and it was organized by Positive
Force.

Realizing they'd be raising relatively small amounts of money, the members of Fugazi reasoned it would be more effective to funnel funds to small organizations for whom even a few hundred dollars would be a significant windfall. And they were local organizations because, as Picciotto puts it, "we're all serious hometowners." (In fact, MacKaye is a sixth-generation Washingtonian.) With D.C. swiftly becoming the drug and murder capital of the nation, corruption rife within the city's government, and residents deprived of voting representation in Congress, social services were sketchy at best and the town was falling into disrepair; there was a lot that needed help. The band decided to focus on helping the downtrodden, donating to prison reform organizations, free clinics, homeless shelters, and AIDS clinics. One of their favorite concerns was the venerable Washington Free Clinic, which provides medical services for the poor and uninsured; MacKaye's father had been involved with the organization for decades.

Like MacKaye's family, Canty's parents were veterans of the civil rights movement of the Sixties and would often put up demonstrators who came through town. "So for us," says Canty, "to me at least, it feels like a continuation from that spirit — to give back to the community that wrought you."

Positive Force hooked up the band with some unorthodox venues, such as the Sacred Heart Church in the racially mixed Mount Pleasant neighborhood and the Lorton Correctional Facility in Virginia, where they played a Boxing Day 1990 show to a few dozen inmates. "They were pretty freaked out," said MacKaye. "They'd never heard anything remotely like us before." Footage of the show from director Jem Cohen's Fugazi documentary *Instrument* reveals that the audience was more amused than "freaked out" by the earnest Fugazi, but the gig was still a bold move.

**M**acKaye may have been the instigator of the band and exerted a strong pull on its aesthetics in the early stages, but he had learned from bitter experience with Minor Threat to make sure there was band unanimity every step of the way. "He'd sing every lyric to us to make sure we were cool with the sentiment," says Canty. "He'd realized the importance of that, of making sure everybody was in on every decision and being on the same page aesthetically with him — and behind the sentiment of the song."

Recalling another sticking point with Minor Threat, MacKaye even suggested to the others that they record for his friend Corey Rusk on

Touch & Go instead of Dischord so as to avoid any conflict of interest. "We were like, 'Fuck that, man,'" says Canty, "because part of the thing that we were trying to grow was with Dischord — it was a huge part of our community."

In June '88 they recorded a self-titled seven-song EP at perennial Dischord favorite Inner Ear Studios; local musician Ted Nicely, another Yesterday and Today alumnus, produced the sessions. The EP kicks off with one of Fugazi's most enduring anthems. The way the tense, reggae-inflected verses of "Waiting Room" explode into a heavy metallic chorus, one would assume the song is an impatient call to action. But actually, it is about carefully getting all one's ducks in a row — just like MacKaye had done with Fugazi. "I won't make the same mistakes," MacKaye sings, "Because I know how much time that wastes."

Picciotto sings lead on "Bulldog Front," another tense, subdued verse erupting into a fist-pumping chorus, about tearing down the walls of stubborn apathy and willful ignorance. Like most of Picciotto's lyrics, the words aren't overtly political, but lines like "Ahistorical — you think this shit just dropped right out of the sky" had far-reaching implications — be aware, the song seems to say, that ignorance is slavery. Picciotto's AIDS meditation "Give Me the Cure" takes a different tack, the arty dissonances and novel structure building more and more tension with every change.

MacKaye's "Suggestion" goes in for Gang of Four–ish herky-jerky punk-funk, veering off into false crescendos that ratchet up the verses mercilessly. "Why can't I walk down the street / Free of suggestion?" MacKaye sings, assuming the persona of a sexually harassed woman. (The song was based on the real-life experiences of Dischord scenester Amy Pickering, but some felt MacKaye had no right to sing about a woman's experience. "That's nonsense," MacKaye said. "It's a human issue that we should and will continue to have to deal with." The power of "Suggestion" is undeniable and it has remained a staple of Fugazi live shows ever since.)

**A**fter completing the EP, Fugazi set out on a long European tour. Despite MacKaye's renown, lining up a European tour for a band without a record was quite a feat. But no one had anticipated the draining effects of a lengthy European tour, with its constantly shifting cultures, food, currencies, language, and time zones. The three-month trek was the "hardest thing I'd ever done up to that point," Picciotto says, "just a really harsh tour."

Then again, Picciotto hardly made it easy on himself. He made up for not having a guitar in his hands by running all over the stage like a crazy man. He would get completely carried away, flinging himself about the stage, rolling on the floor, and twisting himself into tortured shapes. At one legendary show at a gym in Philadelphia, he sang a song while hanging upside down from a basketball hoop, then fell in a heap onto Canty's drums. Invariably he'd be a mass of aches and pains the next day, and yet he couldn't help but get up and do it again at the next show. After just a few nights in a row of this, Picciotto was a wreck. And Europe was more than a few nights — it was a few months.

Then there were the accommodations, which were mostly squats. Squats were a legacy of late Sixties underground culture, when unkempt European youths began occupying abandoned buildings in search of cheap housing and a different way of life. Typically squats were run like communes and deeply involved in radical left-wing politics. Many of them made much of their money hosting rock shows.

Squats meant "a series of stinky rooms," says Canty, "and/or a series of rooms where people are staying up all night, smoking hash next to you while you're trying to sleep. Or waking up to Black Flag playing at eight o'clock in the morning."

"There was plenty of times being in Germany and you're playing in some shitty, really awful squat with German punks passed out on the stage in front of you and the whole place reeking because nobody cleaned up all night — somebody vomits on the stage, total squalor," Canty continues. "And then at the end of the night, we say, 'You promised us a place to stay,' and they go, 'Oh yeah, here it is.' And you look over and it's your dressing room, which is right off the stage. So you go and you set up your sleeping bag in a room [where] you just got offstage about an hour before and it still stinks, there's still vomit on the stage right next to where you're sleeping. So you get in your sleeping bag, there are some mattresses back there but they're totally disgusting so you lay them out and you get in your sleeping bag.

"And you get up to go to the bathroom — this is all true — and the toilet is smashed and there are rats running around the toilet. So there's no place to shit or piss. And there's no running water. And you're locked in because they want to lock the place. So we had to piss out the mail slot. And there's rats running around, so we all get in our sleeping bags and we just pull the drawstrings up as close as possible so the rats won't get in."

D.C.'s straight edge reputation dogged the band everywhere they went, especially in the squats, where the hippie drug legacy had never faded. "I'd actually already ingested everything any of these people had ever thought of when they were nine," says Lally. "Not to mention that we weren't flying any flags. We weren't saying *anything*. And we were getting all this . . . stuff."

Canty recalls plenty of times when "somebody in a group house brings you there to sleep and the other members in the group house hate you for Minor Threat or whatever reason." "Or they write things on your bananas," Lally chips in. "Your banana says, 'You guys are assholes.'"


Fugazi had arranged to record their debut album at the end of the tour, in December '88, with John Loder at Southern Studios in London. Unfortunately they hadn't realized the implications of recording first thing in the morning after the final night of the tour. The band was spent. They tracked an album's worth of material, but in the end the performances weren't up to snuff so they trimmed it down to an EP.

Fatigue may have bogged down the performances, but recent events back home were also troubling the band. That November former CIA chief George Bush had won the presidential election, ensuring yet four more years of a Republican in the White House. "That was horrible," Picciotto recalls. "The nausea so many felt when Bush got in, we'd already been through eight years of Reagan and then Bush goes in and he was so creepy, so fucked up. Man, that was terrible."

The dread and anger are all over *Margin Walker*. On the title track, Picciotto reinvents Cupid as a Lee Harvey Oswald–style sniper, riding just ahead of a MacKaye guitar onslaught denser than anything he'd done before. On "Provisional," Picciotto takes to task both a complacent public "Secured under the weight of watchful eyes, lulled to sleep under clear expansive skies" and irresponsible politicos ("We hope we don't get what we deserve, hide behind the targets in front of the people we serve"). And Picciotto's "Lockdown," hectic and teeming, is a typically abstruse indictment of one of his favorite targets, the deplorable U.S. prison system.

MacKaye's lyrics are more direct, more anthemic than Picciotto's sometimes precious verbiage, but they are still largely metaphorical and elliptical. If, as MacKaye says, Minor Threat's lyrics were like one-size-fits-all clothes, Fugazi was more like uncut cloth. "If they want to *make* some clothes, they can use this fabric," says MacKaye. So although MacKaye skirts overt political statements on the PiL-ish "And the Same," a loosely sketched condemnation of force as an instrument of policy, it is still, as MacKaye bluntly puts it, "An attempt to thoughtfully affect / Your way of thinking." On the spitfire reggae verses of the ecological protest "Burning Too," MacKaye warns, "We are consumed by society / We are obsessed with variety / We are all filled with anxiety / That this world will not survive."

**T**hough he was singing more and more, Picciotto was dissatisfied with his role in the band. "I was used to a much more open, democratic musical thing happening," says Picciotto. "I wanted to *play*." So upon returning from the European tour, they all agreed that Picciotto should start playing guitar. The problem was MacKaye's sturdy, rhythmic style meshed seamlessly with Lally's supple, dub-influenced bass; Picciotto couldn't find a way in. Then he realized there was a wide patch of sonic real estate available in the upper frequencies. Using a Rickenbacker, the trebly, chiming guitar made famous by the Byrds, Picciotto could cut through MacKaye's chunky chording like a laser beam. And he did.

Picciotto's move to guitar changed the band profoundly, and not just because two guitars filled out the sound. In the past the band would play MacKaye's songs pretty much as he wrote and arranged them. It was awkward to jam and experiment in rehearsal because the instrumentless Picciotto couldn't participate. But now that Picciotto had a guitar, everyone felt free to improvise; ideas were tossed around as a group, and the band started delving much further into ensemble passages full of startling guitar textures, dissonant chords, and novel approaches to phenomena like feedback and harmonics.

And MacKaye and Picciotto created all those effects without benefit of distortion pedals; MacKaye never varied his equipment: a Gibson SG guitar and a Marshall amplifier. "Even though I know that there's a lot of options, I'm not interested in options," he says. "I'm interested in how far I can take this simple equation, which is an amp, a cord, and a guitar, and how much I can do with it."

The band's less-is-better approach even extended to their diet; they had gone vegetarian, which was a pretty tricky thing to be on the road in the U.S. — the interstates held nothing but meat-intensive fast-food joints. Eventually they discovered that one chain had a veggie cheese melt, but for a long time they would fill up a cooler with decent food from grocery stores and simply picnic in their van.

Like most bands, Fugazi learned the lessons of touring the hard way. For instance, there was the constant matter of where to sleep after the gig. MacKaye had punk rock friends in most towns, but sometimes they were a little *too* punk rock for the rest of the band. "A place where there's cat piss where you lay down your head to sleep, don't go back," advises Lally. "*Do not return to that place.*"

"No matter *what* Ian says," adds Canty.

But after a tour or two, the band rarely had a problem finding nice, urine-free places to stay and were always asked back. "We washed our dishes," Canty explains. "That's the key: when you go to somebody's house, wash your dishes. And then they'll ask you back."

On their first U.S. tour, the summer of '88, they played Olympia's Evergreen State University. Show promoter Calvin Johnson passed a hat so the band could get paid. "It just seemed like paradise being out there," says Picciotto. "It's such a weird sleepy small town and yet there was so much action there — there were so many great bands, so much energy. It was one of the first places we played where we really felt at home, where the kids were dancing and the vibe was just so incredible."

Maybe it was the affinity between two capital cities that were cultural wastelands, but there was also a surprisingly high degree of cross-pollination — Calvin Johnson had lived in the D.C. area in his teens, and Canty's sister had moved to Olympia; Dave Grohl would eventually leave the D.C.-based hardcore band Scream for the Olympia-based Nirvana, and Olympia punk maven Lois Maffeo soon moved to D.C.

The two towns formed a strong cross-continental bond, not only making musical connections but exchanging useful ideas and information, forging a consensus about the way things ought to be in the indie world and beyond. The D.C.-Olympia axis would prove to be an influential force in the years to come. "When we went there, we locked in really hard with those people," says Picciotto. "It was always a really good spot for us."

In September '89 they recorded their first album, once again at Inner Ear with Ted Nicely producing. Nicely was studying to be a chef at the time and had limited time to record the album, so the sessions took place between the decidedly un–rock & roll hours of 9 A.M. and 1 P.M.

It was a pivotal time for Fugazi. By now Canty and Picciotto were contributing substantial musical ideas; the multitalented Canty even wrote some bass lines and choruses. "That's when we all threw ourselves into it really earnestly," says Canty. "It was the first time that both Guy and I could say, 'This is our band.'"

Better recorded than the two EPs and played with the awesome power of a first-class rock band, *Repeater* is a post-punk classic.

The band members' thorough knowledge of rock music compelled them to be as original as possible. When something sounded clichéd, "then comes five hours of trying to put the parts where they're not supposed to go," says Lally. So the songs on *Repeater* veered in all sorts of unexpected directions: squalling noise, tense rhythm breakdowns, static guitar reveries, or a mighty, wall-rattling unison clang. The mix of influences was also unique: a more aggressive take on the reggae-punk fusion that bands like the Ruts had explored, infused with the righteous fervor of the Clash, and driven home with foot-stomping guitar riffs à la MacKaye's old favorites Queen and Ted Nugent. They were also clearly paying a lot of attention to hip-hop; the catchy call-and-response hollering recalls Run-D.M.C. while the repeating guitar squeal on the title track owes much to Public Enemy's epochal "Rebel without a Pause."

The Canty-Lally rhythm section was now red-hot — Canty hits with the force and precision of karate chops, Lally's nimble lines could induce vertigo — and their hectic interplay recedes only for the band's trademark whiplash silences. As ever, pensive passages would suddenly erupt into glorious choruses, as in "Merchandise," where MacKaye thunders,

"You are not what you own!" while an heraldic ascending guitar riff raises the roof.

As six-string adventurists, the band was in a league with Sonic Youth, but most people fixated on the band's politics and policies. And there's no denying that their politics, sharply expressed on *Repeater*, were provocative. The leadoff track, Picciotto's "Turnover," is an extended metaphor about ignoring social ills — to "turn off the alarm" and go back to sleep. Next, the kinetic title track illustrates the effects of that approach — a chilling monologue told from the point of view of a career criminal, it jump-cuts to the point of view of someone hearing gunshots outside. Then the song shifts narrators once again: "We don't have to try it and we don't have to buy it," MacKaye roars.

That last line is echoed throughout the album. *Repeater* is practically a concept album about the notion that one can effect social change by carefully considering the things one buys — and Fugazi extended that idea well beyond the material sense. "Never mind what's been selling / It's what you're buying," sings Picciotto in "Blueprint," echoing a think-for-yourself line at least as old as Black Flag. "Merchandise, it keeps us in line / Common sense says it's by design," MacKaye sings in "Merchandise." Even MacKaye's harrowing OD nightmare "Shut the Door" is a heated meditation on the perils of consumption. "She's not moving! She's not coming back!" he hollers with more rage than terror.

The thing was Fugazi not only talked the talk; they walked the walk. The band had quickly become an ethical lodestar for bands and fans alike, revered bastions of integrity in an increasingly compromised and corrupt world, an impeccable benchmark for everything that pioneering bands like Black Flag and the Minutemen stood for: pragmatism, community, independence, and engagement.

Fugazi existed in an entirely separate realm from what MacKaye calls "college rock" — Dinosaur Jr, Camper van Beethoven, Mudhoney, and the like — which was then in its heyday. They didn't socialize with the SST bands or the so-called "pigfuck" bands on Homestead and Touch & Go. MacKaye even fell out of touch with his old friend Corey Rusk during the late Eighties. "That whole Chicago [scene] — Naked Raygun, Big Black, that crew," MacKaye says dismissively, "were the guys who smoke cigars and eat ribs.

"That whole world, those guys, I think they just were not into punk rock," MacKaye continues. "They grew up on it and then they were growing out of it."

The band toured *Repeater* for virtually all of 1990: after a few local shows in January, they toured the South from February until April, then the rest of the U.S. from May through July; from September through November they were in Europe. Hard touring was not only the crucible in which the band's basic tenets had been formed; it was the main way it won fans. But it was also tough on a band that very much enjoyed their local scene, not to mention their personal lives. "We wanted to play," says MacKaye. "It was rough, physically, but it's like, why do people jog or why do people do anything that involves discipline? I don't know. Bands play music." (MacKaye's sole advice for surviving the rigors of the road: "Drink a lot of water.")

Because they kept playing unconventional venues, touring never stopped being an adventure. In May '90 they played a Dallas warehouse that local punks had converted into a living space. In the ground floor's huge lobby, they had built a stage on top of a crumpled car they had dragged through the front door. The show was packed with about eight hundred people.

Before the show a street fight between two rival skinhead gangs — a Nazi white power outfit and an anti-Nazi group who wore Star of David patches — threatened to spill over into the show. To cool things down, MacKaye went out and met with the leaders of the two groups. "One guy was wearing a Nazi uniform with a swagger stick," MacKaye recalls. "And I swear he was wearing a monocle." MacKaye brokered a peace agreement, pointing out that the warehouse punks had been nice enough to put on the show and it wasn't right to make it into a battlefield.

Finally the first band went on. But then the police showed up and called the fire marshal, who obligingly pointed out various violations. For nearly an hour Fugazi and the show's promoters made exit signs and put lights on them, taped off exit lanes, and cleared exit doors as the crowd grew increasingly restless.

After all the work was completed and Fugazi was getting ready to take to the stage, the fire marshal told MacKaye the place still wasn't up to code. A cop told MacKaye to tell the crowd the show was off. "*I'm* not going to tell them no show," MacKaye replied. "You're going to pull the plug on this, *you* go tell them."

"You're trying to start some trouble with me?" the cop said.

"Sir, I'm not trying to start any trouble with you," MacKaye said firmly. "I'm just telling you that if *you're* going to stop the show, *you* can go tell them. Because I have worked hard to make it happen."

They discussed the situation some more and finally reached a compromise. MacKaye got onstage and, to loud cheering, announced that
the police had decided to let them play. There was only one catch: the
audience had to go outside. "They've closed the street off and we'll have
the doors open and we'll play as loud as we can and we'll sing as hard as
we can," MacKaye told the crowd.

After an initial uproar, everyone filed out onto the street and Fugazi
played to an empty warehouse, with the open doors blocked by a chain-
link fence. "Between songs we would run up and look out the chain-link
fence," MacKaye says, "making sure the police weren't hitting anybody."

By this point there was a raging bonfire in a vacant lot across the way
and hundreds of kids were dancing in the street and stage-diving off
parked cars. "That kind of stuff," MacKaye notes, "is just not going to happen at a rock club."

After *Repeater* the band was routinely selling out 1,000-capacity
shows and yet still hauled their own equipment, booked their own
shows, and slept on people's floors (and they still do). "I love staying with people," says MacKaye. "I love doing the driving. I love having
to load equipment. The experiences are things that a lot of people never
have."

From the very beginning, MacKaye had done pretty much all the administrative work for Fugazi — and wouldn't have it any other way. "He
basically had experience at having done A, B, C, D, E, F, and G," says
Lally. "And he was good at it. And he was pretty insistent on doing it."
MacKaye managed the band, booked the tours, got the money at the end
of the night. He even insisted on driving the van at all times (which he
does to this day). Cutting out managers, booking agents, lawyers, publicists, and road managers is a lot different from the way most bands go
about things. "Yeah, but that's because we stopped to think about
it," Canty says. "We stopped to think about that because it's self-
preservation."

But a lot of bands don't even think about self-preservation. Canty
replies with an analogy about how most people don't think twice about
eating meat, mainly because most food stores don't offer many other options. "Waaaaay in the back, by the scallions, is some tofu," Canty says.

So Fugazi simply went to the back of the store? "We went to a *different* store," Canty says, proudly.

"And we went to the back of *that* one!" Lally chimes in.

"And," Canty adds, smiling and pounding the table, "we bought in bulk!"

**B**oth MacKaye and Picciotto are extremely uncomfortable with connecting the band's business style with something as personal as vegetarianism, but the same sensibility is at work in both cases. MacKaye constantly evaluates every aspect of his life, cutting out unnecessary things that most people unthinkingly accept. "This is what I am trying to do across the board," says MacKaye. "If you're going to see me play music, that's the way it will manifest. If you came over to my house, you'd see the way I live. If I make you dinner, you'll see the food I eat. After trying to be thoughtful about my life and to consider what I've inherited and what I need and what I don't need and what I'll discard and what I want to gain, what's important, what's not important. By going through this checklist and trying to figure all these things out, this is what I've arrived at. And if I'm in a band, it's going to manifest in that presentation."

Fugazi simply cut out the needless clutter in their lives, things most bands accept without ever questioning why. If *Walden* author Henry David Thoreau were to have managed a rock band, it probably would have been run a lot like Fugazi.

Same with Dischord itself. The label almost completely dispensed with promotion to press and radio — the outlay was more trouble and expense than it was worth. Dischord employees "recovered" all the paper they needed from other people's trash. In 1989 a friend got a huge supply of stationery from a marketing company that was throwing it out; it all bore letterheads, but the label simply used the other side of the paper. Dischord was still using the paper ten years later and has never bought an envelope in its entire existence. And the savings got passed on to the consumer: Dischord albums were never more than $10, even on CD.

**O**n January 12, 1991, Fugazi played in the freezing cold rain at Lafayette Park, across the street from the White House, on the day Congress gave the OK to begin bombing Iraq. "When Operation Desert Storm happened," says Picciotto, "people were petrified in this town." Two thousand people showed up and pogoed so hard that they sent up clouds of steam drifting over the stage. Four days later the bombs began falling on Baghdad.

By the summer, *Repeater* had sold well over a hundred thousand copies, an astounding number for a small indie label, especially one with such minimal promotion. Word of mouth about the band had spread widely through the indie community, and the record was selling far beyond just the hardcore crowd. Unswerving integrity was one thing, but it was their live shows that made Fugazi an underground legend. Already masters of tension and release, they could mesmerize a crowd with a tightly coiled rhythm vamp, add in some fraught guitar interplay, and then blow it all away with gale-force explosions of thunderous volume. A song like "Shut the Door" might get stretched out to nine minutes or more as the band leaned into extended but riveting improvisations, showing off an uncanny musical telepathy honed by endless roadwork. Fugazi never worked with a set list, which meant they could vibe off the crowd and each other in perfect synchrony.

Studious-looking in his nerdy glasses, Canty slapped out the band's funkified rhythms as Lally paced around by his amp, casually eyeing the crowd from under the brim of his watch cap. But it was Picciotto and MacKaye's show, the two of them lunging and lurching around the stage, twisting their bodies like wet washcloths, violently swinging the necks of their guitars as if to knock the previous chord unconscious.

The two frontmen were a study in contrasts: while MacKaye would go in for anything from a knock-kneed Lindy hop to Townshendian guitar leaps, Picciotto chewed the scenery — he fell all over the place, humped the stage, climbed the amps, contorted his body like a Gumby doll. MacKaye dressed in drab, baggy clothes; Picciotto would sport tight black jeans and, invariably, a red shirt. MacKaye's sober athleticism found its polar opposite in Picciotto's almost hammy sensuality, a formidable yin and yang that powered the band's galvanic performances.

**B**y this time even the Meat Puppets and Mike Watt's band fIRE-HOSE had signed to majors, and about half a dozen major labels wanted to sign Fugazi. But the band felt their music was already being distributed adequately. Sales bore that out. And with Dischord, they definitely knew who they were dealing with. Of course, there were also the inevitable noble reasons. "Big bands that stay independent lend weight to the indie movement," MacKaye said. "People are forced to deal with indies to get big names. That gives a lot of other bands access, it spreads the wealth."

Spreading the wealth was important to Fugazi — the band always gave opening slots on tours to independent bands who didn't necessarily draw crowds but merited the high-profile gig. And even on longer tours, they usually kept an opening band on the bill for no more than a half dozen shows or so, in order to give exposure to as many bands as possible.

The band was now routinely committing rock & roll heresy by turning down big interviews with major national music magazines like *Rolling Stone*, *Details*, and *Spin*, partly because they carried tobacco and alcohol advertising. "Some magazines just make us uncomfortable," MacKaye explained to the zine *Noiseworks*. "As we've gotten bigger, there's choices we've had to make, and we don't like things out of our control. We're trying to maintain that right." "I don't trust those mags to reflect us accurately or honestly," Picciotto added. "I certainly don't need a mag that puts 'for men' on the cover like *Details*." But Picciotto singled out *Rolling Stone* for the most opprobrium: "I can't see," he said, "what in God's name they have to do with rock & roll."

The old "belly of the beast" argument didn't wash, either — "I can see there's a point to getting good ideas into *Rolling Stone*," Picciotto added, "but when you're sandwiched between a thousand bad ideas, I don't think it translates."

**F**or their second album, they again requested the services of Ted Nicely, but Nicely was now a full-time chef and treasured his free time, so he reluctantly turned down the job. Then the band figured that since they did everything else themselves, they might as well do their own recordings as well.

The approach had another benefit. None of them, not even the veteran MacKaye, had ever been in a band that had stuck together this long. "We were kind of hitting a plateau," says Picciotto, "where we needed to find a way to keep pushing it so it didn't feel static." Making their own record seemed to be one way of doing that. So in January '91, they enlisted the trusty Don Zientara as engineer and went to it.

But the timing wasn't right. The band had been on the road constantly that year and it showed. "Within the band, our communication at that point was kind of weird," Picciotto says. "I think it had to do with that we'd been around each other a fuck of a lot."

Many bands would snipe at each other under such circumstances, but the members of Fugazi did something else almost as deadly to creativity — they treated each other with kid gloves. "Here's four people who have a fairly good idea of how to make a salad," says MacKaye, "and yet

everybody was so concerned about insulting other people's taste that
no one dared to pick up a head of lettuce or chop a tomato or anything.
We all just sat there and let it sit in the middle of the room. No one
wanted to take control because it seemed like it would be offending
someone else."

On top of it all, the band had little grasp of the full capabilities of a
recording studio. So they simply decided to make a very straightforwardly
recorded album, an unadorned document of the songs so people could
sing along by the time the band came to town. "Our position was that the
records were the menu and the shows were the meal," MacKaye says,
echoing the Minutemen's earlier "flyers and gigs" philosophy. Neverthe-
less, it wound up to be a very powerful record.

**S**teady Diet of Nothing continues in the vein of Repeater, with
tense, sinuous rhythms, novel guitar textures, big sing-along choruses, and dramatic dynamic contrasts, but this time with more
sense of space — and darkness. All the roadwork had not only strained relations within the band, but they felt out of touch with their beloved local
scene. All this took place in the midst of the Gulf War, when yellow rib-
bons, "I Support Our Troops" bumper stickers, and breathless media coverage of so-called smart bombs all signaled overwhelming public
approval of the U.S.'s gunboat diplomacy. "I think we all started to feel
that America was just becoming a madhouse," says Picciotto, "and it depressed us a lot."

Picciotto's "Exeunt" starts things off with a great rotating bee-hum of
feedback that lapses into a slow-galloping reggae-fied groove topped off
with angular caterwauling guitar. The song is about as elliptical as it gets,
but then MacKaye follows it up with another classic Fugazi anthem.
"Reclamation" declares its intentions in direct terms: "Here are our demands: We want control of our bodies," MacKaye announces amidst
pointillistic guitar harmonics. "You will do what looks good to you on
paper / We will do what we must." In a singsong roar, MacKaye chants
the word "reclamation" over a guitar hyperstrum at once frenetic and
grand.

In pointed opposition to the "Reagan Sucks" approach of hardcore,
Steady Diet addresses charged politics in oblique ways; this fact spoke
nearly as many volumes as the lyrics themselves. Picciotto's chant-along
"Nice New Outfit" neatly limns the West's "Might makes right" philosophy: "You can pinpoint your chimney and drop one down its length / In

your nice new outfit, sorry about the mess." He addresses "Dear Justice Letter" to famed liberal Supreme Court Justice William Brennan, bemoaning the fact that the great judge had retired the previous year, leaving the Court stacked with conservative Reagan/Bush–era appointees.

It wasn't all political, though — MacKaye's forlorn "Long Division" examines the slow, no-fault disintegration of a friendship; in "Latin Roots" Picciotto comes to terms with his Italian ancestry, and on "Runaway Return" he recasts the age-old prodigal son story in a modern context. But the last words on the album, from MacKaye's "KYEO" ("keep your eyes open") leave no doubt as to the band's focus: "The tools, they will be swinging," MacKaye defiantly hollers, "but we will not be beaten down."

The album enjoyed some fortuitous timing. Because *Steady Diet of Nothing* came out in 1991, the Year That Punk Broke, it emerged as a big seller and the first Fugazi record that most people heard.

**F**ugazi went on to release three more albums in the Nineties, and although the crowds at their shows fell off a bit as the alternative rock phenomenon waned, Fugazi never failed to sell out the rooms they played, continuing to make challenging, exciting music and progressing even further as an improvising ensemble. They kept their ticket prices at $5 (all the more impressive considering ten years of inflation) and never compromised their music — or anything else, for that matter.

That steadfast reluctance to sell out won vast amounts of respect from fellow musicians. Everyone from Joan Jett to Eddie Vedder paid lip service to the band's integrity even as they conducted their own careers in ways that Fugazi never would. Publicly declaring respect for Fugazi, then, was at best a way of sublimating guilt. Much of the rock audience, knowing full well they were complicit in a lot of what Fugazi was opting out of, held the band in high regard for similar reasons.

Despite the alternative gold rush, Fugazi didn't release a follow-up to *Steady Diet of Nothing* until June '93, when they released *In on the Kill Taker*, which actually made the lower rungs of the *Billboard* Top 200 album chart.

Although Fugazi's legend grew even larger in the Nineties, Brendan Canty feels the band's early days tell its truest story. "People might look at us and think we're this icon," he says, "but at the time there was just a couple of hundred people coming to the shows and it wasn't huge and nothing had potential. It was just important to *do it.* And the fact that we all wanted to go on the road and work as hard as possible, and that we were able to, is in itself its own success story. It doesn't necessarily have to be about getting anywhere, but about getting through the process of fulfilling your own possibilities."

# CHAPTER 12

# MUDHONEY

## LOUD BALLADS OF LOVE AND DIRT

### — SUB POP CATALOG DESCRIPTION OF MUDHONEY'S DEBUT ALBUM

In retrospect, Nirvana's legend looms far larger, but it was Mudhoney who spearheaded the Seattle grunge explosion and were Sub Pop's flagship band for the entire time they were on the label. Mudhoney put Sub Pop on the map. "In '88, '89, Mudhoney would blow Nirvana off the stage," says Sub Pop founder Bruce Pavitt. "They were the great band. They blazed the trail for Nirvana."

Beginning with Sonic Youth, the American indie underground had become increasingly concerned with approval from England. And for a British press fascinated with the pigfuck bands' unsparing portrayals of America's more brutish and provincial aspects, the next step was to find bands who actually embodied them. And what better place to find them than the rugged Pacific Northwest, then unfamiliar territory even to most Americans; it was a region that still held remnants of the frontier and was known for little more than building airplanes and logging. The idea of blue-collar mountain men making Sasquatch rock appealed directly to the British press; the enthusiasm quickly echoed back across the Atlantic.

Sonic Youth had a powerful effect on Mudhoney in other ways as well, as Mudhoney became only the latest in a series of connections the New York band had built up over the course of the decade. But the Re-

placements also figured in the story of Mudhoney and Sub Pop. Not only
had the Replacements opened up the floodgates of Seventies arena rock,
but Sub Pop bands, especially Mudhoney, took the Replacements' beer-
sodden self-deprecation and irony and ran with it. Irony also enabled Sub
Pop and its bands to quest for ever-higher levels of exposure and income
and still be able to laugh it off as a joke about questing for ever-higher levels of exposure and income.

Another strand of Mudhoney's sound came out of the entire aesthetic
spawned by the seminal *Nuggets*, a 1972 compilation of proto-punk Sixties garage bands, not to mention the Northwest's rich tradition of garage
rock. Garage, like punk, was a young white male genre, aggressive and
full of orthodoxy. Many of the first fanzines to write about punk rock had
originally focused on garage rock (others had featured science fiction,
which appealed to a roughly similar type of person, but that's another
story). Half of Mudhoney were record collectors, which might account
for the band's alternating currents of self-consciousness and abandon. In
that sense, and several others, Mudhoney was a metaphor for Sub Pop itself.

Sub Pop was more calculated than any previous American underground indie. Pavitt and his partner Jonathan Poneman had closely studied the history of independent labels, particularly those of the preceding
ten years, and learned from their successes and mistakes, and put everything they had gleaned into promoting their local scene. No more was indie rock a matter of making it up as you went along — the road map was
now pretty clear. Marketingwise, Sub Pop was the culmination of a
decade of blood, sweat, and tears. But as such, it was also the beginning
of the end.

**B**ruce Pavitt grew up in the comfortable Chicago suburb of Park
Forest, Illinois, and attended a progressive high school, then in
1977 moved on to Illinois's Blackburn College, a place he once described as "a Socialist Utopia." In between classes at Blackburn, Pavitt
would visit Chicago's Wax Trax Records store and pick up the latest punk
singles and zines. One zine in particular made a strong impact — *Cle*
from Cleveland, a city best known for being the butt of jokes. "That made
me realize," Pavitt said, "that an underground cultural renaissance could
happen in any part of the country."

For junior year Pavitt transferred to the progressive Evergreen State
College in Olympia, Washington, in 1979 and started working at the col-

lege's radio station KAOS and at *Op*, KAOS's newsletter. At KAOS he
met fellow punk fan Calvin Johnson, who soon began contributing to a
fanzine Pavitt was doing for college credit called *Subterranean Pop*,
which focused exclusively on American independent label rock music.

Pavitt's goal was to build a national network of like-minded people to
fend off what he called "the corporate manipulation of our culture" by
the media centers of New York and Los Angeles. As Pavitt wrote in another manifesto, "A decentralized cultural network is obviously cool. Way
cool."

*Subterranean Pop* was one of the first zines to view the independent
scene as a nationwide phenomenon. Through KAOS and *Op's* unparal-
leled record collections, Pavitt had access to piles of American independent releases and reviewed them by region, which tended to highlight
localized musical trends — trendy new wave bands in Boston, acid-
damaged party bands in Texas, art student noise outfits in New York, and
so on. In *Subterranean Pop* #2 Pavitt declared a philosophy that he
would take to dizzying heights later in the decade. "EXPLOSIVE artistic
hanky-panky is everywhere," he wrote. "Sometimes it just needs a little
support."

Pavitt particularly favored bands from the Midwest and Northwest
because the hip East Coast music magazines largely ignored them. "They
seemed to think that no American band that didn't live in New York
could possibly stand on its own," said Calvin Johnson. "They had an An-
glophile attitude and looked down their noses at California and the rest of
America."

The music Pavitt championed was hard to find, so after four issues he
shortened the name to *Sub Pop* and began alternating printed issues with
sixty-minute compilations of music from around the U.S., encouraging
the consumer to buy an inexpensive cassette of American bands rather
than "spending big bucks on the latest hype from England." Nineteen
eighty-two's *Sub Pop* #5 featured twenty-two bands, including Pell Mell
(Portland, Oregon), Oil Tasters (Milwaukee), the Nurses (D.C.), Sport of
Kings (Chicago), the Embarrassment (Wichita, Kansas), the Beakers
(Seattle), and Pavitt himself.

Pavitt was smart — he made sure to include regionally popular
bands; that way he'd be guaranteed some sales in their hometowns. The
gambit worked — Pavitt sold a remarkable two thousand copies of *Sub
Pop* #5. "I paid my rent for, like, a year and a half with that tape," Pavitt
says. He also got brilliant underground illustrator Charles Burns to do the
cover art, shrewdly surmising that magazines would be happy to repro-

duce Burns's striking black-and-white artwork. Says Pavitt, "I was always looking at the big picture as far as promotion and marketing and stuff like that."

**S**eattle's punk scene had been mobilized by a March '77 Ramones show in the ballroom of the tony Olympic Hotel; the place endured a trashing and the hotel never hosted a rock show again, but punk bands soon started popping up all over town. A few years later Black Flag started playing places like the Mountaineer's Club and the Eagle's Nest, and hardcore raged through the city for several years, spurred by visits from bands such as the Dead Kennedys, D.O.A., and the Subhumans, as well as the usual SST acts.

But punk rock wasn't the only kind of music with a foothold in Seattle — early Northwest garage rockers like the Sonics, the Wailers, and the Kingsmen had never gone out of style there. Commercial metal was also popular — one of AC/DC's first U.S. strongholds, Seattle was home to Heart and later Queensrÿche. But most bands who wanted to make it left town at the earliest opportunity, usually winding up in Los Angeles and failing miserably. This sense of futility gradually gave way to a sense of freedom, though — Seattle bands could do whatever they wanted, since no one was looking. Sure, there were lots of bands who just wanted to be Joy Division, others who were fifth-rate Minor Threat imitators, but there were others who just didn't give a hoot.

And there was plenty of local support: KJET-AM played plenty of area bands from the mid-Eighties up until 1988; they'd even play cassettes. Dawn Anderson's newsprint zine *Backlash* offered cogent and comprehensive coverage, as did the respected local giveaway paper the *Rocket*. Several key punk stores were happy to take 45s on consignment. It was a nice little setup.

**P**avitt moved to Seattle in early 1983. He was so broke he had to sell his blood twice a week; his diet consisted mainly of a case of sardines a friend had lifted from her father's fishing boat. After squeezing out one last *Sub Pop* tape (#9), he quickly established himself as a player in the emerging Seattle underground scene — by April he was writing a monthly column called "Sub Pop U.S.A.," for the *Rocket* as well as DJing at the University of Washington station KCMU. By 1984 he was working at an indie record store called Bomb Shelter Records and oversaw the store's release of an EP by local visionaries the U-Men that quickly sold out its 1,000-copy run.

He was also DJing at the all-ages punk club the Metropolis, where he made friends with a bunch of musicians around town who would always ask him to play Minor Threat. Sometimes he'd hang out with one of them, acid-tongued University of Washington English major Mark McLaughlin, and listen to records.

McLaughlin had also befriended future Soundgarden guitarist Kim Thayil, who coincidentally had been close to Pavitt's family in high school. McLaughlin and Thayil first met at an early Eighties T.S.O.L. show, when Thayil strode up to him and said, "Hey, you're in my philosophy class."

"Dude," McLaughlin replied incredulously, "you're at a punk rock show and you have a *mustache?*"

**M**cLaughlin, an Eagle Scout raised in a strict household, began life as a real straight arrow. "I think I was really drawn to rock & roll because it was so forbidden to me," he recalled. Still, he managed to form a band of school chums called Mr. Epp and the Calculations, who put up posters for fictitious shows before they had even learned how to play instruments. McLaughlin took the punk name Mark Arm, chosen basically as an absurdist joke about insulting people by calling them a body part. In 1982 the band released a seven-inch EP called *Of Course I'm Happy, Why?* (on the local Pravda Records) and got reviewed in *Maximumrocknroll*, who described the disk as "weirdly structured guitar raunch crammed with cynicism."

Arm was already tapping into the national indie scene: he and bandmate Jeff Smith copublished a fanzine called *The Attack*, whose readers included members of Sonic Youth and the Butthole Surfers; Mr. Epp appeared on a New Alliance compilation called *Mighty Feeble* with a quick hardcore outburst called "Jaded"; their "Mohawk Man" had even gotten some airplay on Rodney Bingenheimer's show on L.A.'s KROQ. But Mr. Epp remained quite obscure and broke up in early '84.

Arm and a lanky, bespectacled guitarist named Steve Turner first met at the same 1982 T.S.O.L. show where Arm had bumped into the fecklessly mustachioed Kim Thayil. They'd been introduced by a mutual friend who had assumed that Arm and Turner were both straight edge and therefore should meet each other. But it was instantly apparent that neither Arm nor Turner was straight edge, and as soon as they laid eyes on each other, they both burst out laughing. "And we've been trapped together ever since," says Turner with a wry chuckle. "I think there's one six-month period where we weren't in at least one band together in the last sixteen years."

Turner's dad worked in international trade for the city of Seattle, his mother worked for Boeing, and he grew up in the affluent Seattle suburb Mercer Island. Like Arm, he didn't really have much to do with rock music until his teens, when he found punk rock and the early Northwest garage rockers, as well as L.A. garage legends the Seeds, and ravenously began making up for lost time. By 1980 Turner was a certified skate punk; that epochal summer he saw Devo on one night and Black Flag the next. At the public Northwestern School for the Arts, he and his friend Stone Gossard played in the short-lived Ducky Boys. Soon after meeting Arm, Turner joined Mr. Epp — as well as Arm's other band the Limp Richards — in the last six months of its existence.

**A**fter Mr. Epp broke up, Turner and Arm decided to soldier on together and began eyeing potential candidates for their next band. They settled on bassist Jeff Ament because he jumped around a lot and played through a distortion pedal. But Ament had detested Mr. Epp, so Turner went so far as to get a job at the same restaurant where Ament worked just to befriend him. The scam worked. Turner brought in his old bandmate Stone Gossard, and Turner and Arm's friend Alex Vincent got the drum seat. Arm put down the guitar and assumed frontman duties, basically because all his equipment was broken.

The band was called Green River, after the Green River Killer, a serial murderer responsible for the deaths of nearly fifty women around the Northwest in the early Eighties. (It probably didn't hurt that "Green River" was also the title of a Creedence Clearwater Revival hit either.) By then Turner had discovered the sludgy Sixties powerfuzz of Blue Cheer as well as the first Stooges album. Arm had begun working his way from Northwest garage rock and the Stooges right up through Alice Cooper, Black Sabbath, and Aerosmith, bands he'd disavowed when he first discovered punk rock. Their new band plied a mixture of punk, proto-punk, and classic scarf-on-the-mike-stand rock & roll.

Ament was a longhaired jock from Montana who wore flannel shirts, although he underwent a surprising metamorphosis for Green River's first gig, a house party. "He shows up with kind of a rock outfit on and white makeup on his face," recalls Turner. "I was like, 'Ohhhhh nooooo. . . .'" From then on, Turner says, it was makeup every night for Arm, Gossard, Ament, and Vincent. Turner quickly became disenchanted with the band's increasingly glammy style and left that August, but not before playing on the six-song *Come on Down* EP, a strange collision of mid-Eighties metal and the Stooges' *Funhouse* LP, released on Homestead in 1985.

Turner continued to play with Arm in a goofy side band called the Thrown Ups, who wore wacky costumes and improvised all their songs onstage, making music that the band once said "sounds like vomit looks." The idea, says Turner, "was to see how stupid we could act and have people still watch us." They actually recorded three EPs and an album for a small local indie called Amphetamine Reptile, their finest moment being a song entitled "Eat My Dump." The band's singer, an unhinged Australian graphic artist named Ed Fotheringham, later claimed the band was actually a conceptual statement about DIY — if the Thrown Ups could put out a record, *anybody* could.

Green River replaced Turner with Bruce Fairweather, took whatever jobs they could find, and saved their money so they could tour. They pulled out of town that summer in Gossard's parents' station wagon, U-Haul trailer in tow. Unfortunately, *Come on Down* didn't come out until they reached New York, where they headlined CBGB to about six people; when they opened for ghoul-punks Samhain in Detroit, Arm and Ament almost got mauled by the crowd when Ament appeared onstage sporting big, poofy hair and a skimpy pink tank top that said "San Francisco."

On their first trip to Seattle, Sonic Youth played an in-store at the record shop where Pavitt worked, Fallout Records. They hit it off and on their next visit, in January '85, they took Pavitt's suggestion that Green River open for them. Recognizing a fellow hipster Iggy fan and obsessive record collector, Moore particularly hit it off with Arm. It was the beginning of a beautiful friendship. Sonic Youth liked Green River so much that they requested them as opening band every time they played Seattle. After one July '86 show, Thurston Moore wrote in his tour diary, "Local band Green River split the night with volumatic Ig-pow glamkore. 'Twas hot. Sorta like very ultra."

Later that year Green River opened for Public Image, Ltd., at Seattle's landmark Paramount Theatre and finally gave John Lydon some payback for the hard time he'd given bands like the Minutemen, Mission of Burma, Minor Threat, and who knows how many others. At the end of their set, Arm told the crowd, "If you want to see what happens to somebody who's completely sold out, just wait." Green River had already trashed PiL's dressing room and were kicked out of the building right after their set. Lydon further retaliated by writing the withering PiL classic "Seattle" after the show.

E ven if the Seattle underground scene was small, it was also quite a motley crew. "There were guys in ski jackets with long hair and mustaches and then there were freaky punk rockers with spikes," says Seattle scenester Bob Whittaker. "And that was really cool. No one would bat an eye at some freak that didn't fit the look."

"It was real small and it was a lot of fun," agrees Steve Turner. "Hard rock and metal was never that much of an enemy of punk like it was for a lot of other scenes. Here, it was like, 'There's only twenty people here, you can't really find a group to hate.'"

Metal and punk had started mixing in Seattle around 1984, much of the credit going to the U-Men. When the U-Men landed a deal on Homestead, a lot of lightbulbs went on over a lot of heads around town. Locals got a further inkling that there was a possibility of wider success when the 1985 Young Fresh Fellows album *Topsy Turvy*, on the fledgling local label PopLlama, got a glowing review in *Rolling Stone*. The Fellows began touring the U.S., as did the U-Men, and gradually an invisible barrier around Seattle began to crumble.

But as things in the wider world started looking promising, back home Seattle's infamous Teen Dance Ordinance was passed, making it extremely difficult to stage all-ages shows by, among other things, raising insurance rates to astronomical heights and requiring excessive amounts of security. The move crippled the Seattle music scene until the first wave of punks hit twenty-one and began playing and/or patronizing a small handful of taverns around the city.

The music scene didn't totally die: local bands like Soundgarden, Skin Yard, Green River, and Malfunkshun were all playing Seattle, and the Melvins were regularly coming up from the humble fishing and logging town of Aberdeen. But there were not many places to play and no record labels to speak of, and most bands didn't even think of trying to play other cities. So they stayed in town, developing material, chops, and stagecraft.

As hardcore further mutated into speed metal, others, especially Seattlites, preferred to wallow in the deepest sludge possible after Black Flag's *My War* tour hit town. "A lot of other people around the country hated the fact that Black Flag slowed down to their 'creepy-crawl' thing," Steve Turner says, "but up here, it was really great — we were like, 'Yay!' They were weird and fucked-up sounding." The new Seattle sound was officially christened on April 1, 1986, when the *Deep Six* compilation was released on the small Seattle label C/Z. The six bands — Green River, Malfunkshun, the Melvins, Skin Yard, Soundgarden, and the U-Men — had a mostly heavy, aggressive sound that melded the slower tempos of heavy metal with the intensity of hardcore. *Deep Six* isn't a particularly good record and it took three years to sell out its original 2,000-copy pressing, but if three people make a conspiracy, six *bands* constituted a movement, especially in a small city like Seattle. "People just said, 'Well, what kind of music is this? This isn't metal, it's not punk. What is it?'" recalls Skin Yard's Jack Endino. "People went, 'Eureka! These bands all have something in common.'"

Green River, Malfunkshun, the Melvins, and Soundgarden all started hitting the clubs (all two or three of them) at about the same time. And since they had some stylistic features in common, a mutual admiration society formed. "We used to jam together a lot, we talked about each other's bands, what we liked about 'em, what we hated about 'em," says Soundgarden's Chris Cornell. "You'd just go to a club and see a band that somebody you'd know started or was coming in from out of town and you'd drink beer and watch the music."

Steve Turner has a less altruistic theory about the togetherness of the early Seattle scene. "It all grew out of MDA [ecstasy's chemical cousin] parties," he says. "They were all standing around saying how much they loved each other as bands. There was a lot of that. I never took MDA — it scared me, watching these people on this love fest."

Bruce Pavitt agrees that MDA and ecstasy had a huge impact on the embryonic Seattle scene. "To walk into a Soundgarden show and there's only nine other people in the room, it exaggerated the sense of community there and the sense of drama," says Pavitt. "It made everything that came out of the speakers sound like the voice of God."

And MDA was far from the only mind-altering substance the Seattle scene enjoyed. The other major intoxicant in the equation was beer. Perhaps because Seattlites tend to be a bit uptight, they need a few more belts than most in order to unwind. All this combined to produce a strong, if perhaps artificially induced, sense of community in Seattle.

In 1986 Pavitt did a vinyl version of his U.S. underground compilations, releasing the grandiosely titled *Sub Pop 100*, which featured Sonic Youth, Naked Raygun, the Wipers, and Scratch Acid, as well as Japan's Shonen Knife and a brief spoken word piece by Steve Albini. The limited edition of five thousand sold out in months. With a staff of one and no recording budget, profits were sizable: "I made enough money," Pavitt says, "to go to Amsterdam and party for a couple of weeks."

Although the album might have seemed a one-shot deal, the cryptic message on the spine indicated quite differently: "The new thing: the big thing: the God thing: a mighty multinational entertainment conglomerate based in the Pacific Northwest." Nothing could have sounded more preposterous, but Pavitt was clearly thinking big — in a 1986 year-end wrap-up in his "Sub Pop" column in the *Rocket*, he predicted, "The Seattle scene is gearing up for a major explosion. . . . Expect great records to come out of this region in '87." Seattle rock scenester Jonathan Poneman was on the same wavelength: a month earlier he had written in the *Rocket*: "The town right now is in a musical state where there is an acknowledgment of a certain consciousness. . . . Something's gonna happen."

Unhappy with Homestead, Green River moved to their friend Pavitt's new label and recorded the *Dry as a Bone* EP in June '86, although Pavitt couldn't afford to release the record until June of the following year. With a hyperbole that became his signature, Pavitt described the record in an early Sub Pop catalog as "ultra-loose GRUNGE that destroyed the morals of a generation." Although the word "grunge" had been used to describe various kinds of rock music for years, this was the first known application of it to the grinding, sludgy sound of Seattle.

By now Pavitt had worked in just about every facet of the music business — press, retail, radio, and DJing, not to mention producing several nationwide compilations. He put everything he'd learned into that first release.

Pavitt settled on the EP format over the LP for a couple of reasons beyond the simple fact that it's cheaper. First, a six-song EP would guarantee that wherever a fanzine reviewer or college radio DJ dropped the needle, there would be strong material. Secondly, the EP, with its wider grooves, sounded better, which was essential for music that depended so much on physical impact. And drawing on his retail experience, Pavitt

knew that powerful cover art could help sell records; a twelve-inch EP —
instead of a seven-inch — meant the cover graphics would be larger. "My
first inkling of Sub Pop was at a New Music Seminar where I was working the Homestead booth and Sub Pop were the booth across the aisle,"
recalls former Homestead cochief Craig Marks. "They had insanely great
graphics. And I knew we were in trouble."

Pavitt used big, bold lettering and Charles Peterson's gritty photographs to magnify the power of what was pressed into the vinyl inside.
Peterson shot mostly at shows, not in a studio. "His photos were not four
guys standing in front of a white wall — no, that's not where the action is,"
says Pavitt. "The action is down at the tavern where people are drinking
and blowing off some steam." Peterson's photographs were black and
white, mostly because most fanzines couldn't reproduce color (or perhaps because that was the only kind of film he could lift from his day job),
and anyway monochrome tends to look more arty. They were full of blurs
and streaks of light, which conveyed both the action onstage and in the
pit — as well as the disorientation produced by beer and MDA — but they
were also carefully composed, lending a subtle sense of classical order to
the chaos of flying hair and contorted bodies.

Invariably, Peterson's pictures included the audience as well as the
band, something which played into the egalitarian punk ethos that Sub
Pop embraced. "What you're trying to do at these shows is break down the
division between the performer and the audience," says Pavitt. "You're advertising the fact that there's a community here — it's not just this industry that's manufacturing bands, it's a happening scene where people are
feeding off each other."

Pavitt wanted a consistent graphic look for Sub Pop's record covers,
posters, and ads, so he gave Peterson plenty of work in the years ahead.
"We were extremely conscious about trying to piece it together so there
was some kind of unity in marketing and presentation," says Pavitt. "It
helped unify the scene and made it seem larger than it actually was."
Pavitt, no doubt, was thinking back to the unity of the early SST bands,
and the way Black Flag, the Minutemen, Hüsker Dü, and others all
seemed to form a social and aesthetic cabal. But while SST had cultivated an outlaw image that captured the natural antiestablishment fantasies of the 16-to-25 set, "Sub Pop figured out a cleaner, more graphic,
more collegiate way to do it," says Bob Mould. "It was more wholesome."

The funny thing was many of the shows in Peterson's classic early
Sub Pop photographs weren't attended by more than a few dozen people.
"Bruce loved those Charles Peterson photos because it made it look like

more of an *event*," says Bob Whittaker. "Instead of sitting around a stinky club with a bunch of ugly people, it looked like this . . . *scene*. And we're standing around, all smelly, going, 'Huh? What's the big deal?'"

On a fall '87 tour, a stylistic rift in Green River widened to a canyon. Arm says the rest of the band was playing things like Whitesnake and Aerosmith's wretched *Permanent Vacation* in the van, while he was vainly trying to turn them on to garage-inflected Australian underground bands like Feedtime and the Scientists. What's more, Ament and Gossard were urging Arm to take singing lessons. Green River disbanded that Halloween. "There was a tension in the band for a while and then it just got to be too great — it was punk rock versus major label deal," says Arm. "It was obvious that things weren't happening the way certain people wanted them to happen. So we broke up."

Ament, Fairweather, and Gossard then formed Mother Love Bone and signed with PolyGram; after that band fell apart, Ament and Gossard formed Pearl Jam.

Jonathan Poneman (pronounced PON-a-mun) grew up in Toledo, Ohio, and went to the University of Washington. Poneman also booked club shows and had a KCMU show that exclusively featured Seattle bands. One night he happened to catch a set by Soundgarden and was blown away. "I saw this band that was everything rock music should be," says Poneman. "It was very immediate, very raw, very intense, and just completely brazen. There was no feeling of artiness or pretense; it was just in your face."

He offered to finance a record and the band accepted, but Kim Thayil thought Poneman should team up with Thayil's old buddy Pavitt, who had a little experience with these things. So Thayil arranged a meeting between Pavitt and Poneman and they agreed to work together. Despite the fact that Thayil was a dear friend, Pavitt was not very sanguine about Soundgarden, but, as Pavitt puts it, "The fact that Jonathan was offering to throw $20,000 into the pot kind of sweetened the deal."

In July '87 Sub Pop released "Hunted Down"/"Nothing to Say." Soundgarden's *Screaming Life* EP followed in October of that year, this time financed essentially by Poneman. "Sub Pop, unlike most of these other labels, nailed it musically from the get-go," says Scott Byron, then editor-in-chief of the college radio tip sheet *CMJ*. "I remember getting the *Screaming Life* EP in the mail and just being blown away. And it wasn't because they had hyped it or anything — they just sent us the record." The following week Soundgarden achieved the rare distinction of making the cover of both *CMJ* and *Rockpool*. Sub Pop was off to a phenomenally flying start.

Although Poneman's initial role was just as an investor in the Soundgarden record, he quickly became a full partner. Generally speaking, Pavitt was the creative side of Sub Pop, handling more of the A&R work as well as overseeing artwork and ad copy; the more pragmatic Poneman focused on business and legal issues (although he wound up signing by far the label's best-selling band). "So many of the crazy ideas were Bruce's," says Turner, "and then Jonathan would figure out ways to make it work."

There were other differences between the two young men as well. Pavitt had plenty of underground cool and preferred artier bands whereas Poneman had more populist tendencies. (It was often said that Pavitt was the "Sub" and Poneman was the "Pop.") This echoed a basic schism in the Seattle scene. Green River's Jeff Ament had made no bones about the fact that he wanted a major label career, but Mark Arm remained avowedly indie punk; Soundgarden vocalist Chris Cornell assiduously worked the rock god angle while bandmate Kim Thayil, a Butthole Surfers fan, did an underground show on KCMU (and later on, Nirvana's Kurt Cobain would vainly try to resolve both impulses within himself). Poneman felt this tension was the engine behind something that would become very big on a national and perhaps international level. At first Pavitt disagreed — "I'd say, 'Jon, I've been following this indie thing for ten years, it's just not going to happen. Let's deal with this roots music — it's going to be small — maybe it's elitist but it's pure.'"

But Pavitt had something of an epiphany when he started working at Yesco, a "foreground music" company that was eventually swallowed up by the Muzak corporation. By the fall of '87, Pavitt had gotten jobs there for many of his musician friends, including Mark Arm, whose deep musical knowledge and cutting wit had made him a respected arbiter of cool and an influential tastemaker.

Pavitt had favored more cerebral stuff like Television and the Butthole Surfers, but Arm introduced him to the charms of more primordial bands like the Stooges and Alice Cooper. "He was just a huge influence on me, helping to focus my tastes and opening my mind up to music that didn't sound like Sonic Youth," says Pavitt. So when he and Poneman were brainstorming the label, they decided they wouldn't just sign any old band they liked. "We wanted," says Pavitt, "to focus on this primal rock stuff that was coming out."

There was no avoiding the fact that hard rock and metal bore a lot of undesirable baggage, but Big Black had shown a way through. "Albini showed how a band could be 'alternative,'" wrote Clark Humphrey in the Seattle rock history *Loser*, "without abandoning the larger than life passion of hard rock, preserving the heroics and volume levels of metal without the hairspray clichés." When Big Black played their August '87 swan song at Seattle's Georgetown Steamplant, Mark Arm was standing in the audience, front row center.

S teve Turner wasn't enjoying college very much, so he dropped out after the fall '87 semester and started playing in bands again. He still had the jokey Thrown Ups, but, as he recalls, "I was kind of getting the bug to be in a band that actually practiced."

One night at a drunken party, Turner and Ed Fotheringham jammed with one of the most sought-after drummers in town, Dan Peters. It went so well that Turner asked Peters if he wanted to rehearse with him and Fotheringham and eventually maybe record a single. They were surprised when the highly overbooked Peters accepted. "We didn't know it at the time," says Turner, "but he was flying high on MDA when we asked him."

Fotheringham soon dropped out — "He didn't want to be in a band that actually practiced," Turner says, smiling — so Turner invited Mark Arm in. (Peters had met Arm before, when they both found themselves in the bathroom line at a club in Seattle. "He kept saying, 'Green River just broke up!'" Peters recalled. "He was really excited about it. Then he cut in line in front of me and puked all over the toilet.") Now they found that they totally clicked — and the combination clicked — Turner and Arm's garagey guitar gnashing meshed well with Peters's rolling 'n' tumbling, machine gun–style drumming.

Arm and Turner had known bluff, gravelly voiced Matt Lukin for years, when he began driving up to Seattle punk shows from Aberdeen with his Melvins bandmate Buzz Osborne and their friend Chris Novoselic. They'd become fans of Lukin's playing, not to mention his fabulous Gene Simmons stage moves and prodigious beer intake, so when they heard he'd recently been left behind when the rest of the Melvins moved down to San Francisco, they invited him in, too. They all played together for the first time on New Year's Day 1988. (Although one would expect such a hard-drinking band to be hopelessly hung over that particular day, they had laid off on New Year's Eve — "Amateur Night," as Lukin calls it.)

Everyone liked what they heard and decided to make a go of it. Arm suggested the name "Mudhoney," after a 1964 movie by mammocentric B-movie director Russ Meyer, whose work had developed a hipster cult following by the early Eighties. Turner liked the name. "It was slightly cheesy and corny," he says. "And from the Sixties."

However, Lukin still lived two hours away in Aberdeen, where he worked as a carpenter; Peters was already in two other serious bands, so Mudhoney clearly had only limited prospects. "We knew that we weren't going to be taking it that seriously or anything," Turner says. Their only goal was to maybe put out a single and have a little fun. "We could write some songs, record them, and, chances are, we could release it on Am Rep," Turner remembers thinking, "or at least Pavitt's thing."

**A**rm played some boom box tapes of Mudhoney as an audition for Pavitt. The tapes were virtually inaudible and the band hadn't even played a show yet, but Pavitt trusted Arm's taste implicitly and, besides, Mudhoney had an outstanding pedigree. So in March '88 Sub Pop paid $160 for Mudhoney to record five songs with Jack Endino. Pavitt and Poneman were especially keen on working with Mudhoney, since Green River's dissolution and Soundgarden's recent move to SST had gutted their roster. Mudhoney decided to go with Sub Pop. After all, Pavitt was a friend — they knew and trusted him and he lived right in town. Besides, Sub Pop had just gotten an *office*. "They had high hopes and dreams," Turner remembers wistfully.

That spring Pavitt and Poneman decided they would quit their day jobs and make a serious go of Sub Pop. They incorporated in April, with $43,000 of seed money cobbled together from a loan, family, friends, and Poneman's savings. "Of course that was spent in, like, thirty days," says Pavitt. "We almost went bankrupt after a month."

**B**y early summer Mudhoney had developed a buzz in their hometown and lived up to it with a savage live show. "It was incredible from the very first time they performed," says Pavitt. "I've never seen anything like it. . . . Emotionally, a lot of the music was very menacing and intense, very physically expressive. The way they moved . . . they fell down on the floor and who cares if you miss a few guitar chords — the looseness of it was really pretty revolutionary. It really projected a 'fuck it' attitude."

After playing their first shows opening for visiting New York bands Das Damen and White Zombie, they opened for Seattle Neanderthal-rockers Blood Circus that July. "It was sold out, lines around the block, fire marshals were there," said Turner. "The interest in these brand-new bands that didn't have any [records] out took people by surprise. The local scene was starting to explode all of the sudden."

"It was really incredibly easy for us," says Turner, still sounding a little amazed about it. "We basically said we were a band and we had two labels that would put stuff out and we could get shows any time we wanted them — at the two places that had shows. It was that easy."

"Touch Me I'm Sick" and "Sweet Young Thing Ain't Sweet No More" make up Mudhoney's debut single, and everyone was sure that "Sweet Young Thing," an almost dirgey blues-based number complete with slide guitar, was the hit. "It was so slow and gross and weird," agrees Bob Whittaker. "And 'Touch Me I'm Sick' was this little jingle on the other side." But things didn't work out that way; maybe it had something to do with the fact that "Sweet Young Thing" is a vivid depiction of a mother finding her young drug-abusing daughter vomiting into a toilet bowl.

Not that the flip side is so soft and fluffy — "Touch Me I'm Sick" is mainly a nasty, brutish, and short guitar riff powered by Turner's fuzz pedal, more a rhythmic noise than a melodic figure. (The riff itself harks back to the Stooges' "Sick of You," which in turn bore more than a passing resemblance to the Yardbirds' "Happenings Ten Years' Time Ago.") The song was suffused with self-loathing and anger, although in a typical disavowal Arm claims the chorus line was just a catchphrase that they built a song around. But a review of the single in the *Rocket* questioned why a bunch of white middle-class guys from Seattle could be so angry, whereas groups like Public Enemy and the Sex Pistols had legitimate reason. "You can be pissed off and bored anywhere," Arm retorts.

The single was delayed until August so Pavitt could fulfill his dream of pressing the record on turd-brown vinyl. More important, it was released in a limited edition (of eight hundred), an idea they borrowed from Amphetamine Reptile. Limiting supply, Pavitt and Poneman reasoned, would increase demand; that and their customized inner labels, colored

**MUDHONEY CLOWNING
AT THEIR FIRST PHOTO
SHOOT.** LEFT TO RIGHT:
**MATT LUKIN, STEVE
TURNER, DANNY
PETERS, MARK ARM.**

MICHAEL LAVINE

vinyl, and bold artwork would automatically make Sub Pop releases col-
lectible fetish objects. Lo and behold, the pressings sold out and then
shops would put the records on display for exorbitant prices, providing invaluable validation for the bands, the label, and the nascent Seattle scene
in general. When that first pressing of "Touch Me I'm Sick" sold out almost immediately, Sub Pop did a reissue of three thousand copies, getting
around the limited edition tag by using a different shade of vinyl, also ensuring that a certain percentage of collectors would buy the single again
just for the new color. The scam would be copied by countless other indie labels in the years to come.

The second run of the "Touch Me I'm Sick" single also contained a
key piece of image making. At some expense, Sub Pop flew out
photographer Michael Lavine, one of Pavitt's old Evergreen buddies, from New York for Mudhoney's first photo shoot. As with so many
Seattle bands, beer loomed large in the Mudhoney mythos, and the shoot
had them piling on top of each other, shirtless, longhaired, and clutching

cans of Rainier beer (the official Seattle rocker beer at the time simply because it was the cheapest). The images compiled what would become Sub Pop archetypes: male bonding, shaggy locks, and beer.

The members of Mudhoney were quite optimistic about their future — Arm and Peters vowed they'd never work again and quit their day jobs (Arm at Muzak, Peters as a messenger) solely because they had a single out. Turner could always come back to his job as an usher at a performance art space; Lukin could do his carpentry part-time.

Then Sonic Youth entered the picture. They'd kept in touch with Pavitt ever since that first visit to Seattle, and musical knowledge had passed freely between the two camps. Bob Whittaker recalls working at Sub Pop one day and reading a note from Moore on the bulletin board: "Hey you guys, check out this all-girl group from L.A. called Hole." "And everyone was given the heads-up," says Whittaker. "There was constant communication between everyone."

Before the Mudhoney single had even been released, Pavitt sent Sonic Youth the Mudhoney five-song tape for their comment and immediately Sonic Youth proposed a split single, with each band playing a song by the other. The single, with Sonic Youth doing "Touch Me I'm Sick" and Mudhoney doing "Halloween," was released in December '88.

Early on, Minneapolis and New York were Sub Pop's biggest fans. Minneapolitans got it because the loud, heavy music and beery nonchalance was clearly descended from what they'd already been enjoying for several years. But New Yorkers cottoned to Sub Pop because Sonic Youth had talked up its bands so much. "We owe, and the music scene of this city owes, a lot to Sonic Youth, because Sonic Youth spent years touring around the country, making records, and cultivating a real grassroots independent movement. It served them well to reinvest their interests and their endorsements into the various scenes across the country," says Poneman. "They developed this influence and this clout and they shared it. It's a very inclusive movement."

T hen came a great stroke of luck. In July '88 Pavitt and Poneman attended the New Music Seminar in New York and bumped into their friend Reinhardt Holstein, who ran a German label called Glitterhouse. Holstein told them they should get in touch with a friend of his who was putting together a government-sponsored music convention in East Berlin called Berlin Independence Days. And somehow, even though the band was barely seven months old and very obscure, Pavitt and Poneman managed to get Mudhoney a show at the convention in October. "And they went over there," says Pavitt, "and blew people away."

"Hi! Hi! It's great to be here! Hi! We're from America! Howdy!" an excited Arm told the crowd before the band started playing. Later in the set he instructed the crowd to "pull down your pants if you like us." No one did. A mock-dejected Arm quipped, "No one likes us." But a number of key promoters did and soon a big European tour was arranged. It wasn't just a big break for Mudhoney; it was a big break for Sub Pop. Suddenly the label was literally all over the map.

Mere days after they returned, Pavitt and Poneman having cleaned out their personal bank accounts in order to buy the group a van, Mudhoney was off on their first American tour. Along for the ride was their new buddy Bob Whittaker.

Whittaker had known Pavitt and Poneman from the Seattle punk rock circuit. One day he'd sat down to lunch with them and listened to them complain about not getting paid by distributors. "You guys should hire me — I'll strong-arm those bastards," Whittaker joked. "And they kind of looked at each other," says Whittaker, "and went, 'OK!'" And so, along with Charles Peterson and Steve Turner, Whittaker worked at Sub Pop, dunning delinquent distributors, pestering radio stations and record stores, packing up boxes of records, and serving as "refreshments coordinator" at Sub Pop parties; he'd get paid in lunches, records, and, occasionally, some cash.

A party animal par excellence, Whittaker was a loudmouth with a heart of gold, a master of uproariously buffoonish humor, and very bright to boot. So Mudhoney invited him to tour with them. "We didn't have anything for him to do," says Turner. "We didn't have T-shirts, he didn't know how to run sound, he didn't know how to change a guitar string. He just came along largely as entertainment." Pavitt and Poneman begged Whittaker not to leave the office for such a long time, but he went anyway, enduring Lukin's Lynyrd Skynyrd tapes for the sake of seeing America with a rock & roll band.

Unfortunately, Mudhoney was touring on the strength of one single and were quite unknown; posters for the shows resorted to noting "ex-Melvins" or "ex–Green River," which really wasn't much of a hook. Attendance, needless to say, was light — usually no more than a few dozen people. "We'd show up and there'd be the odd, really excited couple of kids that worked at the college radio station," recalls Whittaker.

And in best indie tradition, their van was a nightmare. "You'd shift and the linkage would drop out," Whittaker says. "You'd have to send somebody running down the freeway to get parts of it." To make matters worse, the heating ducts had been pulled out, so air blew into the van with gale force. Even after stuffing coats and rags into the holes, the two people sitting up front would have to stuff themselves into sleeping bags and wear funny Norwegian hats with ear flaps. Exhaust streamed into the back of the van so that, as Turner puts it, whoever was in the loft bunk "would get very sleepy."

Whittaker refused basic touring responsibilities like carrying amps. "Basically all he was doing was finding us places to stay, going out in the crowd and finding the weakest one in the pack and convincing them to let us stay at their house by promising them a fun party," says Turner. "It was fun for the first two weeks, but after that we were just grumpy and exhausted." Then it became a nightly battle over who got to sleep in the van instead of putting up with the raging party at the house.

The first show of the tour, in Salt Lake City, was a disaster — they'd driven for hours through pouring rain, sat through something like eight local bands, and then played terribly. To top it off, Whittaker got so drunk that he started pouring beer on Arm and Turner while they played.

But the tour's low point was a show in Lexington, Kentucky, where they played to virtually nobody. The guitarists actually set up on the floor of the club and slam-danced with the handful of kids who showed up. The club could only afford to pay the band $14, two packs of cigarettes, and a six-pack of Sprite. Mudhoney never returned to Lexington.

In Kansas City they played a show at a YMCA for perhaps twenty-five people, then went to a party some hardcore kids were throwing down the street. The band arrived to find a basement full of skinheads who had wrapped themselves in big cardboard boxes and were happily bashing each other around the room. "People were inventing their own scenes because there was nothing else going on," says Turner, adding that by the time of their next U.S. tour, regional variations in things like slam dancing had gotten erased by MTV. "It went from each town having its own little story to it being kind of the same group of people in every town."

Just to break up the boredom, Whittaker picked up a long blond wig, a fake mustache, and some greasepaint. A few shows into the tour, in Kalamazoo, Michigan, when depression and monotony were already beginning to set in, he put on the disguise, along with a blacked-out tooth. Soon, a drunken older woman, also with a missing tooth, took a shine to this tall blond stranger and attached herself to him. "I love this band!" she shrieked over and over throughout the set, and proceeded to write lyrics for the band on napkins all night long.

When they reached Maxwell's in Hoboken, writer R. J. Smith did a piece on the band for the *Village Voice*. A piece in the *Voice* was a big deal for a fledgling label like Sub Pop. "That tour really put Seattle on the map because prior to that, nobody cared about Seattle, there weren't any bands from Seattle touring that anybody cared about," says Pavitt. "Mudhoney went out in that crappy van and blew people away."

All things considered, the going was far easier than on the early Green River tours. "There was all this groundwork that had been done before," says Arm. "By the time Mudhoney was up and going, there was a complete network of local promoters all over the country. Even though our first tour was $100 shows, we were able to *do* these shows, whereas Green River just a few years earlier didn't have anything out and didn't have a booking agent; we just spent a lot of our own money calling up various venues and trying to get in and watch that fall through as we're driving to the places that we *think* we're playing."

And things started to click, especially when the *Superfuzz Bigmuff* EP came out halfway through the tour, in October '88. (The title came from the fact that Turner played the Big Muff distortion pedal and Arm played one called the Superfuzz — both were long out of production and considered uncool, antiquated technology; you could only find them in junk stores. But Arm says the attraction was obvious: "It was like, 'This is cheap, let's buy it!'") The record was wall-to-wall garage blues; tough stop-and-start riffs punctuate Arm's abraded yowlings, strafed by Turner's leering slide guitar chords. "In 'n' Out of Grace" features a minute-long bass-and-drum solo followed by a full-fledged wah-wah guitar freak-out. The hell-for-leather garage attack was tempered by beery sing-along choruses — one critic described the sound as "the Banana Splits meet the MC5," which was hilariously on target.

Contrary to the band's rowdy wiseguy image, Arm's lyrics were filled with dark imagery — of damaged lovers, emotional suffocation, self-hatred, alienation, and tons of guilt. But Arm steadfastly denies any heavy meaning. "They're just observations or experiences," says Arm. "Nothing's straight, though — I mean, why let the truth get in the way of a good story? Not that I think any of the stories are particularly good. They're just there to fill in the space between guitar solos and drum breaks." But Arm's denials of any particular import to his lyrics were at odds with the paint-peeling vitriol of their content and delivery. (Many of Arm's songs somehow mentioned either dogs or sickness, but he never did quite put it all together: "We kept hoping he'd come in with a song about a sick dog," says Turner drily, "but he never did.")

Arm's vocals leaped between a snide whine, an anguished holler, and a caustic shriek that could singe eyelashes at fifty paces; as even he acknowledged, he didn't *sing* so much as "howl and stuff." Arm's and Turner's guitars combined to make a caustic, distorted grind; Lukin provided an innard-rattling low-end throb; and Peters — the band's secret weapon — barked out spectacular, speedy rolls that seemed to shoot the songs' rhythms out of a cannon.

The band readily acknowledged that they borrowed ideas rather than making up their own. "That's all you can do today," Turner explained. "I think you're kinda fooling yourself as a rock band if you think you're doing something really original." The band veered widely between parodying primal forms like Sixties garage and biker rock and reveling in them — they seemingly couldn't decide if they were a joke or not. "There is room for real emotion in music," Turner said, "but I don't know if that's what we are. I don't really care." But there was no denying their chemistry, especially live. When Mudhoney set aside their self-consciousness and just put their heads down and rocked, they could be one of the best rock & roll bands on the planet.

The nation's fanzines seemed to agree and gave *Superfuzz Bigmuff* a rousing thumbs-up. A *Flipside* review enthused, "The children born during the Summer of Love are getting drunk in dingy bars, peace man. Take a trip to get this record. Tune in, turn it up."

They returned to Seattle barely long enough to catch their breath before heading out for a tour of the West Coast and Southwest with Sonic Youth.

*Superfuzz* was now in stores and winning consistent raves in the fanzines, there were many more people in the front row singing along to the songs, and the general buzz on the band was strong. But the band was still a bit nervous about performing, and Arm and Turner would work off the tension by cutting up onstage — tossing their guitars to each other across the stage midsong, striking silly ballet poses, making absurd between-song banter, or just rolling on the floor — then launch right into another dark and fuzzy musical psychodrama.

Sonic Youth did more than provide an influential endorsement. Mudhoney needed $150 a night to stay on the road, and Sonic Youth would always make up the difference if Mudhoney fell short some nights. And even better, Sonic Youth invited Mudhoney on their upcoming tour of England, which was a godsend — Mudhoney had lined up a European tour, but the U.K. remained notoriously difficult for American under-ground bands to crack.

The two-week tour with Sonic Youth kicked off at the end of March '89. Blast First had recently released the Sonic Youth/Mudhoney split single in the U.K., and very smartly included an itinerary for the tour with every record. Even better, ultra-influential BBC DJ John Peel was now raving about Sub Pop and Mudhoney in particular and played "Touch Me I'm Sick" constantly; the English music weeklies were also enthralled by the band and rarely wasted an opportunity to use variations on the phrase "Touch Me I'm Sick" for headlines. *Superfuzz Bigmuff* sold about five thousand copies in Europe and wound up staying on the U.K. indie charts for a year, virtually unheard of for an American label.

The first show of the tour was in Newcastle. The crowd had been hyped into a frenzy by the advance publicity and the Sonic Youth endorsement — many surely recalled Dinosaur Jr, the last band Sonic Youth got behind. The first thing Arm did was wade into the audience, where he was promptly swarmed by fans. Then Thurston Moore stage-dived right after him. "The crowd is fucking going apeshit," recalls Turner. "It was the greatest reception we've ever gotten. And it was because nobody'd seen us yet."

In Manchester some of the audience starting spitting on Mudhoney, apparently thinking the old punk custom still prevailed in the States. Arm deadpanned into the mike that although gobbing was not a Seattle thing, it was very much appreciated in Sonic Youth's hometown of New York. The hail of saliva stopped, then resumed tenfold when Sonic Youth hit the stage. By one report, Thurston Moore's hair was matted with spit and he would periodically have to flick the spew off his hands.

The somewhat older, relatively straitlaced members of Sonic Youth were practically aghast at Mudhoney's behavior. "It was almost like they were on a trail of carnage," recalls Lee Ranaldo. "They were completely living out the life of the kind of the rock & rollers they were supposed to be. They were constantly fucked up, constantly on the edge of chaos and collapse and all that stuff. . . . Mudhoney were just real heavy dopers and boozers, and they would go at it until literally they were not able to be conscious anymore. . . . They would polish off a couple of cases of beer before getting onstage." Ranaldo says his quintessential Mudhoney memory is of Matt Lukin standing on a chair at one after-show party, completely drunk, stripped down to his undershorts, his body covered with felt-pen drawings of penises. "They were really living it to the bone," says Ranaldo. "We were all astounded."

Throughout the tour Mudhoney joined Sonic Youth for the encores, jamming on the Stooges' "I Wanna Be Your Dog"; Lukin would invariably show up with tambourine in hand and pants around ankles. "He discovered his body and suddenly started dropping his pants and getting completely naked," Turner says, with more wonderment than scorn.

"Matt became a cartoon one day," he adds. "And stayed that way for a good while."

Afterward Mudhoney went on to do six more weeks in Europe, where they were virtually unknown. The German dates went well because of Sub Pop's licensing deal there, as well as the buzz from the first Berlin show. But the rest of the Continent was a different story, and they played tiny venues and dirt-floor basement squats for little or no money. In France "we played for, like, twenty people in some kind of government-funded youth camp," Turner recalled. "There was no stage; we just played in the corner of the room. After we finished our twelve songs or whatever, they actually locked arms and said, 'You cannot leave this corner.' So we had to play some of the songs again."

"Then they made us eat casserole," Arm grumbled.

About three weeks into the tour, Turner somehow managed to slice his hand open on a broken car antenna in Hamburg. By the time he was discharged from the hospital, it was touch and go as to whether they'd make it in time for their show with Sonic Youth in Nijmegen, the Netherlands, that night. Their driver floored it to the show, with Arm, Lukin, and Peters all slugging vodka in the back of the van the whole way, distressed about Turner's hand, which was now encased in a huge wad of gauze. They arrived at the venue ten minutes before show time.

"The next thing I knew, we were onstage in front of hundreds of Dutch people politely waiting for us to finish so they could see Sonic Youth," said Arm. "Well, I was having none of that. These motherfuckers were gonna rock if I had to beat up everyone in the place. I jumped into the crowd, threw a few drunken, waterlogged punches, and got back onstage. No response, except maybe confusion, so I cursed 'em and stormed off the stage, expecting my boys to follow. They didn't. They were as baffled as the audience. So I'm backstage and they're playing the rest of 'You Got It . . .' then they go into 'Need.' I'm thinking, 'Great, they're going to play the rest of the set without me. I could stay here like an ass or I could go out there like an ass and continue on like nothing happened.' After they played another song I sheepishly went out and joined the band. . . . Nijmegen never invited us back."

But by the time they returned to England in May for a final handful of dates, Sub Pop mania was in full bloom and things got amped up even further thanks to a Peel Session that was broadcast all over the United Kingdom. A reported 150 journalists were on hand to witness the sold-out 1,000-seat show at a university in London; two notes in, Arm and Turner dived into the audience with their guitars on. A couple of songs later, Arm jokingly invited the audience onto the stage and a huge throng of kids accepted, promptly collapsing the stage. No one was hurt, but Arm and Turner were left stranded out in the crowd while bouncers cleared the

A DEFINITIVE CHARLES PETERSON PHOTO OF MUDHONEY LIVE AT THE BACKSTAGE, SEATTLE, 1991.

CHARLES PETERSON

stage. In the melee the stage monitors disappeared. Techs tried to fix the PA but were too busy keeping the speakers from falling over onto the crowd. Naturally, Arm invited everyone to climb on top of the speakers, and many did, then he dived off into the crowd. Arm then asked people to throw money onto the stage, but few accepted that particular invitation.

The next day the London papers reported that a riot had taken place. Mudhoney's U.K. fame was assured.

**B**ruce Pavitt and Jonathan Poneman understood that virtually every significant movement in rock music had a regional basis, from Memphis to Liverpool to San Francisco to Minneapolis to Manchester, England. They'd studied the successes of early indies like Sun, Stax, and Motown as well as contemporaries like SST and Touch & Go, and deduced that what helped make them successful was having a consistent sound and look. Pavitt and Poneman then transferred these features to Sub Pop.

The idea was to develop the kind of brand loyalty that SST had enjoyed in its heyday — the confidence that if you bought anything with the Sub Pop logo on it, it was not only going to be good, but good in about the same way everything else on the label was. One thing Sub Pop did was to take out ads that promoted a label identity over the identity of any one band, the basic message being that if it was on Sub Pop, it rocked.

Key to this was Jack Endino, who would record seventy-five singles, EPs, and albums for Sub Pop between 1987 and 1989 and served much the same role as Spot had with SST and Steve Albini and Butch Vig had with Touch & Go. Endino had a talent, as Bruce Pavitt once put it, for "making the guitars bleed," and could do so on an exceedingly modest budget — he could record an entire album for about $1,000. In order to crank out recordings at the pace Sub Pop required, Endino soon developed some standard setups. This also meant the records had similar sounds, but that's exactly what Pavitt and Poneman wanted — a "Seattle sound," just like there'd been a "Memphis sound" and a "Liverpool sound."

But to locals, there *wasn't* a "Seattle sound" — Mudhoney's garage-fuzz didn't really sound much like Soundgarden's gnarled neo-Zeppelinisms; TAD's aggro steamroller rock didn't sound much like the thrashy Swallow. But to the objective observer, there were some distinct similarities. "The sound that I hear from bands that are walking in my door comes from fuzzy guitars, bashing drums, screaming vocals, no keyboards, and a general loud intent," Endino said. Said Kim Thayil, "It's kind of this sloppy, smeary, staggering, drunken music."

Pavitt and Poneman were very keen on identifying the label and its bands with Seattle. "It's a regional chauvinism that you find in sports," Pavitt explains. "People relate to that. They get pumped up by that." And Seattle was then fairly obscure, so they had an open field as far as defining its image. Sub Pop would further the "decentralized cultural network" Pavitt had been championing since the earliest days of *Subterranean Pop*. Take Sub Pop's motto "World Domination," for instance. "When we say 'World Domination,'" Pavitt explained, "we're saying, 'Fuck you, we're from Seattle, and we don't care if the media machines are in L.A., we're going to create our own.'"

And Pavitt and Poneman had done their homework on the independent label rock business. "We're using a precedent set by Tamla-Motown and Stax, where you have the scene that is being born in a particular region and then you just have a machine that you use to refine and perfect your product," Poneman said. "You create a sensation, like Great Britain in 1962 through 1965. All of a sudden there are all these bands coming out of this part of the world, there's good press, it's romantic. Everybody likes the idea that there's this burgeoning, happening scene somewhere in the world. If you're a teenage kid living in Dullsville, U.S.A., maybe someday you can go to Seattle and join a rock band and maybe play the Central."

What further united the Sub Pop bands in people's minds were the visuals — the bold lettering and monochrome photos on the record covers combined for a very definite, evocative sensation of gritty, sweaty machismo. And the musicians themselves had a look to match — no matter what kind of music they played, everybody seemed to wear flannel shirts, torn jeans, and long hair.

Shaggy SST bands like Black Flag and the Meat Puppets, says Turner, were the main inspiration for long hair in Seattle. "They started growing their hair, and so did Seattle — that's an easy answer," says Turner, "and the fact that a lot of people secretly were heshers anyway and just cut their hair once to be punk but secretly liked the metal long hair to begin with."

Mudhoney favored shoulder-length hair, horizontally striped velour T-shirts, Mardi Gras beads, blue guitars, and trucker's wallets chained to their belt loops (useful for holding on to your cash while you got passed around the mosh pit). The beads and striped T-shirts never really caught on, but everything else became de rigueur alt-rock attire within the year, especially the hair — long, greasy, sweaty . . . grungy. (Still, there was one grunge fashion statement that Mudhoney never went in for. "There was a look where people would wear shorts and long underwear and Doc Martens," says Arm. "I could never figure that one out. I was like, 'Hey, your underwear is showing!'")

At the beginning of the decade, embracing arena rock was antithetical to the underground scene. But now it was the next logical step after the undeniable classic rock elements of bands like the Replacements (the Faces), the Butthole Surfers (Grand Funk Railroad), and Dinosaur Jr (Neil Young). Pavitt and Poneman had seen this phenomenon developing and succeeding, and knew that the Seattle bands were in a position to capitalize on it.

The Seattle bands' long hair was just one manifestation of their disdain for both the strictness of hardcore and the pointy-headed pretensions of East Coast art-rock. So was their heretical embrace of decadent metal and proletarian hard rock. And what was more punk than to throw this shameful musical lineage right in people's faces. "Ultra HEAVY Zep rip-off," crowed a Pavitt-penned Sub Pop mail order catalog about the *Screaming Life* EP. "The very thought that you could put out a band that even remotely resembled Led Zeppelin was just *hideous*," Pavitt recalls. "People stopped talking to me. So I thought, 'People in the underground are offended, and people aboveground are offended, too. This is *great!*'"

One day in early '88, Jack Endino got a call from some Aberdeen band who wanted to record. They were friends with the Melvins, so Endino told them to come right up. A really tall guy and a small blond guy with piercing blue eyes arrived with Melvins drummer Dale Crover and the trio recorded ten songs in an afternoon. Endino thought the stuff was so good that he asked if he could make some cassettes for some people he knew. He called up Poneman and raved, "Dale Crover from the Melvins came in with this guy from out in Aberdeen, and the guy looks like he could be pumping gas or be some sort of grease monkey, but, man, he opens his mouth and Jesus fucking Christ I can't even believe it. I don't know what to make of this music — I don't know whether it's good or bad — but you have to hear it."

Poneman flipped over the music and brought it to the Yesco crew for an appraisal. No one liked it very much — "too rock" was the general opinion; besides, Nirvana (what a corny name!) were from out of town. And Pavitt just couldn't see an angle. TAD's Tad Doyle was a 300-pound professional butcher from Idaho; Soundgarden had a hunky lead singer and fused Led Zeppelin and the Butthole Surfers; Mudhoney was a local supergroup. But Poneman was crazy about Nirvana, so Pavitt began to cast about for a hook for selling the band. He found it in the band's semi-rural blue-collar background. "It really started to fit in with this TAD thing," Pavitt says, "the whole real genuine working class — I hate to use the phrase 'white trash' — something not contrived that had a more grass-roots or populist feel." And that was the key to promoting the band in the U.K. — "If you want to sell records in England, you want to sell them something American, you don't want to sell them something that sounds British," Pavitt says. "And these guys seemed very authentic and that's what appealed to me about the group."

Still, it was a whole year before Sub Pop got around to releasing Nirvana's "Love Buzz"/"Big Cheese" single in a limited edition of a thousand copies in November '88. (Sub Pop mail order department worker Hannah Parker painstakingly hand-numbered every copy. Perhaps because of such dedication, Pavitt soon asked her to marry him. She accepted.) It was the inaugural entry in the Sub Pop Singles Club, a venture that helped rescue the label from one of its many flirtations with financial oblivion.

Sub Pop had started to get letters complaining that their limited-edition singles (a) were hard to find and (b) sold out too quickly. "We put the two conditions together," says Poneman, "and realized we had a great marketing tool." The Sub Pop Singles Club was born. For $35 a year, subscribers got a single a month — a pretty good deal, but the brilliant part was that Singles Club subscribers paid *before* they got their records, which gave the label a significant financial boost. "On a limited budget, if you have the desire to sell a lot of records," Pavitt says, "you have to figure out ways to scam and manipulate the public." With typical Sub Pop irony, the teaser line was "We're ripping you off big time."

Sure enough, collectors pounced on the singles. Sub Pop took the seven-inch single, a format the major labels had abandoned because it was more trouble than it was worth, and turned it into a modest cash cow. At its peak in 1990, when the annual fee hit $40, the Singles Club topped two thousand subscribers. A host of other indie labels followed their lead, and the seven-inch single enjoyed a renaissance for several years, with every Tom, Dick, and Mary indie label pressing up "collectible" 45s on colored vinyl like they were going out of style (which, of course, they were).

And while Sub Pop was issuing 45s in the U.S., their German licensee Glitterhouse was putting out twelve-inch editions of the same releases, usually with different packaging. Many Glitterhouse releases got imported to the U.S., effectively doubling the exposure for the records, an excellent tool for creating what Pavitt calls "a celebrity culture" out of Sub Pop. Also, Pavitt was a big believer in having plenty of publicity photos taken of each band, which meant that Sub Pop raised its profile simply by having more photos in magazines than its competitors.

**B**oth extremely well spoken, Poneman and Pavitt did copious amounts of interviews, more than any artist on the label. Most label owners avoided such things, but the way Pavitt looked at it, it was free advertising — "What label in their right mind wouldn't take the opportunity to hype its product?" he says. "You can spend $500 on a full-page ad or you can spend ten minutes on the phone." American zines and the British music press were more than happy to run the interviews — Pavitt and Poneman made great copy.

Pavitt and Poneman soon realized that the press, particularly the typically young fanzine writers, would eagerly swallow whatever hype they tossed out. They were free to establish a mythos about the label based on exaggeration. "It's a very luxurious, opulent, prestigious office," Pavitt boasted of Sub Pop headquarters to one fanzine. But in truth it was just a couple of rooms in a nondescript old office building on the edge of one of Seattle's seedier neighborhoods. The elevator didn't even go all the way to their floor. "Our technology was a phone, a pencil and pad of paper," Pavitt reveals. "For our first year, our records were warehoused in the bathroom, so you'd have to step over *Superfuzz Bigmuff* to take a piss."

In December '88 came another successful piece of hype: *Sub Pop 200*, a triple-album, twenty-band label compilation complete with sixteen-page booklet. The cover art, by Charles Burns, depicts a demonic guitarist with, presciently enough, a monkey on his back. In an inside photo, Pavitt and Poneman are dressed in suits and gave themselves titles like "Executive Chairman of Supervisory Management." Sub Pop was going to be important, if only because Pavitt and Poneman were going to make it so.

The tracks, by such local luminaries as Mudhoney, Nirvana, TAD, the Fastbacks, Steve Fisk, Screaming Trees, the Walkabouts, and Seattle's underground poet laureate Steven Jesse Bernstein, could easily have fit on two LPs. "But no, we wanted to take a more lavish approach," Pavitt says. "It was just overkill — sheer overkill and maximum hype." It worked — to out-of-towners, the set gave the impression of a teeming, vibrant scene in Seattle, when in fact the Seattle scene appeared to be in trouble as venues closed right and left, police hassled the places that dared to soldier on, and local radio stations grew increasingly unsympathetic to Seattle bands. The album caught some ears, and some hugely influential ones at that. Wrote John Peel in the *London Observer*, "It is going to take something special to stop *Sub Pop 200* being the set of recordings by which others are judged for some time to come."

**N**ational American music press was beyond the reach of all but the largest indie labels. So, mindful of what it had done for Sonic Youth, the Butthole Surfers, and Dinosaur Jr, Pavitt and Poneman set their sights on the U.K. press. To a struggling new label looking for some publicity, the English music weeklies were a very attractive prospect. "They were willing to be bought," explains former Homestead employee Craig Marks, "and these were established music papers, not erratic zines — they were long, lavish articles written by journalists. And it was very glamorous to be accorded acclaim by 'the English.' They knew how to make stars." So Sub Pop went to England. Or rather, they got England to come to them.

In March '89, Sub Pop flew *Melody Maker* writer Everett True all the way to Seattle and plied him with all the free drinks, shows, and interviews he could handle. "Insane stuff," Pavitt says, "and that's what made us look like this ridiculous little label trying to act like a major." True obliged with a glowing, if slightly condescending, roundup of Sub Pop's roster in one week's issue and a front-page feature on Mudhoney the next. It was a huge coup. Suddenly the other two English music weeklies were calling up for interviews, then a host of American fanzines.

Pavitt's hunch that Sub Pop's "white trash" aesthetic would win over the English panned out just as he'd hoped. "I really felt that the Brits and the Europeans wanted to see something that was unruly and that was more of an American archetype — something that was really primal and really drew from the roots of rock & roll, which was very American," says Pavitt. "I think their Americanness, their unruliness and their spontaneity and their lowbrow sense of humor really won people over. They weren't trying to be really conceptual or pretentious or anything. They just went out there and rocked."

The U.K. press believed that such raw rock & roll could only be made by Neanderthals, and Sub Pop obligingly played to their preconceptions. "Our bands were all lumberjacks," Poneman declared. "Or they painted bridges." And if they didn't, Sub Pop made it seem like they did — for instance, they never mentioned the fact that TAD's Tad Doyle had a music degree from the University of Idaho and instead made him pose in the woods with a chain saw.

To a certain degree, Mudhoney's music played into this stereotype, but it also transcended it: the music was actually well constructed, the lyrics were razor sharp, and Mudhoney boasted ample wit and sarcasm, things to which the British press could easily relate even as they continued to celebrate their prejudices about Americans. "They were the ultimate American rock & roll band," says Pavitt. "They were intelligent, sophisticated, and witty, but they were also very primal." Even the makeup of the group reflected the split nature of the music (and indeed of Sub Pop itself): Arm and Turner were educated and middle to upper-middle class while Lukin had grown up in redneck Aberdeen and Peters had a trailer home childhood. Sometimes the differences in the band members' backgrounds did show. During one early interview, Arm stated that "unless you're omniscient, you're going to be prejudiced of something." Peters, in all seriousness, added, "but even Amish people are prejudiced."

"Not 'Amish,' *omniscient*," Arm corrected him.

Peters was so embarrassed that he rarely did an interview again.

Arm says the class schism never caused any friction: "It was all about who you thought played well and who you wanted to be in a band with and who you got along with instead of 'What does your daddy do?'" But the class-fixated English were entranced with the idea of blue-collar Americans making rough-and-ready rock music and bent over backward to fit bands into that concept. So Everett True felt compelled to state: "Mudhoney are laconic, wry, intelligent and working class. They don't wash their clothes a great deal." Of Lukin, he wrote, "A carpenter by trade, Matt is an All-American working class guy who drinks beer, watches sports and fixes cars" — actually, Lukin didn't watch sports or fix cars, but why let the truth get in the way of a good stereotype?

"All he wants to do," True wrote of Turner, the thoughtful anthropology major, "is 'rock out' and have a good time."

June '89 saw a big breakthrough for Sub Pop and the Seattle scene in general. "Lamefest," with Mudhoney, TAD, and Nirvana, was the first time a local show had sold out Seattle's landmark 1,400-seat

Moore Theatre. The Moore was a local institution, and the feat was almost beyond comprehension by anyone around town. "Throughout the history of Seattle music, local music was never taken seriously," says Pavitt. "After that show, local music was taken seriously."

The manager of the Moore was so dubious about the turnout that he failed to hire enough security to contain the overwhelming crowd that showed up. "Kids were just going insane," Pavitt recalls. Mark Arm kicked one overzealous bouncer, sending him sprawling into a maelstrom of moshers. Afterward, Arm almost got mauled by the security team, and for a long time Sub Pop bands were banned from the venue.

But the point had been made. "You knew that the music was real when you weren't playing in front of ten of your drunk, ecstasy-imbibed friends but playing in front of fourteen hundred kids who were just going absolutely nuts," Pavitt says. "And we were thinking we were right — 'These guys *are* great.'"

Success was not something that a lot of people in the underground were comfortable with. In the late Eighties, twenty-something people had little hope of participating in the Baby Boomer yuppie celebration. Baby Boomers had barricaded them from corporate culture and its attendant rewards. Besides, indie bands weren't supposed to be successful, and if they were, they were surely doing something wrong. Like the Replacements before them, Mudhoney seemed embarrassed by their success, sabotaging themselves with drinking, stage tomfoolery, and obtuse interviews even as they went through the motions of pursuing their career. By the summer of '89, Sub Pop was selling T-shirts with the Sub Pop logo on the back and on the front, in big bold letters, the word "Loser." "The loser," as TAD guitarist Kurt Danielson explained to the *Rocket*, "is the existential hero of the Nineties."

It was more than a word on a T-shirt: Poneman's business card read "Corporate Lackey" and Pavitt's "Corporate Magnate." "Why bother to say, 'Die Yuppie Scum,'" says Pavitt, "when you can parody all the corporate mania that's been going on all these years?" Sub Pop's jokey big-business posture simultaneously mocked and embraced that culture, self-promotion disguised as self-deprecation. "This way you could kind of have your cake and eat it, too," says Pavitt. "You could promote yourself as brashly and as loudly as possible, but you're poking fun at yourself so people couldn't really give you shit."

**M**udhoney recorded a self-titled debut album with Jack Endino in July '89 — it came out only three months later, with the first three thousand copies packaged in a gatefold sleeve and poster specially for what a Sub Pop press release affectionately called "collector scum."

It was a good record, but the band was treading water, trapped in the classic predicament of making a crucial follow-up record while vigorously promoting the previous release. One of the album's best songs was "You Got It (Keep It Out of My Face)," but a different, superior version had already been released as a single months before. Even Arm admits the album was "just kind of more of the same but not quite as good." Despite some powerful moments and improved musicianship, it could not beat the six-song EP for getting to the point.

By this time Mudhoney was the height of cool in the United Kingdom. English band-of-the-moment Transvision Vamp was so eager for some hipness points that they ever so casually threw copies of *Superfuzz Bigmuff*, Bob Dylan's *Highway 61 Revisited*, and a book on the Velvet Underground into the cover photo of their new album. The hip thing to do was to grow your hair long like the guys in Mudhoney.

But the whole band took a dim view of the trendy English music scene, so they found it ironic — even a little confusing — that they had become its darlings. Arm notes that the Replacements briefly considered calling their *Hootenanny* album "England, Schmengland." "Which was the general feeling amongst most American underground people of the day — it's all hype, what a load of crap," says Arm. "And next thing you know, *we're* the load of crap. It was kind of goofy."

The buzz on Seattle and Sub Pop was starting to break through to the American mainstream media, too. *Chicago Sun-Times* writer Michael Corcoran did a long piece on the scene, noting Seattle and its "distorted marriage of heavy metal and punk called 'grunge.'" "Influential music magazines from Europe and the United States have called 'The Seattle Sound' the best thing to happen to new music since the advent of New York's CBGB's," Corcoran wrote.

And then came the deluge. It had been a very isolated scene until A&R people started flying up to check out Soundgarden. Everybody was excited about the prospect of their friends Soundgarden cracking the big time, but there was also worry that their little scene was being co-opted. Soundgarden's SST album *Ultramega OK* came out at the end of 1988; they signed to A&M within a year, and by the spring of '90 Seattle was crawling with major label A&R execs angling for bands like the Posies and Screaming Trees. Seattle was everyone's darling from the underground to the overground.

Well, almost everybody's. "You go see Mudhoney or one of those bands and it's silly how great they think they are," said Steve Albini in a *Maximumrocknroll* interview. "It's almost offensive to me. And the thing is, when Mudhoney started out they were a real cool, real fucked up band. Their first single, I think, is really great. And now it's sort of like a hard rock version of the Beatles."

A lbini wasn't the only naysayer. Mudhoney toured Australia twice in 1990, playing everything from pubs to theaters. That year's *Rockpool* poll of American college radio programmers named Mudhoney their favorite band. But once the band hit the U.K., it was a different story. The British music press is nothing if not fickle, and many writers, including Everett True, had turned against them, partly because of Sub Pop's overblown hype barrage, partly because the band had gotten too big for their liking, and partly because of the band's new look, which got mentioned in virtually every live review of the tour: "We had cut our hair," Turner explains. "That made them reassess us a little bit."

And the U.K. press was upset that a couple of the guys in Mudhoney were not exactly the backwoods savants they had been making them out to be. "That was the thing — they found out that Mark and Steve had gone to college," says Bob Whittaker. "They weren't the working-class freak show that everybody thought they were."

"This one guy, the only damning evidence he could call us was 'harmless history students' — I was like, 'Well, that's pretty much me in a nutshell,'" says Turner with a shrug. "I mean, yeah, we *aren't* white trash mountain men. We *told* them that from the beginning, but they never printed it — they'd just print their imaginations of what we said."

"Mudhoney are not the pig-fucking sulphate-rotten greasy biker Viking stormtroopers with one foot in the grave and the other in a nun's entrails that their music suggests," wrote *NME*'s Steven Wells. "If Mudhoney had been sent to Vietnam they would have all been Radar from M*A*S*H. Mudhoney are geeky motherlovers, all matchstick arms and legs and horn-rimmed glasses and small bottoms and boyish fun. They are far too intelligent as individuals to believe in the rock 'n' roll woah, they seem to be making a career out of one huge, elongated piss-take (albeit a piss-take that kicks some serious three guitar all-out attack bottom).

No journalist has ever penetrated their facetious facade, none has ever managed to slice them down to the bone."

**B**y the summer of '90, speculation that Mudhoney was splitting up was filtering through the press. Reports of the band's demise were, however, greatly exaggerated. Turner was burned out from constant touring and wanted to take a break by returning to college.

The break also meant that the band could recharge its creative energies. The others were content to hang fire for a while, but the more enterprising Peters toured with Screaming Trees and, for an eye blink, was a member of Nirvana, playing one landmark show and recording one landmark song ("Sliver") with the band before they jettisoned him in favor of Dave Grohl. In reaction to President Bush's Gulf War, Arm released a solo single, a cover of Bob Dylan's "Masters of War."

**B**y 1990 Sub Pop was so hip that it was attracting one-off singles by what were or would soon become some of the biggest names in what was now being called "alternative rock": Dinosaur Jr, Rapeman, Fugazi, Rollins Band, Hole, Smashing Pumpkins, and Soundgarden. Sub Pop itself was landing features in places like the *Los Angeles Times* and on National Public Radio.

As early as March '89, Pavitt had been bracing for a backlash from the English press. "It's only a matter of time," he told *Maximumrocknroll*. "That's the way it works. The English press build you up, only to tear you down." And yet Pavitt and Poneman seemed to be getting a bit carried away, as if they were believing their own hype. Poneman's liner notes from *Fuck Me, I'm Rich*, an Australian Sub Pop compilation, declared, "I don't play rock music, I 'play' rock bands! The same way others 'play' the horses." Not to be outdone, Pavitt added, "Once upon a time, Seattle opened it's [sic] legs and fucked the world. YES! Loud powerfuzz and muff shagging hair action . . ." Meanwhile, the label was releasing either a single or an album a week. In letting what Poneman once called Sub Pop's "calculated arrogance" get out of hand, Pavitt and Poneman had forgotten one thing: Pride goeth before a fall.

"Will Sub Pop be able to stay on top of its scene and meet an expanding market for its product, or will it become overloaded, overextended and ineffective as so many promising independent labels have before it?" asked writer Richard T. White in a 1989 *Pulse!* profile of the label. Pavitt's cocky reply: "I've been doing this forever. It's like breathing. Quiz me — I know this shit."

Unfortunately, Sub Pop was relying on what Pavitt called "intuitive accounting." Pavitt and Poneman got too bound up in the more glorious processes of signing bands and recording, designing, and promoting their records while the business end fell by the wayside. "We were an awesome promotional machine," admits Pavitt, "but at the expense of the nuts and bolts."

Sub Pop had also gone into the distribution business — at one point distributing a dozen or so other labels, most of them Northwest micro-indies — and was not doing it very well. The label was losing vast amounts of money and couldn't pay their clients. And in the spring of '90, Sub Pop was hit with two coffer-draining lawsuits. One was from the Pepsi Corporation, which was upset that TAD's "Jack Pepsi" single featured a close approximation of their logo; the other was by a couple whose mildly compromising photo was used without permission on the cover of TAD's 8-Way Santa album.

More problems came when Pavitt and Poneman began to feel they'd hit a sales wall — and had an inkling that Nirvana's second album would be a bigger success than they could handle — and started looking for ways of breaking through it. So they began the expensive process of negotiating a major distribution deal with CBS Records.

At the same time, major label A&R scouts were courting more and more of Sub Pop's artists. That and the talk of an impending major label distribution deal for the label prompted its bands to ask for bigger advances; since few of them had contracts with the label, they were free to walk. So in order to keep their bands happy, Pavitt and Poneman starting handing out drastically higher advances, even though they couldn't actually afford it. And, as Pavitt put it to the *Rocket*, "That's what fucked us."

Ironically, the CBS deal fell through in the summer of '90, but not before Sub Pop had spent tens of thousands of dollars in legal fees.

As the Seattle phenomenon widened, bands began moving to Seattle from all over the country, dressing up in "grunge" clothes and playing "grunge" rock. "It was really bad," says Turner. "Pretend bands were popping up here, things that weren't coming from where we were coming from."

Pained by the grunge overkill, the original Seattle bands were doing what they could to distance themselves from the flock of arrivistes. TAD was getting more melodic, Screaming Trees' Mark Lanegan released a second solo album of moody balladeering, and Nirvana was writing more or less straightforward pop songs; Sub Pop itself was diversifying into power-rockabilly (the Reverend Horton Heat), spoken-word-meets-sampledelica (Steven Jesse Bernstein's brilliant *Prison*, a collaboration with producer Steve Fisk), and naive pop (Beat Happening).

And Mudhoney took an appreciable change in direction on their next album, *Every Good Boy Deserves Fudge* (the name is a mnemonic for the notes of the musical staff). Even the cover speaks volumes: instead of a shaggy, sweaty black-and-white shot by Charles Peterson, the cover art is a colorful, cartoonish illustration of a sinking ship by the band's old friend Ed Fotheringham — visually, quite a break from the usual Sub Pop look, but still very Seattle. And instead of Sub Pop mainstay Jack Endino, they recorded with Conrad Uno, who ran Seattle's tiny PopLlama Records, the Young Fresh Fellows' label.

They'd done some demos with Endino at the relatively upscale twenty-four-track Music Source, but they hadn't turned out very well. Realizing they were repeating themselves, they figured it was time for a change. It was clear that their best work, the "Touch Me I'm Sick" single, was done on an eight-track board. Girl Trouble had just recorded a great album at Egg Studios with Conrad Uno on an eight-track board that had once been used at Stax's studios in Memphis. So Mudhoney went to Egg and ran down eleven covers — songs by key influences like Black Flag, Devo, Elvis Costello, and others — in one day, with the idea of releasing an entire punk covers album. "But then Guns N' Roses did one," says Turner, "and that idea was over."

But they liked the way the tracks sounded, so they recorded their second album at Egg (so named for the soundproofing egg cartons nailed to the walls), a cozy little room in the basement of Uno's house in an unassuming corner of the suburban University District. The whole thing cost $2,000.

Uno, a droll, kindly gent who had played in various Seattle art bands in the Seventies, had never heard a Mudhoney album until he recorded them. He quickly came to a realization about Arm's talents: "He's a terrible singer," said Uno. "But he's a great singer." Uno also came to appreciate the band's sense of spontaneity. "With Mudhoney, I would say, 'Uh, guys, you kinda missed that one part,'" he said. "And they would say, 'Aw, it's OK.' If they made it through the song and it had a good energy to it, that's enough."

**M**udhoney's self-titled album had sold thirty thousand copies in the U.S. and about fifty thousand in Europe, and the catchy *Every Good Boy* was sure to sell more. But Sub Pop kept delaying its release, saying there wasn't enough money to put it out. The label was also getting behind on royalty payments. "We'd meet with them and they'd say, 'Come down tomorrow and we'll cut you a check,'" says Peters. "And we'd go down there the next day and they'd say, 'I didn't say that. You must have misunderstood me.'"

Finally Mudhoney decided to force the issue and booked a September tour to support the still unreleased new album. Pavitt and Poneman insisted they would come up with the money soon, but no one believed them. "The honesty wasn't really there," says Peters. "They would say things, and maybe they truly meant them, but they were, like, outlandish."

"And then they flew out the Afghan Whigs, who they were trying to sign," says Bob Whittaker, who was now taking on some managerial duties for the band. "And basically spending the money they'd gotten from [Glitterhouse] for the advance for *our* record to fly the Afghan Whigs out. They were thinking too far ahead. To our minds, they should have been concentrating on us and the record that was about to come out that was going to sell a lot."

"Whereas before we had been in an all-for-one, one-for-all state of mind, we were [now] trying to save our asses," says Poneman. "We didn't do it at the expense of Mudhoney, but Mudhoney had been accustomed to a certain kind of consistency and favoritism from us that we simply could not provide because we were simply trying to keep the organization afloat."

By early '91 Sub Pop was bouncing checks all over town; they couldn't pay their employees, bands, the pressing plant, even their landlord. Any one party could have pushed them into bankruptcy by insisting on their money. *Seattle Weekly* ran a story on the label's financial woes; a couple of weeks later so did the *Rocket*, with a cover photo of a dejected-looking Pavitt and the cover line "Sub Plop?"

In response, Pavitt and Poneman made up T-shirts that said "Sub Plop" in the Sub Pop logo style, with the legend "What part of 'We have no money' don't you understand?" on the back. And then they sold them to raise money.

But privately Pavitt and Poneman were increasingly at odds over how to cope with the crisis: Poneman preferred to think things would blow over eventually, but Pavitt, upset about letting down so many people, many of whom were good friends, was taking it very hard. "I was medicating myself," he says. "I was under incredible stress. My god, just having to deal with that kind of stuff was very hard."

In the name of preserving his friendship with Pavitt, Arm preferred not to know how much money Sub Pop owed Mudhoney. But one day Steve Turner stopped by Pavitt's office and mentioned that Poneman had promised they'd get $5,000 the following day. Pavitt, stressed nearly to the breaking point, just burst out in a fit of nervous laughter. After he calmed down, he explained to Turner that much as he would love to pay the band, the label was broke and the money simply would not be there the next day. Turner was mortified at Pavitt's outburst; Arm called Pavitt the next day and said that the incident had so upset Turner that they had decided right then and there to go looking for a new label. "I always have really respected and liked Bruce," says Turner. "And so we just thought, 'Let's get out of here before we just tear their heads off or something.'"

"I remember seeing Steve the next day and trying to talk to him and being so at the end of my rope that I broke down and started crying," says Pavitt. "What hurt me more than anything was that he felt like I didn't respect him. I didn't care if they went to a major — whatever. But the fact that he would misread what I was trying to communicate . . . I was simply trying to be honest. It was such a low point for me, just standing there crying in front of this guy. I just said, 'I'm sorry.'"

Asking for their master tapes and artwork back would have set off legal action neither side could afford. And more important, Arm and Turner didn't want to ruin their friendship with Pavitt, while everyone in the band simply felt an allegiance to Sub Pop itself. "If Sub Pop hadn't put out our records, we'd probably still be playing down at the Vogue," said Peters. "We probably wouldn't have lasted through the summer," Arm added.

Mudhoney had no desire to cash in on the Seattle gold rush and would have gladly stayed with Sub Pop if not for the financial irregularities. "They were very smart to leave," Pavitt concedes, "because at the time we were bordering on bankruptcy."

Out of loyalty and friendship, Mudhoney let Sub Pop release one last album, so at long last *Every Good Boy* finally came out on July 1, 1991. It was, as everyone knew it would be, a big hit, going on to sell an estimated seventy-five thousand copies worldwide — a huge success for an indie label — and peaking at number thirty-seven on the U.K. album charts. The album single-handedly lifted Sub Pop out of its financial doldrums.

And when it rained for Sub Pop, it poured. In the spring of '89 Nirvana had insisted on a contract, which Poneman hastily drew up. "I just remember them being in the office, sitting around signing this contract," says Poneman. "I remember thinking, 'This could be important.'"

Nirvana's 1990 "Sliver"/"Dive" single sold an amazing 15,000-plus copies, and at an estimated thirty thousand copies, their first album *Bleach* had become one of Sub Pop's best sellers ever. The British music press ate the band up, spinning a tale — with Pavitt and Poneman egging them on — of a trailer-trash rock savant. Some demos the band made with Butch Vig were making the rounds of the majors, and, strongly urged by their mentors in Sonic Youth, Nirvana signed to Geffen Records in April '91, becoming one of Sub Pop's earliest and most painful defections.

The news hit Pavitt hard. "It came as a complete and total shock," he says. "It really scarred me. It made me a lot more guarded and a lot more cynical about what I was doing. I felt that all problems aside, I'd given every drop of blood to making this organization work and making the bands work and it seemed like an incredible betrayal at the time. I wept publicly. I was really, really crushed."

Nirvana still owed Sub Pop two albums, for which Geffen paid Sub Pop about $75,000, in addition to three "points" (a point being 1 percent of the list price) on sales of the next two Nirvana albums. Upon its release in September '91, Nirvana's major label debut *Nevermind* began selling at a phenomenal pace, netting Sub Pop hundreds of thousands of dollars; then *Bleach* started selling, too — the label made an estimated $2.50 on each copy sold, and the record eventually went gold (half a million copies).

"Had we not had that agreement," said Poneman in 1993, "Bruce and I would probably be washing dishes at this moment."

**W**hittaker, who had been Mudhoney's de facto manager anyway, formally proposed that he become the hub of the negotiations for a new label. The band enthusiastically accepted — they wanted someone who knew where they were coming from. "Plus," Turner says of their colorful manager, "it made a good story."

At first they thought they'd go to another independent label, so they met with Caroline Records, a big indie that also distributed Sub Pop. Caroline told them they'd have to tour nine months a year "just like Smashing Pumpkins" and that they'd have to "sweeten up the guitars." Also, side projects like Arm and Turner's band Monkeywrench were out of the question. All this made the band furious. "We're just like, 'Fuck you, how dare you,'" says Arm. "'How dare you tell me how to live my life?'" If even indies were thinking that way, the band figured, why not just go to a major. So they talked to some majors, although they were wary of what had happened to bands like Hüsker Dü and the Replacements.

By this time *Nevermind* was exploding, Seattle was "the new Liverpool," and Mudhoney was one of the last key Seattle bands available. Even though the band was fiercely independent and probably had little commercial potential, majors were interested because in those heady times no one knew what would sell anymore. Eventually they went with Warner Brothers' Reprise label. "We just asked ourselves, 'Who had the foresight to sign Devo?'" says Arm, half joking. "And went with that."

Instead of a high advance that they'd have to sell a lot of records to recoup, Mudhoney asked for a higher royalty rate, control of the cover art, the music, and the recording process. Since the label hadn't invested very much money in them, the band was under less pressure to make commercial records. (Of course, it also meant the label didn't have as much incentive to push them.) The individual members of Mudhoney could play and record with all the outside projects they pleased. (Ironically, none of the band's major label releases ever recouped their advance, meaning that it probably would have been wiser to take a higher advance and a lower royalty rate.)

For the press, Pavitt tried to put the best face on Mudhoney's exit in typically entrepreneurial terms. "Mudhoney going to Warner Brothers? Great!" he exclaimed. "If Warner Brothers wants to spend hundreds of thousands of dollars promoting our act, and we sell the back catalog, I have no problems with that at all." But privately he knew that an era had ended.

*Bleach* and *Nevermind* had put Sub Pop far into the black, but Sub Pop was never as much fun for Pavitt and Poneman again after the traumas of nearly going bankrupt and then losing Nirvana. "That actually soured their outlook on things," says Mark Arm. "They were never the same after that. Innocence was lost."

"I realized that I was in a very sick business — at least in the majors, you know from the get-go that you're going to be fucking people over," says Pavitt. "To develop these meaningful interpersonal relationships and then having them ripped apart through business was hard enough one time around, but over and over again, I really started to kind of retreat. I became a lot more jaded. I stopped really trying to get to know the musicians. And it was all done from a distance. I wasn't going to put myself through that anymore."

Seattle had become a much different place. In the wake of the major label feeding frenzy that hit the town, a second, far more massive influx of bands from all over the country moved there to hit it rich, further diluting the community. There was a changing of the guard as the original scenesters either aged out of the action or were on tour too often to participate. "It [wasn't] the tight little circle of friends it once was," Arm says. "But nothing's going to stay forever."

Sub Pop itself changed, too. "The purity of intention, I think, slipped by the wayside," says Arm. "And they started second-guessing, started getting a little more cynical about trying to sign up things that they thought might sell — and working like a 'real' label should instead of just putting out stuff because they really liked it." Despite the commercial success of some thoroughly nongrunge releases — Sebadoh, Combustible Edison, the Spinanes, the Reverend Horton Heat, the Afghan Whigs, Mark Lanegan, Beat Happening, and Sunny Day Real Estate — in the ensuing years Sub Pop never again captured the imagination of the record-buying public.

**M**udhoney tried to emulate *Every Good Boy* with their major label debut, *Piece of Cake*, but it was a rush job and sounded it. The band got off on the wrong foot with the label and never recovered — after three low-selling albums, Mudhoney was dropped in 1999. Lukin left the band shortly afterward and Mudhoney took an indefinite hiatus.

The hard truth was Mudhoney never equaled the greatness of "Touch Me I'm Sick." Even Arm feels the single is the best thing they ever did. "It's a glorious 'Here we are, this is what we sound like,'" he says. "And we never sounded like that again.

"Steve always likes to say that we're a footnote," Arm continues. "And probably in the greater scheme of things, that's at best what we will be remembered as."

# CHAPTER 13

# BEAT HAPPENING

. . . NOW, I'M NOT JUST YOUR AVERAGE "I KNOW ALL
THE PUNK BANDS" KID. AFTER FIFTEEN MONTHS AT *THE
GOOD RADIO STATION* (KAOS-FM IN OLYMPIA,
WASHINGTON) PLAYING GREAT TEENAGE MUSIC, I FEEL
THAT I KNOW ROCK 'N' ROLL. I MEAN, I *KNOW* IT. AND I
KNOW THE SECRET: ROCK 'N' ROLL IS A TEENAGE SPORT,
MEANT TO BE PLAYED BY TEENAGERS OF ALL AGES —
THEY COULD BE 15, 25 OR 35. IT ALL BOILS DOWN TO
WHETHER THEY'VE GOT THE LOVE IN THEIR HEARTS,
THAT BEAUTIFUL TEENAGE SPIRIT . . .

— CALVIN JOHNSON, "THE TEENAGE RADIO STAR,"
*NEW YORK ROCKER* (CA. 1979)

Sub Pop wasn't actually the first bastion of indie rock in the Northwest. Long before Bruce Pavitt and Jonathan Poneman set up shop, Calvin Johnson was spreading the independent gospel throughout the region and indeed the world with his label K Records and his band Beat Happening, both based in humble Olympia, Washington.

In *K Newsletter* #1, a comic strip depicts the K logo with arms and legs, facing down a monster: "Our hero battles the many-armed corporate ogre," the caption reads, "breaking the spell of musical repression." But that was about as explicitly political as K got. Everything else the label and its flagship band did was far more action than talk.

Like so many K bands, Beat Happening looked at the established rules and said, "Why?" They were resolutely unmacho and played melodic, downright quaint-sounding music. They could barely play or sing. Implicit in Beat Happening's music was a dare: If you saw them and said, "Even I could do better than that," then the burden was on you to prove it. If you did, you had yourself a band, and if you didn't, you had to shut up. Either way, Beat Happening had made their point.

The plainly collegiate Beat Happening had the temerity to call themselves punks; that took a little nerve in the mid-Eighties underground, which favored the loud, the aggressive, the noisy. But having a little nerve, they felt, was what punk was really all about. (Besides, Johnson just didn't have a hardcore type of voice — he *had* to find some other way to be punk.) And as it turned out, Beat Happening and K were a major force in widening the idea of a punk rocker from a mohawked guy in a motorcycle jacket to a nerdy girl in a cardigan.

By the late Eighties, the indie underground had expanded so much that it could support subgroups that had almost no use for any other kind of music, and K Records represented one such pocket. Something that cloistered couldn't help but erect a cult of personality, and Calvin Johnson was that personality, someone whose first name sufficed, like Whitney or Michael did for mainstream music fans. Thanks to Johnson's charisma, K Records wrought a small but intensely devoted following of people who felt that any friend of Calvin's was a friend of theirs.

Johnson built a consensus around himself, leading a veritable children's crusade out of the doubt that his approach wasn't valid. In his little universe, it was acceptable to act fey or childlike, like a softball league in which it's OK to "throw like a girl." In the process he fostered a noncompetitive, unintimidating atmosphere that reclaimed the kind of people who had been pushed out of punk rock by the more aggressive, conformist aspects of hardcore.

A lot of those people were women. And a lot of them saw Johnson, the band's other singer Heather Lewis, and even the band's retiring guitarist Bret Lunsford and decided that they, too, could play in an underground rock band. It's no wonder Olympia became the epicenter of the riot grrrl movement.

In the Nineties, Beat Happening became the godparents of a whole fleet of bands who flaunted rudimentary musicianship and primitive recordings, a retro-pop style, and a fey naïveté in a genre that became known as "twee-pop" or "love rock." And as several of the early indies expanded far beyond what anyone could have predicted, K kept the flame of small-scale do-it-yourself alight.

And it did so even as the flame of their counterparts in Seattle began to sputter out. It's illuminating to compare the Sub Pop and K mottoes. Sub Pop's catch-phrase was "World Domination" and K's was "The International Pop Underground"; Sub Pop was about developing regionally and conquering globally in an aggressive, flamboyant, quasi-corporate way, while K was about networking, uniting kindred spirits in a benign conspiracy of outsider geeks. "It was a communications channel, a CB radio channel where people my age were sending up smoke signals all around the world," says former Olympia scenester Rich Jensen. "It was like, 'Hey! We're over here in Olympia!' And 'We're here in Athens!' And 'We're here in Minneapolis!' "

The two labels had a bit of a tortoise-and-hare relationship, so it's not terribly surprising that K's philosophy, as perfectly exemplified by Beat Happening, has endured, while grunge, pigfuck, and other Eighties indie genres have faded into memory. After all, K proposed an approach too welcoming and accessible not to be influential for a good long time to come.

A bout sixty miles southwest of Seattle is Olympia, Washington, a peaceful, immaculate town of thirty thousand, all clean streets and pristine little parks. Like so many state capitals, its cultural life is a bit wanting, but just a few miles out of town is the Evergreen State College. The school, which keeps no grades and urges students to determine their own courses of study, has attracted free thinkers, self-starters, and neo-hippies from all over the country ever since its founding in the early Seventies.

The school also hosts community radio station KAOS. Back in the mid-Seventies, few people differentiated between the steady trickle of music that appeared on independent labels and music on majors; KAOS music director John Foster was one of the first to attach a sociopolitical significance to the distinction. The concept would resonate for at least the next two decades.

At the time, the main genre of independently released music was grassroots folk, which happened to dovetail into two of the key ideas of the American independent rock movement: regionalism, as in the idea that a localized sound would both serve the tastes and needs of its community and defy the homogenizing effects of mass media; and egalitarianism, in that music didn't need to be made by professionals, as the big-time entertainment business would have the public believe.

Foster championed independent music at KAOS, instituting a rule that 80 percent of the music the station broadcast had to be on independent labels. He also founded the Lost Music Network (LMN), an "educational non-profit organization with members all over the world doing their part to educate others about musics that are not widely known." To that end, Foster founded *Op* magazine, which started out as an insert in the KAOS program guide and became a freestanding publication in August '79. Each issue featured subjects whose names began with successive letters of the alphabet; the first issue was "A," the second "B," and so on. (Foster packed it in after the "Z" issue in 1984 and joined the Peace Corps.) The idea was resolutely anticommercial — the self-imposed restriction of the alphabet kept the magazine out of the music industry's hype loop. *Op* treated independent labels as ends in themselves, not as mere stepping-stones to major labels, and made a point of reviewing the lowly cassette format, providing a key boost to the small but bustling underground cassette scene in the Eighties. The writing was varied and often excellent: Evergreen grad Matt Groening wrote a definitive piece on rap in the "R" issue, famed experimental guitarist Fred Frith was a frequent contributor, and Olympia high school student Calvin Johnson wrote an article about the San Francisco punk band the Avengers for the first issue.

Johnson had spent a good chunk of his childhood in Olympia — his late father had been press secretary to Washington governor Albert Rosellini in the early Sixties — and had gotten his first KAOS DJ gig at the age of fifteen, thanks to the station's community outreach program. The station was still dominated by hippie types who were into what Johnson called "really bad music," but Johnson got a weekly slot playing punk rock and quickly discovered U.K. post-punk groups like Delta 5, the Raincoats, the Slits, and Young Marble Giants, all of whom were on England's Rough Trade Records. Those bands prized creativity above technique; women played prominent roles in all of them.

Not only did Johnson avidly embrace his mentor John Foster's ideas about circumventing the big-money media and keeping culture closer to the people; he also held up Foster as a key musical influence. As a singer, the normally low-key Foster would let it all hang out in his a cappella performances. "You should have seen him in Portland last spring," Johnson wrote in a 1982 issue of *Op*. "Wow, made my heart skip a crazy beat. . . . He was going out on a limb there, singing some crazy song about Los Angeles or something. It was embarrassing. That's how good it was."

When Johnson and his family moved to Maryland for his senior year of high school, he discovered the thriving D.C. punk scene and was mightily impressed with the independence and drive of the teenagers who, against all odds, had created their own community. He met Ian MacKaye just one day before he moved away again, excited to have come across someone who thought about music the way he did.

Bruce Pavitt, then an Evergreen student, took over Johnson's punk rock slot at KAOS. When Johnson returned to Olympia in 1980 as an Evergreen freshman, he and Pavitt became fast friends. "He just had *presence*," says Pavitt of Johnson. "He had presence and vision. As we all were, he was really caught up in the possibility of expanding the power of regionalism in independent music. . . . Calvin was a very early supporter of Dischord and all-ages shows and all those DIY punk philosophies. He got it, and he got it from day one."

Rich Jensen met Johnson in the fall of '81 at Evergreen and was immediately fascinated by Johnson's provocative nature — Johnson was "a Nietzschean personality," says Jensen, "who constantly tested everyone around him to engage their intelligence to the point of neurosis — just right *there* — and then back down a little bit. And then go at them again later."

The Lost Music Network and Olympia's food co-op made a big impression on Johnson. "Those are institutions that are about decentralizing the economy, decentralizing the modes of production and . . . localizing your spending habits," he explained in a 1998 interview. "They are about people creating something for themselves and for their own community. And those were both big models for me. About how you could create your own culture, how to voice your opinions or communicate with people."

"Calvin," Jensen summarizes, "had purified the social ideas of the Sixties revolution but had tossed out a lot of self-luxuriant and decadent aspects." Given all this, coupled with his love of punk rock, it seemed like the most natural thing in the world was to start an independent label. It would be a sort of Dischord West, a label that would document bands from Olympia, an even more unlikely music town than D.C.

Noting the success of Pavitt's *Sub Pop* cassettes, Johnson decided to use the cassette format as well. For one thing, cassettes were easy to manufacture and could be made in small batches, as opposed to records, which had to be ordered at least a thousand at a time. They're a very egalitarian format, too — with the cassette, musicians didn't need any technicians to mediate between them and their recordings — "If you've got something to say, you can go for it," says Jensen. "Turn the cassette on and *do it.*" Cassettes supported the idea that culture could be easily produced and didn't have to be made by unreal "stars" and served up by faceless, faraway corporate entities. "The origins of a lot of the things that came out of Olympia," Johnson said, "had to do with demystifying the tools of media so access was not restricted due to fear."

Johnson named his label K Records. Johnson has said the "K" stands for "knowledge"; others note that "K" is at the other end of the alphabetical LMN (Lost Music Network) and *Op* sequence started by John Foster. The label's logo, Johnson's own crayon rendering of a "K" inside a shield, is said to come from the insignia of the KB movie theater in Washington, D.C., where Johnson worked as an usher one summer.

Quiet and shy, Heather Lewis came from the affluent New York suburb of Westchester County to attend Evergreen (second choice: Yale) in 1980. Before that Lewis had never considered being in a band. "When I was in high school, a girl growing up in the suburbs didn't think about being in a band," she says. "When I got to college, I started going to shows and seeing people that I knew playing music and playing their own songs — that was a completely new thing to me."

During the summer of '82, Olympia scenester Gary May turned his downtown apartment into a popular rehearsal/party space. One day Lewis dropped by and started goofing around on the drums. May suggested that she join a band — *his* band, in fact, and together with Doug Monaghan, they formed a sax, guitar, and drums trio called the Supreme Cool Beings, which attracted a hipster party crowd.

K's first release was the Supreme Cool Beings' 1982 *Survival of the Coolest* cassette. The recording had been made during a live KAOS broadcast hosted by Johnson, but the tape had gotten mangled so Johnson simply used a cassette a friend had made off the air on his home deck. He tried selling *Survival of the Coolest* by mail order, but nobody ordered it. He tried selling it through distributors, but no distributors wanted it. But he also sold it to local stores on consignment and managed to move about a hundred copies that way. "It was the most exciting thing that had ever happened in my life," Johnson said.

In 1983 K released its second tape, *Danger Is Their Business*, a compilation of a cappella tracks sung by just regular folks around town, people who didn't normally perform music. The title was an oblique reference to the fact that Olympia rednecks would hassle punk rockers in the street. A cappella singing, the reasoning went, was as dangerous — and as punk rock — as walking down the street with one's hair dyed purple. "We had this idea that it was actually *dangerous* not to conform, not to go along with consumer culture," says Jensen, who compiled the collection with Johnson. And using local nonmusicians made another point: "It's not just consumption; it's [a] process of involvement. We're not just buying somebody's ideas," Gary May said in a 1982 *Sub Pop* interview. "We write songs about ourselves, and people who know us have a shot at understanding what we're talking about." The label later issued a 1985 sequel called *Dangerous Business International*. "If the point of punk was to let it all out and be yourself," as a K bio put it, "the logical extension of that was to break it down to the extreme bare essentials, a person and their voice."

According to Jensen, issuing cassette compilations of a cappella singing was part of "the idea of propagating a resistance to the technically mediated way of consuming your lifetime, from going to school to doing your job and dying, to buying that house to being suburban to studying how appropriately you should play music, how you should entertain yourself and in fact, just leave it to some experts, leave it to some people who have the means to take care of some very expensive equipment who need to know what they're doing, the idea of instead coming up with a strategy by which you might, through an act of bravery — demonstrable, jaw-dropping, minimalist *bravery* — provoke people to see that there was a *behavioral* barrier, not a technical or financial barrier, to being up onstage and making the culture happen *right now* with you and everybody else in the room."

By early '81, Johnson had begun fronting the Cool Rays, who appeared on one of Pavitt's *Sub Pop* compilations. "The two main features of the Cool Rays," wrote Geoff Kirk in *Op*, "were a weird tension (caused by the fact that one was never sure if the rhythm section would make it through the song) and Calvin's unique brand of personal magnetism." Even then, around Olympia, Johnson was a star — a fearless performer who liked to show off the lower ranges of his uncertain baritone like a teenager whose voice had just changed.

Johnson started another band called Jungle Action, then played rudimentary guitar in a duo called 003 Legion — a "neo-beat, minimalist, rhythm/poetry act," wrote Geoff Kirk — which featured artist Stella

Marrs, who played the drums with a pair of high heel shoes. "The way she worked was by not remembering things," Johnson recalled. "She would play it when it was happening; then it was out of her mind. So all we could plan ahead was the tempos. Like, the first song we'll play fast, then slow, then fast again; on the second, just slow. It ended up we never performed anything we practiced and we never practiced anything we performed.

"After that," Johnson added, "I thought the next step would be to work with someone who remembers."

In January '83 Johnson hooked up with Heather Lewis and Laura Carter to form Laura, Heather and Calvin. The trio played three shows before they even rehearsed, preferring to wed music and lyrics on the fly.

A couple of hundred people showed up when Laura, Heather and Calvin opened for regional favorites the Wipers at a storefront space Johnson had rented for the night in downtown Olympia in early spring of '83, one of the first punk shows in town. It was a key development, since punk shows usually happened at Evergreen, which turned over its entire student population every four years. If a scene could develop downtown, punk would gain a permanent foothold in Olympia, which was important to Johnson, who was from there and intended to stay.

Later that spring they played a show at the Smithfield Cafe, a small café/performance space/gallery in downtown Olympia. In the audience was Bret Lunsford. The bright, soft-spoken Lunsford grew up in Anacortes, a remote fishing, lumber, and refinery town in northern Washington. He was the second youngest of eight children; his oldest siblings were ten and fifteen years older and had been full-fledged hippies. "They showed by example that there were alternatives to staying in town and working at a fish cannery or working on a fishing boat or lumber mill or something like that," Lunsford says.

In 1982 Lunsford traveled around the country after graduating from high school, winding up in Tucson, where he was visited by Lois Maffeo and Calvin Johnson, who were friends of his Evergreen girlfriend. Johnson brought some issues of *Sub Pop*, and Pavitt's and Johnson's writings struck a deep chord in Lunsford. "What they were saying there really resonated with what I was thinking about punk rock as an alternative," he says, "a real attempt to change the social order of the world."

Lunsford eventually decided to go to Evergreen and arrived just in time for Laura, Heather and Calvin's show at the Smithfield. "I said, 'Man, this band strikes a spiritual chord in me,'" Lunsford recalled. "I just knew something was brewing." Lunsford had seen amazing bands like Minor Threat, Hüsker Dü, and Black Flag, but this was very different. "That performance was so riveting," says Lunsford. "It was amazing how naked the band let themselves be and yet normal at the same time — as much as you can say that Calvin onstage is normal."

Laura Carter moved away to Seattle that summer; that fall Johnson, Lunsford, and some friends played a couple of songs at a show at a former railroad depot in Anacortes; Lunsford played drums and guitar. It was basically a messy jam, but there was a spark. Johnson invited Lunsford to join a band he was starting with Lewis.

Lunsford was a novice guitarist at best, but that mattered little to Johnson — he just wanted to play with Lunsford. "You should be in this band," Johnson declared. "We should call it Beat Happening and we should go to Japan." Japan, Johnson reckoned, was "the last place on earth where it's still cool to be American." He figured all they had to do was move there, play in a rock & roll band, "and we'd become teen idols overnight."

The mild-mannered Lunsford's first reaction was that he just didn't think of himself as a guy who played in a rock group. "My experience of it," says Lunsford, "was having a feeling like there are people who are destined to be rock & roll stars and those are the people that make the music. It's a special breed that feels it in them to scale the stage and climb up to be with the gods. I didn't feel like I was capable of that.

"But he asked me," says Lunsford, "so I just thought, 'Well, I'll play along with this.'"

The band name was strongly reminiscent of early Sixties teen pop combos; Johnson probably got the name from a student film Lois Maffeo had been planning called *Beatnik Happening*. Although they found its rampant sexism repugnant, the Olympia crew found a lot to like about the Beat movement. "There's a lot of really great ideas about exploring and unpeeling the structure of the way things have to be — or ought to be — based on larger society's views," says Lunsford. "That's a constant inspiration."

T he trio started rehearsing at Lunsford's apartment that September. True to their macaroni-and-cheese lifestyle, their drum kit was usually a couple of yogurt containers; they played on a thrift-store electric guitar with no amplifier. They'd all switch between guitar and

**A 1992 PUBLICITY PHOTOS OF BEAT HAPPENING.** TOP PHOTO LEFT TO RIGHT: **CALVIN JOHNSON, BRET LUNSFORD, HEATHER LEWIS.**

BRET LUNSFORD

drums, although only Lewis and Johnson sang. "I was very much afraid of [singing]," says Lunsford. "It was a big enough accomplishment for me to be onstage and still be able to move enough to play guitar or drums. And a lot of that I credit to Calvin's ability to capture the biggest percentage of attention so I could just be off to the side, in the shadows."

The first Beat Happening show was in somebody's kitchen in Olympia later that fall. "It hit me immediately as one of the greatest artistic spectacles of my lifetime," says Bruce Pavitt. "Calvin was magnetic and the lyrics were so inspired. I recall Calvin jumping to the top of the kitchen table, bending to his knees, and rocking to 'I Spy.' It was minimal, it was lo-fi, and it was genius."

Soon Johnson proposed making a record. Lewis, for one, was a little incredulous. "Calvin definitely was the one who felt, 'If you make a song, you record it and you release it,'" Lewis says. "Whereas I was thinking, 'Can you *do* that? Are we *allowed* to do that?'"

One mid-December Sunday afternoon, they set up in a band practice room in a former Evergreen campus firehouse; Rich Jensen had bor-

rowed a reel-to-reel four-track and some microphones. Nobody quite
knew how to use the equipment, but luckily Wipers leader Greg Sage
had agreed to stop by and wound up engineering the recording. The
band had never really been able to play a song correctly all the way
through, but by doing it piecemeal with multitracking they were able to
conquer their lack of technique.

Sage quickly mixed down the four-song tape and played it back to the
band. "We were like, 'Oh wow, that sounds really good!'" says Lunsford.
"I was seriously shocked and amazed. And proud. It was like, 'Oh man,
we might really have something here!'"

A lot of the credit, Lunsford feels, goes to Sage. "He just had a magical ear," Lunsford says. "We were not aware of what we were doing. We
couldn't hear ourselves, but he heard it."

But after hearing the tape, some of their friends and supporters felt
Beat Happening was now going in a slicker direction that wasn't as interesting. "But friends of ours who were more musically adept were happy
for us," says Lunsford. "'Oh man, you managed to play through a song
without flubbing it!'"

**T**he first thing that struck most listeners about Beat Happening's
music was that the band could barely sing or play their instruments, which was quite a statement back in the days when hardcore and speed metal were taking the punk motto "loud fast rules" to new
extremes. The music couldn't have been more different from what was
going on in the underground at the time. The vocals sounded like someone singing with their Walkman on; the often out-of-tune guitars could
have been played by a ten-year-old; the drums were shaky, even on the utterly bone-simple beats. And since there was no bass guitar, it all sounded
just plain . . . *dinky.*

But the songs were *good* — great melodies propelled by early Sixties
surf music guitar-drum rhythms that induced almost involuntary frug-
ging and swimming. Johnson played up the ominousness of his baritone
in a B-movie kind of way while Lewis, with her girlish singsong, took a far
more straightforward, unguarded approach.

One role model was clearly the original straight edge naive pop-
punker, former Modern Lovers leader Jonathan Richman, the man with
the head-cold voice who wrote deceptively amateurish ditties with titles
like "I'm a Little Dinosaur," "Hey There Little Insect," and "I'm a Little
Aeroplane" and was known to record in bathrooms and tour by Greyhound bus.

Elsewhere Beat Happening copped the skeletal horrorbilly sound of the Cramps, while Johnson's wayward baritone recalled Lee Hazlewood and Johnny Cash; their sparse, lightweight tunes also had roots in the songs Maureen Tucker sang with the Velvet Underground and, way back, the earnest, spartan pop of Buddy Holly. With the campy swingin' beach party vibe, bare-bones arrangements, and male baritone alternating with female singer, the early B-52's also came to mind; so did the playful, inchoate noise of bands like Half Japanese and the Shaggs.

With their less-than-rudimentary musicianship, Beat Happening might have been making a conceptual point, but it was also the best they could manage. The way the music harked back to sounds from throughout the rock & roll timeline said much more about the inherent characteristics of rock music than it did about the breadth of the band's record collection. They had simply tapped into something classic.

The band's first release, a self-titled cassette, featured four songs from the Sage session and one recorded live on KAOS later that same night. The initial hundred-copy pressing sold out early the following year. "Things were really starting to happen in Olympia," said Johnson. "More people were into it than just enough to fill up a party."

**T**o Lunsford, Johnson's Japan scheme "sounded like one of those crazy things you wouldn't ever really do, but you wait to see who backs down first," said Lunsford. But nobody backed down. So in March '84 they found themselves setting out for a two-month visit to Japan. After wandering around Tokyo for the first month, checking out clubs and soaking up the exotic streets, they eventually played a high school and a few clubs with names like Rock Maker and Rock House Explosion. According to Johnson, at one club a Japanese musician approached him and said, "You radical band-o! Your guitar need tune-ah!!" It was pretty apparent that Japanese teen idolhood was not imminent.

Not only was Johnson getting college credit for the trip (studying how the Japanese managed their energy use), he was on assignment for *Op* to write about Japanese underground music. But he'd been there for weeks and hadn't managed to find any. Then one day, in the music section of a department store, he found a bin labeled "Power Station." Power Station, it turned out, was a Japanese label specializing in punk and new wave. Johnson bought a bunch of their records and sent letters to the label and the bands.

One of the bands was the Osaka pop-punk trio Shonen Knife. The three women in the band worked as secretaries by day and had to keep their band a secret from their families and employers, since it was considered unseemly in Japan for women to play rock music. Perhaps because of that kind of repression, Shonen Knife's music radiated a joyful sense of release. K eventually released the band's first album, *Burning Farm*, on cassette in the U.S. the following year, and Shonen Knife's unsullied pop joy was to become a major part of what K Records was all about. The band actually became a kind of shibboleth in the indie community — if you got them, you were in.

While in Japan, Johnson, Lewis, and Lunsford recorded some songs on two boom boxes, making low-rent overdubs by singing into the second boom box while the first one played, titling the resulting cassette EP *Three Tea Breakfast*. "It seemed like, hey, if we record all these songs while we're in Japan, we got a great gimmick for selling this cassette," said Johnson. "We can come back and say, 'Hey, *recorded in Tokyo.*'"

When the band came back and played a show in Anacortes, Johnson tried out his marketing gambit. "I went around and I tried to sell — 'Hey, *recorded in Japan,*'" said Johnson. "And people were like, 'Oh yeah? Big deal.'"

Still, the Japanese trip was empowering — "We said, 'If we can do this, we can do anything,'" said Lunsford — and confirmed that playing in a band was what Johnson, Lewis, and Lunsford wanted to do with their lives for the foreseeable future.

In November '84 K released its first vinyl, Beat Happening's "Our Secret"/"What's Important" single, drawn from the original five-song cassette. A wistful one-chord singsong chant with primitive drumming, a bit of percussion, and one guitar, "Our Secret" is a simple tale, imbued with the disingenuous sexuality that would become a Johnson trademark. "She said that she liked me and we could be friends," Johnson drones, "in our special secret way." But her family doesn't approve and the couple runs away together, inaugurating a forbidden love motif in Johnson's lyrics that had roots at least as far back as doo-wop. With several chords this time, the flip, "What's Important," has a stiff, shuffling rhythm, like a bunch of twelve-year-olds approximating Iggy Pop's "The Passenger." Lewis sings in a high, girlish voice, "Sing me a song about the place you see / We can go there, just you and me." It was a far cry from Black Flag, whose singer, Henry Rollins, was then howling, "Myyyy warrrrrr!"

In performance the band would switch instruments constantly and have lengthy onstage discussions about what to play next; their cheapo equipment would often break or go out of tune. By just getting up there and being normal, fallible people, they were ignoring some deeply entrenched notions. "We were very aware at the time that there was a dividing line between musicians and nonmusicians," says Lunsford. "Part of what we were doing in that context was saying, 'Well, we're not musicians, but that doesn't mean we can't play music and can't be performers and can't enjoy ourselves and entertain an audience all at the same time.' In fact, we could perhaps do it more effectively than something that's heavy into technique and very light — if nonexistent — in action."

But Lewis and Lunsford were indeed the sort of shy, retiring people who normally would never walk onto a stage. So the reality was that the band still required that hoariest of rock archetypes, the charismatic frontman. And Johnson, in his own quirky way, was up to the task. In concert he'd contort himself affectedly, like a four-year-old, reaching his hand back to his shoulder blades or clutching at his too-small T-shirt, grinding his hips, then pogo with fey abandon, now and then coyly flashing his chubby belly, much to the delight of his female fans. At most shows he'd launch into one of his semi-improvised a cappella numbers, gesticulating eccentrically, his eyes theatrically bulging out of his head as he extemporized rhyming couplets sung with little or no regard for Western tonality. Some called it rank exhibitionism; some considered it provocative and confrontational, a way of forcing the audience to grapple with their insecurities and prejudices (i.e., wanting to kill the prancing prat on the stage). It was probably both.

Digging Beat Happening took a leap of faith. "He wasn't afraid of being laughed at — but he wasn't being comical," Lunsford says of Johnson. "It wasn't uncommon for him, especially more in the early years, for him to be shedding tears while he was singing, at certain songs. That was just what the song did to him. That was pretty impressive to me. I knew it wasn't fake."

*Newsletter* #1 (written by Johnson) proclaimed: "The new Beat Happening 7" 45 is one of the most important audio documents of today's hip young teen subculture." Even though Johnson, Lewis, and Lunsford were in their early twenties, the teen concept ran very deep in Olympia. Being a teen was a metaphorical state that could be prolonged indefinitely, a way of being in which one was unspoiled, blame-less, enthusiastic, and sincere.

The straight edge (drugs, drink, and smoking, anyway) Johnson be-gan by framing his vision of youth culture in quaint terms, casting his own little hipster utopia as a kind of punk rock *Ozzie and Harriet*, an even more wholesome variation on the D.C. scene. Who would hassle a sober, clean-cut kid in a cardigan?

To be sure, the straight-arrow Eisenhower/Kennedy-era style was partly a product of what was available in thrift stores at the time, but it dovetailed perfectly with the times, both embodying the nation's prevail-ing air of nostalgic conservatism and countering its sleaze and greed by signifying an impeccable purity. It was also a reaction to Evergreen's pre-dominantly post-hippie culture — to the Olympia punks, hippies were sexist, ineffectual, drug-addled fools with bad taste in clothes and music; then there was the age-old town/gown conflict, which pitted the area's large blue-collar population, aggrieved by the poor local economy, against the affluent left-wing Evergreen bohemians. The Olympia scene-sters did everything to differentiate themselves from the mulleted, mus-tachioed redneck who would drive by them in his primer gray Camaro and yell, "Fuck you!"

In Olympia, following Johnson's lead, the retro sensibility caught on in a big way. Much of the music had a kitschy streak a mile wide, while its romantic discourse was couched in terms of crushes and coy adoles-cent yearnings. People in their early twenties were having pajama parties and tea parties and Twister parties. The men dressed like extras in *Dobie Gillis*, and in their frumpy dresses, clunky bob hairdos, and old-lady glasses, the women looked like punk librarians. Johnson himself, with his vintage cardigans and short-back-and-sides haircut, even spoke in collo-quialisms from an era gone by — asked why he missed an epochal Big Black show in Seattle, he replied, "I was washing my hair that night," a corny old locution women used to use for turning down dates.

"You can tap into a lot of creativity if you step into that — there's an innocence and a warmth and a sense of family — you can really tap into those feelings," Bruce Pavitt explains. "So it's a legitimate artistic point of view and it's small town, baking pies, slumber parties, fetishizing this ro-mantic, old world, small-town fifties culture. Instead of getting together for speedballs, you'd get together and make a pie or something." (Despite the devotion to wholesome pastimes of bygone teen eras, there was also plenty of drinking and drugs in Olympia, not to mention a never-ending game of sexual musical chairs, all of which was kept strictly under wraps.)

"It turned into this weird little *Peyton Place* utopia where everyone fucked one another and they had cakewalks and they'd put on shows in weird places like the steps of a building or in a hallway or in a back alley somewhere," said Kurt Cobain in 1992.

A lot of it sprang from the nature of Olympia itself. "Not a whole lot happened there," says Lewis, "so it was what you made of it." Many people, when faced with such a situation, simply retreat to the mindless comforts of the Great American Tranquilizer: the couch, a beer, and the TV. "It made me shudder to think of that as a cultural alternative," says Lunsford. "That was the road we were *supposed* to go down. The powers that be wanted us to do that, so we would be surrendering our revolutionary cause if that's what we did."

So the Olympians created a whole little world for themselves, which was relatively easy: Olympia is a tiny place — the downtown is about twelve square blocks and the entire underground music scene was housed in two or three small apartment buildings. Johnson was the lead instigator, the Pied Piper, of this cloistered mini-subculture. "He'd pull out a yo-yo and start playing with it and go, 'Hey, we're having a pie-baking party at my house tonight — bring your pajamas,'" Pavitt recalls. "Part of me has to wince, like, 'Oh my god, will the affectations never end?' But it's performance art."

Soon the charismatic Johnson attracted a following. "I'd like to call them Calvinists," said Cobain. "All of a sudden, Calvin found himself the leader of these doe-eyed young kids who looked and talked like Calvin and were into the same music and tried to carry on the traditions of the Calvinist regime. They did it pretty well. They started up their own little planet. They had their own coffee shop and their own record store. They dominated the town. They basically just took over."

In some ways it seemed Johnson's role bordered on cult leader, with all the perks and quirks that position tends to entail. "Calvin had a lot of rules," says Jensen. "Besides not smoking, not drinking, just drinking tea — *no* onions. That was one of the craziest rules — no onions. You'd go to somebody's house and they'd make this wonderful dinner and obviously it would be pasta and obviously there would be onions in it, but he would be like, 'I hate onions.' There would be rules." But Johnson's affectations stood him in good stead. "He believed that would be a good strategy to promote his own significance and make an interesting life for himself," says Jensen. "If he wants to talk to [important people like] Thurston Moore, they think he's funny and they remember him."

By 1984 Olympia was producing cool bands like Girl Trouble, the Wimps, and the Young Pioneers, all K Records artists. Yet the only all-ages venue in Olympia remained Gary May's apartment. Beat Happening would have to organize shows in offbeat places, like the monthly "acoustic punk" shows in an alley behind the Martin Apartments.

The scene got a tremendous boost when the all-ages Tropicana club opened in March '84 in a downtown Olympia storefront. Local punk rockers helped run the place, and the Tropicana quickly became known to touring underground bands as a friendly way station between Seattle and Portland run by like-minded folks and filled with kids who loved to dance; bands often found themselves at raging after-parties that were far wilder than the shows. But the Tropicana was constantly hassled by punkphobic jocks and rednecks who would drive by and heave rocks through the windows; when the town passed a strict antinoise ordinance seemingly targeted at the club, the Tropicana closed, in February of the following year.

Riding the same wave of enthusiasm that begat the Tropicana, Beat Happening enjoyed one of its most active years in 1984 — they played in town over a dozen times, mostly at the Tropicana, where they opened for Black Flag in September. In retrospect it's an extremely odd pairing, but in some ways the two bands weren't so very far apart. "Back then, Calvin and Henry Rollins, or even *Heather* and Henry Rollins probably came from similar standpoints about how they felt about themselves and independence and freedom," says Candice Pedersen, who was in the audience. "So then you could perform together because you were coming from the same places in your heart. You may not make the same music, but you feel about music the same way."

But as Beat Happening played, at least one person on the bill didn't feel any kinship with the band whatsoever. "You could see Rollins behind the stage looking increasingly incredulous," wrote Lois Maffeo. "Was Johnson mocking Rollins' macho stage presence by offering the exact opposite? Was Rollins being upstaged?"

Eventually Rollins planted himself in the front row and began heckling Johnson. But Johnson, already quite used to such treatment, simply ignored an increasingly frustrated Rollins. "Finally, in exasperation, Rollins reached up and placed his hand over Johnson's crotch," Maffeo recalled. "Johnson merely took a step back, looked Rollins in the eye, and said, 'Didn't your mother teach you any manners?'"

Johnson continued the show unmolested.

The ten tracks of Beat Happening's first album came from several sources: most came from a second Greg Sage session, but there was one track from a live show in Portland and even a home boom box recording. Johnson did the cover art himself — a smiling stick-figure kitty flying by in a crudely drawn rocket ship, all against K's trademark yellow background.

The songs have a studied air of innocence, but closer inspection reveals darker, deeper aspects. With its surfy guitar line and faux mysterioso vocals, Johnson's "I Spy" seems merely a corny espionage spoof until the last line: "I wear Spanish boots and Brooks Brothers suits / And I don't know how to cry," Johnson rumbles, hurling a parting barb at machismo. Johnson's latest rebel/forbidden love anthem "Bad Seeds" pointedly alluded to the Sixties counterculture: "The new generation for the teenage nation / This time, let's do it right."

On "Fourteen" Johnson juxtaposes childhood imagery with some seriously grown-up romantic alienation, while on "In Love with You Thing," accompanied only by a distant maraca and what sounds like a drumstick hitting a cardboard box, he sings, "If I could touch those parted lips / Your swinging little hips just gotta be kissed." It wasn't just kid stuff.

Lewis's four songs tended toward elemental tales of unrequited love and heartbreak, and the Buddy Hollyesque romp "Down at the Sea" celebrates a beach party thrown by "Mr. Fish" and "Mistress Lobster."

"What we were doing wasn't about being really good musicians," Lewis says. "It always seemed to me it was about making a song. We're just making a song." By Lewis's estimate they had rehearsed perhaps twenty times in their entire career by 1988. And not only did it not matter if you couldn't play your instrument; it barely even mattered if you had an instrument at all. For much of their existence, the band didn't own their own drum set and would simply borrow one from another band on the bill. And if no one wanted to lend their drums, it wasn't a big deal. "Our attitude was if people don't let us borrow drums then we can go grab a garbage can or a cardboard box and that will do," says Lunsford. "And that was seriously our attitude. We were like, well, whatever, we can still make music."

By borrowing drums and purposely avoiding mastery of their instruments, "we were, on some level, maybe just being obnoxious and presumptuous," Lunsford admits, "but we were challenging the idea of how you were supposed to do things in a band."

And Beat Happening was even challenging the idea of how you were supposed to do things in an *underground* band. Switching instruments tended to flummox soundpeople, who were also perplexed by the band's lack of a bassist. "A lot of people just used it as another example of how we just didn't get it," says Lunsford. "'Poor Beat Happening, they don't know how to write songs, they don't know how to play their instruments, and they don't even have *enough* instruments.'"

Beat Happening refused to play the game on several other levels, too. "We were dismissed because we weren't macho," says Lunsford. "A lot of the success of indie bands was based on this kind of macho revolutionary stance or macho alcoholic stance or whatever. And we didn't have that kind of presentation."

I n 1985 a sharp, articulate Evergreen junior named Candice Pedersen began interning at K, earning college credit at Evergreen and $20 a week. The first Beat Happening album was then in the pipeline. K corporate headquarters was a table in Johnson's bedroom; business was transacted on a Snoopy telephone. Work consisted of filling about a half dozen (on a good day) mail orders, calling stores, doing accounting with a ledger and pencil, doing production work for upcoming releases.

Neither Johnson nor Pedersen had any business training, so they made it up as they went along, with occasional advice from other indie entrepreneurs from around the country such as Ian MacKaye, Bruce Pavitt, and Corey Rusk. Besides, Johnson and Pedersen could afford to be a little naive about finances since overhead was low (Johnson's apartment was $140 a month), and they could turn a profit after selling only about 250 singles. "It would be like, 'Wow, we need some money. We should make those phone calls we never made,'" says Pedersen.

Their business plan was simple: "Put out what you like, keep it cheap, and then put it back into the company," says Pedersen, an approach the label has followed ever since. The idea behind K, as Johnson put it, was to strike "a good balance between running a business and helping people get their thing done." As he wrote in one of K's catalogs, "There are many different ways to measure success besides with a calculator."

At first K didn't have a distributor, so they simply sold direct to stores. Back then that was possible because chains did not yet dominate the retail industry and mom-and-pop stores were still players. "There was just less money being thrown around, so you didn't have to compete as much with everybody to get into a store," Pedersen explains. "There were also fewer labels, so you could create a personal relationship — you might be one of only thirty-five things that aren't on one of the big six labels."

Taking the idea directly from Dischord, they established a fifty-fifty split after expenses for albums and a flat rate of thirty-five cents per single sold, generous even today. Low expenses and modest packaging meant the bands would see income that much sooner.

**J**ust as they released their debut album in early '85, Beat Happening decided to take some time off. Lewis had moved to Seattle and Lunsford to Anacortes, a three-hour drive from Olympia. So the band practiced rarely, getting together on infrequent weekends. And even then the priorities for these three good friends were making food and renting videos, with rehearsing a distant third. "It's always been sort of like a tea party kind of thing," Lewis explains.

The following year Johnson wanted to resuscitate Beat Happening and proposed a tour. Lunsford was up for it, but not Lewis. "It's really hard for me to sing for people," she explains. "Some people are natural performers. I'm not a natural performer."

Where Johnson would often assume a persona in his songs, as in "Gravedigger" or "I Spy" or "Hangman," Lewis's lyrics always cut close to the bone (perhaps closer than even her bandmates imagined). "That's why it was so hard for me to sing those songs," says Lewis. "In a lot of his songs, Calvin could kind of be this *thing*. It's not like he's not himself, but I think in some of his songs he didn't feel vulnerable, whereas I often did."

Then again, Johnson may have had a motivation for performing as old as rock & roll itself. Mudhoney's Steve Turner recalls a show his band played with Beat Happening, a college gig in Vancouver. "As we were loading our gear in," Turner recalls, "Calvin came up to me, put his arm around my shoulders, and said something like, 'Ah yes, a college show. You know what that means, don't you? Lots of young girls in striped T-shirts and no bras.'"

Johnson and Lunsford simply taught Lunsford's girlfriend (later his wife), Denise Crowe, how to play drums. For transportation they hooked up with a company that hired people to drive cars across the country and hit the road for a string of all-ages dates, starting in Seattle and going straight to a coffeehouse in Columbus, Ohio. From there it was to places like New York's underground punk shrine ABC No Rio, playing to a few dozen people.

ohnson and Australian musician/critic David Nichols had begun corresponding in 1984 after Nichols read a review of the first Beat Happening cassette and Johnson read about Nichols's fanzine in the
same issue of *Op*. Nichols's band the Cannanes had also released their
first album on cassette, and when the two found they were kindred spirits, the connection was strong. The Cannanes were one of several bands
(the Pastels and the Vaselines in Scotland and a few bands on New
Zealand's Flying Nun label were others) around the world who had independently adopted a musical approach like Beat Happening's. Maybe
it's no coincidence that they all sounded similar — with severely limited
technique, musical resemblances were inevitable — but the sensibility,
the impulse behind the approach, was cause for serious bonding.

In 1986 Nichols picked up several copies of Beat Happening's album
when he stopped off in Olympia on his way to England. At the time Johnson wasn't feeling very upbeat — Beat Happening was still just an obscure
regional band with two self-released cassettes, a single, and an album,
none of which had sold particularly well. "It just was a very emotional
time for me because I had put out this record," said Johnson. "It was kind
of not doing anything. Nobody had bought the record. I was trying to do
K and nobody seemed to really care about it."

But shortly afterward the Snoopy phone rang and on the line was
someone from Rough Trade Records, the home of so many of Johnson's
favorite records. One of the Beat Happening albums Nichols had picked
up had found its way to the label; they wanted to release it in the United
Kingdom that November. Johnson was ecstatic.

Unfortunately, Rough Trade never accorded Beat Happening the
first-class treatment enjoyed by their big bands, like the Smiths and the
Go-Betweens, but the initial excitement irrevocably buoyed the band's
spirits. And through Rough Trade, like-minded U.K. bands like the Pastels, Teenage Fanclub, Heavenly, and the Vaselines all discovered Beat
Happening. Soon the Pastels issued a couple of Beat Happening records
on their label 53rd & 3rd, and K released a Cannanes cassette and records
by Heavenly and Teenage Fanclub.


ohnson's childlike stick-figure rendering of a smiling kitty adorned
virtually everything K made. In a funny way, it was a very punk rock
gesture. "They drew pictures of bunnies and kitties while everybody
else was trying to do these slick graphics or at least something that looked

BEAT HAPPENING
Girl Trouble
Screaming Trees
Nisqually Delta Podunk
     Nightmare
live at Capitol Lake Park
Downtown Olympia
Saturday Aug. 8, 1987
4:00pm FREE

Sponsored by steel Moon prods.
and
Olympia Parks and Recreation

A CLASSIC BEAT
HAPPENING SHOW
POSTER FEATURING K'S
SIGNATURE KITTY.

DESIGN AND ILLUSTRATION:
CALVIN JOHNSON

professional," says Northwest underground mainstay Steve Fisk. "Independent rock was struggling to look professional — the Eighties had created this idea that good graphics were *slick* graphics. So Calvin drawing everything and Xeroxing it or doing really crude Macintosh art, that was just another way of being rude."

And the kitty cat fulfilled another function, of taking punk rock ideas about inclusion seriously. "It's very embracing," Candice Pedersen explains. "You allow people to not be scared of something or feel like they have to pass some test to become a part of something." The kitty became the universally recognized symbol of what Some Velvet Sidewalk's Al Larsen jokingly dubbed "love rock." The term stuck.

Sure enough, the smiley-face approach attracted a following of outcasts — not the mohawked malcontents of years past, but the kind of people who were into the Smiths; a nerdier, more sensitive bunch who weren't interested in perpetuating the malice and exclusion they had felt growing up. "People made me feel bad when I was a kid," says Pedersen, "so why would I want to go out of my way to make people feel rotten, like somehow they don't belong or they don't cut the mustard?"

The cutesiness extended to the way Beat Happening used only their first names in album credits. But even though K imagery and language were couched in naïveté and innocence, Johnson was just as savvy and calculating as his old friend Bruce Pavitt. "We're both mythmakers," Pavitt explains. "We just created a different myth."

Even in the midst of his most abandoned live performances, Johnson was fully aware of the shapes he was throwing. "He goes into this psycho dancer state of mind and is still really focused on what's happening," says Lunsford. "He's kind of channeling things that are important to him and then giving them out in varying degrees of articulateness." And there was no doubt that he was becoming an astute businessman.

Johnson had a formidable charisma, too. "He's one of those people who walks into a room," says Lewis, "and people notice him." The other two were quite happy to cede Johnson the limelight — that was the way they worked as friends, so why should it be any different as a band? Johnson took to the role gladly with his navel-baring performance style and dominance of lead vocal duties. In press photos he often partially hid behind a fellow band member or even a statue, coyly, cagily drawing attention to himself.

In person Johnson could be haughty, brusque, and cutting, and would not take kindly to people who tried to move in on his turf, that is, Olympia. "A lot of people are really surprised when they meet him," says Lunsford, "because they expect him to be Mr. Rogers and he's not."

But plenty of people bought the cutesy, naive image, hook, line, and sinker, one writer even describing Johnson as "our personal Elvis (and Hello Kitty's human counterpart)." But that didn't do Johnson justice. Sure, Elvis had his hips and Johnson had his belly button, but Johnson had a bit of Colonel Parker in him, too. And as for the Hello Kitty part, forget about it — the man was no one's toy.

In the spring of '87 Beat Happening promoted and played a series of shows in obscure towns around Puget Sound like Mount Vernon, Bellingham, and Anacortes, and down as far as Corvallis, Oregon, with Girl Trouble and Screaming Trees — "the Screaming Trouble Happening tour." Such was the togetherness of the tiny Northwest underground scene at the time that Beat Happening and the rowdy, hard-drinking aggro-psychedelic Screaming Trees soon did an EP together.

By 1988 Johnson, his brother Streator, and Lunsford had founded a nonprofit organization called Sound Out Northwest. The following summer they took Northwest punk bands out on tours of rural Washington — towns like Astoria, Aberdeen, Port Angeles, Port Townsend, Bellingham,

Sequim, Ellensburg, and Everett. "And just say, 'Hey, here's what rock bands look like that aren't cover bands,'" says Lunsford. "We tried to take our band feeling about what we should be doing politically into what can we do in the world we're in, which is rock & roll and the Northwest and small towns around here, what can we be doing? . . . And let's just go out and show some punk rock to these kids and see how they take it."

As it happened, the Beat Happening/Mudhoney/Mecca Normal show at the Eagles Hall in sleepy Anacortes created quite a stir. The conservative Eagles didn't like funny-looking punk rockers invading their sanctum and refused to book a punk rock show again. Months later Lunsford tried to arrange a Beat Happening/McTells/Nation of Ulysses show in Anacortes. He booked the local railroad depot, put up posters all over town, and then was informed he couldn't hold the show; he moved it to a nearby grange hall, but that was rejected, too. "Punk in small towns in '88, '89 was just too dangerous to the normal way of doing things," Lunsford explains. "We found out how many walls there were in this free society that were blocking self-entertainment. Something as simple as being able to entertain yourself, if it wasn't happening in a business that was either selling alcohol or a successful nightclub for all ages, which are usually short-lived, then it was suspect."

They wound up having the show in the backyard of a friend's house in the woods and passed a hat so the bands could get paid.

A fter a stint in the legendary West Coast instrumental combo Pell Mell, Johnson's old KAOS crony Steve Fisk became the house engineer at Albright Productions, a small studio in Ellensburg, some hundred miles from Olympia in the cow-friendly flatlands of eastern Washington. Screaming Trees had already done some excellent recordings at Albright with Fisk, and it was there that Beat Happening recorded *Jamboree*. Released in early 1988, it's widely considered their best album.

Everyone sings and plays with far more confidence; on "In Between" the guitars are strummed so hard they go out of tune halfway through the song. The ultra-spare arrangements (three songs are basically just vocals) suggest far more than what is on the track; the songwriting sharpened immeasurably, the melodies are even more affecting.

As ever, Johnson's lyrics lean heavily on the terminology of late Fifties/early Sixties teen pop, given an extra childlike frisson with a nearly constant mention of sweets: hot chocolate, baked Alaska, apple pie, honey, cider, sugar cubes, bananas, molasses, etc. All of this would lead a lot of listeners to take them at face value, but Johnson's world also encompassed death, transgression, jealousy, and lust.

While Johnson's darker *Jamboree* songs sound like elemental variations on the *Munsters* theme, Lewis's two tunes are more sweet: she ponders mortality with an uncommunicative boyfriend in "In Between" and tries to engage another silent Sam on the live a cappella "Ask Me": "And oh hey, well OK / Aren't you going to ask me what I did today?" she sings in a plaintive, girlish singsong that audibly gathers confidence over the song's one-minute duration.

But the album's classic is Johnson's supremely wistful "Indian Summer," a song that was covered several times over the next few years. In a nifty feat of minimalist composition, the vocal melody sounds all the changes against the subtle alternation of two guitar chords. It's seemingly a tale of innocent rural romance, of picnicking in a graveyard, although naturally Johnson works in some sexual double entendre ("Boy tasting wild cherry . . .") and the whole food/sex/death scenario is a Freudian field day. On the chorus the couple vows, "We'll come back for Indian summer / And go our separate ways," but the song's melancholy says otherwise; the couple's teen idyll is lost forever.

*Jamboree*'s finale is the electrifying "The This Many Boyfriends Club," recorded live in a hall in Ellensburg. In yet another Johnsonian tale of outcast love, the narrator comforts a girlfriend who's been mocked by classmates. "It makes me mad / When I see them make you sad," Johnson sings, with both the sincere, off-key cadence of a five-year-old singing to himself and alternating currents of very adult love and rage, all echoed by the caterwauling guitar feedback that is the song's only accompaniment (aside from the hysterical screaming of a couple of female fans in the audience). It is a positively astonishing performance.

Writing in his *Conflict* fanzine, Gerard Cosloy called *Jamboree* "the most sexually charged rock LP since some Bauhaus disc I forgot the name of. . . . The secret to Beat Happening's complete domination of rock lies not in the music's simplicity, nor what some fuckheads see as feigned innocence or eccentricity; Calvin, Heather and Bret take on situations and ideas, not 'cause they think it's funny or strange to feel the way they do — Beat Happening truly live in the world they convey . . . it's not a sense of wonder they convey, it's the truest sense of abandon anyone's created in way too long."

**T**he band did their first proper U.S. tour, this time with Lewis back in the lineup, in the spring of '88, traveling around the country in a compact car for three and a half weeks. On their next tour they lived it up and rented a Lincoln Town Car; for another tour they landed cheap airfares to New York, played a few lucrative college shows there, and then came right back.

In the several years since Lewis had last been on the road, the indie circuit had literally changed its tune. "It just seemed like there were more bands that were — not necessarily like us — but they weren't like hardcore bands," Lewis says. "It was more melodic music."

But some things remained the same. There were still extremely few women on the indie circuit, and even though she was traveling with two of her best friends, Lewis felt a bit lonely. "It was also comfortable, too," says Lewis, "because it was what it was — I wasn't *expecting* there to be girls out there."

Thanks to all their international connections, they were able to put together a European tour in the summer of '88, visiting England, Holland, Germany, and Scotland. They played the Scottish dates with the Pastels and the English dates with the Vaselines; the London shows were met with varying degrees of enthusiasm, but even the least enthusiastic crowds were more polite than anything they'd encountered in the States outside of their hometown.

Unfortunately one English journalist pounced on the band and said some nasty things about Lewis's appearance. "It was some asshole," says Lunsford, "someone that was out to personally attack somebody who they thought was vulnerable." Johnson's reaction was to call up the writer and, pretending he hadn't seen the review, ask him if he was interested in profiling the band. They wound up doing a cordial interview.

And there was some good press, too. *Melody Maker*'s influential Simon Reynolds reviewed a sparsely attended club show that July in Brixton. On the hyperextended "whyyyyyyy" in "Our Secret," Reynolds noted, "The lack of fluency in Calvin's voice, his callow, chesty drone is infinitely more affecting than the deftly frantic signification of emotion practised by 'accomplished' singers.

"In search of 'purity,' Beat Happening reduce rock to its barest rudiments, chord changes almost mystically asinine," Reynolds continued. "Beat Happening know that the *deep* moments in our lives don't extract profundities from us; rather, it is clichés that are the endless, involuntary spew of the lover's discourse."

fter graduating in '88, Lunsford worked in the fish-packing industry around Anacortes, then began working at a bookstore. After
graduating in '85, Lewis made her living cooking in restaurants or
painting the occasional house; Johnson eked out a living from K, albeit
helped along by the occasional check from Mom.

K was now distributing releases by Sub Pop; Ellensburg, Washington's Velvetone; England's Bi-Joopiter Expressions; Eugene, Oregon's
Dunghill; Scotland's 53rd & 3rd and Beatkit. The label had released
records by White Zombie, Half Japanese, and Shonen Knife on singles
and a series of compilations called Let's Together, Let's Kiss, and Let's Sea.
The international labels and bands gave K an extra cachet, while carrying
the smaller, struggling labels earned K much respect and gratitude. The
label also released records by future indie starlets like Girl Trouble, the
Flatmates, Some Velvet Sidewalk, Mecca Normal, the Pastels, and Unrest, among many others, as part of its long-running International Pop
Underground series of singles, which debuted in early 1987.

Despite its international signings, the label's core bands came from
such unknown, unfashionable Washington towns as Montesano, Ana-

BEAT HAPPENING AT
THE INTERNATIONAL
POP UNDERGROUND
CONVENTION IN
OLYMPIA, AUGUST
1991. LEFT TO RIGHT:
CALVIN JOHNSON,
HEATHER LEWIS, BRET
LUNSFORD.

CHARLES PETERSON

cortes, Ellensburg, and Tacoma. Johnson was fascinated by these bands — "They are so isolated, they can't help but develop their own sound," he told Pavitt in a *Seattle Rocket* "Sub Pop" column. K recordings, Johnson felt, were "folk music, music made by peasants." The label had turned out exactly as Johnson had hoped.

Right in line with that grassroots sensibility, K releases tended to be recorded on old tube equipment, partly because that was all they could afford and partly because the label and its bands didn't think pristine corporate productions were actually an improvement. The K bands and Beat Happening in particular got identified with "lo-fi," an approach whose foremost exponent was Lou Barlow's Sebadoh. Ironically, only Beat Happening's first album actually had low audio fidelity; the term referred to wobbly performances as much as sonic imperfections. But at any rate, the indie underground had once again turned a liability into a virtue — "lo-fi" signified authenticity.

Mecca Normal, a Vancouver, B.C., guitar-and-voice duo that melded poetry and performance art with six-string pyrotechnics, debuted on K in 1988 as did Olympia's own Some Velvet Sidewalk. Girl Trouble's record sold about fifteen hundred copies — a big success — and the Beat Happening record sold a bit more than that. The indie world was still small enough that critics weren't overwhelmed by the sheer number of releases and would actually notice what was happening on even a tiny outfit like K, and the label began attracting some attention from a small group of critics, chief among them Cosloy and Ira Robbins.

At the same time, a small following formed around the label, mostly college kids. "Back then you kept coming across the same names all the time — everyone knew who everyone was through the mail order," says Pedersen. "And you'd write back and they'd write back and you'd have a correspondence — and they were kept very regularly back then."

The label couldn't afford to send out many promo copies, which meant that even indie big-wigs had to fork over money for K releases. "I remember thinking, *'Thurston Moore* is buying records and he's ordering them just like everybody else?'" says Pedersen. "But that's what people did if they wanted to get anything."

After returning from Europe, Beat Happening recorded their next album, *Black Candy*. Working once again with Steve Fisk, the band retained their signature "Hey, kids, let's start a band!" allure while making much darker music than before. Lewis's cover art features a stylized sketch of a hard candy wrapper against a black background; at the center is a vortex that suggests the record's spectral pull.

If the earlier stuff was what Steve Fisk affectionately calls "tom-tom I-love-you rock," this was more sophisticated, from the opening "Other Side" with its vocal harmonies and honest-to-goodness middle eight to the closing "Ponytail," which builds ever-spiraling drama on a layered guitar sound as expansive as the eastern Washington plains.

Besides scarecrows, bonfires, and crowns of barbed wire, Johnson's lyrics are more sexual than ever — "Can't live unless I have her sin dripping down my chin," he sings on the title tune. Then there's the (even) more direct approach — the singsong "Playhouse" sounds like a kids' song, but it's actually a direct sexual come-on: "We'll just take off all our clothes," Johnson sings, "In our playhouse, that's how it goes." Or how about "Let me rummy on your tummy / It shines yummy" on "Pajama Party in a Haunted Hive" amidst a chaotic swarm of distortion and feedback.

Once again the band's conceptual reach was long — the lighter-hearted songs like the catchy, lovestruck "Cast a Shadow" and Lewis's "Knick-Knack" only serve as sunny exceptions that prove the album's shadowy rule, and even those are cloaked in dank reverb. Right down to the forbidding title track, *Black Candy* is all of a piece.

Black Candy's 1989 release began to expand Beat Happening's tiny but very devoted national following, but then came yet another period of inactivity. By now Lewis was pursuing a career as an artist, Lunsford was working up in Anacortes, and Johnson was busy with his informal side project the Go Team, not to mention running K.

They did play a quartet of shows in Seattle that year, including the memorable "Nine for the 90's" show, which featured nine area bands —

including Alice in Chains — at Seattle's landmark Paramount Theatre, the first chance most of the Seattle rock scene had gotten to see Beat Happening live. Seattle was not yet the trendy, prosperous hub it would later become and hence was a bit insecure about its place in the world — bands from the suburbs, much less a boondock town like Olympia, were massively uncool. Beat Happening had their work cut out for them.

After a couple of staid performances, it was Beat Happening's turn; Johnson immediately walked to the edge of the stage, looked straight into the crowd, and said, "We're not like the other acts on this bill, we're punk rock. So fuck you."

"Any doubts that my friends from Seattle had about the power of Beat Happening evaporated at that moment," recalls Bruce Pavitt. "With one guitar and one minimal drum set, they rocked the house."

Near the end Lunsford's amp conked out. Most bands would have stopped the show to deal with the problem, but Johnson and Lewis simply plowed through the remainder of the song, just voice and drums, as if nothing was wrong. "They weren't about to stop and play with the amp for ten minutes and ruin the momentum of the show," Pavitt says. "That lo-fi gesture of not giving a fuck about the guitar or the sound but being fully in the moment was true punk rock."

The show not only convinced the Seattle hipsters that Beat Happening was a band to be reckoned with, but it also helped cement the crucial division between their grassroots indie ethos and the slick rock careerism of "alternative" groups like Alice in Chains, a philosophical chasm that would widen dramatically in the coming years.

**B**eat Happening started up yet again in 1990, recording the "Nancy Sin" single and playing a few shows, including a mini-tour with Fugazi and a handful of shows with Nation of Ulysses and the McTells. They played a show in Houston where virtually the entire audience left after the opening band. One person stayed. "And we played," says Lunsford proudly. "We did the show for one person."

For such playful music, Beat Happening would make some people extremely angry. "A lot of times, we would play and people would just say, 'Who the fuck *are* you? You *suck!*'" recalls Lewis. "We just didn't have that sound that was easy for people to latch on to. Some people loved it, but a lot of people didn't."

And Johnson, with his fey performance style, received the brunt of the abuse. "The hostility that he created so simply, so easily, was just amazing," recalls Fugazi's Joe Lally. "You'd be in the crowd and people next to you would just be like, 'Fuck this guy!' They'd be plotting how to kill him. How does he do it? He was getting them so angry — it was amazing to see. And the next thing you know, shit is flying at him."

Johnson knew just how provocative he was. "Calvin was prepared for the ugliness that people would throw at him," says Lunsford. "He was aware that he was challenging people with his performance." In fact, Johnson practically relished the abuse. "Calvin will always say the best shows were the weirdest ones," says Lewis. "For me, those were always hard. It was hard to get spit on, it was hard to have these people yelling at you and throwing things at you. That was hard for me. It was easier for me if they liked us."

Despite the cutesy perception of the band, Beat Happening was one of the most confrontational groups on the indie circuit. "It wasn't because we were clueless that we were going up onstage and playing songs that we might have been able to perform better if we really wanted to," says Lunsford. "We *knew* we weren't doing what people wanted to hear. We were forcing our music on them."

At no time was this more apparent than on a May '90 West Coast mini-tour with Fugazi. "They were really interested in having us play with them because they recognized what we were doing as a subversion of macho straight edge," Lunsford says. "And so [to] that element that was still coming to their shows expecting Minor Threat revisited, in a way, they were saying, 'Get through *this*. Let's see you get through this, and then you'll be broken in a little bit to what we're going to do that's different from Minor Threat.'" Fugazi's Ian MacKaye disputes this motive, but the effect was just as Lunsford describes.

At a show in the Los Angeles suburb of Reseda, a certain segment of the audience did not like Beat Happening at all. At first they just heckled the band, then they started throwing paper wads and paper cups and wound up heaving the glass ashtrays that were placed on the tables. The band ignored all this and played on.

Then at one point Lunsford glanced over and saw that Johnson had blood streaming down his face — he'd been struck on the nose by an ashtray. Lewis saw it, too, and wanted to stop the show and take Johnson to the hospital. "But he didn't stop the song at all," says Lunsford. "He didn't miss a lyric."

After the last song of their set, Johnson threw the mike down and walked off the edge of the stage, straight through an awed audience that parted like the Red Sea, and right out the front door.

"That was some courageous punk rock," says Fugazi's Guy Picciotto. "They were an unsettling band. People think of them as being fey and poppy and all this stuff, but they were really delivering some hard science on those tours. It was powerful, really inspirational for us."

"It really was amazing," agrees Picciotto's bandmate Brendan Canty. "You don't have to sound like the Sex Pistols, all you have to be is different to provoke such animosity."

**B**eat Happening recorded a single with Sub Pop, "Red Head Walking," in the summer of '90, and thanks to Sub Pop's huge notoriety at that moment, the record made more of an impact than any previous Beat Happening release. By the end of the year they were in the studio with Steve Fisk, recording their fourth album, *Dreamy*, also for Sub Pop.

The move from K was surprising, but the band figured that they could sell more records with a larger label, and going with Sub Pop was an easy call since Bruce Pavitt was such an old friend. Sure enough, *Dreamy*, released in February '91, enjoyed more public and critical acclaim than ever before: Johnson has estimated it sold over ten thousand copies, their best seller ever.

The songs were even more melodic and confidently played than ever, although no one would ever in a million years mistake Beat Happening for a slick bunch of L.A. studio hacks. Lewis's "Fortune Cookie Prize" is sweet as pie, while, as ever, Johnson delves into dark sexuality, like the bondage imagery of "Me Untamed." There is a Shonen Knife homage in "Hot Chocolate Boy," doleful countryish pop in "Cry for a Shadow," a Feelies homage in "Collide."

There was also an ominous song that seemed directly about the indie community. By 1990, with virtually every major label scouring the region for the next Soundgarden, much of the joy had been drained out of the scene. Shows had become ritualized macho-fests accompanied by grim, turgid music. "Five years ago we were intense," Johnson intones on "Revolution Come and Gone." "The rest have caught up, the world is a mess."

After touring the U.S. some more that year, they began making preparations for a very special event, one that would provide one last burst of the kind of excitement Johnson missed so acutely.

**T**hanks to Johnson and Pedersen's tireless networking, K had become the undisputed headquarters of what had become informally known as the International Pop Underground: a community of "naive pop" bands from around the globe, like Japan's Shonen Knife, Germany's Bartlebees, and their old friends the Pastels and the Cannanes. The bands of the I.P.U. had created their own movement simply by assiduously seeking each other out and pooling resources and information. K and Beat Happening had formalized the notion of proudly amateurish, shambling music as a way for independent-minded kids to escape the prefabricated, focus-group culture that confronted them from all sides. Somehow it seemed time to consolidate those massive gains.

In July '90 K threw a dance party at a local grange hall, inviting not only Olympia friends but friends from Tacoma and Seattle, too. "It was just a really fun party," says Pedersen. "And then it seemed like, 'Why don't we have a party for *everybody?*'" Johnson liked the idea, too — they'd developed a far-flung network of phone and pen pals whom they'd never met in person. "I thought it would be neat," Johnson said, "to have a place for them to get together and all hang out."

By the following January, they had set the dates — August 20–25, 1991. By March invitations were out, and it was already clear that this convocation, which had been dubbed the International Pop Underground Convention, was to be a major event.

**U**sing his customary quaint neo-beatnik locutions, Johnson's manifesto for the convention invited "hangman hipsters, new mod rockers, sidestreet walkers, scooter-mounted dream girls, punks, teds, instigators of the Love Rock Explosion, editors of every angry grrrlzine, plotters of youth rebellion, Midwestern librarians, and Scottish ski instructors who live by night." And, he was sure to add, "No lackies to the corporate ogre allowed."

Registrations numbered more than four hundred, with conventioneers arriving from not just all over the country, but all over the world. Eventually about nine hundred indie rockers flooded the tiny town. Writer Gina Arnold compared the atmosphere to "a cross between your high school cafeteria and CBGB's."

Although big music conventions like the New Music Seminar and CMJ were touted as being "alternative," they were hardly that — they were expensive to attend, dominated by major labels, and really not that much fun. The I.P.U. Convention couldn't have been more different, being what Ira Robbins, covering the event for *Rolling Stone*, described as "rock & roll summer camp." There was a peace vigil and a screening of all five *Planet of the Apes* movies; one of the more popular events was a series of disco dance nights at the Northshore Surf Club.

Folks from bands pitched in with all aspects of the convention; Ian MacKaye took tickets for a couple of hours at Friday night's show at the Capitol Theatre. "Ian MacKaye, to this day I don't think I've ever seen him happier," says Pedersen. Otherwise, most musicians just hung around and caught shows like everyone else.

When the Melvins played a free outdoor show at Capitol Lake Park on Saturday, their parents and grandparents all showed up in Melvins T-shirts and took in the band's pants-leg-rattling set. "Here you have this incredibly unpretentious environment where people are respectful of each other," says attendee Bruce Pavitt, "bonding together in a way that was so different from these other seminars. The atmosphere, the feeling, the vibe, emphasized camaraderie and cooperation. And it was very special."

A majority of the groups in attendance weren't on K; they were just people the K folks knew. The fifty-plus bands included the L7, Jad Fair, the Fastbacks, Beat Happening, Scrawl, Spinanes, Fugazi, Nation of Ulysses, Unwound, and Seaweed. There were five international bands: Scotland's Pastels, England's Thee Headcoats, and Canada's Shadowy Men on a Shadowy Planet, Mecca Normal, and the Smugglers. Not bad for a tiny label in a tiny, out-of-the-way town.

All the bands were on indie labels except L7 (who had just signed with Slash/Warner Brothers), and the convention dispensed with the usual panels, seminars, and booths. The only nod to commerce was a kiosk at the Capitol Theatre that sold records and T-shirts. Unlike major music biz conventions in New York, bands got paid for their performances. No free passes were given to the media. "It was not about business," says Pedersen. "It was about really loving music."

Everything went smoothly, except for some substandard sound at the Northshore and Jarvis, the Capitol Theatre cat, peeing in a box of medium-size Beat Happening T-shirts. And the Sub Pop barbecue.

That spring Bruce Pavitt had accepted his friend Johnson's invitation to host a barbecue for two hundred people on the Evergreen campus; but in the intervening months, the convention more than doubled in size while Sub Pop slid to the edge of bankruptcy. "I thought I should have been given a *trophy* for providing free food for two hundred people when I could barely pay my own rent," Pavitt says. Instead, Sub Pop got

jeered in virtually every account of the convention. How the mighty had fallen.

The most memorable and influential show was the very first of the convention.

A group of women from the indie community had been holding meetings to discuss feminist issues and ideas. Calling themselves riot grrrls, they had proposed the idea of a women-only night at the I.P.U., to be called "Love Rock Revolution Girl Style Now." But the hard line was soon dropped and they decided to allow males into the show after all. The evening featured a long list of female-centric bands — including Bratmobile, Seven Year Bitch, and Rose Melberg — playing brief sets. Heavens to Betsy, which included future Sleater-Kinney singer-guitarist Corin Tucker, played their first show ever; they had to play early because their parents were driving them home afterward. The event galvanized the riot grrrl community, which in turn spawned countless female-centric punk rock bands and fanzines all over the country.

THE SCENE OUTSIDE
THE CAPITOL THEATRE
IN OLYMPIA AFTER
FUGAZI CLOSED OUT
THE INTERNATIONAL
POP UNDERGROUND
CONVENTION.

CHARLES PETERSON

Beat Happening's aesthetic loomed large — many bands had no bass player, musical technique was largely irrelevant, and naïveté was on proud display. It hardly mattered that for most bands that night the urge to rock apparently outstripped the ability to do so. *Puncture* writer Robert Zieger noted, "My friend Mark summed it up best; as we watched yet another ultra-minimalist band combine simple riffs, steady drumbeat, a heavy-handed affectation of child-like innocence, and half-formed stories of yummy food and being nervous around a really neat boy, he leaned toward my ear and groaned, 'Beat Happening have a lot to answer for, don't they?'"

Gina Arnold rightly called the International Pop Underground Convention "the culmination of years of alternative fandom united," but it was also the end of an era for the indie underground. As it happened, the convention couldn't have been held at a more auspicious time: it was four weeks before *Nevermind* was released and the first Lollapalooza tour was well under way. Nineteen ninety-one, as one film documentary so quotably put it, was the Year That Punk Broke. Just as the indie community was reaching its highest expression, huge, irrevocable changes were just over the horizon.

"You're talking about a festival that was unconsciously somewhat of a culmination of all things Eighties, the independent scene in the Eighties," says Brendan Canty, "which was inherently unselfconscious and unappreciated back then, so when it finally got to that point, it felt like a community. But it didn't necessarily feel like it was going anywhere or that we were using it as a launching pad for the Nineties. It felt a lot more like a celebration of what people were doing in their town, independent of each other and yet somehow with each other's help, too."

"It was the first time you got to be king — the freaks got to be king," says Candice Pedersen. "And you could take that home with you."

But the I.P.U. was a one-shot deal — they'd made their point. "This is *the* International Pop Underground Convention," Johnson told *Rolling Stone*, "and I don't see that we need to have another one." And there never was.

**B**y 1992's *You Turn Me On*, Beat Happening had gone as far as they could go — they couldn't play any fancier so they just extended the songs, firmed up the arrangements, and made cleaner recordings. Some tracks were recorded by Steve Fisk and some were recorded with Stuart Moxham, formerly of Young Marble Giants, one of the Rough Trade bands that had exerted such a tremendous influence on Johnson back when he was first DJing at KAOS. A lot of *You Turn Me On*, especially the Fisk tracks, was the result of laborious digital editing. But the album, all eloquent poetry and lambent guitar drones, is extraordinarily, heartbreakingly beautiful, as strong a valedictory as any band could hope for.

**A**s the years passed, Beat Happening's audiences had gotten a little larger and more enthusiastic; the band, and Lunsford in particular, began to get more comfortable onstage. "It's the rock cliché," says Lunsford, "but you can feel the energy from the crowd, and it inspires you to give back, to become a musical conduit for that energy. That was intoxicating."

But at the same time, the band was divided on the prospect of slipping into what Lunsford calls "more of a classic business and a rock show dynamic." "It wasn't my goal to be doing that," he says. "I don't think it was Heather's either." And they weren't kids anymore — they were pushing thirty; even more important, Lunsford had become a proud papa in 1990. "I had to say, 'What are my primary commitments?'" he says. "Being in a seriously touring rock & roll band is difficult to do as a parent."

Even after the Northwest explosion, Kurt Cobain's outspoken advocacy of the band, and the frequent press attention paid to his K tattoo, Beat Happening's approach ensured that they were never touted as the Next Big Thing From The Northwest. On September 20, 1992, the new Seattle platinum factory Pearl Jam played a free concert in Seattle's Magnuson Park for thirty thousand jam-shorted, backward-baseball-hatted, stage-diving alternative rock fans. That same day, way on the other side of town, Beat Happening played a show at the Fantagraphics warehouse, with no stage, for 150 people and countless boxes of comic books.

They played their last show on Halloween of '92 in Lawrence, Kansas, at the end of a fall U.S. tour. A couple of weeks earlier, they had sold out Maxwell's. The audience was mostly true-blue fans, with few of the arrivistes who had recently flocked to so many other Northwest bands — the grunge gold rush had bypassed Beat Happening, which was more than fine with them. "There was a looming anxiety about that possibility in us as a band," Lunsford says. "That would have been a big departure from what our initial goals were, unstated as they were. So here we are, playing Maxwell's to a packed house, and we're loving it and everyone's loving it. So I guess we won."

# EPILOGUE

It was bound to happen. The records out of the indie subculture were now selling in sufficient numbers to merit more than just token acknowledgment by the music industry; the underground had grown into a sophisticated, well-organized network that reached into virtually every pocket of America. And the baby boomer regime that had long dominated the music industry could no longer afford to ignore the new music consumer demographic welling up behind it.

Something like this had happened before. Hippies were once a bona fide counterculture, too, but then somebody figured out how to mass-market the phenomenon, and before you could say "Jefferson Airplane" a sanitized version of hippie rock was all over the airwaves and peace signs were used to sell everything from jewelry to beach towels.

But this time the process took a lot longer. In the mid-Seventies the Ramones, the Sex Pistols, and their peers had also made a creditable effort to foment an alternative youth culture. Although a denatured punk style did make it to the malls and to MTV, it never stood a chance of dominating popular culture the way the hippies did. That's because the arithmetic was against them: the plain and simple fact was there were far more hippies in the Sixties than there were punks in the Seventies and Eighties. "That's the reason this revolution took so long to complete a cycle that should have been done in three years," says Mission of Burma's Roger Miller. "And it's still not done. It's just this slobbering mess."

If baby boomer cultural dominance was like a dam holding back the generation after it, that dam finally burst the day of *Nevermind*'s release in September of 1991. At the time, Fugazi was on tour in Australia promoting *Steady Diet of Nothing*. "It was like our record could have been a hobo pissing in the forest for the amount of impact it had," says Guy Picciotto. "*Nevermind* was so huge, and people were so fucking blown away. We were just like, 'What the fuck is going on here?' It was so crazy. On one hand, the shows were bigger, but on the other hand, it felt like we were playing ukuleles all of a sudden because of the disparity of the impact of what they did."

With only minimal promotion to begin with, *Nevermind* hit number one, blanketed MTV with several videos, and went on to sell more than ten million copies. The funny thing was the album was a fairly complete compendium of the music the industry had been largely ignoring for the previous ten years, synthesizing underground bands like Black Flag, Hüsker Dü, Dinosaur Jr, the Pixies, Scratch Acid, the Melvins, and others. But it made that sound palatable to the mainstream with strong melodies and slick production. "That record changed everything," says Corey Rusk. "That record started the avalanche of the mainstream of America at least superficially becoming interested in independent music. I don't think anything will ever be the same after that record came out. I'm not saying for better or for worse, but it's undeniable that that was the record that extended what so many people had felt and been a part of, and extended it to people who had never thought those thoughts before, or thought to be a part of something like that before."

The infrastructure that the underground community had been building for ten years was now in place. The progressive-leaning *Spin* magazine was well established, and even *Rolling Stone* was paying more attention to the music. Indie distributors were finding their way into the chain stores. And everybody wanted a piece of the action. "I saw a lot of friends and acquaintances turn their bands which were previously something that they did out of passion into a shot at a small business," Steve Albini told the venerable zine *Punk Planet*. "In the course of doing it, they ended up hating their bands in a way that I used to hate my job, because it became something they had to do: it was an obligation."

For a time the underground community lost all sense of scale. Indie's commercial hopelessness had been the very thing that united the scene and kept it from being the shallow, mercenary snake pit the majors had long been. Because it was such a small world, cooperation and straight shooting had been imperative. But much of that was demolished now that the sky, not the basement, was the limit.

Every facet of the underground was affected. The success of R.E.M. and U2 had already proven that college radio was a viable stepping-stone to larger commercial success, but the alternative explosion sucked college radio far deeper into the belly of the mainstream music industry. Labels plowed even more money into college radio promotion, and the collegiate airwaves accordingly became more formatted, competitive, and compromised.

The music industry viewed indie rock as little more than a marketing path. Bands and labels painstakingly developed grassroots national followings and then, once all the hard work had been done, a major could snatch them up and cash in. The more established labels soon skimmed off the cream of the indie crop, but a slew of well-heeled start-up labels — including Charisma, SBK, Giant, DGC, Imago, Hollywood, and Def American — also needed bands to fill out their rosters. So they raided whatever was left, plucking up many bands who had released only a 45 or two — as long as they sounded at least a little bit like Nirvana — and handing them gigantic advances that they could never possibly hope to earn out. Failure was almost inevitable.

(One way to break these bands while maintaining their "indie cred" was to release their music on "fake indie" labels, outfits that posed as free-standing operations but were in fact wholly owned subsidiaries of major labels. The problem was that anyone who cared about such things knew which were the fake indies, and everyone else couldn't care less whether a band was on an indie or not. The tactic disappeared quickly.)

As majors raided more and more indie bands, the trust and close personal connections between indie labels and their bands waned. Indies put less and less emotional capital into their bands, realizing that some major label would probably reap the benefits of their hard work (of course, the indie labels retained the bands' back catalog, paying off handsomely for some). Some bands were even signed by indies for purely speculative reasons, on the hunch that a major would soon buy out the band's contract for a hefty sum.

Very suddenly and very improbably, this music that had been so thoroughly ignored by the mainstream music business for more than ten years had become big business. "Ian once said this thing, and I think it's really true: The conversations changed after '91," says Guy Picciotto. "Before, people talked about ideas and music. And then after that, people talked about money and deals."

One upside was that a few independent labels did quite well in the wake of the alternative rock explosion. In particular, Gerard Cosloy got the success he so richly deserved. Matador Records, the label he began running with founder Chris Lombardi, became an indie powerhouse (although it eventually struck a succession of major label affiliations in the Nineties). Matador bands like Pavement, Yo La Tengo, Liz Phair, Superchunk, Guided by Voices, Cat Power, and the Jon Spencer Blues Explosion dominated the underground landscape for most of the decade.

Chapel Hill's Merge Records, the label run by Mac McCaughan and Laura Ballance of Superchunk, one of the foremost indie bands of the early Nineties, also became a major force, thanks to bands like Magnetic Fields, Neutral Milk Hotel, Polvo, and Versus. Berkeley's Lookout Records prospered as well; Green Day, one of their leading bands, brought the sounds of early English punk rock to the masses twenty-five years after the fact. L.A.'s Epitaph Records had several staggering successes, including Offspring, NOFX, Bad Religion, and Rancid, all of whom went gold or platinum. Excellent regional labels like Drag City, Simple Machines, and Teen Beat all blossomed in the Nineties.

But not every indie label got to bask in the warm sun of Nevermind's success. After Gerard Cosloy left Homestead, the label languished for years before briefly becoming a hotbed of free jazz, then disappearing. Once the Replacements and Soul Asylum left Twin/Tone, the label lapsed into obscurity, subsisting on its venerable back catalog. Despite a massive influx of cash from sales of Nirvana's pre–major label album Bleach, a huge increase in other back catalog sales, and some very good new releases, Sub Pop was not able to capitalize on its initial success, mostly due to dissent between its principals and an inability to shake its grunge associations.

But the SST story is by far the most pathetic. In the late Eighties the label began issuing far more records than even a major could profitably promote, and the quality of the music plummeted, destroying the label's hard-won cachet. By 1989 Sub Pop had plainly stolen SST's fire.

Even worse, SST stood accused of not paying proper royalties to some of its most important bands, and eventually the likes of the Meat Puppets and Sonic Youth successfully sued to get their masters back. Another black eye came with Negativland's infamous "U2" record, which sampled the Irish rock superstars of the same name and dared to put the letter "U" and the numeral "2" on the cover along with an illustration of the well-known U.S. spy plane of the same name. Thanks to an ugly exchange of lawsuits between Negativland, SST, and U2's label, SST's reputation was irreparably tarnished, and by 1990 the label was completely off anyone's radar.

Labels with a strong commitment to integrity, taste, and community continued to thrive in the post-Nevermind era. Dischord flourished throughout the Nineties, thanks mostly to the still highly active Fugazi but also to fine bands like Jawbox, Lungfish, Make-Up, Shudder to Think, Slant 6, and the Warmers. The ever-righteous Touch & Go went on to even greater success with beloved bands like the Jesus Lizard, Girls Against Boys, Tar, Didjits, Urge Overkill, and Steve Albini's new band,

Shellac. Thanks partly to the fervent testimonials of Kurt Cobain and partly to a whole bunch of kids who were repulsed by the macho breast-beating of the grunge scene, K Records expanded its cult following even as its newly founded Olympia neighbor Kill Rock Stars Records carved its own niche with critically lauded post–riot grrrl punks Sleater-Kinney.

But just as the music struggled to absorb a huge influx of new fans, it also struggled to accommodate a huge influx of labels. There were now so many indie labels and bands that the original tight-knit community had become severely diluted. It seemed that the DIY ethos that gave birth to the indie rock movement was threatening to become its undoing. Now *everyone* was doing it themselves — and a lot of it was mediocre. And like an oversize herd of deer, there was simply too much of it for all to thrive.

**T**aking music away from corporate labels and putting it in the hands of local practitioners demystified the process of making and selling records. One of the dividends of that was helping people feel OK about not fitting into mainstream culture. So it makes sense that freaks and outcasts were the first to be drawn to this concept. But gradually the idea radiated into the more conventionally minded precincts of society: people who perhaps didn't need that affirmation as badly, people who didn't understand the implications of the do-it-yourself credo, and some-times even the very people who had made the others feel bad in the first place. They had no knowledge of the history and basis of the whole move-ment, nor did they care to find out. There was a lot of resentment.

"People were not as nice and polite," says Steve Fallon, who owned the legendary Hoboken club Maxwell's throughout the Eighties. "The bands still had reverence, but the audience didn't have any kind of rever-ence for anybody or anything. They wanted a part of that music and only that music, and anything that was around it could be shit on and de-stroyed. Those people were handed this music and they were very fortu-nate, but they didn't have any respect for what had come before. It was not a really fun-loving crowd, I have to say."

The scene, once a refuge for original thinkers, was now being over-run by jocks and cheerleaders in underground drag. "If I was walking around somewhere, on the street, it was instant tribal identification," says Ian MacKaye. "I'd see people and immediately be attracted to them — some woman with a shaved head or just something about them, it was just instant identification. And it was really a very important aspect of my community and the larger community that I felt a part of. And a few years ago, when punk rock spread everywhere, it became really hard for me.

Suddenly it was like some weird horror movie. I kept seeing people who
I'd identify with instantly and then I realized, wait a minute, they're just
normal people. It's like some old World War II movie where you're in a
whole town of regular Americans but they're actually all Nazi spies.
That's what it felt like. Kind of freaked me out a little bit."

Not everyone was upset about the way Nirvana had crashed the
mainstream gates. "It felt great," says J Mascis. "It was so validating. It was
just cool that some music I actually liked was on the radio. People were
getting it. It was a big breakthrough. It just felt like your buddy has succeeded. Suddenly the country somehow gets it a little bit. Just that something that didn't suck was on the radio was amazing."

But the music, particularly grunge, had lost touch with what the underground had tried to do at the beginning of the decade. "Most of those
bands, I couldn't feel anything for," says Mission of Burma's Peter
Prescott. "I heard in it the kind of stuff that I had always wanted to get
*away* from. Not that I hate Kiss and AC/DC and Led Zeppelin, because
I think they were sort of hovering in the background of a lot of that stuff,
but that's what I played in my basement in high school. . . . So to see
punk rock mutate into this different version of that was not a grand thing
to me. I felt out of that."

Ironically, in the early Nineties the stylistic palette of American indie
rock had become quite limited. Indie largely discarded all sorts of ideas
that the original punks had introduced — early AM pop (Ramones),
transcendental guitarism (Television), funk and world music (Talking
Heads), agitprop (the Clash), mystical poetry (Patti Smith), media manipulation (Sex Pistols), performance art (Pere Ubu). What remained was
solipsistic and clichéd, a phenomenon so presciently forecast by Sebadoh's Lou Barlow in the definitive loving/scathing send-up "Gimme Indie Rock" in 1991. Punk had winnowed its heritage down to one single
inbred white gene, working hairsplitting variations on a simple theme.

The alternative phenomenon deluged the media landscape, from
fashion runways to a 1993 car ad in which a grungy young man crowed,
"This car is like punk rock!" The indie community of the Eighties had developed largely outside the withering media spotlight, where it could
hatch and thrive unmolested. That situation simply didn't exist anymore.
For a while, there effectively *was* no underground. "I thought that was the
end of what you might call punk rock," says Peter Prescott, "because punk
rock is unique and individual and is not for everybody. So almost *by defi-
nition* it can't be popular."

Which underground music appealed to the mainstream and which didn't seemed to be determined along class lines, with the more proletarian sounds of the Seattle grunge scene (Nirvana, Alice in Chains, Soundgarden) conquering the masses. Since nothing with that blue-collar sound could be underground anymore, indie rock became increasingly the preserve of the more privileged strata of American youth, who favored cerebral, ironic musicians like Liz Phair, Pavement, and Palace Brothers. Perhaps to make up for the seeming elitism, such musicians placed even less of a premium on musical technique than ever. But maybe that was just a flip of the bird to the traditionally working-class emphasis on artisanal values like chops, speed, and power.

Punk confrontation was largely gone from the indie world; in its place was a suffocating insularity, whether it was Cat Power's depressive mutterings or Pavement's indie rock about indie rock, however beautiful or evocative they might have been. Sticking your neck out too far was verboten. There was a distinct sense of tactical retreat, of lying low until the storm passed. Many musicians sought refuge in irony, where nothing was revealed and all could be denied.

By the mid-Nineties, the indie community began to cast about for new sounds. Some defected to techno and the rave scene, while others explored spoken word and poetry slams. Some musicians delved into the past; classic artists as disparate as Johnny Cash, Leonard Cohen, and the Beach Boys became very hip. The trend eventually bubbled back into indie as "record-collector rock," an extended game of spot-the-influence. Sure enough, the music started to diversify, but instead of a thriving, united counterculture, the indie scene was now just a small segment of the music market catering to ever more minute and rarely overlapping subgenres: Twee pop, math rock, neo-country, riot grrrl, mod, four-track auteurs, emo-core, lounge, garage, love rock, even music made by mentally ill people.

So yes, we won: indie rock was well established, and musicians could now earn a decent living making music even for fairly specialized audiences. And yet the vitality of the music and the community was severely diminished. The revolution had been largely successful, but as it turned out, the struggle was much more fun than the victory.

As the new century dawned, more and more major labels got swallowed up by colossal multinational corporations, and a blockbuster mentality pervaded the music industry. The lowest common denominator prevailed more than ever as corporate bean counters effectively became A&R people, making sales potential an even more critical factor. The situation closely resembled the turn of the previous decade, when flimsy teen-pop acts like New Kids on the Block and Debbie Gibson dominated the charts; this time around it was 'N Sync and Britney Spears, and the marketing was even more fiendishly brilliant.

Since pop history repeats itself with regularity, another underground scene was surely brewing in response to kiddie pop's hegemony, just like it did last time. So where would the "next Seattle" be? Some thought it would be Chapel Hill. At one point it looked as if maybe it was Chicago, or perhaps Berkeley. But maybe the next Seattle will be both nowhere and everywhere — maybe it will be on the Internet.

At the end of the Nineties it became apparent that digital distribution of music was to be the future. Digital recording, laser printers, and home CD burners, not to mention MP3 software, had already become readily available, meaning that anyone — even (gasp) *musicians* — could achieve an unprecedented vertical integration by making, recording, packaging, and distributing their own music. And the networking and word-of-mouth potential of e-mail and linked Web sites is almost too vast to comprehend. This dwarfs the empowering breakthroughs in technology of the early Eighties, when people were suddenly able to photocopy their own magazines, and make their own multitrack recordings and dupe them off on their home boom box. The Internet allows DIY to range far beyond anyone's wildest dreams.

I n the Seventies and Eighties the indie underground reclaimed rock's standing as the sound of a rebellious youth culture founded on deep and far-reaching beliefs. But after 1991 that culture became compromised in both the underground and the mainstream. The mainstream took some of indie rock's righteous zeal and sold a dilute portion of it to the masses. Indie rock also coasted on the work of its Eighties forebears, albeit largely shorn of many of their dearly held principles. The likes of Fugazi and Mike Watt were held up as human talismans of values and virtues that many either took for granted, considered passé, or just felt were too righteous to be workable.

As the indie scene exploded in the early Nineties, principled folks like Watt, Ian MacKaye, Sonic Youth, Steve Albini, Gerard Cosloy, Calvin Johnson, and others were now seen as respected veterans whom the more conscientious newcomers looked to for guidance in defending the ever diminishing distance between the underground and the mainstream. This select group, most of them born in the early Sixties, became elder statespeople just as they turned thirty.

All of these people were also enjoying the fruits of their labor, whether it was a major label deal, a commercially successful label, plum recording jobs, or simply the respect and adoration of not only their peers but a whole new generation of the underground. But unlike in the old days, there was now remarkably little interaction between these king-pins — perhaps they no longer needed each other; perhaps they were re-luctant to be perceived as dwelling in the past; perhaps they enjoyed being a mentor more than being a peer. At any rate, that initial nucleus had split up into several different constellations, each with its own charis-matic center.

Back in the Eighties the indie underground had been a much tougher place to live. Even the top bands lived extremely modestly and depended on one another for anything from club bookings to sleeping ac-commodations. They had the imagination to make it up as they went along, not even knowing where it would all lead. Pioneers like Black Flag, the Minutemen, and Mission of Burma had not a prayer of more widespread success; then again, they couldn't have cared less — the big time was simply out of the question. Other bands, like the Replacements and the Butthole Surfers, had big rock dreams despite some very small rock realities; signing to a major label was the fulfillment of a longstand-ing ambition, whether they admitted it or not. Others, like Big Black, Fugazi, and Beat Happening, found the mainstream repulsive and could never be persuaded to wade into its fetid waters. Still others, like Di-nosaur Jr and Mudhoney, had few political qualms about the majors and simply made the jump when it seemed sensible to.

But they all found a way to make a career in music against some seri-ous odds. They did so by dint of their own initiative, resourcefulness, and probably a fair amount of naïveté. They took the path less taken — a path largely unpaved, far more perilous, and with precious few signposts — but ultimately more rewarding. And in so doing, they lived out a very basic premise of punk: Think for yourself.

# ACKNOWLEDGMENTS

First and foremost, I thank everyone who so graciously consented to an interview for this book. Thank you so much for your time, your reminiscences, your support, your trust, and, most of all, your inspiration. I couldn't have done it without you.

There are a number of people who supplied research materials, advice, encouragement, contacts, or a place to stay, and I thank them profusely for helping out with this project: Mike Appelstein, Matt Ashare, Shelley Barrett and Michael and Lucie O'Clair, Yves Beauvais, Scott Becker, Chris Buck, Melissa Burnel, Catherine and Nicholas Ceresole, Jamie Clark, Steve Connell, Pat Daly, John Davidson, Dave Derby, Ric Dube, Jack Endino and Dawn Anderson, Dave Fisher, Charles Ford, Clif Garboden, Mike Gitter, Fred Goodman, Ted Gottfried, Trevor Grace, David Grad, Bobby Haber, John Henderson, Maureen Herman, Paul Hilcoff, Austin Hughes, Mark Jannot, Streator Johnson, Sonya Kolowrat, Greg Kot, Jessica Letkemann, James Lindbloom, Brian Long, Tristram Lozaw, Dave Markey, Craig Marks, Lynn McCutcheon, Legs McNeil, Mr. Peabody and Sherman, Michael Pietsch, Jack Rabid and *The Big Takeover*, Luisa Reichenheim, Chip Rossetti, Ruth and Ned Rust, Steve Salett, Deborah and Lorenzo and Jacob and Isaac Savona, Geoff Shandler, Kathy Shine, Doug Summa, Johnny Temple, Jenny Toomey, Paul Wehle, Vicky Wheeler, Douglas Wolk, Justin Wood, Howard Wuelfing.

And there are a few people who went way above and beyond the call of duty to help with this project, and I cannot thank them enough. Simply put, the following folks totally rule:
Lori Barbero
Shannon Byrne
Joe Carducci
Cynthia Connolly
Scott Giampino and Ali Hedrick
Peter Jesperson
Ben London and the Experience Music Project
Elizabeth Nagle
Ira A. Robbins
Janet Treadaway
Lydia Wills

This book is for D. Boon and Bob Stinson.

# BIBLIOGRAPHY

## BOOKS

*Banned in DC: Photos and Anecdotes from the DC Punk Underground (79–85)*, compiled by Cynthia Connolly, Leslie Clague, and Sharon Cheslow (Sun Dog Propaganda).

*Confusion Is Next: The Sonic Youth Story*, by Alec Foege (St. Martin's Press).

*Dance of Days: A History of the DC Punk Underground 1975–1994*, by Mark Andersen (Pressure Drop Press, unpublished).

*Five Against One: The Pearl Jam Story*, by Kim Neely (Penguin).

*Get in the Van: On the Road with Black Flag*, Henry Rollins (2.13.61).

*Grrrls: Viva Rock Divas*, by Amy Raphael (St. Martin's Griffin).

*Hardcore California: A History of Punk and New Wave*, by Peter Belsito and Bob Davis (The Last Gasp of San Francisco).

*Hell on Wheels: A Tour Stories Compilation*, by Greg Jacobs (Rockpress).

*I Dreamed of Noise*, by Ignacio Juliá and Jaime Gonzalo (Ruta 66).

*Instant Litter*, compiled by Art Chantry (Red Comet Press).

*jrnls8os*, by Lee Ranaldo (Soft Skull Press).

*Loser: The Real Seattle Music Story*, by Clark Humphreys (Feral House).

*Planet Joe*, by Joe Cole (2.13.61).

*Post Punk Diary: 1980–1982*, by George Gimarc (St. Martin's Griffin).

*Rock and the Pop Narcotic*, by Joe Carducci (2.13.61).

*Rock & Roll: An Unruly History*, by Robert Palmer (Harmony).

*Rolling Stone: The 100 Greatest Albums of the 80's* (St. Martin's Press).

*Route 666: On the Road to Nirvana*, by Gina Arnold (St. Martin's Press).

*The Secret History of Rock*, by Roni Sarig (Billboard).

*Soundgarden: New Metal Crown*, by Chris Nickson (St. Martin's Griffin).

*Spin Alternative Record Guide*, edited by Eric Weisbard with Craig Marks (Vintage).

*The Trouser Press Record Guide* (fourth ed.), edited by Ira Robbins (Collier).

*Turned On: A Biography of Henry Rollins*, by James Parker (Phoenix House).

*Waiting for the Sun*, by Barney Hoskyns (St. Martin's Press).

## VIDEOGRAPHY

*Another State of Mind*, directed by Adam Small and Peter Stuart (Time Bomb).

*The Best of Flipside Video #2: Minor Threat/Minutemen Live!*, director unknown (Flipside Video).

*The Decline of Western Civilization*, directed by Penelope Spheeris (out of print).

*Fugazi: Instrument*, directed by Jem Cohen (Dischord Records).

*The History of Rock 'n' Roll: Punk* (vol. 9) (Warner Home Video/ Time-Life Video & Television).

*Minor Threat Live*, taped by Mitch Parker, Charlie Towne, Gerry Weiss, Tim Kor, Ray Barry, and Dave Wells (Dischord Records).

*Mission of Burma: Live at the Bradford*, directed by Paul Rachman (Ace of Hearts Records).

*The Scott & Gary Show:* Butthole Surfers episode (1984), directed by Scott Lewis and Gary Winter (unreleased).

*The Shield Around the K: The Story of K Records*, directed by Heather Rose Dominic (Northstar Pictures).

*The Slog Movie!: L.A. Hardcore Archives '81*, directed by Dave Markey (We Got Power Films).

*Sonic Youth: Gila Monster Jamboree*, director unknown.

*Sonic Youth: Screaming Fields of Sonic Love*, various directors (Geffen Home Video).

## FANZINES, MAGAZINES, AND NEWSPAPERS

*Action Teen*

*Alternative America*

*Alternative Focus*

*Backlash*

*Bang!*

*The Big Takeover*

*The Bob*

*Brand New Age*

*The Catalogue*

*Chemical Imbalance*

*Chicago Reader*

*Chicago Sun-Times*

*City Pages*

*Clutch*

*D'Art*

*Dakota Student*

*Desperate Times*

*East Bay Express*

*Ego Trip*

*Flesh and Bones*

*Flipside*

*Forced Exposure*

*Gavin Report*

*Goldmine*

*Hard Times*

*Hype*

*L.A. Herald*

*Mac Weekly*

*Matter*

*Melody Maker*

*Minneapolis Star and Tribune*

*Minnesota Daily*

*Minnesota Tribune*

*Motorbooty*

*Musician*

*New York*

NME

*Noiseworks*

*Non-Stop Banter*

*Pages of Rage*

*Paperback Jukebox*

*Publicsfear*

*Pulse!*

*Punk Planet* (PO Box 464, Chicago IL 60690)

*Rockpool*

*Seattle Rocket*

*Seattle Times*

*Seattle Weekly*

*Select*

*Skateboarder's Action Now*

*Sounds*

*Squealer*

*The Stranger*

Sub Pop
Suburban Punk
Suburban Relapse (photocopy)
Suburban Voice
Swellsville
Thrillseeker
Toronto Now
Traffic

Truly Needy
Ultra
Uncle Fester
Uno Mas
U.S. Rock
Village Noize
Writer's Block
Zigzag

## MISCELLANEOUS

"All Things Considered" (NPR Radio show)
Bang Zoom (cassette zine)
Boon & Watt interview tape by unknown
Butthole Surfers bio
Confusion Is Sex liner notes
"Fresh Air" (NPR Radio show)
Interview by Streator Johnson with Calvin Johnson and Bret Lunsford (http://www.geocities.com/Paris/1618/interview.html)
Interview with Bob Mould by "Free" (unpublished transcript)
Online Daily (University of Washington)
Sister interview disc
Sonic Life booklet

# INDEX

*No New York*, 97, 231, 251
Norton, Greg, 161–95, 177, 188. *See also* Hüsker Dü
*Novice*, 15, 19
Novoselic, Chris, 424
no wave, 124, 231, 234, 238
Noxious, Bob, 148, 149
'N Sync, 500
Nugent, Ted, 26, 121, 198, 401
*Nuggets*, 412
Nurses, 413

Obsessed, 384
Oedipus (WBCN DJ), 101
Offspring, 496
O'Flaherty, Mike, 6
One Last Wish, 383
*Op*, 413, 457, 459, 460, 465, 474
*Option*, 201
Ork Records, 16, 77
Osborne, Buzz, 424
Oursler, Tony, 262

Page, Jimmy, 345
Pailhead, 387
Palmer, Robert, 265
Pandora's Box festival, 296–98
Panebianco, Julie, 179, 191, 193
Panic, 17–19
Parker, Hannah, 439
Pastels, 474, 479, 480, 486, 487
Pavement, 495, 499
Pavitt, Bruce, 253, 257, 411–15, 417, 419–29, 436–53, 454, 460, 461, 472, 487–88; background of, 412–15; Beat Happening and, 463, 468, 469, 476, 481, 483, 485; label founded by, 420–22; musical taste of, 423–24; Sonic Youth and, 417, 428; *Sub Pop* column by, 146, 223, 290, 420, 481
Pearl Jam, 422, 490
Pearson, Terry, 264
Pederast, Chavo (Ron Reyes), 21, 22, 24, 32
Pedersen, Candice, 470, 472–73, 475, 482, 486, 487, 489
Peel, John, 433, 441
Pegboy, 344
Pell Mell, 413, 477
*People*, 265
Pepsi Corporation, 447
Pere Ubu, 96, 98, 116, 288, 498
performance art, 275–77, 314

Peters, Dan, 424–53, 427; outside projects of, 446. *See also* Mudhoney
Peterson, Charles, 421–22, 429, 434, 448
Pettibon, Raymond, 19, 21, 40, 51, 52, 54, 187, 261
Petty, Tom, 198, 224, 249
Pezzati, Jeff, 50, 314, 317–29, 320, 330, 343; band left by, 329. *See also* Big Black
Pezzati, Marco, 314
Pfahler, Lisa, 280–81, 283
Phair, Liz, 495, 499
Phillip, Elizabeth, 210, 327
Piccarella, John, 223
Picciotto, Guy, 7, 129, 376, 379–410, 485, 493, 495; background of, 379; in Fugazi, 386–410, 397; personality of, 387; in Rites of Spring, 379–84. *See also* Fugazi
Pickering, Amy, 379, 396
pigfuck bands, 255, 402, 411, 456
Pine, Charlie, 161
Pink Floyd, 82, 84, 97, 308
Pinkus, Jeff, 285, 299–311. *See also* Butthole Surfers
Pirner, Dave, 207
Pitch-a-Tent Records, 4
Pixies, 159, 344, 345, 494
*Planet Joe* (Cole), 58
Plant, Robert, 341, 345
Polsky, Ruth, 247
Polvo, 496
PolyGram Records, 5, 110, 422
Polyrock, 231
Poneman, Jonathan, 412, 420, 422–29, 436–53, 454; background of, 422; musical taste of, 423. *See also* Sub Pop
Pop Group, 67
Popllama Records, 418, 448
Posh Boy Records, 4, 13
Posies, 445
Positive Force, 388, 394–95
Poster Children, 343
postmodernism, 262
post-punk, 13, 58–59, 113, 130, 183–84, 312
Pouncey, Edwin (Savage Pencil), 250
Power Station Studios, 465
Pravda Records, 415
Prescott, Peter, 9, 95, 97–118, 104, 112, 338, 498. *See also* Mission of Burma
Preslar, Lyle, 26, 127–57, 128, 316; Minor Threat left by, 144. *See also* Minor Threat